# AND BOOK TRAINING PACKAGE AVAILABLE

## Exam

Experience realis simulated exams on your own computer with interactive ExamSim software. This computer-based test engine offers knowledge and scenario-based questions like those found on the real exams, and review tools that can show you where you went wrong on the questions you missed and why. ExamSim allows you to mark unanswered questions for further review and provides a score report that shows your overall performance on the exam.

...n a multiple–choice format. Answer treatments not only explain why the correct options are right, they also tell you why the incorrect answers are wrong.

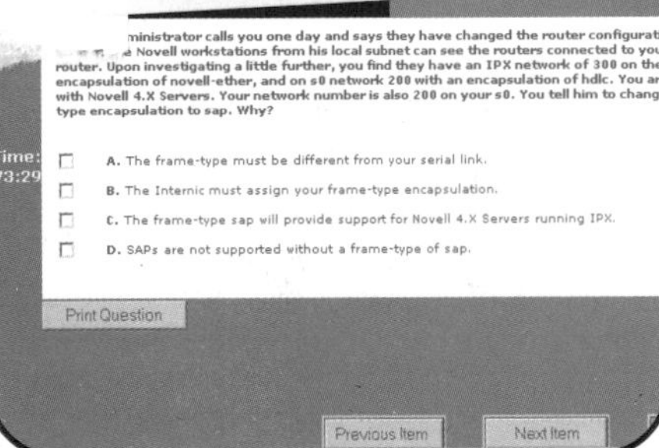


## SCENARIO-BASED QUESTIONS

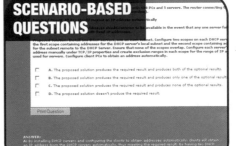

Applied **scenario-based questions** challenge your ability to analyze and address complex, real-world case studies.

## Additional CD-ROM Features

Complete hyperlinked **e-book** for easy information access and self-paced study.

**DriveTime** audio tracks offer concise review of key exam topics for in the car or on the go!

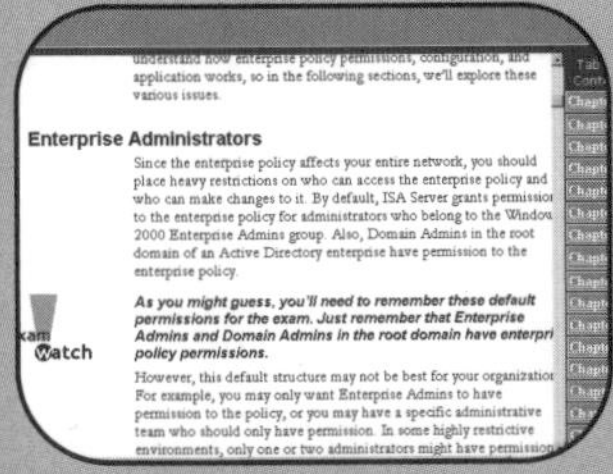


The **Score Report** provides an overall assessment of your exam performance as well as performance history.

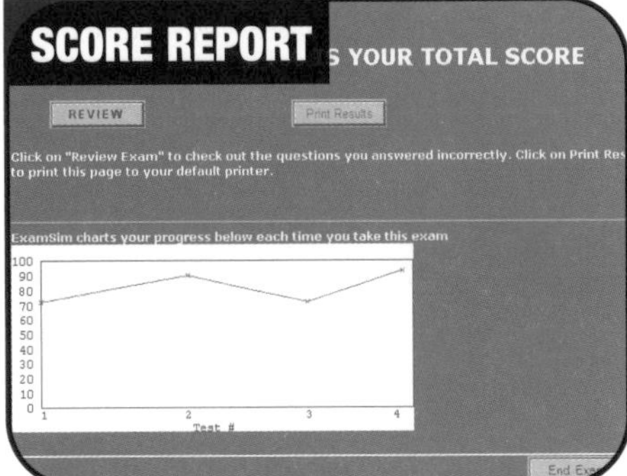


### System Requirements:

A PC running Microsoft® Internet Explorer version 5 or higher

# MCSE Designing Windows® 2000 Web Solutions Study Guide

(Exam 70-226)

# MCSE Designing Windows® 2000 Web Solutions Study Guide

## (Exam 70-226)



Osborne McGraw-Hill

New York Chicago San Francisco Lisbon London Madrid
Mexico City Milan New Delhi San Juan Seoul Singapore Sydney Toronto

U.S.A.

To arrange bulk purchase discounts for sales promotions, premiums, or fund-raisers, please contact Osborne/**McGraw-Hill** at the above address. For information on translations or book distributors outside the U.S.A., please see the International Contact Information page immediately following the index of this book.

**MCSE Designing Windows® 2000 Web Solutions Study Guide (Exam 70-226)**



1234567890 DOC DOC 01987654321

Book p/n 0-07-219129-5 and CD p/n 0-07-219136-8
parts of
ISBN 0-07-219128-7

**Publisher**
Brandon A. Nordin

**Vice President & Associate Publisher**
Scott Rogers

**Editorial Director**
Gareth Hancock

**Acquisitions Editor**
Timothy Green

**Project Manager**
Jenn Tust

**Acquisitions Coordinator**
Jessica Wilson

**Editorial Management**
Syngress Media, Inc.

**Technical Editor**
Melissa Craft

**Technical Reviewer**
Jarret W. Buse

**Production**
Apollo Printing and Typesetting

**Series Design**
Roberta Steele

**Cover Design**
Greg Scott

This book was published with Corel VENTURA™ Publisher.

# FOREWORD

## From Global Knowledge

At Global Knowledge we strive to support the multiplicity of learning styles required by our students to achieve success as technical professionals. In this series of books, it is our intention to offer the reader a valuable tool for successful completion of the Designing Windows 2000 Web Solutions Certification Exam.

As the world's largest IT training company, Global Knowledge is uniquely positioned to offer these books. The expertise gained each year from providing instructor-led training to hundreds of thousands of students worldwide has been captured in book form to enhance your learning experience. We hope that the quality of these books demonstrates our commitment to your lifelong learning success. Whether you choose to learn through the written word, computer-based training, Web delivery, or instructor-led training, Global Knowledge is committed to providing you the very best in each of those categories. For those of you who know Global Knowledge, or those of you who have just found us for the first time, our goal is to be your lifelong competency partner.

Thank you for the opportunity to serve you. We look forward to serving your needs again in the future.

Warmest regards,

Duncan Anderson
President and Chief Executive Officer, Global Knowledge

## The Global Knowledge Advantage

Global Knowledge has a global delivery system for its products and services. The company has 28 subsidiaries, and offers its programs through a total of 60+ locations. No other vendor can provide consistent services across a geographic area this large. Global Knowledge is the largest independent information technology education provider, offering programs on a variety of platforms. This enables our multi-platform and multi-national customers to obtain all of their programs from a single vendor. The company has developed the unique Competus™ Framework software tool and methodology which can quickly reconfigure courseware to the proficiency level of a student on an interactive basis. Combined with self-paced and on-line programs, this technology can reduce the time required for training by prescribing content in only the deficient skills areas. The company has fully automated every aspect of the education process, from registration and follow-up, to "just-in-time" production of courseware. Global Knowledge Network through its Enterprise Services Consultancy, can customize programs and products to suit the needs of an individual customer.

## Global Knowledge Classroom Education Programs

The backbone of our delivery options is classroom-based education. Our modern, well-equipped facilities staffed with the finest instructors offer programs in a wide variety of information technology topics, many of which lead to professional certifications.

## Custom Learning Solutions

This delivery option has been created for companies and governments that value customized learning solutions. For them, our consultancy-based approach of developing targeted education solutions is most effective at helping them meet specific objectives.

## Self-Paced and Multimedia Products

This delivery option offers self-paced program titles in interactive CD-ROM, videotape and audio tape programs. In addition, we offer custom development of interactive multimedia courseware to customers and partners. Call us at 1-888-427-4228.

## Electronic Delivery of Training

Our network-based training service delivers efficient competency-based, interactive training via the World Wide Web and organizational intranets. This leading-edge delivery option provides a custom learning path and "just-in-time" training for maximum convenience to students.

## ARG

American Research Group (ARG), a wholly-owned subsidiary of Global Knowledge, one of the largest worldwide training partners of Cisco Systems, offers a wide range of internetworking, LAN/WAN, Bay Networks, FORE Systems, IBM, and UNIX courses. ARG offers hands on network training in both instructor-led classes and self-paced PC-based training.

# Global Knowledge Courses Available

## Network Fundamentals

- Understanding Computer Networks
- Telecommunications Fundamentals I
- Telecommunications Fundamentals II
- Understanding Networking Fundamentals
- Implementing Computer Telephony Integration
- Introduction to Voice Over IP
- Introduction to Wide Area Networking
- Cabling Voice and Data Networks
- Introduction to LAN/WAN protocols
- Virtual Private Networks
- ATM Essentials

## Network Security & Management

- Troubleshooting TCP/IP Networks
- Network Management
- Network Troubleshooting
- IP Address Management
- Network Security Administration
- Web Security
- Implementing UNIX Security
- Managing Cisco Network Security
- Windows NT 4.0 Security

## IT Professional Skills

- Project Management for IT Professionals
- Advanced Project Management for IT Professionals
- Survival Skills for the New IT Manager
- Making IT Teams Work

## LAN/WAN Internetworking

- Frame Relay Internetworking
- Implementing T1/T3 Services
- Understanding Digital Subscriber Line (xDSL)
- Internetworking with Routers and Switches
- Advanced Routing and Switching
- Multi-Layer Switching and Wire-Speed Routing
- Internetworking with TCP/IP
- ATM Internetworking
- OSPF Design and Configuration
- Border Gateway Protocol (BGP) Configuration

## Authorized Vendor Training

### *Cisco Systems*

- Introduction to Cisco Router Configuration
- Advanced Cisco Router Configuration
- Installation and Maintenance of Cisco Routers
- Cisco Internetwork Troubleshooting
- Cisco Internetwork Design
- Cisco Routers and LAN Switches
- Catalyst 5000 Series Configuration
- Cisco LAN Switch Configuration
- Managing Cisco Switched Internetworks
- Configuring, Monitoring, and Troubleshooting Dial-Up Services
- Cisco AS5200 Installation and Configuration
- Cisco Campus ATM Solutions

### *Bay Networks*

- Bay Networks Accelerated Router Configuration
- Bay Networks Advanced IP Routing
- Bay Networks Hub Connectivity
- Bay Networks Accelar 1xxx Installation and Basic Configuration
- Bay Networks Centillion Switching

### *FORE Systems*

- FORE ATM Enterprise Core Products
- FORE ATM Enterprise Edge Products
- FORE ATM Theory
- FORE LAN Certification

## Operating Systems & Programming

### *Microsoft*

- Introduction to Windows NT
- Microsoft Networking Essentials
- Windows NT 4.0 Workstation
- Windows NT 4.0 Server
- Advanced Windows NT 4.0 Server
- Windows NT Networking with TCP/IP
- Introduction to Microsoft Web Tools
- Windows NT Troubleshooting
- Windows Registry Configuration

## UNIX

- UNIX Level I
- UNIX Level II
- Essentials of UNIX and NT Integration

## Programming

- Introduction to JavaScript
- Java Programming
- PERL Programming
- Advanced PERL with CGI for the Web

## Web Site Management & Development

- Building a Web Site
- Web Site Management and Performance
- Web Development Fundamentals

## High Speed Networking

- Essentials of Wide Area Networking
- Integrating ISDN
- Fiber Optic Network Design
- Fiber Optic Network Installation
- Migrating to High Performance Ethernet

## DIGITAL UNIX

- UNIX Utilities and Commands
- DIGITAL UNIX v4.0 System Administration
- DIGITAL UNIX v4.0 (TCP/IP) Network Management
- AdvFS, LSM, and RAID Configuration and Management
- DIGITAL UNIX TruCluster Software Configuration and Management
- UNIX Shell Programming Featuring Kornshell
- DIGITAL UNIX v4.0 Security Management
- DIGITAL UNIX v4.0 Performance Management
- DIGITAL UNIX v4.0 Intervals Overview

## DIGITAL OpenVMS

- OpenVMS Skills for Users
- OpenVMS System and Network Node Management I
- OpenVMS System and Network Node Management II
- OpenVMS System and Network Node Management III
- OpenVMS System and Network Node Operations
- OpenVMS for Programmers
- OpenVMS System Troubleshooting for Systems Managers
- Configuring and Managing Complex VMScluster Systems
- Utilizing OpenVMS Features from C
- OpenVMS Performance Management
- Managing DEC TCP/IP Services for OpenVMS
- Programming in C

## Hardware Courses

- AlphaServer 1000/1000A Installation, Configuration and Maintenance
- AlphaServer 2100 Server Maintenance
- AlphaServer 4100, Troubleshooting Techniques and Problem Solving

# ABOUT THE CONTRIBUTORS

## About Syngress Media

**Syngress Media** creates books and software for Information Technology professionals seeking skill enhancement and career advancement. Its products are designed to comply with vendor and industry standard course curricula, and are optimized for certification exam preparation. You can contact Syngress via the Web at www.syngress.com.

## Contributors

**Jada Brock-Soldavini** (MCSE) is a Senior Network Services Administrator for the State of Georgia. With over seven years in the Information technology field, Jada has a very diverse background. Her experience includes a number of years building and supporting desktop clients and network servers as well as network administration and architecture development in both Windows NT/2000 and Exchange 5.5/2000, as well as Cisco Technologies. Prior to her current job, she worked as a Consultant for a business ISP firm in Atlanta, primarily with Linux, Unix and Apache Web Servers.

Jada graduated from Massey Business College in Atlanta, Georgia with an AS in Computer Information Systems and holds a membership with the Network Professional Association and the IEEE Society. Jada lives in the suburbs of Atlanta, Georgia with her husband Michael and two children Alyssa and Daniel. She is currently working on her CCNP certification. Jada is a published author who enjoys writing technical articles and technical books in her spare time. Her e-mail address is jadasoldavini@ hotmail.com.

**Chris Broomes** (MCSE, MCT, MCP+I, CCNA) is a Senior Network Analyst at DevonIT (www.devonitnet.com), a leading networking services provider specializing in network security and VPN solutions. Chris has worked in the IT industry for over eight years and has a wide range of technical experience.

Chris is also founder and President of Infinite Solutions Group Inc. (www.infinitesols.com), a network consulting firm located in Lansdowne PA, specializing in network design, integration, security services, technical writing and training. Chris is currently pursuing the CCDA and CCNP certifications, while mastering the workings of Cisco and Netscreen VPN and security devices. He can be reached at cbroomes@infinitesols.com.

**Jarret W. Buse (MCT, MCSE+I, CCNA, CNA, A+, Network+)** is a technical trainer and consultant specializing in Microsoft products. He has worked in the computer field for nine years and instructs students in the use of various Microsoft products as well as different computer certifications. With a degree in programming, he is still working toward his MCSD, but has not has not yet found time to complete the certification. He can be reached at jarretbuse@hotmail.com.

**Melissa Craft (CCNA, MCSE, Network+, CNE-5, CNE-3, CNE-4, CNE-GW, MCNE, Citrix CCA)** designs business computing solutions using technology to automate processes, and using business process reengineering techniques.

Early on in her career, Melissa threw herself at the task of truly understanding network engineering, gaining a myriad of technology certifications and, at the same time, deploying projects for clients. Over the years, Melissa has successfully designed, implemented and integrated networks ranging in size from a few nodes to over 100,000 nodes. This consulting experience incorporated extensive project management, needs-analysis, LAN and WAN design, deployment and operational turnover.

In 1997, Melissa began writing magazine articles regarding networking and the technology industry. In 1998, Syngress Media hired Melissa to contribute to an MCSE certification guide. Since then, Melissa has continued to write about various technology and certification subjects.

Currently, Melissa works on Microsoft Solutions for CompuCom Systems, Inc. CompuCom is a systems integrator headquartered in Dallas, Texas. CompuCom provides business services, IT design, project management and support for distributed computing systems. Melissa is a key contributor to the business development of Microsoft technology-based solutions. As such, she develops enterprise-wide solutions and methodologies focused on client organizations. These technology solutions touch every part of a system's lifecycle—from network design, testing and implementation to operational management and strategic planning.

Melissa holds a bachelor's degree from the University of Michigan, and is a member of the IEEE, the Society of Women Engineers and American MENSA, Ltd. Melissa currently resides in Glendale, Arizona with her family, Dan, Justine and Taylor, and her two Great Danes (a.k.a Mobile Defense Units), Marmaduke and Apollo as well as her Golden Retriever (a.k.a. Mobile Alarm Unit) Pooka. Melissa can be contacted via e-mail at mmcraft@compuserve.com.

**Michael Cross** (MCSE, MCPS, MCP+I, CNA) is the Network Administrator, Internet Specialist, and a Programmer for the Niagara Regional Police Service. He is responsible for network security and administration, programming applications, and Webmaster of their Web site at www.nrps.com. He has been consulted and assisted in computer-related/Internet criminal cases, and is part of an Information Technology team that provides support to a user base of over 800 civilian and uniform users. His theory is that when the users carry guns, you tend to be more motivated in solving their problems.

Michael also owns KnightWare, a company that provides consulting, programming, networking, Web page design, computer training and various other services. He has served as an instructor for private colleges and technical schools in London, Ontario, Canada. He has been a freelance writer for several years, and published over two dozen times in numerous books and anthologies. He currently resides in St. Catharines, Ontario, Canada with his lovely wife Jennifer, and two slightly neurotic cats.

**George D. Hoffman** (MCSE, MCT) resides in Stoneham, MA with his wife Ann-Marie, a native of Dublin, Ireland. After graduating from Boston College, George served as a Navy Officer and subsequently operated his own advertising and marketing business before "joining the crowd and moving to the world of computers." In addition to teaching applications and Microsoft technical classes in the United States, he has taught and consulted extensively in Ireland. In his spare time, while not preparing for the next Microsoft exam, George enjoys woodworking and golf, much more successful at the former than the latter.

## Technical Editor

**Melissa Craft** (CCNA, MCSE, Network+, CNE-5, CNE-3, CNE-4, CNE-GW, MCNE, Citrix CCA) designs business computing solutions using technology to automate processes, and using business process reengineering techniques.

Early on in her career, Melissa threw herself at the task of truly understanding network engineering, gaining a myriad of technology certifications and, at the same time, deploying projects for clients. Over the years, Melissa has successfully designed, implemented and integrated networks ranging in size from a few nodes to over 100,000 nodes. This consulting experience incorporated extensive project management, needs-analysis, LAN and WAN design, deployment and operational turnover.

In 1997, Melissa began writing magazine articles regarding networking and the technology industry. In 1998, Syngress Media hired Melissa to contribute to an MCSE certification guide. Since then, Melissa has continued to write about various technology and certification subjects.

Currently, Melissa works on Microsoft Solutions for CompuCom Systems, Inc. CompuCom is a systems integrator headquartered in Dallas, Texas. CompuCom provides business services, IT design, project management and support for distributed computing systems. Melissa is a key contributor to the business development of Microsoft technology-based solutions. As such, she develops enterprise-wide solutions and methodologies focused on client organizations. These technology solutions touch every part of a system's life cycle—from network design, testing and implementation to operational management and strategic planning.

Melissa holds a bachelor's degree from the University of Michigan, and is a member of the IEEE, the Society of Women Engineers and American MENSA, Ltd. Melissa currently resides in Glendale, Arizona with her family, Dan, Justine and Taylor, and her two Great Danes (a.k.a Mobile Defense Units), Marmaduke and Apollo as well as her Golden Retriever (a.k.a. Mobile Alarm Unit) Pooka. Melissa can be contacted via e-mail at mmcraft@compuserve.com.

## Technical Reviewer

**Jarret W. Buse (MCT, MCSE+I, CCNA, CNA, A+, Network+)** is a technical trainer and consultant specializing in Microsoft products. He has worked in the computer field for nine years and instructs students in the use of various Microsoft products as well as different computer certifications. With a degree in programming, he is still working toward his MCSD, but has not has not yet found time to complete the certification. He can be reached at jarretbuse@hotmail.com.

# ACKNOWLEDGMENTS

We would like to thank the following people:

- Richard Kristof of Global Knowledge for championing the series and providing us access to some great people and information.
- All the incredibly hard-working folks at Osborne/McGraw-Hill: Brandon Nordin, Scott Rogers, Timothy Green, Gareth Hancock, and Jessica Wilson.

# CONTENTS AT A GLANCE

# CONTENTS

# PREFACE

This book's primary objective is to help you prepare for the MCSE Designing Windows 2000 Web Solutions exam under the Windows 2000 certification track. As the Microsoft program continues to transition from Windows NT 4.0, it will become increasingly important that current and aspiring IT professionals have multiple resources available to assist them in increasing their knowledge and building their skills.

At the time of publication, all the exam objectives have been posted on the Microsoft Web site and the beta exam process has been completed. Microsoft has announced its commitment to measuring real-world skills. This book is designed with that premise in mind; its authors have practical experience in the field, using Windows 2000 operating systems in hands-on situations.

Because the focus of the exam is on application and understanding, as opposed to memorization of facts, no book by itself can fully prepare you to obtain a passing score. It is essential that you work with the software to enhance your proficiency. Toward that end, this book includes many practical step-by-step exercises in each chapter that are designed to give you hands-on practice as well as guide you in truly learning MCSE Designing Windows 2000 Web Solutions, not just learning *about* it.

## In This Book

This book is organized around the actual structure of the 70-226 exam administered at Sylvan Prometric and VUE Testing Centers. Microsoft has let us know all the topics we need to cover for the exam. We've followed their list carefully, so you can be assured you're not missing anything. Each chapter covers a major aspect of the exam, with an emphasis on the "why" as well as the "how to" of designing Windows 2000 web solutions as a network administrator or engineer.

## In Every Chapter

We've created a set of chapter components that call your attention to important items, reinforce important points, and provide helpful exam-taking hints. Take a look at what you'll find in the chapters:

- Each chapter begins with the **Certification Objectives**—what you need to know in order to pass the section on the exam dealing with the chapter topic. The Certification Objective headings identify the objectives within the chapter, so you'll always know an objective when you see it!

EXERCISE

- **Certification Exercises** are interspersed throughout the chapters. These are step-by-step exercises. They help you master skills that are likely to be an area of focus on the exam. Don't just read through the exercises; they are hands-on procedures that you should be comfortable completing. Learning by doing is an effective way to increase your competency with the language and concepts presented.
- **From the Classroom** sidebars describe the issues that come up most often in the training classroom setting. These sidebars give you a valuable perspective into certification- and product-related topics. They point out common mistakes and address questions that have arisen from classroom discussions.

- The **CertCam** icon that appears in many of the exercises indicates that the exercise is presented in .avi format on the accompanying CD-ROM. These .avi clips walk you through various system configurations and are narrated by George D. Hoffman, MCSE, MCT.
- **Scenario & Solution** sections lay out specific scenario questions and solutions in a quick and easy-to-read format.

| SCENARIO & SOLUTION | |
|---|---|
| I need to ensure that my Web site is still accessible, even if my Internet connection goes down. How can I accomplish this goal? | Work with your ISP to provide you with another Internet connection and configure it as a load-balancing and failover connection to your site. |
| What components should I consider to make redundant in my network topology? | All components of the infrastructure that it is feasible to make redundant, including network devices, server CPUs, power supplies, disks, or RAID arrays. |
| How can I ensure that the services provided by my Web infrastructure are redundant? | Hosting copies of the back-end applications such as database applications on multiple servers and creating a cluster using Windows Cluster Services will create a redundant architecture. |

- The **Certification Summary** is a succinct review of the chapter and a restatement of salient points regarding the exam.

- The **Two-Minute Drill** at the end of every chapter is a checklist of the main points of the chapter. It can be used for last-minute review.

Q&A

- The **Self Test** offers questions similar to those found on the certification exam. The answers to these questions, as well as explanations of the answers, can be found at the end of the particular chapter. By taking the Self Test after completing each chapter, you'll reinforce what you've learned from that chapter, while becoming familiar with the structure of the exam questions.
- The **Lab Question** at the end of the Self Test section offers a unique and challenging question format that requires the reader to understand multiple chapter concepts to answer correctly. These questions are more complex and more comprehensive than the other questions, as they test your ability to take all the knowledge you have gained from reading the chapter and apply it to complicated, real-world situations. These questions are aimed to be more difficult than what you will find on the exam. If you can answer these questions, you have proven that you know the subject!

## Some Pointers

Once you've finished reading this book, set aside some time to do a thorough review. You might want to return to the book several times and make use of all the methods it offers for reviewing the material:

1. *Re-read all the Two-Minute Drills*, or have someone quiz you. You also can use the drills as a way to do a quick cram before the exam.
2. *Review all the Scenario & Solution sections* for quick problem solving.
3. *Re-take the Self Tests.* Taking the tests right after you've read the chapter is a good idea, because it helps reinforce what you've just learned. However, it's an even better idea to go back later and do all the questions in the book in one sitting. Pretend you're taking the exam. (For this reason, you should mark your answers on a separate piece of paper when you go through the questions the first time.)
4. *Complete the exercises.* Did you do the exercises when you read through each chapter? If not, do them! These exercises are designed to cover exam topics, and there's no better way to get to know this material than by practicing.
5. *Check out the Web site.* Global Knowledge invites you to become an active member of the Access Global Web site. This site is an online mall and an information repository that you'll find invaluable. You can access many types of products to assist you in your preparation for the exams, and you'll be able to participate in forums, on-line discussions, and threaded discussions. No other book brings you unlimited access to such a resource. You'll find more information about this site in Appendix B.

# The CD-ROM Resource

This book comes with a CD-ROM that includes test preparation software and provides you with another method for studying. You will find more information on the testing software in Appendix A.

# MCSE Certification

This book is designed to help you pass the MCSE Designing Windows 2000 Web Solutions exam. We wrote this book to give you a complete and incisive review of all the important topics that are targeted for the exam. The information contained here will provide you with the required foundation of knowledge that will not only allow you to succeed in passing the 70-226 exam, but will also make you a better Microsoft Certified Systems Engineer.

The nature of the Information Technology industry is changing rapidly, and the requirements and specifications for certification can change just as quickly without notice. Microsoft expects you to regularly visit their Web site at **http://www.microsoft.com/mcp/certstep/mcse.htm** to get the most up-to-date information on the entire MCSE program.

*Windows 2000 Certification Track*

| Core Exams | | |
|---|---|---|
| **Candidates Who Have Not Already Passed Windows NT 4.0 Exams<br>All 4 of the Following Core Exams Required:** | OR | **Candidates Who Have Passed 3 Windows NT 4.0 Exams (Exams 70-067, 70-068, and 70-073)<br>Instead of the 4 Core Exams on Left, You May Take:** |
| **Exam 70-210:** Installing, Configuring, and Administering Microsoft® Windows® 2000 Professional | | **Exam 70-240:** Microsoft® Windows® 2000 Accelerated Exam for MCPs Certified on Microsoft® Windows NT® 4.0<br><br>The Accelerated Exam will be available until December 31, 2001. It covers the core competencies of exams **70-210**, **70-215**, **70-216**, and **70-217**. |
| **Exam 70-215:** Installing, Configuring, and Administering Microsoft® Windows® 2000 Server | | |
| **Exam 70-216:** Implementing and Administering a Microsoft® Windows® 2000 Network Infrastructure | | |
| **Exam 70-217:** Implementing and Administering a Microsoft® Windows® 2000 Directory Services Infrastructure | | |

| ***PLUS – All Candidates – 1 of the Following Core Exams Required:*** |
|---|
| *Exam 70-219: Designing a Microsoft® Windows® 2000 Directory Services Infrastructure |
| *Exam 70-220: Designing Security for a Microsoft® Windows® 2000 Network |
| *Exam 70-221: Designing a Microsoft® Windows® 2000 Network Infrastructure |
| ***PLUS – All Candidates – 2 Elective Exams Required: For a full listing of elective exams that apply, please see www.microsoft.com/trainingandservices*** |
| *** Note that some of the Windows 2000 Core Exams can be used as elective exams as well. An exam that is used to meet the design requirement cannot also count as an elective. Each exam can only be counted once in the Windows 2000 Certification.* |

Let's look at two scenarios. The first applies to the person who has already taken the Windows NT 4.0 Server (70-067), Windows NT 4.0 Workstation (70-073), and Windows NT 4.0 Server in the Enterprise (70-068) exams. The second scenario covers the situation of the person who has not completed those Windows NT 4.0 exams and would like to concentrate ONLY on Windows 2000.

In the first scenario, you have the option of taking all four Windows 2000 Core Exams, or you can take the Windows 2000 Accelerated Exam for MCPs if you have already passed exams 70-067, 70-068, and 70-073. (Note that you must have passed those specific exams to qualify for the Accelerated Exam; if you have fulfilled your NT 4.0 MCSE requirements by passing the Windows 95 or Windows 98 Exam as your client operating system option, and did not take the NT Workstation Exam, you don't qualify. Please note that as of this writing the Accelerated Exam is scheduled to be retired on December 31, 2001.)

After completing the Core requirements, either by passing the four Core Exams or the one Accelerated Exam, you must pass a "design" exam. The design exams include Designing a Microsoft Windows 2000 Directory Services Infrastructure (70-219), Designing Security for Microsoft Windows 2000 Network (70-220), and Designing a Microsoft Windows 2000 Network Infrastructure (70-221). One design exam is REQUIRED.

You also must pass two exams from the list of electives. However, you cannot use the design exam that you took as an elective. Each exam can only count once toward certification. This includes any of the MCSE electives that are current when the Windows 2000 exams are released. The 70-226 exam counts towards one of your Windows 2000 elective exams. In summary, you would take a total of at least two more exams, the upgrade exam and the design exam. Any additional exams would be dependent on which electives the candidate may have already completed.

In the second scenario, if you have not completed, and do not plan to complete the Core Windows NT 4.0 exams, you must pass the four Core Windows 2000 exams, one design exam, and two elective exams. Again, no exam can be counted twice. In this case, you must pass a total of seven exams to obtain the Windows 2000 MCSE certification.

## How to Take a Microsoft Certification Exam

If you have taken a Microsoft Certification exam before, we have some good news and some bad news. The good news is that the new testing formats will be a true measure of your ability and knowledge. Microsoft has "raised the bar" for its MCSE Windows 2000 Certification Exams. If you are an expert in the Windows 2000 operating system, and can troubleshoot and engineer efficient, cost effective solutions using Windows 2000, you will have no difficulty with the new exams.

The bad news is that if you have used resources such as brain-dumps, boot-camps, or exam specific practice tests as your only method of test preparation, you will undoubtedly fail your Windows 2000 exams. The Windows 2000 MCSE Exams will test your knowledge, and your ability to apply that knowledge in more sophisticated and accurate ways than was expected for the MCSE exams for Windows NT 4.0.

In the Windows 2000 exams, Microsoft uses a variety of testing formats which include product simulations, adaptive testing, drag-and-drop matching, and possibly even "fill-in-the-blank" questions (also called "free response" questions). The test-taking process will measure the examinee's fundamental knowledge of the Windows 2000 operating system rather than his or her ability to memorize a few facts and then answer a few simple multiple-choice questions.

In addition, the "pool" of questions for each exam will significantly increase. The greater number of questions combined with the adaptive testing techniques will enhance the validity and security of the certification process.

We will begin by looking at the purpose, focus, and structure of Microsoft Certification tests, and examine the effect that these factors have on the kinds of questions you will face on your certification exams. We will define the structure of exam questions and investigate some common formats. Next, we will present a strategy for answering these questions. Finally, we will give some specific guidelines on what you should do on the day of your test.

## Why Vendor Certification?

The Microsoft Certified Professional program, like the certification programs from Cisco, Novell, Oracle, and other software vendors, is maintained for the ultimate purpose of increasing the corporation's profits. A successful vendor certification program accomplishes this goal by helping to create a pool of experts in a company's software and by "branding" these experts so companies using the software can identify them.

We know that vendor certification has become increasingly popular in the last few years because it helps employers find qualified workers and because it helps software vendors like Microsoft sell their products. But why vendor certification rather than a more traditional approach like a college degree in computer science? A college education is a broadening and enriching experience, but a degree in computer science does not prepare students for most jobs in the IT industry.

A common truism in our business states, "If you are out of the IT industry for three years and want to return, you have to start over." The problem, of course, is *timeliness*; if a first-year student learns about a specific computer program, it probably will no longer be in wide use when he or she graduates. Although some colleges are trying to integrate Microsoft Certification into their curriculum, the problem is not really a flaw in higher education, but a characteristic of the IT industry. Computer software is changing so rapidly that a four-year college just can't keep up.

A marked characteristic of the Microsoft Certification program is an emphasis on performing specific job tasks rather than merely gathering knowledge. It may come as a shock, but most potential employers do not care how much you know about the theory of operating systems, networking, or database design. As one IT manager put it, "I don't really care what my employees know about the theory of our network. We don't need someone to sit at a desk and think about it. We need people who can actually do something to make it work better."

You should not think that this attitude is some kind of anti-intellectual revolt against "book learning." Knowledge is a necessary prerequisite, but it is not enough. More than one company has hired a computer science graduate as a network administrator, only to learn that the new employee has no idea how to add users, assign permissions, or perform the other day-to-day tasks necessary to maintain a network. This brings us to the second major characteristic of Microsoft Certification that affects the questions you must be prepared to answer. In addition to timeliness, Microsoft Certification is also job-task oriented.

The timeliness of Microsoft's certification program is obvious and is inherent in the fact that you will be tested on current versions of software in wide use today. The job task orientation of Microsoft Certification is almost as obvious, but testing real-world job skills using a computer-based test is not easy.

## Computerized Testing

Considering the popularity of Microsoft Certification, and the fact that certification candidates are spread around the world, the only practical way to administer tests for the certification program is through Sylvan Prometric or Vue testing centers, which operate internationally. Sylvan Prometric and Vue provide proctor testing services for Microsoft, Oracle, Novell, Lotus, and the A+ computer technician certification. Although the IT industry accounts for much of Sylvan's revenue, the company provides services for a number of other businesses and organizations, such as FAA pre-flight pilot tests. Historically, several hundred questions were developed for a new Microsoft Certification exam. The Windows 2000 MCSE exam pool contains hundreds of new questions. Microsoft is aware that many new MCSE candidates have been able to access information on test questions via the Internet or other resources. The company is very concerned about maintaining the MCSE as a "premium" certification. The significant increase in the number of test questions, together with stronger enforcement of the NDA (Non-Disclosure Agreement) helps ensure that a higher standard for certification is attained.

Microsoft treats the test-building process very seriously. Test questions are first reviewed by a number of subject matter experts for technical accuracy and then are presented in a beta test. Taking the beta test may require several hours, due to the large number of questions. After a few weeks, Microsoft Certification uses the statistical feedback from Sylvan to check the performance of the beta questions. The beta test group for the Windows 2000 certification series included MCTs, MCSEs, and members of Microsoft's rapid deployment partners groups. Because the exams have been normalized based on this population, you can be sure that the passing scores will be difficult to achieve without detailed product knowledge.

Questions are discarded if most test takers get them right (too easy) or wrong (too difficult), and a number of other statistical measures are taken of each question. Although the scope of our discussion precludes a rigorous treatment of question analysis, you should be aware that Microsoft and other vendors spend a great deal of time and effort making sure their exam questions are valid.

The questions that survive statistical analysis form the pool of questions for the final certification exam.

# Test Structure

The questions in a Microsoft form test will not be equally weighted. Essentially different questions are given a value based on the level of difficulty. You will get more credit for getting a difficult question correct than if you got an easy one correct. Because the questions are weighted differently, and because the exams use the adapter method of testing, your score will not bear any relationship to how many questions you answered correctly.

Microsoft has implemented *adaptive* testing. When an adaptive test begins, the candidate is first given a level three question. If it is answered correctly, a question from the next higher level is presented, and an incorrect response results in a question from the next lower level. When 15 to 20 questions have been answered in this manner, the scoring algorithm is able to predict, with a high degree of statistical certainty, whether the candidate would pass or fail if all the questions in the form were answered. When the required degree of certainty is attained, the test ends and the candidate receives a pass/fail grade.

Adaptive testing has some definite advantages for everyone involved in the certification process. Adaptive tests allow Sylvan Prometric or Vue to deliver more tests with the same resources, as certification candidates often are in and out in 30 minutes or less. For candidates, the "fatigue factor" is reduced due to the shortened testing time. For Microsoft, adaptive testing means that fewer test questions are exposed to each candidate, and this can enhance the security, and therefore the overall validity, of certification tests.

One possible problem you may have with adaptive testing is that you are not allowed to mark and revisit questions. Since the adaptive algorithm is interactive, and all questions but the first are selected on the basis of your response to the previous question, it is not possible to skip a particular question or change an answer.

## Question Types

Computerized test questions can be presented in a number of ways. Some of the possible formats are used on Microsoft Certification exams and some are not.

### True/False

We are all familiar with True/False questions, but because of the inherent 50 percent chance of guessing the correct answer, you will not see questions of this type on Microsoft Certification exams.

### Multiple Choice

The majority of Microsoft Certification questions are in the multiple-choice format, with either a single correct answer or multiple correct answers. One interesting variation on multiple-choice questions with multiple correct answers is whether or not the candidate is told how many answers are correct.

> EXAMPLE:
> Which two files can be altered to configure the MS-DOS environment? (Choose two.)
>
> Or
>
> Which files can be altered to configure the MS-DOS environment? (Choose all that apply.)

You may see both variations on Microsoft Certification exams, but the trend seems to be toward the first type, where candidates are told explicitly how many answers are correct. Questions of the "choose all that apply" variety are more difficult and can be merely confusing.

### Graphical Questions

One or more graphical elements are sometimes used as exhibits to help present or clarify an exam question. These elements may take the form of a network diagram, pictures of networking components, or screen shots from the software on which you are being tested. It is often easier to present the concepts required for a complex performance-based scenario with a graphic than with words.

Test questions known as *hotspots* actually incorporate graphics as part of the answer. These questions ask the certification candidate to click on a location or graphical element to answer the question. For example, you might be shown the diagram of a network and asked to click on an appropriate location for a router. The answer is correct if the candidate clicks within the *hotspot* that defines the correct location.

### Free Response Questions

Another kind of question you sometimes see on Microsoft Certification exams requires a *free response* or type-in answer. An example of this type of question might present a TCP/IP network scenario and ask the candidate to calculate and enter the correct subnet mask in dotted decimal notation.

### Simulation Questions

Simulation questions provide a method for Microsoft to test how familiar the test taker is with the actual product interface and the candidate's ability to quickly implement a task using the interface. These questions will present an actual Windows 2000 interface that you must work with to solve a problem or implement a solution. If you are familiar with the product, you will be able to answer these questions quickly, and they will be the easiest questions on the exam. However, if you are not accustomed to working with Windows 2000, these questions will be difficult for you to answer. This is why actual hands-on practice with Windows 2000 is so important!

## Knowledge-Based and Performance-Based Questions

Microsoft Certification develops a blueprint for each Microsoft Certification exam with input from subject matter experts. This blueprint defines the content areas and objectives for each test, and each test question is created to test a specific objective. The basic information from the examination blueprint can be found on Microsoft's Web site in the Exam Prep Guide for each test.

Psychometricians (psychologists who specialize in designing and analyzing tests) categorize test questions as knowledge-based or performance-based. As the names imply, knowledge-based questions are designed to test knowledge, while performance-based questions are designed to test performance.

Some objectives demand a knowledge-based question. For example, objectives that use verbs like *list* and *identify* tend to test only what you know, not what you can do.

EXAMPLE:
*Objective:* Identify the MS-DOS configuration files.
Which two files can be altered to configure the MS-DOS environment? (Choose two.)

A. COMMAND.COM

B. AUTOEXEC.BAT

C. IO.SYS

D. CONFIG.SYS
**Correct answers: B, D.**

Other objectives use action verbs like *install*, *configure*, and *troubleshoot* to define job tasks. These objectives can often be tested with either a knowledge-based question or a performance-based question.

EXAMPLE:
*Objective:* Configure an MS-DOS installation appropriately using the PATH statement in AUTOEXEX.BAT.

*Knowledge-based question:*
What is the correct syntax to set a path to the D: directory in AUTOEXEC.BAT?

A. SET PATH EQUAL TO D:

B. PATH D:

C. SETPATH D:

D. D:EQUALS PATH
**Correct answer: B.**

*Performance-based question:*

Your company uses several DOS accounting applications that access a group of common utility programs. What is the best strategy for configuring the computers in the accounting department so that the accounting applications will always be able to access the utility programs?

A. Store all the utilities on a single floppy disk and make a copy of the disk for each computer in the accounting department.

B. Copy all the utilities to a directory on the C: drive of each computer in the accounting department and add a PATH statement pointing to this directory in the AUTOEXEC.BAT files.

C. Copy all the utilities to all application directories on each computer in the accounting department.

D. Place all the utilities in the C: directory on each computer, because the C: directory is automatically included in the PATH statement when AUTOEXEC.BAT is executed.
**Correct answer: B.**

Even in this simple example, the superiority of the performance-based question is obvious. Whereas the knowledge-based question asks for a single fact, the performance-based question presents a real-life situation and requires that you make a decision based on this scenario. Thus, performance-based questions give more bang (validity) for the test author's buck (individual question).

# Testing Job Performance

We have said that Microsoft Certification focuses on timeliness and the ability to perform job tasks. We have also introduced the concept of performance-based questions, but even performance-based multiple-choice questions do not really measure performance. Another strategy is needed to test job skills.

Given unlimited resources, it is not difficult to test job skills. In an ideal world, Microsoft would fly MCP candidates to Redmond, place them in a controlled environment with a team of experts, and ask them to plan, install, maintain, and troubleshoot a Windows network. In a few days at most, the experts could reach a valid decision as to whether each candidate should or should not be granted MCDBA or MCSE status. Needless to say, this is not likely to happen.

Closer to reality, another way to test performance is by using the actual software and creating a testing program to present tasks and automatically grade a candidate's performance when the tasks are completed. This *cooperative* approach would be practical in some testing situations, but the same test that is presented to MCP candidates in Boston must also be available in Bahrain and Botswana. The most workable solution for measuring performance in today's testing environment is a *simulation* program. When the program is launched during a test, the candidate sees a simulation of the actual software that looks, and behaves, just like the real thing. When the testing software presents a task, the simulation program is launched and the candidate performs the required task. The testing software then grades the candidate's performance on the required task and moves to the next question. Microsoft has introduced simulation questions on the certification exam for Internet Information Server 4.0. Simulation questions provide many advantages over other testing methodologies, and simulations are expected to become increasingly important in the Microsoft Certification program. For example, studies have shown that there is a very high correlation between the ability to perform simulated tasks on a computer-based test and the ability to perform the actual job tasks. Thus, simulations enhance the validity of the certification process.

Another truly wonderful benefit of simulations is in the area of test security. It is just not possible to cheat on a simulation question. In fact, you will be told exactly what tasks you are expected to perform on the test. How can a certification candidate cheat? By learning to perform the tasks? What a concept!

## Study Strategies

There are appropriate ways to study for the different types of questions you will see on a Microsoft Certification exam.

### Knowledge-Based Questions

Knowledge-based questions require that you memorize facts. There are hundreds of facts inherent in every content area of every Microsoft Certification exam. There are several keys to memorizing facts:

- **Repetition** The more times your brain is exposed to a fact, the more likely you are to remember it.
- **Association** Connecting facts within a logical framework makes them easier to remember.
- **Motor Association** It is often easier to remember something if you write it down or perform some other physical act, like clicking on a practice test answer.

We have said that the emphasis of Microsoft Certification is job performance, and that there are very few knowledge-based questions on Microsoft Certification exams. Why should you waste a lot of time learning filenames, IP address formulas, and other minutiae? Read on.

### Performance-Based Questions

Most of the questions you will face on a Microsoft Certification exam are performance-based scenario questions. We have discussed the superiority of these questions over simple knowledge-based questions, but you should remember that the job task orientation of Microsoft Certification extends the knowledge you need to pass the exams; it does not replace this knowledge. Therefore, the first step in preparing for scenario questions is to absorb as many facts relating to the exam content areas as you can. In other words, go back to the previous section and follow the steps to prepare for an exam composed of knowledge-based questions.

The second step is to familiarize yourself with the format of the questions you are likely to see on the exam. You can do this by answering the questions in this study guide, by using Microsoft assessment tests, or by using practice tests on the included CD-ROM. The day of your test is not the time to be surprised by the construction of Microsoft exam questions.

At best, performance-based scenario questions really do test certification candidates at a higher cognitive level than knowledge-based questions. At worst, these questions can test your reading comprehension and test-taking ability rather than your ability to use Microsoft products. Be sure to get in the habit of reading the question carefully to determine what is being asked.

The third step in preparing for Microsoft scenario questions is to adopt the following attitude: Multiple-choice questions aren't really performance-based. It is all a cruel lie. These scenario questions are just knowledge-based questions with a story wrapped around them.

To answer a scenario question, you have to sift through the story to the underlying facts of the situation and apply your knowledge to determine the correct answer. This may sound silly at first, but the process we go through in solving real-life problems is quite similar. The key concept is that every scenario question (and every real-life problem) has a fact at its center, and if we can identify that fact, we can answer the question.

### Simulations

Simulation questions really do measure your ability to perform job tasks. You must be able to perform the specified tasks. There are two ways to prepare for simulation questions:

1. Get experience with the actual software. If you have the resources, this is a great way to prepare for simulation questions.
2. Use official Microsoft practice tests. Practice tests are available that provide practice with the same simulation engine used on Microsoft Certification exams. This approach has the added advantage of grading your efforts.

## Signing Up

Signing up to take a Microsoft Certification exam is easy. Sylvan Prometric or Vue operators in each country can schedule tests at any testing center. There are, however, a few things you should know:

1. If you call Sylvan Prometric or Vue during a busy time, get a cup of coffee first, because you may be in for a long wait. The exam providers do an excellent job, but everyone in the world seems to want to sign up for a test on Monday morning.
2. You will need your social security number or some other unique identifier to sign up for a test, so have it at hand.
3. Pay for your test by credit card if at all possible. This makes things easier, and you can even schedule tests for the same day you call, if space is available at your local testing center.
4. Know the number and title of the test you want to take before you call. This is not essential, and the Sylvan operators will help you if they can. Having this information in advance, however, speeds up and improves the accuracy of the registration process.

# Taking the Test

Teachers have always told you not to try to cram for exams because it does no good. If you are faced with a knowledge-based test requiring only that you regurgitate facts, cramming can mean the difference between passing and failing. This is not the case, however, with Microsoft Certification exams. If you don't know it the night before, don't bother to stay up and cram.

Instead, create a schedule and stick to it. Plan your study time carefully, and do not schedule your test until you think you are ready to succeed. Follow these guidelines on the day of your exam:

1. Get a good night's sleep. The scenario questions you will face on a Microsoft Certification exam require a clear head.
2. Remember to take two forms of identification—at least one with a picture. A driver's license with your picture and social security or credit card is acceptable.
3. Leave home in time to arrive at your testing center a few minutes early. It is not a good idea to feel rushed as you begin your exam.
4. Do not spend too much time on any one question. You cannot mark and revisit questions on an adaptive test, so you must do your best on each question as you go.
5. If you do not know the answer to a question, try to eliminate the obviously wrong answers and guess from the rest. If you can eliminate two out of four options, you have a 50 percent chance of guessing the correct answer.
6. For scenario questions, follow the steps we outlined earlier. Read the question carefully and try to identify the facts at the center of the story.

Finally, we would advise anyone attempting to earn Microsoft MCDBA and MCSE certification to adopt a philosophical attitude. The Windows 2000 MCSE will be the most difficult MCSE ever to be offered. The questions are at a higher cognitive level than seen on all previous MCSE exams. Therefore, even if you are the kind of person who never fails a test, you are likely to fail at least one Windows 2000 certification test somewhere along the way. Do not get discouraged. Microsoft wants to ensure the value of your certification. Moreover, it will attempt to so by keeping the standard as high as possible. If Microsoft Certification were easy to obtain, more people would have it, and it would not be so respected and so valuable to your future in the IT industry.

MCSE

MICROSOFT CERTIFIED SYSTEMS ENGINEER

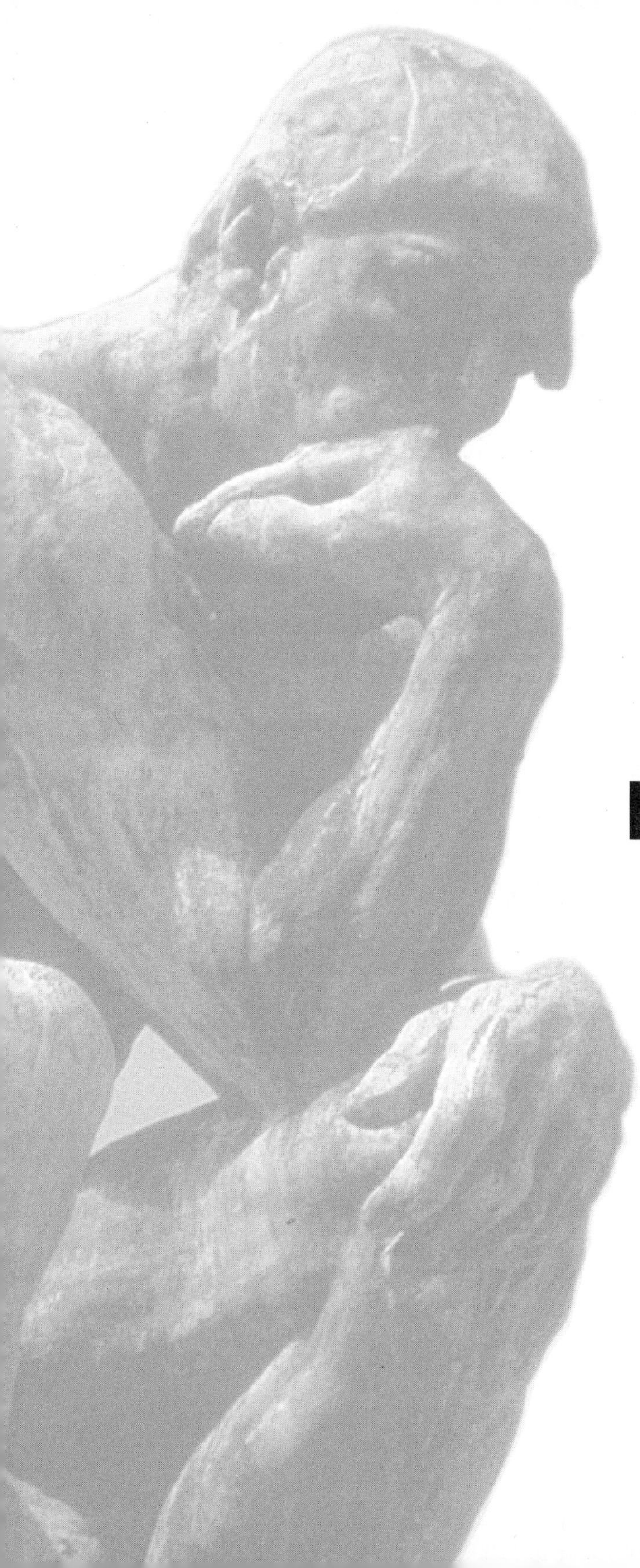

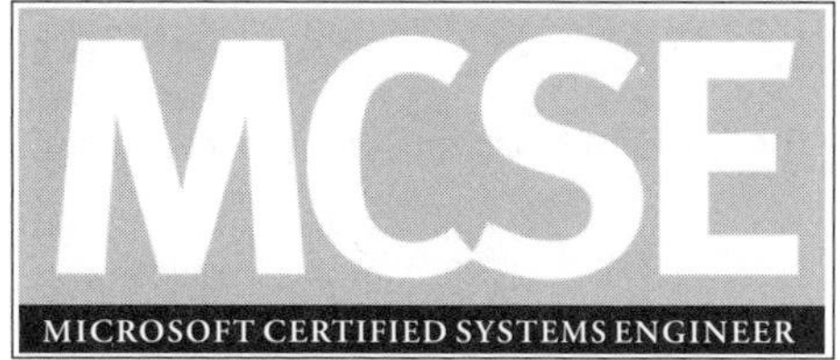

# 1

# Introduction to Designing Windows 2000 Web Solutions

## CERTIFICATION OBJECTIVES

1.01 What is Designing Windows 2000 Web Solutions?

1.02 Overview of Exam 70-226

1.03 What We'll Cover in This Book

1.04 Windows 2000 Server and Web Solutions Terminology

✓ Two-Minute Drill

Q&A Self Test

Welcome to the study guide for Exam 70-226, Designing Windows 2000 Web Solutions. This exam marks a change in the infrastructure technology workplace. More network administrators are building and managing Web servers than ever before. With this exam, Microsoft officially recognizes the need for Microsoft Certified Systems Engineers (MCSEs) capable of designing and establishing Web solutions based on its cornerstone server technology: Windows 2000.

Businesses are investing more resources in Web solutions to remain competitive as well as keep up with their clients' demand for Internet services. In order to get the most returns on their investments, these organizations must use cost-efficient solutions that are available when Internet users need them and can grow as demand for Web services increases.

Organizations that do business on the Internet are learning that high availability of their Web sites keeps visitors coming back. On the Internet, even a minor delay in a site's performance can cost a company customers. A solid Web solution design can ensure that an organization's needs are met in the critical areas of scalability, manageability, and availability.

**CERTIFICATION OBJECTIVE 1.01**

# What is Designing Windows 2000 Web Solutions?

Microsoft built Windows 2000 Server for the Internet, recognizing that many businesses today are adapting to the opportunities—and the challenges—involved with doing business on the Internet. Organizations have found different ways of using the Internet to reduce their costs or increase the bottom line, so every Web solution tends to be unique to the business that develops it. As Web solutions become increasingly varied and complex, so do the skills required to design and maintain them. For this reason, designing highly available Web solutions with Microsoft Windows 2000 Server technologies is an essential skill.

Some of the Web solutions that companies are implementing include:

- Virtual private networking (VPN) for secure intranet and extranet communications

- E-commerce solutions
- Business-to-business (B2B) applications to gain efficiencies between two or more organizations
- Business-to-consumer (B2C) applications to provide individual customers services and/or products via the Internet
- Informational or educational material distribution to the public

In order to provide these types of Web solutions, Windows 2000 supports emerging technologies such as Extensible Markup Language (XML), streaming media, and Internet Protocol Security (IPSec). In order to support a highly performing, available, and scalable Web solution, Windows 2000 also supports Symmetric Multiprocessing (SMP), network load balancing (NLB), cluster services, and Redundant Array of Inexpensive Disks (RAID). These technologies enable you to scale up a server. Web sites can also be scaled out by using multiple servers to provide a single Web solution designed in *n*-tier fashion, as shown in Figure 1-1. The value of scaling out, rather than scaling up, is that a single server cannot become a single point of failure.

Windows 2000 Server is delivered in three versions: Windows 2000 Server, Windows 2000 Advanced Server, and Windows 2000 Datacenter Server. Each version of the operating system supports increasingly scalable server platforms. The maximum supported components for each version are detailed in Table 1-1.

**TABLE 1-1** Windows 2000 Supports a Variety of Scalable Hardware

| | Server | Advanced Server | DataCenter Server |
|---|---|---|---|
| CPU | 4 processors | 8 processors | 16 processors<br>32 processors for OEMs |
| RAM | 4GB | 8GB | 64GB |
| Clusters | Not supported | 2 nodes | 4 nodes |

FIGURE 1-1 Scaling Up or Scaling Out

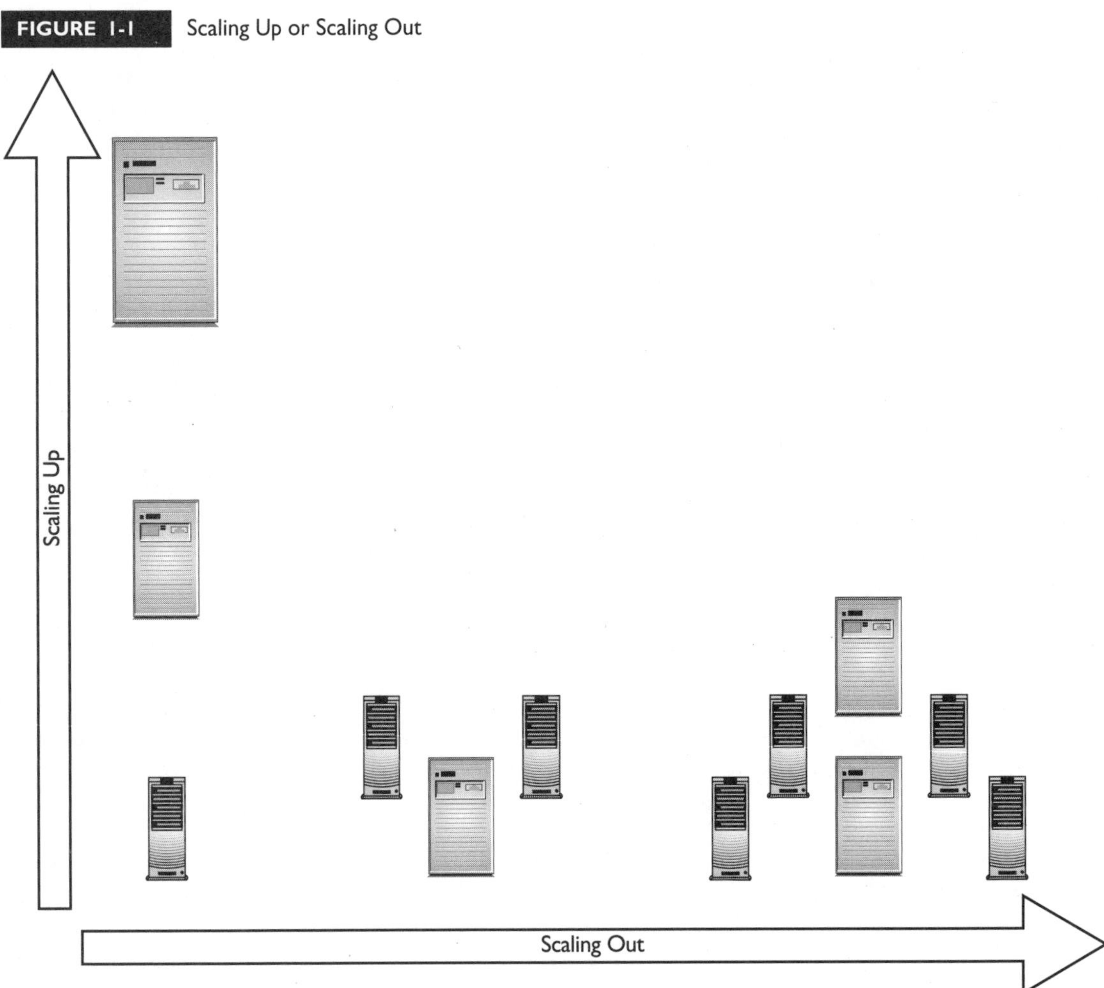


## EXERCISE 1-1

### Determining the Correct Windows 2000 Server Version

Your Web solution design will consist of the following:

- Server 1: A single processor, 2GB RAM, not clustered
- Server 2: Dual processors, 6GB RAM, a two-node cluster

- Server 3: Dual processors, 6GB RAM, not clustered
- Server 4: Sixteen processors, 8GB RAM, a two-node cluster

Here are the steps to follow to determine the correct version of Windows 2000:

1. You must determine the version of Windows 2000 you need to install on each platform.
2. Referring to Table 1.1, look at the processor requirements for each server. The table reveals that Server 4 must be DataCenter Server.
3. Referring to Table 1.1, look at the RAM requirements for Servers 1, 2, and 3. The table reveals that Servers 2 and 3 must both be Advanced Server.
4. Referring to Table 1.1, look at the cluster requirements for Server 1. The table reveals that Server 1 can be installed with Windows 2000 Server.

---

For any data traveling across the Internet, the main concern for an organization is the security of that data. Not only do organizations need to protect data from corruption; they also need to prevent malicious attacks on their production networks and their confidential data. Since the Internet is universally accessible, there is no practical way to keep hackers but not customers or suppliers away from the Internet. This leaves network designers with the monumental task of putting content on the Internet, enabling access to data for authorized users, and keeping that content and that data safe from tampering.

Windows 2000 was developed with a number of security capabilities that are geared to maintaining secure communications on the Internet. These capabilities include:

- Certificate services to enable use of digital "keys" for secured data access
- Smart cards for physical security elements
- IPSec for securing data as it is transmitted
- Encrypting File System (EFS) for securing data stored on a hard disk
- Kerberos for authenticating users

exam Watch

***The name* Kerberos *is derived from the three-headed dog that guarded the gates of Hades in Greek mythology. As this name implies, Kerberos is very secure and is integral to Windows 2000 Active Directory, including both Active Directory authentication and interdomain trusts. Kerberos is not used for trusts between forests or between Active Directory domains and Windows NT domains.***

Now that you've seen a little information about the security features that Windows 2000 supports, the following are a few scenarios for their use.

| SCENARIO & SOLUTION | |
|---|---|
| You need to use a digital key for data access. What feature in Windows 2000 Server can you install to provide this key? | You can install Certificate Services to provide digital keys to your users for data access. |
| Your company is purchasing a security system. The president wants to integrate the new system with the network. What type of feature can be used with Windows 2000 Active Directory to verify a user's identity? | Smart cards can be used with Windows 2000 Active Directory to verify a user's identity. |
| Your company loses 100 laptops per year. You want to ensure that certain data files on the laptops' hard drives cannot be read by someone who comes across or steals one of these laptops. What can you use? | You can install laptops with Windows 2000 Professional and train end users to encrypt the data using the Encrypting File System. |

One of the attractive features of using Microsoft Windows 2000 Server to build a Web solution is that the platform is enterprise-capable. An organization can use Windows 2000 servers for file and print services, application services, and database services as easily as for Web services. This all-around capability enables Windows 2000 Web solutions to leverage any data or application that exists on a Windows 2000-based production network. Not only that, but when an organization uses Windows 2000 Server across all areas of the network, the organization does not require additional administrative skill sets.

Regardless of how many different network operating systems exist on a production network, the key to developing a successful Web solution lies in a single best practice: Design to meet the business requirements. Typically, the main requirements for a Web solution are scalability, high performance, reliability, security, and manageability. If each of these five requirements is met, the Web solution will be highly available.

## FROM THE CLASSROOM

### Tips for Designing Highly Available Web Solutions

Highly available Web solutions are only as available as the hardware they rely on. If that hardware has fails, the Web solution fails. If the hardware is redundant and fails, the Web solution continues to be available. Two features within Windows 2000 Server can contribute to underlying redundant hardware and should always be considered when you develop your design: network load balancing and clustering.

You can increase the performance of a Web solution using two or three tiers of servers. Front-end servers provide Web services via Internet Information Services (IIS). Back-end servers provide data services via SQL Server. You can add a middle tier for Component Object Model (COM+) application services.

A failure in a Web solution can be fatal to business, especially when the Web site *is* the business. In Windows 2000 Server, you can use Performance Monitor to keep tabs on the Web servers.

Scaling up has an upper limit. In addition, as you scale up, you still only have a single server that becomes a single point of failure. Scaling out by adding multiple servers to provide a single Web solution is more desirable.

Test your designs in a lab before putting them into production. A paper design, even one created using network modeling software, is a theory. The actual implementation of that theory in the lab will prove that the design will work or will expose areas for improvement.

A Web site application drives design requirements. The network itself is intended to facilitate the application. If you cannot support the application's requirements, the design will not fulfill its purpose.

Practical, hands-on experience plus theoretical understanding of IP networking are the two fundamental areas of knowledge for a Web site designer. Always design to meet business requirements. There is little likelihood that you can design a network that is everything to everyone. You'll need to make trade-offs in which you need to decide whether to change the implementation dates, the cost of the project, or some factor in the Web site's performance. When you reach a point where a trade-off must occur, refer to the business's requirements, and your design will be successful.

*—Melissa Craft, MCSE, MCNE, CCNA, CCA, Net+*

CERTIFICATION OBJECTIVE 1.02

## Overview of Exam 70-226

Exam 70-226 tests you on the skills required to design highly available Web solutions with Windows 2000 Server. This test takes on a different format compared with the traditional MCSE exams. This exam's questions are based on case studies in order to test your performance capabilities. Case study-based exams more accurately reproduce the scenarios that you will encounter on the job.

The exam presents you with a case study of a hypothetical organization that has a set of business requirements and technical specifications. The case study is followed by a series of questions that build on each other to test your knowledge of design, specifically when presented with companies that have similar business and technical requirements. The test then presents a second case study of a different organization with another set of business and technical specifications, another series of questions, and so on. You don't need to worry about confusing one case study with another, because you can access the case study from each question and refer to it to validate your answers before going forward. Once you have completed all the questions for one case study, you might not be able to return to that case study if you have moved on to the next.

exam Watch

***Always refer to the case study for details before you complete a question and move on to the next one.***

The exam is so different from other Microsoft exams that you should download a demo from

www.microsoft.com/trainingandservices/default.asp?PageID=mcp&PageCall=tesinn&SubSite=examinfo

and run through a practice test before you take the actual test at a testing center. Unlike the standard exams, the case study-based tests do not include tutorials, so you will not be able to run through a tutorial at the testing center.

You should consider taking this exam if you are planning to attain your MCSE, work in medium-sized to large networks with Web solutions based on Windows 2000, and have at least two years of experience in designing Web solutions. Exam

70-226 does grant you credit toward the MCSE certification, in either the core or the elective portions. If this is the only test that you take and pass from Microsoft, you will achieve the Microsoft Certified Professional (MCP) certification.

Exam 70-226 measures your design skills for the following components of a Web solution:

- Cluster solutions, including network load balancing and component load balancing
- Data storage
- System management and monitoring
- Disaster recovery
- Network infrastructure, Transmission Control Protocol/Internet Protocol (TCP/IP), and server configurations
- End to end bandwidth requirements, especially when considering an *n*-tier environment
- Network, server, and cluster capacity
- Upgrade strategies for servers and clusters
- Directory services
- Security, including authentication, encryption, and firewalls
- Exchange Server messaging for Web integration
- Database for Web integration
- Content and application topology, including application management and monitoring

All these skills can be used for designing a highly available Web site. The advantage of a highly available Web site is that it retains Internet users. When users find that a site does not delay them from getting the information they're interested in, they are more likely to return to that site. Of course, the Internet is an unforgiving place—a 30-second delay can result in loss of Internet users. Good design techniques can ensure that your Web site is available. In addition, you will find that the network will be predictably consistent in its performance and fault tolerance. Mission-critical Web sites require zero downtime, and ideally, your design will achieve zero downtime for the Web site, even if individual servers are down periodically for maintenance or other reasons.

Another benefit of good design is the scalability of the Web site. You should be able to grow a Web site to meet end users' demands, especially during peak usage periods. For example, an e-commerce Web site might need to scale up during the holidays and return to scale for regular use at other times. By contrast, a services Web site that grows only as usage increases needs to scale up to meet performance demands. Designs for scalability need to take into account the bandwidth requirements as well as the transaction costs of the Web site applications. A good design will not need fundamental changes made to the network topology when growth occurs but will be flexible enough to add server components, additional servers and storage, or increased bandwidth to the Internet as needed.

on the Job

***Building some growing room into your Web solution is usually a good idea. To do this, you first buy a large server platform—one that is capable of supporting multiple processors, multiple storage systems, multiple network interface cards, and the like. Then you put only the components into the server platform that will suffice for your needs over the next few months. If your Web solution is successful and you need to scale up the server, you can purchase more RAM, more processors, or more storage as you need. These components are more easily absorbed into your budget than purchasing an entirely new server.***

Finally, a good Web site design can stabilize administrative overhead costs. Wide area network (WAN) costs, remote access costs, downtime costs, and support costs can all be minimized, depending on the Web site design. For example, you might need fault tolerance for an Internet connection, but a design that selects two links that are identical in bandwidth will not maximize the investment in those links. A design that selects a lower-bandwidth backup circuit for use only to ensure resilience of the network to remain connected to the Internet for short periods of time can be more cost effective. Not all designs are developed for stabilizing costs. If a company required high performance of its Web site as a priority, the design would be best configured with two identical Internet links.

Now that you have an idea of the benefits of design techniques, here are some scenarios that can help you identify them.

## SCENARIO & SOLUTION

| | |
|---|---|
| Your new Webmaster designs a multimedia flash page that takes 40 seconds to load and run before people can reach the home page. It looks very cool. Should you keep it or remove it? | You should remove the multimedia element that would cause such a delay. Users might find it looks cool, but they probably won't wait long enough for it to load. |
| You are given the task of creating a Web solution that is always available, but your boss wants you to keep costs low. What can you do? | You can invest in an Internet connection with a slower backup link so that the main expenditure is in the link that is used daily, not the one that is mostly used on failure of the first link. |

## EXERCISE 1-2

### Establishing Design Needs

Company A has a mission-critical application that is currently accessed by customer businesses via remote access phone lines. The application produces more than $12,000 per hour in income for Company A and is used 24 hours, seven days a week, 365 days per year. Company A wants to implement a VPN solution and remove the remote access phone lines. Your job is to determine whether the following needs are met by a particular design:

- Reduce costs by removing phone lines.
- Ensure continuous uptime for the application.
- Ensure availability of Internet connections.

You produce a design that removes all but four of the phone lines, retaining those as backup links in case the Internet connections fail. You include two Internet connections so that if one fails the other can still function. You design a single server with no redundant features to house the application. Did you meet all three design objectives?

1. Look at the detsign to see if you have reduced costs by removing phone lines. You will see that you have done so.

2. Look through the design to see if you have ensured continuous uptime for the application. Because your application will be placed on a single server with no redundant features, the answer is no, you have not.
3. Look at the design to see if you have ensured availability of the Internet connections. Because you have two Internet links, you have done so.

---

You can register for Exam 70-226 through Sylvan Prometric (www.2test.com) or VUE. During the registration, you will select a testing center where you will take the exam. On the date that you take the exam, you should bring to the testing center two pieces of identification, at least one of them with a photograph, so that your identity can be validated. You will also be required to accept a nondisclosure agreement. If you refuse to accept the agreement, you will not be allowed to take the exam.

**CERTIFICATION OBJECTIVE 1.03**

## What We'll Cover in This Book

This book will provide you with the information and skills that you need to design a network infrastructure to support Web solutions. Each chapter provides a key skill area that builds on the preceding skill area. Since Web solutions vary according to business requirements, the types of Web solutions you develop will incorporate a variety of elements. For example, you could design a Web solution with Exchange Server 2000 to meet one set of business requirements for electronic messaging. However, for another set of business requirements, you could design a Web solution with SQL Server 2000. As you read through each chapter in this book, you will be introduced to design skills and concepts that you can use to build a solution based on an organization's needs.

When you have completed this book, you will be able to:

- Describe the attributes used to define a network services design using Windows 2000 networking services.

- Identify the fundamental TCP/IP functions required by a solution and use them to establish security, availability, and performance.
- Strategize for efficient data transmission.
- Use Dynamic Host Configuration Protocol (DHCP) and Domain Name System (DNS) and optimize their design for performance.
- Connect to the Internet using Network Address Translation (NAT).
- Design an extranet using IPSec, Layer 2 Tunneling Protocol (L2TP), or Point-to-Point Tunneling Protocol (PPTP).
- Design a remote access solution using Windows 2000 Server services.
- Develop a network management strategy.
- Analyze and create solutions for e-commerce, distributed sales organizations, virtual offices, and Internet service providers (ISPs).

Building a highly available Web site requires more than just a network operating system. It requires applications and services that will work together to provide Web services to Internet users. Depending on an organization's needs, a Windows 2000-based Web site will consist of a combination of the products listed in Table 1-2. We will mention these products in cases where they are required for a Windows 2000-based Web site, but they do not comprise a majority of what you will need to know for this exam.

## Chapter 2 Overview

Chapter 2 focuses on the server platform aspect of a Web solution. In this chapter, we discuss the basics of Network Load Balancing (NLB), which is incorporated into the Windows 2000 Server operating system. NLB can be used in a Web solution to improve availability as well as scalability and fault tolerance. NLB is a form of clustering in which client connections are distributed across multiple servers. A *cluster* is a set of two or more servers that can provide the same service. Generally, clusters require shared data storage and direct connectivity between the servers. (This rule is excepted by the case of a software cluster such as that provided by Application Server 2000.) In failover clustering, client connections are only provided by a primary server in the cluster. If the primary server fails, the secondary server detects the failure and takes over the primary server's tasks.

**TABLE 1-2** Applications Used in Building a Highly Available Web Solution

| Product | Solution Use | Function |
|---|---|---|
| Application Center 2000 | Scalability of multiple servers to increase availability | Deployment and management tool for high-availability Web applications built on Windows 2000 Server |
| BizTalk Server 2000 | Interoperability and security of services | Business process tool to develop secure, reliable B2B applications and e-commerce applications using XML and EDI |
| Commerce Server 2000 | Performance via a Web site development kit | Application framework to build e-commerce solutions |
| Host Integration Server 2000 | Scalable connectivity to enterprise hosts | Gateway between enterprise hosts, such as mainframes and minicomputers, and other network systems |
| Internet Security and Acceleration (ISA) Server 2000 | Manageable and secure Internet connectivity | Firewall and high-performance Web cache to build a secure connection between a production network and the Internet |
| Mobile Information 2001 Server | Extensibility of Web solution to mobile devices | Application server for Web solutions in order to enable mobile device accessibility. |
| SQL Server 2000 | Data storage | Database server for data storage and analysis |
| Exchange Server 2000 | Electronic messaging | Provides a reliable, scalable, and high-performance messaging and collaboration platform |

From a user's perspective, a cluster appears to be a single logical server or single Web site address. However, NLB maintains individual names for each member of the cluster so that the load can be dynamically redistributed as changes are made to the cluster. This takes into account the addition of new cluster members to handle spikes in traffic as well as NLB's automatic detection of a failed cluster member.

**exam Watch**

***Users see a cluster using NLB as though it were a single server. They only need to know a single IP address and/or hostname in order to access the resources provided by the cluster.***

In addition to teaching how to design a Web solution using clusters and NLB, this chapter reviews various types of data storage. Data storage is important to a Web solution's design. You will learn design concepts surrounding RAID and Storage-Area Networks (SANs). Depending on the type of data storage you select, you can increase your solution's reliability, availability, and performance.

## Chapter 3 Overview

Chapter 3 focuses on designs for server topology and network management. Designing a network management system requires that you have a disaster recovery strategy, which can change depending on your server topology. These topics are interdependent in your design.

Starting with the server topology, you will learn how to design servers so that they can either scale up or scale out, according to the Web site's needs. The placement of the servers across the network can ensure the Web site's availability. Redundancy in the server topology will provide fault tolerance as well as scalability by design.

Once the servers have been implemented, you can begin monitoring them. However, you should plan to monitor and audit events that will make sense for your network. For instance, if you want to ensure security of your Web servers, you should audit the servers for those events in which a person gains access to a resource that should remain secure.

on the job

***Be sure to put audits of events only where they are necessary to be reviewed and investigated. A network administrator I knew decided that he needed to see evidence of every logon and network resource access, even if it was an authorized one. The security logs on his servers filled up quickly, and then, because he had configured the logs so that they would not overwrite old data, they filled up the free space on the drive and stopped the servers, one by one.***

Monitoring your network can prevent some types of disasters. For example, monitoring for performance of the Web site can indicate increasing faults in a component that can be replaced before the server fails completely. Some disasters are not preventable but can be corrected by a well-designed disaster recovery plan. Given that businesses depend on Web servers for income, the recovery of those servers is extremely important in case of disaster.

## Chapter 4 Overview

In Chapter 4, you learn how to design a highly available network topology and plan the server configurations. A good network topology design ensures that your Web site is available. You will learn when to design redundant links and determine bandwidth requirements.

When determining the server configuration, you will design server components to ensure high availability. You can use redundant server components such as these:

- Processors
- Power supplies
- Network interface cards
- Cooling fans

Redundant components can be used to increase a server's capacity. For example, the load of network traffic can be distributed across multiple network interface cards, all connected to the same network segment. Redundant components can also be used to provide fault tolerance such that a component is not used until the primary component has failed.

Let's look at some scenarios for using redundant components.

| SCENARIO & SOLUTION | |
|---|---|
| You have had three hard disks go bad in the past couple of years. If a hard disk goes bad on your Web server, it will cause a loss of productivity for the company. What can you use to reduce this risk? | You can use a RAID array in which a single disk failure will not interrupt the server's ongoing operations. |
| Your server does not start. You find that the power supply has failed. What can you do to stop this from happening in the future? | You can install dual power supplies in your servers. |
| Your network interface card is reaching 100 percent utilization, but the server's processor and memory are only 30 percent utilized. What can you do to increase the server's performance? | You can install a second network interface card on the same network segment, then configure it to share the load of network traffic. |

## Chapter 5 Overview

To communicate on the Internet, you must use Transmission Control Protocol/Internet Protocol (TCP/IP); to translate between computer names and IP addresses, you should use the Domain Name System (DNS). Dynamic Host Configuration Protocol (DHCP) can reduce administrative overhead of those IP addresses as well. Each of these Internet protocols and services is described within Chapter 5 so that you can learn how to design a TCP/IP infrastructure.

TCP/IP is a comprehensive suite of protocols and services. These protocols and services enable communication between computers on an internetwork, such as downloading a Web page via HyperText Transfer Protocol (HTTP) or copying a file via File Transfer Protocol (FTP). Electronic messaging in the TCP/IP suite can use Simple Mail Transfer Protocol (SMTP), Post Office Protocol 3 (POP3), or others.

When you design a TCP/IP network infrastructure, it is imperative that you work to meet your design objectives. You need to identify performance parameters and obtain the Web site application's requirements to put those design objectives into action. For example, if you are designing a Web site that will connect both to the Internet and to a network that uses other protocol suites, you should define whether your Web site can be segmented away from the other protocols so that bandwidth to and from the Web site is based on pure TCP/IP. If the Web site application is particularly bandwidth intensive—for instance, as a video application would be—you should definitely segment the Web site traffic away from the other protocol traffic.

**exam Watch**

***A TCP/IP infrastructure includes DNS servers, DHCP servers, and servers that provide Web services via HTTP.***

## Chapter 6 Overview

Chapter 6 will help you determine the optimal size for your design components. Sizing is a skill that requires an understanding of growth. Not only must you design for today's capacity needs—you must plan for tomorrow's needs as well.

*Capacity* refers to the number of users or transactions that can be supported. When the number of transactions is larger for one component than for another, a bottleneck is created.

## EXERCISE 1-3

### Calculating Capacity

Your dual-processor server can handle 100 transactions per second if it has 2GB of RAM. You have only 1GB of RAM, and the server can support only 50 transactions per second. You should determine what your bottleneck is—whether it is a factor for a Web application that demands only 30 transactions per second or whether it is a factor for a Web application that grows to 80 transactions per second after six months.

1. You have a dual-processor machine that can handle 100 transactions per second for your particular Web site application, but you have only enough memory to support 50 transactions per second. The memory is the bottleneck.
2. If the Web site application never reaches 50 transactions per second due to user demand, the bottleneck doesn't matter.
3. However, if you estimate that you will grow to 80 transactions per second during the first six months of usage, you should increase the server's capacity by adding more memory.

Per-server capacity is not the only concern that you will deal with in Web site designs, however. You will likely develop multiserver Web sites. Not only will multiple servers provide resilience for your Web site, but you will have a much larger amount of capacity to deal with. As the number of servers scale out in clusters that are dedicated to various tiers for your application, you can realize a huge capacity for users and their transactions.

In this chapter, you will learn how to calculate the capacity needs for your network bandwidth and Internet connections. You will also learn how to size these components of a server:

- Memory
- Processor
- Cluster size
- Storage needs

## Chapter 7 Overview

For this exam, Microsoft Web solutions are placed on Windows 2000 servers. Doing so requires a thorough understanding of the Windows 2000 operating system, Active Directory, infrastructure upgrade needs, and methods of upgrading from Windows NT. Chapter 7 is dedicated to the upgrade and design of the Windows 2000 operating system and directory service.

When you upgrade the infrastructure to support the Web application, you will likely upgrade services on Windows NT Servers. For example, if you are upgrading a Windows NT Server that runs DNS, you need to plan a DNS upgrade. This can be tricky, considering that Windows 2000 Active Directory requires DNS features that are not available on Windows NT DNS. In some cases, you might have a Windows NT Server that is running routing or remote access services or that is working in a cluster. These services might not need to be upgraded only due to connectivity changes but also to work under the Windows 2000 operating system.

**exam Watch**

***Windows 2000 Active Directory requires Service Resource Records (SRV RRs), a DNS feature that is not available in Windows NT DNS. If you are using a version of DNS that does not support SRV RRs, you need to plan and execute a DNS upgrade first in order to install Windows 2000 Active Directory.***

Active Directory services provide the basis for authentication on a global scale for Windows 2000. Active Directory uses DNS as the organizational basis for domains. It also uses DNS for locating domain controllers. This requires a DNS design.

The organization of Active Directory begins with designing at least one or more forests. Each forest plan has a separate domain design. Each forest also requires its own site plan. The final design will be of organizational units, security, and policies. You will learn how to put together a complex directory service design and to integrate it with your Web application.

## Chapter 8 Overview

Security is of critical importance for any system that is connected to the Internet. Web applications are, by nature, Internet connected and therefore require a focus on security. Chapter 8 provides you with the skills needed to plan security for your Web site application.

There are several areas of security that you will need to examine and design for a Web site:

- **Authentication** How will people log on to the Web site? Where will their authentication information be stored? How will people register to become authenticated users?
- **Authorization** What information will be available to the public? What information will be available only to authenticated users? How will users be authorized to access information?
- **Encryption** What information is too sensitive to send over the Internet as plain text? How will you encrypt that information? How will users decrypt that information? Is there a need for a VPN?
- **Firewalls** What information should be prohibited from being sent over the Internet? What type of firewall can prevent that information from being accessed across the Internet?
- **Audits** How will you ensure that the security of your network is functioning? How often should you audit your security to ensure that it is protecting data?

You will learn how to use the Active Directory for your authentication method and when to use anonymous authentication so that information is available publicly. You will discover how to apply rights to groups so that the member users of those groups are authorized to access information.

When you learn about encryption and firewalls, you will start looking at the protocols that travel across the Internet. You will learn how to apply IPSec and when to use the Secure Socket Layer (SSL) to encrypt and secure data. You will learn how to filter out specific TCP and User Datagram Protocol (UDP) ports in a firewall scheme. You will also learn how to audit your security plan to ensure that it is performing well.

## Chapter 9 Overview

Messaging, data, and applications are the technical drivers for Web site development. People access the Internet not only to download information in the form of hypertext but also to communicate with other people, purchase products and services, access entertainment in various multimedia formats, and use both personal and business applications. When you design a Web site with Windows 2000, you should consider the integration of that Web site with these other applications.

For example, most Web sites—even those created solely to provide information—include a "Contact" page. This page typically includes addresses, phone numbers, and e-mail addresses. In some cases, Web site designers provide an HTML form through which the Internet user can create and send an e-mail to the Webmaster or other contact person. This form links directly to an electronic messaging system such as Exchange Server 2000. This is not the only way that Exchange Server 2000 can integrate with a Web site application, however. Exchange Server 2000 now provides a Web storage system and supports workflow applications natively. With these capabilities on top of its rich messaging resources, Exchange Server 2000 can be fully integrated in a Web site application. This chapter prepares you for the design needs of such an application.

**on the Job**

***One research company I worked with had scientists located all over the world in remote locations. They used the Internet to connect and had a VPN to ensure data privacy. However, they encountered a great many problems managing day-to-day business tasks such as hiring, approving vacations, and submitting expenses. The successful solution used Exchange Server 2000 and Outlook Web Access, implementing a workflow application that could be viewed through a browser window. It reduced the company's administrative overhead 20 percent.***

Chapter 9 also prepares you to design database services and applications into your Web site. Data can be stored in an organized database such as Microsoft SQL Server 2000. You need to store a variety of types of information, depending on the type of Web site application. For example, an e-commerce site needs to store information about users' purchases.

## Chapter 10 Overview

Chapter 10 helps pull all the design skills together so that you will be able to design an *n*-tier, component-based topology. You will learn about the Component Object Model (COM+) applications and how they are used by Windows 2000 and its Internet Information Services. You will also learn how to design COM+ servers in a tiered model so that COM+ applications can reside on servers separate from the

Web servers and even on servers separate from database and messaging servers. This construction is the *n*-tier model, displayed in Figure 1-2.

When you design an *n*-tier Web application, you will place database services on a separate set of servers from the ones you use for content and COM+ applications. This type of a design ensures availability of the Web site over the long term. Once

**FIGURE 1-2** The *n*-Tier Model

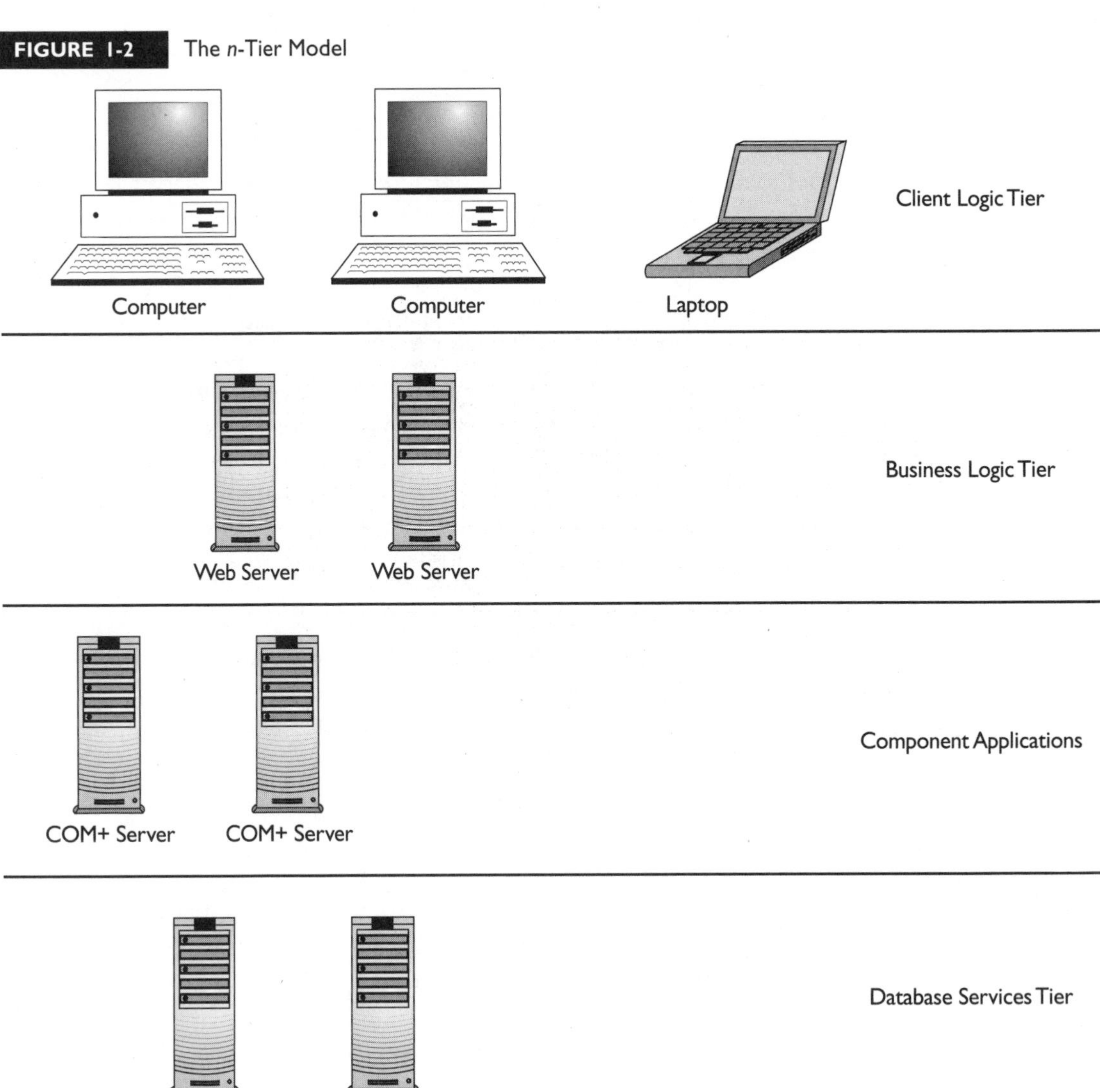

that Web site is running, you need to manage and monitor the applications to ensure that they are online and available when users request them.

CERTIFICATION OBJECTIVE 1.04

## Windows 2000 Server and Web Solutions Terminology

Not only will you need to know Web terminology for this exam—you will also need to understand Windows 2000 specific terminology. The terms and definitions in Table 1-3 provide a basic starting point.

**TABLE 1-3** Web and Windows 2000 Terminology

| Subject Area | Term | Definition |
|---|---|---|
| Security | Kerberos | Kerberos is a secure authentication method developed at the Massachusetts Institute of Technology (MIT). In the Kerberos method, a user is granted a ticket, which enables that user to access network resources and services. |
| | IPSec | Internet Protocol Security (IPSec), which is used in VPNs, is a method of securing data at the packet level. This means that data is secure as it is being transmitted across an internetwork. |
| | L2TP | Layer 2 Tunneling Protocol (L2TP) is used for VPNs. It creates a tunnel through the Internet through which secure data can pass. |
| | SSL | Secure Socket Layer (SSL) secures data transmitted across the Internet. *Socket* refers to the method of passing data from a specific application on one computer to a specific application on another computer. SSL uses public and private key encryption. |
| | VPN | Virtual Private Networking (VPN) is the ability to use a public network, such as the Internet, as though it were an extension of a private network. This is typically executed using tunneling protocols, encryption, and secure authentication. |
| Management | MMC | Microsoft Management Console (MMC) is a graphical console that is used for Microsoft utilities. The MMC can be customized with multiple utilities, according to an administrator's preferences. |

**TABLE 1-3** Web and Windows 2000 Terminology *(continued)*

| Subject Area | Term | Definition |
|---|---|---|
| | Disk quotas | Disk quotas are a feature of the Windows 2000 operating system whereby an administrator can limit the amount of storage space to a specified amount per user. This allocation of space can be performed only on volumes formatted with the NTFS file system. |
| TCP/IP | DNS | Domain Name System (DNS) is a hierarchical method of organizing names and mapping them to IP addresses. DNS servers are required to provide the query service to DNS clients. In a traditional DNS server, the administrator must input each name and address mapping for the DNS zone that the server has authority over. |
| | DDNS | Dynamic Domain Name System (DDNS) allows computers to register their own names and IP addresses mapping in a DNS server. This reduces administrative overhead. |
| | NAT | Network Address Translation (NAT) enables a private network to use one set of IP addresses and translate them to a public IP address. This enables the network to have more hosts than the public IP address(es) set might support. |
| | DHCP | Dynamic Host Configuration Protocol (DHCP) servers assign IP addresses to DHCP clients. By assigning IP addresses only as needed, administrative overhead for IP address management is greatly reduced. |
| | HTML | HyperText Markup Language (HTML) provides the tags or codes to be inserted into a text file so that it can be read by a Web browser. Markup tags create links to other files and reveal how to display text and graphics in the browser window. |
| | HTTP | HyperText Transfer Protocol (HTTP) is the protocol used to download HTML pages from the Internet. |
| | XML | Extensible Markup Language (XML) provides a special set of markup tags to specify, describe, and display datasets. |
| Fault Tolerance | NLB | Network Load Balancing (NLB) provides a form of clustering so that clients can connect to any available server in a cluster of multiple servers. |
| | Cluster | Clusters are a set of servers configured to act as a single server. |
| | RAID | Redundant Array of Inexpensive Disks (RAID) is a set of hard disks that are configured to function as a single hard disk. |

**TABLE 1-3** Web and Windows 2000 Terminology *(continued)*

| Subject Area | Term | Definition |
|---|---|---|
| Storage | DFS | Distributed File System (DFS) is the ability to distribute files across multiple servers but publish those files in a hierarchy that appears to be located on a single server. |
| | Dynamic volumes | Dynamic volumes are a new type of disk partition supported by Windows 2000. Dynamic volumes are more flexible than traditional partitioning and support software-level RAID. |
| Directory Services | Active Directory | Active Directory is the directory service available with Windows 2000 Server. |
| | Domain Controller | Domain Controllers (DCs) are the servers that contain a copy of the Active Directory domain partition. |
| | Global catalog | The global catalog is the index of partial information about users, groups, and other resource objects that exists in every domain in a single forest. |
| | Forest | An Active Directory forest is the largest unit of Active Directory. It contains member domains, a common global catalog, plus a common schema and configuration. |
| | Domain | A domain is a partition of Active Directory that contains users, computers, servers, groups, and other resource objects. The domain is a single security boundary. Every domain must contain the same security settings within the domain. |
| | Site | A site is a collection of well-connected IP subnets. Sites are defined by an administrator and can be configured to optimize traffic across heavily utilized, costly, low-bandwidth and wide area network (WAN) links. |
| | OU | An organizational unit (OU) is a container that can be nested into a tree within a domain. An OU can contain user, group, computer, and other objects as well as other OUs. |
| | Multimaster replication | Replication, or synchronization, of the objects within the domain partitions and the global catalog is considered "multimaster." Each DC is considered a master, or authoritative, for the information in its partition. When the DCs replicate, the objects are updated between the DCs. If two DCs have conflicting updates for the same object, multimaster replication uses an algorithm to determine which update is the latest. |
| | Transitive trusts | Trusts between Active Directory domains are transitive so that if Domain A trusts Domain B, and Domain B trusts Domain C, then Domain A also trusts Domain C. |

# CERTIFICATION SUMMARY

Today's Internet-integrated world requires network administrators and engineers capable of designing, implementing, and managing Web solutions. Exam 70-226, Designing Highly Available Web Solutions with Windows 2000 Server, was developed specifically to test for these skills. This certification requires an understanding of the following:

- Designing a highly available network topology
- Designing servers for high availability
- Using clusters in your Web solution
- Designing an *n*-tier solution
- Securing the internetwork
- Planning for ongoing management and monitoring of your environment
- Integrating database, messaging, applications, and content into your design

As you complete each chapter in this book, you will learn the design skills and basic knowledge required to implement a Web solution in your environment. This book will prepare you for Exam 70-226 as well as provide you with information that you can use in a production network environment.

# TWO-MINUTE DRILL

## What is Designing Windows 2000 Web Solutions?

- ❑ Microsoft built Windows 2000 with the capabilities required to support Web solutions.
- ❑ Businesses use Web applications to reduce their costs and to increase productivity.
- ❑ Scaling out by using multiple servers to provide a single Web solution increases availability because there is no single point of failure.
- ❑ There are three versions of Windows 2000 Server: Windows 2000 Server, Windows 2000 Advanced Server, and Windows 2000 DataCenter Server. Each version supports an increasing scale of hardware.

## Overview of Exam 70-226

- ❑ Exam 70-226 is a case study based exam.
- ❑ You can download a demo from www.microsoft.com/trainingandservices/default.asp?PageID=mcp&PageCall =tesinn&SubSite=examinfo to practice on the case study test format.
- ❑ You should take Exam 70-226 if you are pursuing an MCSE and work in a medium-sized to large environment that includes Web solutions.
- ❑ This exam tests your design skills that cover cluster solutions, server topologies, network infrastructure designs, applications and content, *n*-tier Web designs, directory services, security, and Windows 2000.

## What We'll Cover in This Book

- ❑ The book covers the attributes used to define a network services design using Windows 2000 networking services and fundamental TCP/IP functions required by a solution.
- ❑ The book looks at DHCP, DNS, and NAT.
- ❑ You will learn about designing an extranet using IPSec, L2TP, or PPTP.

- You will learn how to integrate applications such as messaging and database into your Web solution design.

## Windows 2000 Server and Web Solutions Terminology

- One security-related term is Secure Socket Layer (SSL), which secures data transmitted across the Internet. SSL uses public and private key encryption.
- Microsoft Management Console (MMC) is a graphical console that is used for Microsoft utilities and that can be customized according to an administrator's preferences.
- Dynamic Domain Name System (DDNS) allows computers to register their own names and IP address mappings in a DNS server.
- Trusts between Active Directory domains are transitive, so that if Domain A trusts Domain B, and Domain B trusts Domain C, then Domain A also trusts Domain C.

# SELF TEST

The following questions will help you measure your understanding of the material presented in this chapter. Read all the choices carefully because there might be more than one correct answer. Choose all correct answers for each question.

## What is Designing Windows 2000 Web Solutions?

**1.** Which of the following is *not* a Web solution?

A. Virtual private network

B. Business-to-business applications

C. Printing services for a private branch office

D. Printing services provided to customers across the Internet

**2.** Which of the following server platform options is supported by Windows 2000 Advanced Server?

A. SMP

B. RAID

C. NLB

D. All of the above

**3.** You are designing a Web solution and you do not want to have your Web server become a single point of failure. Which of the following design methods will be optimal for you to employ?

A. Scale up a server with SMP

B. Scale up a server with RAID

C. Scale up a server with redundant power supplies

D. Scale out the solution with a cluster

**4.** Which of the following design guidelines will ensure a successful Web solution?

A. Design with the latest technology

B. Design to use redundancy in every network link

C. Design to meet the business requirements

D. Design with redundant internal server hardware components

5. You are presenting a design for a Web solution that is based on Windows 2000 Server. The business already has implemented Windows 2000 Server for all its enterprise network needs, such as file and print services. Which of the following is one of the advantages of using Windows 2000 Server for your Web solution?

   A. The business will not need to hire a different skill set for managing the Web solution.

   B. The business will have multimedia delivered to all its Windows 2000 Professional clients.

   C. The business will have reduced administrative overhead through the use of DDNS and DHCP.

   D. The business can reap the benefits of UNIX and Novell integration features.

## Overview of Exam 70-226

6. BusyBees Co. wants to develop a Web solution that will replace its current remote access systems provided by Windows NT remote access servers and 300 separate phone lines accessible through an 800 number. BusyBees has 5000 users, 3000 of whom are remote sales associates with their own laptops. BusyBees wants to have a Web solution if possible and has asked you for a solution that will stabilize costs. Which of the following will you present?

   A. Reduction of servers to reduce administrative costs

   B. A Windows 2000 Server VPN with Internet connection

   C. A hardware replacement solution to upgrade laptops to a standard image

   D. An e-commerce Web site

7. Which of the following subjects is covered in Exam 70-226?

   A. Installing a ROM BIOS chip

   B. Programming a shopping basket on an e-commerce site

   C. Planning for disaster recovery

   D. Monitoring a Web solution from a UNIX server

8. The managers of BusyBees Co. were so pleased with the VPN solution that you presented that they have requested your services in designing a new Web solution. A developer has developed a SQL Server 2000 database application for BusyBees, and now the company wants it to be installed on a highly available server topology. Which of the following solutions will you present?

   A. A cluster server for the SQL Server 2000 database application, with a separate cluster for the Windows 2000 Internet Information Services

B. Redundant network links to the Internet with a single server that has one processor and a single hard disk

C. Proxy services for BusyBees users to go through in order to access the Internet

D. A firewall and an encryption system

**9.** You are designing a solution for a phone company. The CIO tells you that the application is mission critical. He further states that if the application fails, the company loses $10,000 per minute in logged minutes that users spend on their telephones. What would be the top design goal for a Web solution that integrates with this application?

A. Achieve security so that no one can hack into the application.

B. Reduce the administrative overhead of the solution.

C. Stabilize the costs of running the application.

D. Achieve zero downtime for the application and Web solution.

**10.** BusyBees has called you in on another mission. The SQL database application is such a success that the company's Internet user base has grown to quadruple the number that they had originally anticipated. The traffic that they are experiencing is maxing out the servers and the Internet links. What design feature did you incorporate into your design that would make BusyBees happy to have hired you in the first place?

A. Security

B. Performance

C. Scalability

D. Manageability

## What We'll Cover in This Book

**11.** YellowJackets Inc. is a manufacturing corporation with 40,000 employees. Management has decided to implement a Web solution that will enable customers to create a custom emblem online and order jackets with that emblem sewn on. The application requires an electronic messaging feature to send information over the Internet using Simple Mail Transfer Protocol (SMTP). Which of the following Microsoft products can supply messaging?

A. Application Center 2000

B. Exchange Server 2000

C. Commerce Server 2000

D. Internet Security and Acceleration Server 2000

12. You have configured a server with dual network interface cards so that each card connects to the same network segment. In your configuration, you have configured traffic to be distributed across both the cards. If one of the cards fails, the other card will take on the full load of network traffic. What will this system provide for your server? (Select two answers.)

   A. Manageability

   B. Security

   C. Availability

   D. Performance

13. What type of security is used to ensure that data is not readable while it is transmitted across a public network?

   A. Authentication

   B. Authorization

   C. Encryption

   D. Firewalls

14. Which of the following Windows 2000 Server features provides user authentication?

   A. Active Directory

   B. Domain Name System

   C. Dynamic Host Configuration Protocol services

   D. Security Account Manager for the domain

15. YellowJackets recently purchased another company, BlackWasps. The BlackWasps Web applications run on Windows NT Servers. YellowJackets corporate managers want to keep the existing domain name of BlackWasps because of brand recognition, but they want to upgrade the BlackWasp Web servers to Windows 2000 and include them in their Active Directory forest. Which of the following do you need to upgrade first on the BlackWasp servers?

   A. DNS

   B. DHCP

   C. SSL

   D. MMC

## Windows 2000 Server and Web Solutions Terminology

**16.** Which of the following provides a secure method for authentication in which a user is granted a ticket with which to access resources?

A. IPSec

B. L2TP

C. PPTP

D. Kerberos

**17.** You have been hired by a SpydRWeb, a Web hosting company, to audit its Web hosting servers, which run on Windows 2000. Upon monitoring disk usage, you determine that more than 30 percent of SpydRWeb's customers are using more disk space than they are paying for. Which of the following can you use to ensure that SpydRWeb's customers can use only the space that they have been allocated?

A. Dynamic volumes

B. Disk partitions

C. Disk quotas

D. RAID

**18.** SpydRWeb has a Class C address, which affords it 254 individual IP addresses without using subnetting. However, SpydRWeb has more than 500 users on its network. Which Web solution can be used to provide an IP address to each user on the network?

A. NAT

B. DNS

C. DHCP

D. SSL

**19.** How do Active Directory domain controllers synchronize data?

A. They all download the information from the primary domain controller (PDC).

B. They use multimaster replication.

C. They use transitive trust relationships.

D. They use network address translation.

**20.** SpydRWeb has a single domain within its Active Directory. A new client has requested to be able to administer its own servers remotely, and SpydRWeb wants to put those servers in a separate domain to maintain security. What feature will ensure that SpydRWeb can still query information about users and resources from Active Directory, even though it uses a separate domain?

A. Forest

B. Domain controller

C. Site

D. Global catalog

# LAB QUESTION

YellowJackets has implemented a Web solution. The growth of the solution is faster than originally anticipated, just reaching 100 transactions per second. Given the current growth rate, it is likely that the solution will reach 200 transactions per second in two months and 400 transactions per second in six months. In a year, it should reach 600 transactions per second. This is what you know:

- **Current state** The six servers in the solution can handle 300 transactions per second, or 50 transactions apiece.
- **Scenario 1** If they double the RAM in the servers, the servers should be able to handle 450 transactions per second, or 75 transactions apiece.
- **Scenario 2** If they add a second processor to each server, the servers should be able to handle 480 transactions per second, or 80 transactions apiece.
- **Scenario 3** If they double the RAM and add another processor, the servers will support 720 transactions per second, or 120 transactions apiece.
- **Scenario 4** If they add two more servers, they will be able to handle 400 transactions per second, or 50 transactions apiece.

Which scenario should you recommend for YellowJackets?

# SELF TEST ANSWERS

## What is Designing Windows 2000 Web Solutions?

1. ☑ **C.** Printing services for a private branch office is not a web solution. When printing locally, you are not sending data across the Web.
   ☒ **A** is incorrect because a VPN is considered a Web solution, since it provides private network access across the Internet. **B** is incorrect because a B2B application is a Web solution between two corporate entities. **D** is incorrect because printing services provided to customers across the Internet is an example of a B2C application that is conducted across the Internet.

2. ☑ **D.** Windows 2000 Advanced Server supports SMP, in which there are multiple processors in a single server to provide more processing power, RAID, in which there are multiple hard disks configured to work as a single storage system, and NLB, in which client connections can be distributed to multiple servers in a cluster.
   ☒ **A, B,** and **C** are incorrect because because Windows 2000 Advanced Server supports all three of these technologies.

3. ☑ **D.** Scaling out the solution with a cluster is the optimal method because there are multiple servers in a cluster and none of the servers becomes a single point of failure.
   ☒ **A** is incorrect because multiple processors in the SMP server only provide more processing power, but the server remains a single point of failure. **B** is incorrect because a RAID array provides more hard disk redundancy, but the server itself remains a single point of failure. **C** is incorrect because redundant power supplies do not change the fact that the server is a single point of failure for the Web solution.

4. ☑ **C.** Designing to meet business requirements is a best practice that ensures a successful Web solution.
   ☒ **A** is incorrect because using the latest technology does not mean that the technology will be successful in a Web solution. **B** is incorrect because some Web solutions do not require redundancy in network links. **D** is incorrect because redundant internal server hardware components will not necessarily ensure success if there are other priorities for the business to meet in its Web solution.

5. ☑ **A.** One advantage for using Windows 2000 Server as part of a Web solution in a network that already uses Windows 2000 Server for other services is that the business does not need to have a new type of skill set to manage the Web solution.

☒ B is incorrect because the question did not mention that there were Windows 2000 Professional clients. C is incorrect because the question did not mention that DDNS or DHCP would be used in the Web solution. D is incorrect because the question did not state that UNIX or Novell servers were required for integration.

## Overview of Exam 70-226

6. ☑ B. You should present a Windows 2000 Server VPN solution with an Internet connection that will replace the Windows NT remote access servers and a majority, if not all, 800-number phone lines. This solution will stabilize costs by funneling remote access services through a single Internet link.
☒ A is incorrect because it is not a Web solution and if BusyBees has a minimal number of servers, it could have a negative rather than positive effect on costs. C is incorrect because it is not a Web solution and there was no mention of cost issues resulting from laptop images. D is incorrect because an e-commerce Web site will not stabilize costs.

7. ☑ C. Planning for disaster recovery is a subject that is covered by Exam 70-226. This is a skill that is required for highly available Web solutions, since high availability demands uptime, even in the face of disasters.
☒ A is incorrect because installing a ROM BIOS chip is not a skill required for Web solution design. B is incorrect because programming skills are not covered by this exam. D is incorrect because integration with UNIX is not a skill set covered by this exam.

8. ☑ A. The solution that best meets BusyBees' requirements for a highly available server topology is one using cluster servers for the database application and a separate cluster for Windows 2000 Web servers, provided by native Internet Information Services.
☒ B is incorrect because redundant network links do not affect the server topology, and the single server with a single processor and hard disk is not highly available. C is incorrect because proxy services will not be useful for the server topology of the SQL database application. D is incorrect because, although a firewall and an encryption system are probably a good solution for any Web application, this solution does not meet the need for the highly available server topology.

9. ☑ D. The top design goal for a Web solution that integrates this type of mission-critical application would be to achieve zero downtime. Each minute costs the company more money than some servers cost, so adding servers to the solution will be an easily absorbed cost.
☒ A is incorrect. Security would be a high-priority goal for the Web design, but it would not be as high a priority as a goal of zero downtime. B is incorrect because it is highly unlikely that

administrative overhead is as costly as downtime would be, so this is not a top design goal. **C** is incorrect. Given that the costs of running the application are not mentioned, it is unlikely that this would be the top design goal of the Web solution.

**10.** ☑ **C.** Scalability is a feature that enables you to grow a Web solution to meet changing needs.
☒ **A** is incorrect because security will not help you with growth in application usage. **B** is incorrect because the performance of the Web solution will degenerate as usage increases. **D** is incorrect because manageability will not help the Web site grow to meet increased demand from users.

## What We'll Cover in This Book

**11.** ☑ **B.** Exchange Server 2000 can supply messaging functions. It integrates with Windows 2000's Internet Information Services to send e-mail over SMTP.
☒ **A,** Application Center 2000, is incorrect because it is used to extend the scale of a Web solution. **C,** Commerce Server 2000, is incorrect because it is used to provide an e-commerce solution. **D,** Internet Security and Acceleration Server 2000, is incorrect because it provides both security and proxy services for Web solutions.

**12.** ☑ **C** and **D.** By configuring both cards to take on network traffic simultaneously, you increase the performance of the server. By configuring one card to take over if the other card fails, you increase the availability of the server.
☒ **A** and **B** are incorrect because dual network interface cards will not affect the manageability or security of the server.

**13.** ☑ **C.** Encryption is the type of security that ensures that data is not readable while it is being transmitted.
☒ **A** is incorrect because authentication is used to validate the user who is attempting to access resources. **B** is incorrect because authorization is used to grant access rights to resources on the network. **D** is incorrect because a firewall protects data while that data remains within a private network, but it does not protect data that transmits across a public network.

**14.** ☑ **A.** Active Directory is the directory service for Windows 2000 Server. It provides user authentication.
☒ **B** is incorrect because the Domain Name System provides hostname-to-IP address mapping. **C** is incorrect because Dynamic Host Configuration Protocol services assign IP addresses to client computers. **D** is incorrect because Windows 2000 Server does not include a domain Security Account Manager (SAM). SAM is a legacy Windows NT feature.

**15.** ☑ **A.** You should plan to upgrade DNS servers first. Windows 2000 Active Directory is not compatible with legacy Windows NT DNS because it does not support Service Resource Records (SRV RRs).
☒ **B** is incorrect because DHCP services are unlikely to be used on Web servers. **C**, SSL, is incorrect because it will be unaffected by the upgrade. **D**, MMC, is incorrect because there is no Microsoft Management Console on a Windows NT server, and it is installed by default as part of Windows 2000.

## Windows 2000 Server and Web Solutions Terminology

**16.** ☑ **D.** Kerberos is a secure method of authentication. When using Kerberos, a user is granted a ticket that is then used for resource and service access.
☒ **A**, IPSec, is incorrect because it provides a packet level of encrypting data as it crosses the internetwork. **B** and **C** are incorrect because both L2TP and PPTP provide methods of tunneling across the Internet to reach a private network. **A**, **B**, and **C** are all used in various implementations of a VPN.

**17.** ☑ **C.** You can implement disk quotas on the Windows 2000 Servers so that the space used by each of SpydRWeb's customers is only the space that they have purchased.
☒ **A**, **B**, and **D** are incorrect because dynamic volumes, disk partitions, and RAID offer no means of managing the space used by individuals on a Windows 2000 Server.

**18.** ☑ **A.** Network Address Translation can translate external IP addresses to a different set of internal IP addresses, thus enabling a network to have more hosts than the number of external IP addresses it has registered.
☒ **B**, **C**, and **D** are all incorrect because DNS, DHCP, and SSL will not provide more IP addresses.

**19.** ☑ **B.** Active Directory domain controllers synchronize their domain partitions through multimaster replication.
☒ **A** is incorrect because this is the method used in legacy Windows NT. **C** is incorrect because the trust relationships will not affect the method of data synchronization.
**D** is incorrect because network address translation is used to map internal IP addresses to external IP addresses.

**20.** ☑ **D.** The global catalog is an index of partial information about the users and resource objects in the entire Active Directory forest. The global catalog is used for queries across the entire Active Directory.

☒ A is incorrect because the forest is a group of domains that share a common schema, configuration, and global catalog. **B** is incorrect because the domain controller is a server that contains a copy of a domain partition. **C** is incorrect because a site is a collection of well-connected IP subnets that are configured by an administrator for the purpose of managing replication.

# LAB ANSWER

You should recommend Scenario 3. In order to reach the scale of transactions that YellowJackets will need in one year's time, you should recommend that the servers should each have doubled RAM and an additional processor.

MCSE

MICROSOFT CERTIFIED SYSTEMS ENGINEER

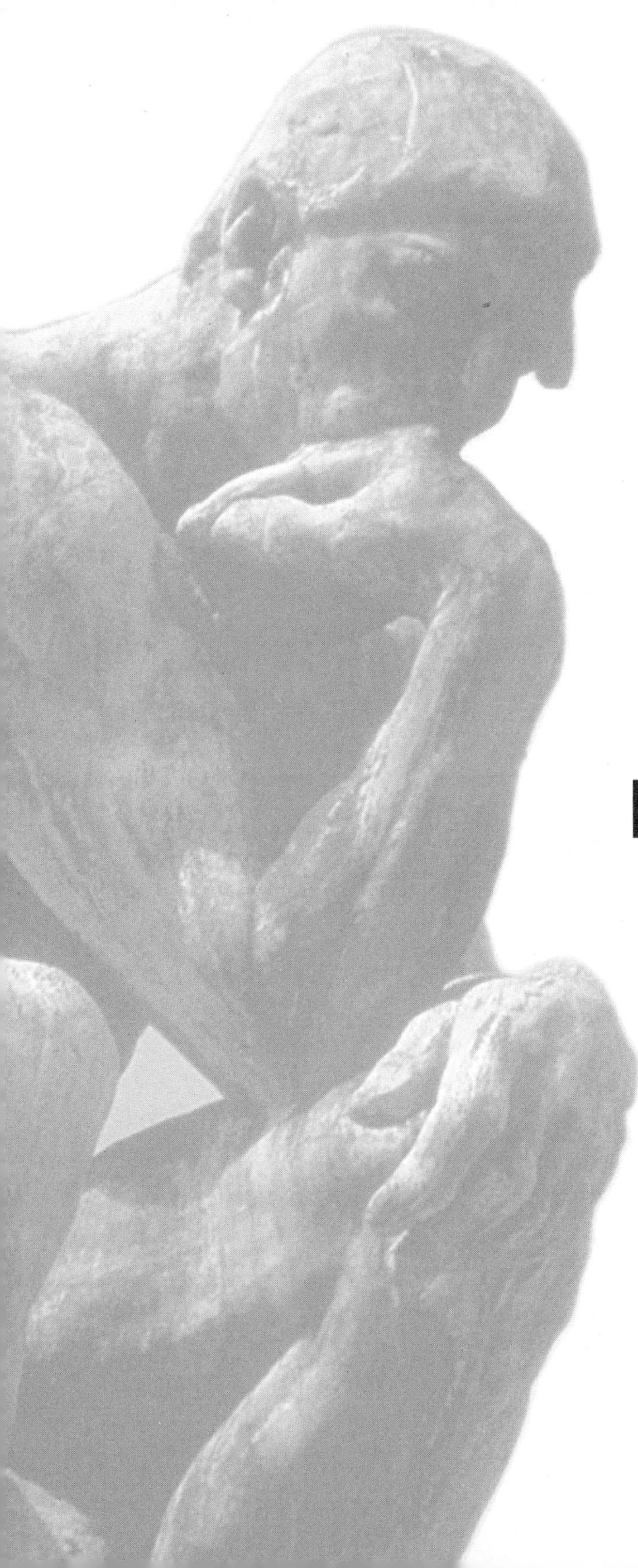

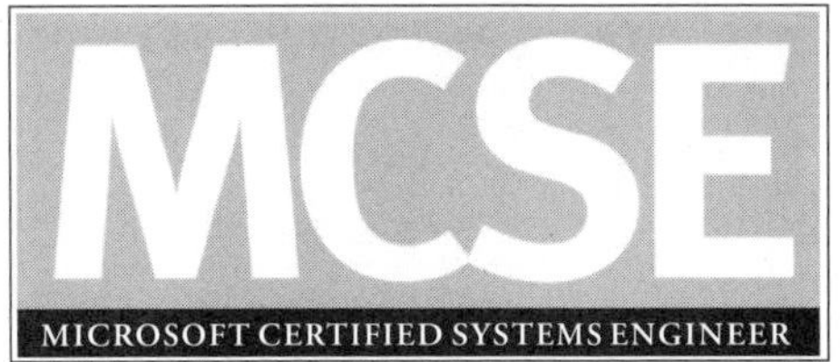

# 2

# Designing Cluster and Server Architectures for Web Solutions

## CERTIFICATION OBJECTIVES

| | |
|---|---|
| 2.01 | Designing Network Load-Balancing Solutions |
| 2.02 | Designing Server Cluster Solutions |
| 2.03 | Designing Data Storage |
| ✓ | Two-Minute Drill |
| Q&A | Self Test |

Highly available Web infrastructures are required to be reliable, fault tolerant, and able to perform at a high level of efficiency. In order to make this possible in most cases, two or more servers must be combined and made to function as one unit. This unit is known as a *cluster*. The cluster's sole purpose might be to serve up Web pages, process data and store it in a database, or coordinate activities between two different server layers. Whatever functions the group of servers is responsible for, they must be made to always be on the job without failure.

Windows 2000 Advanced Server and Datacenter Server both have the ability to form server clusters to provide high availability and reliability to the tune of 99.999 percent uptime. Microsoft has designed these services to be robust and intelligent enough to handle the most demanding Web service environments needed today.

In this chapter, we discuss cluster and network load-balancing solutions and the factors that determine their configuration. We look at how factors such as the number of hosts available for network load balancing and clustering affect the configuration of a cluster as well as affecting how many clusters are necessary to provide the high level of service needed. We also look at how the ability to use multicast packet transmissions and unicast transmissions affects the cluster architecture. In addition, we discuss failover strategies and how they can be built into the clusters. Finally, we learn about disk storage and how the two most widely used types, Redundant Array of Inexpensive Disks (RAID) and storage area networks (SANs), add power and redundancy to our cluster architecture.

## CERTIFICATION OBJECTIVE 2.01

# Designing Network Load-Balancing Solutions

The Windows Network Load Balancing (NLB) service was first included in Windows NT 4.0 Enterprise Edition. NLB allows an administrator to distribute incoming TCP/IP traffic intended for a specific TCP/IP address across multiple servers. This distribution of load allows for faster response and a higher level of availability of the particular address to clients that request services from it. NLB is ideal for use in environments in which many requests for services are made to a particular IP address and greater availability and a faster response time are paramount.

NLB is best suited for increasing the availability and reducing the response time of Web sites in high-performance Web infrastructures. On the local area network (LAN), it is suitable for increasing the availability of Dynamic Host Configuration Protocol (DHCP) services for Transmission Control Protocol/Internet Protocol (TCP/IP) address assignment. Windows 2000 Advanced Server and Datacenter Server bring an improved, more mature NLB service. This service is capable of creating near-zero downtime if implemented properly.

The NLB service is actually a network-level driver that sits directly below the Windows 2000 TCP/IP protocol stack and directly above the network interface card (NIC) drivers. All traffic that a NIC picks up is filtered by NLB and handled based on the type of packet it is. Figure 2-1 displays the Windows 2000 network protocol architecture, showing where the NLB driver sits.

**FIGURE 2-1**

An NLB Driver Functions as a Layer Between TCP/IP and the NIC Driver

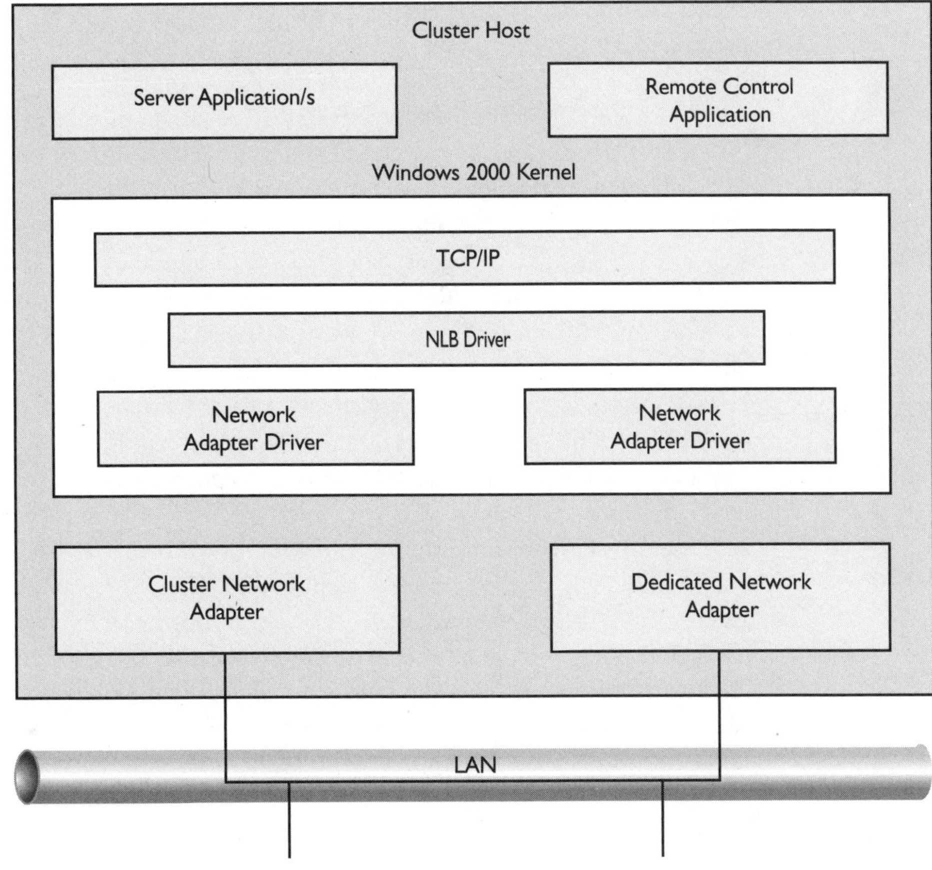

NLB works specifically on incoming TCP, User Datagram Protocol (UDP), and Generic Routing Encapsulation (GRE) traffic. Throughput of incoming traffic is maximized by the NLB architecture since it uses the broadcast subnet to deliver packets to all hosts in a cluster. Furthermore, the service's filtering mechanism eliminates the need to route packets to any specific host, thus increasing efficiency.

The unique distributed architecture of an NLB cluster also affords it the luxury of not having a single point of failure, like some of the other load-balancing technologies for which a centralized unit acts as a dispatcher, coordinating and redirecting traffic flow. Instead, each member of an NLB cluster runs the NLB driver so that load balancing continues despite the failure of one of the members of the cluster, as long as there are at least two surviving cluster hosts.

Another feature of the NLB architecture is that it overlaps delivery and reception of packets on the NIC driver as opposed to waiting until a driver's transmission of a packet is complete. This system allows for faster overall processing of packets, because the drivers don't have to wait for the packets to come in; they can process them "on the fly." Figure 2-2 illustrates these features.

This system is possible because the TCP/IP stack can process a packet while the NIC driver is receiving another packet without the NIC driver having to wait until TCP/IP is done processing the packet. This process significantly increases throughput and efficiency in network transmission, because the time lag between packets leaving a client or server and arriving at their destination, also known as *latency,* is reduced and the number of packets that can be transmitted at one time is increased.

When an NLB cluster is created, we must assign an IP address to which all the hosts in the cluster respond. This IP address is known as the *primary IP address* or *virtual IP address.* A cluster can have many different virtual IP addresses but only one primary address. For example, we might want to partition a Web server that serves many clients or networks by assigning different IP addresses to the same server. This way, different clients can be served different Web pages via different IP addresses to relieve overload on any particular IP address.

The primary IP address is used to identify the cluster for remote control operations and is used in the heartbeat messages that are emitted by all functioning cluster hosts. The primary IP address and any other virtual IP addresses that clients use to identify the cluster are bound to the *cluster adapter.* The cluster adapter is the NIC that is responsible for handling all cluster network traffic. If there is only one NIC in the host, a dedicated IP address for network operations that does not involve

**FIGURE 2-2** NLB Cluster Traffic-Handling Properties

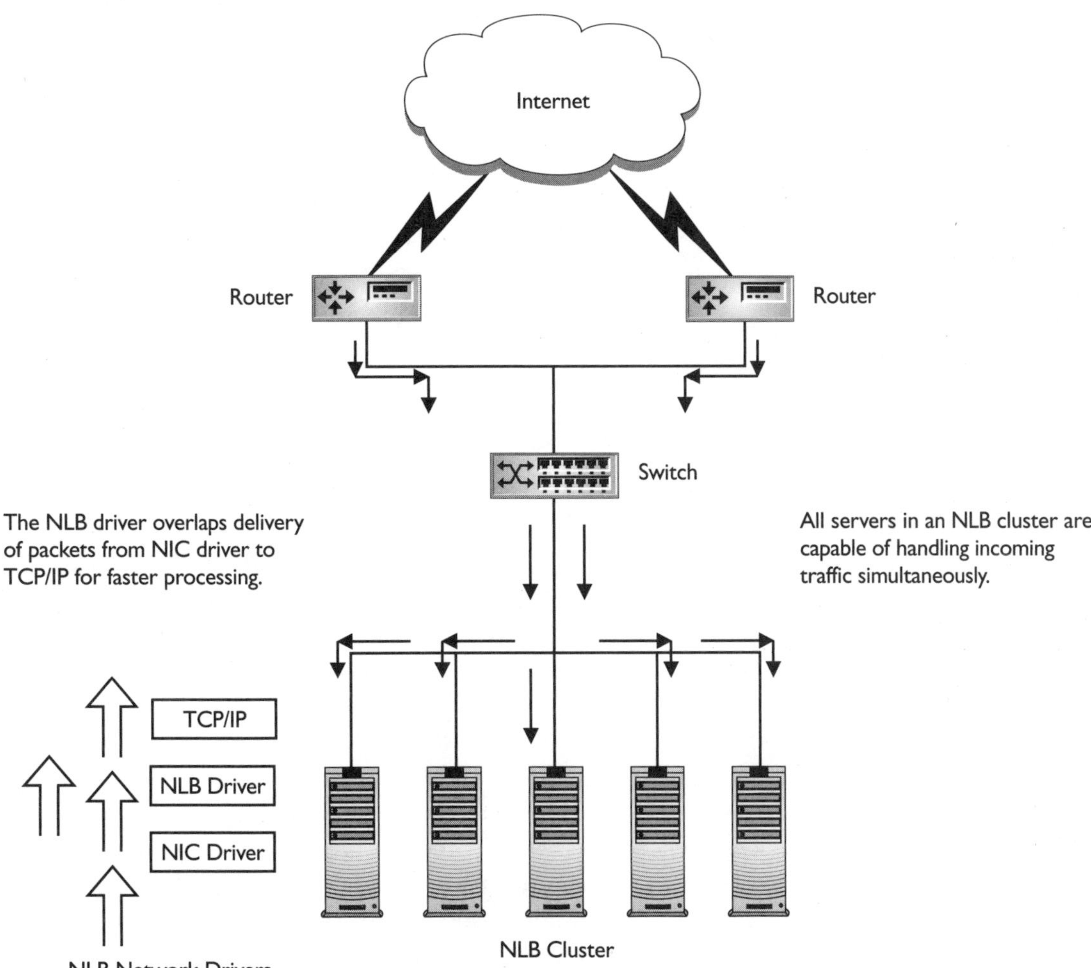
Internet
Router
Router
Switch
The NLB driver overlaps delivery of packets from NIC driver to TCP/IP for faster processing.
All servers in an NLB cluster are capable of handling incoming traffic simultaneously.
TCP/IP
NLB Driver
NIC Driver
NLB Network Drivers
NLB Cluster

clustering might also be bound to the cluster adapter. Optionally, we can have another NIC in the cluster host that allows the server to communicate with other cluster hosts and other servers on a separate network.

exam Watch

***NLB filters only incoming TCP, UDP, and GRE traffic. It does not filter any other traffic such as Internet Protocol (IP) but passes it untouched to the TCP/IP software of all the hosts in the cluster. We cannot use NLB to create high availability for any other network services that do not use these types of IP packets.***

In the following sections, we discuss the leading factors that affect the architecture and deployment of NLB clusters. We examine how each of these factors affects the design of an NLB cluster solution, and we attempt to gain an understanding of the components of a sound NLB cluster solution design.

## Number of Hosts

In order for a cluster to exist, whether an NLB cluster or a Cluster Service cluster, more than one computer must be available to create the cluster. Windows 2000 Advanced Server is capable of forming an NLB cluster of up to 32 servers and a Cluster Service cluster of two servers. Windows 2000 Datacenter Server is also capable of forming NLB clusters of up to 32 servers but is capable of forming Cluster Service clusters of up to four servers. The servers participating in an NLB cluster are referred to as *hosts,* whereas servers participating in a Cluster Service cluster are referred to as *nodes.* You can overcome the 32-server limit of the NLB service and the four-server limit to Cluster Service by combining clusters using Microsoft's Application Center 2000. Application Center 2000 allows you to stack clusters to a theoretically limitless number of hosts for one Web site.

The number of hosts in an NLB cluster should be sufficient to support the estimated number of clients that will be requesting services from the cluster. This is an important point, because underprovisioning for the anticipated load will lead to lower levels of availability of each host and thus lower levels of service than required for the infrastructure. NLB does provide our infrastructure with scalability; we simply have to add more hosts to the cluster until performance is acceptable. However, it would be much more cost-saving (and possibly job-saving as well) to design the infrastructure with the appropriate number of hosts to begin with.

Adding more servers to mitigate the effects of the load would in turn improve performance. The NLB service uses a statistical algorithm for calculating which host receives incoming traffic from which client. The service also uses load percentage, which can be set for each host in the cluster in the NLB Properties window, to determine which host accepts incoming traffic and how much traffic it accepts. On the other hand, the load-balancing algorithm works better with the more incoming client traffic we have. The algorithm tends to improve the distribution of load as more requests come in. This effect is a result of the nature of the algorithm and service, which causes a tendency toward the statistical distribution of the load.

NLB also uses a feature called *handling priority* to help decide which host handles incoming traffic from the next client that makes a request to the cluster. In a cluster, hosts are assigned priority numbers ranging from 1 to 32; the lower the number, the higher the handling priority. This feature is triggered via the NLB Properties dialog box. The host with the highest handling priority is known as the *default host.* Despite the load-balancing algorithm, hosts with higher priorities still receive the new client connections before lower-priority hosts. In the event of default host failure, the host with the next highest priority assumes the position of the default host and, if it has the capacity, takes on the processing of the traffic that was formerly handled by the previous default host. Usually the NLB algorithm recalculates and redistributes the traffic among the other hosts.

## Number of Clusters

The number of clusters in our design is also a factor of anticipated load. Some Web infrastructures might require NLB clusters in both the front-end Web server network and the back-end application or database server network. Security requirements could also play a part in the design decision to include more than one NLB cluster. In some Web infrastructures, it might be feasible to have an NLB server cluster to handle Secure Hypertext Transfer Protocol (HTTPS) requests that is separate from the cluster that handles unsecured Hypertext Transfer Protocol (HTTP) traffic. In this scenario, illustrated in Figure 2-3, once a client makes an HTTPS request, the client is redirected to the HTTPS cluster.

## Multicast Versus Unicast

NLB uses Data Link layer (OSI model Layer 2) broadcast or multicast to distribute incoming TCP/IP traffic to all hosts in the cluster simultaneously. NLB has two modes of Layer 2 configurations for accepting incoming traffic: unicast mode and multicast mode.

FIGURE 2-3 Two Server Clusters Separate HTTP Traffic from HTTPS

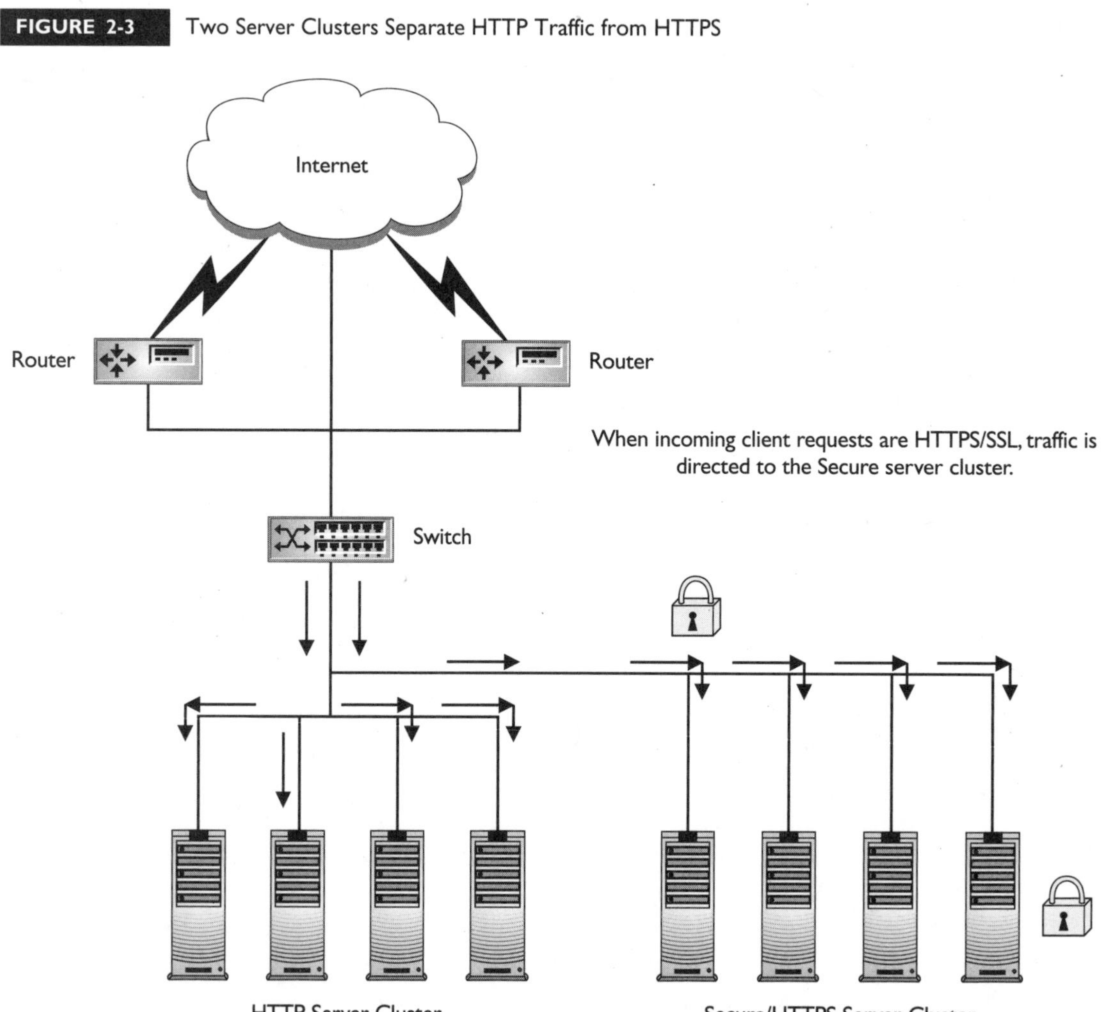


In *unicast mode*, NLB assigns all the hosts in the cluster the same Media Access Control (MAC) layer address. The original MAC address that belonged to the particular NIC is still there; however, NLB has reassigned it in favor of the unicast address. The unicast addressing scheme allows all members of the cluster to receive incoming packets. The traffic is then passed up to the NLB driver, where it is filtered and processed. Although the cluster uses a unicast address for all its member hosts, the address remains unique because it is derived from the primary IP address of the cluster.

exam Watch

***NLB modifies the cluster adapter's MAC address by setting a registry key value and then reloading the NIC driver. The host does not have to be rebooted.***

Because most clusters should be connected to a switch, another problem arises that NLB must resolve . Since switches are primarily Layer 2 devices, the unicast MAC address used by every host in the cluster would cause a conflict in the switch. NLB eliminates this problem by modifying the cluster's source MAC address for outgoing traffic. NLB replaces one of the values in the MAC address with the value of the handling priority of the particular host that is transmitting packets through the switch. This prevents the switch from learning the true MAC address of the NIC that is transmitting packets through the switch, and thus the switch is forced to use the cluster MAC address that NLB gives it so that incoming traffic can be transmitted through all the switch ports simultaneously.

## FROM THE CLASSROOM

### Problems Arising from Unicast Mode Transmission

If the cluster is attached to a hub instead of a switch, there is no need for NLB to modify the cluster MAC address. Masking the cluster MAC address could actually result in the flooding of any switches that are upstream in the network topology, thus inadvertently compromising network performance. The modification of the cluster MAC address is a default feature of NLB. We can disable this feature and avoid the switch-flooding problem by changing the NLB MaskSourceMAC registry key value to 0.

—*Chris Broomes, MCSE, MCP+I, CCNA*

The drawback to NLB in unicast mode is that cluster hosts cannot communicate with the other hosts in the cluster using the cluster adapters. This is true because a host that attempts to send data to another host is sending data to its own MAC address due to unicast mode's masking of all cluster members' MAC addresses with the same MAC addresses, as is illustrated in Figure 2-4. The host is, in essence, sending data to itself in an infinite loop, and the data is never transmitted through the network medium. Adding a second NIC to each host in the cluster rectifies this situation, as shown in Figure 2-4. In this configuration, NLB is bound to the NIC configured for the network that receives the incoming client requests, while the other NIC is configured for a separate network that the hosts can use to communicate with each other and back-end application or database servers.

In *multicast mode*, NLB assigns a Layer 2 multicast address to the cluster adapter instead of masking the MAC address on each host. The multicast address is based on the cluster's primary IP address in the format *03-BF-x-x-x-x* for a cluster of primary IP addresses of *x.x.x.x*. This system allows each cluster host to retain its unique MAC address and thus allows communication between hosts within the cluster, without the need for a second NIC. Additional system overhead is not incurred for a separate dedicated IP address on the cluster hosts because the address is on the same NIC.

Multicast mode floods network switches, just like unicast mode. However, configuring a virtual local area network (VLAN) within the switch that includes the ports to which the cluster hosts are connected can limit switch flooding in multicast node. Some routers will not resolve multicast MAC addresses from multicast mode cluster hosts. In order to resolve the multicast MAC addresses static entries for the IP-address-to-MAC-address mapping must be entered into the router's Address Resolution Protocol (ARP) table.

## Failover Strategy

Windows 2000 NLB is designed to provide failover protection within a cluster as well. All hosts in a cluster emit and listen for packets called *heartbeat packets* on their dedicated networks. Once a cluster host goes down, its heartbeat messages stop. The NLB algorithm detects this stoppage and recalculates and redistributes the load among the surviving servers within 10 seconds. If a dedicated TCP/IP service was running on the downed server, another server automatically assumes the service. Figure 2-5 illustrates the failover response of NLB.

FIGURE 2-4 A Host With Two NICs Can Overcome Unicast Mode's Limitations

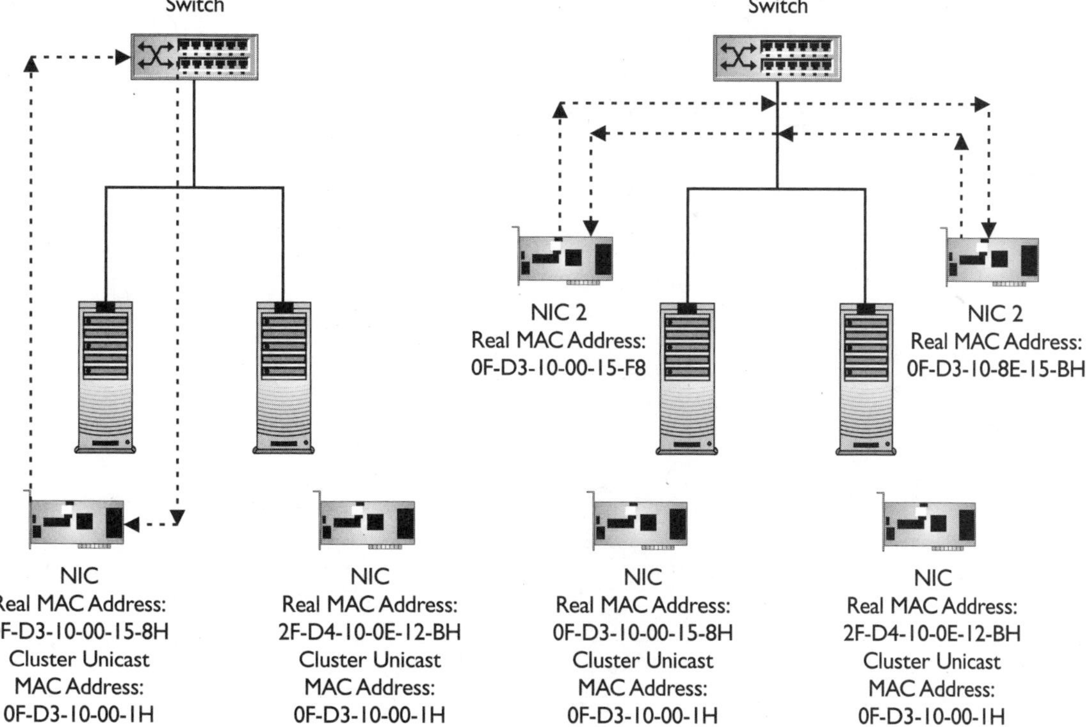


NLB employs what is known as an *N–1 way* architecture for failover. This means that in a cluster of *N* number of hosts, if one or more members of the cluster fail, failover will take place with the surviving hosts until only one cluster host is left.

## Priority

NLB clusters have a hierarchy of hosts within the cluster. NLB enforces a priority on all the members of a cluster. Priority runs in the cluster from 1 to a maximum of 32, with the server with the lowest number having the highest priority. As mentioned

**FIGURE 2-5** The NLB N–1 Failover Mechanism

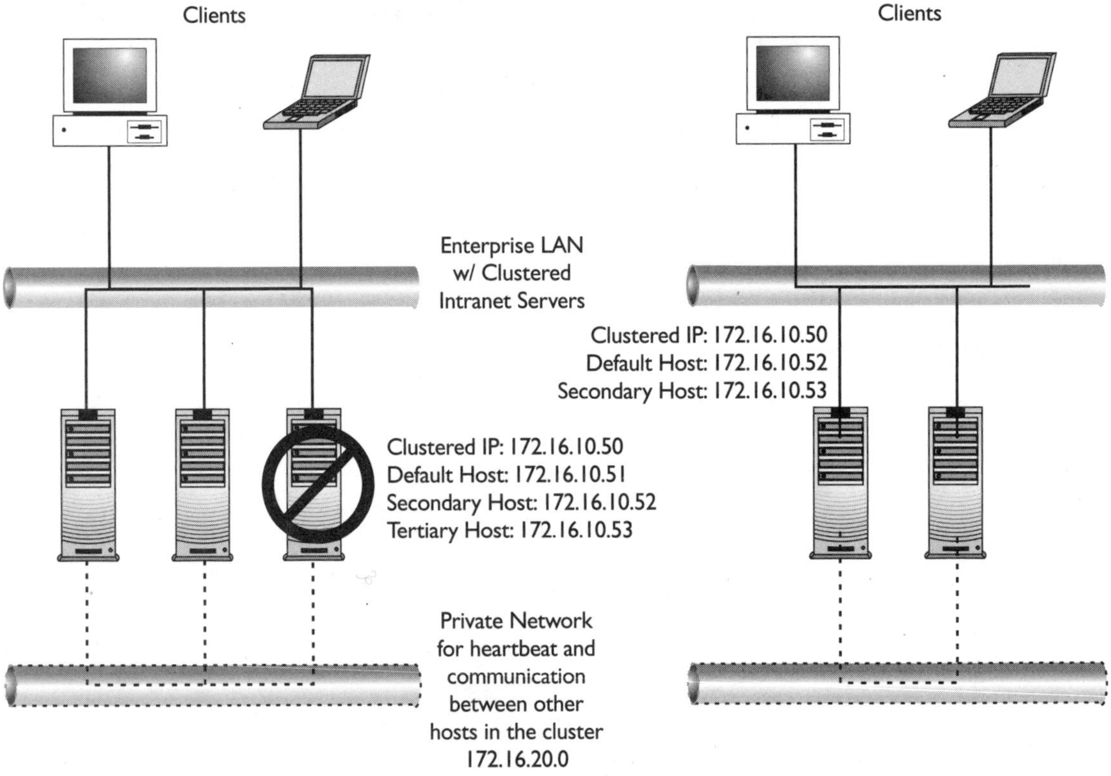

previously, the host with the highest priority is known as the *default host.* The default host is the preferred host for handling new network traffic. If the default host goes offline, the host with the next highest priority takes over handling the incoming traffic that the default host handled. This system ensures fault tolerance for network services supported by NLB.

Host priority can be overridden by creating *port rules*—rules for handling network traffic based on the specific ports involved—through which it is possible to configure load balancing for specific port ranges. Port rules can also be used to block traffic that uses certain ports. Port rules can employ one of two load-balancing policies: single-host or multiple-host load balancing.

The *single-host load balancing policy* directs all incoming client requests to the host with the highest *handling priority.* The handling priority is associated with the port rule and is different from the host priority. Using port rules and handling priorities enables different hosts in the cluster to handle all client traffic for specific applications.

*Multiple-host load balancing policies* spread incoming traffic from clients across multiple hosts in the cluster. Multiple-host load balancing employs one of three client affinity modes: single-client affinity, class C client affinity, and no affinity. We discuss client affinity in the next section. By default, NLB is configured with one port rule that spans all TCP/IP ports from 0 to 65,535 with multiple-host load balancing and single-client affinity.

on the Job

***If you attempt to add a host to a cluster and that host has the same priority as a host already in the cluster, you will not be able to add the host and an error message will be created in the Event Log.***

## Affinity

In NLB, *client affinity* refers to the ability of NLB to direct traffic from a specific client or network to a single member of the NLB cluster. The effect is that the same server services all the requests of a particular client, as opposed to randomly selecting the responding server based on the NLB distributed algorithm. This does not mean that the server cannot respond to other requests; it simply means that a particular client whose IP address matches the one configured in the NLB client affinity properties always sends to and receives from one particular server.

There are three modes of client affinity: None, Single-client, and Class C. *None client affinity mode* is in actuality the "no affinity" mode for NLB. In this mode, any server can receive and respond to requests from any client, as calculated by the algorithm. If any particular client and server communicate with each other multiple times, it is only a result of chance. This affinity mode configures client traffic to be distributed across multiple ports on multiple cluster hosts. *Single-client affinity mode* configures a single cluster host to always communicate with and service the requests of a client that matches a particular IP address. This is the default client affinity setting. *Class C affinity mode* configures a single cluster host to respond to any client within a particular Class C IP address range. Figures 2-6 a through c illustrate the differences between the three client affinity modes.

Client affinity has a negative effect on cluster performance. In some cases (as in Class C affinity), affinity most likely ensures that one server is dedicated to a certain client or group of clients, therefore robbing the rest of the cluster of the full measure

FIGURE 2-6a

Single-Client Affinity

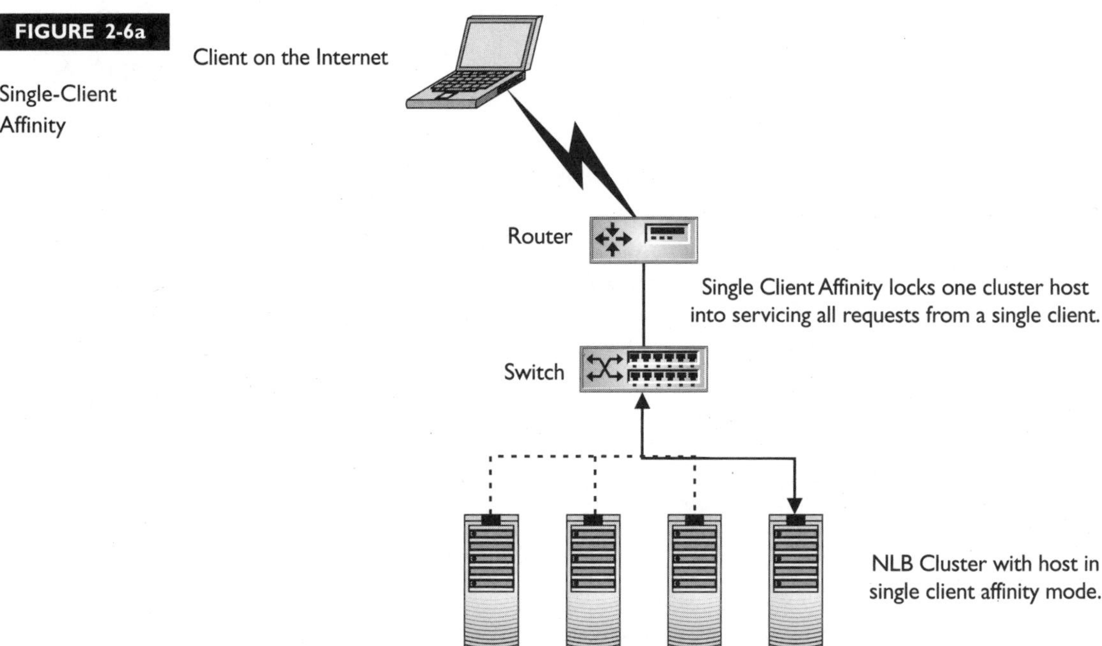
Client on the Internet
Router
Single Client Affinity locks one cluster host into servicing all requests from a single client.
Switch
NLB Cluster with host in single client affinity mode.

of that individual server's processing power, memory, and network resources. Disabling client affinity tends to improve network performance in an NLB cluster because client requests are fully distributed across the cluster's hosts.

## Filtering

A feature closely related to affinity is the filtering mode of a cluster host. The *filtering mode* is the method by which network traffic on a specific port is handled. The filtering mode is applied to traffic on specific ports through configuring a port rule. Three filtering modes are available in NLB: single host, multiple host, and disabled.

*Single-host filtering* specifies that a single cluster host handle network traffic for an associated port rule. The host that handles the traffic is determined by its handling priority. Therefore, changing the handling priority of the hosts in the cluster can change the host that handles the traffic over a specific port or a specific range of ports.

*Multiple-host filtering* specifies that multiple cluster hosts handle the traffic for the particular port rule. This filtering mode is the more desirable of the modes since it

**FIGURE 2-6b**

Class C Client Affinity

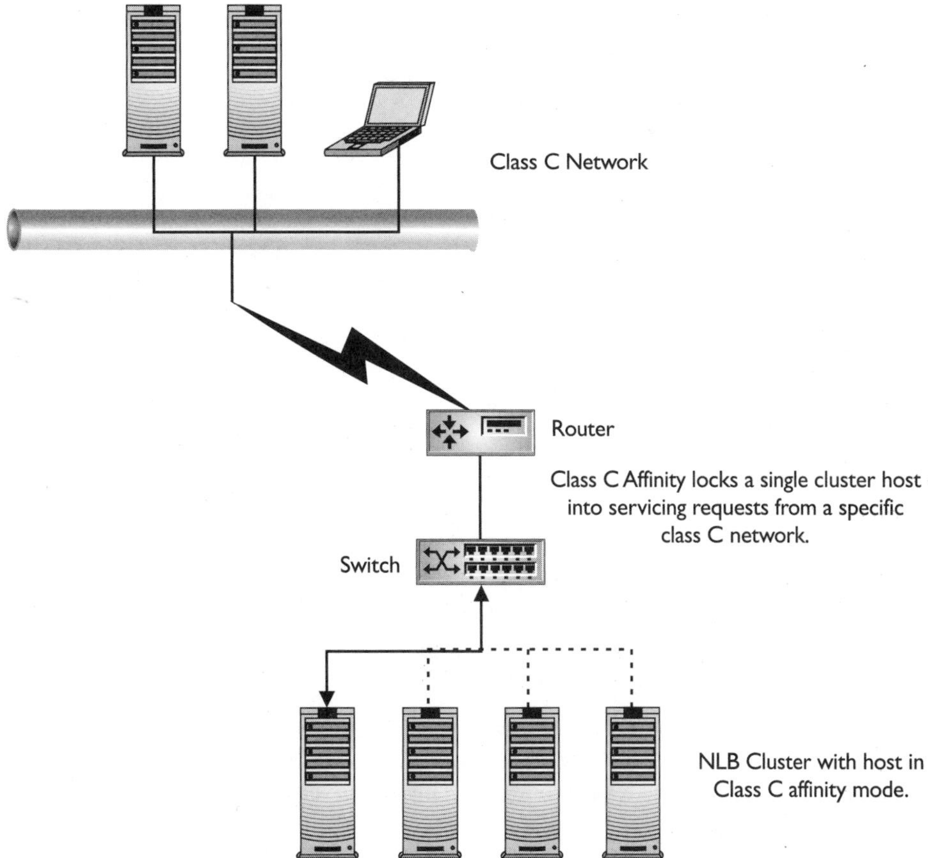
Class C Network
Router
Class C Affinity locks a single cluster host into servicing requests from a specific class C network.
Switch
NLB Cluster with host in Class C affinity mode.

provides scalability of performance as well as fault tolerance because multiple hosts are servicing a client request. Load weighting can be configured within this mode so that cluster hosts can receive as much traffic as they can service optimally. Traffic load is distributed among the cluster hosts on a per-connection basis for TCP traffic and on a per-datagram basis for UDP traffic. Load distribution via filtering can be restricted when single- or class C client affinity is configured.

The *disabled filtering mode* serves to block all network traffic for an associated port rule from being handled by any cluster host.

**FIGURE 2-6c** None Client Affinity

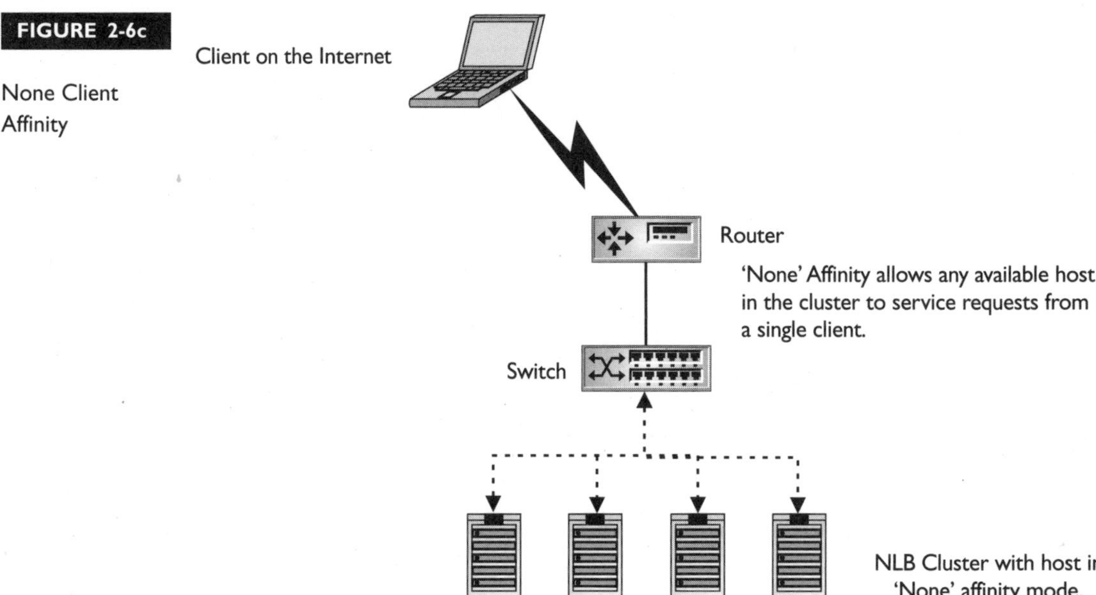
Client on the Internet
Router
'None' Affinity allows any available host in the cluster to service requests from a single client.
Switch
NLB Cluster with host in 'None' affinity mode.

exam Watch

***Take care to understand the differences between host priority and handling priority, and filtering modes and client affinity. The terms are very similar and should not be confused. The exam will probably include questions involving the differences between these terms.***

## Load Weighting

*Load weighting* is the parameter that determines how much traffic a single-cluster host is configured to filter or process for a particular port rule when a cluster employs multiple-host filtering mode. A load weight value of 0 blocks all traffic from a single-cluster host. However, a single host cannot have a value of 100 because that would imply that no load balancing is taking place. The total load weights for all hosts in a cluster can also not equal 100 because the percentage of the load weight that a single member handles is calculated by dividing that host's local load weight value by the sum of all the values in the cluster. Since hosts can dynamically enter or leave the cluster, the sum of the load weight values is never fixed. The traffic load can be evenly distributed across all hosts in a cluster using the Equal Load Distribution option in the port rules configuration.

## Application Types

NLB is useful for providing reliability, maintaining and increasing responsiveness to client requests, and providing high availability of service. The applications to which NLB provides these advantages are primarily TCP/IP-based applications that are capable of maintaining multiple TCP/IP sessions that write to a common data storage area. Applications such as Microsoft SQL Server that have their own methods of updating and maintaining the application state between a client and a server should not be scaled by NLB in its affinity-disabled mode.

NLB provides the best benefit for network and server applications that are robust and can tolerate inconsistencies in services such as Web services, streaming media, VPN services, and terminal services. NLB provides the mechanisms that application monitors use to control cluster operations. This is how one host can assume the load of a failed host in a cluster. NLB enables detection of the failed host providing a particular service and facilitates starting that service on another host in the cluster.

**EXERCISE 2-1**

### Installing Network Load Balancing

For this exercise, we will use three servers running Windows 2000 Advanced Server. The servers are NLBSRV1, NLBSRV2, and NLBSRV3. Do the following:

1. Open **Network and Dial-up Connections.**
2. Right-click the **Local Area Connection** on which Network Load Balancing is to be installed.
3. Click **Properties.**
4. Under Components Checked are used by this Connection, one of the components listed should be Network Load Balancing. At this point, this option should not be selected, only listed.
5. Select the **Network Load Balancing** check box.

6. Click **Properties**.
7. The Network Load Balancing Properties dialog box appears. You'll see three tabs: Cluster Parameters, Host Parameters, and Port Rules. The default is Cluster Parameters.
8. On the Cluster Parameters tab, specify the name **cluster.syngress.com**.
9. Under Cluster's Primary IP address, enter **172.16.10.68**.
10. For the Subnet Mask for the cluster, enter **255.255.255.0**.
11. For the Dedicated IP address, enter **172.16.10.69**.
12. For the Subnet Mask, enter **255.255.255.0**.
13. Select **Enabled** for Multicast Support.
14. In the Remote Password field, enter **Password01**.
15. Reenter the password of **Password01** in the Confirm Password field.
16. Select **Enable** for Remote Control.
17. In the Host Parameters section, assign priority IDs 1, 2, and 3 to the three hosts NLBSRV1, NLBSRV2, and NLBSRV3, respectively.
18. In the Configuring the Initial State tab, check the box to have Network Load Balancing start when Windows 2000 starts.
19. Leave the Port Rules section as its default.
20. Leave the Filtering mode as its default.
21. For the Affinity, the options are None, Single, or Class C. Select **None**.
22. Select **Equal load Distribution** to have each host accept an equal portion of the load.

---

Now that we understand how Network Load Balancing works and how we can use it, let's look at a few NLB scenarios and solutions.

| SCENARIO & SOLUTION | |
|---|---|
| What is an ideal example of an environment for which NLB is a good solution? | NLB is ideal for environments in which many requests for services are made to a particular IP address and greater availability and faster response time are paramount. |
| Is it possible to create a server cluster using NLB with only one server? | No, there must be at least two servers present to create a server cluster. Additionally, there can be up to 32 servers in a cluster. |
| Is Windows 2000 Network Load Balancing designed to provide failover protection within a cluster? | Yes. All hosts in a cluster emit and listen for packets on their dedicated networks; these packets are called *heartbeat packets*. If a heartbeat stops because a cluster host has gone down, the NLB algorithm detects this stoppage and recalculates and redistributes the load among the surviving servers within 10 seconds. |
| Can host priorities be overridden? | Yes. Host priorities can be overridden by creating port rules—rules for handling network traffic based on the specific ports involved—through which it is possible to configure load balancing for specific port ranges. |
| In NLB, what is *client affinity*? | *Client affinity* refers to the ability of NLB to direct traffic from a specific client or network to a single member of the NLB cluster. |

**CERTIFICATION OBJECTIVE 2.02**

# Designing Server Cluster Solutions

Windows 2000 Cluster Service is an improvement of the Microsoft Cluster Server (MSCS) first introduced in Windows NT 4.0 Enterprise Edition. Like MSCS, Cluster Service's goal is to provide fault tolerance and redundancy for enterprise-level server applications that must have little or no downtime.

Cluster Service, a complimentary component of Windows 2000 Advanced Server and Windows 2000 Datacenter Server, can be enabled any time after installation. At present, Windows 2000 Advanced Server Cluster Service can support only two-node clusters, and Datacenter Server Cluster Service can support only four-node clusters. However, the cluster members can be as powerful as eight-way processor servers, with 8 gigabytes (GB) of memory in Windows 2000 Advanced Server and 32-way processors with 64GB of memory in Windows 2000 Datacenter Server. Cluster Service was designed as separate, isolated components that work alongside the operating system.

In the following sections, we discuss the factors considered in the design of Cluster Service clusters. We also examine the factors that influence the number of hosts per cluster, the number of clusters, failover and failback strategies, application types, and dependencies in order to gain an understanding of factors that influence cluster design.

## Number of Nodes

As mentioned in the chapter introduction, Cluster Service is available in two levels: two-node clusters in Windows 2000 Advanced Server and four-node clusters in Windows 2000 Datacenter Server. Cluster Service's architecture allows applications and services to be hosted on each node in the server cluster. The number of applications or services that can be hosted on a single node in a server cluster depends on the system overhead incurred by the applications or services as well as the specifications of the server computer that will host them. Thankfully, as we mentioned, Windows 2000 Advanced Server can support up to eight processors and 8GB of memory, and Datacenter Server supports up to 32 processors and 64GB of memory—more than enough for today's most demanding environments.

The number of hosts in a cluster depends on the largest number of applications and services that we intend to host on a single node in the cluster. Number of hosts is an important factor in the design of a cluster because, should a server fail or be taken offline for maintenance, the remaining nodes need to have sufficient capacity to handle all the applications and services to be hosted by the cluster without a significant interruption or degradation in quality of service.

For example, if we have a two-node cluster and one of the nodes goes offline for any reason, the remaining node must have the capacity and processing power to host all the services for the cluster that were shared by the two hosts. In essence, the remaining node must have at least twice the capacity and processing power that is desired. Therefore, the more servers we have in a cluster, up to the maximum limit in Windows 2000 Datacenter Server, the less load that each of the cluster's remaining nodes must handle.

## Cluster Resource Groups

A *resource group* in Windows 2000 Cluster Service is a logical collection of software and hardware components that work together to provide a service in the cluster. A resource group usually contains all the relevant resources and components needed by a specific application or service-providing server in the cluster and the clients that are serviced by that server. However, a resource group can also consist of elements that bear only an administrative relationship to each other. Resource groups are managed by the Cluster Service on the cluster's behalf.

A resource group can be owned by only one node in a cluster at a time; that node must possess individual resources of that cluster group. No node can own resources in the same cluster resource group other than what it originally owned. This caveat is a result of the *shared-nothing architecture* of Cluster Service. This architecture ensures that resource groups can be owned by individual nodes and eliminates the need for any special apparatus to connect the nodes to the resource group beyond the default Windows 2000 Small Computer Serial Interface (SCSI) or Fiber Channel drivers.

Each of the resource groups has an associated policy that specifies which node the resource group prefers to be hosted by and which node the resource group is moved to in the event that its preferred node fails. This policy is enforced across the entire cluster. Resource groups also have their own network service names and addresses that the clients use to communicate with the cluster or at least the node that is servicing a client.

## Failover and Failback Strategy

Cluster Service's primary feature is its failover capability. If an application, resource, resource group, or entire node in the cluster fails, the services that were being provided by the unit that failed are taken over and resumed by one of the surviving nodes in the cluster. Failover can be automatic, as in the case of failure of a cluster component, or manually induced by an administrator needing to perform maintenance on a cluster node. Cluster Service possesses a component called the Failover Manager that is responsible for stopping and starting resources. Cluster Service uses an algorithm to determine which cluster node is most eligible to host the resource in the event of a failure. The algorithm is the same one used to determine which host to move a resource to during a manual failover exercise.

If a node in the cluster fails, its resource groups are moved to one or more surviving nodes, depending on how much overhead the resource groups consume. The nodes decide among themselves by relying on the *node preference list,* which is used to assign a resource group to a node. Two failover models are used in Cluster Service: cascading failover and N+1 failover.

In the *cascading failover* model, the node preference can be changed so that one preferred node and one or more backup nodes are assigned high node priority. If the resource on the preferred node fails, it is then moved to one of the backup nodes. If the resource there fails, Cluster Service moves the resource to the other backup node. Hence we have an instance in which a resource was able to survive multiple failures. This strategy assumes that each node in the cluster has extra capacity built into it.

The *N+1 failover* model presents a different scenario. In this model, the node preferences are set so that a group of standby nodes in the cluster is identified. These nodes already exist in the cluster but serve a very minor function within the cluster or possess a far greater capacity for the resources they provide, so they can afford to take on extra load. Unlike cascading failover, the assumption made in N+1 failover is that a standby server is the primary source of extra capacity.

Cluster Service also has a feature called *failback* for restoring a resource to its original cluster node if the node has been recovered and comes back online. In order for a resource to be returned to its rightful place, it must have had the preferred owner defined in the resource group properties. The resource group will be moved from the current owner back to the recovered node. Cluster Service prevents the transfer of resource groups back to their previous owners during peak processing times and if the node has not been properly restored.

## Configuration Schemes

Windows 2000 clusters can be configured in two different generalized clustering/failover schemes: active/active and active/passive. *Active/active configuration* allows us to have all the members of our cluster operational and handling client requests at the same time. If the node with the highest priority goes offline, the resources it was providing are moved to one or more of the surviving nodes and the load is rebalanced. Applications such as Web servers that run in Windows 2000 and would typically benefit from the active/active configuration are those that can recover from lost session-state data and quickly reestablish communications with clients.

In *active/passive configuration,* only one host in the cluster is operational and handling client requests at any one time. All other cluster nodes are simply waiting for failure of the operational node. In the event of node failure, Cluster Service or some other mechanism would decide which node has the next highest priority in the cluster and start the application or resource on that node. Commonly, two-server clusters employ the active/passive strategy. For example, Microsoft Exchange Server 5.5 Enterprise Edition can be set up in an active/passive configuration so that if the primary Exchange server fails, the backup server in the cluster almost immediately comes online and begins servicing redirected client requests.

## Application Types

Applications hosted by server clusters represent themselves as virtual servers to the clients that they serve. Clients connecting to different cluster-hosted applications see only the application with which they are concerned. The fact that a single server may host multiple applications and thus multiple virtual servers is transparent to clients in that the clients don't know that they are connecting to the same server for multiple applications. This is because each virtual server is given its own network service name and IP address on the network.

Client connections to a cluster-hosted application are made to the virtual server IP address or network service name that Cluster Service publishes on the network. In the event of an application or server failure in a server cluster, the entire server application is moved to a surviving node in the cluster that has the capacity to handle the resource group. Clients detect a failure in their connection sessions within the application and attempt to reconnect to the server. Cluster Service redirects the client traffic to the new node that hosts the application. The same IP address and service name are used so that the clients never know that the application has been moved to another node.

This system provides high availability and fault tolerance to the infrastructure. However, one drawback to failover is that unless an application is designed to maintain session data in a disk, the session information is lost. An example of a network application that was designed to maintain session information is Windows Internet Name Service, or WINS. WINS stores session information in a database file on the server. Therefore, the application can be moved to any node in the cluster and be completely recovered because the session information can be retrieved from the database file.

exam Watch

***Most of the cluster solutions we talk about in this chapter and that you will see on the exam are active/active configurations. N+1 failover is the only example of active/passive clustering that you might see on the exam.***

## Dependencies

In the Cluster Service, a *dependency* is a relationship between resources that define which resource needs to be present and available before another resource can become available. Dependencies are defined in the Cluster Service resource group properties and allow Cluster Service to control the order in which resource groups are brought on- and offline.

Let's solidify our comprehension of Cluster Service architecture and design by looking at the following scenarios and their solutions.

| SCENARIO & SOLUTION | |
|---|---|
| Can Windows 2000 Advanced Server Cluster Service support four-node clusters? | At present, Windows 2000 Advanced Server Cluster Service can support only two-node clusters, and Datacenter Server Cluster Service can support only four-node clusters. |
| How many applications or services can be hosted on a single node in my server cluster? | The number of applications or services that can be hosted on a single node in a server cluster is dependent on the system overhead incurred by the applications or services as well as the specifications of the server computer that will host them. |
| How are resource groups within Windows 2000 Cluster Service managed? | Resource groups are managed by the Cluster Service on behalf of the cluster. |
| What are the two different failover models that are used in Cluster Service? | The two failover models used in Cluster Service are cascading failover and N+1 failover. |
| What is failback? | Failback is the feature within Cluster Service for restoring a resource to its original cluster node if the node has been recovered and comes back online. |

**EXERCISE 2-2**

### Installing Cluster Service

Now let's try to install Cluster Service on our servers. In this exercise, we install Cluster Service using the Add/Remove Programs control panel. It is of vital importance that you install the Cluster Service one server at a time. Make sure that Windows 2000 Datacenter Server and the Cluster Service are installed and running on one server before starting the operating system and installing the Cluster Service on a second server. If you start the operating system on a second server before the Cluster Service is running on the original server, the cluster disks can become corrupted. For an exercise that gives a more in-depth tour of installation and configuration of Cluster Service, see Chapter 4, "Designing a Highly Available Network Infrastructure."

1. Click **Start | Settings** and then **Control Panel.**
2. Double-click **Add/Remove Programs.**
3. In the Add/Remove Programs dialog box, click **Add/Remove Windows Components.**
4. In the Windows Components Wizard dialog box, make sure that the Cluster Service check box is selected, and then click **Next.**
5. The Windows Components Wizard begins and runs for a few moments. Then the Cluster Service Configuration Wizard appears. Click **Next.**
6. When prompted, click **Finish.** The Cluster Service Configuration Wizard completes and you return to the Windows Components Wizard, which resumes running.
7. Upon completion of the Windows Components Wizard, click **Finish.**

CERTIFICATION OBJECTIVE 2.03

# Designing Data Storage

No matter how powerful your servers or how fast network hardware and media become, a highly available infrastructure is nothing without a reliable place to store and manipulate the data that travels back and forth between client and server in the cluster. In this section, we examine ways to design the optimal data storage.

## RAID

The use of Redundant Array of Inexpensive Disks (RAID) as a single drive or multiple logical drives is a practice that has been steadily gaining in popularity for over a decade. Part of the reason for the increase in popularity is the fact that RAID can be implemented in a variety of architectures, including those that are designed to deliver greater performance, greater reliability, or both. For several years, many thought that RAID was more suited for mainframe environments, due largely in part to the cost. However, because networks are now vital to an organization's productivity and success and electronic data is essential to virtually every level of business operations, the need for RAID in infrastructures like ours is apparent.

Implementing RAID arrays into our server architecture allows for performance improvements and aids in protecting our important business data. In addition to a network that is available 99.999 percent of the time, we need to ensure increased protection against drive failures for important data. We can help to meet these two requirements using RAID technology.

When we speak of RAID, we need to be familiar with a few relevant terms. The terms defined in Table 2-1 describe certain features and properties of most RAID arrays that we see today.

### Reliability

The most elementary issue in network storage selection is *reliability*. We must consider two major areas of reliability while planning for RAID in our network storage system. They are as follows:

- **Fault tolerance** Fault-tolerant devices are computer systems or components that are designed so that, in the event of a component failure, a backup

**TABLE 2-1** Common RAID Terms

| Term | Definition |
|---|---|
| Disk mirroring | The creation of an exact duplicate of a disk or volume on a separate disk or volume in a system. Disk mirroring is done so that if one volume or disk fails, the system can continue to function without interruption using the remaining duplicate. |
| Fault tolerance | A characteristic of a computer system or component designed so that, in the event that a component fails, a backup component or procedure can immediately take its place, with no loss of service. |
| Striping | The process of dividing a body of data into blocks and spreading the data blocks across several partitions on several hard disks. Each stripe is the size of the smallest partition. |
| Parity | The technique of checking whether data has been lost or written over when it's moved from one place in storage to another or transmitted between computers. |

component or procedure can immediately take the failed device's place, with zero loss of service. RAID technology adds fault tolerance to file systems. Many organizations decide to use disk systems that provide hardware fault tolerance. Server versions of Windows 2000 provide mirroring and RAID 5 in software. Disk mirroring, the most common form of fault tolerance, employs a redundant hard disk that can take over if the primary disk fails. Fault tolerance is covered in greater detail in the RAID 5 section of this chapter.

- **High availability and low frequency of failure** For our server architecture to offer high availability, there must be a low frequency of failure. Microsoft defines a highly available network as a network that is available 99.999 percent of the time. In a storage system, basic RAID (disk mirroring) addresses one threat to availability—disk failure. Other factors, such as a redundant power supply, need to be considered as well. Using redundant components is often first thought of as a method of fault tolerance, but it is clearly a method employed to promote high availability. Additionally, to be classified as a highly available system, the RAID storage device must have hot-swappable components. Our RAID system will be able to maintain its high availability in one of two ways. The first way is if we design it as a complete peripheral subsystem that is external to the file server. Generally, if we design our server architecture so that the RAID system is built into a file server, the chances are very good that if the host crashes, our RAID system will crash, too. This is a result of shared components. Obviously, if we design our infrastructure so that our RAID system is separate from our file server, we will not have this issue. The second method is by employing a clustered configuration implementation. By clustering, we are providing each server with a direct link to the storage system, gaining the benefit of preventing a single system's failure from denying access to the data. Clustering also provides the benefit of performance.

### Performance

In addition to needing highly available servers, we must be concerned with performance. RAID enhances speed by permitting information to be stored across multiple disks rather than a single disk that has to find and deliver information in a sequential manner. Multiple drives in a RAID system simultaneously deliver (or write) segments of the stored information. Access time is improved because RAID has the effect of increasing the storage system's bandwidth.

In reality, the actual increase in performance varies, depending on which RAID system we decide to implement. In a mirrored disk RAID system, data is stored in two places, for both backup and redundancy. Having multiple data channels to the same data improves access time on disk-read operations. The RAID system can access some of the data from one disk and simultaneously access the remainder of the data from the second disk. On the flip side of that coin, when using a mirrored disk RAID system, the write operations essentially slow operation. This happens because both disks must perform the same disk write.

For increased performance on both read and write operations, *disk striping* is a better alternative. Striping involves storing a single data file across multiple disks in an array. However, if we only use striping, although we have gained in performance, we have no fault tolerance.

At the hardware level, one of the most effective methods that we could use to increase performance is to add more hard disks. In most cases, the addition of more hard disks provides us with additional input/output (I/O) bandwidth.

### RAID Levels

Ten different levels of RAID are widely implemented; all are listed in Table 2-2. The Web solution that we are creating using Windows 2000 supports only three of these levels: RAID 0, RAID 1, and RAID 5.

**TABLE 2-2** RAID Levels

| RAID Level | Features | Major Advantages |
|---|---|---|
| RAID 0 | Disk striping. Two or more volumes, each on a separate drive, are configured as a stripe set. Data is broken into blocks, called *stripes*, and then written sequentially to all drives in the stripe set. | Speed and performance |
| RAID 1 | Disk mirroring. Two volumes on two drives are configured identically. Data is written to both drives. If one drive fails, there's no data loss, because the other drive contains the data. RAID 1 does not include disk striping. | Redundancy and write performance |
| RAID 2 | Uses striping across disks, with some disks storing error-checking and correcting (ECC) information. It has no advantage over RAID 3. | Speed and performance |
| RAID 3 | Uses striping and dedicates one drive to storing parity information. The embedded ECC information is used to detect errors. Data recovery is accomplished by calculating the exclusive OR (XOR) of the information recorded on the other drives. Since an I/O operation addresses all drives at the same time, RAID 3 cannot overlap I/O. For this reason, RAID 3 is best for single-user systems with long record applications. | Speed and performance |
| RAID 4 | Uses large stripes, which means you can read records from any single drive. This allows you to take advantage of overlapped I/O for read operations. Since all write operations must update the parity drive, no I/O overlapping is possible. RAID 4 offers no advantage over RAID 5. | Fault tolerance and read performance |
| RAID 5 | Disk striping with parity. Uses three or more volumes, each on a separate drive, to create a stripe set with parity error checking. In the case of failure, data can be recovered. | Fault tolerance and read performance |
| RAID 6 | RAID 6 is similar to RAID 5 but includes a second parity scheme that is distributed across different drives and thus offers extremely high fault and drive-failure tolerance. There are currently few or no commercial examples. | Fault tolerance and read performance |
| RAID 7 | RAID 7 includes a real-time embedded operating system as a controller, caching via a high-speed bus, and other characteristics of a standalone computer. One vendor offers this system. | Speed and performance |
| RAID 10 | RAID 10 offers an array of stripes in which each stripe is a RAID 1 array of drives. This level offers higher performance than RAID 1 but at much higher cost. | Redundancy and write performance |
| RAID 53 | RAID 53 offers an array of stripes in which each stripe is a RAID 3 array of disks. This level offers higher performance than RAID 3 but at much higher cost. | Speed and performance |

## RAID 0

As previously mentioned, RAID 0 offers disk striping. With disk striping, two or more volumes, each on a separate drive, are configured as a stripe set. Figure 2-7 illustrates how disk striping occurs. The stripes are written sequentially to all drives in the stripe set. We have the option of placing volumes for a stripe set on up to 32 drives. Using 32 drives isn't recommended, since we will receive our best performance if we employ somewhere between two and five volumes. Using more than five volumes causes performance to decrease dramatically. The major advantage of disk striping is speed. Data is accessible on multiple disks using multiple drive heads, providing us with a considerable improvement in performance.

If we are working with a tight budget, RAID 0 might not be the best solution for our server architecture, since our increased performance boost will come with a rather significant price tag. Because we are dealing with volume sets in RAID 0, if any hard disk drive in the stripe set fails, the stripe set can no longer be used. Essentially, this means that all data in the stripe set is lost. At that point, we need to re-create the stripe set and re-create the data from backups.

If RAID 0 is the level that we ultimately decide to employ in our network, we need to keep in mind several important points. The first point is that, when we create stripe sets, we want to use volumes that are approximately the same size. Disk management bases the overall size of the stripe set on the smallest volume size. To be more specific, the maximum size of the stripe set is a multiple of the smallest volume size. For example, if we have five physical drives and the smallest volume that we create is 50MB, the maximum size for the stripe set is 250MB. If we want to maximize the stripe set's performance, we can follow these pieces of helpful information:

- We should use disks that are on separate disk controllers, thus providing the ability for the system to simultaneously access the drives.

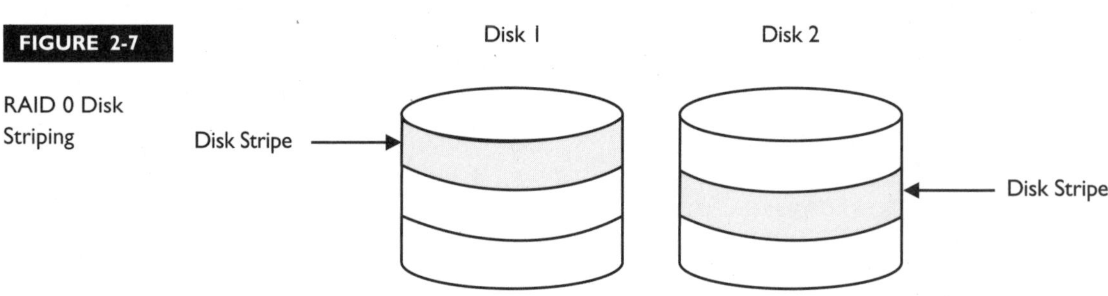


**FIGURE 2-7** RAID 0 Disk Striping

- We should not use the disks containing the stripe set for other purposes. This way, each disk is dedicating all its time to the stripe set.

**EXERCISE 2-3**

## Creating a Stripe Set

Let's walk through the steps to create a stripe set. Note that when setting up RAID in Windows 2000, we use the Disk Management console. However, when we configure RAID hardware, we should always use the software that is provided by the manufacturer. This software is typically accessible via the BIOS. Do the following:

1. In the Disk Management Graphical view, right-click an area marked **Unallocated on a dynamic disk** and then choose **Create Volume**. This starts the Create Volume Wizard. The Welcome dialog box appears. After reviewing the information, click **Next**.
2. Select **Striped Volume** as the volume type. Create the volume. Keep in mind that we need to have a minimum of two dynamic disks to create a striped volume.

Once we have created a striped volume, we can use the volume in the same manner that we would use any other volume we create. Because we are unable to expand a stripe set once it has been created, we need to carefully consider the setup prior to the implementation.

### RAID 1

RAID 1 provides disk mirroring, which enables use of identically sized volumes on two different drives to create a redundant data set. Figure 2-8 illustrates how disk mirroring occurs. The drives are written with identical (mirrored) sets of information, providing a backup if one drive fails. If we decide to use RAID 1 in our server architecture, it is helpful to know that disk mirroring offers about the same fault tolerance as disk striping with parity. Essentially, because mirrored disks don't need to write parity information, they can offer better write performance in most circumstances.

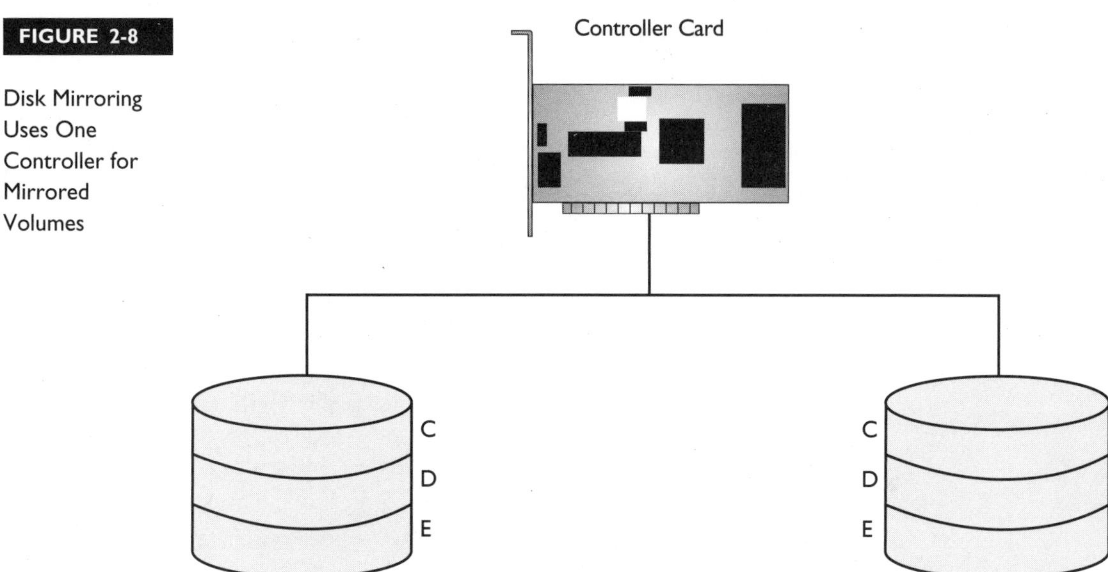


FIGURE 2-8 Disk Mirroring Uses One Controller for Mirrored Volumes

However, disk striping with parity usually offers better read performance, due largely in part to the fact that read operations are spread over multiple drives.

The drawback with disk mirroring that we need to consider is that it effectively cuts the amount of storage space in half. For example, if we need to mirror a 10GB drive, we need an additional 10GB drive. In simple terms, we have just used 20GB of space to store 10GB of information.

One thing that doesn't change between disk striping and disk mirroring is the fact that we want the mirrored disks on separate disk controllers, providing us with extra protection against disk controller failure. If one of the disk controllers fails, the disk on the other controller is still available. This technique is also referred to as *disk duplexing*, illustrated in Figure 2-9. Disk mirroring typically uses a single drive controller, but disk duplexing uses two drive controllers. If one of the mirrored drives fails, disk operation can continue. Here, when users read and write data, the data is written to the remaining disk. We would need to break the mirror before we can fix the mirror. Disk duplexing provides better fault tolerance than disk mirroring.

**FIGURE 2-9**

Disk Duplexing Uses Two Controllers for Mirrored Volumes

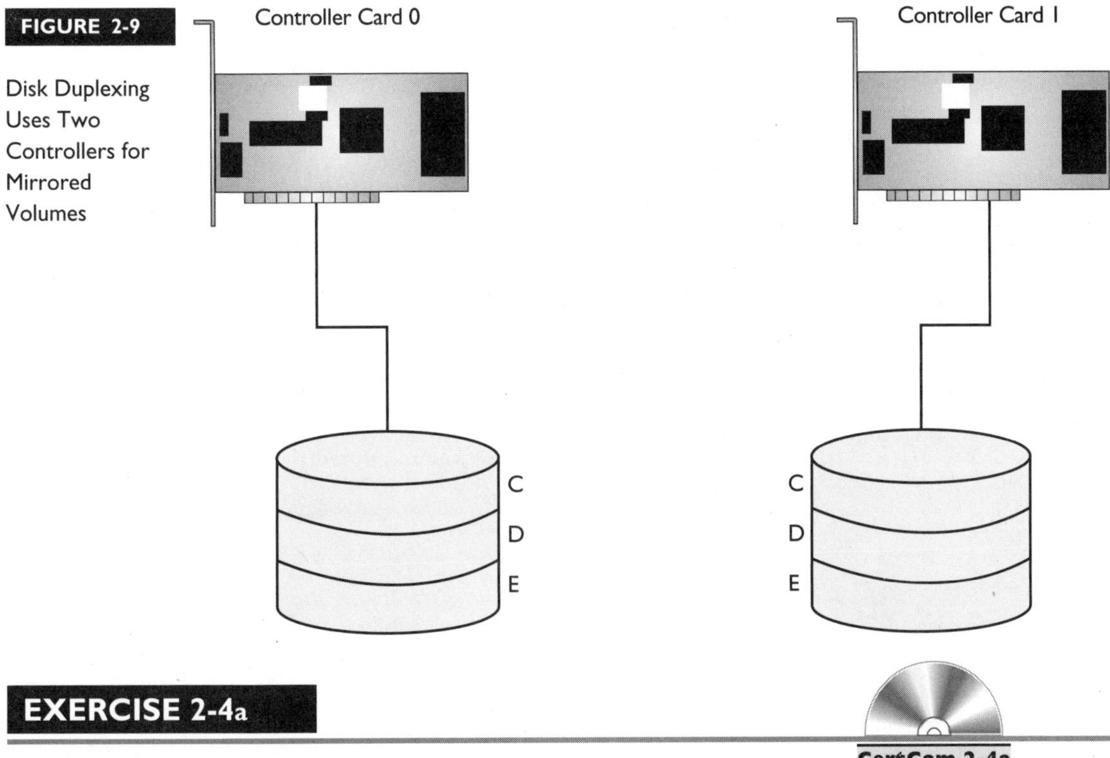


**EXERCISE 2-4a**

CertCam 2-4a

## Creating a Mirror Set

To complete a mirror set, complete the following steps:

1. In the Disk Management Graphical view, right-click an area marked **Unallocated on a dynamic disk**, then choose **Create Volume**. By making this choice, we start the Create Volume Wizard. Once you have read the Welcome dialog box, click **Next**.
2. Select **Mirrored Volume** as the volume type. Create the volume. Remember to create two volumes that are identical in size but that reside on separate dynamic volumes.
3. In typical RAID fashion, mirroring is transparent to users. Users see the mirrored set as a single drive that they can access and use like any other drive.

## EXERCISE 2-4b

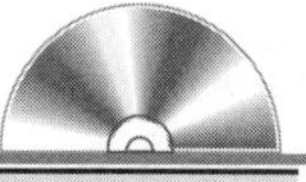


### Mirroring an Existing Volume

Rather than create a new mirrored volume, we can use an existing volume to create a mirrored set. We accomplish this task only if the volume that we want to mirror is a simple volume. We also need to ensure that we have an area of unallocated space on a second dynamic drive with equal or more space than the existing volume. The following two steps complete this task through Disk Management:

1. Right-click the simple volume that we will mirror, then select **Add Mirror**. The Add Mirror Wizard starts.
2. Using the wizard, configure the second volume in the mirrored set.

### RAID 5

RAID 5 is the most common level of RAID used on Windows 2000 servers. RAID 5 offers disk striping with parity. Should we choose to implement RAID 5 in our server architecture, we would need a minimum of three hard disk drives to set up fault tolerance. RAID 5 is illustrated in Figure 2-10. Disk Management sizes the volumes on the drives identically. Again, as with RAID 0, we can place the volumes for a stripe set on up to 32 drives, but we would start to notice performance issues at a severe level after five drives. The best performance improvements occur using between two and five drives.

RAID 5 is really nothing more than an enhanced version of RAID 1, with fault tolerance the enhancement. Fault tolerance gives us the added insurance that a single drive's failure will not bring down the entire drive set. Rather, all operations continue to function normally, with disk operation directed at the remaining volumes in the set. RAID 5 writes parity checksums with the blocks of data to allow for fault tolerance. With this feature, if any of the drives in the stripe set fail, we can use the parity information to recover the data. However, if we have two disks fail at the same time, the parity information would not be sufficient to recover the data, and we would then need to rebuild the striped set from backup.

RAID 5 writes to multiple disks in parallel, with the capacity of one of the disks used to hold parity information, thus providing a general performance improvement. RAID 5 distributes the parity evenly among all drives, thus avoiding a bottleneck.

FIGURE 2-10

RAID 5 Disk Striping with Parity

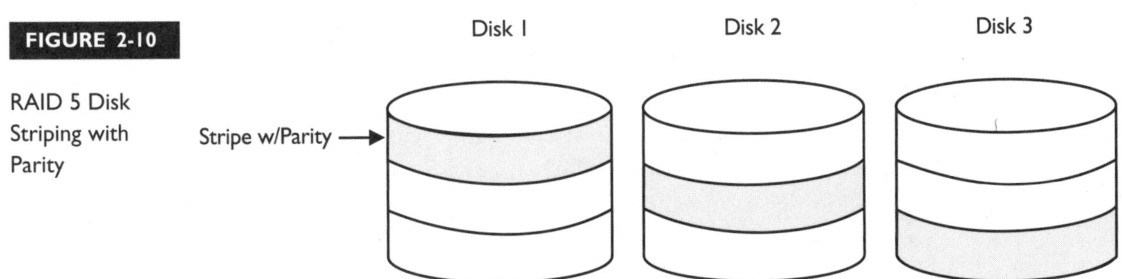


An example is an array of five drives, with 80 percent of each drive data and 20 percent parity.

## EXERCISE 2-5

### Creating a Stripe Set with Parity

In order to create a stripe set with parity in Disk Management, complete the following steps:

1. From the Disk Management Graphical view, right-click an area marked **Unallocated on a dynamic disk** and then select **Create Volume**. The Create Volume Wizard starts. After reading the Welcome dialog box, click **Next**.
2. Select **RAID 5 Volume** as the volume type. Create the volume. Selecting free space on three separate dynamic drives is essential at this point.

Once the stripe set has been created, users can use the set just as they would a normal drive.

***When our budget allows and our particular requirements mandate it, we combine two levels of RAID to increase the level of fault tolerance. For example, we can mirror or duplex two RAID 0 arrays to create a RAID 01 array. This is a mirrored stripe, as is described in Table 2-2. We can do the same with two RAID 5 arrays to create a RAID 51 array. In practice, it is always better to using striping, even though performance is decreased somewhat on write operations. However, performance is improved on read operations. These solutions require more disks and peripheral equipment but are often worth the expense in the reduced downtime and data loss.***

## Storage Area Networks

A Storage Area Network (SAN) is a dedicated high-speed network that consists of multiple storage devices interconnected with each other and with servers that access the data stored in the devices. A SAN usually functions as part of a larger enterprise network or high-availability infrastructure, providing virtually unlimited access to data for its clients. Much like a data center in an enterprise network, a SAN usually consists of collections of fault-tolerant storage devices connected to each other in a centralized location on their own network through a high-speed Fiber Channel switch. This switch makes the network almost impervious to data loss. The storage devices can be RAID array, optical disk libraries, or tape backup.

In essence, a SAN is a LAN that is dedicated to provisioning disk space to accommodate the storage needs of all the clients that are connected to it. Offloading the storage operation from the server to a SAN greatly reduces overhead on all servers attached to the SAN. A SAN can be built using Small Computer Serial Interface (SCSI) connectors as well as coaxial cable, multimode fiber optic connections, and even Shielded Twisted-Pair (STP) wire. Most commonly today, because of its better performance, Fibre Channel is the technology of choice for SANs.

A SAN makes it truly possible to access data 24 hours a day, seven days a week. SANs usually comprise one or more fault-tolerant disk arrays, which make them nearly impervious to data loss. Typically, a SAN is associated with one or more server clusters as well. This is what makes SANs ideal for high-availability environments such as e-commerce infrastructures. Windows 2000 Advanced Server and Datacenter Server include support for all the technologies that are used for connections to SANs, such as SCSI, Fibre Channel, and ATM, either directly or across a network, therefore taking advantage of the unique and powerful storage architecture it provides.

SCSI is the usual medium in the SAN with the capability of transferring data at a rate of about 160MBps. However, SCSI has a limitation of about 40 feet, after which maximum bandwidth falls sharply. Fibre Channel can be used when our SAN is located remotely, since Fibre Channel supports SAN communication up to six miles, without sacrificing its maximum transfer rate of more than 1GBps.

There are three type of Fibre Channel-based SANs: point-to-point, arbitrary loop, and switched. The most common are Fibre Channel arbitrary loop (FC-AL) SANs. FC-AL SANs are similar to SCSI-based SANs but are much faster and have a

127-host limit. Figure 2-11 illustrates the typical components of a high-availability Web infrastructure with a SAN.

on the Job

***So far, only a few of us have been fortunate enough to have seen a SAN at work. Many companies cannot yet recoup the requisite investment in time and money, because only companies with data storage requirements nearing the terabyte (1000GB) range would use it.***

***However, since SAN technology is based on SCSI technology, it could be possible to create a cheaper version of a SAN using the SCSI devices we use today instead of the expensive mainstream Fibre Channel technology via a theory from my old Macintosh computing days. It is possible to daisy chain a series of SCSI-based storage units like RAID arrays and tape drives, with one end point connected to an empty subnet that we create solely for data storage and backup. Typically, the networked end point would be a bare-bones server with only the services needed to share the SAN and make it visible on the network. The performance and reliability would not be as good as Fibre Channel. Neither should you trust critical enterprise data on such a setup. However, this could be a great solution for a few users who need to store considerably large amounts of data for relatively short periods of time.***

A SAN's architecture makes it scalable and better performing than a simple RAID array residing on a single server, much the way that the server cluster is more scalable and better performing than a single server with redundant components. SANs are heterogeneous, capable of supporting a variety of platforms and operating on a variety of network protocols and media. Windows 2000 Advanced Server and Datacenter Server clusters functioning as part of a SAN can easily use the resources a SAN provides. Windows 2000 servers and clients see the storage in a SAN as disk drives. Windows 2000 servers are assigned fractions of the SAN since the servers are most likely sharing the SAN with other platforms such as UNIX.

A SAN runs over a network known as a *system area network*. This network allows any server or cluster that is attached to it to access any of the SAN's components. Data backup can also take place over the systems area network. This is recommended for limiting the amount of traffic on the enterprise network of which the SAN is a part.

FIGURE 2-11

A Typical SAN

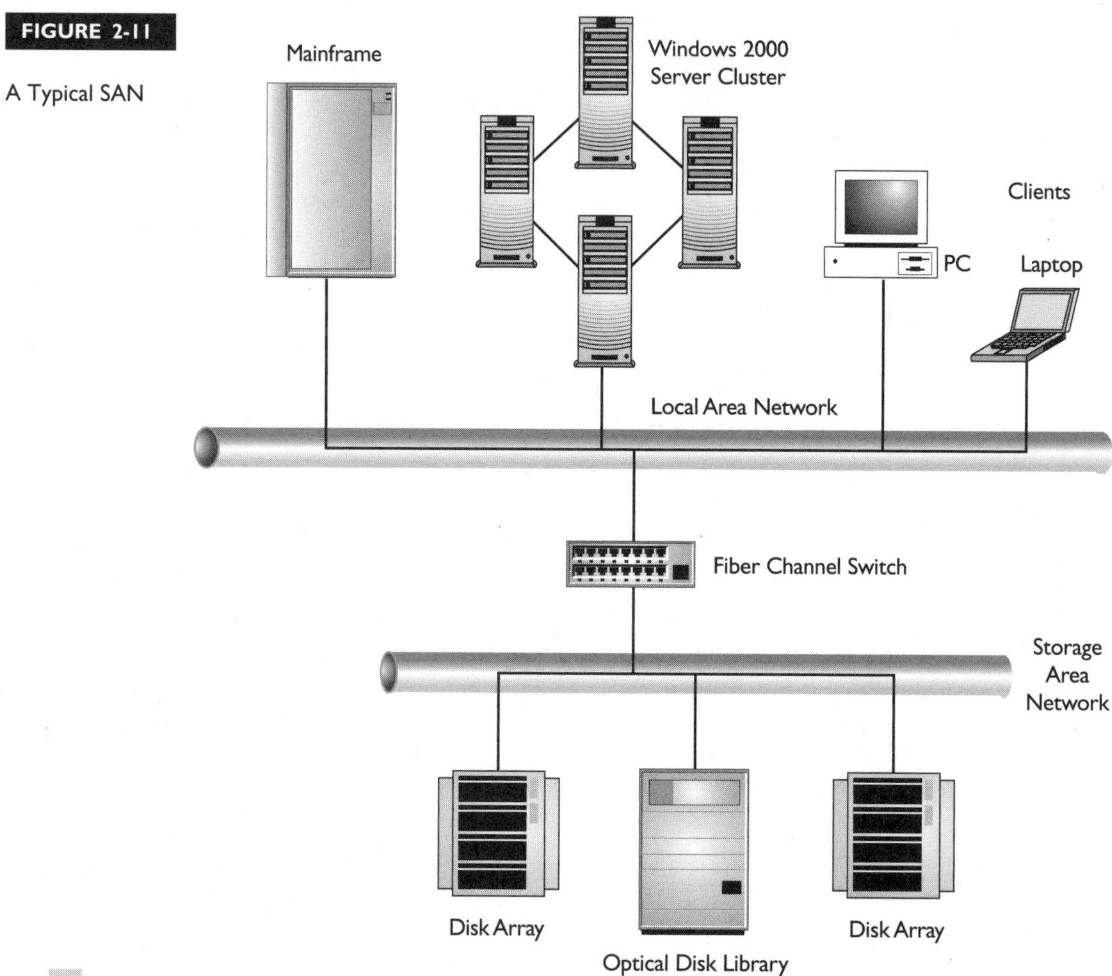


exam Watch

***A systems area network is the network over which a SAN runs. Systems area networks are more versatile and can be used for different applications than a storage network. The terms* SAN *and* systems area network *are not interchangeable.***

Let's take a look at some scenario questions and their solutions to gain a better understanding of SANs and storage.

| SCENARIO & SOLUTION | |
|---|---|
| What is disk mirroring? | Disk mirroring provides the ability to use identically sized volumes on two different drives to create a redundant data set. |
| What are the two major areas of reliability that need to be considered when planning for RAID in a network storage system? | Fault tolerance and high availability/low frequency of failure. |
| What is the difference between RAID 0 and RAID 5? | Both RAID 0 and RAID 5 have disk striping with parity, but RAID 5 also adds fault tolerance. |
| Is a SAN scalable? | Yes. Because of the architecture that is used for SANs, they are scalable, making them desirable for use in high-performance environments. |

## CERTIFICATION SUMMARY

In this chapter, we received an introduction into the architecture of Network Load Balancing and the Cluster Service. We began to look at how they work and where they work in our high-availability Web infrastructure. We discussed some factors that affect which technology we use and the applications for which each is better suited.

We also looked at related components that assist Cluster Service in its task of providing fault tolerance and failover such as RAID and SANs. Since RAID is most widely used, we went into a bit of detail in the different levels of RAID and what each has to offer as a solution that promises high availability and fault tolerance. We then took a brief look at SANs and how they benefit not only high-availability Web infrastructures but corporate infrastructures as well.

# TWO-MINUTE DRILL

## Designing Network Load-Balancing Solutions

- When a Network Load Balancing cluster is created, we must assign an IP address to which all the hosts in the cluster respond. This IP address is known as the *primary IP address* or a *virtual IP address.* A cluster can have many different virtual IP addresses but only one primary address.
- Network Load Balancing has two modes of Layer 2 configurations for accepting incoming traffic: *unicast* mode and *multicast* mode.
- Network Load Balancing employs what is known as an *N–1 way* architecture as a failover strategy.
- There are three filtering modes available in Network Load Balancing: *single host* (specifies that a single-cluster host handle network traffic for an associated port rule), *multiple host* (specifies that multiple-cluster hosts handle the traffic for the particular port rule), and *disabled* (serves to block all network traffic for an associated port rule from being handled by any cluster host).
- Load weighting is the parameter that determines how much traffic a single-cluster host is configured to filter or process for a particular port rule when a cluster is employing multiple-host filtering mode.

## Designing Server Cluster Solutions

- Cluster Service's goal is to provide fault tolerance and redundancy for enterprise-level server applications that must have little or no downtime.
- The number of applications or services that can be hosted on a single node in a server cluster is dependent on the system overhead incurred by the applications or services as well as the specifications of the server computer that hosts them.
- Cluster Service is available in two levels: two-node clusters in Windows 2000 Advanced Server and four-node clusters in Windows 2000 Datacenter Server.
- A resource group in Windows 2000 Cluster Service is defined as a logical collection of software and hardware components that work together to provide a service in the cluster.

- ❑ Applications hosted by server clusters represent themselves as virtual servers to the clients that they serve. Clients connecting to different applications hosted by clusters see only the application with which they are concerned.

## Designing Data Storage

- ❑ Fault-tolerant devices are computer systems or components that are designed so that, in the event of a component failure, a backup component or procedure can immediately take the failed devices place, with zero loss of service.
- ❑ Striping is the process of dividing a body of data into blocks and spreading the data blocks across several partitions on several hard disks. Each stripe is the size of the smallest partition.
- ❑ Only three levels of RAID are functional within Windows 2000: RAID 0, RAID 1, and RAID 5.
- ❑ A storage area network (SAN) is a dedicated high-speed network that consists of multiple storage devices interconnected with each other and with servers that access the data stored in the devices that make up the SAN.
- ❑ SANs are heterogeneous, capable of supporting a variety of platforms and operating on a variety of network protocols.

# SELF TEST

The following questions will help you measure your understanding of the material presented in this chapter. Read all the choices carefully because there might be more than one correct answer. Choose all correct answers for each question.

## Designing Network Load-Balancing Solutions

1. An organization, a high-traffic e-commerce company, is considering using Network Load Balancing servers for the new architecture that it is currently designing. What factors should the company consider when making the decision to use NLB?

   A. How many hits do they anticipate within the next year?

   B. What is the need for response time and availability?

   C. What are the company's security requirements?

   D. Will the company need more DHCP servers?

2. What needs to be done, if anything, to ensure that packets are properly routed using Network Load Balancing?

   A. Install a router on the NLB network segment.

   B. Nothing. NLB already routes the packet to its destination.

   C. Nothing. NLB uses multicast packet transmission to ensure delivery to every NLB cluster host, so routing is not required.

   D. Disable NLB filtering.

3. How are load percentages determined when NLB is employed? (Choose all best answer.)

   A. Load percentages can be determined one of two ways—either by NLB itself, using the algorithm that was created to determine load traffic, or through the use of load percentages, which can be set for each host in the cluster through NLB properties.

   B. The network administrator, when installing NLB, determines load percentages.

   C. The network administrator cannot determine load percentages; these percentages are determined using the algorithm that is a standard feature in NLB.

   D. Load percentages are determined using a combination of rules that are set by the network administrator and with the built-in algorithm feature that is standard with NLB.

**4.** You have built a highly available network infrastructure and used a Layer 2 100MBps switch on your Web server network. Your Web servers all have two NICs connected to the network. You configured your NLB cluster to use unicast mode transmission. Your friend, who is also a network administrator, tells you that there could be address conflict errors on your switch because you are using unicast mode transmission. You check your switch and see no errors. Why is your friend wrong?

A. NLB uses the original MAC addresses of the NIC connected to it so that they are all unique.

B. NLB in unicast mode masks the MAC address of each host in the cluster with the same MAC address for reception of incoming traffic, but it uses a modified version of the MAC address of the server for outbound traffic.

C. NLB uses the network address of the Web cluster instead of the MAC address, so conflicts are avoided.

D. NLB assigns an address to the cluster adapter that is derived from the primary IP address. This allows each host to use its own MAC address, so conflicts are avoided.

**5.** In NLB, what is *N–1 way* architecture for failover?

A. N–1 way is defined as a cluster of *N* number of hosts. If one member of the cluster fails, failover will take place with a surviving host. If more than one host fails at any given time, failover does not work.

B. N–1 way is defined as a cluster of *N* number of hosts. If one or more members of the cluster fail, failover will take place with the surviving hosts until only one cluster host is left.

C. N–1 way is the failover method that is used when client affinity has been enabled on NLB.

D. N–1 way is a failover method used in combination with RAID 5.

**6.** My organization has eight servers in our cluster. We are trying to add another host to the cluster with a priority of 1. What is causing this to happen, and how can this issue be resolved?

A. There is a priority conflict. Do not set the priority until after you have added the host to the cluster.

B. There is probably a MAC address conflict. Assign the cluster MAC address to the host before adding it to the cluster.

C. There is a priority conflict. Change the priority of the new host to a number that hasn't been assigned to the other hosts in the cluster when adding it to the cluster.

D. The host is not authorized. Have the default host authorize the new host before adding it to the cluster.

7. Is there a way to use NLB to assure all network traffic coming from a high-priority client is sent to only one server, receiving high priority on each packet? How would you set this up?

   A. Yes, this can be set up using the Priority feature. The host with the highest priority can be set up to receive traffic from a single source, giving all traffic from that client high priority.

   B. Yes, this can be accomplished by configuring the Client Affinity feature. This feature allows NLB to service all traffic from a specified client with a specific server.

   C. No, this cannot be accomplished with NLB.

   D. Yes, you can accomplish this using a combination of the client affinity and filtering features that are included in NLB.

8. What protocol does NLB use to communicate with a cluster host?

   A. Multicast

   B. Switch flooding

   C. Broadcast

   D. Unicast

## Designing Server Cluster Solutions

9. The organization that you work for is in the process of designing new network architecture based on Windows 2000. You know that you will employ Cluster Service within the architecture. What is the rule you need to follow for the number of nodes that are in a cluster? (Choose all that apply.)

   A. The number of applications and services you need to host on one node

   B. The number of clients requesting services

   C. The throughput of the cluster switch

   D. The processor speed, RAM, and disk configuration of the cluster nodes

10. How does the shared-nothing architecture of Cluster Service work? (Choose all that apply.)

    A. The shared-nothing architecture ensures that resource groups can be owned by individual nodes and eliminates the need for any special apparatus to connect the nodes to the resource group beyond the default Windows 2000 SCSI drivers.

    B. The shared-nothing architecture sets up rules and policies within Console Manager, requiring that resource groups own nodes, releasing them only when a higher priority node is created.

C. The shared-nothing architecture eliminates the need for nodes to share resources.

D. The shared-nothing architecture is based on client affinity and node priority. The higher a node's priority, the less client affinity that is shared. A node with a priority of 1 would be the shared-nothing node.

**11.** How does the failover capability feature work within Cluster Service?

A. Cluster Service does not initiate failover unless the administrator removes the mapping of the failed service in the cluster administration program.

B. Cluster Service removes the failed service from the cluster and informs its clients that the service is no longer available.

C. Cluster Service detects the failure and moves the resource and its mapping to the first available server or servers of the highest priority. The administrator is then required to start the service manually.

D. If an application, resource, resource group, or entire node in the cluster fails, Cluster Service moves the services that were being provided by the unit that failed to one or more of the surviving nodes in the cluster and restarts.

**12.** You are the network administrator for a high-tech, e-commerce organization. The daily demands both internal and external users place on your Web servers are extraordinary. Two weeks ago, you had a failure on a node, and the impact was a loss of revenue. You currently have an N+1 failover set up. Unfortunately, the standby server didn't have the capacity that was needed. What did you do wrong, and how can you prevent something like this from happening in the future? (Choose all that apply.)

A. You underestimated the load the resources would put on the server. The first rule of N+1 failover is that the standby server must have enough capacity to handle the traffic coming to it. Standby servers must be prepared to take on extra capacity. You must also be sure to configure the priority of the nodes in the cluster. To prevent this from happening again in the future, you must reevaluate the server that you have designated as the standby server and ensure that it has the capacity to handle the traffic in the event it is needed.

B. The environment that you have described is one that should be using cascading failover, not the N+1 failover. This allows you the ability to designate one or more backup nodes that are assigned high priority.

C. The only area in which you failed was designating a backup server that did not have enough capacity to handle the traffic coming to it when the primary server failed. Simply reevaluate your backup server's capacity, designate a different one if needed, and then test the server to ensure that it can perform as needed in the event of a true failure. This will help you keep this situation from happening again.

D. None of the above.

13. A company recently finished upgrading its Web servers to Windows 2000. The administrator is only vaguely familiar with the clustering/failover schemes. If the environment has a cluster of four servers, which is a better option: active/active or active/passive, and why?

A. Active/passive is the cluster/failover scheme that you want to employ with a four-server cluster, because having only one host operational and handling client requests at a time provides for the best performance.

B. Active/passive is the solution to employ because it provides a high level of reliability in a four-server environment.

C. Active/active is the ideal solution because it allows you to have all members of the cluster operational and handling client requests at the same time.

D. Either solution is fine. There isn't a great deal of difference regarding performance demands between working with four servers or two servers.

## Designing Data Storage

14. What three levels of RAID are supported by Windows 2000?

A. RAID 0, RAID 3, and RAID 5

B. RAID 1, RAID 5, and RAID 10

C. RAID 53, RAID 7, and RAID 8

D. RAID 0, RAID 1, and RAID 5

15. How does disk duplexing differ from disk mirroring?

A. Disk duplexing is RAID 3, and disk mirroring is RAID 1.

B. Disk duplexing creates two mirrored disks on two different RAID controllers. Disk mirroring creates two mirrored disks on the same controller.

C. Disk mirroring has more stripes than disk duplexing.

D. Disk mirroring creates two mirrored disks on two different RAID controllers, but disk duplexing creates two mirrored disks on the same controller.

16. The organization that you work for is introducing new network architecture. You are at the point of determining which level of RAID to use. The organization is data dependent, with

high performance a must. Disk space is a concern. What level of RAID would be best supported by this environment, and why?

A. RAID 1 is the ideal solution, providing redundancy through disk mirroring.

B. RAID 0 is the ideal solution, bringing high performance (speed) through striping.

C. RAID 5 is the optimal solution, providing high performance through striping and fault tolerance, both of which will provide extra data availability security.

D. Both B and C.

**17.** You have recently accepted a consulting position to assist in the redesigning of an organization's Web infrastructure. One of the tasks that falls under your list of responsibilities is to make the determination of either using RAID or a SAN. You don't have a lot of experience in this area. What you do know is that the solution must be scalable, because huge growth is anticipated over the next three to six years. You also understand that the client is data dependent and cannot afford to have an issue with data availability. What is the best solution for this type of infrastructure?

A. RAID 5 is the best solution for this type of infrastructure because it is scalable and offers 99.999 percent reliability of data availability.

B. A SAN with RAID 5 is the ideal solution for this type of infrastructure. SAN allows for scalability along with the highest likelihood of data availability.

C. RAID 1 is the optimal technology to employ in this type of planned architecture. RAID 1 provides disk mirroring, which ensures no data loss while providing scalability.

D. RAID 0 and RAID 5 combined will help you meet all your client's requirements, with an additional benefit of fault tolerance.

**18.** What is the single biggest difference between RAID and SAN?

A. RAID is scalable, but a SAN is not.

B. SANs are connected to a single server, but RAID arrays are connected to entire LANs.

C. A RAID array is a single group of disks arranged in a fault-tolerant and redundant configuration. A SAN is a collection of varied storage devices and technologies such as RAID, optical storage, and tape libraries.

D. All of the above.

# LAB QUESTION

You are a network architect who works as a consultant. You have just accepted an assignment to design a high-availability Web infrastructure for an up-and-coming e-commerce organization. The following is known about what is available in-house:

- Application with the following three layers:
  - Web front end
  - Middle-layer application focusing on information processing
  - Database back end
- We know the following information about the back-end database:
  - The database fills with records on a consistent basis (approximately every two months).
  - The database information needs to be flushed, without losing any records after it has filled.
  - The sales and marketing team owns the optical tape library.
  - The finance team works with the optical disk library, which is severely underused.
- The information systems team has the following in use or available to use:
  - Backup tape
  - Four RAID arrays, 200GB each, that have just been delivered

The goals the VP of information technology has given you are as follows:

- Infrastructure must be cost effective
- Must provide high availability
- Must provide fault tolerance
- Must offer high performance
- Solution must leverage all storage that is available to the organization

# SELF TEST ANSWERS

## Designing Network Load-Balancing Solutions

1. ☑ **A** and **B**. These are the best answers to this question. When deciding whether or not NLB is needed, capacity, availability, and response time all need to be considered. NLB was designed to improve all three of these.
   ☒ **C** is incorrect because even though security is a valid concern, it is not one of the first questions asked. **D** is incorrect because DHCP cannot be clustered using NLB, nor is it one of the requirements in this situation.

2. ☑ **C**. This is the best answer in this case because NLB uses multicast to ensure that client request packets go through all the switch ports to which the NLB cluster hosts are attached to deliver traffic to all NLB hosts.
   ☒ **A** is incorrect because installing a router on the NLB segment is useless since routers don't help with routing within a single segment. **B** is incorrect because NLB does not route, it multicasts, so routing is not necessary. **D** is incorrect because nothing needs to be done to ensure delivery when packets are multicast.

3. ☑ **A**, **B**, and **D**. These are the best answers to this question. Load percentages can be set by the administrator via the NLB properties windows on each host running NLB or automatically calculated by the NLB algorithm if the load percentage option is not enabled.
   ☒ **C** is incorrect because the network administrator can specify load percentage.

4. ☑ **B** is the correct answer to this question because unicast mode masks each host with a special MAC address, but it uses a modified version of its own MAC address to avoid conflicts in the switch.
   ☒ **A**, **C**, and **D** are incorrect because unicast mode never allows a cluster host to use any of its own addresses, whether MAC or network addresses.

5. ☑ **B** is correct because N–1 way failover works until only one host is left, after which it does not.
   ☒ **A** is incorrect because, if $N = 2$, failover does not work on the remaining host because there is no other host with which to balance the load. **C** is incorrect because affinity is not required to enable failover. **D** is incorrect because RAID 5 is not required for failover to occur.

6. ☑ **C**. If you try to add a host that has the same priority as another host in the cluster, you will not be able to add the host. Changing the priority before we add the host to the cluster will allow us to add the host.

☒ A is incorrect because the priority has to be set when adding the host to the cluster in order for the host to be added. **B** is incorrect because a MAC address conflict does not prevent the host from being added to the cluster. **D** is incorrect because there is no authorization requirement or process for allowing a host into a cluster.

**7.** ☑ B and D are the best answers in this case. Client affinity locks a specific cluster host to a specific client, thus ensuring that the service to that client is high priority.
☒ A is incorrect because the host priority does not specifically specify which client to service. C is incorrect because this is exactly what client affinity is meant to do.

**8.** ☑ A. NLB uses Multicast to communicate with a cluster host.
☒ B is incorrect because switch flooding is actually an error condition caused by unicast MAC addressing. C is incorrect because broadcasting would deliver traffic to all hosts on a network and not just in a cluster. **D** is incorrect because unicast would not deliver traffic to all hosts in the cluster.

## Designing Server Cluster Solutions

**9.** ☑ A and D are the best answers in this case. Since Cluster Service uses the N+1 way failover, we should always scale our cluster based on how many services and applications we can effectively host on our least powerful server in the cluster. Therefore, the physical specifications such as RAM and processor speed are integral to deciding the number of nodes in a cluster.
☒ B is incorrect because even though the number of client requests is a factor to be considered, the number of hosts in an individual cluster is more affected by the number of services hosted per node. C is incorrect because the throughput of the switch does not affect failover.

**10.** ☑ A and C are the best answers here. The shared-nothing architecture enables cluster nodes to manage their own resources such as SCSI disks. This ensures the availability of resources because no resources are shared and no resource groups are lost if a node fails.
☒ B is incorrect because the shared-nothing architecture builds no rules and policies based on priority of any sort. D is incorrect because the shared-nothing architecture and client affinity are not related to each other, nor do they affect each other at all.

**11.** ☑ D. Failed resource groups or applications are moved over to the next eligible node and restarted by Cluster Service.
☒ A is incorrect because failover occurs automatically once failure occurs. **B** is incorrect because Cluster Service does not remove the failed service; it moves it to another node.

C is incorrect because an administrator is not required to restart the moved resource group or application.

**12.** ☑ A and C are the best answers in this case. The server provisioned for use as a standby server must be powerful enough to handle all the services, applications, and resources that are hosted on the cluster.
☒ B is incorrect because even though cascading failover is configured, if all the nodes configured to handle the load fail, the standby server should be able to handle the load. D is incorrect because it does not offer a solution.

**13.** ☑ C. When more than two servers are used, active/active offers the highest performance and reliability.
☒ A and B are incorrect because active/passive is a solution that should be employed when there are only two hosts in the cluster. D is incorrect because active/passive is not an option.

## Designing Data Storage

**14.** ☑ D. Windows 2000 includes software support for RAID 0, 1, and 5.
☒ A, B, and C are incorrect because all other RAID configurations in Windows 2000 must be accomplished via hardware RAID controllers.

**15.** ☑ B. A duplexed disk is a mirror image of a volume or disk that resides on a separate controller in the same server or storage unit. A mirrored disk is a duplicate disk on a volume on the same controller in the same server or storage unit.
☒ A is incorrect because RAID 3 is a form of disk striping with ECC. C is incorrect because neither disk mirroring nor disk duplexing involves striping. D is incorrect because the definitions are reversed. Disk mirroring is done on a single controller.

**16.** ☑ D. High performance is provided through striping, which is a feature of RAID 0 and RAID 5. RAID 5 provides the added data security benefit of fault tolerance.
☒ A is incorrect because if disk space is a concern, mirroring is not the option to use.

**17.** ☑ B. Only SAN is scalable and offers a high level of availability for data.
☒ A, C, and D are all incorrect because scalability is not an option with RAID.

**18.** ☑ C. A SAN contains RAID arrays as well as optical disk libraries or tape libraries.
☒ A is incorrect because a SAN is much more scalable than a RAID array. B is incorrect because a RAID array is connected to a single server, not a LAN. D is incorrect because not all the answers are correct.

# LAB ANSWER

Our solution would consist of three server clusters in addition to the enterprise LAN:

The front end consists of the following:

- Web server cluster using NLB

The middle layer consists of the following:

- Network Load Balancing
- Middle-layer application

The back end consists of the following:

- Database server cluster using Cluster Service

We will design a SAN using the optical disk and tape libraries, the four RAID arrays, and backup tapes. We'll use it as centralized storage for the entire organization. We can dump the database from our back-end servers into the SAN for archiving onto backup tapes or optical disks. If greater capacity is needed, we can simply add more storage media. Figure 2-12 presents a conceptual rendering of the architecture.

**FIGURE 2-12** Lab Exercise Architecture

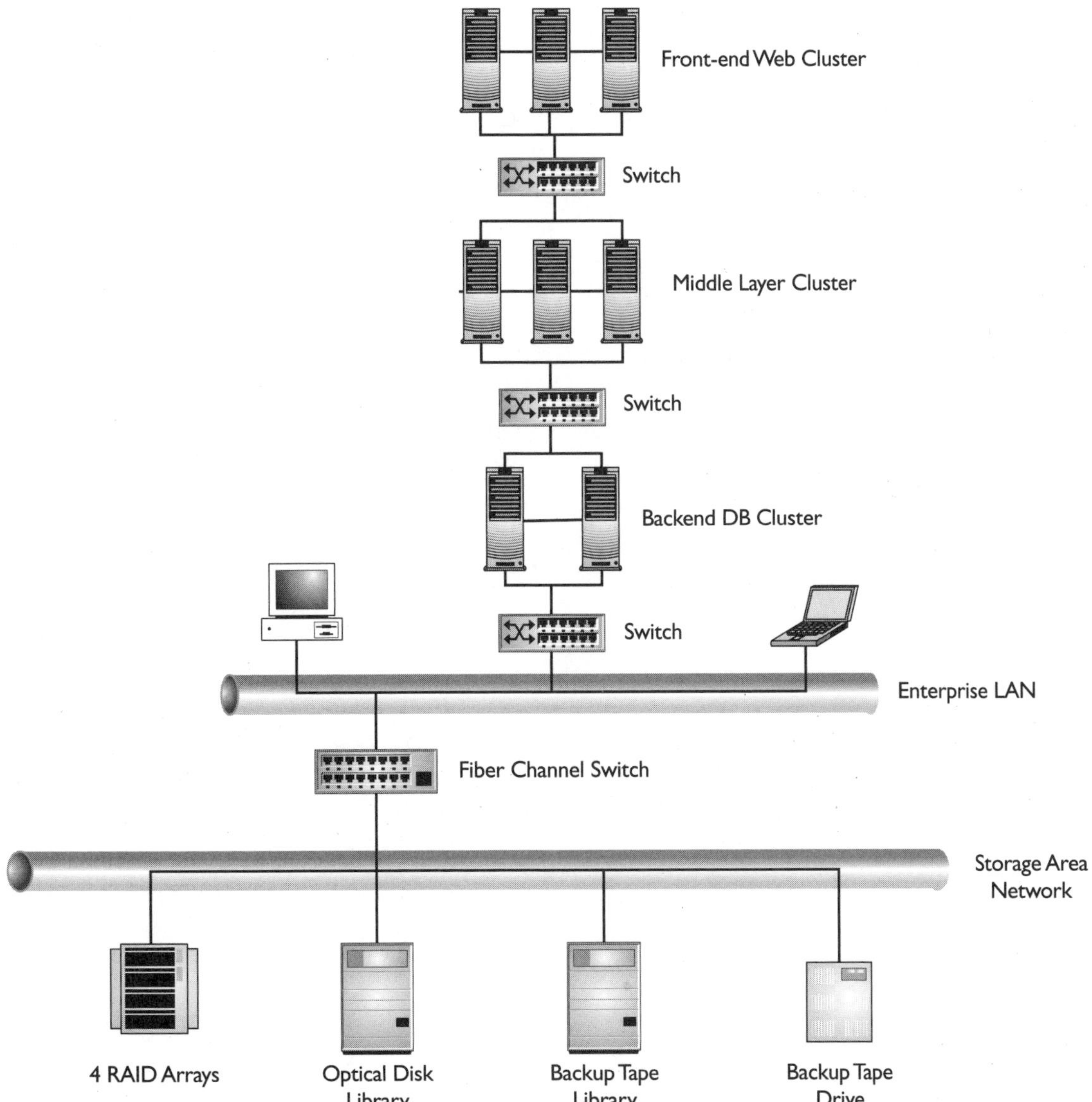

MCSE

MICROSOFT CERTIFIED SYSTEMS ENGINEER

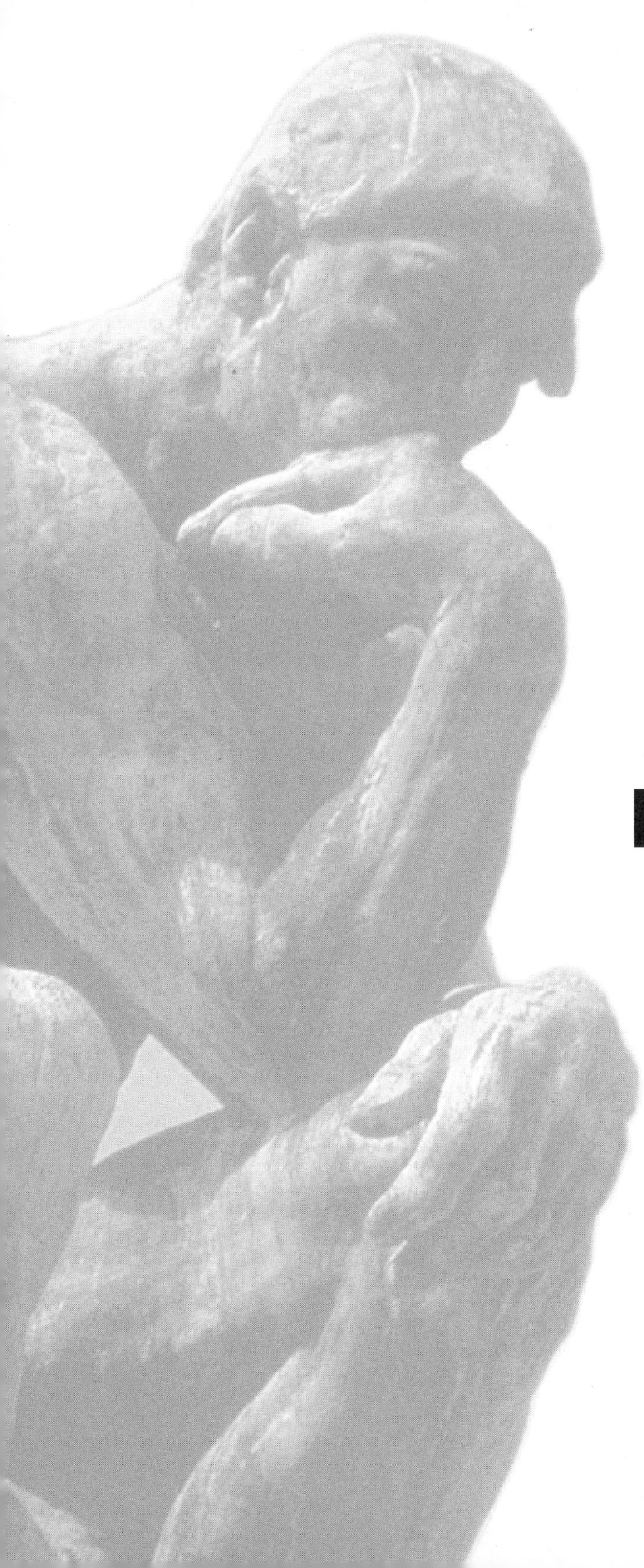

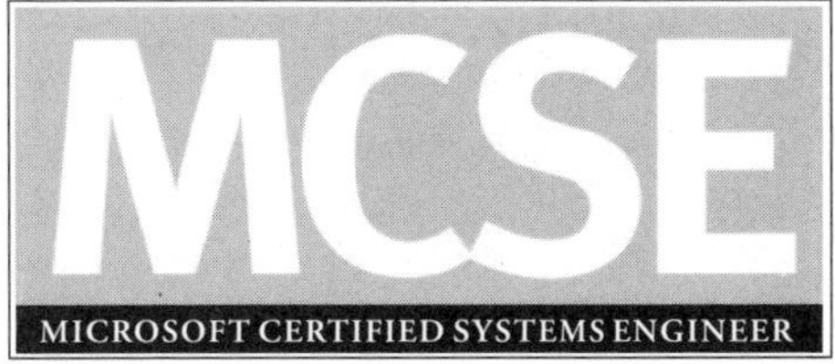

# 3

# Designing Server Topology and Systems Management

## CERTIFICATION OBJECTIVES

| | |
|---|---|
| 3.01 | Designing a Server Topology |
| 3.02 | Designing a System Management and Monitoring Strategy |
| 3.03 | Designing a Disaster Recovery Strategy |
| ✓ | Two-Minute Drill |
| Q&A | Self Test |

Designing a server topology is an important part of networking, because it involves determining where servers should be placed. This determination allows you to improve the performance, availability, and reliability of your network. Once you have set up the network the way you want, you need to monitor your servers to see that they are running properly. Because problems can occur, you should also create a plan that determines what will be done in the event of a disaster.

As we see in this chapter, Windows 2000 provides a number of tools that allow you to monitor your system for problems and others that allow you to troubleshoot and fix your system when problems result. In cases of catastrophic damage, where the server and other equipment are beyond repair, Windows 2000 provides tools that allow you to protect the data and software on the system.

**CERTIFICATION OBJECTIVE 3.01**

# Designing a Server Topology

The term *server topology* refers to the layout of servers on a Windows 2000 network. Servers are important because they authenticate users and provide access to services and resources on a network. If users are unable to access a server, services and resources available to them might be limited. If users can't be authenticated, your network will become a series of useless cabling and equipment, because users will be able to use only the programs and resources on their local machines. Because servers are so vital to your network and its users, it is important that you place servers strategically on your network.

On a Windows 2000 network, *domain controllers (DCs)* are used to authenticate users. The first server designated as a DC on a new network creates the domain. A *domain* is the core unit of the Active Directory (AD) structure and serves as a security boundary. All network objects in AD exist under the domain; these objects can be grouped into one or more domains to reflect the organization of your company. Due to the importance of a domain in the AD structure, you can also see that the layout of DCs is an important factor in your network.

When you first create your Windows 2000 network, the first Windows 2000 server on the network must be a DC. If you didn't make this server a DC, Active

Directory wouldn't be created, and users would need to log on to each server separately. Administrators would also need to manage a different username and password for each server. The reason for these interdependencies is that all servers in the domain are bound to AD. If you create any additional domains, each domain also requires at least one DC.

Although a minimum of one DC is required in a domain, multiple DCs can be used to improve the availability, reliability, and performance of your network. Users can log on to any DC in a domain. If one DC fails or is unavailable for some other reason, users can log on to another DC in the domain. This backup strategy also improves performance because clients are able to connect to either DC when logging on. Rather than everyone attempting to connect to one DC, users can make connections to all DCs in the domain.

In addition to authenticating users, DCs store a replica of the domain's portion of Active Directory. When changes are made to objects in AD, these changes are automatically applied to the DC on which the changes were made. Within 15 minutes of the changes being applied to AD, the changes are replicated to other DCs in the domain. Important updates, such as changes to user accounts, are immediately replicated, whereas less important ones are replicated at regular intervals. However, if the DCs are unable to connect with one another, the replication process cannot occur. This can be a problem because a DC in one location won't be aware of changes made on a different DC in another location.

It is important that a reliable connection is in place so that DCs in different locations can communicate with one another. To illustrate, let's say that a domain is spread across geographical locations. If two DCs are connected with a dial-up connection, and phone lines at one location regularly go down, the two DCs won't be able to replicate Active Directory. If you locked out a user account on one DC, that user would still be able to access the network through the other DC, until the two DCs are able to communicate and the lockout changes to the account can be replicated.

In addition to domains, sites can be used to organize your network more effectively. Sites are made up of one or more subnets that are well connected. The term *well connected* means that they are using a connection that is both fast and reliable. Sites allow you to partition a large domain into more manageable subnetworks, which work on a different set of IP addresses. This is useful if your network is split across a wide area network (WAN) or an unreliable network link is connecting areas of your network together. By adding sites, one site would be on each end of the link. DCs could be added to each site, improving performance.

exam Watch

***Sites are one or more subnets that are well connected. Microsoft recommends that subnets with at least a 512Kbps be combined into a site. If the connection between the subnets is slower than this or the connection is unreliable, the subnets should not be combined.***

The process of determining whether or not to add a DC to a site is based on the number of people in the remote site and the connection between those sites. If there are five users or fewer at a remote site, there is no need to add a DC there. If there are more than five users, you should consider adding a DC. During the logon process, the client attempts to log on to a DC in the local site, which will make authentication quicker. If there is an unreliable connection between the remote site and the main site or if the connection is slow, it is wise to either upgrade the connection or add a DC to the remote site. Doing either will allow users to log on and access resources quickly and avoid downtime that will occur when the connection is down.

When there are more than five users and logon and query performance is poor, you should also make the DC that you add to a site a global catalog (GC) server. With the GC enabled on the DC, users can query the GC rather than AD. The GC consists of objects and a subset of attributes in AD. The GC improves the time it takes to query, because all the attributes for every object in AD aren't included in the GC.

In addition to determining where you position the DCs on your network, you should also consider placement of other servers, files, and other resources that will be accessed. Because DCs are Windows 2000 servers that are designated DCs, they can also be used to provide the same services available through other servers. The DC can act as a file server, provide print services, or act as a DHCP server, a DNS server, a Web server, and so on. Clients are able to use these redundant services on the local site's server, rather than accessing them across a link to another site. Furthermore, if the link between sites goes down, users in the remote site are still able to access those services.

The same is true of data. If a server is placed in a remote site, you should move the files of users in that site to the hard disk of that site's server. If users must access data across a link to another site, performance decreases and network traffic increases. Other data, such as databases used primarily by that site's users, should also be moved. Remember that the farther data is from a user, the longer it will take him or her to access it. The closer data is physically to the user, the faster it will be to access.

Windows 2000 includes Distributed File Sharing (DFS), which allows you to distribute files across your system. DFS allows you to place files in central shares, which are accessed through a single server. This makes it easier for users to find files and easier for network administrators to manage them. When file replication is used, multiple copies of this data can be provided to different sites so that each site has a local copy of the data. This system allows users to access the data more quickly, but it also provides fault tolerance. If one server fails, copies of this data still exist on servers in remote sites.

## IIS and Server Topology

When a network simply has an intranet, the topology of the network won't change dramatically. Internet Information Services (IIS) runs on DCs and servers and is integrated to benefit from the features of the operating system. IIS allows you to implement an intranet on your network so that users can view content and use Web applications over the local network. The network topology will vary dramatically, however, when you connect your network to the Internet. When your local network is connected to the Internet, the first step involves determining what people will be able to access. Your organization will probably want local users to access Internet resources, but you will limit what Internet users can access on the intranet. You can use several different topologies, each of which will affect the access of both Internet users and those on the local network.

The least secure topology is one that allows full access to the Internet. Users of the internal network access the Internet through a server acting as a gateway. This server has a connection to the Internet and routes packets both ways. Users on your internal network will be able to connect to the Internet through the server's connection, whereas Internet users will be able to access resources on the internal network. This accessibility could be useful if there are servers providing applications, data, or other services and resources that the IIS server must use. Windows 2000 security measures protect the internal network so that Internet users are only able to access the data that you feel they should be able to access.

In this topology, TCP/IP routing features on Windows 2000 Server can be used to protect your internal network from hackers and other unauthorized users on the Internet. IP routing determines whether a packet is passed beyond that server to a different network or site. As shown in Figure 3-1, the server acts as a gateway between the networks. It determines what information passes through it and what information is excluded from routing beyond this point.

A benefit of this method is that both users on the internal network and Internet users are able to access the IIS server. The server has two network adapters, one of which communicates with the internal network and another that communicates

**FIGURE 3-1** TCP/IP Routing Enabled

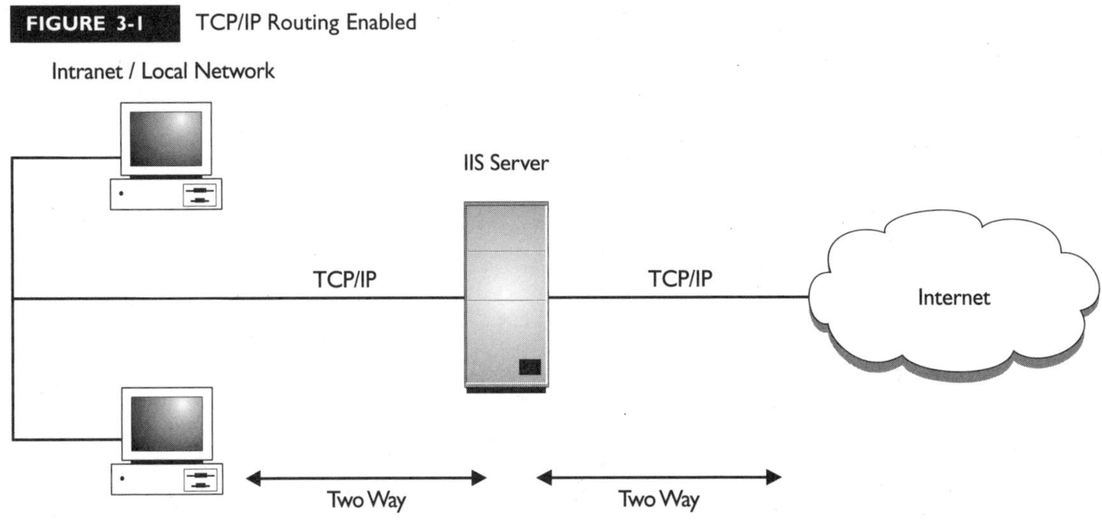


with the external network. You configure each of the adapters with separate IP addresses, and packets from each site are passed through the server to the second card. However, if you don't want to use IP routing on your server, another option might be to use packet filtering on a third-party router.

You can also disable IP routing so that nothing is passed on from the server. As shown in Figure 3-2, if you configure Windows 2000 Server to route no packets;

**FIGURE 3-2** TCP/IP Routing Disabled

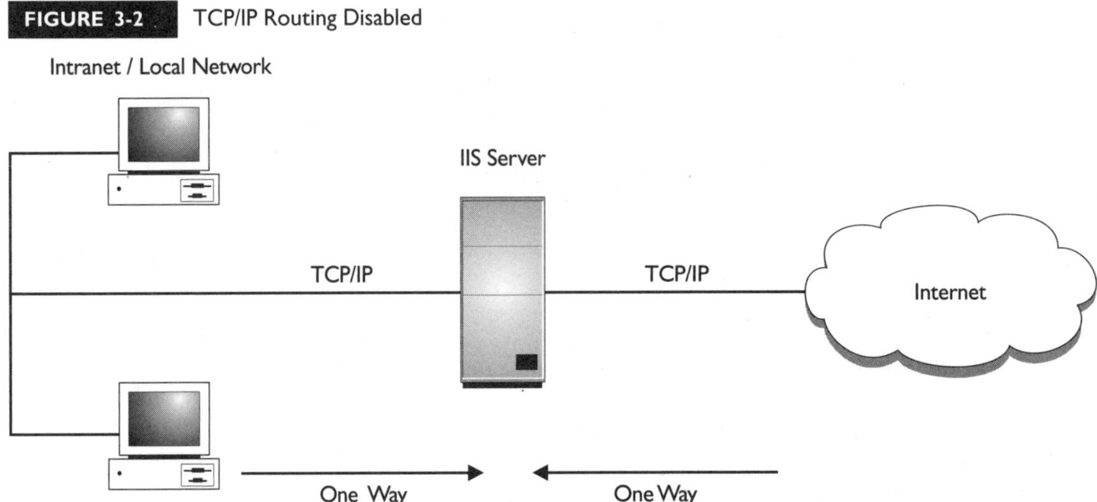

users will only be able to communicate with the IIS server. Packets from the Internet won't be passed on to the internal network, or vice versa.

Third-party routers can also be used to protect your internal network from the Internet. Large companies that use leased-line connections to the Internet commonly use third-party routers. Often, these routers provide packet filtering, which allows you to control what is permitted in and out of your network. You can specify which packets are routed from the internal network and which are allowed to pass on to the internal network from the Internet. Because of this ability, such routers act as an Internet gateway, as shown in Figure 3-3. To configure the router to perform these functions, you need to refer to your router's documentation.

The protocol isolation topology separates the Internet from your internal network using separate protocols. As shown in Figure 3-4, the IIS server uses one protocol to communicate with the Internet, while another is used to communicate with the internal network. Because clients must use different protocols to communicate with the IIS server, the server becomes a barrier between the Internet and the internal network.

In this topology, the IIS server uses two network adapters, each using a different protocol. One adapter is used to communicate with the Internet; the other is used to communicate with the internal network. Because the Internet uses TCP/IP, the adapter connecting to the Internet must use this protocol. The adapter connecting to the internal network must not use TCP/IP but uses any other protocol. Users on

**FIGURE 3-3** Third-Party Routers Can Be Used as a Gateway

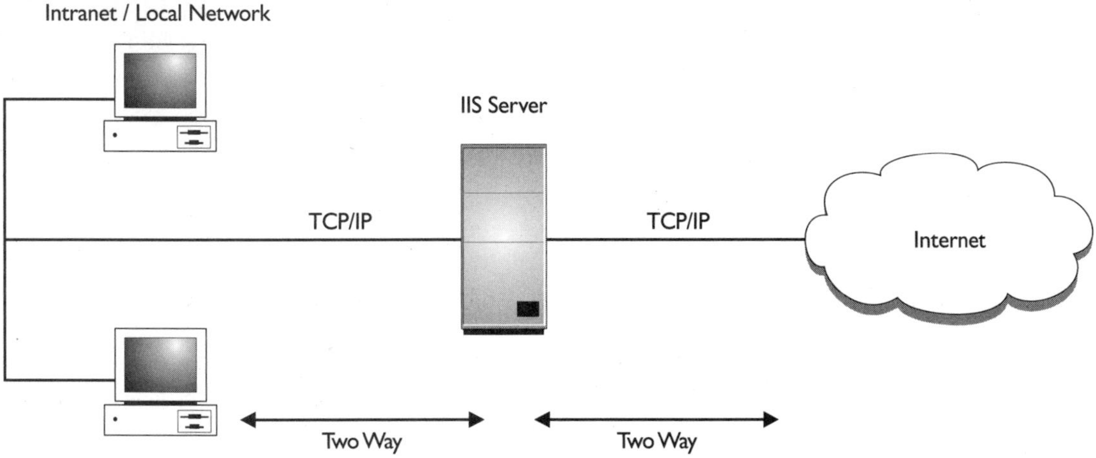

FIGURE 3-4 Protocol Isolation Topology

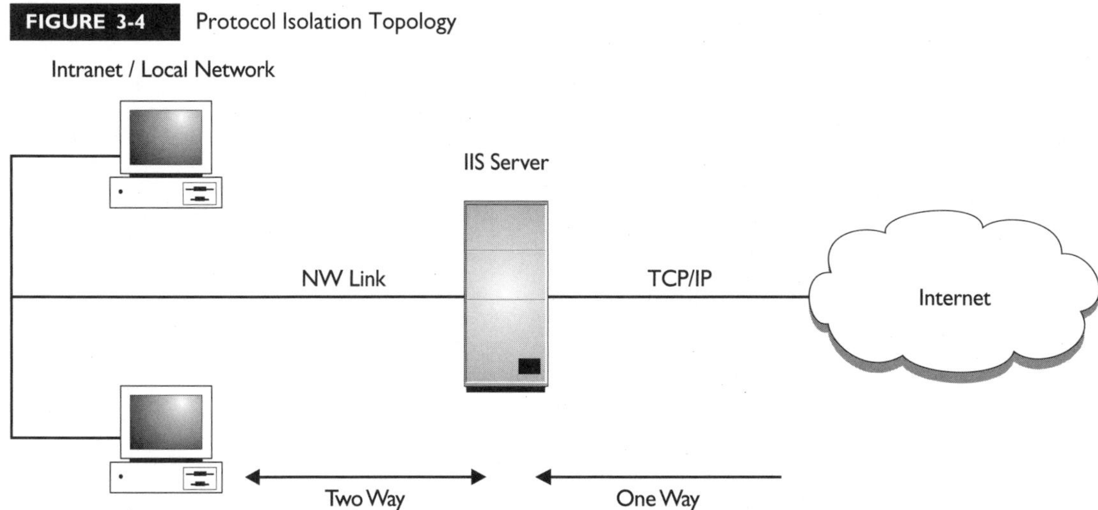


the internal network can use services and resources on the IIS server but won't be able to access IIS because it requires TCP/IP. However, Internet users will be able to access IIS, but they won't be able to see the internal network or access its resources, because it requires a different protocol.

Since users will be excluded from viewing content on the IIS server, you can extend this topology to include two IIS servers. As shown in Figure 3-5, the same topology is used, except that another IIS server is added within the network. Data from the IIS server communicating with the Internet is replicated to the internal IIS server. This allows internal network users to view content and access IIS without causing a security risk.

As shown in Figure 3-5, the additional IIS server uses a protocol other than TCP/IP to communicate with the Internet server and the internal network. This server can communicate with the external IIS server and can be used to replicate its data onto the internal IIS server. The external IIS server uses TCP/IP to communicate with the Internet and another protocol to communicate with the internal network. This system prevents Internet users from seeing and being able to access the internal network.

The best method of keeping your internal network safe from Internet users is to physically isolate the IIS server from the rest of your network. With this method, the

**FIGURE 3-5** Protocol Isolation Topology with an Additional IIS Server

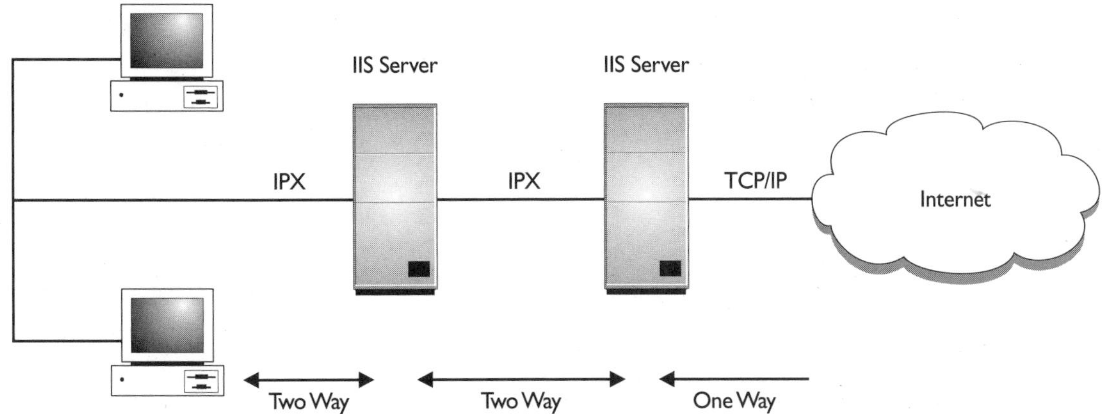


server running IIS isn't connected to the rest of your network. As shown in Figure 3-6, the server runs separately from the network, as a standalone machine.

This topology provides the highest level of security for your internal network. If a hacker successfully broke into the IIS server, he or she would be unable to access data on your internal network. A hacker could get into the IIS server, which requires

**FIGURE 3-6** Physical Isolation Model

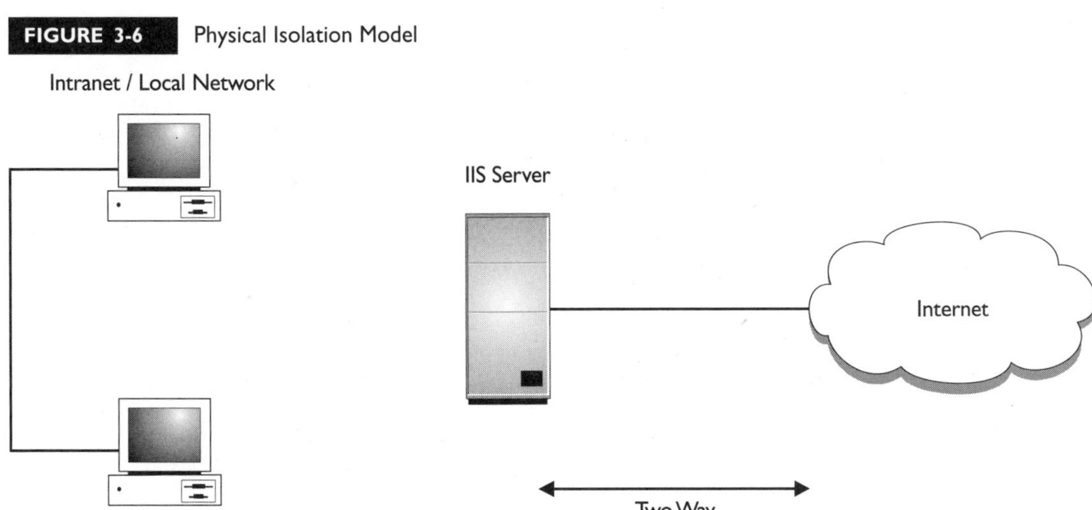

security measures in place, but there is no way for the hacker to obtain sensitive information on the internal network.

A drawback to this topology is that files and other resources cannot be shared between the internal network and the IIS server. Additional servers could be installed and connected to the IIS machine, but these would also need to run separately from the network. If files and resources need to be shared between these servers and the internal network, you could set up temporary connections or use removable media to transfer files between the two.

Another problem with this design is that internal network users won't be able to connect to the Internet with this topology. An option is to have a resource room with workstations connected to the IIS server's connection to the Internet. This solution allows users in this room to use the computers to connect to the Internet and use its resources. It also gives the Webmaster a workstation to use to generate content for the Web site and save it directly to the server. Unfortunately, like the IIS server itself, these workstations won't be able to use internal network resources.

## Scalability

It is doubtful that your network will remain the same size over the years, so it is important to keep scalability in mind when you design your network. As time passes, your organization is likely to hire more employees, so more users will be added to the network. New projects could require creation of new departments or units in your organization; expansion into new geographical areas will create new branch offices. As the structure of the organization changes, these changes will have an impact on your network.

It is important that you make your organization's decision makers aware of your need to be informed of such changes in the company so that you can plan the network accordingly. You should attempt to find out which departments or offices are expected to experience growth so that you can incorporate this growth into your plan. You should also interpret the technological needs of various departments, because some will use the network more than others. Such information is required not only when the network is initially created but also as it grows over time.

As growth occurs, you might need to create new domains. Domains were a distinct limitation of networks in Windows NT 4.0 because they could support only 40,000 user accounts. If the number of users exceeded 40,000, a new domain needed to be created. In Windows 2000, a domain directory can theoretically support up to 10 million objects. In practice, Windows 2000 domains have only been tested to support 1 million objects, but even this number is significantly more than your network will probably ever need.

Rather than more domains being created, it is more likely that new sites will be created. Sites are often created when a company spans a wide geographical area or the organization's scale requires the network's scale to increase. If sites are created, you need to determine whether or not certain sites will need their own DCs. This is the case if performance is an issue and users must wait an unacceptable amount of time to be authenticated or to access resources and services.

DCs aren't necessary for every site on your network. If a site doesn't have a DC, users will be able to connect to a DC in another site and log on to the network. This technique removes traffic from replication, because DCs won't need to replicate information with one another. However, using a DC at another site is an option only if the connection between the sites is fast and reliable and if there is a small number of users at that site. If there is a large number of users, the traffic between the remote site and the main site could bog down as users log on to the network during peak hours, attempt to access large files, or use bandwidth-intensive resources and services. Furthermore, if the connection is unreliable and goes down, users won't be able to log on and access network resources and services.

## IIS Scalability

Scalability is also a major concern for IIS servers. If a company grows, the number of users accessing content and Web applications on the intranet server also grows. If a Web server is at issue, the number of users proportionately increases with the site's popularity. It is important to realize that Web servers often provide vital services to an organization. Web servers can be used to provide mission-critical Web applications, sell a company's product, or provide important information to the public and employees. If an IIS server isn't available or can't perform well, it can cost the company money in terms of lost sales and orders or be a source of embarrassment.

As with files and resources on the network, the performance, reliability, and availability of your intranet or Internet site can also benefit from redundant servers. In this scheme, if the server fails, another server can service requests from users. Such redundancy not only applies to HTML content but to other servers that provide access to Web applications or data.

A method of reducing the number of requests going to a particular server is to separate the services offered among several servers. For example, one server would provide HTML content through one server, news services through another, FTP services through another, and so forth. Because users aren't going to a single server to access all these services, the number of users accessing each server decreases. Not only does this strategy allow you to increase the scale of your Internet servers to meet increases in number of users, it also provides load balancing among the servers.

## Load Balancing

*Load balancing* is a process of distributing between two or more servers the workload a server must perform. This distribution balances the load between the servers so that they can more effectively deal with client requests. In other words, rather than all users attempting to access one server, they are able to use one of several servers, thereby increasing overall performance. The distribution of data between multiple servers can also be used for load balancing, because users are able to access data through more than one server. As we'll see in this section, various methods can be used together to implement load balancing in a Windows 2000 network.

As mentioned earlier in this section, having additional DCs in a domain can also reduce the load that would be placed on a single DC. Rather than users connecting to one DC to be authenticated, they could connect to any of the additional DCs in the domain. This technique reduces the load on a DC during peak hours, when users are logging on at the beginning of the day or logging off at the end of the day.

The Distributed File System (DFS) can be used to redistribute files and shared folders, so users are better able to access and manage files that are scattered across the network. DFS makes these files appear as though they reside in the same location on the network. This eliminates the need to know the exact location of a file on a network, since they all appear to reside on the same server.

Windows 2000 Advanced Server includes a Network Load Balancing Service that works with server clusters. *Clusters* are groups of servers that are configured to work together as a single entity. Clients view the cluster as a single server, even though there may be as many as 32 individual servers making up the cluster. When clients make requests of the cluster, the requests are distributed among the hosts making up the cluster, thereby improving performance. Administration is also made simple because the cluster is managed as a single unit.

exam Watch

***When network load balancing is used, requests can be distributed among a cluster of servers. Up to 32 individual servers can be part of a cluster.***

There are a number of requirements and recommendations for implementing network load balancing on a Windows 2000 network. TCP/IP must be installed, because Windows 2000 is designed to support TCP/IP-based server programs. In terms of space and memory, the requirements are minimal. Windows 2000 uses less than 1MB of hard disk space and between 250KB and 4MB of RAM using the default settings. The variations in memory depend on the network load, which can be increased to allow up to 15MB of RAM to be used. It is also recommended that a second network adapter be installed on each server in the cluster. One card is configured to carry usual traffic to the server so that if users aren't attempting to access the cluster, this first card is used. The second card carries traffic addressed to it as a member of the cluster.

Network load balancing is installed through the Properties dialog box of the Local Area Connection in Network and Dial-up Connections. When you select Network Load Balancing and click the Properties button on the general tab, the Network Load Balancing Properties dialog box appears. As shown in Figure 3-7, this dialog box has three tabs for configuring network load balancing: Cluster Parameters, Host Parameters, and Port Rules.

**FIGURE 3-7**

The Network Load Balancing Properties Dialog Box

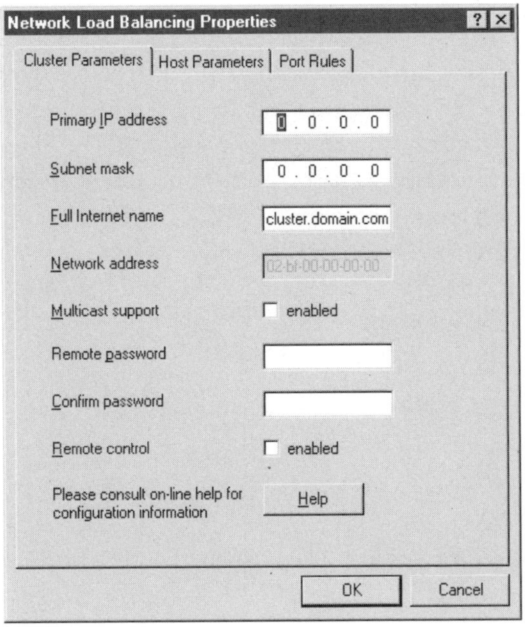

The Cluster Parameters tab allows you to set parameters that apply to the cluster as a whole. The Primary IP Address field on this tab is used to specify the IP address that will be used by the cluster. The Subnet Mask field is used to enter the subnet mask that applies to the IP address you entered in the preceding field. The Full Internet Name filed is used to specify the Internet name (for example, *cluster.mydomain.org*) that will be used to identify the cluster as a whole. The Network Address field might be available to specify the MAC address for the network adapter that will be used for client-to-cluster traffic. The Multicast Support check box is used to change the MAC address so that it uses a multicast MAC address. The Remote Password field is used to enter a password that must be used when the cluster is managed remotely. This password must be reentered in the Confirm Password field, and the Remote Control check box must be checked if the cluster is to be controlled remotely.

The Host Parameters tab allows you to set parameters that apply to the server on which you're installing network load balancing. The Priority (Unique host ID) allows you to specify this server's priority in handling requests. When a server in the cluster becomes unavailable, this setting is used to determine which computer will handle network traffic. The highest priority is the server with the lowest value (ranging from one to whatever number of servers is in the cluster). The Initial Cluster State check box is used to specify whether network load balancing should start automatically on system startup or be started manually. It is checked by default to start automatically. The Dedicated IP Address field is used to specify the IP address that will be used to associate client requests that are specifically for that server. In other words, this IP address is used to connect directly with this server, rather than with the cluster as a whole. The Subnet Mask field is used to enter the subnet mask associated with the dedicated IP address you entered.

The final tab on the Network Load Balancing Properties dialog box is the Port Rules tab. This tab allows you to set parameters that determine how the cluster will function. Via this tab, you can control how network traffic will be handled, based on the rules you create.

## Load Balancing and IIS

If an intranet or Internet site is used by a large number of users, its performance will decrease with increases in the number of users who view content, run Web applications, or use various services available through IIS. A common method of separating the load placed on an IIS server among several servers is to separate the services running on it. This is done by having one server provide FTP services, another provide news services, another provide HTML content, and so forth.

An important method of providing load balancing to IIS is through *clustering*. Clustering allows you to support increases in traffic that are generated by a higher number of users accessing your site and its Web applications. Rather than a single IIS server responding to client requests, the workload is spread across as many as 32 different servers.

One tool that is used for load balancing IIS servers and Web application servers is Microsoft's Application Center. This software is used to create, deploy, and manage both Web and component-based applications. It allows you to implement network and component load balancing across a cluster of servers. As the load on the cluster increases, additional servers can be added to the cluster so that the cluster grows with the demands placed on it.

Application Center provides a management console that can be used to manage the cluster. It allows you to adjust the load on each server in a cluster so that a greater load can be placed on a more powerful server. This is important to many networks since many organizations add servers to a cluster over a period of time. In such situations, one server might have a Pentium II processor while another has a Pentium III and so on. When you can control the load placed on each server, the performance of the cluster as a whole improves.

Regardless of whether you use Application Center or not, the benefits of load balancing for Web servers are varied and impressive. As we discuss further in the next section, another benefit of clustering is that it provides fault tolerance. If one server in the cluster becomes unavailable, the other cluster servers continue servicing client requests. This system allows users to continue accessing Web applications and content material on your site.

**EXERCISE 3-1**

**CertCam 3-1**

### Installing Network Load Balancing on Windows 2000 Advanced Server

1. From the Start menu, select Settings, and then click Network and Dial-up Connections.
2. Right-click the Local Area Connection icon, and then click Properties.

3. When the Properties dialog box appears, you will see a section on the General tab called "Components check are used by this connection." Click the check box beside Network Load Balancing.
4. With Network Load Balancing still selected, click the Properties button. The Network Load Balancing Properties dialog box appears.
5. Set the parameters that apply to your host and cluster on each of the tabs. These will be unique to your machine and your cluster.
6. Click OK to return to the Local Area Connection Properties dialog box, and then click OK again to confirm your settings and exit.

---

## Fault Tolerance

*Fault tolerance* is a system's ability to continue to be functional when a failure occurs. The key to fault tolerance is redundancy. It requires implementing redundant paths, services, and components. For example, if users were unable to access a particular server, they would be unable to be authenticated or access resources if another server wasn't available. Fault tolerance provides an alternate authentication and access method if the normal method is unavailable.

When we talk about fault tolerance, we generally refer to DCs or other servers that aren't related to intranets or the Internet. However, each of the elements dealing with fault tolerance applies to IIS servers as much as to servers for your local network. If an IIS server or a server used by Web applications on an IIS server fails, users of the intranet might be unable to do their work, or money may be lost if it were connected to the Internet. The inability to access the IIS server can be devastating, so it is important to include fault-tolerance options when planning your intranet or Internet Web site.

### Disk Fault Tolerance

When people think of fault tolerance, they generally think of hard disks and disk controllers. In particular, they think of RAID. With this technology, redundant information about the data stored on hard disks can be stored on other disks. There are different levels of RAID, with the basic levels ranging from 0–5. As shown in Table 3-1, each level provides a different degree of performance and fault tolerance.

**TABLE 3-1** RAID Levels

| RAID Level | Description |
|---|---|
| RAID 0 | Disk striping without parity. Data is spread across all disks in an array. No redundant information is stored on other disks, so no fault tolerance is provided. |
| RAID 1 | Disk mirroring. Everything is duplicated on another hard disk. Windows 2000 Server supports disk mirroring. |
| RAID 2 | Disk striping across multiple disks. Error-correction codes are maintained across all disks. RAID 2 isn't as efficient as other levels of RAID that provide fault tolerance, and for that reason it isn't commonly used. |
| RAID 3 | Disk striping across multiple disks. Error-correction codes are stored on one disk. Because all parity information is written to a single disk, it creates a write bottleneck, and all parity information will be lost if the disk containing that information fails. |
| RAID 4 | Disk striping across multiple disks. This is similar to RAID 3 but writes the information in larger blocks. Like RAID 3, this level creates a write bottleneck, and all parity information will be lost if the disk containing that information fails. |
| RAID 5 | Disk striping with parity. Data is written across all disks in the array, and parity information is also written across all disks in the array. Windows 2000 supports this level of RAID. |

Fault Tolerant implementations of RAID supported by Windows 2000 are RAID 1 and RAID 5.

exam Watch

***There are many different levels of RAID. Windows 2000 supports RAID 1 (disk mirroring) and RAID 5 (disk striping with parity). It does not support any of the other levels of RAID.***

*Disk mirroring* in Windows 2000 is called *mirrored volumes* and was called *mirror sets* in Windows NT. With this method of RAID, data on one hard disk is duplicated to another disk, so a mirror image of one appears on the other. Disk mirroring protects you if your primary disk fails, because the data still exists on the mirrored disk. If one of these disks fails, Windows 2000 can use data from the other disk.

Creating mirrored volumes requires two hard disks on your server. The second disk must be the same size or greater than the primary disk used by your system. If the mirrored disk (i.e., the secondary disk) is larger, the remaining space will be shown as free space. When they are mirrored, with the same drive letter used for both volumes, information written to the primary disk will also be written to the second disk.

If your primary disk fails, you would break the mirrored volumes so that the secondary disk becomes an individual volume with its own drive letter. To ensure that your data is safe, you should create a new mirrored volume as soon as possible, rather than rely on only the secondary disk (as an individual hard disk). You should remove the failed hard disk, install a new hard disk, and create a new mirrored volume relationship.

As an added protection, you can also use *disk duplexing*, which is the same procedure as mirrored volumes but one disk controller is used for each hard disk making up the mirrored set. If one disk controller fails, the server can continue to function by reading and writing to the other disk.

RAID 5 (disk striping with parity) can also be used on Windows 2000 servers. With this method, an array of 3 to 32 disks are combined into one volume, and data is stored across all disks in the array. Parity information is written across these disks as well so that data can be rebuilt in the event that one of these disks fails.

### Other Methods of Fault Tolerance

In addition to providing fault tolerance for disk drives, you can also make other elements of your network fault tolerant. As mentioned, although a minimum of one DC is required per domain, you aren't limited to one. DCs can be added to an existing domain, allowing users to be authenticated if one of the DCs becomes unavailable for some reason. For example, a DC might fail completely or might need to be taken offline for maintenance. If your system has multiple DCs, users will still be able to log on and access services and resources, unaware that any problem exists.

This type of fault tolerance applies not only to DCs on a Windows 2000 network but also to IIS servers running on a network. With multiple IIS servers providing content, Web applications, or access to data, users will be able to access these resources even if one of the IIS servers goes down. Many times this is done through network load balancing, by implementing IIS as part of a cluster.

exam Watch

***The key to fault tolerance is that the system can continue to function even though one of its components has failed. To make your network fault tolerant, you should have more than one DC so that users can log on and use resources if one of the DCs fail.***

Network load balancing can also be used for fault tolerance. If one server in a cluster fails, client requests are automatically reallocated to other servers in the cluster. Individual servers in the cluster monitor the availability of one another with multicast or broadcast messages. If one server becomes unavailable or a new server is added to the cluster, a process called *convergence* is started to stabilize the cluster. The server with the highest priority is designated the default host and handles client requests.

Sites can also benefit from different fault-tolerance initiatives, especially when replication is an issue. When sites are used, one of two types of replication, intrasite or intersite, can occur. *Intrasite replication* occurs between DCs within a site; *intersite replication* occurs between DCs in different sites. You should be aware of a number of other differences between the two. With intrasite replication, data that is replicated isn't compressed and, by default, replication occurs every 5 minutes. With intersite replication, data is always compressed, so the amount of data transferred is reduced 88 to 90 percent. By default, replication occurs in intervals of three hours, but it can be set to occur at a specific time. Unlike intrasite replication, which is configured automatically, intersite replication must be configured manually by the administrator.

To provide fault tolerance for intersite replication or to connect between two sites when the normal link is down, you can use multiple connection methods. For example, if your network used a T1 line as a default connection between sites, you could also implement a dial-up network connection for when that line is down. This extra connection provides a redundant link in case of problems. When there is more than one network connection, Active Directory always determines which connection should be used on a per-cost basis. When the default connection (which is logically the cheapest) is available, that is the connection used. If the default connection goes down, Active Directory uses the redundant connection for replication. This redundant link also allows users to connect to other servers on the network and access resources, even though the default connection is unavailable.

Now that we've discussed issues dealing with designing a server topology in such detail, let's look at a number of scenarios and solutions related to these topics.

| SCENARIO & SOLUTION | |
|---|---|
| I have created a network with three sites. One of these sites is remote and is a branch office used by salespeople when they are not on the road. There are 20 salespeople but no more than four or five people in the office at any given time. How many DCs should I place at this site? | None. Microsoft recommends that a DC should be placed in a site if there are more than five users accessing the network. Since five or fewer users work at your site at any given time, there is no need at this time to add a DC to this site. |
| What levels of fault tolerant RAID does Windows 2000 support? | RAID 1 and RAID 5. RAID 1 is disk mirroring, in which data on one hard disk is duplicated to another hard disk. RAID 5 is disk striping with parity, in which data and parity information is stored across an array of hard disks. |

**CERTIFICATION OBJECTIVE 3.02**

# Designing a System Management and Monitoring Strategy

As a system runs for a period of time, problems can occur due to various services failing to respond, events not running properly, bottlenecks, and other issues. Part of managing your system is being able to identify these and other issues that can slow or cripple your server. Fortunately, Windows 2000 includes a number of tools that are useful for monitoring and managing your system.

Designing a systems management and monitoring strategy requires knowledge of the tools available in Windows 2000 Server. As we see in this section, some of these tools provide the ability to notify the administrator of problems, while others require analyzing logged data or information that is generated by various elements of your system and network. To have a firm understanding of your system, you should look at logged information on a weekly basis at the very least, and compare it with previous performance measurements to determine whether any problems exist.

In many cases, monitoring your system will help you ensure that it is performing efficiently. When monitoring performance issues, you should be aware that it is an ongoing process, in which you try to get various aspects of your system to work optimally. Several factors affect performance:

- CPU
- Memory
- Hard disk
- Network

To deal with performance issues in these areas, begin by finding the resource that is slowest on your network. Once this resource is sped up, you can determine whether other areas are affecting speed. This determination might force you to reconfigure components, upgrade hardware and software, add new technologies, or change your network to meet users' needs.

## Performance Monitoring

Windows 2000 Server includes a tool called the Performance Console, which allows you to monitor the performance of local and remote computers. The Performance Console is actually the Microsoft Management Console (MMC) with two snap-ins installed: System Monitor and Performance Logs and Alerts. A *snap-in* is a module that is added to the MMC so that you can perform various functions through a central console program. System Monitor allows you to monitor resource utilization and network throughput; the Performance Logs and Alerts snap-in allows you to log performance data and set remote notification of performance issues.

### System Monitor

System Monitor provides a visual representation of counters. It allows you to view real-time and previously logged data about areas of your system and your network. This data can be presented to you in the form of a graph, histogram, or report so that you can analyze it in a way that's meaningful to you. When System Monitor is first opened, it (by default) opens in graph view, but no information is displayed. This is because counters need to be added.

*Counters,* which are items associated with resources and services on your system, are used to control the system elements System Monitor is to watch. Each object associated with a resource or service can have a collection of counters associated with it. Once the counters are added, data is then displayed in the graph area, as shown in Figure 3-8.

Counters can be added to System Monitor by clicking the toolbar's Add Counters button, which has a plus symbol ("+") on it. This action opens the Add Counters dialog box. The top portion of this dialog box allows you to specify whether you want to use the local computer's counters or specify a particular computer on your network from a drop-down list. Below this section, you will see a section with a drop-down list containing various categories of resources. You can select objects from this drop-down list, exposing the counters for that object. When you select the objects you want to monitor, a list of counters associated with the object appears on the dialog box. These counters allow you to narrow the choice of

**FIGURE 3-8** System Monitor in Performance Console

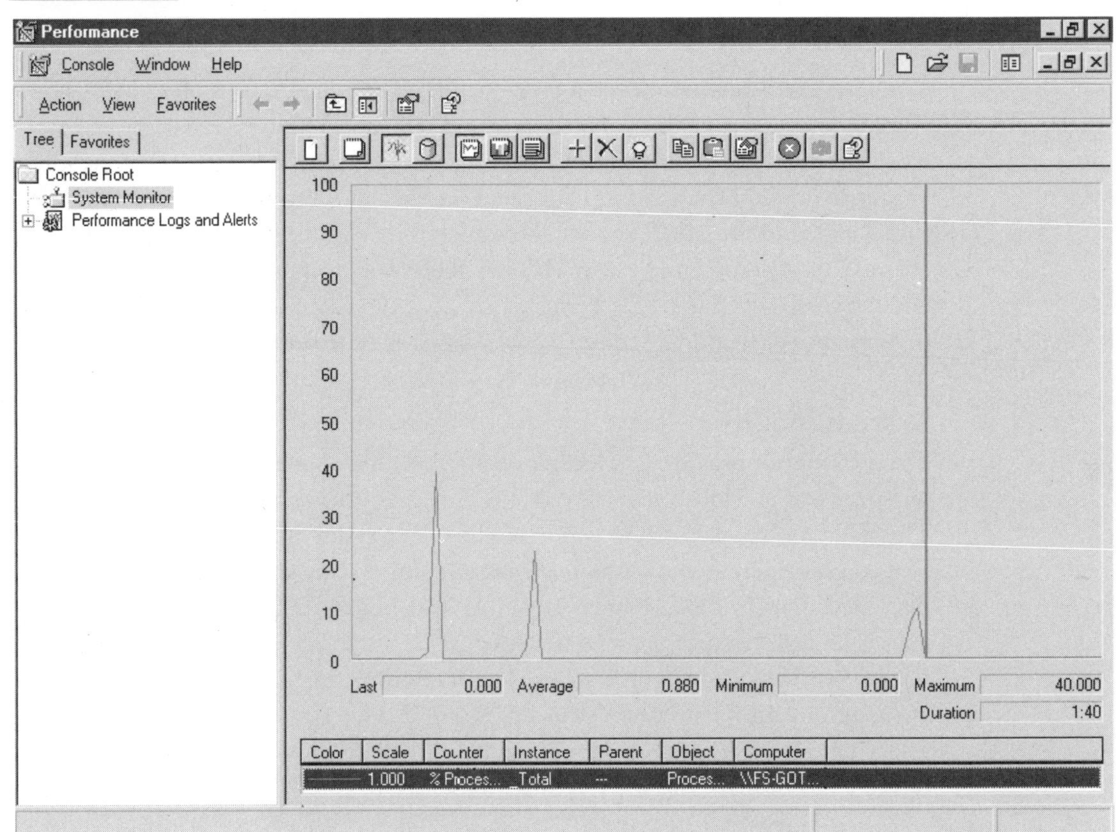

items to be monitored. If you're unsure as to what each counter is used for, you can click the Explain button on the dialog box to display description information.

You can choose a number of objects and counters from the Add Counters dialog box. In many cases, you will select certain ones when you suspect a problem with a certain part of your Windows 2000 server or network. However, Microsoft recommends certain objects and counters be used during normal monitoring. These are shown and explained in Table 3-2.

exam watch

***Don't expect to see questions that specifically deal with knowing which counters to include in normal monitoring on your exam. The information in Table 3-2 is provided for use primarily on your job rather than on the exam.***

**TABLE 3-2** Counters Used During Normal Monitoring

| Object \| Counter | Description |
|---|---|
| Cache \| Data Map Hits % | Percentage of data maps in the system file cache. These are data maps that couldn't be resolved without retrieving a page from the disk, because the page was already in physical memory. |
| Cache \| Fast Reads/sec | Number of reads per second from the file system cache. |
| Cache \| Lazy Write Pages/sec | Number of writes per second in which the disk has been updated after the page has been changed in memory. |
| Logical Disk \| % Disk Space | Percentage of disk space on the logical disk. |
| Memory \| Available Bytes | Number of bytes in memory that are available to processes that are running on the machine. |
| Memory \| Pool Nonpaged Allocs | Number of calls to allocate space in the nonpaged pool. |
| Memory \| Pool Nonpaged Bytes | Number of bytes in the nonpaged pool. |
| Memory \| Pool Paged Allocs | Number of calls to allocate space in the paged pool. |
| Memory \| Pool Paged Bytes | Number of bytes in the paged pool. |
| Processor(_Total) \| % Processor Time | Percentage of time the processor spends executing a non-idle thread. This is the main indicator of processor activity. |
| Processor(_Total) \| Interrupts/sec | Average number of interrupts the processor receives and services each second. |
| System \| Context Switches/sec | Rate at which all of the processors (combined) switch from one thread to another. |
| System \| Processor Queue Length | Number of threads in the processor queue. |

When counters have been added, you will see the timer bar on the System Monitor's graph area begin to move. The movement in the timer bar indicates real-time updates. You will also notice that the value of each counter is shown in both the graph and the value bar, which appears below the graph area. The value bar shows several categories of information about selected counters. It displays the Last, Average, Minimum, and Maximum values of the counter that's currently selected. The value in the Duration field shows the time that's elapsed in the graph. Below the value bar, you will also notice a legend that informs you of what each colored line of the graph represents. This information is useful because more than one counter can be monitored at any given time.

In addition to checking the performance of the server running IIS, you can use specific objects and counters that deal with the services of the IIS Server itself. These objects are the Web Service, Internet Information Service Global, FTP Service, and Active Server Pages.

The Web Service object is used to expose counters dealing with Windows 2000's Web Service. The counters are used to gather information about anonymous and unanonymous HyperText Transport Protocol (HTTP) requests and connections to the HTTP service. It is also used to monitor requests to Common Gateway Interface (CGI) applications or Internet Server Application Programming Interface (ISAPI) extensions. Any such request that has been handled since the Web Service was started can be displayed through the Performance Console.

The IIS Global object is used to expose counters that that report on the usage of a cache that's shared by IIS and on bandwidth throttling. Bandwidth throttling can be set to limit the bandwidth used by IIS. This prevents the network from being bogged down by requests to IIS. The IIS Object Cache is used to store objects that are used frequently so that they don't need to constantly be retrieved. Instead, they are stored in the cache and provided to users or applications needing a particular object. The counters dealing with the IIS Object Cache report on the cache's hits, misses, and effectiveness.

The FTP Service object counters are used to gather information about anonymous and unanonymous connections to the FTP Server. FTP, File Transfer Protocol, is used to exchange files with users who use the service. This system allows users to upload and download files from the IIS server. Counters for the FTP Service allow you to report on a per-site basis so that if multiple FTP sites are used, you can view information on each of them.

Finally, the Active Server Pages object is used to expose counters that report on applications that use Active Server Pages running on the IIS server. The counters provide information on transactions, requests, and other details about usage of Active Server Pages running on the IIS server.

### Performance Logs and Alerts

Performance Logs and Alerts is the second snap-in that's loaded with Performance Console. This tool allows you to log counter data to a file, view existing logs, gather data from counters when a particular event occurs, and be notified of exceeded

## FROM THE CLASSROOM

### Performance of Logical and Physical Disks

Performance Console is a useful tool for troubleshooting your system and monitoring the overall health of your Windows 2000 Server and the network. Using the System Monitor snap-in, you can add counters that allow you to view information about various aspects of your system.

Numerous objects provide counters, but two that often cause confusion are the PhysicalDisk and LogicalDisk objects. PhysicalDisk exposes counters for monitoring the physical hard disk. LogicalDisk exposes counters associated with local drives and storage volumes. By default, the PhysicalDisk object is enabled, but the LogicalDisk object is disabled.

To use the counters for the LogicalDisk, you need to turn the counters on using the Diskperf utility, a command-line utility that allows you to turn the counters for monitoring hard disk activity on and off using switches. By default, Windows 2000 uses the diskperf –yd command to obtain data on physical drives. However, to obtain data on logical drives, you need to run diskperf –yv from the command prompt. To disable the counter, you can run diskperf –n at the command prompt. Once you've turned on the counter and rebooted, you will then be able to collect data about the disk.

*—Michael Cross, MCSE, MCPS, MCP+I, CNA*

performance thresholds. As shown in Figure 3-9, Performance Logs and Alerts has three areas that you can configure for these purposes:

- Counter logs
- Trace logs
- Alerts

*Counter logs* are used to obtain and store data that's collected by the counters you specify. When you use counter logs, data is obtained at specific update intervals. The data can be stored in a comma-delimited or tab-separated format so that it can then be imported into other programs; it can also be stored in a binary log format. This information can be viewed using System Monitor, or it can be exported to other

**FIGURE 3-9** Performance Logs and Alerts in Performance Console

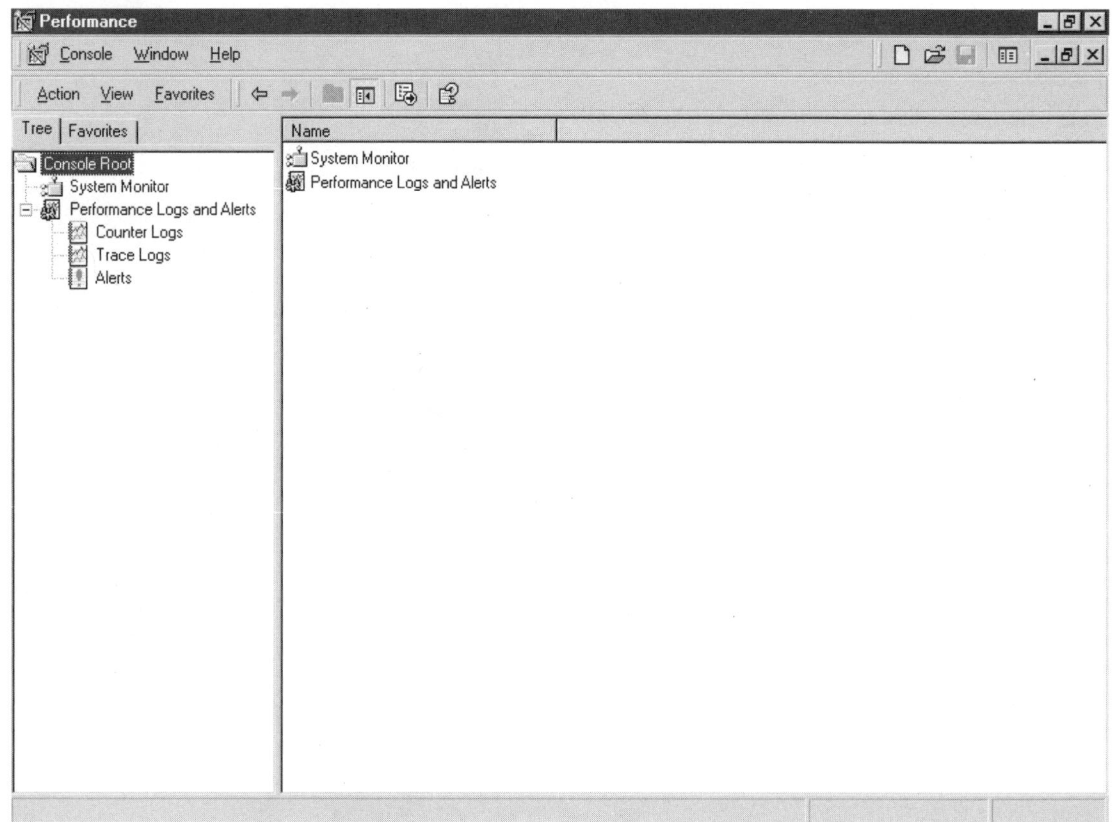

programs for analysis or when creating reports. For example, you could export it to a database to store former data collections or to a spreadsheet program to analyze the results.

on the Job

***It is important to use counter logs to create a* baseline*, which contains results that are logged when your system is performing normally. If you don't take a baseline measurement of your system's performance, you won't have anything to compare current measurements to. Without a baseline to compare current metrics, you might not recognize results that indicate abnormal behavior or increased workloads.***

*Trace logs* are different from counter logs in that they don't obtain data at regular update intervals. Instead, they log data when certain events occur. For example, a trace log might gather data when a page fault occurs. It monitors the activities you specify, and when a page fault happens, it stores the information in a log file.

*Alerts* are notifications that inform you when a particular performance threshold has been exceeded. When you set an alert, you specify an event to occur when a particular counter's value exceeds or falls below a certain value. You can specify that when this event occurs, a message should be sent, information should be logged to a file, or a program should run. Rather than having to watch the value of a counter yourself, alerts notify you so that you can troubleshoot or notify a particular program to deal with the problem without your intervention.

**EXERCISE 3-2**

CertCam 3-2

## Using System Monitor in Windows 2000 Server's Performance Console

1. From the Start menu, select Programs | Administrative Tools, and then click Performance.
2. When the Performance Console appears, select System Monitor from the left pane. The interface for System Monitor will appear in the right pane.
3. Click the button with the plus symbol (+) to display the Add Counters dialog box.
4. When the Add Counters dialog box appears, click the "Use local computer counters" option.

5. Select Processor from the drop-down list of Performance Objects.
6. Select the "Select counters from list" option, and then click the % Processor Time item in the list.
7. Select the "Select instances from list" option, and then click the Total item.
8. Click Add.
9. Click Close and watch as the activity for all processors on that computer appears on the graph on your screen. If it often exceeds 90 percent, your processor could be a bottleneck.

---

## Event Monitoring

Windows 2000 provides the ability to audit various events that occur so that you can track how the system is being used or running. Auditing is used for both network security and for determining problems that exist on your Windows 2000 server. By creating an audit policy, you can monitor the activities of users and various events occurring on the server. You can then view these events through the Event Viewer. The Event Viewer allows you to view information on events that have been logged to various files.

As shown in Figure 3-10, Event Viewer allows you to view events that have been logged to various files on your system. The default log files that can be viewed through Event Viewer are the Security, Application, and System logs. If certain services are installed on your server, such as the Domain Name System (DNS) service, additional log files might appear in Event Viewer.

The *Security log* provides information on audited events. The events that are recorded in this log are determined by the audit policy that is created on your system. You can set an audit policy through the Group Policy snap-in for MMC. Using this tool, you can configure policies to track successful or failed activities on the server, which are then logged to the Security log. Entries that are stored in this log show the user who performed a particular action, the action that was performed, and whether the action was successful or a failure. For example, you can set an audit policy on a user's account, which you suspect a hacker is attempting to use to gain access to the server. Setting an audit policy writes logon attempts to the Security log. Using Event Viewer, you could then view whether the user is unsuccessful. Using

**FIGURE 3-10** Event Viewer in Computer Management

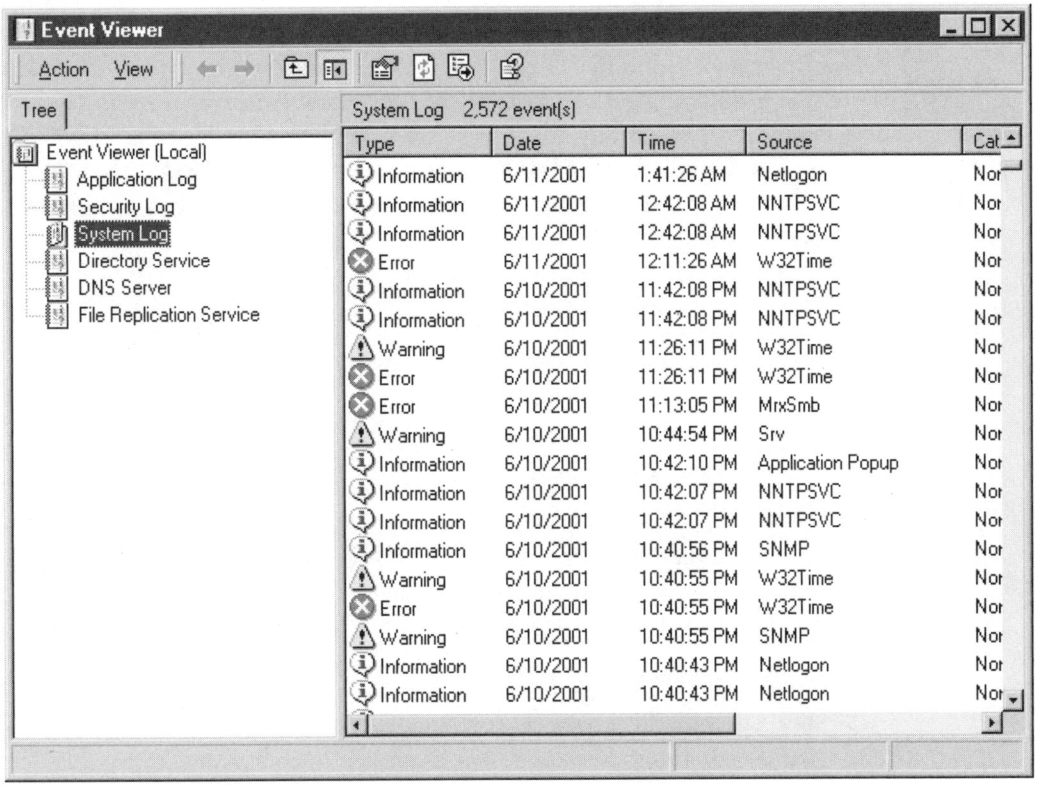

audit policies and the Security log, you can view what users are doing on the server and whether they are posing a threat to security.

The *Application log* provides information on events that are logged by various programs running on your system. These include both programs that are started by Windows 2000 Server when it boots up and applications that you start manually. Unlike the Security log, you don't configure the events logged to the Application log. The programmer who developed the software determines the events that are logged.

The *System log* provides information that is logged by Windows 2000 itself. This information is generated by components that run on the server and reports errors on various drivers and system software that failed to load on startup or experienced problems when running. As with the Application log, the administrator can't control the type of events logged in the System log. The Windows 2000 operating system determines what will be logged.

on the Job

***Administrators commonly look at Event Viewer to view log information when there is a problem. This is a mistake, because problems might not be reported or recognized immediately. For this reason, you should check the logs in Event Viewer on a regular basis. A good way to do this is to check the logs when you are performing a backup on a server. This way, you review logs on a regularly scheduled basis.***

Regardless of the log being viewed, several types of events can be displayed in a log. These events are denoted by various symbols, which indicate the following types of events:

- **Error** This symbol indicates that a particular event failed, such as when a driver fails to load properly at startup.
- **Warning** This symbol indicates a possible future problem. For example, a warning might appear if disk space is low or another DC could not be found to update the time and date.
- **Information** This symbol provides information about a particular event such as when a service successfully starts.
- **Success audit** This symbol provides information about an audit policy that has caused a successful event. For example, if you were auditing a user logging on to the system, a success audit would indicate that the user logged on successfully.
- **Failure audit** This symbol provides information about an audit policy that has caused a failed event. For example, if you were auditing a user accessing files and the user attempted to open a file he didn't have permission to open, a failure audit would indicate that the user couldn't open that particular file.

**EXERCISE 3-3**

CertCam 3-3

### Using Event Viewer

1. From the Start menu, select Programs | Administrative Tools, and then click Event Viewer.

2. In the left pane of Event Viewer, click System Log. Notice that log entries appear in the right pane of the viewer.
3. Analyze the various events that have been logged. When finished, close Event Viewer.

---

## Unresponsive Services

From time to time, you might find that certain services on your Windows 2000 server aren't responding. To deal with this situation, you can use the Services tool to stop the service and restart it or configure recovery actions to occur if the service fails again. Using this method, not only can you deal with problems when they occur, you can take a proactive approach to services that don't respond in the future.

The Services tool is found in the Administrative Tools folder in Control Panel. As shown in Figure 3-11, when the Services tool is opened, you will see a listing of all services currently installed on your Windows 2000 server. Beside each entry is information on the status of this service, how it is configured to start, the account it is to use to log on to the system, and a description of the service.

By double-clicking a service name in the right-pane of Services, you'll see a dialog box for that particular service. The General tab of this dialog box allows you to modify the name and description of the service so that it will appear in a way that's meaningful to you in Services. Below this, you can change the startup type of the service. You have three startup options for a service:

- **Automatic** Causes the service to start automatically when the server boots up.
- **Manual** Causes the service not to start, unless you start it manually.
- **Disabled** Prevents the service from being started unless it is changed to automatic or manual.

Below the startup type, you will see four buttons; these allow you to Start, Stop, Pause and Resume the service. The Start button is used when the startup type is set to Manual and you need to manually start the service. The Stop button stops the service. If the service has stopped responding or you have made changes that require you to stop and restart the service, you can use the Stop button to shut down the service. Clicking Start restarts it.

FIGURE 3-11 The Services Tool

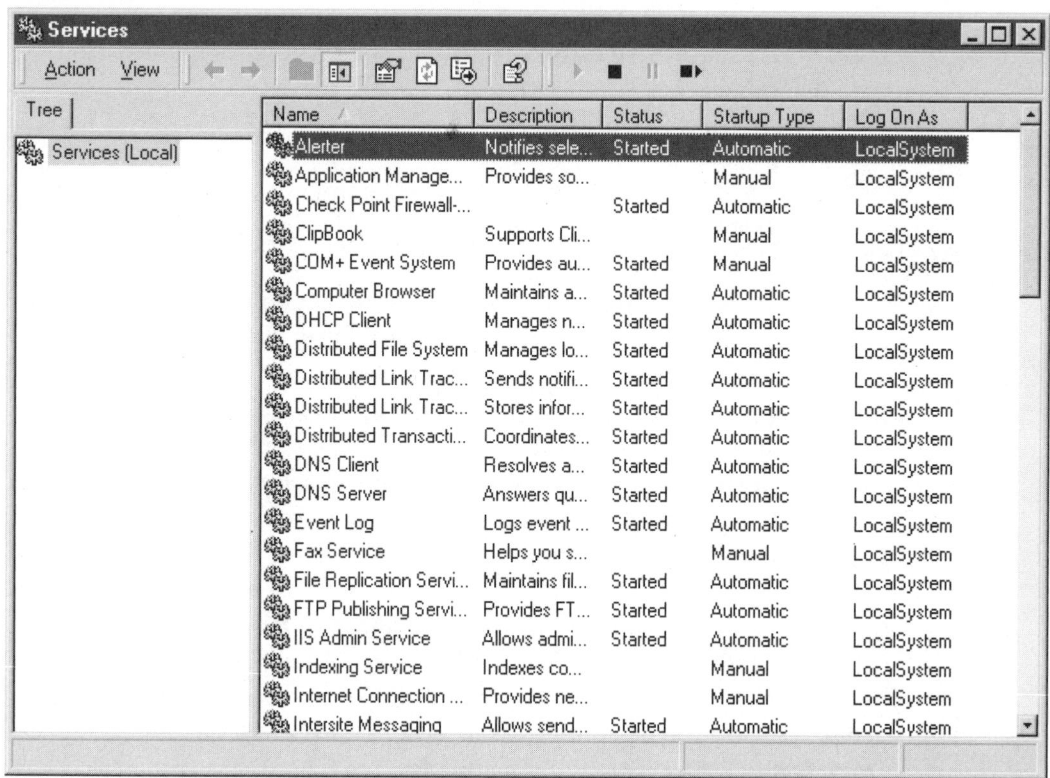


**on the Job** ***When the service is stopped, users connected to the service over the network will be disconnected. For this reason, before you stop the service, you should notify users that the service will be stopped for a specified amount of time. If a service is paused, no new user can use the service but existing users will still be able to access the service.***

The Log On tab is used to specify the account that the service will use. You can choose to use the Local System Account (which is the default account used by services) or specify another account and password that the service should use.

The Recovery tab, shown in Figure 3-12, is used to configure what events should occur when the service fails to respond. You can specify how the server will react to a failure the first time it fails to respond, the second time, and any times after that. You have four options to choose from for each failure option:

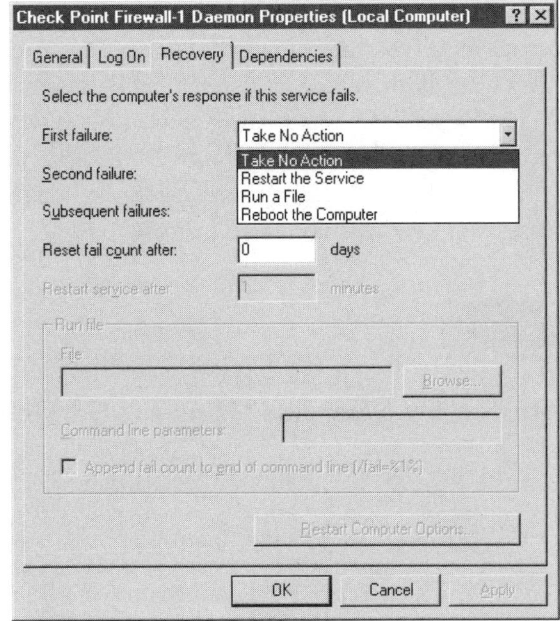


**FIGURE 3-12** Recovery Tab of a Service's Properties

- **Take No Action** Causes the server to do nothing. This is the default action for all failures.
- **Restart the Service** Causes the service to stop and start again. When this option is selected, the "Restart service after" field becomes enabled, allowing you to specify how many minutes the server will wait before restarting the service. It is particularly important that you set IIS to restart to ensure that your IIS server is highly available. If another choice was started for the IIS server, the server might not be available to users when they try to connect to IIS and access resources and Web applications available through it.
- **Run a File** Causes a specified program to run. When this option is selected, the "Run file" section below it becomes enabled, and you can enter the path or browse for the file to run when a failure occurs.
- **Reboot the Computer** Restarts the server. When this option is selected, the Restart Computer Options button on this tab becomes enabled. Clicking this button opens a dialog box that allows you to enter the message that will be broadcast to users before restarting, including how long the server will wait before it restarts.

Below these options is one other field that can be configured. Each time a failure occurs, the server counts how many times the service has failed. The Reset Fail Count After field allows you to set the number of days before the count is reset to 0.

The Dependencies tab is used to view other services on which this service relies to run properly. If the service is stopped and it depends on another service, those other services could be affected. In such cases, the other services might also need to be restarted if they are to function properly.

EXERCISE 3-4

CertCam 3-4

### Stopping and Restarting a Service Using the Services Tool

1. From the Start menu, select Settings, and then click Control Panel. When the Control Panel opens, double-click Administrative Tools. When Administrative Tools opens, double-click the icon labeled Services.
2. When Services opens, double-click the IIS Admin Service that appears in the listing. The Properties sheet for this service should open and should be similar to the one shown in Figure 3-13.
3. On the General tab, reword the description so that it is more meaningful to you.
4. On the Recovery tab, configure the properties to Restart the Service when the first failure occurs.
5. In the Restart Service After field, set the service to restart after 5 minutes.
6. Click OK to confirm your settings and exit the properties.

## Data Analysis

It isn't enough to merely gather information about your system; you must also spend time analyzing it. If you don't check the data gathered on various elements of your server and network, you could remain unaware that a problem exists or that performance is beginning to falter. However, analysis takes more than merely

**FIGURE 3-13**

The Properties Sheet

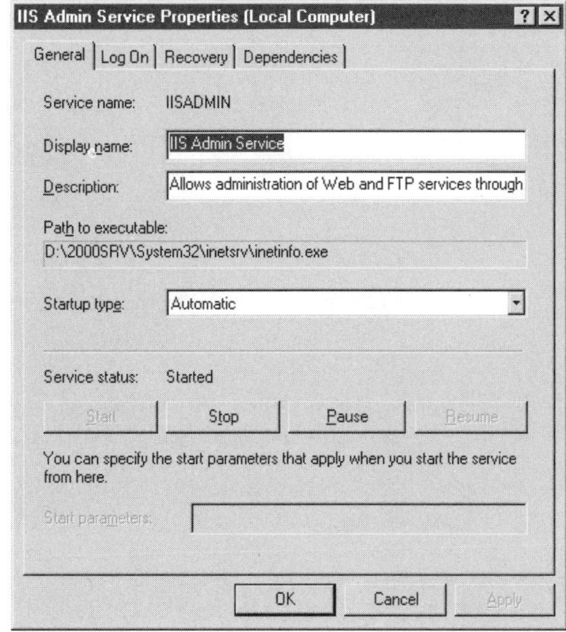


looking at a log file or watching performance metrics change. It requires knowledge of how your server and network run normally.

As we discussed, baselines are recorded information about how your system runs under normal situations. By comparing the baseline to current measurements, you can spot abnormal levels that could indicate bottlenecks or other problems. Creating a baseline requires running monitoring tools at times when the system is running normally, then logging the results to a file. In doing so, you run the tool and log the results over a period of time, at different times of the day, so that you can determine peak hours. A common approach is to set the monitoring program to gather data every minute for three or four days so that you have an accurate picture of how the network and server are being used.

**exam watch**

***The key to a baseline is that it is logged information. Any tools that don't allow you to log results can't be used to create a baseline, because the results cannot be referred to at a later date. Without a baseline, you might be unable to find the source of problems, because you won't have a reference showing how the system runs normally.***

Once the results are logged to a file, you can compare the measurements to those gathered when performance seems sluggish. To illustrate this practice, let's say that you used System Monitor to gather data on your processor. Previously, you used Performance Logs and Alerts to create a baseline, and the processor had a 40 percent utilization rate. Now System Monitor shows current measurements of an 80 percent utilization rate. This information shows you that the processor is either acting abnormally or under greater demands. Without the baseline, you probably wouldn't have noticed the increase in utilization and wouldn't realize that a problem might exist.

In addition to analyzing the data provided by server performance and monitoring tools, you should analyze logs provided by IIS itself. IIS provides a new option that allows you to audit the IIS server's performance. This feature, called *process auditing*, is used to monitor how your Web site uses the server's CPU.

Process auditing is set up through the Microsoft Management Console with the IIS snap-in. On the Extended Properties tab, click the extended log format. Once activated, process auditing will begin for that Web server.

## Windows Management Instrumentation

Windows Management Instrumentation, or WMI, is a set of instructions that allows hardware to communicate with a Windows 2000 server. Using WMI, administrators can be alerted of client hardware and software problems when they occur.

Using WMI, you can communicate with newer hardware devices and thereby monitor and control them. Devices that work with WMI communicate bidirectionally with it, allowing administrators to view alerts that are generated when a device is having problems or is down. WMI is an extension to the Windows Driver Model (WDM). It provides an interface that allows hardware components to provide information and notification to Windows 2000 Server.

Here's how WMI works: When a compliant device needs to communicate with a server, it sends the information to the hardware-specific WDM Mini Driver. The WDM Mini Driver isn't available with Windows 2000 but is instead supplied by the device's manufacturer. This driver passes information to a standard WDM driver that's supplied by Microsoft and passes the information to the WMI interface. WMI gathers together all the information from hardware, drivers, and applications and delivers it to a centralized management store. The administrator is then able to access the information and deal with it accordingly.

Now that we've discussed systems monitoring and management in detail, let's look at some common scenarios and solutions.

| SCENARIO & SOLUTION | |
|---|---|
| I'm not sure what counters I should add to System Monitor. How can I find what each of the counters is used for? | Click the Explain button in the Add Counters dialog box. This button expands the dialog box to show a description of each counter that you select. |
| How can I start Performance Console? | There are two basic ways of starting Performance Console in Windows 2000 Server. From the Start menu, select Programs \| Administrative Tools, then click Performance. The other method is to use the Run command on the Start menu, type **PERFMON**, and click OK. |
| What are the default logs available in Event Viewer, and what are they for? | The Application log shows errors, warnings, and information on various programs that have been started. The Security log shows information on audited events. The System log shows errors, warnings, and information generated by Windows 2000. |

**CERTIFICATION OBJECTIVE 3.03**

## Designing a Disaster Recovery Strategy

Having a disaster recovery strategy is similar to having a good insurance policy. You'd like to think that you'll never fall victim to a fire, flood, or other disaster, but it would be foolish to be unprepared for these events. Losing costly equipment is never as bad as losing the important data contained on a server or certain workstations. Such a data loss can mean the loss of the company's ability to do business.

The focus of a disaster recovery strategy isn't how to prevent a disaster but how to salvage your system once one has occurred. Once the damage has been done, you need to restore the system and data so that the business can continue to function.

Fortunately, Windows 2000 provides a number of features that can be used for disaster recovery:

- Disk fault tolerance
- Windows Backup
- Recovery Console
- Advanced startup options
- Emergency repair disk

The sections that follow discuss each of these areas, allowing you to see where they are useful and how they can be implemented as part of your disaster recovery strategy.

on the Job

***In addition to a disaster recovery strategy, you should also implement a strategy to deal with preventing or protecting yourself from disasters. For example, an Uninterruptible Power Supply (UPS) can be used to protect your server and other equipment from power loss, and might ensure that the power being supplied is also conditioned. You should also have equipment stored in a secure location so that it won't be stolen or tampered with. Such locations should have air conditioning and a fire system in place.***

## Disk Fault Tolerance

Disk fault tolerance is used to recover from the failure of a hard disk that is part of a RAID set. RAID, an acronym for *Redundant Array of Inexpensive Disks*, provides a way for information to be stored on one or more additional hard disks. If a disk in the set is damaged, the data can still be retrieved from the data stored on another disk.

As we saw earlier in this chapter, there are various levels of RAID, but only RAID 1 (disk mirroring) and RAID 5 (disk striping with parity) are supported by Windows 2000. RAID 1 is disk mirroring, or mirrored volumes, as it is called in Windows 2000. When mirrored volumes are used, data on one hard disk is duplicated to another disk, so a mirror image of one appears on the other. RAID 5 is disk striping with parity. With this method, data and parity information are stored across all disks in the array. This system allows data to be recovered from redundant data and parity information stored on other disks in the set.

## Windows Backup

As your server floats away in a flood or melts down to the size of a paperweight in an office fire, it would be particularly bad to say, "Oops, I guess we should have made backups." Backups are copies of data that are written to a tape or other storage devices. Windows 2000 includes a backup program called Windows Backup that allows you to archive files to a medium that can be stored in another location. Then if a file is deleted, a hard disk crashes, or the data is irrevocably damaged, you can restore your data from the backup.

When you use backups as part of your disaster recovery plan, it is important that you keep one set of backups offsite. Remember that if fire, flood, earthquake, or some other disaster destroys your server, the backup media could also be destroyed if it is kept in the same location. By moving one set of backup tapes or other media to a different location, you're protecting yourself from losing your original data.

### Types of Backups in Windows Backup

Windows Backup provides a number of ways to back up data on your computer. The methods are:

- Normal
- Copy
- Incremental
- Differential
- Daily

As we'll see, these methods allow you to control what is to be backed up and how the data is to be treated by Windows Backup afterward.

A *normal backup*, commonly referred to as a *full backup*, is used to back up all your data, all directories and files on a volume, or all volumes on a server. When a normal backup is performed, each file that's backed up has its archive bit modified. An *archive bit* is an attribute of a file and is used to indicate whether files need to be backed up or not. The archive bit is set when a file is modified to show that data within it has changed and therefore needs to be backed up. It is cleared by a full backup to show that the file has been backed up to tape.

A *copy* backs up all files but won't clear the archive bit. In essence, a copy is the same as a normal backup. The important difference between the two is that the archive bit is not cleared in a copy, so any backup processes run afterward will look at these files as though they haven't been backed up before.

*Incremental backups* are used to back up all files that have been modified since the last full or incremental backup. This type of backup looks at the archive bit to see if a file has changed and if it needs to be backed up. It will not back up any files that have not been modified. Once the incremental backup has backed up a file, the archive bit is cleared. This keeps the next incremental backup from backing up the file again if it hasn't been modified.

To restore data from incremental backups, you would first restore files from the most recent full backup. Once this process is complete, you would then add the incremental changes that have been saved to the tape by the incremental backups. This step ensures that files have been completely restored to a system and are completely up to date. If only the full backup were restored, any changes since the time of that backup would be missed. If only the incremental backup were used, files that have not changed since the full backup wouldn't be restored.

*Differential backups* are used to back up files that were modified since the last full backup. In this way, a differential backup is similar to an incremental backup. However, unlike an incremental backup, a differential backup won't clear the archive bit. When data is backed up, the archive bit remains the same.

Differential backups are slower each time they are performed, because the size of the backup grows with each differential backup. This is because the same data plus additional data is being backed up each time. This makes differential backups initially faster to perform than full backups, but slower than incremental backups after the first time a differential backup is performed. Because only modified files are changed, an incremental backup is considerably faster than a full backup (which backs up all files, regardless of whether they've been modified). As the number of files increases on your server, the time it takes to perform an incremental backup increases as well.

The final type of backup that Windows Backup can perform is a *daily backup*, which backs up files that have changed on the day of the backup. However, as in a differential backup, the archive bit isn't cleared.

**EXERCISE 3-5**

### Performing a Full Backup on Windows 2000 Server

1. From the Windows Start menu, select Programs | Accessories | System Tools, and then click Backup.
2. When the Backup program starts, you will see several tabs. The default one that appears should be the Welcome tab. On this tab, click the button labeled Backup Wizard.
3. The first screen of the Backup Wizard is the Welcome screen. Click Next to continue.
4. The next screen allows you to specify what it is that you'll be backing up. The first option allows you to back up everything on your computer, the next allows you to specify what to back up, and the third allows you to back up only the system-state data. Click the second option, labeled "Back up selected files, drives, or network data."
5. When the next screen appears, the left pane allows you to browse the server and network to select files and directories to back up. The right pane shows the files and directories to back up. Select the files and directories to back up, then click Next.
6. The screen that appears allows you to specify the media type to which you want to back up data. If you have no backup device installed, this drop-down list is disabled, and you can only back up to a file. Select the device, then click Next.
7. The final screen shows the options you have selected through this process. On this screen, there is also an Advanced button, which allows you to specify the type of backup to perform. Click the Advanced button.
8. When the Advanced screen appears, you will see a drop-down list containing various types of backups. Normal is a full backup, Copy backs up all files but won't clear the archive bit, Incremental performs an incremental backup, Differential performs a differential backup, and Daily backs up files that have changed today (and doesn't clear the archive bit). Select Normal as the backup type, and click Next.

9. The next screen allows you to specify whether data should be verified after the backup. This verification ensures that data is backed up correctly. However, it also increases the time it takes for the process to complete. Click this check box to select this option. The second check box allows you to use compression and can be used only if a device supporting compression exists on your system. If this check box is enabled, compression can be used. Click Next to continue.
10. The next screen allows you to specify whether data should be appended to an existing backup (if it exists) or the backup data replaced on the media. Select the first option (to append it), and then click Next.
11. The screen that appears allows you to label the backup job. Accept the default label, then click Next to continue.
12. The screen that appears allows you to specify whether the job should be started now or rescheduled for a later time. Click the Now option, and then click Next.
13. The final screen appears again. Click Finish to start the job.

---

## Recovery Console

Recovery Console is a tool that allows you to gain access to the hard disk of a computer running Windows 2000 and perform actions that might enable you to recover your system after a failure. This tool can be started in a number of ways. It can be run from the Windows 2000 Setup floppy disks, the installation CD-ROM, or, if it has been installed on the local hard disk, the Windows 2000 Startup menu. Your ability to start the computer determines whether you can access the Startup menu, however. If you can't access the Startup menu, you will need to run Recovery Console from the Setup floppies or installation CD.

Once started, Recovery Console allows you to access the hard disk, regardless of whether FAT16, FAT32, or NTFS is used as the file system. To protect your system from being hacked with this tool, Remote Console requires you to enter the system administrator password to run it. From this point, you will be able to use various commands to start and stop services and repair a system that isn't starting properly or at all.

exam Watch

***It's important to realize that if the computer doesn't start—such as when the MBR or system volume boot sector has been damaged—the Startup menu can't be accessed. In such a case, you need to run Remote Console from the Setup floppies or installation CD.***

## Advanced Startup Options

The Advanced Startup Options allow you to control how your computer is to start so that you can troubleshoot problems when the machine doesn't start correctly. The Advanced Startup Options are often used when configuration settings have been changed or new hardware has been installed and your system doesn't start properly as a result. For example, you could install a new display driver only to find that you can't see anything properly on your screen. By restarting the computer and using these options, you can access the system and revert to the old driver. The Advance Startup Options allow you to access and restore your system when a problem occurs.

The Advanced Startup Options are accessed at bootup by pressing F8, when the list of available operating systems appears. After you press F8, the Advanced Options menu appears, allowing you to start the computer in the following ways:

- Safe mode
- Safe mode with networking
- Safe mode with command prompt
- Last known good configuration

*Safe mode* is also called *diagnostic mode* because it is used for troubleshooting purposes. When Safe mode is used, Windows 2000 starts with a minimal set of drivers and services. By loading only the drivers and services necessary to run Windows 2000, you are generally able to run the basic operating system. Once Windows 2000 starts in Safe mode, you can then remove or reconfigure any problem software and drivers that are preventing Windows 2000 from starting normally.

When Safe mode is used, it creates a boot log that lists the devices and services that are loaded when Windows 2000 starts. Entries for each device and service indicate whether it loaded successfully or not. By reviewing the information in this text file, you can determine the possible reasons that Windows 2000 isn't starting normally.

Safe mode doesn't provide network support, so your abilities to access files and programs are limited to what you can access on the local computer. Even if your computer is connected to the network, Safe mode leaves your computer as though it were a standalone machine. To acquire network support in Safe mode, you need to select Safe Mode with Networking from the Advanced Startup Options menu. The exception to having network support is if your computer uses PC Cards (i.e., PCMCIA devices). If your computer uses PCMCIA devices, you won't be able to use them when Safe mode with networking is used.

The third version of Safe mode is Safe mode with command prompt. When this option is selected, Windows 2000 starts with its basic drivers and services, but it goes to the command prompt rather than the Windows 2000 GUI. This allows you to enter commands from the DOS prompt, but you will be unable to use any of the graphical tools available in Windows 2000.

The final option in Advanced Startup Options is Last Known Good Configuration. This option is used if you have incorrectly configured a device on your computer and need to restore a previous configuration. When Windows 2000 shuts down properly, it saves that copy of the Registry. When Last Known Good Configuration is selected, this previous copy from the last successful shutdown replaces the current one. The result is the same as if you'd never made the configuration changes, because the system changes are lost and the old ones are restored.

## Emergency Repair Disk

An *emergency repair disk (ERD)* is a floppy disk that contains information about your Windows system settings and can be used to restore damaged or missing system files. The ERD is created using the Windows 2000 Backup utility, which we discussed previously. When Windows Backup starts, the first screen offers a button that allows you to create an ERD from a floppy disk that is inserted into your computer's floppy disk drive.

Using the ERD requires you to start your computer using the Windows 2000 Setup disks or the installation CD. If your system doesn't allow you to boot from the CD, you need to use the Setup disks. When the Setup program starts, you are given the option to repair your system. Pressing *R* allows you to repair the system, and you will be asked whether you'd like to repair it using Recovery Console or an ERD.

The ERD allows you to repair the system manually or use the fast-repair option. If you choose the fast-repair option, the ERD attempts to repair the following areas automatically:

- System files
- Partition boot sector problems on the boot volume

- Startup environment (when dual-boot or multiple-boot systems are being repaired)
- Registry problems

If you use manual repair, you will be able to control whether each of these (except the Registry) is repaired. The Registry can be repaired using only the fast-repair option, which uses a backup copy of the Registry that was created the first time the Setup program was run.

Now that you have a better idea of disaster recovery, let's look at some possible scenarios and solutions.

| SCENARIO & SOLUTION | |
|---|---|
| I want to perform a full backup of my Windows 2000 server, but I can't find an option for a full backup in my Windows 2000 Backup utility. What should I do? | Choose Normal as the backup type. In Windows 2000, the Normal backup performs a full backup of the system. |
| I was considering using Recovery Console to repair my system, but the file system on the Windows 2000 Server uses FAT32. Will Recovery Console support FAT32? | Yes. Recovery Console allows you to access the hard disk regardless of whether FAT16, FAT32, or NTFS is used as the file system. |

## CERTIFICATION SUMMARY

Designing a server topology involves determining the layout of servers on your network and requires you to consider such issues as scalability, fault tolerance, and load balancing. *Scalability* refers to increases in the size (scale) of your network, requiring additional servers to be added to meet the needs of a growing organization. *Fault tolerance* requires providing alternative methods to deal with the possibility that a primary system could fail. As we saw, this area not only includes using fault-tolerant methods for disk drives, it also includes providing redundancy for other systems on your network. Finally, *load balancing* distributes the workload of a server between multiple servers on your network. This increases performance and extends the life of equipment.

Designing a systems management and monitoring strategy involves keeping your system healthy and monitoring for possible problems on your server and network. Performance Console is one tool that can be used in this endeavor. It includes the System Monitor and Performance Logs and Alerts snap-ins. Together, these tools allow you to view real-time data on your system, create and view logged counter data, gather data when a particular event occurs, and be notified of exceeded thresholds. Using Performance Console, you can create a baseline that can be used for data analysis when problems occur. Event Viewer is another tool that allows you to view logged information about audited events as well as information and warnings about system components, security issues, and applications running on the server. Finally, Windows Management Instrumentation (WMI) allows Windows 2000 client hardware to communicate with a Windows 2000 Server. Each of these can be used to monitor your system for problems and manage issues that arise on your server and network.

Designing a disaster recovery strategy involves creating a plan that will allow you to restore data once a disaster has occurred. Windows 2000 provides a number of features that can be used for disaster recovery. Disk fault tolerance provides recovery from hard disk failures. Windows Backup allows you to store data on media so that it can be restored when needed. Recovery Console provides the ability to perform administrative tasks from the command line and aids in recovering your system. The Advanced Startup Options allow you to load the operating system when damage has occurred. Finally, the emergency repair disk, or ERD, allows you to repair problems with the Registry, startup environment, system files, and boot sector. Each of these tools can play a useful part when various disasters have damaged your system.

# TWO-MINUTE DRILL

## Designing a Server Topology

- ❑ At least one DC is required for each domain in your network. Additional DCs can be used in a domain, so users can be authenticated when one of the DCs isn't available. Additional DCs also improve performance because users will be able to connect to any of the DCs.
- ❑ Load balancing is a process of distributing the workload a server must perform between two or more servers. This distribution balances the load between the servers so that they can more effectively deal with client requests.
- ❑ Fault tolerance is a system's ability to be functional after a failure occurs. Fault tolerance requires implementing alternative methods for overcoming a failure, including redundant paths, services, and components.

## Designing a System Management and Monitoring Strategy

- ❑ Performance Console is the Microsoft Management Console that contains two snap-ins: System Monitor and Performance Logs and Alerts. System Monitor allows you to monitor your system's health. Performance Logs and Alerts allow you to create and view logged counter data, gather data when a particular event occurs, and be notified of exceeded thresholds.
- ❑ Event Viewer allows you to view events that have been logged to different files on your system. The default log files that can be viewed through Event Viewer are the Security, Application, and System logs.
- ❑ Windows Management Instrumentation (WMI) is a set of instructions that allows hardware to communicate with a Windows 2000 server.

## Designing a Disaster Recovery Strategy

- ❑ Disk fault tolerance provides a way to recover from the failure of a hard disk that's part of a RAID set.
- ❑ Windows Backup offers several methods of backing up data. Normal is a full backup, Copy backs up all files but won't clear the archive bit, Incremental performs an incremental backup, Differential performs a differential backup,

and Daily backs up files that have changed today (and doesn't clear the archive bit).

- Emergency repair disks (ERDs) allow you to repair Registry problems and provide a way to fix problems with the startup environment, system files, and boot sector.

# SELF TEST

The following questions will help you measure your understanding of the material presented in this chapter. Read all the choices carefully because there might be more than one correct answer. Choose all correct answers for each question.

## Designing a Server Topology

1. Your network consists of two sites that are connected with a T1 line and have a DC in each. Each morning, a user in the sales department logs on to the DC in the site in which he is working, which is called SiteA. On this particular day, work is being done on the T1 line that connects these two sites, so the network connection between the two sites will be down. During this time, you decide to make changes to the user's account in SiteB. Which of the following will occur as a result of these actions?

   A. The user will be unable to log on because the only available DC is in a different site.

   B. The user will be able to log on by connecting and being authenticated by the DC in SiteA, which will have the updated properties for this user's account.

   C. The user will be able to log on but will be unable to access the resources in his local site.

   D. Changes made to the user's account won't be applied to the DC in SiteA until the connection between the two sites is restored.

2. Your network has four remote sites, which are all connected to the main site in which you work. You are deciding whether to add a DC at any of these sites. Which of the following requires a DC? (Choose all that apply.)

   A. Site A has 5 users and a dial-up connection that links the remote site to main site.

   B. Site B has 40 users and a T1 connection that links the remote site to the main site. The connection between these sites has the tendency to go down.

   C. Site C has 10 users and a dial-up connection that links the remote site to the main site.

   D. Site D has 30 users but, on average, only only five workstations at this location are connected to the network. The site is connected to the main site with a dial-up connection.

3. Which of the following would indicate the need to create a new domain on your network?

   A. The network consists of servers running Windows NT 4.0 Server and workstations running Windows 2000 Professional. A Web server is running Internet Information Server on a Windows NT 4.0 server. At present, there are 39,000 users on the network, and an additional 1500 employees will be hired in the next few months.

B. The network is currently running Windows 2000 servers and Windows NT 4.0 workstation. The Web server is running Windows 2000 with Internet Information Services. At present, there are 39,000 users on the network, and an additional 1500 employees will be hired in the next few months.

C. The network consists of servers running Windows 2000 Server and workstations running Windows 2000 Professional. A Web server is running separately from the network on a UNIX computer. At present, there are 39,000 users on the network, and an additional 1500 employees will be hired in the next few months.

D. The network consists of servers running Windows 2000 Server, a Macintosh Web Server, and workstations running Windows NT 4.0, Windows 98, and Macintosh. At present, there are 39,000 users on the network, and an additional 1500 employees will be hired in the next few months.

**4.** Your company's network consists of three sites, called SiteA, SiteB, and SiteC. There is a dial-up connection between SiteA and SiteC and a dial-up connection between SiteA and SiteB. SiteA has 200 users and two domain controllers, SiteB has 100 users and no DCs, and SiteC has 200 users and one DC. All the users in SiteA and SiteB work two shifts, with half of the workers each working on one shift. Users in Site B have an unreliable connection to SiteA, where they log on to the domain. SiteC is a larger complex where all the employees work on a single shift. Users at this site are complaining that the network is slow in the morning and at the end of the workday. Which of the following steps will you take to improve availability and performance? (Choose all that apply.)

A. Install a better connection between SiteA and SiteC so that users in SiteB will be able to log on to the network when their connection with SiteA is down.

B. Install a DC in SiteC so that users can log on to one of two DCs.

C. Install a DC in SiteB so that users can log on to a DC in their local site.

D. None of the above.

**5.** You have decided to implement network load balancing on your network. What is the maximum number of servers that you can group together in a cluster to work together as a single entity?

A. 2

B. 10

C. 25

D. 32

**6.** You have decided to implement fault tolerance on a server that contains sensitive data that's vital to your business. Which of the following levels of RAID does Windows 2000 Server support? (Choose all that apply.)

A. RAID 1

B. RAID 2

C. RAID 3

D. RAID 4

E. RAID 5

## Designing a System Management and Monitoring Strategy

**7.** You are preparing to view performance-related information on your Windows 2000 server. Which of the following tools would you use to view real-time data about elements of your system?

A. System Monitor

B. Event Viewer

C. Performance Monitor

D. Performance Logs and Alerts

**8.** You open System Monitor and attempt to view information on the LogicalDisk. When you try to do so, you find that you can't view any information about your server's logical disk. Which of the following commands would you use to activate this counter?

A. diskperf

B. diskperf -yv

C. diskperf -yd

D. diskperf -n

**9.** You want to log page faults when they occur on your Windows 2000 server. Which of the following would you use in Performance Logs and Alerts to log the information in this way?

A. Counter logs

B. Trace logs

C. Alert logs

D. Event logs

**10.** Which of the following are default log files that can be viewed through Event Viewer and that contain information that is determined by the audit policies that you've created?

A. Security log

B. Application log

C. System log

D. Audit log

**11.** A service isn't running properly on your Windows 2000 server. The service fails to respond, and you have been manually stopping and restarting the service. You open the Services applet and open the Properties for this service. Which of the following tabs on this service's Properties sheet would you use to configure the service to automatically restart?

A. Logon tab

B. Recovery tab

C. General tab

D. Dependencies tab

**12.** You have set up a new network for a company. You are concerned that performance of the network will change over time, and you want to create a baseline of current performance to compare to future measurements. Which of the following tools will you use to create the baseline of your Windows 2000 server's performance?

A. Event Viewer

B. System Monitor

C. Performance Monitor

D. Performance Logs and Alerts

**13.** You have just installed a new device on a Windows 2000 server in a building that's across the road from your office. The device includes a WDM Mini Driver. You want to view information on the device through a Windows 2000 server that's in the server room by your office. Which of the following technologies would you use to monitor and control the device?

A. Windows Management Instrumentation

B. Windows Manager Interface

C. Performance Console

D. System Monitor

## Designing a Disaster Recovery Strategy

**14.** You want to back up all files on your system and have the archive bit modified for when other backups are performed at a later time. Which of the following backup types in Windows Backup will you use?

A. Normal

B. Incremental

C. Differential

D. Copy

**15.** You run a full backup of files on your Windows 2000 server using Windows Backup. Once the backup is run, you modify a spreadsheet and then run a differential backup. Afterward you don't change the spreadsheet and you run an incremental backup. The spreadsheet isn't modified again, and you run another differential backup. Which of the following statements is true?

A. The first differential backup won't back up the spreadsheet.

B. The second differential backup won't back up the spreadsheet.

C. The incremental backup won't back up the spreadsheet.

D. The spreadsheet will be backed up each time.

**16.** You perform a full backup of your system and then perform differential backups each day for the next month. Every day for the next 30 days, a new large file is added to the system. These are the only new files being created, but existing data is modified constantly. Each time the differential backup is performed, it takes longer to complete. What is the most likely reason for this?

A. More files are being added to the system, so it is taking longer to check the archive bit on every file.

B. The tape is filling and is taking longer to respond to the system.

C. The data on the system is growing larger. Since a differential backup is the same as a full backup in Windows Backup, all the files on the system are being backed up each time.

D. The size of the backup is growing with each differential backup, so the differential backup is taking longer to perform.

**17.** You have decided to back up all the data on your system each day. These backups should back up all the data on a daily basis. The backups should clear the archive bit, in case you want to perform other backups that will only back up changed data. Which of the following backup types will you choose?

A. Daily

B. Nightly

C. Normal

D. Copy

18. Which of the following file systems does Recovery Console support?

A. FAT16

B. FAT32

C. NTFS

D. All of the above

19. You want to access the Advanced Startup Options so that you can repair your system. Which of the following keys would you press at bootup to access the Advanced Startup Options?

A. F1

B. F5

C. F8

D. F10

20. You have just installed a new device that has caused problems with your system. You want to restore a copy of the Registry that was saved when the system shut down properly before you installed the new device. Which of the following Advanced Startup Options will you select?

A. Safe mode

B. Safe mode with networking

C. Safe mode with command prompt

D. Last known good configuration

# LAB QUESTION

Asimov Robotics and Housewares runs Windows 2000 servers and Windows 2000 Professional workstations on its network. As shown in Figure 3-14, the company has offices in London, Toronto, and St. Catharines. Each of these cities is a different site on the network, which is a single domain.

The Toronto office has 200 users, London has 500 users, and St. Catharines has 100 users. London and Toronto are connected by a stable T1 connection. Toronto and St. Catharines are linked by a Frame Relay connection. London and St. Catharines are connected by a dial-up connection. While Toronto and London haven't had a problem with their connection, each has had problems maintaining its connection with St. Catharines. There is one DC for the site in London and two DCs in Toronto. London has complained about the speed connecting to the local DC during peak hours of network use.

1. Which of the sites should have a DC installed?
2. You decide to use Event Viewer to view events that are logged by various programs running on your server. Which log file will you check?
3. You are concerned that a driver isn't loading properly when Windows 2000 Server starts. You decide to use Event Viewer to view events that are logged by Windows 2000 Server. Which log file will you check?
4. As part of a disaster recovery program, you decide to implement disk fault tolerance. What levels of RAID can be used for this task?
5. You perform normal and incremental backups on a daily basis. When restoring data to one of your Windows 2000 servers, you restore the full backup and the last incremental backup that was done. What, if any, is the problem with this technique?

**FIGURE 3-14** Asimov Robotics and Housewares

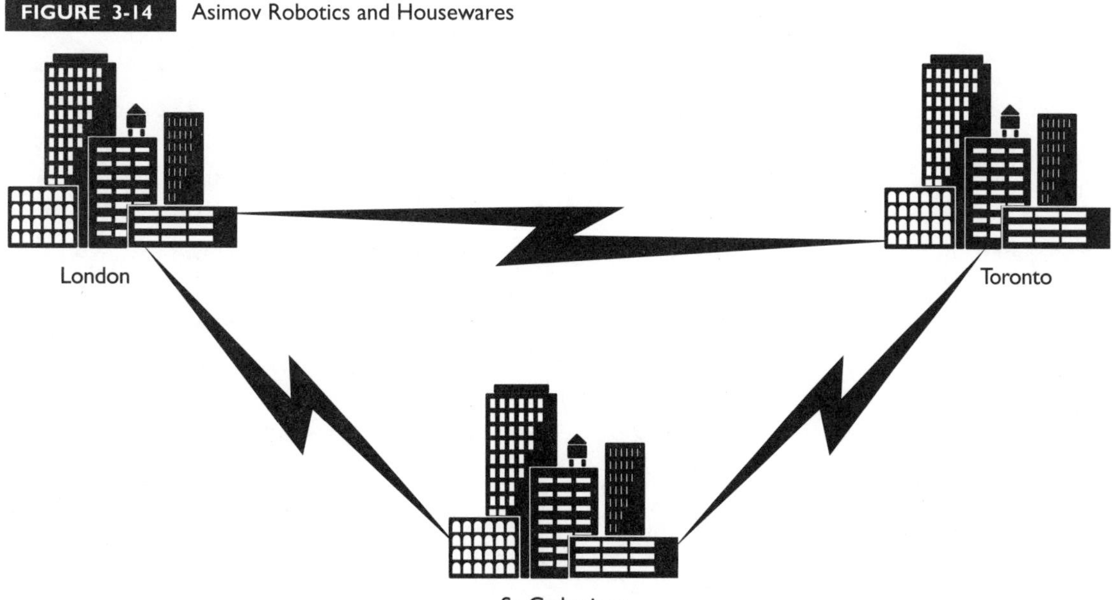

# SELF TEST ANSWERS

## Designing a Server Topology

1. ☑ **D.** Changes made to the user's account will be applied to the DC in SiteA until the connection between the two sites is restored. DCs store a replica of the domain's portion of Active Directory. When changes are made to objects in AD, these changes are automatically applied to the DC on which the changes were made and then replicated to other DCs in the domain. However, if the DCs are unable to connect with one another, the replication process cannot occur. If they can't communicate, a DC in one location won't be aware of changes made on a different DC in another location.
   ☒ **A** is incorrect because the DC in SiteA is still available. Only the connection between the sites is unavailable, so the new properties can't be replicated. SiteA's DC still contains the old information on this user's account as it waits for the new properties for this account to be replicated. **B** is incorrect because SiteA won't have the updated properties for this account. Because the link between the two sites is down, the DCs are unable to replicate and obtain the new properties. **C** is incorrect because the user will be able to log on to the DC in SiteA, which still has the user's old properties.

2. ☑ **B** and **C**. The process of determining whether to add a DC to a site is based on the number of people in the remote site and the connection between those sites. Although Site B has a T1 connection that links the remote site to the main site, it has the tendency to go down. If there is an unreliable connection between the remote site and the main site or if the connection is slow, it is wise to either upgrade the connection or add a DC to the remote site. Either of these steps allows users to log on and access resources quickly as well as avoid downtime that will occur when the connection is down. Site B is also a candidate for a DC, for the same reason that Site C is: Both these sites have more than five users. Microsoft recommends that if there are five or fewer users at a remote site, there is no need to add a DC there. If there are more than five users, you should consider adding a DC.
   ☒ **A** is incorrect because there are fewer than five users at this site. **D** is incorrect because only five workstations are connected to the network. Although there are significantly more users at this site, only five of them can be on the network at any given time. In both cases, Site A and Site D, there is no mention of the link between the site and the main site being unreliable, so this doesn't constitute a need to add a DC.

3. ☑ **A.** The key to this question lies in the kind of server used on the network and whether Active Directory is used. Windows NT 4.0 networks can support a maximum of 40,000 user

accounts. If the number of users exceeds 40,000, you need to create a new domain. Because this choice uses Windows NT 4.0 Servers, Active Directory isn't being used, so the 40,000-user limit exists.

☒ **B**, **C**, and **D** are all incorrect because each of these has Windows 2000 servers running as DCs and Active Directory is used. In practice, Windows 2000 domains have been tested to support 1 million objects. Therefore, the number of users on this network doesn't require addition of another domain.

**4.** ☑ **B** and **C**. Install a DC in SiteC so that users can log on to one of two DCs and install a DC in SiteB so that users can log on to a DC in their local site. If you install a DC in SiteB, users will still be able to log on to the network when their connection with SiteA is down. If you install a second DC in SiteC, users will have an additional DC to log on to, thereby reducing the load that would be placed on a single DC. This step also reduces the load on a DC during peak hours, when users are logging on or off at the beginning or end of the workday.

☒ **A** is incorrect because, when the connection between SiteB and SiteA is down, SiteB is cut off from the network. There isn't a connection between SiteB and SiteC, so when the only connection to SiteB has is down, users are removed from the network. In other words, it doesn't matter what type of connection SiteB and SiteC have, so this choice is incorrect. **D** is incorrect because two of the choices will improve performance or availability.

**5.** ☑ **D**. 32. Clusters are groups of servers that are configured to work together as a single entity. Clients view the cluster as a single server, even though as many as 32 individual servers can make up the cluster. When clients make requests of the cluster, the requests are distributed among the hosts making up the cluster, thereby improving performance.

☒ **A**, **B**, and **C** are incorrect because as many as 32 individual servers can make up a cluster.

**6.** ☑ **A** and **E**. Windows 2000 supports RAID 1 (disk mirroring) and RAID 5 (disk striping with parity). RAID 1 is disk mirroring. In Windows 2000, it is called *mirrored volumes*. With this method of RAID, data on one hard disk is duplicated to another disk, so a mirror image of one appears on the other. RAID 5 is disk striping with parity. With this method, an array of 3 to 32 disks can be used. The disks are combined into one volume, and data and parity information are stored across all disks in the array.

☒ **B**, **C**, and **D** are incorrect because Windows 2000 supports only RAID 1 (disk mirroring) and RAID 5 (disk striping with parity).

## Designing a System Management and Monitoring Strategy

**7.** ☑ **A.** System Monitor allows you to view real-time and previously logged data about areas of your system and network. It provides a visual representation of counters you are watching.
☒ **B** is incorrect because Event Viewer allows you to view information on events that have been logged to various files. **C** is incorrect because Performance Monitor is a Windows NT 4.0 tool, which is now Performance Console in Windows 2000. **D** is incorrect because the Performance Logs and Alerts snap-in allows you to log counter data to a file, view existing logs, gather data from counters when a particular event occurs, and be notified of exceeded performance thresholds.

**8.** ☑ **B.** To obtain data on logical drives, you need to run diskperf –yv from the command prompt. This command activates the LogicalDisk counter associated with local drives and storage volumes.
☒ **A** is incorrect because the –yv switch needs to be used to activate the LogicalDisk. **C** is incorrect because diskperf –yd command obtains data on physical drives, not logical drives. **D** is incorrect because diskperf –n is run at the command prompt to disable the counters.

**9.** ☑ **B.** Trace logs. Trace logs don't obtain data at regular update intervals; instead, they log data when certain events occur. Trace logs monitor the activities you specify, and when an activity occurs, the information is stored in a log file.
☒ **A** is incorrect because Counter logs are used to obtain and store data that's collected by the counters you specify. When counter logs are used, data is obtained at specific update intervals. **C** and **D** are incorrect because there is no such thing as Alert logs or Event logs in Performance Logs and Alerts. However, there are alerts, which are notifications that can be set to inform you when a particular performance threshold has been exceeded.

**10.** ☑ **A.** The Security log provides information on audited events. The events that are recorded in this log are determined by the audit policy that is created on your system.
☒ **B** is incorrect because the Application log provides information on events that are logged by various programs running on your system. **C** is incorrect because the System log provides information that is logged by Windows 2000 itself. These logs are generated by components that run on the server and report errors on various drivers and system software that failed to load on startup or experienced problems when running. **D** is incorrect because there is no Audit log that's a default log that can be viewed through Event Viewer.

**11.** ☑ **B.** The Recovery tab is used to configure the events that should occur when the service fails to respond. You can specify how the server will react to a failure the first time it fails to respond, the second time, and any times after that. The Restart the Service option on this tab causes the service to stop and start again. When this option is selected, the "Restart service after" field becomes enabled, allowing you to specify how many minutes the server will wait before restarting the service.

☒ A is incorrect because the Logon tab is used to specify the account the service will use to log on to the system. C is incorrect because the General tab is used to change such information as the name and description of the service, which appears in the window of the Services applet. D is incorrect because the Dependencies tab is used to view other services on which this service relies to run properly.

**12.** ☑ **D.** Performance Logs and Alerts is used to create baselines. The Performance Logs and Alerts snap-in allows you to log counter data to a file, view existing logs, gather data from counters when a particular event occurs, and be notified of exceeded performance thresholds. Information gathered with this tool can be saved to a log file, which can be referred to at a later date.

☒ **A** and **B** are incorrect because neither provides the ability to store information to a log file. System Monitor allows you to view real-time and previously logged data about areas of your system and network. It provides a visual representation of counters being watched. Event Viewer allows you to view information on events that have been logged to various files. **C** is incorrect because Performance Monitor is a Windows NT 4.0 tool, which is now Performance Console in Windows 2000.

**13.** ☑ **A.** Windows Management Instrumentation (WMI) is a set of instructions that allows hardware to communicate with a Windows 2000 server. Using WMI, you can communicate with newer hardware devices and thereby monitor and control them.

☒ **B** is incorrect because there is no such technology called Windows Manager Interface in Windows 2000. **C** is incorrect because Performance Console is a tool that uses two snap-ins, System Monitor and Performance Logs and Alerts, to gather performance information. It is not used to monitor and control hardware devices. **D** is incorrect because System Monitor is a snap-in that allows you to gather performance information. It is not used to monitor and control hardware devices.

## Designing a Disaster Recovery Strategy

**14.** ☑ **A.** A normal backup, commonly referred to as a *full backup*, is used to back up all your data. When a normal backup is performed, each file that's backed up has its archive bit modified.

☒ **B** is incorrect because an incremental backup is used to back up all files that have been modified since the last full or incremental backup. This type of backup looks at the archive bit to see if a file has changed and if it needs to be backed up. It does not back up any files that have not been modified. **C** is incorrect because differential backups are used to back up files that were modified since the last full backup. When data is backed up, the archive bit remains the same. **D** is incorrect because a copy backs up all files but won't clear the archive bit.

**15.** ☑ **B.** The second differential backup won't back up the spreadsheet. Because an incremental backup clears the archive bit, the differential backup views the file as though it hasn't been modified since the last full backup.
☒ **A** is incorrect because, when the spreadsheet is modified, the archive bit is reset. Therefore, the differential backup will view the spreadsheet as having been changed and needing to be backed up. **C** is incorrect because the differential backup won't clear the archive bit, so the incremental backup will view the spreadsheet as having been modified since the full backup. Therefore, it will back up the file. **D** is incorrect because the spreadsheet won't be backed up each time.

**16.** ☑ **D.** The size of the backup is growing with each differential backup, so the differential backup is taking longer to perform. Differential backups are slower each time they are performed, because the size of the backup grows with each differential backup. This is because the same data and additional data (i.e., modified and newly created files) are backed up each time.
☒ **A** is incorrect because it would not take considerably longer to check the archive bit on 30 extra files. **B** is incorrect because it wouldn't take a significant period of time to cue up the backup tape just because it is being filled. **C** is incorrect because a differential backup isn't the same as a full backup in Windows Backup. A normal backup, however, is a full backup in Windows 2000.

**17.** ☑ **C.** Normal. The trick to this question is that it states that you want to perform backups daily, but the key to the answer is that the archive bit is to be cleared. A normal backup is used to back up all your data. When a normal backup is performed, each file that's backed up has its archive bit modified.
☒ **A** is incorrect because a daily backup backs up files that have changed today but does not clear the archive bit. **B** is incorrect because there is no backup type called a nightly backup in Windows Backup. **D** is incorrect because copy backs up all files but won't clear the archive bit.

**18.** ☑ **D.** All of the above. Recovery Console supports FAT16, FAT32, and NTFS. It allows you to access the hard disk regardless of whether FAT16, FAT32, or NTFS is used as the file system.
☒ **A**, **B**, and **C** are incorrect because Recovery Console supports each of these file systems.

**19.** ☑ **C.** F8. The Advanced Startup Options are accessed at bootup by pressing F8 when the list of available operating systems appears. After you press F8, the Advanced Options menu appears, allowing you to use the Startup Options.
☒ **A, B,** and **D** are all incorrect because the F8 key is used to access the Advanced Startup Options.

**20.** ☑ **D.** Last known good configuration can be used to restore a copy of the Registry from when the computer last shut down properly. When Windows 2000 shuts down properly, it saves that copy of the Registry. When Last Known Good Configuration is selected, this previous copy from the last successful shutdown replaces the current one. The result is as if you'd never made the configuration changes, because the system changes you've made are lost and old ones are restored.
☒ **A, B,** and **C** are incorrect. Safe mode loads Windows 2000 with minimal drivers and services. Safe mode with networking does the same but also provides network support. Safe mode with command prompt loads Windows 2000 with minimal drivers and services but starts the operating system at the command prompt.

# LAB ANSWER

1. London and St. Catharines. St. Catharines has experienced problems with its connection to both London and Toronto, so those users are unable to log on to the network and benefit from resources. Installing a DC at this site would allow the users to log on to the network and use resources when the link to the other sites is down. London should have a second DC installed to reduce the load that would be placed on the single DC. Rather than users connecting to one DC, they could also connect to the additional DCs in the domain to be authenticated. This will reduce the load on a DC during peak hours.

2. Application log. The Application log provides information on events that are logged by various programs running on your system. These include both programs that are started by Windows 2000 Server when it boots up and applications that are manually started by you.

3. System log. The System log provides information that is logged by Windows 2000 itself. These are generated by components that run on the server and report errors on various drivers and system software that failed to load on startup or experienced problems when running.

4. RAID 1 and RAID 5. Windows 2000 supports RAID 1 (disk mirroring) and RAID 5 (disk striping with parity). Windows 2000 supports no other levels of RAID.

5. Data that was backed up between the normal and last incremental backup in the set won't be restored. To restore data from incremental backups, you first restore files from the most recent full backup. Once this is complete, you add the incremental changes that have been saved to the tape by the incremental backups. This ensures that files have been completely restored to the system and are completely up to date.

MCSE

MICROSOFT CERTIFIED SYSTEMS ENGINEER

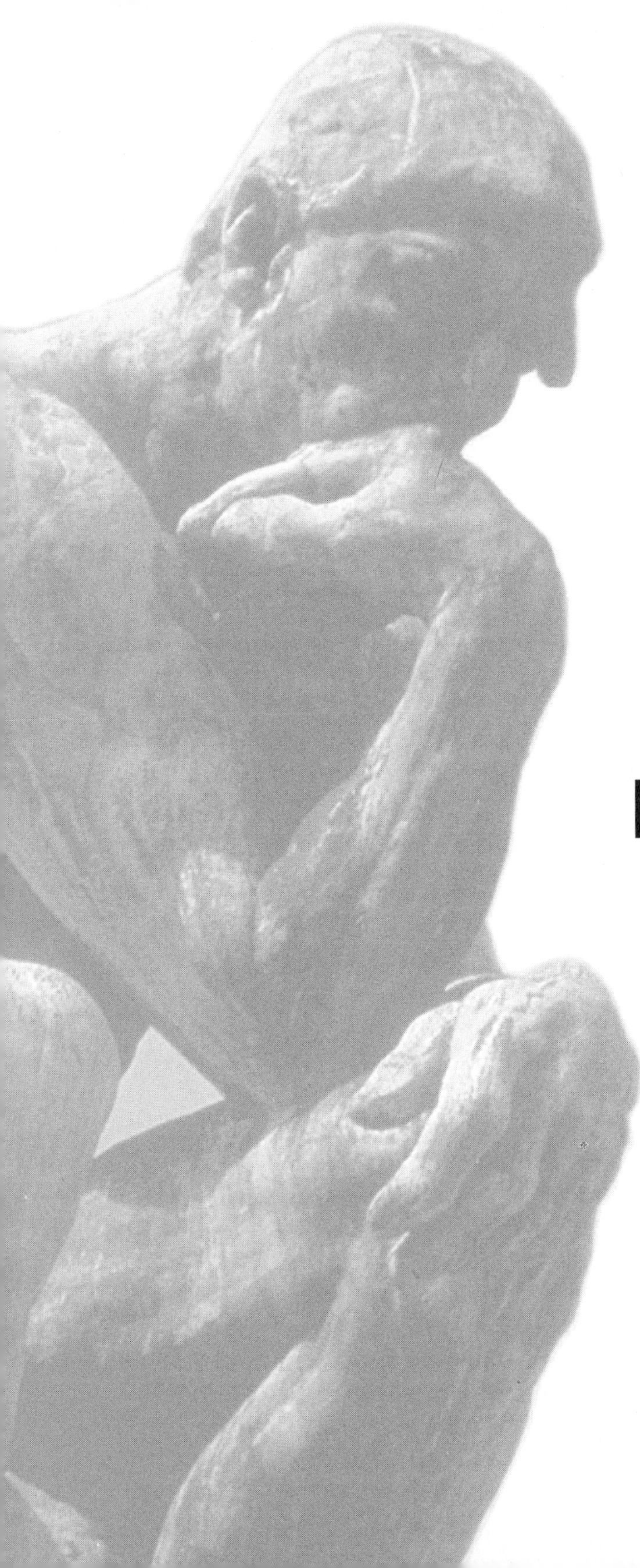

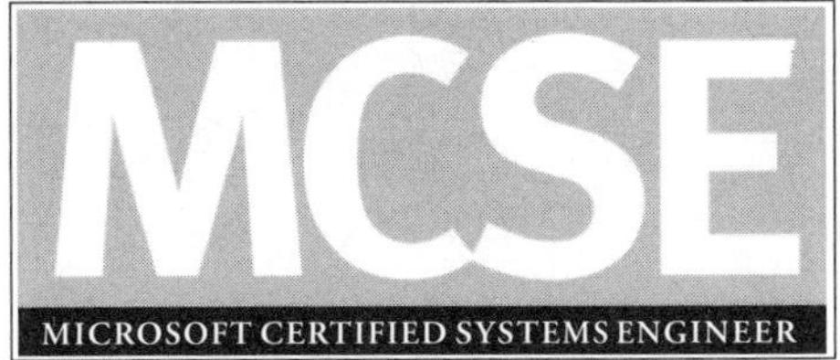

# 4

# Designing a Highly Available Network Infrastructure

## CERTIFICATION OBJECTIVES

4.01 Designing a Highly Available Network Topology

4.02 Planning Server Configurations

4.03 Analyzing and Allocating End-to-End Bandwidth Requirements Throughout an *n*-Tier Environment

✓ Two-Minute Drill

Q&A Self Test

The Internet has grown from an interesting toy to a necessity. Enterprises today must do business over the Internet or risk the threat of being left in the dust and eventually collapsing. How do businesses achieve an Internet presence that is not only significant but also readily available to serve their markets faster than the competition?

One solution is to employ Windows 2000's advanced Web capabilities. Windows 2000 Advanced Server was built for serving large enterprises within corporate LANs, WANs, and over the Internet. Windows 2000's advanced Web services, such as Cluster Services and Network Load Balancing Services, come prepared to respond to the most demanding Web infrastructures. Microsoft's aim was to create a highly reliable and scalable Web solution with Windows 2000 Web servers that serve large enterprises and Internet customers especially. These services were designed to be at least on par with the current leaders in the Internet today and in the future.

The power of Windows 2000 Cluster Services and Network Load Balancing Services can be realized only if the framework on which they work is sufficiently agile and powerful to correctly utilize these services. This chapter covers the steps required to create such a framework. It delves into designing a network topology that allows the Windows 200 Cluster and Network Load Balancing Services to provide the high availability, reliability, and scalability required of Web infrastructures now and in the future.

**CERTIFICATION OBJECTIVE 4.01**

# Designing a Highly Available Network Topology

In this chapter we discuss in detail how we create a highly available network infrastructure. *High-availability networks* are networks that serve customers with 99.999 percent reliability. We cover the principles of redundant paths, services, and components. We also learn how to plan and configure servers that will act as the centerpiece of our infrastructure. During the course of the chapter, we apply what we have learned to build a model of our own high-availability network infrastructure.

We will learn how components such as Network Interface Cards, or NICs, and services such as replication and clustering affect our design and how we can use and/or work around their properties to better our design. We also discuss factors such as bandwidth and connectivity and learn how to include these in our calculations. Lastly, we analyze bandwidth requirements and allocation of bandwidth where it is needed most on our network.

## Redundant Paths

Applying the concept of redundant paths helps us in our design of a true highly available infrastructure in two possible ways. In the first way, with multiple paths to a destination, we can potentially handle more traffic to and from the destination. In the second way, one path can serve as a backup route for the other in the event that one path is broken or congested. Numerous networking vendors have included systems or protocols to provide this sort of reliability. Figures 4-1 and 4-2 illustrate these two advantages of redundant paths.

**FIGURE 4-1** Redundant Paths Ease Traffic Demands

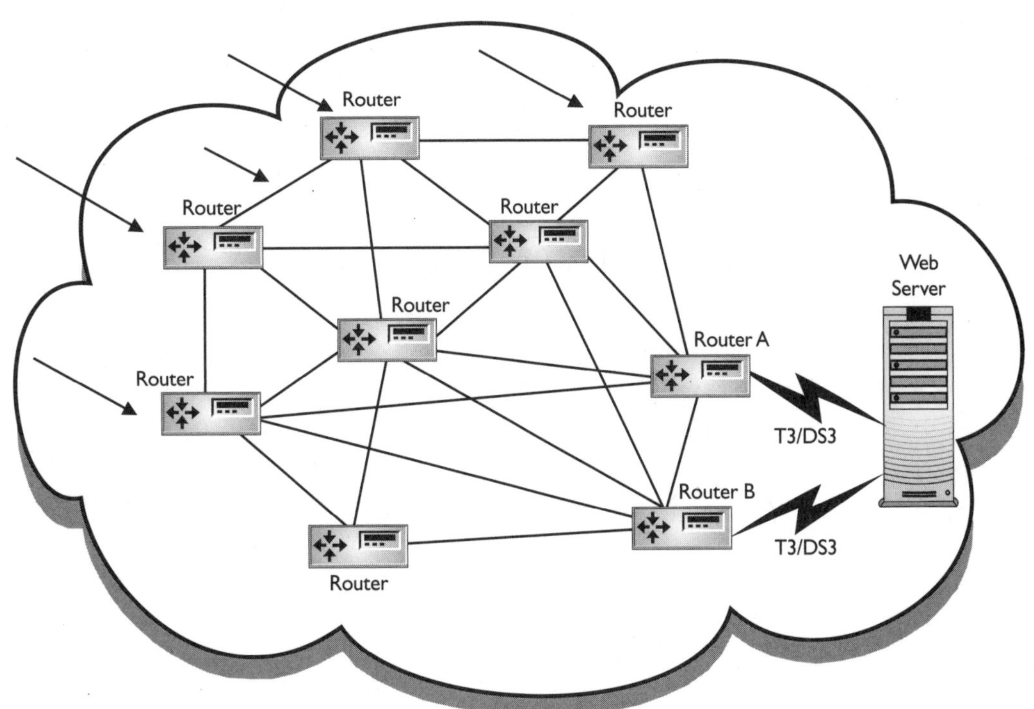

**FIGURE 4-2** Redundant Paths Ensure Availability

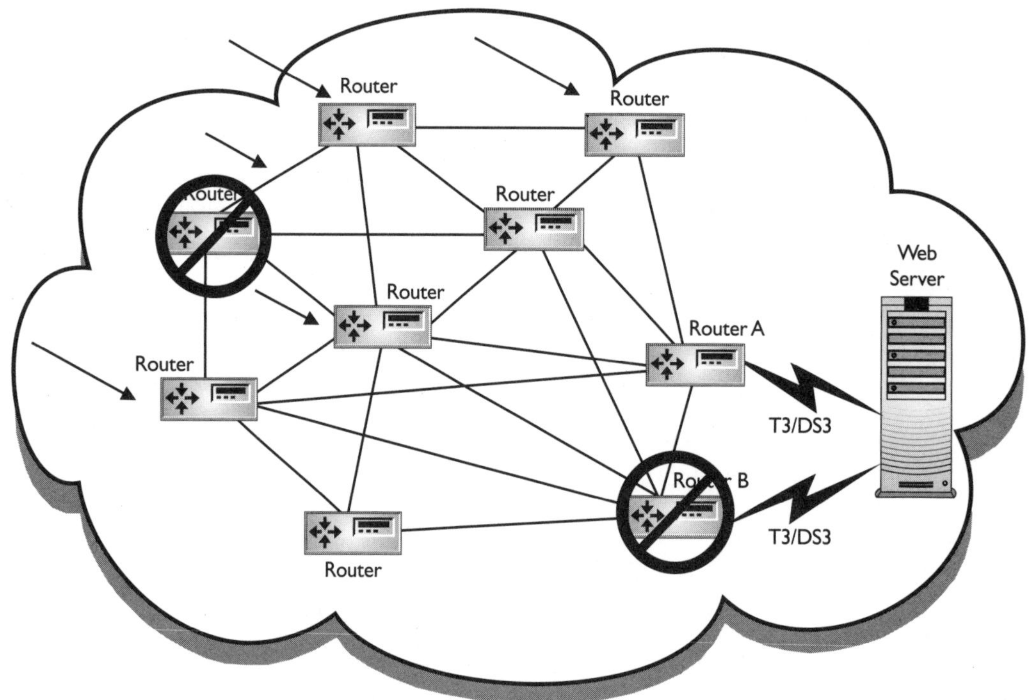


Figures 4-1 and 4-2 both display a routed network topology, with each router having multiple connections to neighboring routers. Router A and Router B represent our redundant Internet connections. These routers are in turn part of a meshed Internet service provider (ISP) network in which multiple paths access each router. In the event that one of the links becomes unavailable as a result of router failure or link failure, alternate paths of varying cost can be taken to arrive at the destination Web site. Many clients making requests to the same Web site or server creates heavy traffic on one path. Redundant paths to the server's redundant Internet routers allow traffic to take the path that is most accessible to it.

In Figure 4-2, one or more of the routers on the path to the Web server are down, so the path to the server is not complete. Redundant paths still allow clients to reach the Web site and be serviced.

How is path redundancy provided? Simple: Just provide and advertise alternate or backup paths to the network via configuration of redundant internetwork routes to the destination, as illustrated Figures 4-1 and 4-2. The backup path could require packets to traverse more routers from source to destination, so we need to consider the cost of the path when developing our redundant path strategy. These are all factors that need to be discussed with our ISP as part of the planning phase of our design.

One way to set up path redundancy in Windows 2000 is to create Windows 2000 IP routers using the Routing and Remote Access Service (RRAS). RRAS allows us to set up a server-based router for use in dial-up remote access, VPN remote access, and LAN-to-LAN IP routing. Redundant paths in RRAS should be set up as static routes. The dynamic routing protocols that are included in RRAS can be used. Static routes are much simpler to manage, however. Figures 4-3 and 4-4 show the addition of redundant static routes in the RRAS console. Creating redundant routes simply involves adding two or more static routes to a destination network through the various interfaces that point to the destination. Note that different gateway interfaces, which are most likely different NICs in the server, are used, and the route

**FIGURE 4-3**

Adding a Redundant Route in RRAS

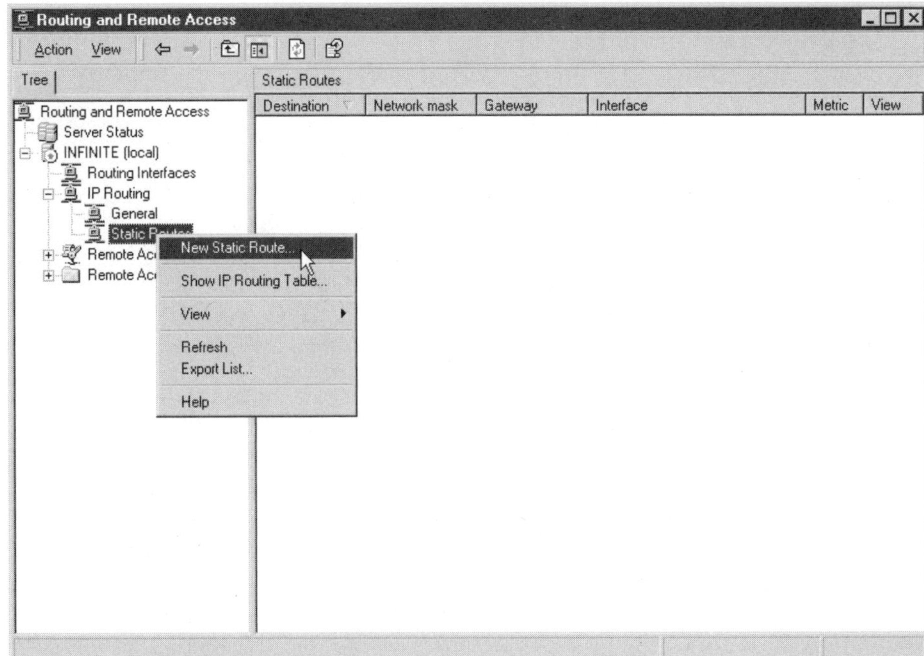

**FIGURE 4-4**

Redundant Routes in the RRAS Routing Table

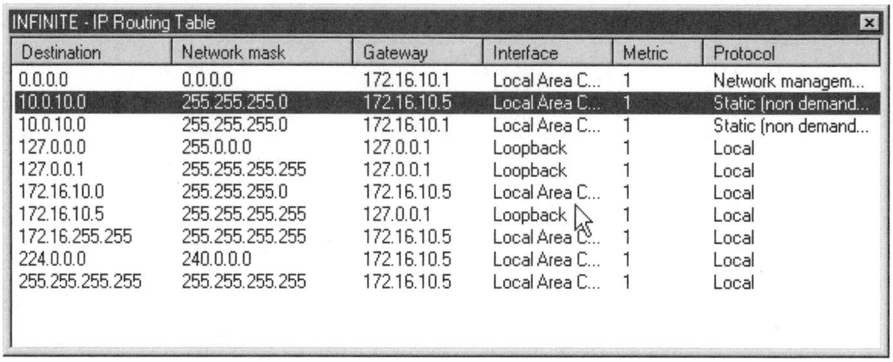

INFINITE - IP Routing Table

| Destination | Network mask | Gateway | Interface | Metric | Protocol |
|---|---|---|---|---|---|
| 0.0.0.0 | 0.0.0.0 | 172.16.10.1 | Local Area C... | 1 | Network managem... |
| 10.0.10.0 | 255.255.255.0 | 172.16.10.5 | Local Area C... | 1 | Static (non demand... |
| 10.0.10.0 | 255.255.255.0 | 172.16.10.1 | Local Area C... | 1 | Static (non demand... |
| 127.0.0.0 | 255.0.0.0 | 127.0.0.1 | Loopback | 1 | Local |
| 127.0.0.1 | 255.255.255.255 | 127.0.0.1 | Loopback | 1 | Local |
| 172.16.10.0 | 255.255.255.0 | 172.16.10.5 | Local Area C... | 1 | Local |
| 172.16.10.5 | 255.255.255.255 | 127.0.0.1 | Loopback | 1 | Local |
| 172.16.255.255 | 255.255.255.255 | 172.16.10.5 | Local Area C... | 1 | Local |
| 224.0.0.0 | 240.0.0.0 | 172.16.10.5 | Local Area C... | 1 | Local |
| 255.255.255.255 | 255.255.255.255 | 172.16.10.5 | Local Area C... | 1 | Local |

metric—usually equal to the cost—can be changed to suit the properties of the redundant connection.

## FROM THE CLASSROOM

### Routing Based on Cost

All hosts on the Internet that need to communicate between two points use the routers that connect the various networks on the Internet. The number of routers you must traverse to arrive at the desired destination measures the distance between two points on the Internet. This distance is known as the *hop count* or *cost*. Obviously, some routers are closer to the desired destination than others; therefore, they have a lower hop count or cost. Routers store the cost to travel to a distant network in their routing tables, along with the networks they know how to get to. The object of any host trying to arrive at a destination network is to get there as quickly as possible. This usually means traversing the lowest number of routers possible. Therefore, routers have been designed to advertise the route to a destination network with the lowest number of hops, or the least cost. Chances are that the more routers present and the more connections among them, the better the chance of finding a shorter route. Routers always direct traffic through the available route with the least cost.

*—Chris Broomes, MCSE, MCP+I, MCT, CCDA*

## Redundant Services

Having more than one computer that provides the same service to our clients is another method that contributes to creating a highly available network infrastructure. Redundant services such as File Transfer Protocol (FTP), Simple Mail Transfer Protocol (SMTP), and Web servers can be accomplished using either Windows Clustering Services or Network Load Balancing Services. Multiple servers acting as one server via one or both of these methods create a fault-tolerant file, mail, or Web service. Figure 4-5 illustrates how Windows Clustering and Network Load

**FIGURE 4-5** Windows 2000 Clustering and Network Load Balancing Services Create Redundant Services

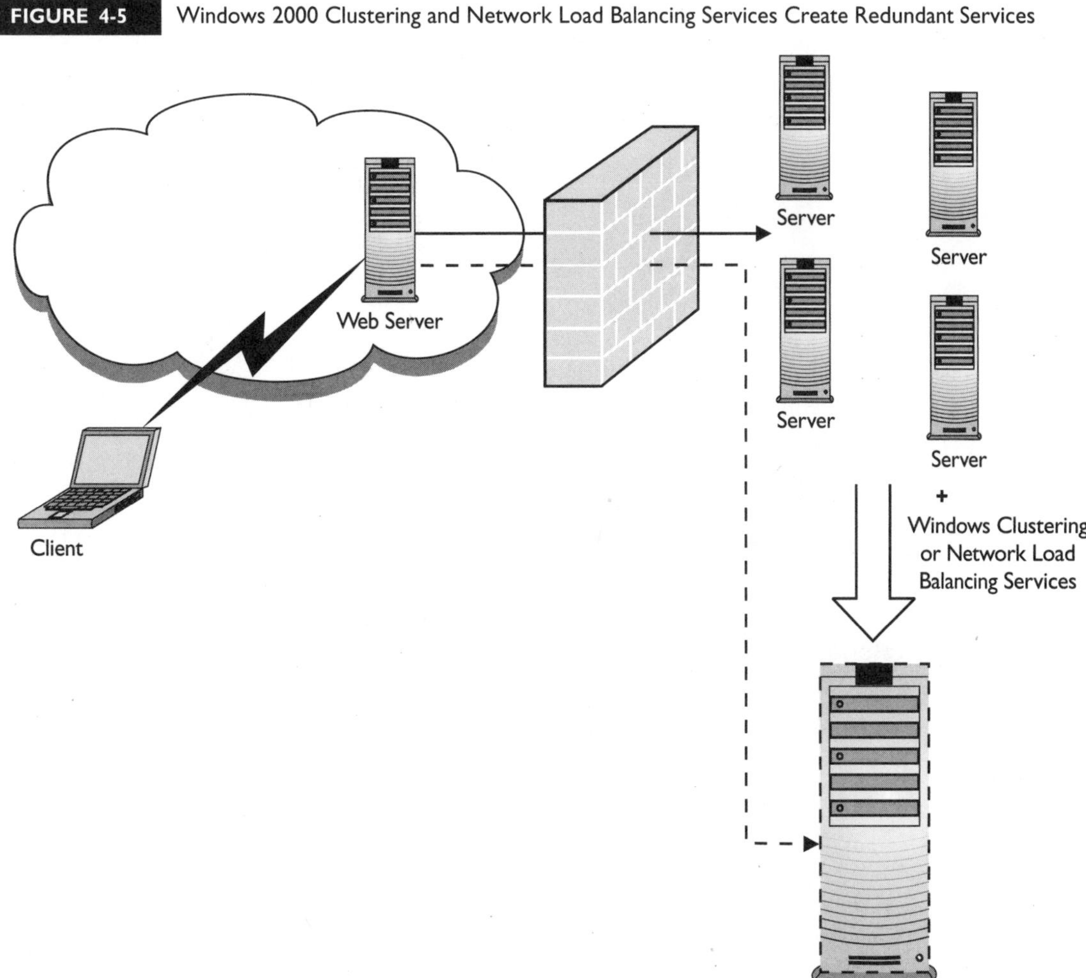

Balancing Services can consolidate multiple servers into one functional unit that provides redundancy and fault tolerance for any Web-based service you are able to offer. Without Windows Clustering and Network Load Balancing Services, the back-end application servers function as separate units. After installing and configuring Clustering and Network Load Balancing Services, the servers act as one unit. The redundancy is apparent in that all servers perform the same functions, so if one or more were to go offline, the others would maintain service to the client or clients. Other services can also be clustered or load balanced, such as Component Object Model Plus (COM+) or Distributed Component Object Model (DCOM) application services.

Windows Clustering Services allow multiple Windows 2000 servers running the same application to share the load of responding to requests from clients. This is accomplished by linking the application instances on the individual servers, thus creating what looks to client applications like one application.

## Redundant Components

How many times have you lost availability of a system as a result of a hardware failure such as the following?

- A hard disk crash
- A small computer system interface (SCSI) or RAID controller failure
- Bad memory chips
- A burned-out network card
- A power-supply failure.

Hardware failure is the most typical source of system failure. The need for information in many different forms and in a hurry takes its toll on Central Processing Units (CPUs), memory, hard disk controllers, and network cards. These devices are not made to last forever. Components must be changed when degradation of performance begins so as to avert the disaster brought about by total failure. Administrators should set a standard or baseline for all systems, depending on function, as well as setting an expected performance level. That way, you have something against which to measure current performance.

Having spare components on hand is a good practice. However, time is still lost in the removal of the old component and installation of the replacement.

The amount of time lost is dependent on whether the components are hot-swappable or whether the system has to be shut down to replace the part. Systems with built-in redundant components eliminate the time spent repairing systems or replacing broken-down components. Many server-class computers come with redundant power supplies as well as options for other redundant components. Designing an infrastructure for high availability must also involve customizing systems to have as many redundant components as possible. All the major computer vendors offer and sell built-to-order systems that can be configured with all the redundant components that we need. The largest, most powerful server platforms may include many of these components as standard features.

Not only must actual computer systems have redundant components, but the entire infrastructure must be as redundant as possible. Hubs, switches, routers, firewalls, and Uninterruptible Power Supplies (UPS) must be available and ready to take over in case of failure of the devices in use or failure of power to the server computers as a whole. Most network device vendors have taken this requirement into consideration and offer features in their devices that can be configured for what is known as *failover*. Failover is the ability of the inactive unit of redundant components to take over the functions of the primary unit in the event of failure of the primary unit.

exam Watch

***Configuring devices for failover protection is an important task in creating a fault-tolerant system. Watch out for exam questions that test your knowledge of the importance of failover.***

**EXERCISE 4-1**

## Surveying Your Network Infrastructure

The following exercise tests your skill at determining the state of your network infrastructure.

1. Take a look at your current network infrastructure. Attempt to identify the areas where it qualifies as redundant or fault tolerant and the areas where it does not. Provide explanations for what you find to be redundant and nonredundant.

2. Carefully examine your servers and their hardware specifications. Identify areas where redundancy could be useful, such as hard disks, network adapters, processors, and control cards. Document your findings and come up with a plan to make the systems redundant.
3. Examine your network devices, such as hubs, switches, and routers. Based on their specifications, determine where redundant components can be installed in them.
4. Examine your server farm as a whole. Identify any server clusters you have. Determine whether the services that are not clustered need to be clustered using Cluster Services for increased service availability or Network Load Balancing Services for TCP/IP load balancing.

---

Now let's look at some scenarios and solutions related to surveying your network infrastructure.

| SCENARIO & SOLUTION | |
|---|---|
| I need to ensure that my Web site is still accessible, even if my Internet connection goes down. How can I accomplish this goal? | Work with your ISP to provide you with another Internet connection and configure it as a load-balancing and failover connection to your site. |
| What components should I consider making redundant in my network topology? | All components of the infrastructure that it is feasible to make redundant, including network devices, server CPUs, power supplies, disks, or RAID arrays. |
| How can I ensure that the services provided by my Web infrastructure are redundant? | Hosting copies of the back-end applications such as database applications on multiple servers and creating a cluster using Windows Cluster Services will create a redundant architecture. |

CERTIFICATION OBJECTIVE 4.02

# Planning Server Configurations

Apart from the layout and components that comprise a redundant network architecture, the configuration of the servers involved in building a highly available Web infrastructure is the single most important factor that we need to consider and control. The servers, of course, are the actual seats of the Web site and the applications and databases that make up the Web site.

What can we do to ensure that the servers that make up our highly available Web site are robust enough to handle the demands that would classify the infrastructure as highly available? We can probably already think of many specifications, such as network interface cards, clustering, and replication services, for such a server. The following sections examine these items in greater detail. Other factors not resident in the server but closely related to it, such as connectivity and bandwidth, will also be discussed.

## Network Interface Cards

The *network interface card (NIC)* is the component that connects a server to the network and allows communication between front-end and back-end servers within a Web infrastructure and between servers and clients on the Internet and on intranets. The maximum throughput that a NIC can allow is directly related to the number of clients a network can support. Even if our server is the most powerful that we can design today, its performance on the network is limited by the NIC's throughput.

Today computers commonly come equipped with network cards capable of a maximum throughput of 100Mbps. However, there are cards available that provide a maximum throughput of 1Gbps (1000Mbps). In most Web infrastructures today, the throughput demanded of a front-end Web server is still limited by the bandwidth of the connection to the Internet. Therefore, a NIC that is capable of 100Mbps throughput is usually sufficient to service the requests that come to the servers.

Servers can also be configured as *multi-homed servers.* That is, they can be equipped with two or more NICs to be used on the same network advertising the same services. However, we cannot create a simple form of load balancing this way as one might expect with two NICs on the same network. In Ethernet networks, two NICs in one server are limited by the same rule as NICs in separate servers: Only one NIC can use the network wire at a time. Therefore, the extra NIC is usually configured as a failover device. This means that if the primary NIC fails, the NIC driver deactivates the failed card and activates the spare automatically. Load-balancing multiple NICs can be configured when Network Load Balancing Services are installed.

How then can we achieve even better performance by manipulating the NIC configuration? The most common way is to equip all our servers in our Web infrastructure with dual 100Mbps NICs. Since the Web servers are usually either connected to some back-end database server or to at least two different Internet access connections, at least one NIC per connection or network subnet should be implemented on each server. Figure 4-6 illustrates an example of a front-end Web server connected to a back-end database server via one NIC and connected to the Internet through a second NIC.

**FIGURE 4-6** Web Server with Two NICs to Support Two Connections

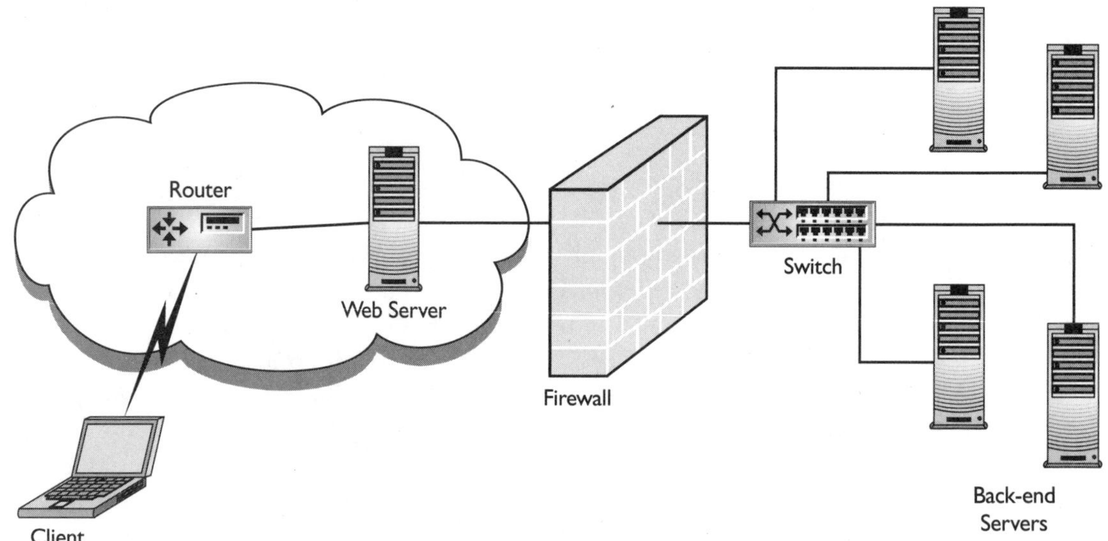

***Most NICs today are equipped with their own processors and memory as well as technology such as bus mastering, which increases the efficiency of their processing of bits. Bus mastering is a method of quickly moving large amounts of data to and from system memory. This method is a form of direct memory access, or DMA. DMA relies on special hardware to move data directly to and from system RAM without processor intervention. During a data move operation, the DMA hardware suspends CPU operation and takes control over the system bus. The hardware then automatically moves the data between system RAM and a buffer in the peripheral controller.*** *Bus mastering* ***is the highest-performance DMA type. Peripheral controllers that support bus mastering have the ability to move data to and from system RAM without the help of the CPU or a third-party DMA controller. Bus mastering allows data to be moved at much higher rates than the other DMA types.***

## Clustering

Earlier in the chapter we talked about configuring redundant services in our Web infrastructure to achieve high availability. We achieve this configuration by employing clustering services. Windows 2000 Advanced Server and Datacenter Server come with two add-on services that provide clustering on the application level and on the network level. These services are Cluster Services and Network Load Balancing Services.

### Cluster Services

Windows 2000 Cluster Services evolved from the Microsoft Cluster Server (MSCS) add-on for Windows NT 4.0 Enterprise Edition. Windows 2000 Cluster Services link two to four Windows 2000 servers and their connected data storage devices together to function as one logical unit. Clients connecting to the applications being run by the servers in the cluster see servers that are part of a cluster as one server and not individual servers. Should any member of the cluster fail, the other servers assume the workload of the failed server without interruption of service.

The members of a cluster are referred to as *nodes.* Cluster Services are ideal for back-end servers such as database servers or COM+ application servers that do not communicate directly with Web clients. In a highly available Web infrastructure, this system allows for more efficient servicing of requests from front-end Web servers than would a single server or even four separate servers running the same application. The applications, disks, and other devices that participate in the cluster are known as *resources.* Windows 2000 Cluster Services are dedicated to ensuring that all resources advertised to clients on a network are always available, even if the original server that housed the application and provided the storage space becomes unavailable.

The services provided by a cluster are grouped logically by type into *resource groups.* More than one node might actually be providing the services contained in the resource group, but only one of the nodes is actually assigned ownership and responsibility for the resource group. The list of services in the resource group, their configuration, and the members of the cluster that contribute to the resources group, as well as the configuration of the entire cluster, are stored in the configuration database on a resource called the *quorum resource.* The quorum resource is a physical disk resource on the common storage resource for the cluster. Each node in the cluster has a local configuration database, but only the quorum resource has the most current configuration for the entire cluster. All recovery information for a cluster is also stored in the quorum resource.

Cluster Services work by first providing a failover mechanism for servers running mission-critical applications, thereby reducing potential downtime and interruption in service. If a member of the cluster that is providing a resource goes down, the entire resource that the node was providing is moved from the failed node to another member of the cluster that is judged able to handle the extra system load of hosting additional resources besides its own, as illustrated in Figure 4-7.

Second, Cluster Services provide scalability for highly available applications. Servers can be added to the cluster to a maximum of four nodes in Windows 2000 Datacenter without interrupting the current service. It is even possible to upgrade server hardware and software components without disturbing the cluster's activity by performing a *rolling upgrade.* A rolling upgrade, as defined by Microsoft, is a process of upgrading cluster nodes, one node at a time, in such a way that services and resources offered by the cluster are always available, even though nodes being upgraded are not available. A rolling upgrade of a server cluster allows the availability of resources and services offered by clustered servers to be maintained during an upgrade. The system downtime associated with the upgrade is reduced to a few minutes—the time needed to move resources from one node to another—compared with the few hours that are usually needed to upgrade a Windows NT–based server.

FIGURE 4-7 Cluster Services Handling Failure of a Cluster Node by Moving the Resource Hosted by the Failed Node to Another Available Node in the Cluster

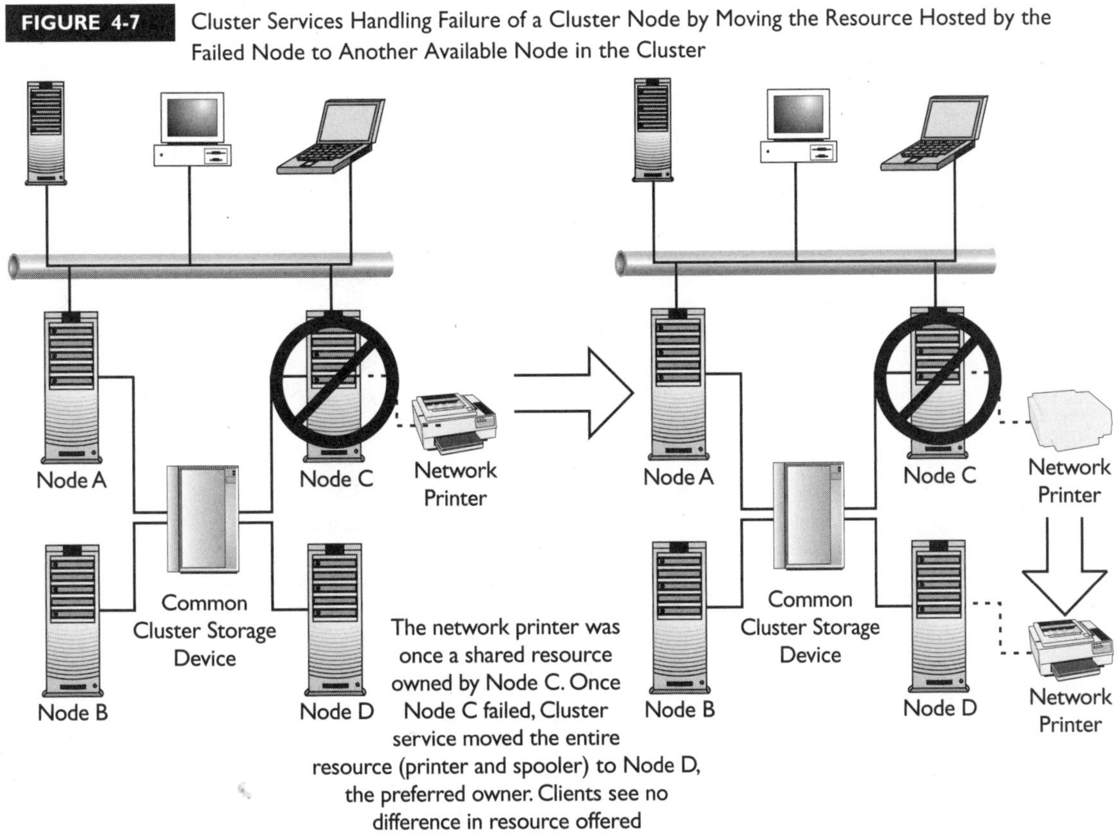
Node A
Node C
Network Printer
Common Cluster Storage Device
Node B
Node D
The network printer was once a shared resource owned by Node C. Once Node C failed, Cluster service moved the entire resource (printer and spooler) to Node D, the preferred owner. Clients see no difference in resource offered
Node A
Node C
Network Printer
Common Cluster Storage Device
Node B
Node D
Network Printer

Third, Cluster Services provide manageability. All the nodes in a cluster and the applications they run are manageable and configurable by administrators, both as an entire cluster and as individual nodes, from anywhere on the network.

Cluster Services create *virtual servers* for each application or service that is hosted on the cluster. Virtual servers are basically representations of each application or service that the servers in a cluster advertise to clients. Clients connect to the applications in a virtual server the same way that they would a normal physical server. Each virtual server has its own separate TCP/IP address and host name that the Cluster Services publish to facilitate communication between the client and the server. Figure 4-8 illustrates the concept of virtual servers.

FIGURE 4-8 Cluster Nodes Hosting Resources That Are Advertised to Clients Via Four Virtual Servers

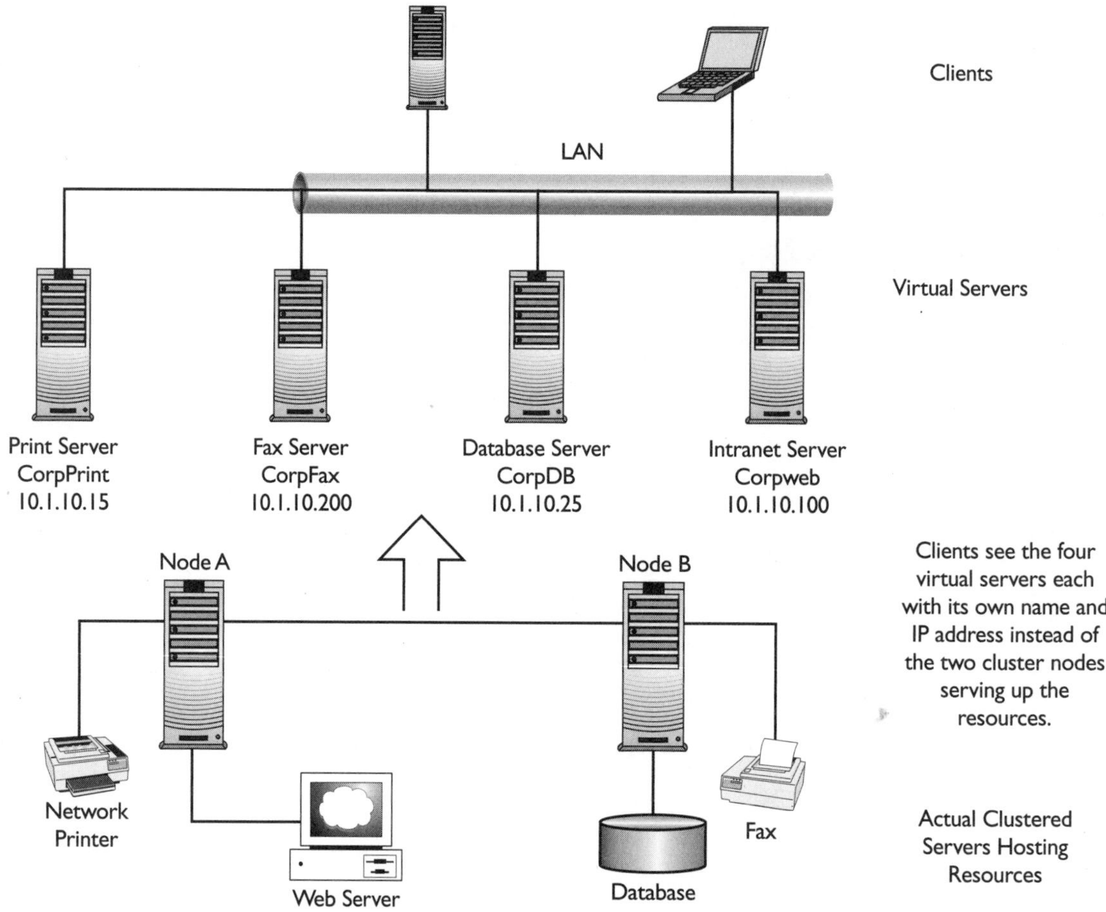


exam watch

***Internet Information Services (IIS) 5.0 also uses virtual servers to host multiple Web sites on the same server or server cluster. Even though the two are conceptually similar, be careful not to confuse IIS's virtual servers with Cluster Services' virtual servers.***

Cluster Services are based on the *shared-nothing* cluster architecture model. This means that any devices that are common to the cluster are actually owned by one of the individual servers in the cluster. In fact, a node in a cluster cannot manage a resource unless it owns at least one of the components of the resource. The shared-nothing model allows for full device compatibility in a cluster because devices require no special hardware or connections outside of the server's normal range of specified devices or connection types. Cluster Services use the standard Windows 2000 drivers for local devices, but external devices that are common to the cluster use only SCSI connections.

Cluster Services consist of components that work together to monitor and manage the cluster and all the resources it advertises. The components take advantage of device drivers, network drivers, and resource instrumentation processes specifically designed for use by Cluster Services. The components are as follows:

- **Communications Manager** The Communications Manager uses remote procedure calls (RPCs) to maintain communication between nodes within a cluster. The Communications Manager provides guaranteed, one-time message delivery between nodes in their correct order and guarantees that any messages sent by offline nodes will be ignored.
- **Configuration Database Manager** The Configuration Database Manager carries out the functions needed to maintain the cluster configuration database. All the information about the physical and logical objects in the cluster is contained in the configuration database. Any changes made to the configuration of the cluster—whether addition or subtraction of a node, relocation of a resource, or change in an IP address—are all written to the configuration database. The Configuration Database Manager on one node coordinates with the Configuration Database Manager on all the other nodes in the cluster to synchronize the database so that it is consistent from node to node. This synchronization is performed via replication using the Global Update Manager.
- **Node Manager** The Node Manager runs on each node of the cluster and maintains a local list of the cluster member nodes. The Node Manager is also responsible for sending periodic heartbeat messages to the other members of the cluster to detect node failures. If a node detects a failure on another node, it broadcasts the failure to the other nodes in the cluster, and they perform what is known as a *regroup event* to verify their views of the cluster membership. The Node Manager orchestrates the moving of the resources hosted on that

node to another active node or the redistribution of the resources among the surviving members of the cluster.

- **Membership Manager** The Membership Manager helps maintain cluster membership as well as monitors the health of member nodes in the cluster.
- **Checkpoint Manager** The Checkpoint Manager is responsible for checking registry keys on a node whenever a resource is brought online and for writing data to the quorum resource when the resource goes offline. This ensures that the Cluster Services can recover from a resource failure.
- **Failover Manager** The Failover Manager is responsible for starting and stopping resources, managing resource dependencies, and initiating failover of resource groups. The Failover Manager makes decisions on which resources to start, stop, or move based on the resource and system information it receives from the Node Manager and from Resource Monitors. The Failover Manager is also responsible for deciding resource group ownership.
- **Event Processor** The Event Processor's task is to facilitate communication between applications and Cluster Services components running on each node of a cluster. This is the mechanism that Cluster Services use to pass information about important events to all the other components of a cluster.
- **Event Log Manager** The Event Log Manager is responsible for replicating event log entries from one node to all other nodes in a cluster.
- **Log Manager** The Log Manager works with the Checkpoint Manager to ensure that the recovery log on the quorum resource contains the most up-to-date configuration data and change checkpoints.
- **Object Manager** The Object Manager supports management of all cluster objects by allowing for search, creation, numbering, and reference counting on cluster objects.
- **Global Update Manager** The Global Update Manager is used by the Configuration Database Manager to replicate cluster changes to the cluster configuration database across all nodes. Any node that does not commit the replicated information from the Global Update Manager to its configuration is forced out of the cluster and put offline.

- **Resource Monitors** Resource Monitors create the interface between the Cluster Services and resource dynamic link libraries (DLLs). When data is needed from a resource, Cluster Services make the request to the particular Resource Monitor for that resource, and the Monitor passes it on to the resource DLL. The reverse happens whenever a resource DLL needs to report an event to the Cluster Services. Many cluster-aware applications, such as Microsoft's DHCP Server, provide their own resource DLLs.

exam Watch

***Two types of failure that can occur in a cluster: a node failure and a resource failure. Heartbeat messages are used to detect node failures, but the Resource Monitors and DLLs are used to detect resource failures.***

Microsoft has included a graphical administration tool for clusters called the Cluster Administrator. The Cluster Administrator enables an administrator to perform failover administration, monitoring, and maintenance on a cluster. This is performed by manipulating any of the cluster component managers mentioned previously.

**EXERCISE 4-2**

## Installing a Two-Node Cluster

The following exercise walks you through the process of installing a simple two-node cluster on two Windows 2000 Advanced servers. To install a cluster, you must have the following hardware configuration on both servers:

- Peripheral Component Interconnect (PCI) storage host adapter, either SCSI or Fiber Channel for the shared storage disks
- Two PCI network adapters on each machine
- A disk storage unit that connects both computers, preferably in RAID configuration
- A unique Network Basic Input/Output System (NetBIOS) cluster name
- Five unique, static Internet Protocol (IP) addresses: two for NICs on the private network for cluster nodes only, two for the public network, and one for the cluster

- A domain service account for the Cluster Services
- All shared disks must be NT File System (NTFS)
- A name resolution method, such as Windows Internet Naming Service (WINS) or Domain Name System (DNS)
- You must be logged on as an administrator to install Cluster Services

**Setting Up the Network** For this exercise, we must first power down all shared storage devices and then power up all nodes. The Cluster Services must be installed on at least one node prior to both nodes accessing the shared storage devices at the same time. Each cluster node requires at least two network adapters; one connects to a public network and the other connects to a private network (which consists of cluster nodes only).

The private network adapter establishes node-to-node communication, cluster status signals, and cluster management. Each node's public network adapter connects the cluster to the public network where clients reside.

Verify that all network connections are correct, with private network adapters connected to other private network adapters only and public network adapters connected to the public network. Run these steps on each cluster node before proceeding with shared disk setup.

**Setting Up the Private Network** Configuring the private network adapter should be performed on the first node of the cluster, and then duplicated on the other node.

**Configuring the Private Network Adapter** *Note:* For the purpose of this exercise, the first network adapter (Local Area Connection) is connected to the public network; the second network adapter (Local Area Connection 2) is connected to the private cluster network. However, this might not be the case with your network.

Perform these steps on the first node in your cluster:

1. Right-click My Network Places | Properties.
2. Right-click the Local Area Connection 2 icon.
3. Click Status. The Local Area Connection 2 Status window shows the connection status as well as the speed of the connection. If the window shows

that the network is disconnected, examine cables and connections to resolve the problem before proceeding. Click Close.

4. Right-click Local Area Connection 2 again, click Properties, and click Configure.
5. Click Advanced. The window shown in Figure 4-9 should appear.
6. Network adapters on the private network should be set to the actual speed of the network rather than the default automated speed selection. Select your network speed from the drop-down list. Do not use an Auto-select setting for speed. Some adapters can drop packets while determining the speed. To set the network adapter speed, click the appropriate option, such as Media Type or Speed.

   All network adapters in the cluster that are attached to the same network must be identically configured to use the same Duplex Mode, Flow Control, Media Type, and so on. These settings should remain the same, even if the hardware is different.
7. Click Transmission Control Protocol/Internet Protocol (TCP/IP).

**FIGURE 4-9**

The Speed of the NIC can be set on the Advanced Tab of the NIC Properties

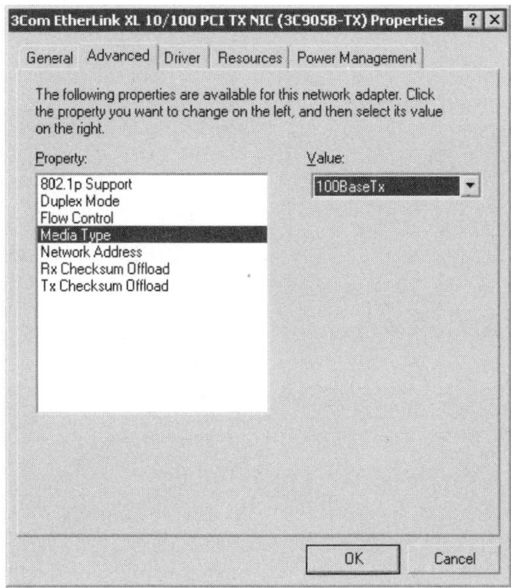

8. Click Properties.
9. Click the radio button for "Use the following IP address" and type the following address: **10.1.1.1**. (Use **10.1.1.2** for the second node.)
10. Type in a subnet mask of **255.255.255.0**.
11. Do this step for the private network adapter only: Click the Advanced radio button and select the WINS tab. Select Disable NetBIOS over TCP/IP, as shown in Figure 4-10. Click OK to return to the previous menu.

    *Note:* Although the public network adapter's IP address can be automatically obtained if a DHCP server is available, this is not recommended for cluster nodes. We strongly recommend setting static IP addresses for all network adapters in the cluster, both private and public. If IP addresses are obtained via DHCP, access to cluster nodes could become unavailable if the DHCP server goes down. If you must use DHCP for your public network adapter, use long lease periods to assure that the dynamically assigned lease address remains valid, even if the DHCP service is temporarily lost. In all cases, set static IP addresses for the private network connector. Keep in mind that Cluster Services recognize only one network interface per subnet.

**FIGURE 4-10**

WINS Configuration for the Private Network

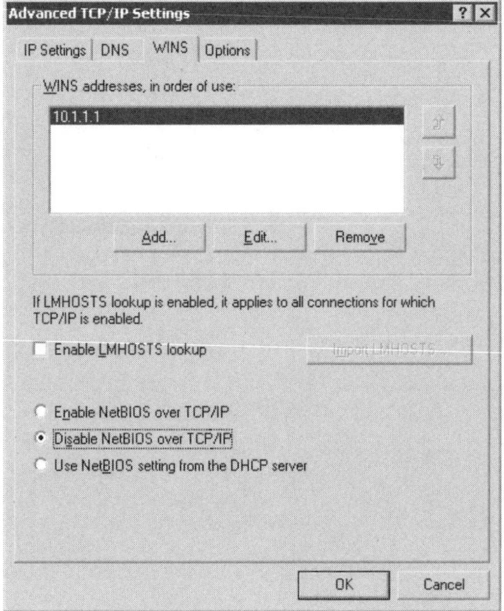

**Renaming the Local Area Network Icons** For clarity purposes, we will rename our network connections. This is a recommended practice to help in identifying a network and correctly assigning its role. Let's rename Local Area Connection to CLSTR_PUB and the Local Area Connection 2 to CLSTR_PRIV:

1. Right-click the Local Area Connection icon.
2. Click Rename.
3. Type **CLSTR_PUB** into the text box and press ENTER.
4. Repeat Steps 1–3 and rename the private network adapter **CLSTR_PRIV**.
5. Close the Networking and Dial-up Connections window. The new connection names automatically replicate to other cluster servers as they are brought online.

**Verifying Connectivity and Name Resolution** The following steps verify that the private and public networks are communicating properly. You should perform the steps for each network adapter in each node. You must know the IP address for each network adapter in the cluster. If you do not already have the information, you can obtain it using the ipconfig command on each node:

1. Click Start, click Run, and type **cmd** in the text box. Click OK.
2. Type **ipconfig /all** and press ENTER. IP information should display for all network adapters in the machine.
3. If you do not already have the command prompt on your screen, click Start, click Run, and type **cmd** in the text box. Click OK.
4. Type **ping ipaddress**, where *ipaddress* is the IP address for the corresponding network adapter in the other node.

   To verify name resolution, ping each node from a client using the node's machine name instead of its IP number. For example, to verify name resolution for the first cluster node, type **ping clstrsrv1** from any client.

**Verifying Domain Membership** All nodes in the cluster must be members of the same domain and able to access a domain controller and a DNS server. They can be configured as member servers or domain controllers. If you decide to configure one node as a domain controller, you should configure all other nodes as domain controllers in the same domain as well. In this exercise, all nodes are configured as domain controllers:

1. Right-click My Computer | Properties.
2. Click Network Identification. The System properties dialog box displays the full computer name and domain. The Domain Name is Syngress.
3. If you are using member servers and need to join a domain, you can do so at this time. Click Properties and follow the on-screen instructions for joining a domain.
4. Close the System Properties and My Computer windows.

**Setting Up a Cluster Account** The Cluster Services require a domain user account under which they can run. This user account must be created before installing Cluster Services, because setup requires a user name and password. This user account should be specifically for the exclusive use of the Cluster Services:

1. Click Start, point to Programs, point to Administrative Tools, and click Active Directory Users and Computers.
2. Click the + to expand Syngress.
3. Click Users.
4. Right-click Users, point to New, and click User.
5. Type in the cluster name as follows:

   First Name =
   Last Name =
   Full Name =
   User logon name = clusterusr@Syngress.com
   Click Next.
6. Set the password settings to User Cannot Change Password and Password Never Expires. Click Next, and then click Finish to create this user. (Some administrative security policies do not allow for the use of passwords that never expire. In that case, you must renew the password and update the Cluster Services configuration on each node before password expiration.)

a) Right-click Cluster in the left pane of the Active Directory Users and Computers snap-in. Select Properties from the context menu.

b) Click Add Members to a Group.

c) Click Administrators, and click OK. This gives the new user account administrative privileges on this computer.

d) Close the Active Directory Users and Computers snap-in.

**Setting Up Shared Disks** *Warning:* Make sure that the Windows 2000 Advanced Server or Windows 2000 Datacenter Server and the Cluster Services are installed and running on one node before starting an operating system (OS) on another node. If the OS is started on other nodes before the Cluster Services are installed, configured, and running on at least one node, the cluster disks will probably be corrupted.

To proceed, power off all nodes. Power up the shared storage devices, and then power up Node 1.

**About the Quorum Disk** The quorum disk is used to store cluster configuration database checkpoints and log files that help manage the cluster. We make the following quorum disk recommendations:

- Create a small partition to be used as a quorum disk. At a minimum, the partition should be 50MB; 500MB is a good recommendation.
- Dedicate a separate disk for quorum resource. Because the failure of the quorum disk would cause the entire cluster to fail, we strongly recommend that you use a volume on a RAID disk array.

During the Cluster Services installation, you must provide the drive letter for the quorum disk. In our example, we use the letter *Q*.

### Configuring Shared Disks

1. Right-click My Computer, click Manage, and click Storage.
2. Double-click Disk Management.
3. Verify that all shared disks are formatted as NTFS and are designated as Basic. If you connect a new drive, the Write Signature and Upgrade Disk

Wizard starts automatically. If this happens, click Next to go through the wizard. The wizard sets the disk to Dynamic. To reset the disk to Basic, right-click Disk # (where # specifies the disk you are working with) and click Revert to Basic Disk.

4. Right-click unallocated disk space.
5. Click Create Partition.
6. The Create Partition Wizard begins. Click Next twice.
7. Enter the desired partition size in MB, and click Next.
8. Accept the default drive letter assignment by clicking Next.
9. Click Next to format and create the partition.

**Assigning Drive Letters** After the bus, disks, and partitions have been configured, drive letters must be assigned to each partition on each clustered disk:

1. Right-click the desired partition and select Change Drive Letter and Path.
2. Select a new drive letter.
3. Repeat Steps 1 and 2 for each shared disk.
4. Close the Computer Management window.

### Verifying Disk Access and Functionality

1. Click Start, click Programs, click Accessories, and click Notepad.
2. Type some words into Notepad and use the File/Save As command to save it as a test file called **test.txt**. Close Notepad.
3. Double-click the My Documents icon.
4. Right-click test.txt and click Copy.
5. Close the window.
6. Double-click My Computer.
7. Double-click a shared drive partition.
8. Click Edit, and click Paste. A copy of the file should now reside on the shared disk.

9. Double-click test.txt to open it on the shared disk. Close the file.
10. Highlight the file and press the DEL key to delete it from the clustered disk.

    Repeat the process for all clustered disks to verify that they can be accessed from the first node.

    At this time, shut down the first node, power on the second node, and repeat the preceding steps to verify disk access and functionality. Repeat again for any additional nodes. When you have verified that all nodes can read and write from the disks, turn off all nodes except the first and continue with this exercise.

**Install Cluster Services Software** We will now install the Cluster Services software. The Cluster Services software is installed just like any other service.

**Configuring the First Node** While we are installing Cluster Services on the first node, all other nodes must either be turned off or stopped prior to Windows 2000 booting. All shared storage devices should be powered up.

During the first phase of installation, use the Cluster Services Configuration wizard to obtain all initial cluster configuration information that must be supplied so that the cluster can be created:

1. Click Start, click Settings, and click Control Panel.
2. Double-click Add/Remove Programs.
3. Double-click Add/Remove Windows Components.
4. Select Cluster Services. Click Next.
5. Cluster Services files are located on the Windows 2000 Datacenter Server or Windows 2000 Advanced Server CD-ROM. Enter **E:\i386** (where *E* is your CD-ROM drive). If Windows 2000 was installed from a network, enter the appropriate network path instead. Click OK.
6. Click Next.
7. Click "I understand" to accept the condition that the Cluster Services are supported on hardware from the Hardware Compatibility List only, as shown on the Cluster Services Configuration Wizard screen.

8. Because this is the first node in the cluster, you must create the cluster itself. Select the first node in the cluster, and then click Next.
9. Enter the name **TestCluster** for the cluster, and click Next.
10. Type the username of the Cluster Services account that was created during the pre-installation. (In our example, this username is *clusterusr*). Leave the password blank. Type the domain name, and click Next. A secure password would normally be provided for this user account. Now that the above steps are complete, the Cluster Services Configuration Wizard validates the user account and password.
11. Click Next.

**Configuring Cluster Disks** *Note:* By default, all SCSI disks not residing on the same bus as the system disk appear in the Managed Disks list. If you do not plan to use these disks as shared devices (an internal SCSI drive, for example), remove them from the Managed Disks list:

1. The Add or Remove Managed Disks dialog box specifies which disks on the shared SCSI bus will be used by Cluster Services. Add or remove disks as necessary, and then click Next.
2. Click Next in the Configuring Cluster Networks dialog box.
3. Verify that the network name and IP address correspond to the network interface for the public network.
4. Check the box "Enable this network for cluster use."
5. Select the option "All communications (mixed network)."
6. Click Next.
7. Verify that the network name and IP address correspond to the network interface used for the private network.
8. Check the box "Enable this network for cluster use."
9. Select the option "Internal cluster communications only."
10. Click Next.
11. For the purposes of our exercise, both networks are configured so that both can be used for internal cluster communication. The next dialog window

offers an option to modify the order in which the networks are used. Because CLSTR_PRIV represents a direct connection between nodes, it is left at the top of the list. In normal operation, this connection will be used for cluster communication. In case of CLSTR_PRIV failure, Cluster Services will automatically switch to the next network on the list—in this case, CLSTR_PUB. Make sure that the first connection in the list is CLSTR_PRIV, and click Next. Always set the connections so that CLSTR_PRIV is first in the list.

12. Enter the unique cluster IP address (**172.32.10.45**) and Subnet mask (**255.255.255.0**), and click Next.
13. The Cluster Services Configuration Wizard automatically associates the cluster IP address with one of the public or mixed networks. It uses the subnet mask to select the correct network.
14. Click Finish to complete the cluster configuration on the first node.
15. The Cluster Service Setup Wizard completes the setup process for the first node by copying the files needed to complete the installation of Cluster Services. Once the files have been copied, the Cluster Services registry entries are created, log files on the quorum resource are created, and the Cluster Services are started on the first node.

### Validating the Cluster Installation

1. Click Start, click Programs, click Administrative Tools, and click Cluster Administrator.
2. The snap-in window should display the cluster tree in the navigational pane, with the different disks and cluster IP address displaying in the main window of the snap-in. We are now ready to install Cluster Services on the second node.

**Configuring the Second Node** When configuring the second node, we should leave node one and all shared disks powered on. Power up the second node. The Cluster Services installation process on the second node requires much less time than on the first node. Setup configures the Cluster Services network settings on the second node based on the configuration of the first node.

Follow the same procedures used for installing Cluster Services on the first node, with the following exceptions:

1. In the Create or Join a Cluster dialog box, select the second or next node in the cluster, and click Next.
2. Enter the cluster name that was previously created (in this example, **TestCluster**) and click Next.
3. Leave "Connect to cluster" unchecked. The Cluster Services Configuration Wizard automatically supplies the name of the user account selected during the installation process of the first node. Always use the same account you used when you set up the first node.
4. Enter the password for the account (if one has been used), and click Next.
5. At the next dialog box, click Finish to complete configuration.
6. The Cluster Services will start. Click OK.
7. Close Add/Remove Programs.

### Verifying Installation

1. Click Start, click Programs, click Administrative Tools, and click Cluster Administrator.
2. Right-click the group Disk Group 1 and select the option Move. The group and all its resources will be moved to another node. After a short period of time, the Disk F: G: will be brought online on the second node. If you watch the screen, you will see this shift. Close the Cluster Administrator snap-in.

---

## Network Load Balancing Services

These services allow up to 32 nodes to be linked together and respond to client TCP/IP requests as one single system with one or more virtual TCP/IP addresses. Network Load Balancing (NLB) ensures that the Web site or back-end server is always available, even if one or more of the actual server computers loses network connectivity. NLB provides scalability in a Web infrastructure because all an administrator has to do to improve or maintain performance is to add more servers to a cluster running NLB up to 32 servers per cluster, thus ensuring that 99.999 percent availability we want to guarantee our customers.

NLB runs as a network-level driver, right between the higher-level TCP/IP applications such as Hypertext Transfer Protocol (HTTP) and the lower-level network adapter drivers. Figure 4-11 illustrates where NLB fits into the Windows 2000 network protocol architecture.

NLB accepts input from the cluster adapter and the true network adapter and passes it up to TCP/IP for further processing. This allows for greater throughput

**FIGURE 4-11** Windows 2000 Network Protocol Architecture, Showing NLB Location and Functions

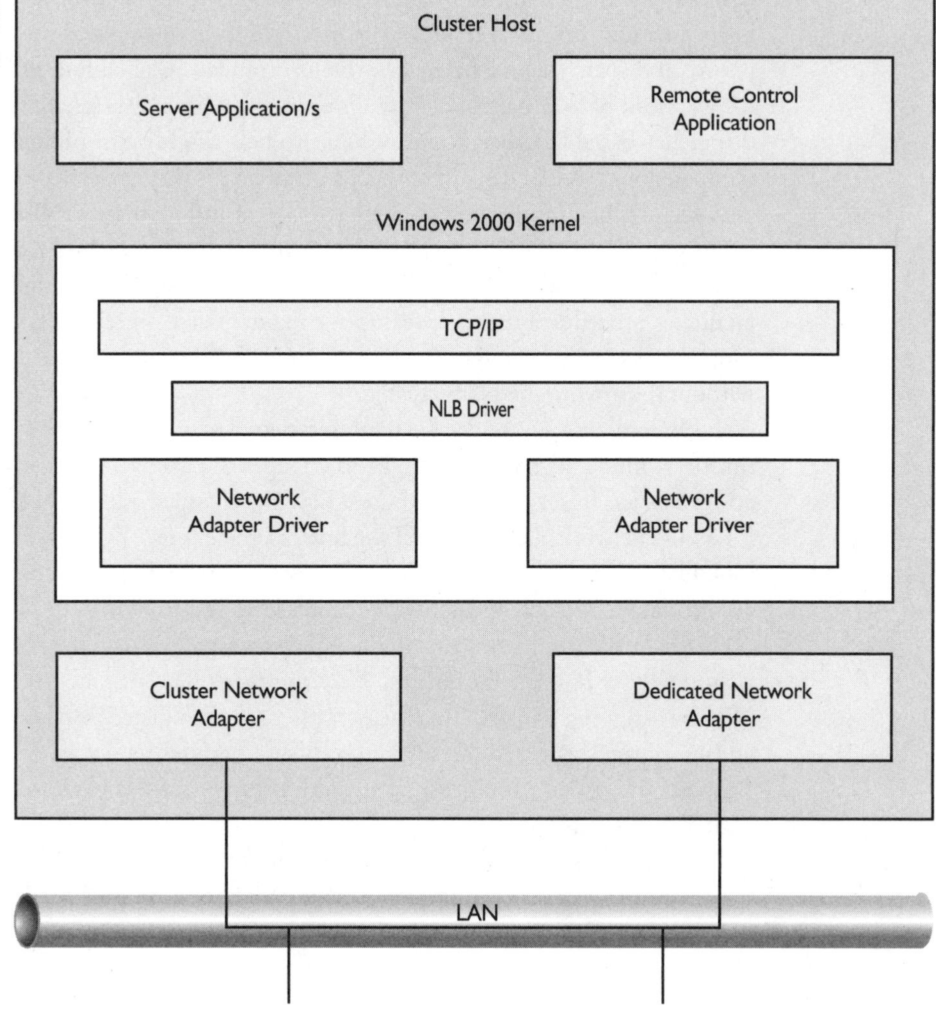

because the NLB driver can accept packets from the network while TCP/IP processes the packets that NLB hands off to it. This system results in increased performance for hosts running NLB as opposed to hosts that are using a dispatcher-based load-balancing technique.

A dispatcher-based load-balancing solution is one that employs a dedicated computer that functions to route TCP traffic to hosts in a network based on port numbers or port rules to more evenly distribute incoming traffic among a group of servers. The load balancing performed by a dispatcher usually involves Network Address Translation (NAT). A *dispatcher* is typically software with multiple components that are meant to coordinate, monitor, and distribute TCP traffic to hosts on a network. As a result of the multiple components and the nondistributed nature of dispatcher load balancers, the load of load balancing itself is not balanced. All the work of load balancing rests solely on the dispatcher itself. This means that dispatcher-based load balancers are liable to be a single point of failure. When compared with NLB, dispatcher-based balancing is very inefficient. As a result of its architecture, besides providing a highly efficient infrastructure, NLB also provides what is known as *(N-1)-way failover*. This means that for a cluster with a number of hosts equaling *N*, all but one host must fail for load balancing to fail. This system facilitates procedures such as preemptive maintenance on servers because one or more servers can be taken offline for upgrade and reintroduced to the cluster without destroying the NLB cluster.

NLB employs two modes for handling network traffic: unicast mode and multicast mode. In *unicast mode*, NLB changes the Media Access Control (MAC) address of its cluster adapter and uses the same changed address as the MAC address for all the network adapters for all the hosts in the cluster. This makes the entire cluster look like one host to the network and allows all the members of the cluster to receive all incoming packets at the network adapter level and pass them to NLB for filtering. A cluster host running unicast mode requires a separate NIC for communicating with the other hosts in the cluster. *Multicast mode* alleviates the need for a second NIC by assigning a Layer 2 multicast address to the cluster based on the primary IP address of the cluster. As a result, each cluster member retains its original address. Both the unicast and multicast MAC addresses are derived from the primary IP address of the cluster.

NLB uses a feature known as a *port rule* to determine how traffic will be handled for any number of ports in the range of the 65,536 ports used in TCP/IP. Port rules can therefore be used to pass certain traffic to certain hosts based on the port number of the packets or to block traffic on certain ports altogether. Port rules employ policies that affect all cluster hosts (multiple-host policies) or a single host (single-host policies).

Multiple-host policies result in traffic distribution among all hosts in the cluster with the ability to specify traffic load percentages; in other words, each host in an

**FIGURE 4-12** NLB Hosts Using Multicast Mode Servicing Clients

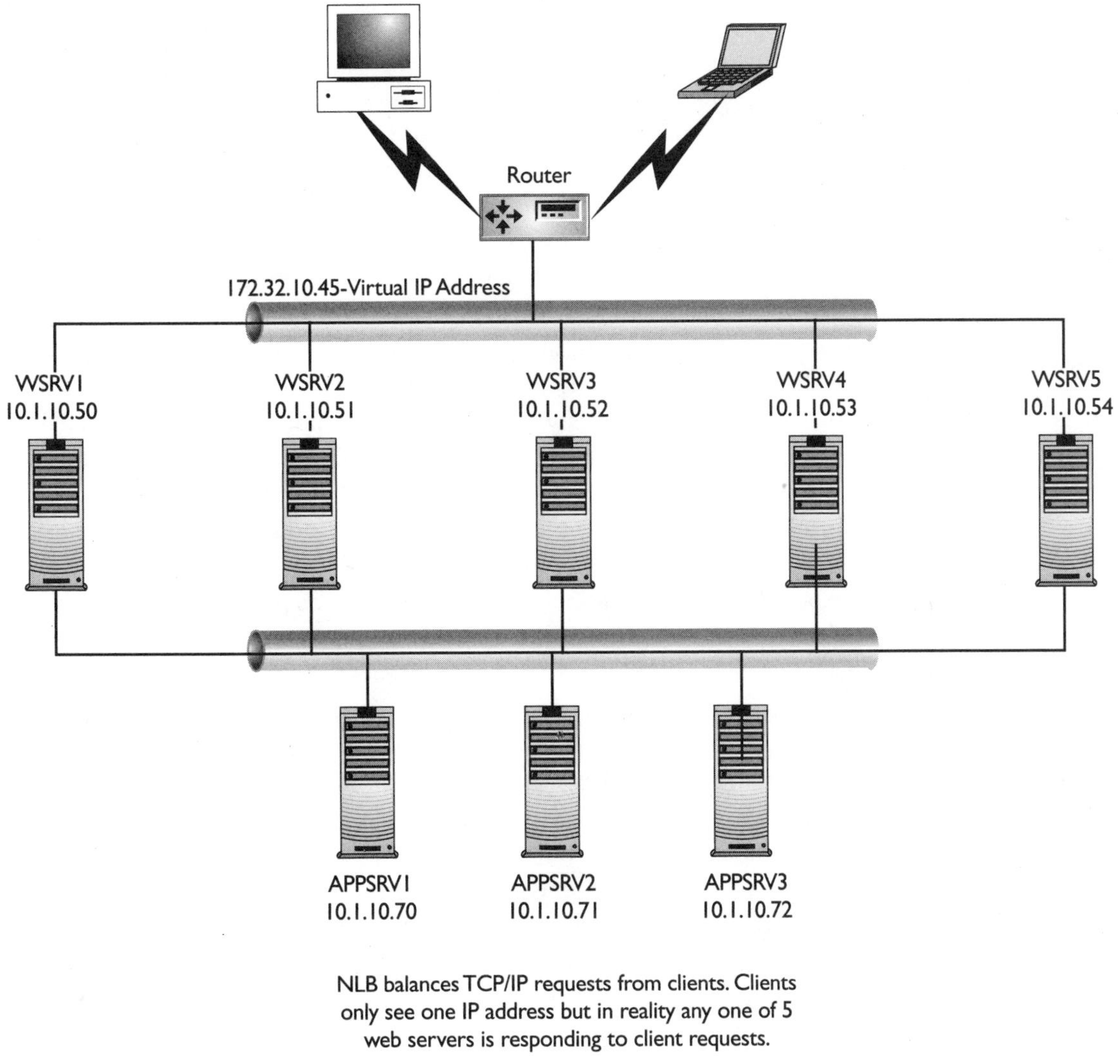
Router
172.32.10.45-Virtual IP Address
WSRV1
10.1.10.50
WSRV2
10.1.10.51
WSRV3
10.1.10.52
WSRV4
10.1.10.53
WSRV5
10.1.10.54
APPSRV1
10.1.10.70
APPSRV2
10.1.10.71
APPSRV3
10.1.10.72
NLB balances TCP/IP requests from clients. Clients only see one IP address but in reality any one of 5 web servers is responding to client requests.

NLB cluster can specify a percentage of the traffic load it will handle. This technique is effective when the members of a cluster are servers of different specifications. A more powerful server with faster processors and network cards can be assigned a higher load percentage. In situations in which all the members are servers of equal specifications, the load can be distributed equally among all members. Figure 4-12 illustrates how Web servers in an NLB cluster service client requests.

exam Watch

***In taking this exam, you would benefit from a sound understanding of IP unicast and multicast communication.***

Single-host policies result in client traffic being directed to the host with the highest handling priority first. This strategy allows specific servers to handle all traffic for specific server-based applications.

NLB uses a fully distributed statistical algorithm for deciding which host in the cluster receives which packets when accepting incoming traffic. The decisions the algorithm makes are not affected by CPU load on a particular server, because NLB is designed to consume only a small percentage of CPU resources and no more. NLB is affected only by changes in network performance of a host, not CPU cycles or memory use. The algorithm basically ensures that the first cluster host that is able to handle the incoming traffic best is the one that receives it. However, a specific host can be selected for certain traffic by enabling a feature known as *client affinity*. This feature creates a direct one-to-one mapping between a particular client and server so that traffic from this client always goes to that particular server.

Servers that are member hosts in an NLB cluster live a dual life. Each server has its own number of client requests to service as quickly as possible. On the flip side, each member of the cluster is also monitoring the cluster and otherwise communicating with the other members of the cluster as well as any back-end servers with which it needs to exchange information. The servers that are members of a load-balanced cluster each emit a "heartbeat" signal to the other nodes in the cluster; this heartbeat is used to monitor their operation. If one of the nodes stops sending the message for some reason, such as in the event of a server outage, NLB redistributes the workload and within 10 seconds the other members of the cluster take over the downed server's workload. The reverse is true when a host has been added to the cluster. NLB redistributes the load to include the new host. The exchange of heartbeat messages among cluster hosts to recalibrate load distribution is known as *convergence*. During convergence, service from the live hosts is unaffected, but traffic to a downed server is not serviced until convergence is complete. A host added to the cluster also does not receive traffic until convergence is complete.

NLB provides a remote-control application that allows administrators to monitor the status of cluster hosts and control cluster operations, such as starting up and shutting down individual hosts or the entire cluster. This remote control can be performed from anywhere on the network without interruption of service.

**EXERCISE 4-3**

CertCam 4-3

### Determining the Status of an NLB Cluster

1. In order to determine node status, you can use the WLBS.EXE command. The syntax is:

   ```
   WLBS command [cluster [:host][remote options]]
   ```

2. For this exercise, we simply want to view the status of the cluster, so we use the QUERY command option. At a command prompt, type **WLBS QUERY**. If you are running this command from a remote computer, you need to connect to a cluster node in order to obtain the WLBS application, then indicate which cluster and host you want to query.
3. Review the output of the command. You should see a status of *converged* if the cluster is fully synchronized and running as a cluster.

## Replication

*Replication* is usually associated with the propagation of domain database information among domain controllers. Replication, however, can be used for updating and synchronizing content on other servers, such as Web servers, or on back-end application or database servers. Windows 2000 IIS can be integrated with Windows Cluster Services and the Microsoft Site Server Content Replication System (CRS) to propagate the configuration of Web and FTP servers within a cluster.

Webmasters who maintain highly available Web infrastructures can use CRS to push content updates to their Web and FTP servers. This technique allows administrators to quickly apply updates in configuration that might be necessary to keep the infrastructure up and running. Not only can we benefit from the stability that clustering and network load balancing provide, we can also use it to update IIS configuration without having to take our Web site offline.

Replication using the CRS is not an automated process, as it is with the Windows 2000 File Replication Service (FRS). It must either be performed manually by running the *iissync utility* or scheduled using the Scheduler service on the first server that is upgraded. Manual replication is achieved by typing the following from the \winnt\system32\inetsrv directory: *iissync <destination server>*. You can schedule the replication of content using either the AT command at a command prompt or the Winat utility.

on the Job

***Content or configuration replication is best performed using the staging server model. The staging server in the Web network is also usually the domain controller and the primary DNS server for the Web server network domain. Content or configuration changes are first uploaded to the staging server and then replicated to all the servers in the Web server domain.***

## Connectivity

*Connectivity* is a serious issue in any Web infrastructure. It is much more important in a highly available Web infrastructure. It is as simple as this: If there is no connectivity or inadequate connectivity, customers receive no service. Connectivity, whether to the Internet or to a private network, can be virtually guaranteed if the correct measures are employed.

As we learned earlier in this chapter, redundant network components such as NICs, switches, and routers guarantee connectivity. Windows 2000 servers can work to help ensure optimal connectivity via the Knowledge Consistency Checker (KCC). The KCC manages the changes in network topology to compensate for limited connectivity. The KCC works closely with the FRS to achieve the network topology that provides the most optimal connectivity and therefore the best network services.

## Bandwidth

*Bandwidth* is the speed or data capacity of a network connection. Bandwidth in a Web infrastructure is important primarily because it determines (to some degree) how the site performs. Bandwidth affects the speed at which a site loads or how quickly data can be downloaded from or uploaded to an FTP site. Bandwidth also affects the speed at which queries are passed from a front-end Web server to a back-end server or the speed at which data from a back-end server is returned to the Web server.

Windows 2000 can help ensure adequate bandwidth via the Quality of Service (QoS). Through QoS, administrators can set thresholds on the minimum bandwidth acceptable before service is noticeably interrupted for particular components of the Web infrastructure, whether back-end databases, front-end Web servers, or some middle-layer application.

Windows 2000 QoS enables administrators and developers to control how much bandwidth a particular component of the highly available Web infrastructure has dedicated to it and maintain the bandwidth via any or all of the following QoS components:

- **802.1p** Flags can be set in the MAC layer header to establish packet priority in shared-media 802 networks.
- **Differentiated Services** Used to specify a packet's transmission priority as it passes through each network device on its journey through the network.
- **L2 Signaling** RSVP objects can be mapped to the OSI Data Link layer (Layer 2) signaling, such as Frame Relay network devices or asynchronous transfer mode (ATM) interfaces.
- **Subnet Bandwidth Manager** Used to manage shared-media network bandwidth.
- **Resource Reservation Protocol** Carries and passes QOS information to QOS-aware network devices between a sender and one or more receivers for a given transmission as well as to senders and receivers.

on the job

***QoS requires that a domain be available to function. QoS attempts to contact a domain controller on startup.***

Now let's take a look at some scenarios and solutions related to the topics covered in this section.

| SCENARIO & SOLUTION | |
|---|---|
| Is replication in a Web infrastructure the same as directory replication? | No. Directory replication is an automatic process that occurs between Windows 2000 domain controllers. Replication in a Web infrastructure is done manually using the Microsoft Site Server Content Replication System. |
| What is the lag time in redistributing network requests to new servers when a member of a cluster using NLB fails? | Less than 10 seconds. |
| If clients are communicating with a particular application on a particular Web server in the cluster and that server crashes, what must the clients do? | Nothing. Cluster Services move the application (virtual server resource) to one of the other computers in the cluster as service is resumed. |

**CERTIFICATION OBJECTIVE 4.03**

# Analyzing and Allocating End-to-End Bandwidth Requirements Throughout an *n*-Tier Environment

As mentioned in the previous section, bandwidth is an integral component of a network infrastructure. Our site cannot be reached, much less be highly available, unless we have adequate bandwidth—not only to serve our customers but also to serve the applications running in our infrastructure. Adequate end-to-end bandwidth is therefore of utmost importance in planning and designing our highly available network infrastructure.

The following section discusses the steps involved in analyzing and allocating adequate end-to-end bandwidth in an *n*-tier environment to sufficiently equip our infrastructure to service the customers we hope to serve at our site and at any one time.

In order to provide adequate bandwidth for our highly available Web infrastructure, we need to consider all the pertinent factors and components that influence the amount of bandwidth we will need. Factors such as number of front-end Web servers and back-end application or database servers, the applications that we are running, and the bandwidth of the Internet connection that the local ISP can provide are all important. The network devices between the front end and back end also play an important part in how much bandwidth we need to achieve 99.999 percent availability. Let's examine the most important factors now.

## Number of Hosts

Each server on our network must communicate with clients and at least one other server. This communication creates network traffic, which consumes bandwidth. If our servers are equipped with high-throughput network adapters (i.e., 100Mbps or higher), the bandwidth consumed is at least 100MB per server. As the number of servers on our networks grows, traffic—and therefore consumed bandwidth—grows. Eventually, a bottleneck will occur as the critical number of servers on our network is reached.

It is therefore recommended that we limit the number of servers per network segment or subnet to reduce traffic and the likelihood of network congestion. Subnetting our network into two or more networks is the most efficacious solution to alleviate congestion. The use of more efficient network devices that reduce latency is also an acceptable solution. The use of multilayer switches that rapidly process and forward traffic from source node to destination is an example of using network devices to alleviate and conserve network bandwidth.

## Applications

Applications employ different protocols to provide their services. For example, Microsoft Exchange Server 5.5 communicates using Simple Mail Transfer Protocol (SMTP), whereas SQL Server communicates using Transact-SQL, and a Web server communicates using HTTP. These native methods of communication eventually are all broken down to some form of TCP/IP packet that travels across a network from one host to another. Before this happens, most application communication takes the form of an RPC. Just about every network application uses RPCs to request data or services from a remote host. Clients use RPCs to communicate with servers, and servers use RPCs to respond to clients as well as to communicate with each other. However, some applications do so more frequently than others and therefore cause increased traffic over the network. Furthermore, some applications also tend to communicate using broadcasts, which consumes significant bandwidth.

The bandwidth allocated on a network must take the communication requirements of the various applications supported on the network into consideration. Additional bandwidth must be allocated for applications that broadcast. Prior to designing a network infrastructure, you should research and plan for the bandwidth requirements for all applications that the network will support.

## Network Devices

The devices that connect the hosts on our network must be able to rapidly and efficiently process and pass data from one node to another. To avoid unnecessary increases in network traffic as a result of retransmission of packets, the intermediate network devices on our network should be able to efficiently handle the throughput of the network adapters on the servers.

As previously mentioned, multilayer switches are an example of efficient network devices. Switches improve on network performance because they improve data transmission rates in two ways: They allow each connected device to transmit packets on their own wire within the switching fabric, and they allow segmentation of a network in Virtual LANs (VLANs). Allowing transmission of packets over their own wires allows devices that are capable to transmit packets in full-duplex mode because they have the bandwidth. Segmenting a network into VLANs reduces network congestion by reducing the number of hosts per network subnet, thus freeing up bandwidth.

As with servers, using devices of sufficient power to handle the job is important. Devices that properly manage the throughput of traffic flow and efficiently utilize available bandwidth are key to achieving high availability.

## Media Type and Access Methods

These days, the minimum standard network medium is Category 5 Unshielded Twisted Pair (UTP) cable. This medium is capable of handling throughput of up to a few hundred Mbps. Our network medium must have a maximum capacity that is sufficient to transport the maximum throughput of the network devices connected to it.

Bandwidth use over a certain percentage of the total available bandwidth results in network saturation. Saturation of network media results in reduction of network performance. The saturation point depends on the media access method being employed. The media access method is basically the technique that protocols use to put data onto the network media. For example, in Ethernet networks using the Carrier-Sense Multiple Access With Collision Detection (CSMA/CD) method, the saturation point is 40 percent. In other media, the saturation point might be higher or lower, depending on the properties of the media.

Higher-capacity media such as fiber optic cable can easily support devices and access methods that have throughputs of 100Mbps and higher. The duplex mode of packet transmission is also important when considering media. Duplex modes are the directions in which network traffic is allowed to travel. The two types of duplex modes are half duplex and full duplex. Full-duplex transmission on media that can support it tends to double throughput.

exam Watch

***There are two methods of media access: CSMA/CD and token passing. Ethernet networks are the primary forms of CSMA/CD-based networks, whereas Token Ring and Fiber Distributed Data Interface (FDDI) are the most prevalent forms of token-passing networks. Knowing the difference between the two methods will be helpful on the exam.***

## Available Internet Bandwidth

So far we have discussed all the factors that are directly under our control. One factor that might not be directly under our control but is important nonetheless is available Internet bandwidth. Local ISPs might or might not be able to provide the bandwidth that is needed to support your infrastructure. Again, you should acquire this information during the planning phase, prior to any actual deployment.

Organizations that can afford it might be able to circumvent this problem by enlisting the aid of a major service provider, such as AT&T, Sprint, or MCI. Most major ISPs offer a colocation service in which customers' Web sites sit on the ISP's redundant and highly available infrastructure. The customer relinquishes direct control of the Web site but receives the advantage of knowing that its Web infrastructure is part of a larger protected and managed infrastructure.

Let's take a look at some scenarios and solutions related to these issues.

| SCENARIO & SOLUTION | |
|---|---|
| My servers are configured with Gigabit Ethernet cards. What type of network medium will give me the maximum performance from these NICs? | High-throughput NICs such as Gigabit Ethernet cards require a high-bandwidth network medium such as fiber optic cable. |
| How does the number of servers affect bandwidth? | Each server that transmits packets over the network medium uses a percentage of the bandwidth. During a network broadcast, for example, significant bandwidth is used. The more hosts on the network, the more traffic and therefore the more bandwidth is consumed. |

## CERTIFICATION SUMMARY

This chapter gave us the skills to begin thinking about planning and designing a high-availability Web infrastructure with Windows 2000 technologies. In this chapter, we discussed the elements of a high-availability infrastructure such as redundant Internet paths and redundant services and components. We learned how redundant components reduce server and network device downtime by reducing component repair and replacement time. Redundant paths increase availability of our Web sites by providing an alternate route for clients to travel through to get to our sites as well as acting as a failover mechanism in the event that the primary Internet connection fails.

We learned about Windows 2000's two clustering technologies, Cluster Services and Network Load Balancing Services. Cluster Services provide failover and fault-tolerant protection for vital applications and resources on a highly available Web infrastructure. Cluster Services can employ the N+1 architecture, which maintains a host available to accept resources from a failed node. Cluster Services detect failures in server clusters and move resources from failed nodes to surviving nodes to maintain the service to customers. Network Load Balancing (NLB) distributes TCP/IP traffic among the hosts in the NLB cluster so as to service client requests quickly and more efficiently. NLB Services reside between the TCP/IP layer and the network adapter driver layer in the Windows 2000 networking protocol architecture. Both cluster services use a heartbeat system to detect cluster member failure and prompt redistribution of server load.

Finally, we looked at the factors influencing end-to-end bandwidth allocation for a high-availability Web infrastructure. Factors that influence bandwidth allocation are number of hosts on the network, types of network devices, types of applications, and type of network media. All these factors are within the control of the individual or organization designing the infrastructure. Some organizations are able to fulfill the requirements of the infrastructure themselves, while for others, colocation might be a viable solution.

# TWO-MINUTE DRILL

## Designing a Highly Available Network Topology

- ❑ A highly available network is available to serve clients with 99.999 percent reliability.
- ❑ A highly available network topology consists of redundant paths, redundant services, and redundant components.
- ❑ Redundant paths allow for handling of more traffic and offer a backup route in the event one path is broken or congested.
- ❑ Windows Cluster and Network Load Balancing Services can consolidate multiple servers into one functional unit that provides redundancy and fault tolerance for any Web-based service offered.
- ❑ Server or network device hardware with redundant components greatly reduces downtime due to repair and/or service.

## Planning Server Configurations

- ❑ Windows 2000 Cluster Services can contain a maximum of four servers per cluster on Datacenter Server or two nodes in a cluster for Advanced Server. Cluster Services are not available on the standard version of Windows 2000 Server.
- ❑ Network load balancing can handle a maximum of 32 servers per cluster.
- ❑ Cluster Services compensate for a downed cluster node by moving the node's resource applications to another server or servers in the cluster.
- ❑ Resource groups are logical collections of related components in a cluster.
- ❑ Clustered servers emit heartbeat messages to each other when fully functional. Additionally, when they go down, no heartbeat message is transmitted.

## Analyzing and Allocating End-to-End Bandwidth Requirements Throughout an *n*-Tier Environment

- ❑ Limit the number of servers per network segment or subnet to reduce traffic and the likelihood of network congestion.

- The bandwidth allocated on a network must take the different communication requirements of the various applications supported on the network into consideration.
- Prior to designing a network infrastructure, you should research and plan for the bandwidth requirements for all applications that the network will support.
- The devices that connect the hosts on our network must be able to rapidly and efficiently process and pass data from one node to another. Devices that properly manage the throughput of traffic flow and efficiently utilize available bandwidth are key to achieving high availability.
- The minimum standard network medium is Category 5 UTP cable. This medium is capable of handling throughput of up to a few hundred Mbps.
- Available Internet bandwidth is a factor that is generally out of our control, but it is one that needs to be recognized and planned for when building a highly available network.

# SELF TEST

The following questions will help you measure your understanding of the material presented in this chapter. Read all the choices carefully because there might be more than one correct answer. Choose all correct answers for each question.

## Designing a Highly Available Network Topology

**1.** High-availability networks are networks that serve customers with what percentage of reliability?

A. 97.6 percent

B. 99.999 percent

C. 98.5 percent

D. 89.9 percent

**2.** Your Web site has an intermittent availability issue. NLB is employed as a method to ensure availability on your Web front end, yet for some reason your Web site continues to return "Page cannot be displayed: HTTP 500—Internal server error" messages to some clients intermittently at the highest peaks of activity. What are possible solutions for this problem? (Choose the *best* answer.)

A. Provide a redundant path that can be used when the bandwidth of the default path is saturated.

B. Have your ISP increase your Internet bandwidth.

C. Install a switch on your public network.

D. Upgrade your Web servers.

**3.** What are the three possible ways that redundant paths help in the design of a true highly available infrastructure? (Choose all correct answers.)

A. Redundant paths provide failover protection in case your primary Internet connection fails.

B. Redundant paths increase your outbound Internet access bandwidth.

C. Redundant paths provide a type of load balancing by supporting incoming clients on a different connection.

D. Redundant paths increase the speed of your Web servers.

**4.** What is the difference between redundant paths and load balancing? (Choose the *best* answer.)

A. Load balancing provides an alternate route for client connections, whereas redundant paths do not.

B. Redundant paths provide an alternate route for client connections, whereas load balancing distributes TCP/IP traffic from only one route.

C. Redundant paths enable Web servers to distribute their workload, whereas load balancing does not.

D. Load balancing enables Web servers to distribute the incoming TCP/IP traffic load from one or more paths. Redundant paths provide backup or failover paths for the infrastructure.

**5.** When working with redundant paths, what effect does an unavailable link or router failure have on Web site performance?

A. Performance degrades permanently.

B. Performance is not affected.

C. Performance degrades temporarily until the router is restored.

D. Performance degrades temporarily until the alternate route is advertised.

**6.** What is the importance of having redundant components in your network? (Choose the three *best* answers.)

A. Redundant components duplicate the work of your existing components and are therefore unnecessary.

B. Redundant components reduce downtime due to repairs and prevent data loss in the event of a hardware failure.

C. Redundant components are important for disaster recovery.

D. Redundant components are necessary for fault tolerance.

## Planning Server Configurations

**7.** You recently purchased five new servers for your e-commerce Web infrastructure running Windows 2000 Advanced Server. Your network is a fiber optic network with a 10Gbps maximum bandwidth. Each machine has dual Pentium 4 1.4GHz processors and 1GB of RAM—more than enough to handle the front-end Web sites and the back-end database application you plan to run on your new site. During tests on your Web site performance, you notice that the new servers' network throughput is approximately 10 times lower than the expected 1000Mbps. You have already optimized Windows 2000 for performance. What could be the problem, and how would you rectify it? (Choose the *best* answer.)

A. The NICs on the new servers are only 100Mbps NICs. Replace them with 1000Mbps NICs.

B. The Server service has not been optimized for network applications. Change the setting in the Network Properties window.

C. The speed and duplex mode were not configured on the NICs. Configure the NIC for full duplex and maximum throughput in the Local Area Connection Properties window.

D. The router between the front-end network and the back-end network is not powerful enough. Upgrade to a router with higher throughput.

**8.** You are administering a cluster of three servers. You want to move a cluster resource from one node to another, but you receive an error message stating that the resource cannot be moved to that node. Why? (Choose all that apply.)

A. The node with the resource is not in the same cluster as the node to which you want to move the resource.

B. The node to which you want to move the resource does not own any of the components of the resource to be moved.

C. The node to which you want to move the resource is not the preferred node on which to host the resource.

D. The node to which you want to move the resource is too busy.

**9.** In Windows 2000 Cluster Services, how many Windows 2000 servers can be linked together to form a cluster?

A. Cluster Services can link a maximum of two Windows 2000 Advanced Servers and four Windows 2000 Datacenter Servers, for a maximum of six servers per cluster.

B. Cluster Services can link a maximum of four servers for both Advanced Server and Datacenter Server.

C. Cluster Services can link a maximum of two servers for both Advanced Server and Datacenter Server.

D. Cluster Services can link a maximum of two servers for Windows 2000 Advanced Server and a maximum of four servers for Windows 2000 Datacenter Server.

**10.** How do Cluster Services provide more efficient service for a network? (Choose all that apply.)

A. Cluster Services distribute application resources across multiple servers, thereby reducing the load on any one server.

B. Cluster Services can reduce the number of nodes required on a network by hosting multiple services on one cluster.

C. Cluster Services increase the fault tolerance of network resources by moving resources to functioning cluster nodes in the event of a node failure.

D. Cluster Services improve application response time because multiple servers handle client requests and are able to deliver a response faster than a single server would.

**11.** What is one advantage of running NLB versus dispatcher-based load balancing?

A. Hardware TCP/IP load balancing is faster and more efficient than software load balancing.

B. Network load balancing requires no special hardware aside from the Microsoft HCL-approved server hardware.

C. Dispatcher-based load balancing usually has higher throughput than NLB.

D. Dispatcher-based load balancing eliminates many of the constraints of hardware load balancing.

**12.** You are building an NLB cluster of five servers. You have only enough in your budget for one high-performance NIC per server. Should you be running in unicast or multicast mode, and why?

A. Unicast mode because it conserves addresses on the network

B. Multicast mode; all the servers use the same MAC address, thus communication is more efficient

C. Unicast mode because each server can have multiple IP addresses on the high-performance NICs

D. Multicast mode because the same Layer 2 address is used for the cluster but each server retains its original address for intracluster communication

**13.** Your Web infrastructure has seven servers that are configured on the network using Cluster Services. Three of the servers are Pentium 4 dual 1.4GHz with 2GB of RAM, one 1000Mbps NIC, and a 100Mbps NIC; an additional three are Pentium III dual 866MHz with 1GB of RAM and dual 100Mbps NICs. The remaining one server is Pentium III 750MHz with a 100Mbps NIC. The 750MHz server cannot handle the same amount of traffic that the other servers can handle. What would possibly be the most appropriate way to have it function in the cluster? (Choose all that apply.)

A. Build the 750MHz server as the +1 server in case of failure.

B. Use Cluster Administrator to move the less demanding resources to the 750MHz server and keep the higher-demanding services on the more powerful servers.

C. It makes no sense to add the server to the cluster.

D. Add the server to the cluster, but set its node preference to low.

**14.** One of your servers in your cluster fails. Cluster Services moved the resources they were managing to another node in the cluster. How was the decision made as to which node to move the resources to?

A. Cluster Services always move the resources to the node that manages the quorum resource.

B. Cluster Services always move the resources to the node with the fastest processor.

C. Cluster Services are designed to move the resources to the node with the lowest node preference number.

D. Cluster Services are designed to move the resources to the node with the highest node preference number.

## Analyzing and Allocating End-to-End Bandwidth Requirements Throughout an *n*-Tier Environment

**15.** What are some of the pertinent factors that need to be taken into consideration when planning to provide adequate bandwidth for our highly available Web infrastructure? (Choose all that apply.)

A. The number of servers on your network

B. The network media

C. The available Internet bandwidth

D. The number of RAID arrays

**16.** Your employer has a traffic issue on the Web site network. Congestion and bottlenecks are a regular problem. What is one possible solution to this issue? (Choose the *best* answer.)

A. Install more powerful hubs.

B. Install more powerful multilayer switches.

C. Subnet the network.

D. Remove redundant hosts from the network.

**17.** What is a remote procedure call (RPC), and what is its function in the network?

A. RPC is a protocol that is used between servers to transfer data.

B. An RPC is a protocol that reduces available network bandwidth.

C. RPC is a protocol that clients and servers use to request services across a network.

D. RPC is a protocol that increases available network bandwidth.

**18.** How does the use of multilayer switches on our network result in an increase in efficient bandwidth usage? (Choose all that apply.)

A. Switches allow you to transmit data in full-duplex mode, provided that your media allows for it.

B. Switches reduce network collisions by allowing each NIC connected to them to transmit over its own wire within the switch fabric.

C. Switches use Layer 2 and 3 addressing, which is more efficient.

D. Switches separate higher- and lower-speed network traffic from each other.

**19.** You are upgrading your servers from 486 to Pentium III with 100MB network cards. You notice that performance is not as good as you expected it to be after the upgrade. You examine your network cable and discover that it is Category 3 UTP cable. How do you achieve better performance?

A. Install switches on your network to improve performance.

B. Upgrade the network media to Category 5 or better.

C. Configure your network adapters to transmit in full-duplex mode.

D. Add an additional network card in each machine.

**20.** If available Internet bandwidth is not within our control, what measures can we take to ensure that it is not an issue on our network? (Choose the *best* answer.)

A. There is nothing we can do. It is out of our control.

B. Contact one of the larger ISPs such as AT&T, Sprint, or MCI for service through a local ISP.

C. Move our company to a more urban location with better Internet access.

D. Colocate our site at a major ISP location.

# LAB QUESTION

Your organization is about to launch a new Web venture that requires a robust, highly available Web infrastructure to support it. You have been tasked with the network infrastructure design. You must design a network that can support upward of 500,000 hits per day and 300,000 client requests to a back-end application. The application uses a Microsoft SQL Server database to store its data. The infrastructure must be fault tolerant and allow you to administer it remotely. You have been given a sizable budget to carry out this project. You must give a presentation outlining your plans, so you decide to first build a model in diagram form so that you can more closely examine the details. Create this diagram and explain the components.

# SELF TEST ANSWERS

## Designing a Highly Available Network Topology

1. ☑ **B.** High-availability networks serve customers with 99.999 percent reliability.
   ☒ **A**, **C**, and **D** are incorrect because high availability is defined as a 99.999 percent uptime.

2. ☑ **A.** Providing a redundant path is the best answer in this case because the problem is being experienced at the Web front end, where the clients are not gaining access to the Web server. The "Error 500" message gives a clear indication that the problem is with available Internet bandwidth.
   ☒ **B** is close to the best answer but it is not fault tolerant. **C** and **D** are incorrect because they affect only the physical infrastructure and don't address the bandwidth issue hinted at by the server error message.

3. ☑ **A**, **B**, and **C.** These three answers are correct because redundant paths are partially meant as failover mechanisms. Redundant paths are also meant to increase the bandwidth that Web server have to service client requests as well as to balance the TCP/IP traffic load from Web clients.
   ☒ **D** is incorrect because simply having more bandwidth or a redundant path does not affect the system performance of your Web servers.

4. ☑ **D.** This is the best answer to this question because servers use load balancing to distribute more traffic to hosts that can process more traffic and less traffic to hosts that cannot handle much traffic. This is done with traffic coming from any number of sources. Redundant paths provide the alternate pathways through which the clients and servers communicate.
   ☒ **A** is incorrect because load balancing does not provide alternate routes. **B** is incorrect because load balancing can distribute traffic from multiple routes. **C** is incorrect because redundant paths do not in themselves provide load balancing.

5. ☑ **D.** If a site with redundant paths has a failure on one of the paths, performance will degrade or the site will be momentarily inaccessible until the redundant route is put into production and advertised by the routers that know of the route.
   ☒ **A** is incorrect because performance degrades only until the redundant path is put into production. **B** is incorrect because performance will be affected if the primary Internet connection fails. **C** is incorrect because since the site has redundant paths, we do not have to take it offline until we can replace failed hardware. We can simply put the other circuit into production.

**6.** ☑ **B, C,** and **D.** These are the best answers because redundant components can either eliminate downtime and data loss by immediately taking over in the event of a failure or reduce downtime by being easily put into production if failure occurs. Redundant components are also necessary for disaster recovery and fault tolerance, which ensures reliability.
☒ **A** is incorrect because redundant components are essential to a highly available Web infrastructure simply because they duplicate the function of production components.

## Planning Server Configurations

**7.** ☑ **A.** A throughput of 10 times less the expected throughput of 1000Mbps hints that the NICs installed in the servers are only 100Mbps NICs. Replacing them with 1000Mbps NICs should improve throughput.
☒ **B** is incorrect because not optimizing the Server service would not produce that kind of performance drop. **C** is possible but not likely since most NICs are configured to automatically detect the available bandwidth and adjust their throughput accordingly. A duplex mismatch wouldn't produce sub-par performance of a factor of 10. **D** is also possible but not likely because, as stated in the question, the performance measured was on the local network, not between two networks.

**8.** ☑ **A, B, C,** and **D.** These are all possible reasons. Cluster resources cannot be transferred from one cluster to another. A node can manage a resource only if it owns at least one of the components of the resource. Cluster Services move resources to the node that it designates as having the highest preference first. Cluster Services will not move a resource to a node if the node is too busy to accept the resource at the time.

**9.** ☑ **D.** Cluster Services can link only two Windows 2000 Advanced Servers but can link up to four computers running Windows 2000 Datacenter Server.
☒ **A** is incorrect because it says that Cluster Services can link six servers in a cluster. **B** is incorrect because Advanced Server can form only two node clusters. **C** is incorrect because Datacenter Server can form four node clusters.

**10.** ☑ **A, B, C,** and **D.** Cluster Services provide efficiency by reducing the number of different resource servers required on a network if multiple services run on one cluster. Cluster Services also provide failover protection; in the event that one of the nodes fails, Cluster Services move the resources that node was managing to a node that can handle the load. Server performance is increased because the processing power of more than one computer is combined to service client requests.

**11.** ☑ **B.** This is the correct answer because NLB does not require additional hardware aside from the Microsoft-recommended HCL to function.
☒ **A** is incorrect because it does not address this question. **C** is incorrect because NLB load-balanced servers have been observed to have greater throughput than hardware-based load-balancing solutions. **D** is incorrect because dispatcher-based load-balancing solutions are usually hardware solutions.

**12.** ☑ **D.** Multicast mode NLB allows you to use one NIC for communicating on both public and private networks.
☒ **A** is incorrect because, even though unicast mode conserves Layer 2 addresses, hosts with one NIC cannot communicate on both the public and private networks. **B** is incorrect because servers use the same MAC address to communicate on the public network in both unicast and multicast modes, but multicast mode still allows hosts to use their NIC MAC addresses to communicate on the private network.

**13.** ☑ **B** and **D.** Since the server is not powerful enough to handle the higher-demand resources, moving less demanding resources to it will efficiently use it and save system resources on the more powerful servers, thus improving performance. The node preference could also be set on the server to make it the last designated server that would assume management of resources.
☒ **A** is incorrect because configuring the server as the +1 node assumes it has enough capacity to handle any of the resources in the cluster, which is untrue. **C** is incorrect because we want to add the server to the cluster.

**14.** ☑ **D.** Cluster Services are designed to move the resources to the node with the highest preference number.
☒ **A** and **B** are incorrect because the node that manages the quorum or the system with the fastest processor might not necessarily be the node with the highest preference. **C** is incorrect because the node with the highest preference is the one to which the resources are moved in the event of failure.

## Analyzing and Allocating End-to-End Bandwidth Requirements Throughout an *n*-Tier Environment

**15.** ☑ **A, B,** and **C.** These answers are correct because the number of servers, the available Internet bandwidth, and the type of network media all affect network traffic and availability, which needs to be considered in planning.
☒ **D** is incorrect because the number of RAID arrays does not affect the Internet bandwidth.

**16.** ☑ **C.** This is the best answer because congestion could be occurring due to the number of computers and the traffic they generate exceeding the network's capacity. Subnetting the network into two separate networks would reduce network traffic by reducing the number of hosts per network segment.
☒ **A** is incorrect because installing a shared media device such as a hub only increases congestion. **B** is incorrect because if multilayer switches were installed, the network would already be subnetted and there would be no congestion problem. **D** is incorrect because removing redundant hosts from the network would decrease availability and fault tolerance.

**17.** ☑ **C.** Clients and servers use RPCs to request services over a network from a remote host.
☒ **A** is incorrect because RPCs do not transfer data between servers. **B** is incorrect because RPCs do not consume much network bandwidth. **D** is incorrect because RPCs do not increase network bandwidth.

**18.** ☑ **A, B,** and **C.** These are the best answers because switches do allow each connected device to travel over its own wire within the switch frame, which allows the device to transmit data in full-duplex mode if the media allows it. Multilayer switches use Layer 2 and 3 addressing, which is more efficient than a hub.
☒ **D** is incorrect because switches do not separate higher-speed traffic from lower-speed traffic.

**19.** ☑ **B.** Category 3 cable is only capable of a maximum data rate of 16Mbps, whereas Category 5 cable is capable of data rates of 100Mbps.
☒ **A** is incorrect because installing switches will not improve bandwidth, since it is inherent in the media properties. **C** is incorrect because CAT 3 cable is not capable of transmitting in full-duplex mode. **D** is incorrect because another network card in each computer will only cause bottlenecks in the network due to traffic congestion.

**20.** ☑ **B** and **D.** Larger ISPs might be able to work with smaller local ISPs to provide higher-bandwidth Internet connections in some cases. Colocation is an option that allows a customer to share a major ISP's high-availability infrastructure.
☒ **A** is incorrect because most if not all ISPs offer some type of service to overcome the barrier of limited-bandwidth Internet access. **C** is almost a good answer but is not feasible, since moving a business is much more expensive than moving a few servers.

# LAB ANSWER

For an infrastructure that will support that many hits and transactions per day, our infrastructure must be quite formidable. Let's start with a front-end Web server cluster of five dual to quad

Pentium Xeon processor servers with 2GB of RAM, dual 1000Mbps NICs, and a RAID 5 hot-swappable disk array running Windows 2000 Advanced Server and the NLB and QoS Services for efficient IP traffic distribution and prioritization.

Our back-end application server farm will consist of a cluster of four eight-way Pentium Xeon processors or eight-way Pentium 4 1.4GHz processor servers with 2GB of RAM and dual 1000Mbps NICs. The common cluster storage unit is also hot swappable and in RAID 10 configuration and has a capacity of 150 percent—the maximum estimated storage for the SQL Server database.

Underlying it all, we have chosen to build an optical fiber network with high-performance optical multilayer switches and high-performance routers at the edge of our network. We have also purchased two DS3 Internet connections from a major ISP. All our servers and network devices are connected to dedicated UPS for power protection. Figure 4-13 illustrates our Web infrastructure design.

**FIGURE 4-13** Web Infrastructure Design

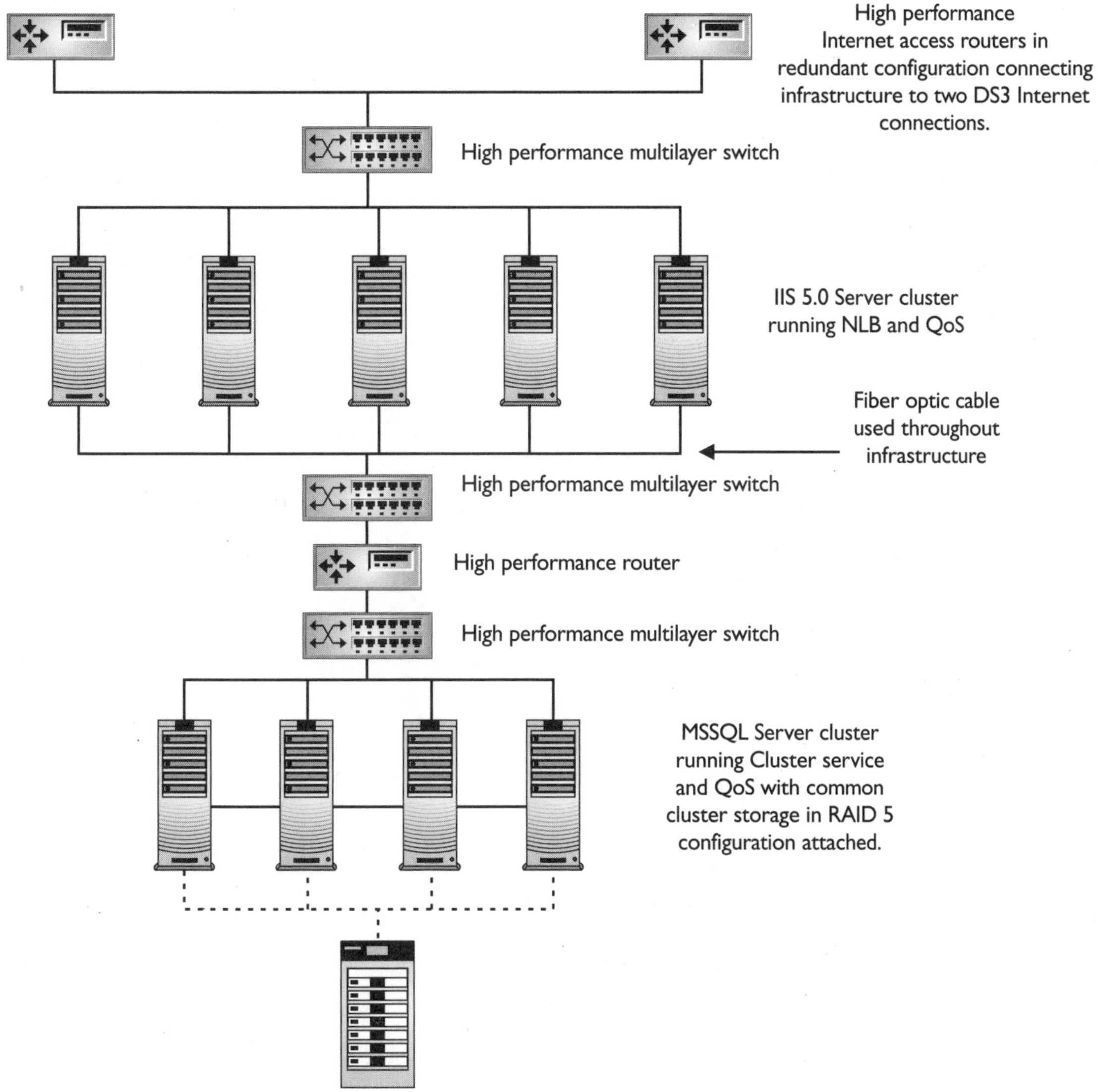

High performance Internet access routers in redundant configuration connecting infrastructure to two DS3 Internet connections.

High performance multilayer switch

IIS 5.0 Server cluster running NLB and QoS

Fiber optic cable used throughout infrastructure

High performance multilayer switch

High performance router

High performance multilayer switch

MSSQL Server cluster running Cluster service and QoS with common cluster storage in RAID 5 configuration attached.

MCSE
MICROSOFT CERTIFIED SYSTEMS ENGINEER

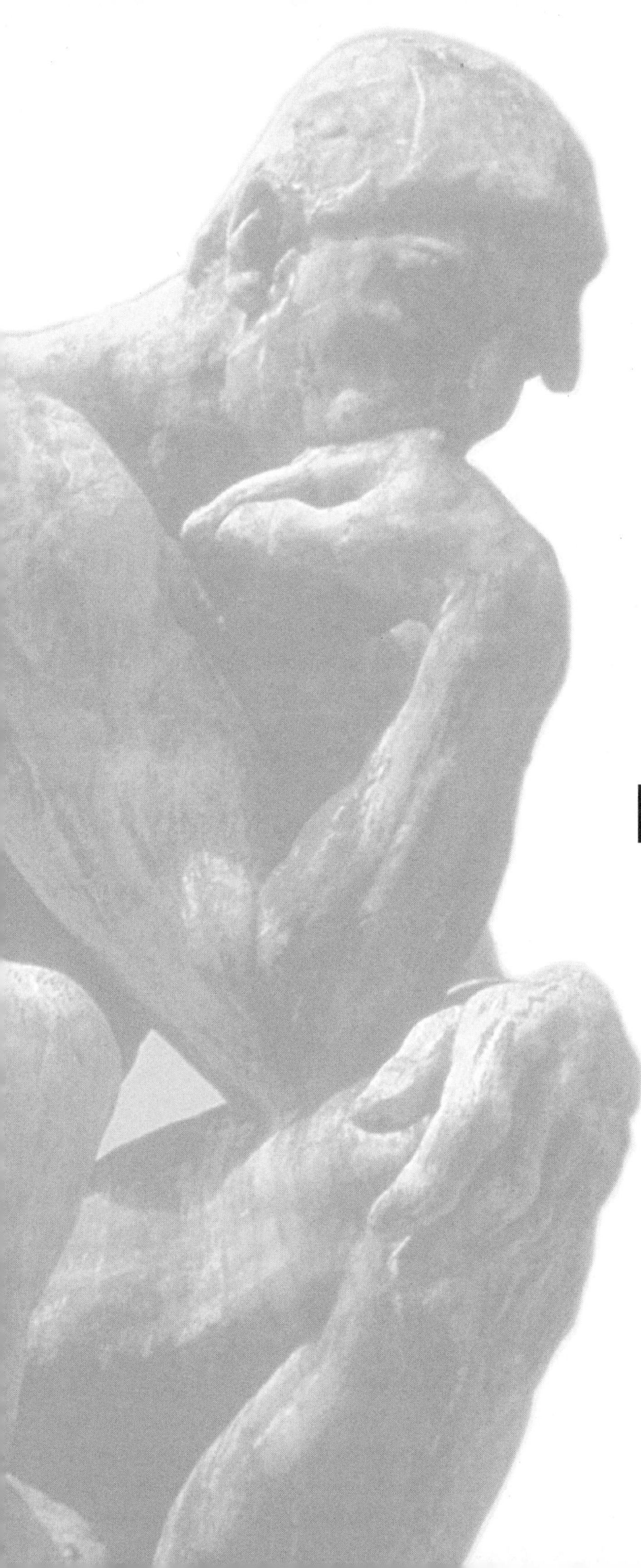

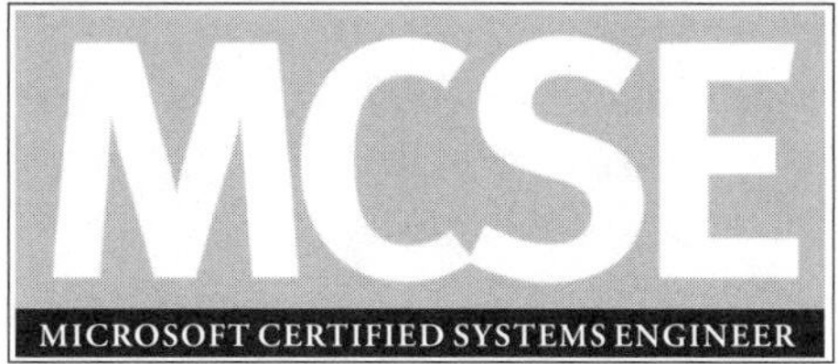

# 5

# Designing TCP/IP

## CERTIFICATION OBJECTIVES

| | |
|---|---|
| 5.01 | Designing a TCP/IP Network Infrastructure |
| 5.02 | Understanding DNS |
| 5.03 | Understanding DHCP |
| 5.04 | Designing Other TCP/IP Services |
| ✓ | Two-Minute Drill |
| Q&A | Self Test |

No matter how many methods there are for connecting a host or a network to the Internet, all hosts and all networks still use Transmission Control Protocol/Internet Protocol (TCP/IP) to communicate. Since the Internet's inception more than 20 years ago, TCP/IP has been the protocol of the Internet. During the life span of the Internet, TCP/IP has been refined and enhanced to allow new services and features to be offered over the Internet. One service that has benefited the most from the evolution of TCP/IP is the World Wide Web. Individuals use the Web to communicate to masses of people all over the world, every hour of every day. The ability to provide this functionality in a fast, efficient, and reliable manner is due in part to the elegant, efficient design of this one protocol on which the entire Internet runs.

Chapter 5 takes you through the process of designing a TCP/IP network infrastructure that can provide the type of performance, redundancy, and reliability needed to power a highly available Web environment. The chapter examines the critical role that Domain Name System (DNS) and Dynamic Host Configuration Protocol (DHCP) play in a sound TCP/IP implementation. The chapter also discusses how the enhancements of the TCP/IP services offered add power to a network infrastructure. Finally, the chapter looks at how other TCP/IP services that Windows 2000 has brought into play influence performance and availability on the network infrastructure.

**CERTIFICATION OBJECTIVE 5.01**

# Designing a TCP/IP Network Infrastructure

Windows 2000 TCP/IP is Microsoft's latest iteration of the industry-standard network communications protocol. Windows 2000 TCP/IP is more compliant with the Internet Engineering Task Force's (IETF) Requests for Comments (RFCs) than TCP/IP in Windows NT 4.0. Microsoft has greatly enhanced its version of TCP/IP to make Windows 2000 a truly Internet-ready operating system.

Numerous additions and improvements to Microsoft TCP/IP make it more compliant with industry standards as well as more compatible with the major networking and Internet technology vendors. The list of additions and improvements pertaining to enhanced network performance in the version of Microsoft TCP/IP introduced in Windows 2000 is as follows:

- **Quality of Service (QoS) and Resource Reservation Protocol (RSVP) support** Enables the reservation of a certain amount of network bandwidth between an individual client and a server based on type to prioritize network traffic.
- **Asynchronous Transfer Mode (ATM) services support** Support for IP over high-speed, high-performance ATM media.
- **Internet Group Management Protocol version 2 (IGMP) for IP multicasting** Support for IP multicasting, which is the transmission of an IP datagram to a *host group*—a set of hosts identified by a single IP destination address.
- **IP security (IPSec)** TCP/IP security standard for encrypting information for secure transmission over the Internet.
- **Multiple default gateways** The ability to have multiple default gateways enables a host to selectively choose through which of a number of gateways it should communicate. This allows a Web server administrator to configure redundant connections to the Internet as well as to other internal networks, which results greater reliability and failover protection.
- **Dead gateway detection** Support for TCP detection of a nonresponsive gateway and the calculation of an alternate route (as provided by multiple default gateway support). This also contributes to the failover protection scheme.
- **Increased default TCP window size** A larger TCP buffer so that more information can be transmitted and received per packet during each communication between hosts. This results in greater efficiency in communication.
- **Selective acknowledgments (SACK)** The ability to correctly identify and acknowledge packets that belong to a specific data transmission. SACK identifies that packets have been dropped or are out of sequence and facilitates their retransmission or re-sequencing and defragmentation.

- **TCP fast retransmit** A timer setting in TCP that waits for acknowledgments of packets passed down to IP. If an acknowledgment is not received in time, the packet is resent.
- **Improved performance for management of large numbers of connections** This is extremely helpful when designing a Web site to which thousands of clients are expected to connect. This is actually a by-product of employing QoS/Differentiated Services (Diffserv) features in our TCP/IP configuration. Diffserv uses a header field called the Diffserv Code Point (DSCP) to define scheduling or packet queuing behaviors in network communications. This allows Web servers to queue traffic instead of simply ignoring it during high-traffic periods.
- **Automatic Path Maximum Transmission Unit (PMTU) detection** Facilitates easier detection of the MTU of a host to which we are connected. This speeds up data transmission through the use of an automatic discovery algorithm that detects the MTU of the devices in the transmission path and simply selects the smallest value so that no fragmentation occurs.

Even with all these enhancements, Windows 2000 TCP/IP continues to support all the services available in the previous versions of TCP/IP, such as Windows Sockets, RPCs, and NetBIOS.

Windows 2000 TCP/IP introduces a new version of the Network Device Interface Specification (NDIS) version 5, which facilitates communication with the network interface card. Figure 5-1 shows the Windows 2000 TCP/IP model. A basic understanding of this model gives us a clearer view of how components in the TCP/IP architecture work with each other to provide services on a network.

The fact that Windows 2000 TCP/IP supports many more features, media types, and protocols gives us a lot more flexibility in choosing components when designing a highly available TCP/IP network infrastructure.

To design a robust but flexible network infrastructure from the ground up, we must first examine our requirements for the network and come up with a design plan that provides an idea of what this network should look like. It is essential that our network be fast and reliable; it must also be flexible, to accommodate change. We should examine factors such as the number of hosts we need on our network and the number of subnets we should have to properly manage network traffic. We need to consider the kind of network medium and access methods that we are

**FIGURE 5-1** Windows 2000 TCP/IP Model

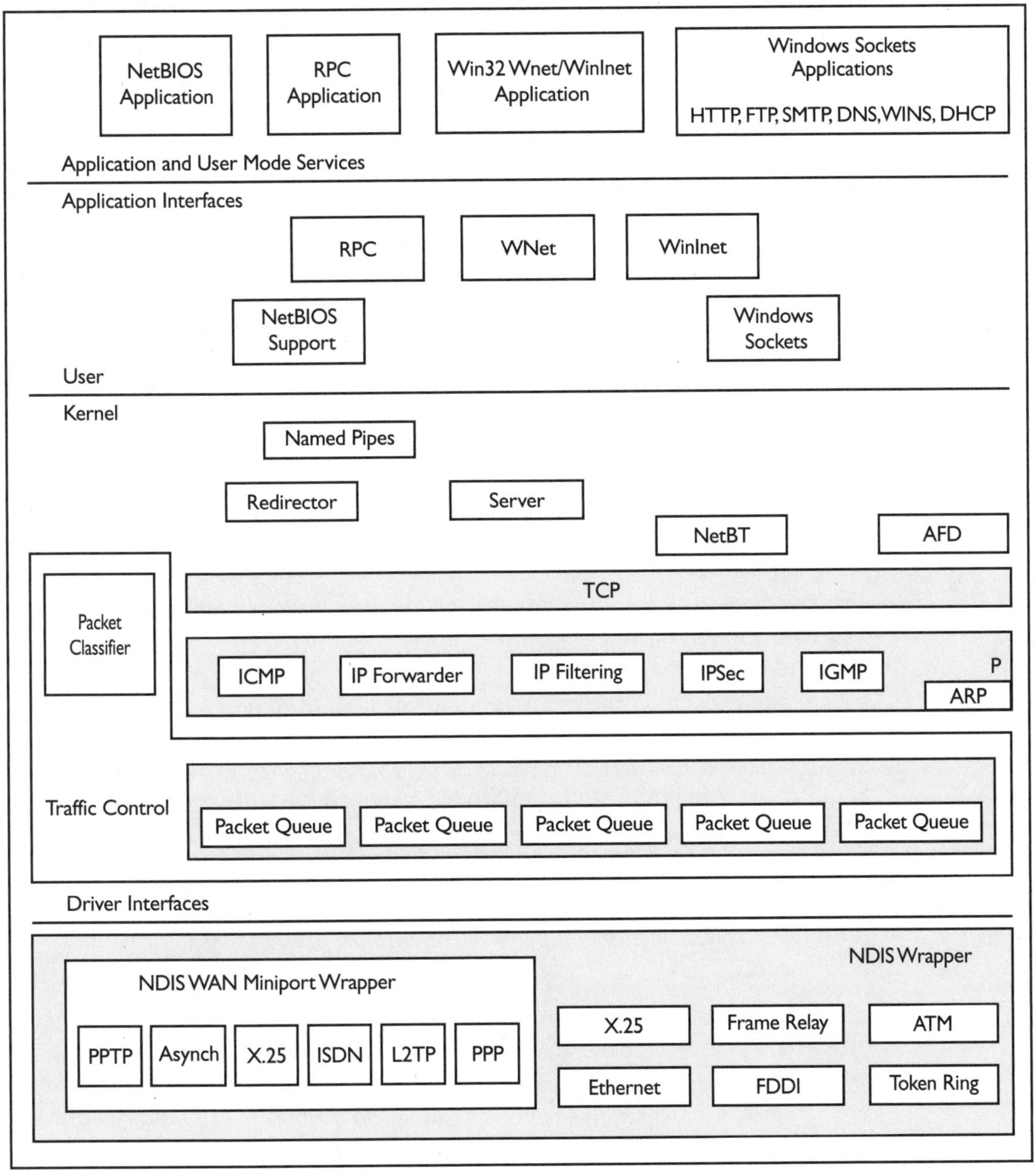

NetBIOS Application
RPC Application
Win32 Wnet/WinInet Application
Windows Sockets Applications
HTTP, FTP, SMTP, DNS, WINS, DHCP
Application and User Mode Services
Application Interfaces
RPC
WNet
WinInet
NetBIOS Support
Windows Sockets
User
Kernel
Named Pipes
Redirector
Server
NetBT
AFD
TCP
Packet Classifier
ICMP
IP Forwarder
IP Filtering
IPSec
IGMP
P
ARP
Traffic Control
Packet Queue
Packet Queue
Packet Queue
Packet Queue
Packet Queue
Driver Interfaces
NDIS Wrapper
NDIS WAN Miniport Wrapper
PPTP
Asynch
X.25
ISDN
L2TP
PPP
X.25
Frame Relay
ATM
Ethernet
FDDI
Token Ring

dealing with. It is always an excellent idea to draw a diagram of the proposed network to help determine the exact topology and configuration of the network.

This section discusses designing a TCP/IP network infrastructure from the perspective of addressing and locations where hosts reside on the network. We look at subnet addressing in detail to get a good idea of what works best when designing a high-performance network.

## Subnet Addressing

The number of hosts on a network segment significantly affects the performance of the network. More hosts mean more traffic and a greater risk of creating bottlenecks in the network because of that increased traffic. For example, in an Ethernet network, having too many hosts can bring the network to a crashing halt as packets transmitted from one host collide with packets from other hosts more frequently. This section on subnet addressing will delve into how we can reorganize our networks so that there are fewer hosts per segment and therefore less traffic—which ultimately provides us with less likelihood of a traffic bottleneck.

Understanding how TCP/IP addressing works is essential to successfully designing a TCP/IP network. A clear understanding of addressing allows the network designer to accurately size the network for the desired number of subnets and hosts and to provide a flexible design with room to grow and evolve as the demands on the network increase.

The addresses with which we are concerned, TCP/IP version 4 addresses, are 32-bit addresses consisting of four octets of binary numbers. TCP/IP addresses are represented in dotted decimal form, such as 123.119.174.16, and in 32-bit binary form, such as 01111011 01110111 10101110 00010000. A TCP/IP address consists of three parts—the network number, the host ID, and the subnet mask, as follows:

- The *network number* identifies the network that any particular host is a part of.
- The *host ID* identifies the specific host on the network.
- TCP/IP addresses have a third component known as the *subnet mask*, which, when used with the address, enables us to determine whether a host belongs to a local or a remote network. The subnet mask consists of two parts: the network portion and the host portion. In the subnet mask, the network portion is the part that consists of all 1s and the host portion is the part that contains all the 0s.

TCP/IP addresses that are used in networks are divided into five classes:

- *Class A networks* use the network numbers between 0 and 126 in their first octet and have a default subnet mask of 255.0.0.0. The address 123.0.0.16 with a subnet mask of 255.0.0.0 is an example of a Class A address.
- *Class B networks* use any number from 128 and 191 as their first octet and have a default subnet mask of 255.255.0.0. The address 168.24.11.2 with a subnet mask of 255.255.0.0 is an example of a Class B address. Notice that Class B networks do not include 127 in the first octet; **127.0.0.0** is a nonroutable TCP/IP network used only for monitoring the state of a network interface card. It is also referred to as the *loopback* address.
- *Class C networks* use any number from 192 to 223 as their first octet and have a subnet mask of 255.255.255.0. The address 222.219.20.53 255.255.255.0 is an example of a Class C address.
- *Class D networks* use any number from 224 to 239 as their first octet. Class D addresses are used for multicast purposes. In fact, only a few Class D networks in the 224.0.0.0 range are free for use.
- *Class E networks* use any number from 240 to 255 as their first octet. Class E addresses are reserved strictly for experimentation and are not to be used in private networks.

Class A addresses, by virtue of their subnet masks, are able to provide a much greater number of addresses than a Class B or C network. However, as we mentioned, having too many hosts on our network can affect performance and availability adversely due to network traffic congestion. Even in a Class C network, depending on the number of hosts we need to support and the level of network performance and availability we are looking to achieve, we might need to subnet our network into smaller segments that work better for us.

exam Watch

***Knowing how to convert from decimal to binary and back to decimal quickly is important in this exam. The decimal values in a binary octet, from left to right, are 11111111 = 128, 64, 32,16, 8, 4, 2, 1. Memorize this conversion.***

*Subnetting* is the creation of multiple networks from one network by manipulating the host portion of the subnet mask of the network address. This is also usually accompanied by the physical act of introducing a router or a multilayer switch and splitting our larger network into smaller segments or subnetworks. In order to create subnets, we must calculate and create subnet addresses. Subnet addressing is actually the mathematical division of one network into many smaller networks by manipulating the bits in the host portion of the subnet mask.

To perform subnet addressing, we must first know the size and number of segments we are trying to arrive at. If we have a Class C network—for example, 194.245.17.0 255.255.255.0—we can have a maximum of 254 hosts in this one network. However, what if we plan to create a highly available and fault-tolerant Web infrastructure of two networks with only 20 or 30 servers per network segment? In this case, a single network of 254 hosts would not work for us. Therefore, we can subnet this network by swiping the first three bits from the last octet of the subnet mask to create six segments of 30 hosts each. Figure 5-2 shows our Class A network before and after subnetting has been performed.

**FIGURE 5-2** Network Before and After Creating Subnets

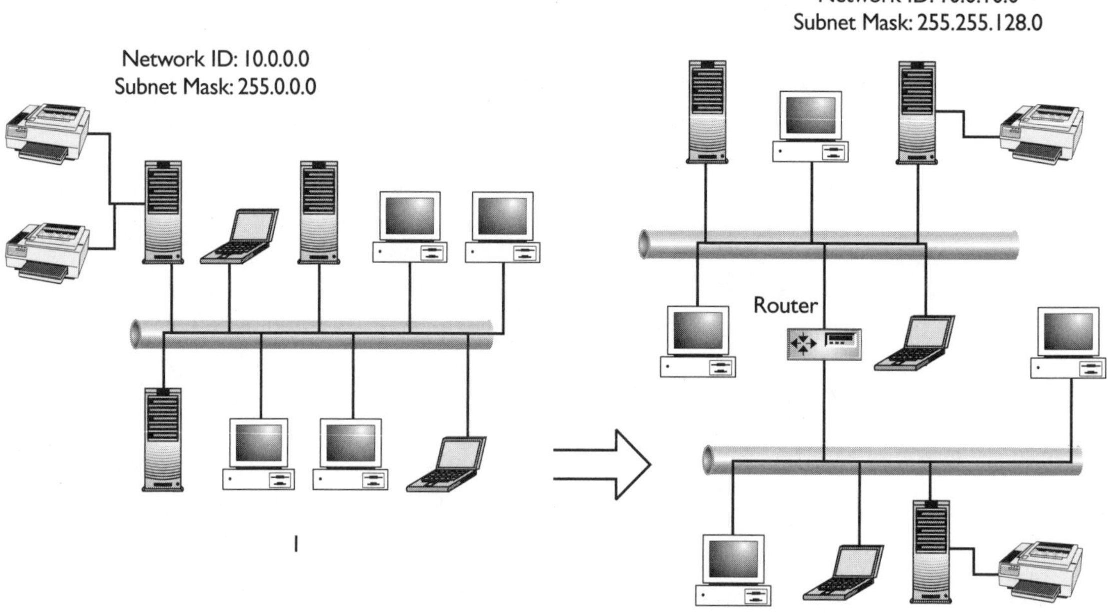

Additionally, if we had a Class B network and needed to subnet it so that we had at least 16 subnets and at least 4000 hosts per subnet, we could calculate the network numbers and the subnet masks that would satisfy such a requirement. We go about this by performing the following steps:

1. Determine the number of subnets that are required. Creating a conceptual diagram of the network is recommended to accomplish this task.
2. Convert the number of subnets required from decimal to binary to see how many bits in an octet are used to represent the number. The number of bits used is the number of high-order host bits we need to borrow to create these subnets.
3. Convert the number of bits to high-order bits and then back to decimal to determine the value of the subnet number for the new network.
4. Replace the first 0 octet in the default network mask of the current network with the subnet number to create the new subnet mask.
5. Use the new mask to determine address ranges for the new subnets.

exam Watch

***It is also important that we understand the concept of logical ANDing that is used to determine network address ranges by using the subnet mask.***

Exercise 5-1 shows how to calculate the number of hosts and the number of subnets.

## EXERCISE 5-1

### Calculating Subnets from Hosts

1. Our Class B network 172.16.0.0 255.255.0.0 needs to be subnetted so that there are no more than 126 hosts per subnet. This exercise shows how to perform the reverse calculations to find the number of subnets once you know the number of hosts per subnet. Since we know we need 126 hosts or less, convert the number 126 to binary.
2. Remove these bits from the number of available bits in the default subnet mask, starting with the lowest bit in the fourth octet. If 255.255.0.0 = 11111111 11111111 00000000 00000000, the number of available bits is 16. If we remove the number of bits that equals 126 from the available bits

(7 bits), we should be left with a value for the subnet number of our network. In this case, the only host bit left is the high-order bit in the fourth octet.

3. Since we've already identified the host bits, all the remaining 0 bits become subnet bits. Convert the remaining bit from 0 to 1 so that the subnet mask looks like this:

```
11111111 11111111 11111111 10000000
```

4. Convert the binary octets to decimal to see what the subnet mask is. Notice that the subnet mask in this example looks like a modified Class C mask 255.255.255.128. This mask reduces the number of hosts allowed per subnet to 126. Since the network address is a Class B network, the default subnet mask is 255.255.0.0. This means that we have possibly 512 subnets of 126 hosts per subnet. Since we cannot use a subnet of all ones or a subnet of all zeros we actually have only 510 subnets that we can use.

## FROM THE CLASSROOM

### Calculating Hosts and Networks Using $2^n - 2$

The equation $2^n - 2$ can be used to calculate the number of networks we will create, depending on how many subnet bits we swipe from the subnet mask. *n* is the number of bits swiped. For example, a Class A network 12.0.0.0 with 6 bits swiped from the next available octet would result in $2^6 - 2 = 64 - 2 =$ 62 networks. Additionally, we can find the number of hosts we now have per network using the same formula, but this time *n* is the number of remaining bits in the subnet mask. The result is $2^{18} - 2 = 262144 - 2 = 262142$ hosts for each network.

—*Chris O. Broomes, MCSE, MCP+I, CCNA*

Now let's look at some scenarios and solutions related to the material discussed in this chapter.

| SCENARIO & SOLUTION | |
|---|---|
| I have a very important client whose company needs specific network traffic to travel first at all times. He actually wants a specified bandwidth allotted just for his company, from my network to his. Is this possible with Windows 2000 TCP/IP? | Yes, with QoS and RSVP support, which enables the reservation of a certain amount of network bandwidth between an individual client and a server to ensure prioritized communication, that request can be accomplished. |
| My company has just completed the specs on what is needed to build a highly available network infrastructure. Is there anything specific we should do prior to building this network? | Yes. You should always draw a diagram of the proposed network plans prior to beginning any work on the infrastructure. This diagram will help you identify any possible holes or trouble areas, as well as a physical example of the topology and configurations that you will be working with. |
| What is the benefit of subnetting? | Having too many hosts on a network could bring your network to a crashing halt as packets transmitted from one host collide with packets from other hosts more frequently. Subnetting creates fewer hosts per segment and therefore less traffic and less likelihood of a traffic bottleneck. |
| What are the decimal values in a binary octet from left to right? | They are:<br>11111111 = 128, 64, 32,16, 8, 4, 2, 1 |

## CERTIFICATION OBJECTIVE 5.02

# Understanding DNS

The *Domain Naming System (DNS)* is the name resolution service of choice for Windows 2000. By design, DNS is a highly reliable, hierarchical, distributed, and scalable database. Windows 2000 clients use DNS for service location, including locating domain controllers for logon, as well as for name resolution. Microsoft's DNS is derived from the Berkeley Internet Name Domain (BIND) system and is therefore BIND compliant. As a matter of fact, Windows 2000 DNS is compatible or compliant with the standards for a name resolution system on the Internet.

on the Job

***Although the DNS service itself can function with other DNS services that are BIND compliant (or even BIND itself), problems can arise when you use Windows 2000 DNS with older DNS programs. These problems specifically relate to the fact that Windows 2000 DNS can support the latest DNS advancements such as Dynamic DNS (DDNS) and Service Location Reservation Records (SRVRR), but an older DNS server might not. If you configure Windows 2000 DNS to use these advancements, you could find that the system is incompatible or that those services simply do not function. For example, BIND 8.1.1 is compatible with Windows 2000 DNS but does a core dump when it receives certain updates from Windows 2000 clients. The flaw is fixed in version 8.1.2.***

DNS is used to map "friendly" hostnames to IP addresses. Your enterprise network has a domain name. It is the responsibility of the network administrator to maintain the database. When the Internet was very small, a manually edited, static host file was the only mechanism required to update names to IP addresses. All the information was kept on each computer in a Hosts file that had to be manually updated every time a computer was added to or removed from the Internet. In some places, the Hosts file was maintained in a centralized location. After the file was updated, each computer had to download a copy of the Hosts file. This method became inefficient as the Internet grew in size. Obviously, one or a few persons could not be responsible for keeping track of millions of computers on the Internet, especially if this tracking had to be done manually. There was no doubt that a better, more advanced way to resolve hostnames to IP addresses had to found. DNS is that more advanced way.

Down-level client operating systems using their respective TCP/IP versions (Windows NT 3.5 and 3.51, Windows NT 4.0, Windows 95, and Windows 98), however, rely on Network Basic Input/Output System (NetBIOS), which uses either a NetBIOS Name Server (NBNS) such as Windows Internet Naming Service (WINS) or a broadcast or flat LMHOSTS file. In particular, the NetBIOS name service is used for domain controller location.

Since DNS as implemented in Windows 2000 is Windows Internet Name Services (WINS) aware, a combination of both DNS and WINS can be used in a mixed environment to achieve maximum efficiency in locating various network services and resources. Additionally, WINS in a legacy or mixed environment plays an important interoperability role while also preserving current investment. Windows NT 4.0-based clients can register themselves in Windows 2000 WINS, and Windows 2000-based clients can register in Windows NT 4.0 WINS. Therefore, if we cannot upgrade all our servers at the same time, we can leverage our current Windows NT 4.0 Server or Windows NT 4.0 Workstation computers to continue to serve our end users while we upgrade incrementally.

## DNS Hierarchy

As we mentioned earlier, the DNS namespace is a hierarchical structure with a meaningful name resolution. What exactly does that mean? In simple terms, it has to do with the method that is used to organize domains. To obtain a better mental image of this concept, imagine the folder structure of your Windows 2000 Explorer window, which is also a hierarchical design. With domains, they can contain hosts or other domains. The highest level of the hierarchy is the root, which is managed by the Internet Name Registration Authority (INRA). The INRA manages the domains such as COM or NET and demands the management of subdomains to those who request a particular namespace. DNS is based on a naming scheme consisting of a hierarchical and logical tree structure. This structure, stored as a database, is called the *domain namespace.*

The root domain is usually shown as a period or a dot, as shown in Figure 5-3. The next level contains the top-level domains. This level is the level that is most familiar to users. This level contains the .com, .net, .org, .gov, .edu, and .mil domains.

The next level down is called the *second-level domain.* Microsoft.com and Cisco.com are considered second-level domains. Second-level domains are obtained through the *Domain Registrars* organization. Domains located below the second level are often referred to as *subdomains.* The DNS administrator is responsible for designing, allocating, and maintaining subdomains.

Because we are designing a highly available network, we should take subdomains one step further and discuss the benefit of creating subdomains within our network. Subdomains are used to split up DNS domains for quicker search results. Think in the context of a phone book: If you were looking for a name that begins with the letter *T,* it wouldn't be very efficient to search through the *A*s, *B*s, and so on until you reached the *T*s. In fact, it would be very time consuming to perform a search in that manner. DNS subdomains serve the same purpose. When a request is made of

FIGURE 5-3

DNS Hierarchy

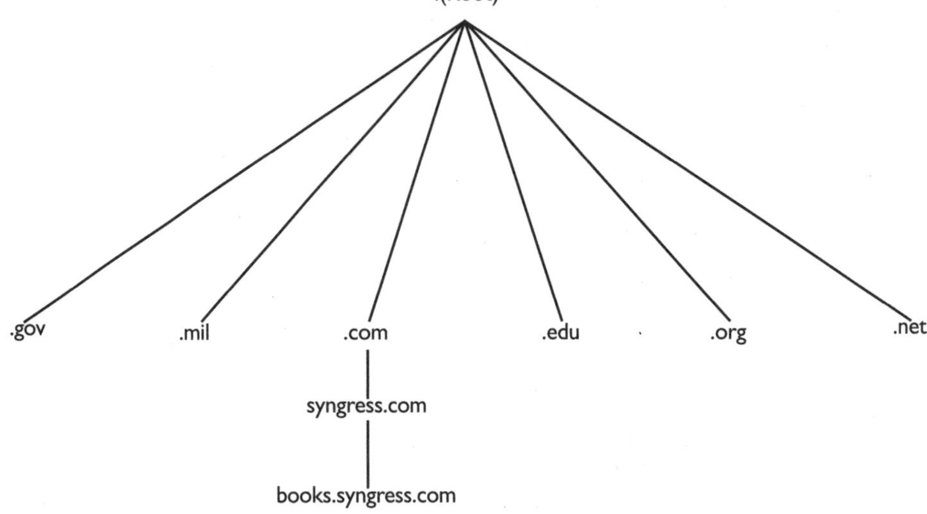


the DNS domain, if subdomains have been created, the response time on the query is much quicker.

Here is some additional information that will come in handy:

- The only limitations to the number of subdomains that can be managed from a single DNS server are the memory and disk space of the server.
- Each domain contains resource records. These resource records represent the hostnames and IP addresses contained on that domain.
- A group of domains managed from a single DNS is called a *zone.* A zone is a portion of the DNS database that is responsible for domains contained within it. Zones are classified as either primary or secondary.
- A *primary zone* contains the records managed by the DNS server that is authoritative for those records.
- *Secondary zones* are copies of the primary DNS zone that balance out the DNS name queries for the hosts in the domain.
- Windows 2000 introduces the Active Directory Integrated zone. The Active Directory Integrated zone is a zone stored within Active Directory under the domain objects container.

Table 5-1 provides a full listing of DNS domain names used and the type of organization that uses such domain names.

## DNS Naming

Prior to Windows 2000, Microsoft networks were typically based on the NetBIOS naming standard. In order to establish a session, the NetBIOS must know the NetBIOS name of the target computer. For this to happen, each computer required a NetBIOS name. On TCP/IP-based networks, the NetBIOS name had to be converted to an IP address. This led to additional broadcast traffic on the Internet.

With NetBIOS, no two computers can share the same NetBIOS name. If this happens, the computer attempting to use the same NetBIOS name will not be able to access the network. This is because NetBIOS presents itself as a "flat" network.

When you use DNS, two computers can share the same hostname on the network, even on the Internet. This is because DNS is not flat. Rather, it's hierarchical. Unlike DNS, NetBIOS uses a flat namespace. This means that all NetBIOS names consist of a single part. This is different from DNS in which names are fully qualified in a hierarchical *name.domain.domaintype* format.

The fully qualified domain name (FQDN) includes the hostname and the domain membership of that computer. With an FQDN, we can have two computers that share the same hostname—for example, we can have two FQDNs for two

**TABLE 5-1** Top-Level Domains and Their Uses

| DNS Domain Name | Type of Organization |
|---|---|
| .com | Commercial |
| .edu | Educational institutions |
| .gov | Nonmilitary government |
| .org | Nonprofit |
| .net | Networks |
| .mil | Military government |
| Num | Phone numbers |
| Arpa | Reverse DNS |
| Xx | Two-letter country code |

computers with the hostname of *Fred.* Although the two different computers use the same hostname (Fred), they reside in two different neighborhoods:

```
Fred.flintstone.bedrock.com
Fred.rubble.bedrock.com
```

## Domains

A domain locates (or specifies) an organization (or other entity) on the Internet. Continuing with our example of *bedrock,* if we want our company *Bedrock* to connect to the Internet namespace, we need to request INRA for a second-level domain name of *bedrock.com.*

## Hosts

*Hosts,* also known as *subdomains,* are located below the second-level domains. As mentioned previously, the DNS administrator is responsible for designing, allocating, and maintaining subdomains. Subdomains are used to efficiently set up network architecture. Again, using our previous example, one host in the bedrock.com domain could be barney.flinstone.bedrock.com, as shown in Figure 5-4.

**FIGURE 5-4**

DNS Console Showing Hosts and Domains

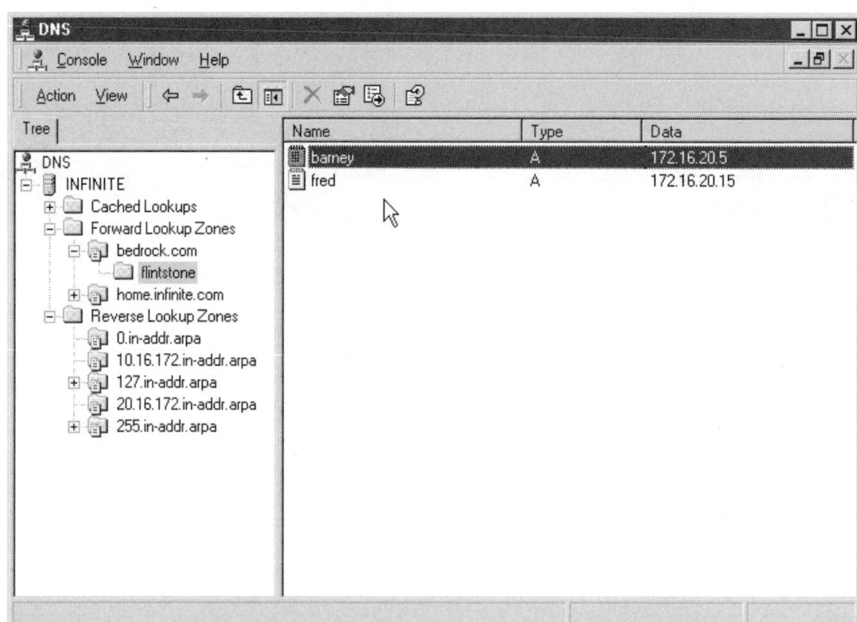

## Dynamic DNS (DDNS)

Windows 2000 DNS introduces a new feature called Dynamic DNS update (DDNS). DDNS overcomes the need to manually update DNS address (A) records and pointer (PTR) records every time a DHCP client changes its IP address or a static host is assigned a new IP address by an administrator. A records are hostname-to-IP address resolution records, or what is also known as *forward lookup zone records. Fred.bedrock.com* is an example of an A record. PTR records are IP address-to-hostname resolution records, or reverse lookup zone records. *10.20.16.127.in-addr-arpa* is an example of a PTR record.

DDNS is enabled by default in Windows 2000 DNS clients but can be disabled by unchecking the "Register this connection's address in DNS" option in the Advanced TCP/IP settings window in the Properties window of our local network connection, as shown in Figure 5-5. DDNS is disabled by default in Windows 2000 DNS servers.

DDNS works by a host sending A record and PTR record updates to the DNS server when a change in the hostname or IP address of a host occurs. For instance,

**FIGURE 5-5**

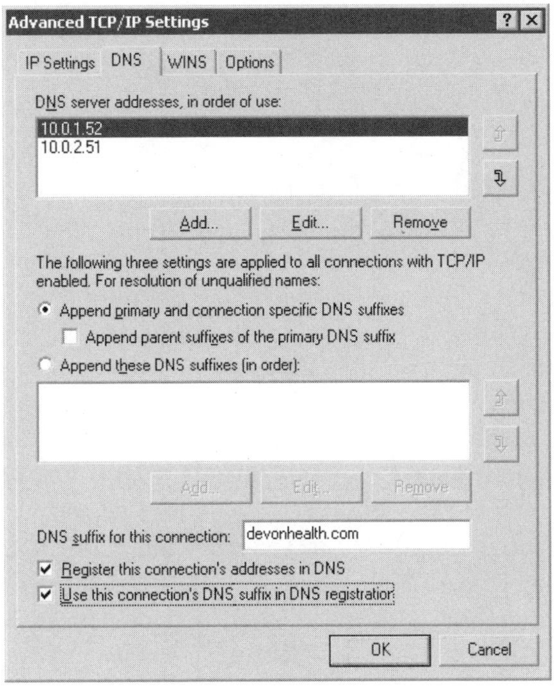

Dynamic DNS Update Settings Are Controlled by Check Boxes on the DNS Tab

when a Windows 2000-based client starts, the DHCP client software (not the DNS client software) sends a Start Of Authority (SOA) message to locate the primary DNS server. The primary DNS server responds to the message, then the client sends an update request to the server. The server receives and processes the request and adds records for the host. This process occurs each time TCP/IP information changes for the client.

## DNS Design Options

As we design the architecture for our highly available network, we really need to consider the various design options DNS offers. The ultimate goal is to have our network available 99.999 percent of the time, and part of achieving that standard requires that we consider security during our implementation. Obviously, any flaws in security could ultimately result in the network being unavailable. One security method that can be employed using DNS to heighten security is split-brain DNS.

A second area that requires attention when designing our infrastructure is the method by which queries are handled. This area might not seem critical for a low-traffic site, but for a site that receives a sizable number of requests (anything over 100,000), this is a critical function of DNS. In the same fashion as Network Load Balancing Services, we discuss the employment of round-robin DNS for the handling of queries.

### Split-Brain DNS

*Split-brain DNS,* or *split DNS,* refers to using separate internal and external DNS views of your domain's network using internal and external DNS servers. Using the same DNS server for both the internal and the Internet side of the network, a company increases the risk of exposing the structure of its internal network to intruders.

By setting up separate DNS servers that are updated independently, the risk is virtually eliminated. The internal server contains the database of all the DNS names within the organization, and the external server knows only how to resolve names dealing with the external presence, such as Web servers. With the split DNS, the internal DNS server is inside the firewall, and the external DNS server is set up outside of the firewall. The disadvantage to split-brain DNS is that you have double the administrative overhead for DNS because there are twice as many DNS servers to manage.

To set up a split DNS structure, the internal name servers must be configured to forward queries they can't resolve to the external name server. The external DNS records are configured to contain only a small zone file for the domain, which lists Web and FTP server addresses and any translated server addresses that can be published for anyone to see. The internal servers contain only the DNS records for the internal networks. If an internal user looks up a hostname, the internal DNS server answers the query. The internal DNS server will answer an internal user's query, regardless of whether that request is forwarded to an external DNS server for resolution.

When an external user (Internet user) queries for a hostname inside the domain, the query is answered by an external DNS server that contains only information about hosts external to the local network. Figure 5-6 shows the layout of a split-brain DNS configuration.

### Round-Robin DNS

If we want our network to be considered highly available, we must be prepared to service each request as it is received. Choosing a method that is efficient and accurate is critical for our network to function as a highly available network. One solution is *round-robin DNS (RRDNS)*, a process in which a single FQDN is resolved into a single IP address from a pool of available machines. A different IP address from the pool is returned each time the machine name is looked up, in round-robin fashion. The round-robin method is considered a simple, fast, and an inexpensive choice for handling requests that are received by a network, in an efficient and accurate manner.

RRDNS functions when the domain tables are filled with multiple address records (called A records) that have the same hostname but point to one or more IP addresses that serve the same Web content. We accomplish this task by editing the DNS configuration file on the server (for our example, bedrock.dns). As the DNS request looks for your DNS server, the Web server responds to the client with the next address from the list. The client uses that DNS address for as long as the time-to-live (TTL) value that has been assigned in that domain's zone file (i.e., a file that contains all the DNS records and configuration files for that DNS domain). You can optionally assign specific TTL values to individual records as well.

RRDNS is comparable to Network Load Balancing Service (NLBS), which requires you to configure multiple IP addresses on one server. Although the cost of RRDNS might be attractive, there is one significant drawback to this service: DNS really has no way of knowing whether the Web server is answering properly. DNS isn't sensitive to the state of a Web server and will continue to route traffic to it,

**FIGURE 5-6**

Split-Brain DNS Servers Provide Name Resolution for Internal and External Networks Separately

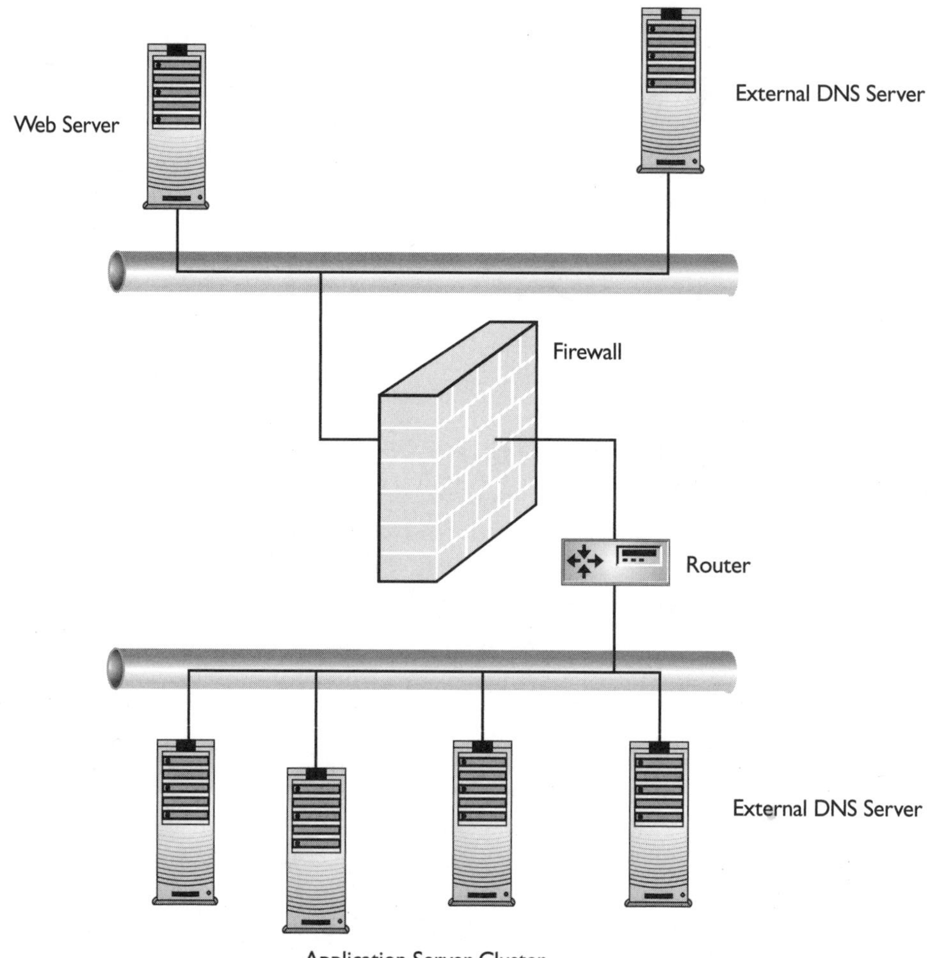


even if the server is down. One other significant drawback that should be mentioned is that round-robin works only with static content. If the pages being called have dynamic content and code, requiring a session to be maintained when it is opened, RRDNS will not work. A DNS configuration using NLB would be more favorable in those circumstances.

**EXERCISE 5-2**

CertCam 5-2

### Setting Up Split DNS Servers

For this exercise, you need two Windows 2000 servers, each configured for a different network, as shown in Figure 5-6 in the split-brain DNS section.

On the external DNS server:

1. Click Start, select Settings, and then select Control Panel.
2. Double-click Administrative Tools, and then double-click the DNS icon to launch the DNS Manager.
3. Under DNS Manager, the server name appears. Click the Action menu and select "Configure the server."
4. The DNS Configuration Wizard is launched, as shown in Figure 5-7.
5. Create a forward lookup zone so that hostnames can be resolved to IP addresses.
6. Create the forward lookup zone file.

**FIGURE 5-7**

DNS Server Configuration Wizard Used to Configure DNS Zones

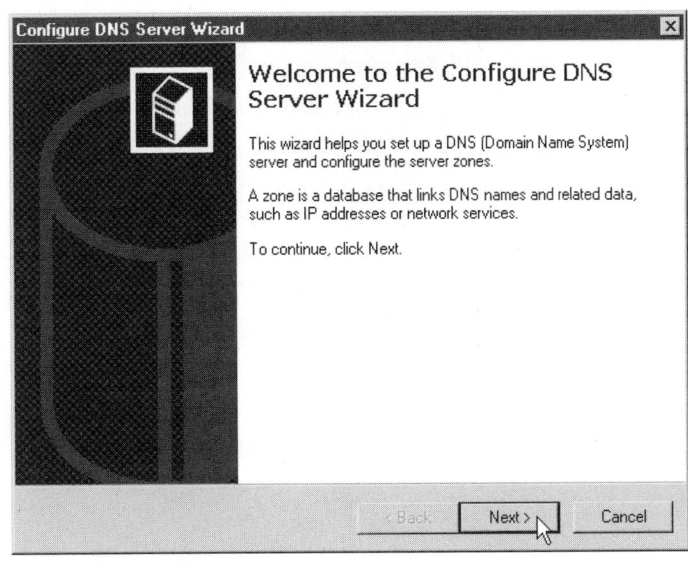

FIGURE 5-8

Configure Forwarders to Resolve Queries This DNS Server Cannot Resolve

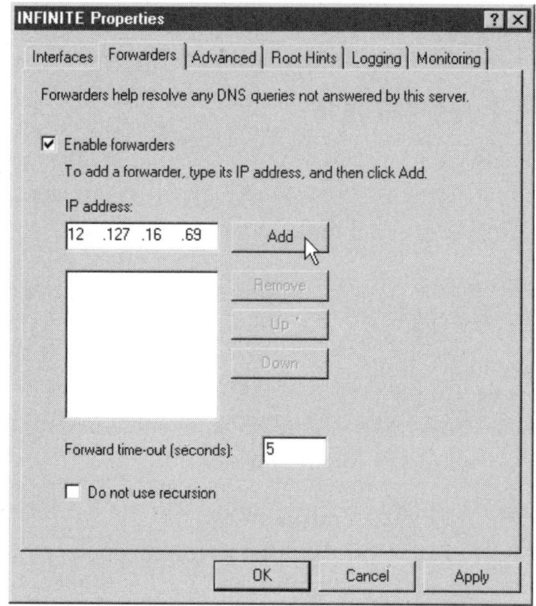


7. Create the reverse lookup zone so that IP addresses can be matched to hostnames.
8. Create the reverse lookup zone file.
9. Highlight the DNS server, then right-click and select Properties.
10. Click the Forwarders tab and add other external DNS servers that this server will query if it receives a request for a name it cannot resolve, as shown in Figure 5-8. Click Apply.

---

Let's take a look at the following scenario and solution examples.

| SCENARIO & SOLUTION | |
|---|---|
| What is a benefit of creating subdomains within our network? | The benefit of creating subdomains is that by creating them, we split up DNS domains, which provides us with quicker search results. |
| What is split-brain DNS? | Split-brain DNS (also known as *split DNS*) refers to using separate internal and external DNS views of your domain's network using internal and external DNS servers. |
| With DNS can I have two computers use the same hostname on the network? | Yes. When you use DNS, two computers can share the same hostname on the network, even on the Internet. This is because DNS is not flat. You can have two machines with the same hostnames but not the same NetBIOS name or the same FQDN. |

## CERTIFICATION OBJECTIVE 5.03

# Understanding DHCP

*Dynamic Host Configuration Protocol (DHCP)* was derived from the Internet standard Bootstrap Protocol (BOOTP), which allowed dynamic assignment of IP addresses. DHCP eliminates the need for manually configuring IP information within your enterprise. The only exception to this rule is for servers that require static IP addresses. With DHCP, the TCP/IP information is automatically given to the client when the system boots. DHCP helps significantly reduce the stress of managing TCP/IP in an enterprise network.

DHCP for Windows 2000 Server is a significant enhancement over DHCP in Windows NT 4.0. These enhancements make Windows 2000 DHCP easier to deploy, manage, and maintain. The enhancements are as follows:

- **Integration with DNS** This could be the single most important improvement in DHCP for Microsoft to date. Integration of DHCP with DNS results in true dynamic IP address management. The DHCP server is able to update pointer (PTR) records for DHCP clients in the DNS hierarchy. DHCP clients are able to receive FQDNs from DNS as well. This allows the DHCP server to be configured to perform the name registration of down-level clients such as Windows NT, Windows 95/98, and Windows 2000 DDNS by registering an A record and a PTR record for the client on its behalf.

- **New vendor-specific options and user class support** Vendor-specific options allow Windows 2000 DHCP server to be aware of various features available in vendor devices. DHCP looks up the configuration that best suits a certain vendor and supplies the options to the device on address assignment. User class support allows DHCP clients to specify whether they are a workstation, a laptop, a desktop, or a handheld device. An administrator can then use this information to configure the DHCP server to assign options to clients based on the type of device they are.
- **Multicast address allocation** A DHCP server can now assign addresses to multicast groups as well as unicast (single-host) addresses. These addresses are used to communicate with specific groups of hosts on a network—for example, with server clusters using the NLBS.
- **Unauthorized DHCP server detection** When a DHCP server is installed, it must be manually authorized to provide service to client on a network. An administrator manually assigns the DHCP server in Active Directory as a valid DHCP server that services client requests. When a DHCP server comes online, it contacts the Active Directory database to find out whether it is on the list of authorized DHCP servers. If it is, the server then broadcasts a DHCPINFORM message to find out if it is authorized in other directory databases as well. If it either does not contact another database or is not on that directory's list of authorized servers, it will not service client requests from that directory. A Windows 2000 DHCP server will service only those clients in the directory it is authorized to service. All other requests will be ignored.
- **Clustering** DHCP is one of the native Windows 2000 services than can benefit from the reliability of Windows 2000 Cluster Services. DHCP servers can be clustered to provide increased availability. Cluster Services can work with DHCP so that if a DHCP server in a cluster fails, the scope and namespace information is rewritten on a surviving node transparently. Clustering also precludes the need to split scopes between DHCP servers, as was previously done to provide fault tolerance and availability.

All these enhancements make for a much more powerful and efficient addressing mechanism using DHCP.

Several requirements must be met when installing DHCP in a Windows 2000 network. First, any computer that runs the DHCP Server service must be either a Windows NT 4.0 server or a Windows 2000 server. Static IP addresses must be used on the server running the DHCP Server service. The DHCP server must have a static IP address so that it is not possible for its own IP address to change. If the IP address were to change on the DHCP server, the clients would be forced to register repeatedly, because they would be unable to find the server.

When the DHCP service is installed, a DHCP scope must be configured and activated. The scope can have certain IP addresses excluded, as well as make reservations for other IP addresses. Reserved IP addresses are usually specifically set aside for infrastructure servers and network devices. For a client to be DHCP enabled, the operating system must be one of the following, and all must be configured to use TCP/IP:

- Windows 2000, Windows 95 or later, or Windows NT 3.51 or later
- Windows for Workgroups 3.11 running TCP/IP-32
- MS-DOS with the Microsoft Network Client 3.0 (with real mode TCP/IP driver)
- LAN Manager 2.2c for DOS

To understand more fully how DHCP dynamic address allocation works, you must be aware of the four-phase process, known as the *DHCP IP address acquisition process,* and what occurs during each phase of that process. The four phases are actually four "conversations" that take place between the client and the DHCP server. The four phases are Discover (DHCPDISCOVER), Offer (DHCPOFFER), Request (DHCPREQUEST), and Acknowledgment (DHCPACK). If the address assignment process is not successful, the fourth phase is a negative acknowledgment (DHCPNACK), which we also briefly discuss in this section.

*DHCPDISCOVER* consists of a client broadcasting to the network in an attempt to communicate with the DHCP server. The broadcast packets always contain the Media Access Control (MAC) address and the computer name. Additional information is included in the broadcast: a parameter request list, which includes the DHCP option codes that the client supports; a message ID that is sent with each message that the client and server send regarding this particular request; and the type of network interface card that the client is running. Because the client does not know where the DHCP server is located and does not have an IP address itself , it uses 0.0.0.0 as the source and 255.255.255.255 as the destination. As you are aware, broadcasts cannot be routed, so there must either be a local DHCP server, or a relay agent of some type must exist on the local subnet. Usually a DHCP relay agent, in every subnet, will route DHCP broadcasts to the nearest DHCP server.

*DHCPOFFER* is the second phase of the four-phase process. Once the server has been located through the DHCPDISCOVER process, the following configuration information is broadcast to the client: the IP address that is being offered to the client, the subnet mask, the lease length—which can be changed to whatever length is desired in the DHCP Administrator MMC snap-in—and the IP address of the DHCP server. As soon as the configuration information has been sent to the client, the IP address is flagged to ensure that it is not given out to another client.

In the third phase of the process, known as *DHCPREQUEST*, the client returns a message to the DHCP server acknowledging that it accepts the IP configuration information that was received in the DHCPOFFER. If other DHCP servers also offer IP addresses, their offers are denied; the IP addresses that they offered are released, and those IP addresses are put back in the pool of available IP addresses.

In the final phase, the *DHCPACK* phase, the DHCP server sends one final message to the client. This message is a response to the client's acceptance of IP information, and it contains the TCP/IP configuration data from WINS or DNS servers.

As mentioned previously, the fourth phase could also be a negative response called *DHCPNACK*, which does not always occur. This phase occurs when the DHCPREQUEST fails. This could happen when the client is trying to lease an old address that is no longer available or is being used. In this case, the server sends a negative broadcast, the DHCPNACK, and the process is starts over. Figure 5-9 illustrates the DHCP addressing process.

The lease renewal begins when 50 percent of the lease time is up. After 50 percent of the lease time has been used, the client sends a DHCPREQUEST to the DHCP server to renew its lease. If the DHCP server allows the lease to be renewed, the lease time in its internal database will be updated and the DHCPACK will be sent with the updated lease time. If the client is unable to contact the DHCP server when 50 percent of the lease time is up, the client will attempt to make contact once again when 50 percent of the remaining lease time has been exhausted. This equates to

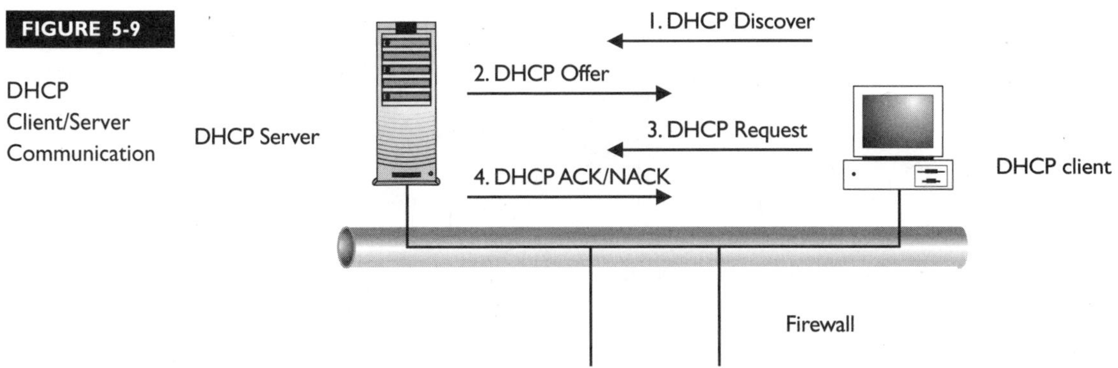


FIGURE 5-9 DHCP Client/Server Communication

87.5 percent of the total lease time. If the lease expires or a DHCPNACK is received, the client's current IP address is released and the lease process begins again.

## Planning DHCP Servers

There are a few factors to consider when planning a DHCP server deployment. The network topology, number of hosts per DHCP server, and placement of the DHCP server are all critical determinants of a DHCP server configuration. Network topology is discussed in the section on DHCP in routed and switched environments. In this section, we examine the other two factors.

The first factor we need to consider is the number of DHCP servers we need to configure and the addressing scheme we will use. The number of DHCP servers we decide to use depends on the number of clients we intend to support, the number of subnets we are servicing, and the IP address class we plan to use. On a small LAN, with 254 hosts (the numerical limit for a Class C network) or less, using a Class C addressing scheme, one DHCP server with one configured address scope is adequate. However, if more than 254 hosts exist on the network and the media can handle the traffic, we could use a Class B addressing scheme (which has a numerical host limit of 65534) or multiple Class C address scopes on a single DHCP server.

Another way to deal with having more clients than a single scope can accommodate is to use *superscopes.* A superscope is basically a series of contiguous scopes organized into one logical group. Multiple DHCP servers can also be used to service larger numbers of clients. If we are using at least two servers, we might want to configure them with overlapping scopes in an 80/20 fashion. This means that each machine is responsible for 80 percent of its scope and 20 percent of the other server's scope.

This helps balance the DHCP traffic load and creates some measure of redundancy in the network. Figure 5-10 shows the DHCP Manager console of a server that is configured to use superscopes.

The placement of DHCP servers is another critical factor that influences our deployment. To avoid added configuration, DHCP clients must have a local DHCP server with which they can communicate. For networks that are segmented, each segment should ideally have its own DHCP server. This is advisable especially if the segments are separated by slow WAN links. In situations in which a DHCP server cannot be provided to the remote network, a computer can be configured as a DHCP relay agent to pass DHCP traffic it collects from its local network to the remote network that hosts the DHCP server.

on the Job

***For networks that use superscopes, all contiguous subnets can use the same default gateway unless separated by a router. For instance, the subnet shown in Figure 5-10 can use the same default gateway (172.16.10.1).***

**FIGURE 5-10**

A DHCP Server That Uses Superscopes

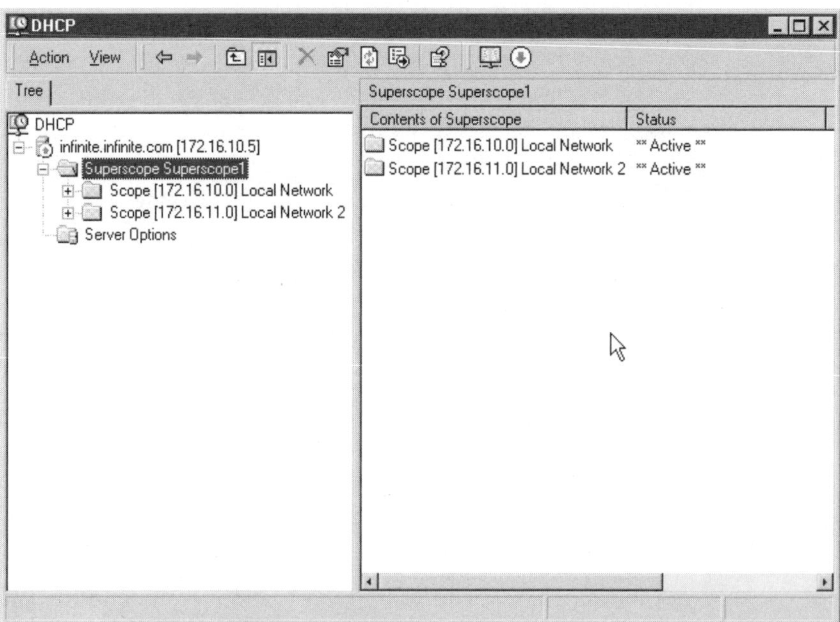

## Routed and Switched Environments with DHCP

Things can get pretty interesting when you are deploying DHCP in a routed and switched network environment. Since DHCP clients use broadcasts to initially locate the local DHCP server, special modifications might have to be made for DHCP in a routed environment, where the DHCP server might be on a different subnet from the client. Since routers are designed by default to ignore broadcasts and not pass them on, a DHCP client that is separated from the DHCP server by a router will not be able to contact the DHCP server and will have to resort to automatic client configuration. Figure 5-11 illustrates this scenario.

**FIGURE 5-11**

By Default, Routers Reject DHCP Broadcast Messages from Clients on Remote Subnets

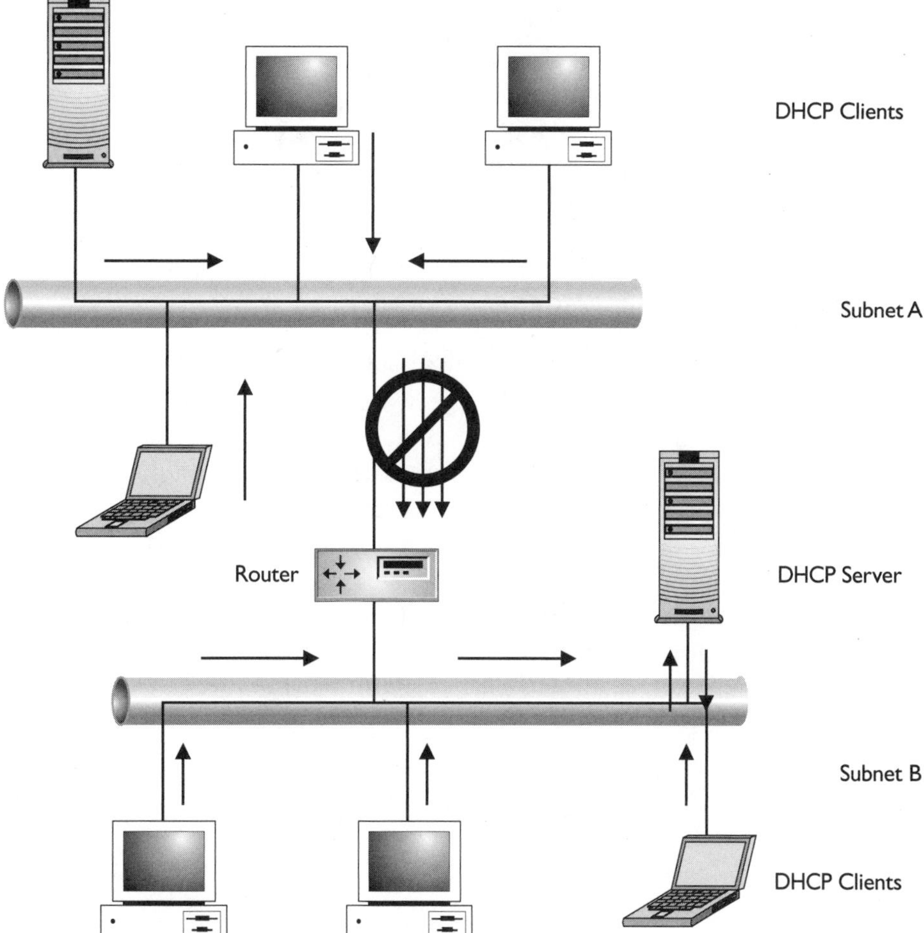

As we can see in Figure 5-11, unless the router is specifically configured to do so, it will not forward the DHCP/BOOTP broadcast messages that DHCP clients initially send.

exam Watch

***Automatic client configuration is also known as*** *automatic IP addressing*. ***This is an addressing technique used only by Windows 2000 Professional and Windows 98 clients when they are unable to contact a DHCP server. The clients automatically assign themselves an IP address in the range 169.254.0.0 with a subnet mask of 255.255.0.0.***

There are three remedies to this dilemma. The first resolution is to configure a computer on the subnet as a DHCP relay agent; this computer is remote from the one that the DHCP server is on. The relay agent accepts broadcasts from DHCP clients on its local subnet and forwards them in a directed unicast to the remote DHCP server. The DHCP server replies to the agent, which then broadcasts the address of the DHCP server to the client on its local subnet. Once the clients know the address of the DHCP server, they can communicate with the server directly across the router.

exam Watch

***For the DHCP relay scenario to work, your router must be able to forward BOOTP or DHCP relay traffic.***

The second remedy is to install another Network Interface Card (NIC) into the DHCP server and configure it with an address on the remote subnet. This extra card should then be connected to the remote subnet so that the DHCP server has an interface that is local to that subnet and is therefore able to directly service that subnet. This is not the most practical remedy, however, since there is a limit to how many NICs a server will hold. In addition, the physical distance between subnets might be too great to enable a physical connection.

The third solution would be to configure the router that separates the networks to forward DHCP/BOOTP messages. If the router is not capable of doing this, an OS upgrade that will enable the router to pass on these messages should be researched and applied to the router if possible. Otherwise, a router capable of forwarding BOOTP messages should be used in its place. Figures 5-12, 5-13, and 5-14 illustrate each of the three remedies.

**FIGURE 5-12**

Using a DHCP Relay Agent to Forward DCHP Traffic

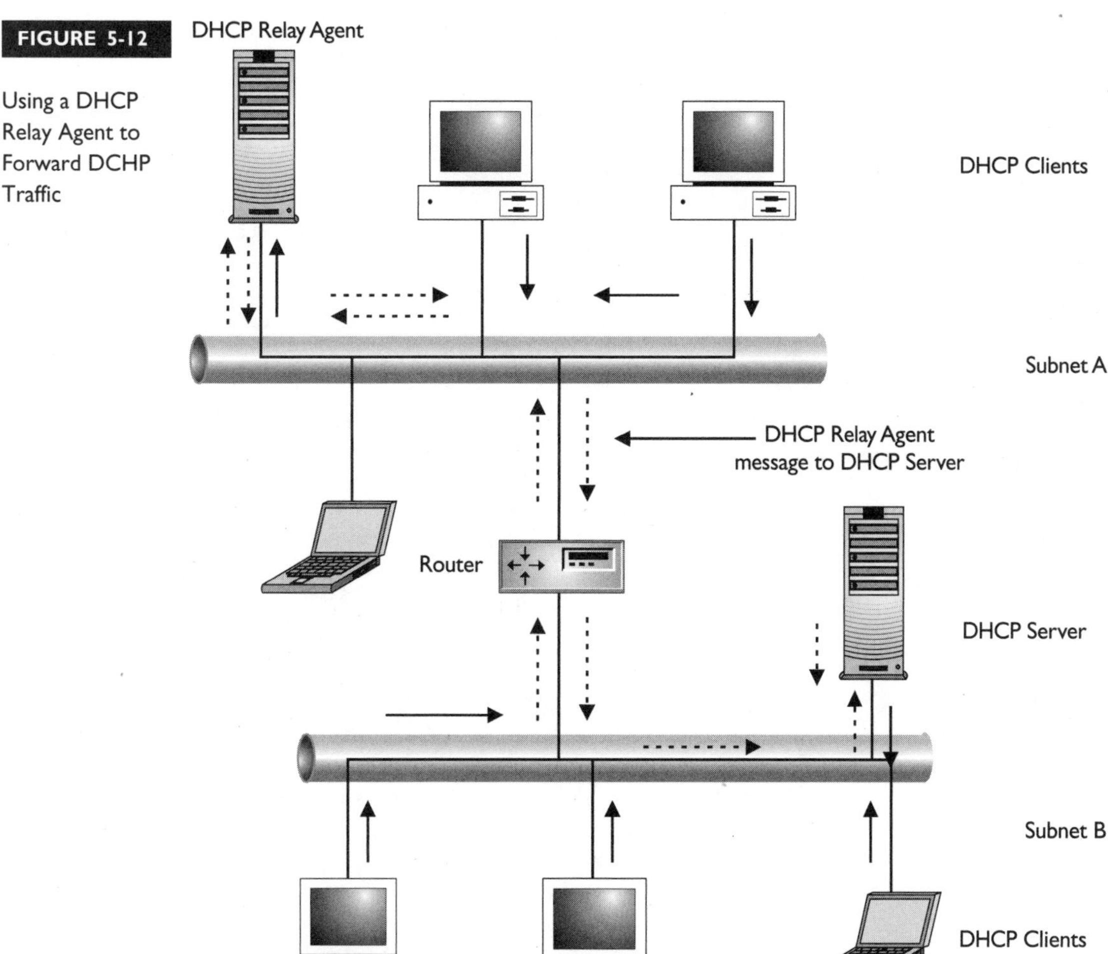

FIGURE 5-13

A Second NIC Can Create an Interface on a Remote Subnet for DHCP Server

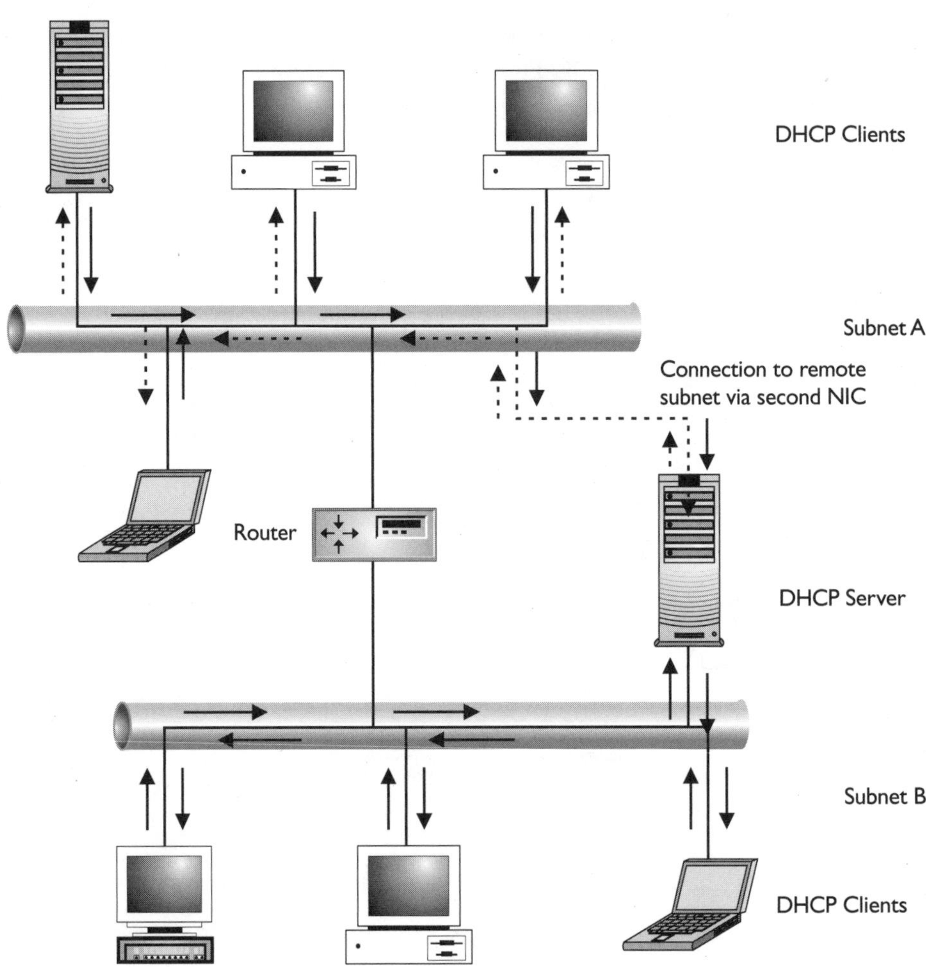

**FIGURE 5-14**

Configuring a Router to Forward BOOTP/DHCP Messages

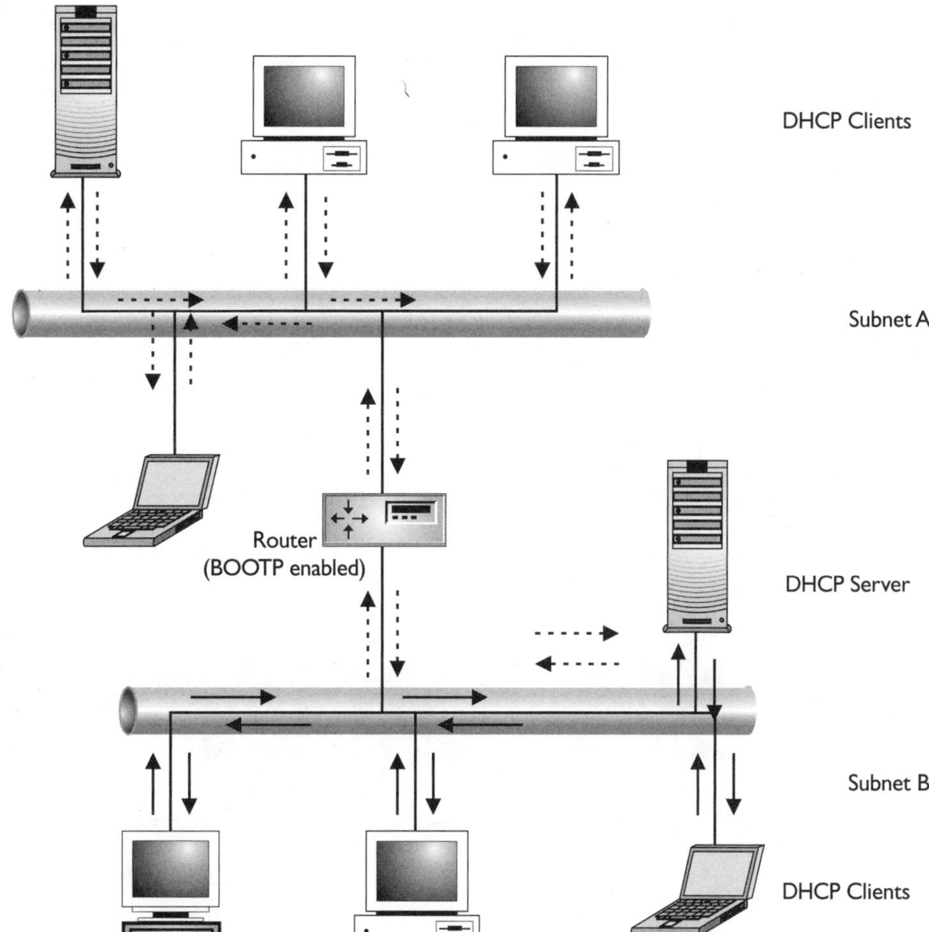

**EXERCISE 5-3**

## Setting Up a Simple DHCP Scope

This exercise involves setting up a DHCP server and one scope for a small, Class C network. You'll configure the DNS, WINS, and default gateway options in addition to the IP address range in the scope. Do the following:

1. Click Start, click Settings, and then click Control Panel.
2. Double-click the Add/Remove Programs icon.
3. Click the Add/Remove components button.
4. Click Next to run the Installation Wizard.

Now let's look at some scenarios and solutions related to DHCP.

| SCENARIO & SOLUTION | |
|---|---|
| How does the client receive the TCP/IP information when using DHCP? | When using DHCP, the TCP/IP information is automatically given to the client when the system boots. |
| What are the four phases of the lease process in DHCP? | The four phases are:<br>Discover (DHCPDISCOVER)<br>Offer (DHCPOFFER)<br>Request (DHCPREQUEST)<br>Acknowledgment (DHCPACK) *or*<br>Negative acknowledgment (DHCPNACK) |
| How can I provide DHCP service to clients on remote subnets with only one DHCP server? | Any of three ways:<br>1. Configure a DHCP relay agent on each remote subnet.<br>2. Add a NIC in your DHCP server for each subnet.<br>3. Configure the router between the subnet to forward BOOTP/DHCP traffic. |

CERTIFICATION OBJECTIVE 5.04

# Designing Other TCP/IP Services

Our discussion on designing a TCP/IP infrastructure that is capable of servicing a highly available Web infrastructure will have no meaning unless we discuss the very services we are building an infrastructure to support—the actual Web services.

Windows 2000 sports a new version of HTTP server, Internet Information Services 5.0 (IIS 5.0). IIS 5.0 brings all the functionality that was possessed by its predecessor, IIS 4.0. IIS 5.0, however, also brings new capacities and new features and enhancements on old features to maximize its performance.

In the following sections, we look at IIS 5.0 as well as its companion services, File Transfer Protocol (FTP) and the Simple Mail Transport Protocol (SMTP). We will see how they function and learn about their enhancements that increase their reliability and robustness.

## HTTP

Keeping top performance, scalability, reliability, and security in mind, let's discuss the importance of *HyperText Transfer Protocol (HTTP)* in our highly available network infrastructure. HTTP, which is an application protocol, is the set of rules used for exchanging files on the Internet. HTTP is implemented over TCP/IP. In building a highly available Web solution, HTTP is a critical success factor. If we are going to build a highly available Web infrastructure, we need a high-performance HTTP server at the center of it. Windows 2000 IIS 5.0 provides such a high-performance HTTP server.

IIS 5.0 includes all the features of its predecessor, IIS 4.0, such as the ability to host different Web sites on different virtual Web servers. Virtual Web servers can even use folders on other servers to host the files for a Web site. This allows for a Webmaster to host multiple Web sites or Web domains on the same server, either all with the same IP address or each with its own IP address. It provides the ability to use different port numbers for different Web sites or Web pages. For example, a Web site can have its public information on pages hosted on the default port 80 and confidential information on pages hosted on the Secure Sockets Layer (SSL) port 443. Figures 5-15 and 5-16 give examples of the Web server using virtual servers, virtual folders, and the SSL port.

**FIGURE 5-15**

A Web Server That Uses a Virtual Directory

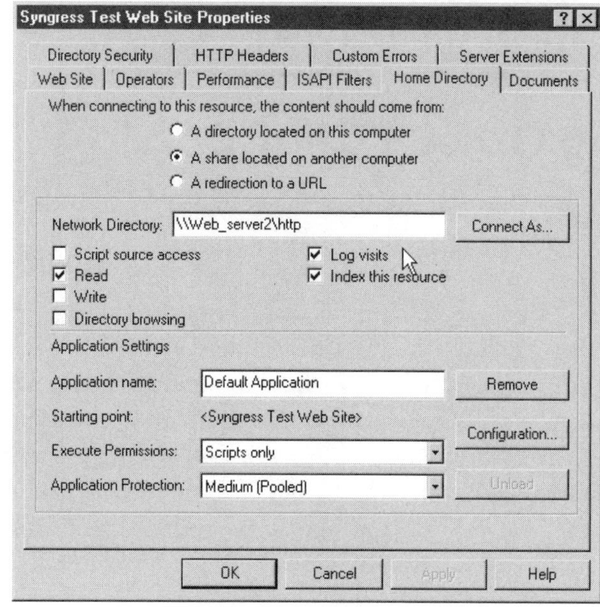


**FIGURE 5-16**

A Web Site That Uses the SSL (443) Port

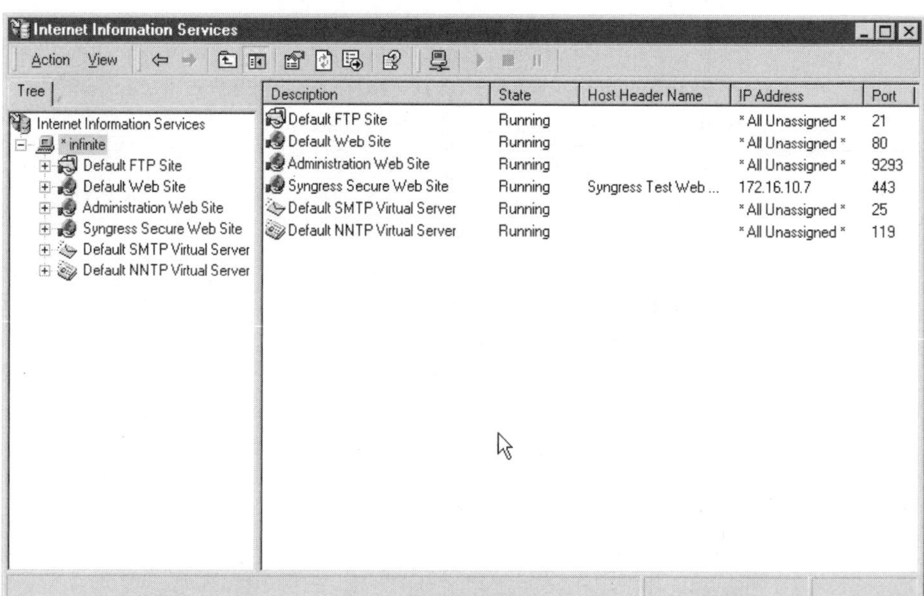

IIS 5.0 runs within Windows 2000 and incorporates advanced features to improve reliability, performance, management, security, and application services above that offered in IIS 4.0. These are all features that we need to consider when designing our infrastructure. IIS 5.0 is fully integrated at the operating system level, which allows organizations to quickly and easily add Internet capabilities that mesh directly into the rest of the infrastructure.

Let's examine reliability and performance more in depth with IIS 5.0. A number of significant features help make IIS more reliable and enhance performance. The reliable restart feature is one aspect of IIS that allows for easier and faster restart of Web services without rebooting. An added feature, application protection, helps improve reliability, providing the ability to run applications in a pool, separate from Web services. Another feature that helps to improve reliability is the CPU throttling and socket-pooling feature, which helps control resource consumption. Administrators can allocate the amount of CPU bandwidth available to processes and the amount of network bandwidth available to sites.

Performance is a huge concern in our network. If our organization is to be successful, we must run at peak performance. If there is a problem with an application, we can't take the risk of having that problem affect everything. To protect ourselves from that type of problem, we might want to consider using the process isolation feature that is a standard option within the Internet Service Manager (ISM) console. Using the process isolation feature protects our main IIS process by having Web applications run in their own memory space. This provides us with an improvement in server stability. Prior versions of IIS did not offer the ability to set isolation levels, but IIS 5.0 allows the user to set the levels at low, medium, or high, under the application protection setting in the ISM console. The medium setting is the default for Active Server Pages (ASPs) in IIS 5.0. The medium setting functions so that every Web application set to medium shares the same instance of DLLHOST.EXE.

With IIS 5.0, the reliable reset feature is a significant improvement for reliability. In the past when there was a system failure, the system would have to be rebooted, starting up four separate services after every stoppage. The administrator needed specialized knowledge of the syntax of the Net command. With the reliable reset feature, the administrator is able to restart Web services without rebooting the computer. The new feature is used to restart services automatically if they fail. This obviously helps with reliability, because there is no delay between the time a service goes down and the time it restarts. The drawback to such a feature is that an administrator might not be immediately aware of a potential problem because the service is automatically reset. The Event Log must be monitored regularly for such issues to ensure that a serious problem isn't at the root of the restart.

The many features included with IIS 5.0 are only enhanced when IIS 5.0 is clustered for availability, performance, and fault tolerance. IIS 5.0 servers can be clustered using either Network Load Balancing Services, Cluster Services, or a combination of both to dramatically increase performance, reliability, and fault tolerance in a Web infrastructure. A server cluster created using Network Load Balancing enables a Webmaster to create an extremely high-availability Web site across multiple servers using a single or multiple IP addresses. In Chapter 4, we saw that the preferred topology for a high-availability Web infrastructure is a two-network configuration. This configuration consists of a front-end Web server network, where Web server clusters reside outside a firewall or a router with packet filtering configured, and a back-end application/database server network, where clustered database or application servers reside. The front-end Web servers are configured to communicate with the back-end servers through the firewall and across a router separating the two networks.

This configuration—besides being efficient—is very secure and protects the data stored by the application/database servers. The Web servers and any applications they host contain no critical data, so if they are compromised, no serious damage is done. Additionally, since the Web servers are clustered, they are made fault tolerant.

Other areas of IIS 5.0 provide benefits as well. In addition to the reliability and performance features that we discussed, management of IIS 5.0 is also important to note. IIS 5.0 is easier to install and maintain than previous versions. We all know what a benefit that is, especially when it comes to installation. IIS 5.0 has a simplified installation process, a new security task wizard, flexible remote administration, and the ability to account for time used by processes. IIS 5.0 is now installed as part of the Windows 2000 installation process. This allows for the simplification of maintenance tasks because administration utilities are accessed from a central location, there are remote administration options, and administrators can delegate tasks to selected users. All of these features make an administrator's job much easier.

We can't really talk about building a highly available Web solution and not mention security. Although this topic is not the focus of this particular chapter, it certainly does fit into this section. As mentioned previously, traditional security on a Web server was implemented using SSL on port 443 on IIS. IIS 5.0 adds support for industry-standard security protocols besides SSL. These protocols include Kerberos v5 authentication, Transport Layer Security, Digest Authentication, Server Gated Cryptography, and Fortezza. In addition, security task wizards aid an administrator in managing a site's security settings. Table 5-2 provides a brief overview of the five major security mechanisms that are used in IIS 5.0.

Knowing how important performance, reliability, security, manageability, and scalability are within our infrastructure, IIS 5.0 fits nicely into our planned architecture. By employing IIS 5.0, our Web server will be able to support a broad range of requirements.

## FTP

*File Transfer Protocol (FTP)* has been the protocol of choice for transmitting large amounts of data over a TCP/IP network since it was included in the TCP/IP suite in the early 1970s. An FTP server has been part of Microsoft's IIS server since its original iteration in 1995. Over the years, FTP has become the most popular file transfer mechanism on the Internet. FTP uses TCP at the Transport layer; therefore, all data that is exchanged between the FTP server and the client is assured to be delivered, both intact as originally sent and in a timely manner. A similar file transfer protocol, Trivial File Transfer Protocol (TFTP), uses the connectionless Transport layer protocol UDP to upload and download data. FTP is the transport mechanism that many (if not most) Internet content management solutions use.

**TABLE 5-2** Security Mechanisms Used in IIS 5.0

| Mechanism | Meaning |
|---|---|
| Authentication | Verifies user identity. IIS 5.0 employs the following four types of authentication:<br>Anonymous<br>Basic FTP<br>Anonymous FTP<br>Integrated Windows |
| Access control | Protects access to contact. |
| Auditing | Monitors security-related activity on Web site. |
| Encryption | Prevents tampering of content. |
| Certificates | Securely send/receive site identity information. |

## FTP Architecture

Understanding an FTP server's architecture will assist us in both configuration and troubleshooting, so let's cover the basics. Figure 5-17 shows the position that FTP occupies in the Department of Defense (DoD) TCP/IP and the Open Systems Interconnect (OSI) models.

The FTP application resides in the Application layer but uses the Transport layer protocol TCP through ports 20 and 21 to actually perform the file transfers. FTP uses TCP port 21 for session control and port 20 for data transfer. Any requests sent to the FTP server are completed through port 21. Data transfer is handled by TCP port 20 since port 21 is already in use. We need to connect to another port because only one service at a time can use a port.

**FIGURE 5-17** **FTP Architecture**

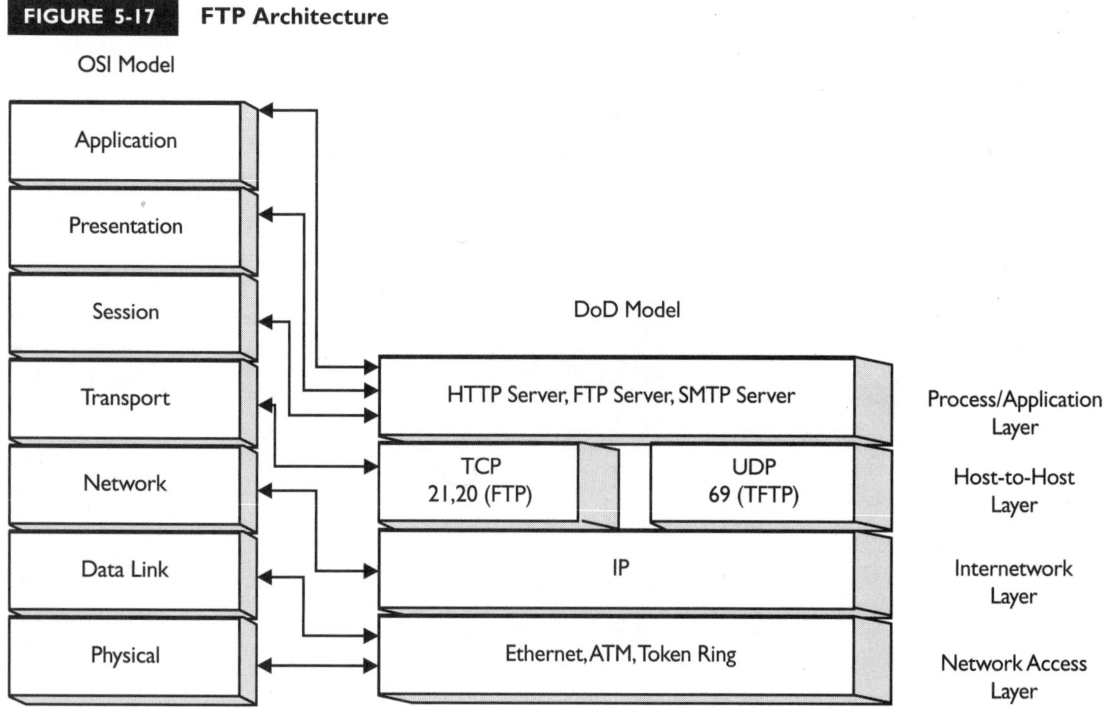

**EXERCISE 5-4**

## Configuring FTP

In this exercise, you will perform a little advanced configuration on an FTP server to automatically place a user using this server into his own directory and limit access on the FTP server to the FTP directory. Do the following:

1. In Windows Explorer, place the FTP directory under the \inetpub\wwwroot directory.
2. In the IIS snap-in, point the FTP server to the FTP directory.
3. Also in the IIS snap-in, create a second FTP server under the first and give the second one the same name as the username of the client who wants to upload files.
4. Point the second FTP server to the FTP directory (the same one as in Step 2).
5. In Windows Explorer, set the following NTFS permissions on the FTP directory: Give Anonymous FTP User Full Control on the FTP directory and Deny All Permissions on the root directory.

   After a user logs on, IIS places the authenticated client in the virtual FTP site of the same name. The client has full control over directory content and can upload files. An anonymous user who logs on can read the files but will have no control over them and won't be able to browse outside the virtual FTP directory.

**exam Watch** ***FTP server security can also be assured by assigning the correct NTFS permissions to grant the IUSR_computername account only the file and directory access we want to grant.***

### FTP Site Properties

The default FTP server that IIS 5.0 installs is configured and ready to go with anonymous access immediately after installation. Let's take a quick look at two options that are important in the FTP Site Properties tab. The first option is IP Address. The IP Address option allows for FTP virtual servers, a configuration that is available only in IIS 4 and 5. This feature allows us to configure multiple FTP virtual servers on one server machine. Since FTP does not consume many system resources, this is an advantageous option. Figure 5-18 displays the FTP Site Properties window with the IP address field using the (All Unassigned) option.

Chances are that when configuring virtual servers, you will configure one FTP virtual server for each Web virtual server that is configured. As with Web virtual servers, only one FTP virtual server can be configured with the IP address of All Unassigned. What this means is that IIS can support a single default FTP site for any IP address that is not specifically assigned to an individual virtual server. The All Unassigned option refers to all IP addresses configured in Windows 2000 that are not assigned to a specific FTP virtual server. If an IP address is assigned to a Web virtual server but not to an FTP virtual server, it is still unassigned for the FTP service and will be a part of the All Unassigned category when configured for another FTP virtual server.

As mentioned earlier, FTP listens on TCP port 21 by default, but it is possible to change the port for the FTP service, which is the second option that we want to examine. By changing the listening port, we successfully accomplish one thing: We provide basic security. If a user on the Internet knows our Web address and wants to get into our file list, the person could realize that he or she can use the FTP protocol

**FIGURE 5-18**

The FTP Site Properties Screen

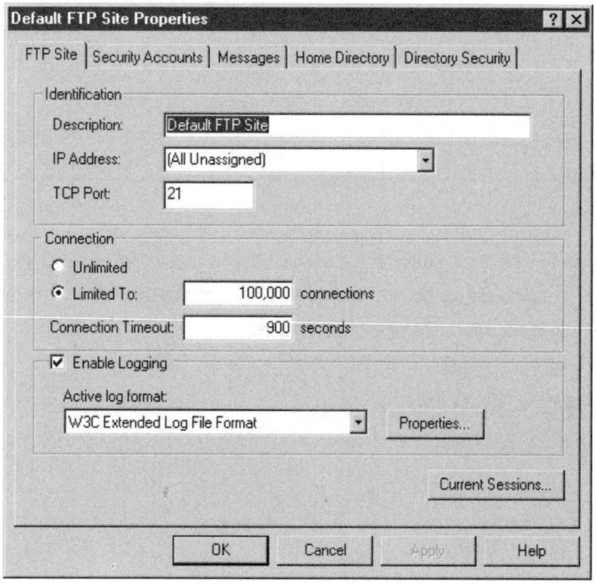

to access the same data. Because most FTP ports request TCP port 21 when attempting to access the data, if we change the FTP listening port, we have taken away the wild guesses. The two possible locations to modify the listening port are as follows:

- The Services file located in the winnt_root\system32\drivers\etc directory
- The Internet Information Services Metabase

Once the listening port has been modified, we need to save the Services file in the same directory, and we cannot give it a file extension name. If we only want to change the FTP listening port for all FTP clients and not the requesting port, we need to change the port in the IIS Metabase. If we want to change the FTP listening port for an individual FTP site, we also need to make that change in the IIS Metabase. Remember that the Metabase stores configuration information for IIS and all its virtual servers as well as virtual directories. To change the FTP listening port in the Metabase, use the FTP Site tab on the FTP Site Properties dialog box. It is important to mention that anyone with a port scanner could determine the new listening port with relative ease.

With IIS 5.0, if the IIS Metabase is configured with a different FTP listening port than is configured in the services file, the result will be that the FTP listening port used by a specific FTP site is the one configured in the IIS Metabase. Let's say that we have the FTP port configured for port 21 in the Services file; we then use the ISM to configure the FTP port for our own Web site to port 1089. When the FTP service starts for our FTP site, it listens on port 1089. This happens because the Metabase overrides the Services file. This also provides us with the ability to configure a different FTP listening port on each individual FTP site. One huge benefit of this functionality is that we are not required to use multiple IP addresses for multiple FTP sites. Rather, we can use one IP address and numerous listening ports for the FTP service. This helps considerably in the event that we would be limited in the number of IP addresses that would be available to us. We are still able to configure and host multiple FTP sites using the same IP address.

In the event that hardware is in short supply and demand for the FTP service is low, the FTP server can be maintained on the same server computer as the Web (HTTP) server. The server can still be used to service clients, either with multiple IP addresses or through different ports. If our FTP server and Web server share the same hardware, we should host the FTP home directory on another computer, perhaps even a back-end network computer, to maintain a high level of performance.

The placement of FTP servers on a network also has significance when it comes to performance and security. FTP is basically a program that allows a user to transfer data between two computers. Leaving a server unprotected on the Internet, outside a firewall, is simply asking to have your server hacked. How then do we create a FTP resource that is both visible and available to clients, yet protected from unwanted exploits?

Microsoft FTP server can be configured to allow anonymous access (the default configuration) or to allow access to only valid members of the computer's or domain user account database. If the Allow Anonymous Connections check box is unchecked, only user accounts on the server (or Active Directory, if the server is part of a Windows 2000 domain) are allowed to log in. This scheme provides some measure of security to the FTP site in that all users who log in to the site must be authenticated. They can also be tracked and audited using the Event Viewer. FTP servers also possess a Directory Security page that can be used to grant or deny access to single hosts, networks, or DNS domains. Figures 5-19 and 5-20 show the Security Accounts page, where user access is defined, and the Directory Security page, where network access is defined.

**FIGURE 5-19**

Security Accounts Tab Showing the Anonymous Access Setting

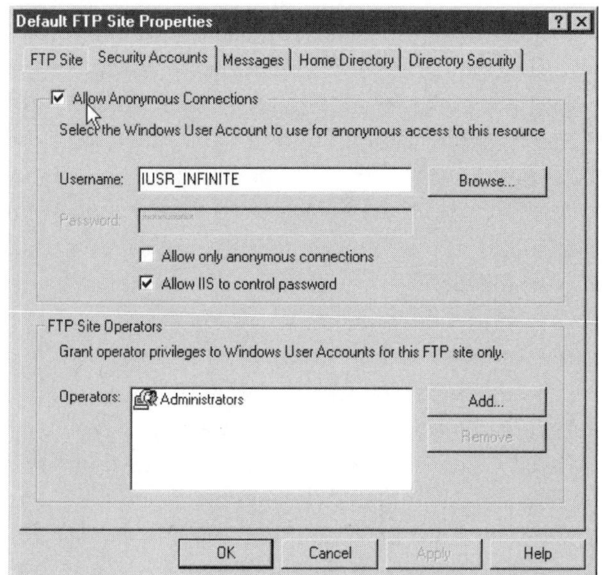

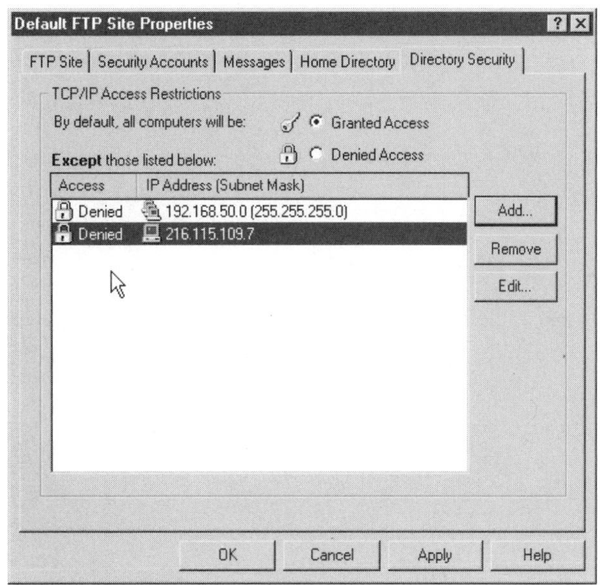


**FIGURE 5-20** Directory Security Is Used to Grant or Deny Access to an FTP Server

**Demilitarized Zones** The term *Demilitarized Zone* or *DMZ* refers to a place on a network where hosts are both visible to the Internet and separate from the rest of the network. Commonly, DMZs are used for securing Web, Internet mail, and FTP servers while giving them accessibility from the Internet. A DMZ is usually a separate network "grown" from a firewall or router interface that is not routed to or through an enterprise's private network. Physically, the server computer sits in the same place as the other computers on your network, but it is logically isolated.

Apart from isolation from a private network, the other factor that secures the DMZ is that filters can be applied to the firewall or router from which the DMZ originates. All unnecessary ports can be closed, leaving open only the ports that clients need to communicate with the server. In addition, certain networks can be blocked at the router or firewall via access lists. Figure 5-21 illustrates the concept of a DMZ with Web and FTP servers in relation to a private network.

## SMTP

*Simple Mail Transfer Protocol,* or *SMTP,* is the protocol that allows a server to accept, process, and forward electronic mail (e-mail) over networks. SMTP is the standard mail protocol for TCP/IP as originally defined in RFCs 821 and 822.

**FIGURE 5-21** Web and FTP Servers Reside in the DMZ to Make Them Safe But Available

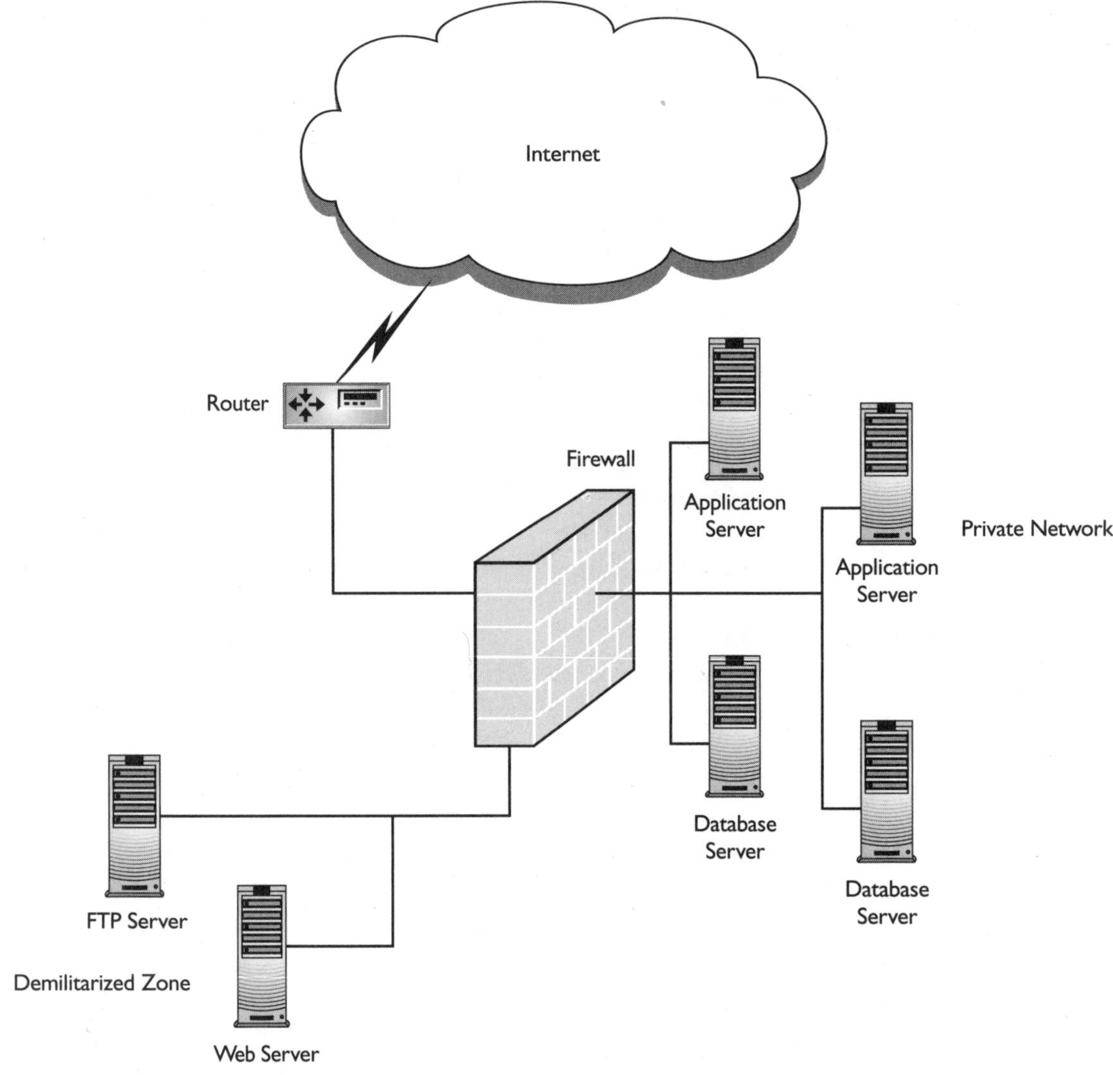


SMTP uses TCP port 25 to send and receive data; therefore, it is a connection-oriented service. Webmasters use SMTP servers as part of Microsoft IIS 5.0 to give Web sites e-mail functionality. An SMTP server is capable of delivering e-mail both locally and

remotely over the Internet to Web clients. Web applications can easily be designed to take advantage of the functionality of the SMTP service—for example, to send registration confirmation e-mails from a registration page on a Web site. The SMTP service included with IIS 5.0 is not an enterprise-level mail solution. For an SMTP solution that is capable of providing service to an enterprise, Microsoft Exchange Server is a great choice.

When Exchange Server 2000 is used, the ideal situation is to offload the SMTP service from the Exchange 2000 server to the IIS server. As with an FTP server, if hardware is available so that a separate server can be used for offloading the SMTP function, the server hosting the SMTP service should be outside the private network on the other side of the firewall. In this case, since the SMTP server must transfer mail to and from the Exchange server, the server can be immediately outside the firewall on the same network as the Internet router. Having the servers separate, on different networks, both protects the Exchange server from attack and improves on performance, since each machine is running only dedicated functions.

SMTP is configured as a virtual server on IIS 5.0. We can create more virtual servers as the need arises, as is the case with HTTP and FTP servers. Figure 5-22 shows the default STMP virtual server.

**FIGURE 5-22**

A Default SMTP Virtual Server

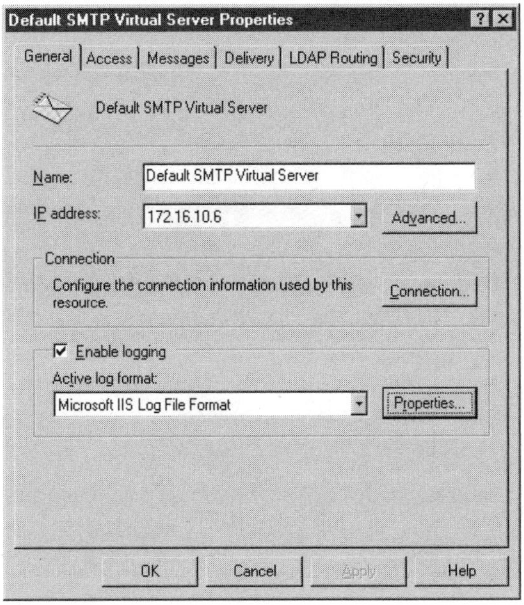

The SMTP server uses a directory called MailRoot in the \inetpub\ directory to contain and process e-mails that it receives or sends. The MailRoot directory contains subdirectories, each of which is concerned with a particular process or function of the SMTP service. The functions associated with each subdirectory are as follows:

- **Drop** The Drop subdirectory is where all incoming messages are placed. Messages for all the domains hosted on a Web server are placed in this directory by the SMTP service.
- **Pickup** The Pickup subdirectory is where outgoing messages are processed. Messages are received into the Pickup subdirectory, which places them in a queue, where they await delivery.
- **Queue** The Queue subdirectory is where messages are sent to from the Pickup delivery to be delivered to recipients. If a message cannot be delivered for some reason, it is held in the queue and delivery is reattempted at designated intervals.
- **Badmail** The Badmail subdirectories store undeliverable mail that cannot be returned to the sender.

Let's take a look at some scenarios and solutions related to the topics covered in this section.

| SCENARIO & SOLUTION | |
|---|---|
| What is considered one of the most important functions of IIS? | Linking clients accessing the system through HTTP to other Windows application services. |
| What port does FTP listen on? | Port 21. |
| Why is the SMTP service included with IIS 5.0? | SMTP is included to enable Web designers to provide basic e-mail functionality in Web sites. |
| What happens to a message that cannot be delivered by the SMTP service? | It gets sent to the Badmail subdirectory. |

# CERTIFICATION SUMMARY

In this chapter, we discussed the elements of designing TCP/IP for a highly available network infrastructure. We learned about the enhancements and new features in Microsoft TCP/IP that Windows 2000 brings and the advantages they afford. We learned about improving network performance and reducing traffic by subnetting networks into small units. We came to understand the concept of subnet addressing and how it is performed. We gained some understanding of how factors such as network topology, network media, and access methods affect the design of a TCP/IP infrastructure.

We examined the major components of a TCP/IP network such as DNS and DHCP, and we talked about the options we could employ to optimize these components in a variety of scenarios. We also touched on the central protocol involved in a Web infrastructure, HTTP, as part of Microsoft's IIS 5.0. We briefly discussed the functionality of FTP and SMTP, the two most widely used services on IIS, next to HTTP. We learned about the features included in IIS 5.0 such as application protection and reliable restart that optimize its performance and make it a much more reliable Web platform than its predecessors.

# TWO-MINUTE DRILL

## Designing a TCP/IP Network Infrastructure

- The first step in designing a robust and flexible network infrastructure from the ground up is to have a design plan that illustrates the completed network. This planning phase should include a drawing of a network diagram.
- One method used to improve performance on networks is to use subnetting, which is done by reducing the number of hosts per network segment by introducing a router or multilayer switch and splitting a larger network into smaller networks.
- Class A networks use the network numbers between 0 and 126. A Class B network uses the numbers between 128 and 191. A Class C network uses the numbers between 192 and 223.
- The number of subnets and the number of hosts per subnet can be calculated using the equation $2^n - 2$, where for subnets $n$ is the number of high-order bits swiped from the default subnet mask and, for the number of hosts, $n$ is the number of remaining bits.

## Understanding DNS

- DNS, by design, is a highly reliable, hierarchical database that is both distributed and scalable.
- The highest level of the DNS hierarchy is the root. The next level is referred to as the top-level domain, this level contains the .com, .gov, .edu, .mil, .org, and .net domains. The next level is the second-level domain. Microsoft.com is an example of a second-level domain. Domains that fall under the second-level domain are called *subdomains*.
- Split DNS is the method of using different servers to handle external and internal queries and information. Employing this method helps eliminate the threat of exposing the structure of the internal network to intruders.
- Round-robin DNS (RRDNS) is one possible method for responding to server queries in the most immediate time frame possible. RRDNS functions in virtually the same manner as Network Load Balance Services.

## Understanding DHCP

- ❑ Dynamic Host Configuration Protocol (DHCP) was derived from the Internet standard Bootstrap Protocol (BOOTP), which allowed dynamic assignment of IP addresses.
- ❑ DHCP helps significantly reduce the stress of managing TCP/IP in an enterprise network by having the TCP/IP information automatically given to the client when the system boots.
- ❑ Automatic client configuration, also known as *automatic IP addressing*, is an addressing technique used by Windows 2000 Professional and Windows 98 clients when they are unable to contact a DHCP server. The clients automatically assign themselves an IP address in the range 169.254.0.0 with a subnet mask of 255.255.0.0.
- ❑ Some factors to consider when planning a DHCP server deployment are network topology, number of hosts per DHCP server, and placement of the DHCP server.

## Designing Other TCP/IP Services

- ❑ IIS 5.0 is fully integrated at the operating system level, which allows organizations to quickly and easily add Internet capabilities that mesh directly into the rest of the infrastructure.
- ❑ The process isolation feature of IIS 5.0 allows applications to run in their own memory space so as not to corrupt the server.
- ❑ FTP uses TCP port 21 for session control and port 20 for data transfer. Unless an administrator specifies a different listening port through the IIS Metabase, any request sent to the FTP server will be completed through port 21.
- ❑ If a change is made to the listening port in the Metabase but not in the Services file, the change will still be valid because the Metabase overrides the Services file in FTP.
- ❑ SMTP is configured as a virtual server on IIS 5.0.

# SELF TEST

The following questions will help you measure your understanding of the material presented in this chapter. Read all the choices carefully because there might be more than one correct answer. Choose all correct answers for each question.

## Designing a TCP/IP Network Infrastructure

**1.** In the design stage of building a robust network infrastructure, what are the key factors that determine the number of hosts that will be needed on the network and the number of subnets needed to properly manage network traffic? (Choose all that apply.)

A. Media type

B. Network bandwidth

C. Network access method

D. Throughput of NICs

**2.** You have just accepted a position with a flourishing company. Business is extremely good—in fact, *too* good. Over the past 90 days, network response time on your Web site network has decreased 20 percent as a result of all the network traffic, and the situation is only getting worse. The first project you are assigned to work on is to improve network performance on the Web site network. After a thorough investigation of the existing network, you notice that there are 400 hosts on each network segment. You immediately determine that this is the reason for the slow network response. How do you remedy this situation? (Choose the two *best* answers.)

A. Add multilayer switches to the segments to break up the collision domains.

B. Further segment the network by adding more routers and changing the addressing.

C. Add more Web server to the network to handle client requests.

D. Create server clusters to consolidate network services to single groups of servers.

**3.** What are the two critical pieces of information that we must know prior to performing subnet addressing? (Choose two.)

A. The IP address class

B. The number of subnets we are trying to create

C. The number of hosts per subnet we are trying to arrive at

D. The default subnet mask of the network we are subnetting

**4.** An organization is having network performance issues—slow response times and trouble accessing the network. The company is a Class C organization and runs with no routers or multilayer switches on its network because, when the original architecture for the infrastructure was being planned, the company was advised that Class C organizations do not use subnetting. The company has only 150 hosts on the network. Is subnetting a viable solution to this problem, and why or why not? (Choose the *best* answer.)

A. Yes. Subnetting always increases network performance.

B. No. Subnetting will not solve the problem if there are so few hosts. There could be other issues, such as the media type or network access method that is employed on the network or even the type of traffic that is generated from applications run on the network. The fact that the company uses shared media hints that the installation of a switch might rectify the problem.

C. No. The company should consider supernetting instead because it actually needs more hosts on the network to improve performance.

D. Yes. Subnetting is an alternative for nonswitched networks that usually improves performance.

**5.** Convert the binary address 1111100110110 to decimal. Which of the following is the correct conversion?

A. 7990

B. 4096

C. 512

D. 8192

## Understanding DNS

**6.** The company you work for is having some network problems on its e-commerce Web site. Nobody is able to fully diagnose the problem and determine what is happening. When the infrastructure was in the planning stages, the anticipated number of daily hits was listed as 5000. After 18 months in business, it is apparent that the estimate was off by almost 400,000 hits per day. The good news is that you are in business to stay. The bad news is that your network can't handle that amount of traffic. Your manager asks you what you see as a solution to the problem. You determine, based on the network employing DNS and RRDNS, that the solution is to add more servers. Your manager disagrees; he thinks the solution is to switch to

Network Load Balancing Services and that will remedy the situation. What is the best possible solution for this problem, and why?

A. Use Network Load Balancing Services. The network load will be redistributed.

B. Use Network Load Balancing Services. Servers will then have more addresses with which to respond to clients.

C. Add more Web servers. You need more servers to respond to clients.

D. Add more Web servers. RRDNS works better the more Web servers you have.

7. You want to register two new subdomains, pebbles.bedrock.com and bambam.bedrock.com, to your bedrock.com domain. The administrator reads the request incorrect and enters the domains as bedrock.pebbles.com and bedrock.bambam.com. What sort of issues would arrive from that mistake, and how could the situation be fixed?

A. The inability to find hosts on the pebbles subdomain. Delete the incorrect subdomain and recreate it using the correct syntax.

B. The inability to find hosts on either subdomain. Leave the subdomains as is; DDNS will fix the problem.

C. The inability to locate hosts on the bambam subdomain. Integrate DNS with DHCP to fix the problem.

D. The inability to locate hosts on either domain. Delete the incorrect subdomains, update the server records, and then recreate the subdomains with the names in the correct order.

8. You have just been promoted to network administrator at your company. The first thing you are asked to do is clean up the domain structure on your network. What you quickly discover is that there are no subdomains created within your entire organization. How do you go about changing the majority of the second-level domains into subdomains?

A. Delete the secondary domains, and then recreate them as subdomains within the remaining secondary domains.

B. Unregister the secondary domains with the InterNIC, move all the hosts under them to another domain or subdomain, and then delete them. Recreate the domains as subdomains of the remaining secondary domains.

C. Right-click the secondary domain folder, then select Properties and select subdomain on the Domain Type tab of the Domain properties screen.

D. Create the subdomains within the secondary domains, and then rename the secondary domains.

**9.** Which of the following describes the benefit of DNS and its hierarchical structure over NetBIOS and the flat structure on which it is based?

A. DNS allows for two hosts to have the same name as long as they are in different subdomains.

B. DNS has a "friendlier" naming system than NetBIOS.

C. DNS allows you to easily find hosts and services on very large networks.

D. DNS in Windows 2000 is dynamically updated.

**10.** Your organization is employing RRDNS to service queries of hosts on the network as they are received. This solution works very well for the amount of requests that are received, and everyone seems satisfied with the response times of the network. The only problem is that occasionally requests are not handled in an immediate manner. There are no notifications sent when this happens. What is the issue? (Choose all that apply.)

A. There is no problem. Sometimes all the DNS serves are busy.

B. RRDNS hosts cannot tell if a host for which they have a record is online or not.

C. The notification options were never set.

D. The requests are for hosts outside the local network.

**11.** Is there a limit to the number of DNS subdomains you can create and manage?

A. Yes, DNS is limited by the number of letters in the alphabet.

B. Yes, the number of DNS subdomains cannot exceed the number of hosts on the network.

C. No, there is no theoretical limit.

D. Yes, the number of subdomains is limited by the network bandwidth.

## Understanding DHCP

**12.** A company is having some difficulties with its network. It runs DHCP on a Windows 2000 network. The company went with this particular infrastructure because it wanted to avoid having to manually configure any IP addresses. The problem is that clients keep losing the servers so that they can't access any services. What can be done to remedy this situation?

A. Use static IP addresses for all servers.

B. Create an LMHOSTS file with the servers' names to IP address mapping and download it to all clients.

C. Create a HOSTS file with the FQDN to IP address mapping for the servers and download it to all clients.

D. Go back to static IP addressing for all computers.

13. What are the operating system requirements for a client to be DHCP-enabled?

A. Windows 2000, Windows 95 or later, or Windows NT 3.51 or later

B. Windows for Workgroups 3.11 running TCP/IP-32

C. Windows 98

D. All of the above

14. What special considerations need to be made when considering a DHCP server deployment? (Choose all that apply.)

A. Whether or not the server has a static IP address

B. The network addressing scheme

C. Network topology

D. The number of DHCP servers needed

15. An organization employs DHCP. It is experiencing some problems because its DHCP server is on a different subnet from the clients. What can the company do to remedy this situation? (Choose all that apply.)

A. Put a DHCP server on every subnet.

B. Configure a DHCP relay agent on each subnet without a DHCP server.

C. Configure the routers between subnets to forward BOOTP/DHCP traffic.

D. Move the DHCP server to the client subnet.

16. You have just installed a new DHCP server to service clients on a new subnet. However, the DHCP server does not seem to be assigning any addresses to clients on the subnet. What most likely could be the problem here?

A. The DHCP options were not properly configured.

B. The DHCP scope was not configured.

C. The DHCP scope was not activated.

D. The DHCP server was not authorized in Active Directory.

## Designing Other TCP/IP Services

17. A company is having a problem with its Web server needing to be rebooted. This is a huge issue, because sometimes it happens in the middle of the night, which causes one of the administrators to be paged and have to make a trip into the office. It doesn't happen every day, but it happens often enough that it is becoming an issue. The manager would like you to come up with a list of possible solutions. The company is currently running IIS 4.0 on a RAID 5 disk array and Windows NT 4.0 Enterprise Server. What are some possible solutions? (Choose the *best* answer.)

    A. Create a server cluster using network load balancing for fault tolerance.

    B. Create a server cluster using Cluster Services for redundancy.

    C. Upgrade the server to Windows 2000 server and IIS 5.0 and enable the reliable restart option.

    D. Rebuild the server and use a RAID1 disk array instead.

18. An organization is having continuous problems with one application that is running on its Web server. Unfortunately, that one application is affecting the company's entire Web server farm. There are constant performance issues. Employees often have unexpected downtime as a result of the server crashing due to application failure. The company plans to rebuild the application, but it won't be finished for at least three months. Until that happens, is there anything that the organization can do to lessen the impact on its entire network?

    A. Run the application on a standalone server.

    B. Create a server cluster with two servers running the application and Windows 2000 Cluster Services.

    C. Use the process isolation feature to have the application and its associated components run in their own memory areas.

    D. Run the application on a server in a different subnet.

19. What does *anonymous access* mean within the FTP architecture? (Choose all that apply.)

    A. The person who logs in cannot be identified.

    B. Anyone is able to log in using the username *anonymous.*

    C. The person who logs in is using the local IUSR_computername account.

    D. Anyone who logs in has restricted access.

**20.** Recently a company added a new domain on its Web server with a registration page. The company wants to be able to automatically send confirmation and thank-you messages to clients who register on the site. How can the company do that?

A. Create a virtual mail domain in the SMTP server for the new domain and configure the Web page to use SMTP to send messages whenever a client registers.

B. Use the logs on the Web site to get a list of people that registered and send them each san e-mail.

C. Create a link to the Drop directory on the SMTP virtual server. The Web server will automatically e-mail the client once the user clicks the link.

D. It is not possible to send mail from the Web server. Configure your enterprise e-mail application to send the mail for you.

**21.** You have changed the listening port in the Services File from port 21 to port 2121. Each time you make the change, the listening port always reverts back to port 21. You save your changes prior to exiting the Services file, yet the changes are still not being maintained. You know that nobody else is physically going in and changing the listening port back to port 21, because you are the only administrator with access to make this change. Why is this happening, and what can you do to fix it?

A. The settings in the IIS Metabase overwrite changes made to the Services file. Change the port number in the FTP Site Properties window.

B. The FTP port cannot be changed. There is nothing you can do to fix it.

C. The settings in the IIS Metabase overwrite changes made to the Services file. Change the port number using the Metabase editor.

D. The settings in the IIS Metabase supercede the Services file settings. Reinstall FTP and select a different port during the installation.

# LAB QUESTION

You have been given the task of designing a robust, highly available TCP/IP-based network infrastructure for a highly available Web site. The network should initially consist of seven Web servers clustered using Network Load Balancing Services and will support 250 domains and five back-end applications on five different back-end server clusters. The network should be flexible enough accommodate a maximum of a 500 percent increase in the number of clustered Web servers and back-end application servers at a moment's notice. The Web segment should be dedicated to the Web servers only, with a separate segment for the back-end servers.

You must design an infrastructure that supports the ideal number of hosts on two subnets. The infrastructure must also support dynamic addressing of servers, but the addresses cannot change once they have been assigned. Some of the applications require e-mail notifications to be sent to clients and administrators when certain events occur. How would you go about handling this task?

# SELF TEST ANSWERS

## Designing a TCP/IP Network Infrastructure

1. ☑ **A, C,** and **D.** Media type, network access method, and NIC throughput all contribute to the performance level of the network.
   ☒ **B** might seem like a correct answer, but it isn't, because the media type and, to some extent, the network access method determine network bandwidth.

2. ☑ **A** and **B.** These are the best answers. Adding multilayer switches will help lessen congestion because hosts connected to the switch can transmit in full-duplex mode. Further segmenting by adding more routers will also reduce the number of hosts per segment and thus reduce collisions and improve response time.
   ☒ **C** is incorrect because adding more Web servers means adding more hosts to an already congested network segment. **D** is incorrect because clustering does not solve the problem of network congestion. It only improves the availability of services, which would be cancelled out by the network congestion.

3. ☑ **B** and **C.** In order to appropriately subnet our network using the formula $2^n - 2$, we need to know how many subnets we want and how many hosts per subnet will give us the best performance.
   ☒ **A** and **D** are incorrect because the IP address class and subnet mask will already be known to us.

4. ☑ **B.** This is the best answer in this case. There are too few hosts on the network to warrant further subnetting. In addition, as **B** states, the fact that media is being shared indicates the need for a switch to reduce collisions.
   ☒ **A** is incorrect because subnetting does not automatically increase performance. **C** is incorrect because supernetting would have no effect on the network. **D** is incorrect because in this instance there are too few hosts to effectively subnet the network.

5. ☑ **A.** If we count only the 1s in their respective positions and add them up, we arrive at 7990.
   ☒ **B** is incorrect because 4096 is the value of the highest bit. **C** is incorrect because 512 is the value we would get if we discarded all the 0s and counted the 1s out of place. **D** is incorrect because 8192 is the value we get if we simply raise 2 to the power of the number of bits present.

## Understanding DNS

6. ☑ C. DNS is working fine, so the bottleneck here is in the number of Web servers to respond to client requests.
   ☒ A and B are incorrect because NLB redistributing the TCP/IP load will not improve performance if there are not enough servers to handle the client requests. Additionally, NLB does not automatically assign multiple IP addresses to a cluster host. D is incorrect because the number of Web servers does not affect RRDNS in any way.

7. ☑ D. If both subdomains are named incorrectly, none of the hosts in them will be reachable. In fact, the domains are actually totally different domains from the root domains. Deleting and recreating the subdomains is a sure bet to rectify the problem.
   ☒ A and C are incorrect because both domains are affected, not just one or the other. B is incorrect because Dynamic DNS (DDNS) does not fix subdomain inconsistencies.

8. ☑ B. Second-level domain registrations are handled by InterNIC. You should send a request to InterNIC to cancel those domains before you delete them from your infrastructure.
   ☒ A and D are incorrect because, if you simply delete or rename a second-level domain, all the hosts in it are affected because their FQDNs don't match the domain they are in. C is incorrect because the domain type can only be switched from primary to secondary and vice versa.

9. ☑ A, C, and D. As a result of its distributed hierarchical structure, DNS allows two or more hosts to have the same computer name as long as they are in different zones or subdomains. DNS's distributed and hierarchical nature allows for easier locating of hosts since contacting the authoritative DNS server for a specific zone is all that is required. In addition, DNS in Windows 2000 comes with Dynamic DNS update support.
   ☒ B is incorrect because NetBIOS names are actually shorter than DNS names and thus more friendly.

10. ☑ A, B, and C. RRDNS cannot detect whether a host is online or not when it issues a query. The fact that response time is bad only occasionally also supports A. C is correct because if notification had been set in the DNS Notify field in the DNS properties, an administrator would have received a message.
    ☒ D is incorrect because notification that the hostname could not be resolved would be sent to the querying party.

11. ☑ C. Theoretically, the number of supported DNS domains is only dependent on server capacity. The more powerful the server, the more domains that can be supported.

☒ A, B, and D are incorrect because neither alphabetical restraints nor number of hosts, nor decreased network bandwidth determines the number of domains.

## Understanding DHCP

**12.** ☑ **A.** All servers on a network, especially the ones that provide core services such as DHCP and DNS, should have a static IP address so that they can always be located.
☒ **B** and **C** are incorrect because using a file with a name-to-IP address mapping will still result in the server being unreachable because it changed its address. **D** is incorrect because you are attempting to move away from static addressing.

**13.** ☑ **D.** All these clients with the options noted are viable DHCP clients.

**14.** ☑ **B, C,** and **D.** When you are considering a DHCP server deployment, the network addressing scheme, the network topology, and the number of DHCP servers needed are important factors to determine.
☒ **A** is incorrect because it is more a requirement that the DHCP servers have static addresses during the implementation than it is a predeployment consideration.

**15.** ☑ **A, B, C,** and **D.** All answers are correct. Placing a DHCP server on every subnet to service the clients there, configuring a relay agent, or configuring the routers between the subnets to forward BOOTP/DHCP traffic are all viable options. In addition, if you have only one client subnet, moving the DHCP server to the client subnet so it is local to the clients will solve the problem.

**16.** ☑ **B, C,** and **D** are all correct answers. The DHCP server cannot service clients if a scope is not configured or activated. Furthermore, the DHCP server will not be able to service clients if it is not an authorized DHCP server in Active Directory.
☒ **A** is incorrect because even if DHCP options have not been properly configured, as long as a scope is configured and active and the server is authorized, it will still service clients even if it gives them incorrect information.

## Designing Other TCP/IP Services

**17.** ☑ **C.** The reliable restart feature in IIS 5.0 should restart the server when necessary.
☒ **A** and **B** are both good possible answers but they are not the best answer, because they might all need to be rebooted at the same time. **D** is not correct because disk mirroring will preserve the data but it will not handle the rebooting issue.

18. ☑ C. IIS 5.0's process isolation feature works to assign and keep the application in its own memory area, where it does not affect other applications or the operating systems if it fails or generates an error.
☒ A would be a viable option if the application didn't need to work with other servers. **B** is incorrect because the application itself is problematic. Running multiple instances of the application in a cluster simply means that there will be multiple failures. **D** is incorrect because even if the application were run on a server on a different network, the application failure would still affect the server and thus the network.

19. ☑ A, B, and C. Anonymous access on an FTP server means that clients can log on using the user name *anonymous,* which translates to the IUSR_computername user account on the FTP server, no matter who logs in, so the actual user is never identified.
☒ D is incorrect because the IUSR_computername account access level can be any level of access a normal user account can have.

20. ☑ A. SMTP supports the creation of virtual mail domains alongside Web domains. SMTP was designed to add the ability to send and receive e-mail from a Web site.
☒ B is incorrect because we want to send mail automatically, but this method involves sending mail manually. **C** is incorrect because the Drop directory is where incoming mail is delivered. Simply creating a link to it will not send e-mails. **D** is incorrect because SMTP was designed for the very purpose stated in the question—responding to clients via e-mail.

21. ☑ A. Simply changing the port setting in the FTP Site Properties window will change the settings in the Metabase, which overwrites all the settings in the Services file.
☒ B is incorrect because we can change the port number permanently via the Metabase. **C** is incorrect because there is no such thing as the Metabase editor in IIS 5.0. **D** is incorrect because we do not have to reinstall FTP server to change the listening port number.

# LAB ANSWER

We decided to build an ATM-based fiber optic network based on the requirements for performance. We calculate that the Web server segment should support at least 42 Web servers based on the estimation of a 500 percent increase in the number of servers. The back-end network should support at least 120 servers based on the same estimate, with four servers per cluster running Windows 2000 Datacenter Server. Our addressing scheme based on this configuration was to have a Class C network subnetted to use two subnets of 127 hosts each (192.168.1.0 and 192.168.1.128 with a subnet mask of 255.255.255.128). We configured four DHCP servers, two per subnet, clustered for failover protection and network load balancing, to service the servers, each with half the Class C scope 192.168.1.0 active. We also configured split-brain DNS on the DHCP servers and integrated DHCP and DNS for more efficient hostname registration. We created the Web domains on the DNS server in the Web network and registered all the domain names with the InterNIC. We finally configured virtual SMTP mail domains for all the domains that required it and configured Drop folders that reflect the individual domain names. A diagram of the network appears in Figure 5-23.

**FIGURE 5-23** Diagram for Lab Question

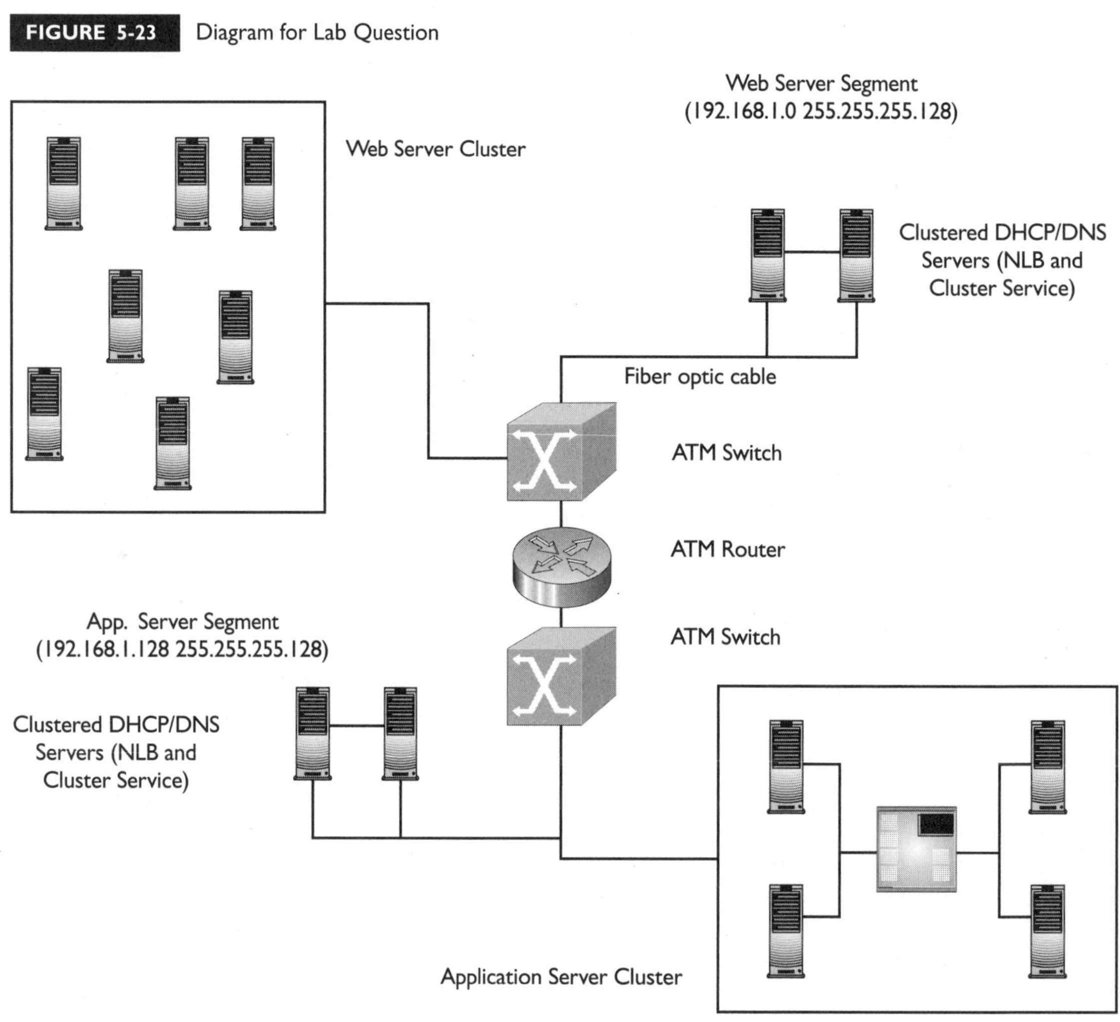

MCSE
MICROSOFT CERTIFIED SYSTEMS ENGINEER

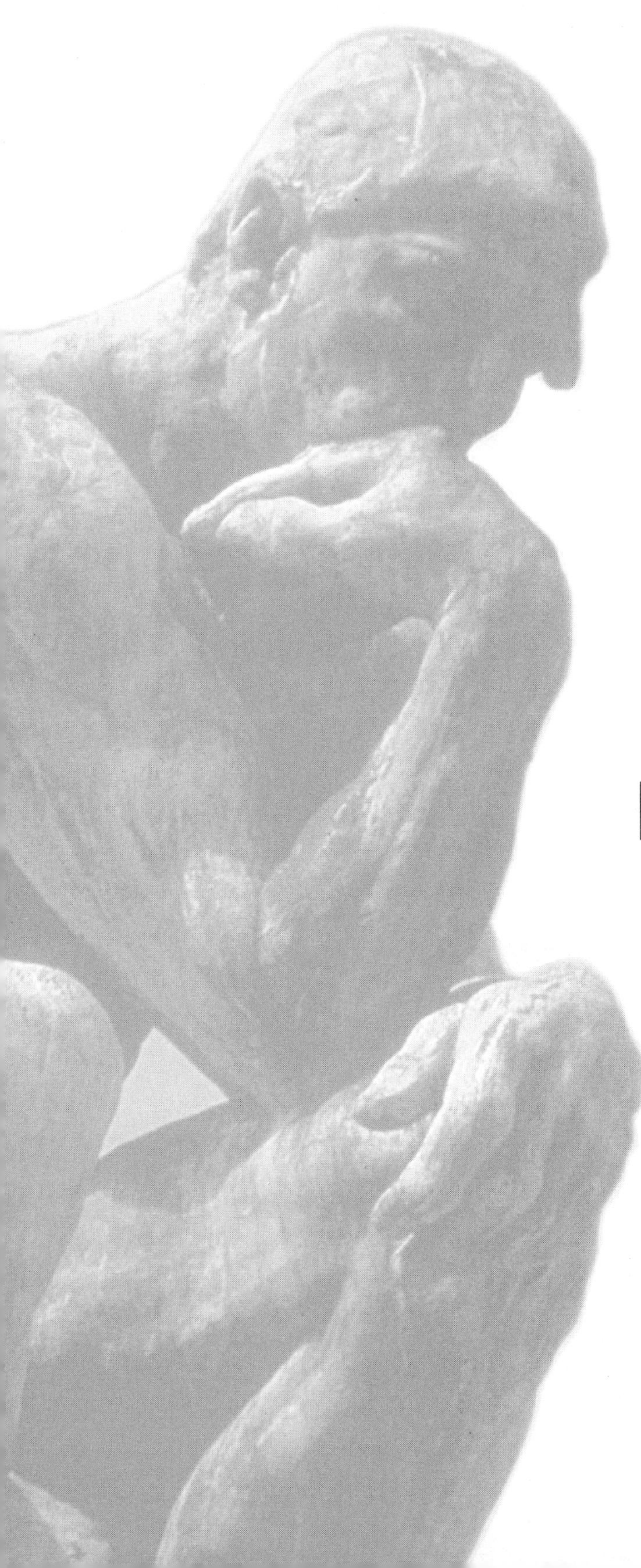

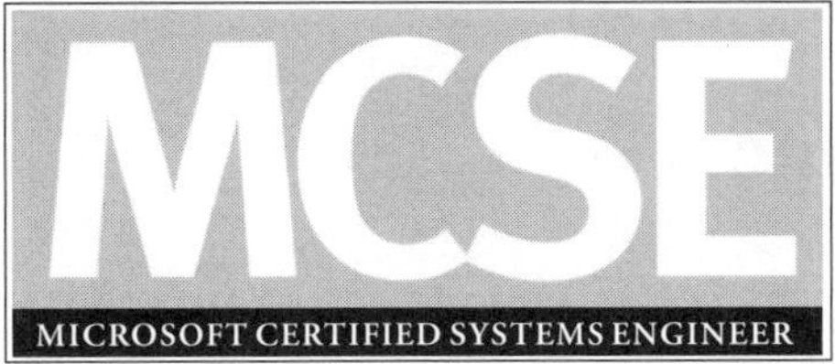

# 6

# Planning Capacity Requirements

## CERTIFICATION OBJECTIVES

| | |
|---|---|
| 6.01 | Calculating Network Capacity |
| 6.02 | Calculating Server Capacity |
| 6.03 | Calculating Cluster Size |
| 6.04 | Calculating Storage Requirements |
| ✓ | Two-Minute Drill |
| Q&A | Self Test |

Capacity planning for your IIS 5.0 Server involves many processes. Administrators must determine current needs as well as scalability for the future. Capacity-planning issues involve managing traffic with connection capacity, software, and hardware. If you make decisions regarding equipment and software to purchase for an IIS 5.0 Web site, this chapter shows you how to measure performance and see where the bottlenecks occur so that you can make the necessary adjustments. Calculating network capacity involves many different processes. Follow the network capacity-planning checklist outlined in this chapter to obtain an in-depth look at your IIS 5.0 site.

Topics covered in this chapter include:

- Creating installation checklists
- Connection capacity
- Traffic analysis
- Tools available in IIS 5.0 to measure site performance
- Throttling server bandwidth for better performance

Since Internet needs are changing so rapidly, capacity planning is important in choosing your hardware and software. Hardware and software need to be scalable and redundant.

**CERTIFICATION OBJECTIVE 6.01**

## Calculating Network Capacity

Before you begin purchasing hardware and software for your Web site, you need to make a few installation determinations. We begin with the basics, such as:

- What is the function of the site?
- Will customers upload and download from this site?
- Will the server provide Domain Name Services (DNS)?
- Will any other servers, such as e-mail, Network News Transport Protocol (NNTP), or Simple Mail Transport Protocol (SMTP), run on this server?
- If clients connect, will they access large database languages such as Simple Query Language (SQL)?

- What is the customer base and potential expansion now, in one month, in six months, and next year?

If you have the means to do so, set up a lab and use the Web Capacity Analysis Tool (WCAT) tool provided by Microsoft. WCAT runs simulated workloads on client/server configurations. With WCAT, you can test how your IIS and network configuration respond to a variety of client requests for information. You can use results of these load tests to determine the server and network configuration for your Web server. WCAT is designed to evaluate how Internet servers respond to various client workload simulations. When you change your hardware and software configuration and repeat the prepared tests, you can identify how the new configuration affects server response to the simulated client workload. You can use WCAT to test servers with single or multiple processors and servers that are connected to multiple networks. A minimum of two computers are needed for the lab. Use one as the Web server and the other to access the lab server information and monitor performance on the server. WCAT may be downloaded from http://webtool.rte.microsoft.com/.

## Connection Capacity

You should choose the proper Internet connection based on the amount of time users are willing to wait to access the site and the type of file users will request. Bandwidth determines how quickly the data will arrive at the target computer. Too little bandwidth on a network can result in site delays or crashes. The IIS 5.0 Web server connects to the Internet via a NIC, modem, or Integrated Services Digital Network (ISDN) adapter. When you are connecting with a NIC, take into consideration the card's manufacturer and its available drivers. Always maintain the latest drivers that are available for your NIC. Using older versions of drivers for your NIC can cause problems with network performance. Table 6-1 presents a listing of connections and maximum bandwidth.

### Estimating File Transmission Time

Generally, a basic HTML page without audio, video, or extensive graphics should load in about 5 seconds. If the site has external files such as audio, video, or graphics, they should load within 30 seconds. If your Internet users are connecting to your server via a modem and the Internet, it is a good idea to keep the graphics, video,

**TABLE 6-1** Internet Connection Categories and Bandwidth

| Connection Type | Maximum Bandwidth |
|---|---|
| Dedicated PPP/SLIP | Limited to modem speed |
| 56K Frame Relay | 56.0Kbps |
| ISDN (using PPP) | 56.0–64.0Kbps |
| T1 | 1.54Mbps |
| Fractional T1 | Varies |
| T3 | 45.0Mbps |
| ATM | 155Mbps |

and audio to a minimum. A faster line connection will take 0.1 or 0.2 of a second per connection to send a data packet and a modem will take nearly 1 second per connection.

Imagine a server that has only basic HTML pages, a few graphics, and a little audio. Each HTML file is approximately 5 kilobytes (KB) in size. This is the average size of a file with no graphics, audio, or video. The Web server has T1 line connections to the Internet at a transmission speed of 1.544Mbps. It is impossible to actually transfer data this quickly due to protocol overhead during transmission. Overhead occurs when data divides into packets when it is sent on the network. Each packet includes around 20 bytes of header information in addition to the data that transmits. The 5KB page we are requesting in this example has significant TCP/IP overhead—roughly 30 percent. For larger files, overhead becomes smaller in terms of percentage. Table 6-2 shows the traffic produced by a 5KB page.

**TABLE 6-2** Traffic Produced by a 5KB Page

| Type of Traffic | Approximate Number of Bytes Sent |
|---|---|
| TCP/IP overhead | 1360 |
| Generic text file | 5000KB |
| GET request | 250 |
| TCP connection | 180 |
| Total | 6790 |

To find the number of bits in the page, just multiply the total bytes by 8 (remember 8 bits equals 1 byte): 6790 x 8 = 54,320. The T1 line can transmit at roughly 1.54Mbps. Divide 1,540,000 by 54,320 and we find that the maximum rate is roughly around 28 pages per second. Remember, if you are using a modem, that adds a start and stop bit to each bit, so it would be slower than these figures show. When viewing Table 6-3, which shows data sent per second by connection type and speed, keep in mind that the page requested is a small 5KB page with text only.

Please make note that the connection speed and pages sent per second are best-case figures. The download time will double on these text files if you add a graphic to the file. If you need to keep to a quota of a higher number of pages per second, you can achieve this goal by compressing your larger pictures, using smaller pictures, removing images from the page, or connecting to the Internet with a quicker connection type.

The association between bandwidth and the central processing unit (CPU) is that if your server has a site that has a transactional database with dynamic pages, your server is more prone to CPU bottlenecks and generally would experience more processor and memory issues than running out of bandwidth. However, a site with mostly static pages would actually be more likely to run out of bandwidth than have processor and memory troubles.

**on the Job**

***If you have a T1 line for your connection and 150 users request the same page simultaneously, your connection is now saturated. At a connection speed of 28.8Kbps, it only takes around 52 clients to saturate your line.***

**TABLE 6-3** Pages Sent Per Second by Connection Type and Speed

| Connection Type | Connection Speed | Data Sent Per Second |
|---|---|---|
| PPP/SLIP | 28.8Kbps | Half a page |
| Modem | 56Kbps | Nearly 1 page |
| ISDN | 128Kbps | 2+ pages |
| T1 | 1.5Mbps | 26 Pages |
| 10Mb Ethernet | 8Mbps | 136 pages |
| T3 | 44.7Mbps | 760 pages |
| 100Mb Ethernet | 80Mbps | 1360 pages |
| 1Gbps Ethernet | 800Mbps | 13,600 pages |

### Client Perception

Let's look at an example of client perception. Your site, Ticketworld.com, is selling tickets to the hottest concert in the last five years, but so is another company, Getaticket.com. The Ticketworld.com site looks awesome because a graphic artist has filled the home page with many new options and cool graphics. The tickets went on sale at 10:00 AM and requests are flooding your hot new site. Time to purchase these tickets is limited because it should be a sold-out event. Your network administrator is monitoring traffic; after a while, he notices that the T1 line is saturated and clients are dropping the connection to the site. Bandwidth is not available on the network. The administrator decides to visit the competitor site; he easily hops on the index page and maneuvers to the purchasing page via a navigational menu.

What is going on here? Clients are impatient when they try to access a Web site. In general, a download should take no longer than 30 seconds at maximum. If you place a substantial number of graphics on a page and suddenly have a heavy load of user bandwidth, the graphics download will be delayed. This means that users will get impatient and will possibly go somewhere else to purchase their goods. The moral of this story is, keep your pages simple and in tune with the goods or service the Web site plans to sell.

## Measuring Performance

This section discusses the tools and methods needed to determine network bandwidth and traffic using System Monitor. Microsoft IIS 5.0 has included various tools and settings that allow the administrator to tune for performance. The WCAT tool mentioned earlier and the Web Application Stress Tool allow you to "stress test" your Web environment. These tools are available on the Microsoft Web Site at http://webtool.rte.microsoft.com/.

Windows 2000 includes Performance Monitor (Perfmon), Network Monitor, and Task Manager to analyze traffic, bandwidth usage, and server performance. In this section, we learn how to estimate bandwidth usage and traffic on a Web server using Performance Monitor.

## Using Perfmon.exe

The IIS 5.0 system continually changes depending on connections maintained, file sizes, number of files requested, and use of security and logging. This process and the variables involved refer to the *Inetinfo working set*. Because of the numerous variables involved, the Inetinfo working set has no fixed size. It is important that your servers have enough working Random Access Memory (RAM) to accommodate the user-mode process Inetinfo.exe. The IIS 5.0 server should have enough RAM installed to keep the Inetinfo.exe process in memory at all times. Performance on an IIS 5.0 server will suffer if part of the Inetinfo.exe process pages to the hard disk. The Inetinfo.exe process handles the Web, File Transfer Protocol (FTP), and SMTP services. Remember that each current connection is also allocated 10KB of memory in the Inetinfo working set. Also keep in mind the following:

- Performance Monitor allows you to monitor real-time performance in chart, histogram, or performance mode.
- Performance Monitor includes an alert feature that allows you to start an action based on an event that the administrator defines (for example, when counters reach a maximum level for performance).
- You can use Performance Monitor to monitor counter logs to monitor performance on a local or remote Windows 2000 system.

Open the Performance Monitor snap-in. Performance Monitor is an Microsoft Management Console (MMC) snap-in found by clicking Start | Programs | Administrative Tools | Performance. Alternately, click Start | Run and type **Perfmon.exe** in the text box. Figure 6-1 shows the Performance Monitor screen.

To get an estimate of traffic on the server, you need to add two counters. The counters are located in the Web Service object. The counters you should select are:

- Total Connection Attempts (all instances)
- Current Connections

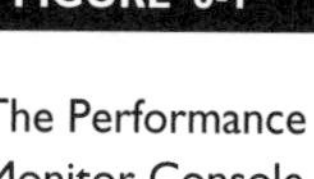
FIGURE 6-1

The Performance Monitor Console

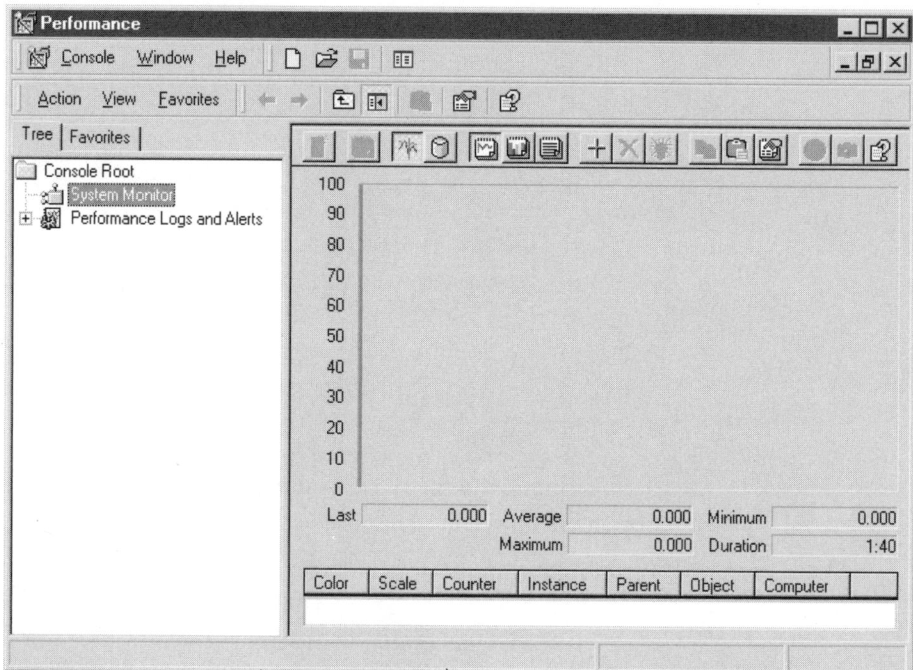


## EXERCISE 6-1

### Monitoring Traffic on the Web Server

In this exercise, you learn how to analyze traffic on the Web server. Do the following:

1. Verify that you are logged on to your domain as administrator.
2. Start Performance Monitor by clicking Start | Run, then type **perfmon.exe**.
3. To add figures, click the + symbol on the Perfmon toolbar.
4. Use Select Counters from Computer.
5. Choose the server you are monitoring.
6. Choose the Performance object.
7. Select the Web Service.
8. Select Counters from the list.
9. Choose Total Connect Requests.

10. Select Add.
11. Choose the Current Connection counter.
12. Select Add.
13. Choose Close.
14. Monitor the traffic over a period and analyze the data. What does it tell you?

    The Total Connection Requests counter also includes connection requests that have failed. Consider this when you are estimating traffic on your server. Manage your logs for at least a week to capture a good estimate. After you have successfully collected traffic data for the server, you need to set the number of daily connections on the Web site from your estimate. To do this, use your IIS snap-in. Select the Web site, click Properties, and set the value under Performance Tuning to a value larger than you anticipate receiving.

---

Now that you have an understanding on analyzing network traffic on your Web server, let's take a look at some other counters that you can use in Performance Monitor. Table 6-4 shows Objects, Counters, and Values available to you when you are using System Monitor to view Web traffic and bandwidth.

When using the Performance Monitor console, be cautious in adding objects and counters. The more objects and counters assessed, the higher the CPU usage power needed from your system. The Performance Monitor console should be used only to pinpoint performance bottlenecks. Do not cause additional problems by using this tool continuously.

Microsoft IIS 5.0 has many more counters you can use to monitor your site for performance issues. For more information on using Performance Monitor, refer to your Windows 2000 documentation by clicking Help on the Start menu.

on the job

***Allow the process to run over a certain amount of time and view the results. The total bandwidth monitored should not use more than 50 percent of the total network bandwidth.***

You might find that you are having performance issues due to bandwidth restrictions. You can throttle bandwidth on your Web server to allow the server to perform better. The next section explains how to throttle the bandwidth on the Web server.

**TABLE 6-4** Objects, Counters, and Values Used to Observe IIS 5.0 with Performance Monitor

| Object | Counter | Ideal Value |
|---|---|---|
| Web Service | Active Server Pages\Request wait time | Low as possible |
| Web Service | Active Server Pages\Requests queued | None |
| Web Service | Active Server Pages\Transactions/sec | High as possible |
| Network Interface | Bytes Total/sec | Less than 50 percent of total bandwidth |
| Network Interface | Bytes Sent/sec | Low as possible |
| Network Interface | Bytes Received/sec | Low as possible |
| Web Service | Disk (Logical or Physical) percent disk time | Low as possible |
| Web Service | Disk (Logical or Physical) Queue Length | Less than 2 |
| Web Service | Disk (Logical or Physical) Average Disk Bytes/Transfer | High as possible |
| Web Service | Internet Information Services Global\ Cache Hits % | High as possible |
| Web Service | Memory/Pages/sec | 0–20 (more than 80 is too high) |
| Web Service | Memory Available Bytes | A minimum of 4MB |
| Web Service | Memory\Committed Bytes | Not greater than 75 percent of physical memory size |
| Web Service | Memory\Pool non paged bytes | Stable; if you see a gradual rise you could have a memory leak |
| Web Service | Processor\% Processor Time | Less than 75 percent |
| Web Service | Processor\Interrupts/sec | 486/66 processors up to 1000<br>P90 up to 3500<br>P200 more than 7000 |
| Web Service | Web Service/Bytes Total/sec | High as possible |

## Throttling Bandwidth Used by Web Server

From the IIS snap-in, select the server running IIS 5.0. Right-click the server, click the Performance Sheet tab, and select the Enable Bandwidth Throttling box. Enter the maximum network use amount. Choose Apply, then choose OK.

**Throttle Individual Site Bandwidth** From the IIS snap-in, select the server running IIS 5.0. Choose the Web Site. Click the Performance Sheet tab and select the Enable Bandwidth Throttling box. Enter the maximum network use amount. Choose Apply, then choose OK. Figure 6-2 shows the properties for individual Web Site bandwidth throttling.

**Using HTTP Compression** You can enable HTTP compression to provide faster transmission speeds between the Web server and browsers that support compression. Applications or static files may be compressed. The folder that will hold the compressed file or application must be on an NTFS partition. The temporary folder used for this function may not be shared or compressed. There is a tradeoff, however, when you use HTTP compression in that more CPU resources are required for the compression.

***Test the Processor counter of the Processor object using System Monitor over a period of a few days before using HTTP compression. If your baseline shows the % Processor Time as 80 percent or greater, compression is not a good idea for this server.***

**FIGURE 6-2**

Enable IIS 5.0 Server Bandwidth Throttling on Individual Web Sites

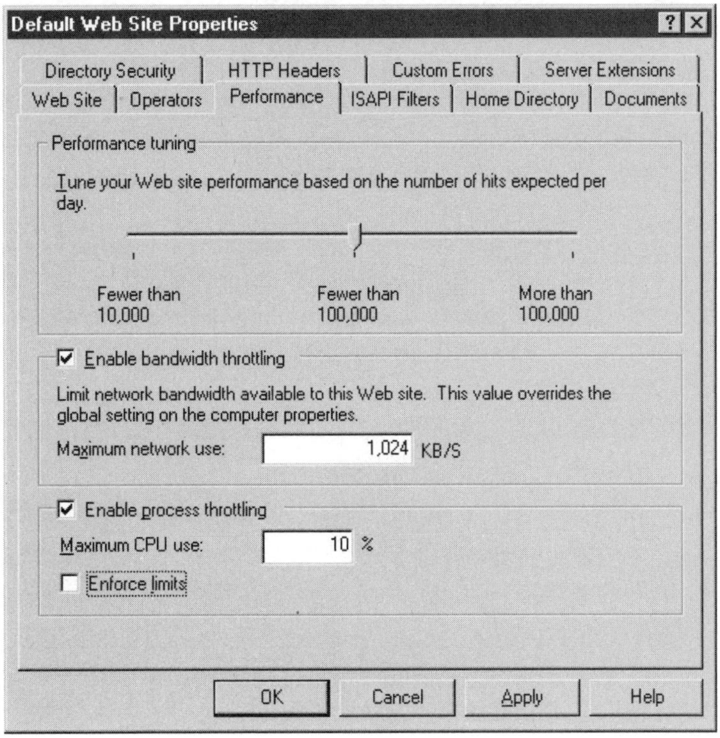

**Enabling HTTP Compression** Use the IIS MMC snap-in. Choose the computer icon and click the Properties button. Select Master Properties, then select WWW Service. Click Edit. Select the Service tab, then select Compress static files. Select Compress application files. Type a path or browse to the local temp folder.

Choose Apply, then click OK. If you choose to enable HTTP compression on individual Web sites, this will override any global computer settings that have been entered via HTTP compression.

**HTTP Keep-Alives** Web browsers prompt the Web server to keep the connection open across multiple requests. This allows enhanced server performance because the client machine is not making multiple requests to the server. The feature is enabled by default in IIS 5.0. It is not a good idea to disable this feature in IIS 5.0 because additional requests and connections will affect server resources and performance. The client browser would also become less responsive. Figure 6-3 shows the HTTP keep-alives enabled on this Web server.

**FIGURE 6-3** Configuring the HTTP Keep-Alives on the IIS 5.0 Server

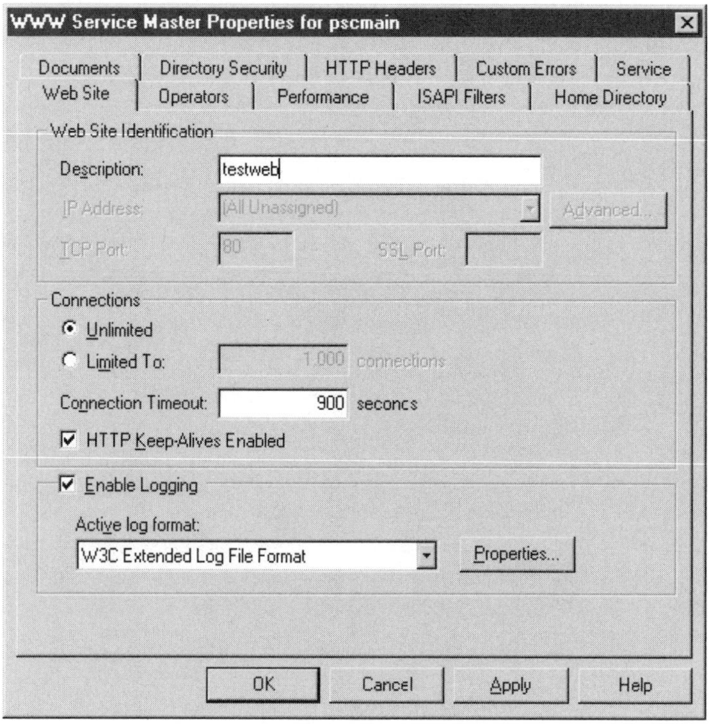

**Limiting Connections in IIS 5.0** You can conserve bandwidth on IIS 5.0 by setting connection limits on the Web server. This technique allows other services that might run on the server to maintain a certain bandwidth amount.

Open the IIS MMC snap-in. Select the Web site and click Properties. Choose the Web site Properties tab and choose Connections. Enter the number of simultaneous connections you want to limit on the server. Enter the connection timeout value, then click apply and click OK.

When the connection limit is met, all other connections are rejected. The server will continue to process data until the timeout value is reached.

### Logging Web Server Connections

To monitor Web server connections, open Performance Monitor. Choose the Web Service object. Add the Current Connections, Maximum Connections, and Total Connection Attempts. Log for a week at a minimum to create a good snapshot of connections on the server.

Once you have a traffic estimate on your site for both normal loads and usage spikes, you can get an overall average of your network capacity. If you are running an ISP, it might be a good idea to set standards regarding what is permissible to run on sites. Let customers know that certain items are allowed and others might not be allowed.

## Network Monitor

Network Monitor is a tool used in Windows 2000 to analyze network traffic. Network Monitor captures network traffic for display and analysis. The version of Network Monitor shipped with Windows 2000 Server is a "lite" version. If you have Microsoft Systems Management Server, it has a Network Monitor version that includes additional features:

- Source address of the computer that sent the frame
- Destination Address of the computer that received the frame
- Protocols used to send the frame
- The portion of the message being sent

Network Monitor collects data by performing a "capture" on packets being sent on the network. The server or system using Network Monitor should have a NIC that supports the promiscuous mode (the NIC adapter passes on frames sent on the network). If you are capturing data across a network, use the Network Monitor Agent to capture information using a remote computer. The Network Monitor Agent collects statistics from a remote computer and sends the information to your local computer. The captured data can be saved to a text file or a capture file to be opened later for inspection. A NIC that supports *promiscuous mode* can capture and analyze all network traffic. Without this type of support, you would not get a clear picture of actual network traffic.

**Using Network Monitor to View Traffic** You need to build an address database to use address pairs in a capture filter. To do this, open Network Monitor by clicking Start | Programs | Administrative Tools | Network Monitor. Alternatively, you can click Start | Run and type NETMON. A view of Network Monitor is shown in Figure 6-4.

Select Start from the Capture menu, or press F10 to start the capture.

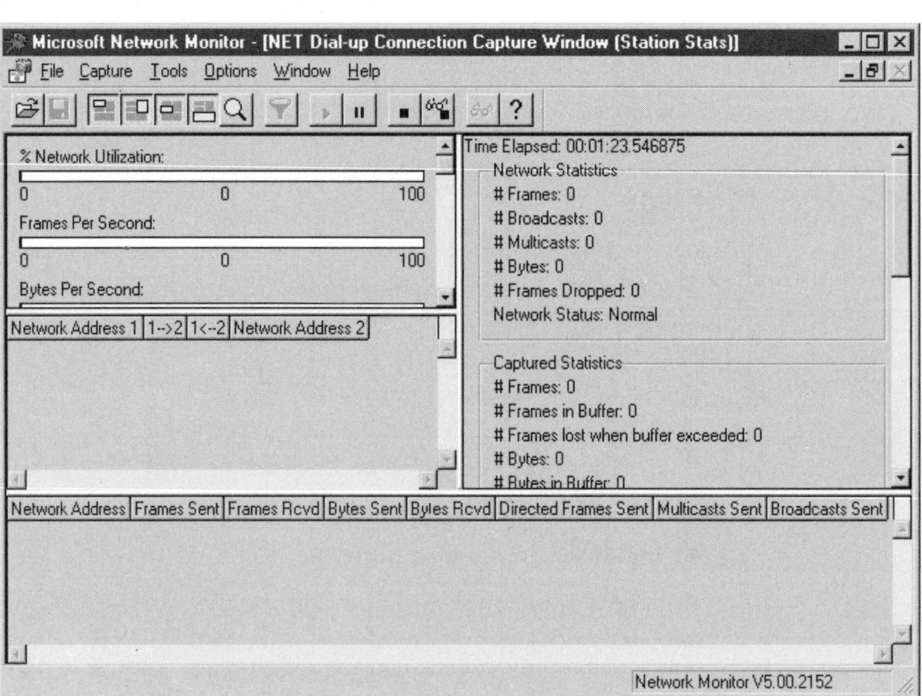


**FIGURE 6-4** Using Network Monitor to Analyze Server Traffic

To stop and view information from the capture, you can either select Capture | Stop and View or press SHIFT-F11. After you capture and observe the data, you can filter the information based on various sections such as protocol, computer name, address, and even traffic direction. You can choose to save a captured file by clicking File | Save As | Filename | Save.

When using Network Monitor, you can enable security by installing the Network Monitor driver on the Windows 2000 server. The Network Monitor driver automatically verifies that a user attempting to make a connection has administrative privileges. For more information regarding Network Monitor, click Help | Index and type the keyword **Network Monitor**.

### Task Manager

Task Manager in Windows 2000 allows you to assign and view processes running in real time. You can stop a process or even assign it a new priority if it is taking up a high level of CPU and/or memory. Task Manager may be accessed by pressing CTRL-ALT-DEL and clicking the Task Manager button.

If you need to perform monitoring tasks on your IIS 5.0 Web server, use Table 6-5 as a quick reference tool.

## Client/Server Communications

*Universal data access* is Microsoft's way of providing access to all types of information across an organization. The Microsoft Data Access Component (MDAC) comprises the data technologies that enable Universal Data Access/Open Database Connectivity (ODBC), Object Link Embedding Database (OLE DB), and Microsoft Active-X Data Objects (ADO).

**TABLE 6-5** Choosing IIS 5.0 Tools for Particular Tasks

| To Perform This Task | Use This Tool |
|---|---|
| View network traffic | Network Monitor (Netmon) |
| Reassign a process that's overutilizing CPU | Task Manager to reassign the process |
| Create a baseline for a server | Performance Monitor and counters pertaining to the issue. |

## ODBC and OLE DB

ODBC is a widely recognized method of accessing data in various relational databases. OLE DB is designed to communicate with any database, whether relational or nonrelational. Applications that use OLE DB fall into two categories: providers and consumers. A *provider* application allows any consumer to access data through OLE DB; a *consumer* application uses data through the OLE DB interface.

## Active Directory Objects and Remote Data Services

Microsoft Active-X Data Objects (ADO) and Remote Data Services (RDS) use OLE DB to communicate with remote and local databases. ADO is used to access both client-side and server-side data. ADO is an OLE DB consumer. Not all ADO applications are supported by providers. RDS is a feature of ADO that optimizes the transfer of data between the client and the ADO components. Advanced Data Connector (ADC) is the parent of RDS. It is less flexible than RDS and has been integrated into ADO to give uniformity to the access of remote data. The relationships between data access components are shown in Figure 6-5.

**FIGURE 6-5** Data Access Components and IIS 5.0

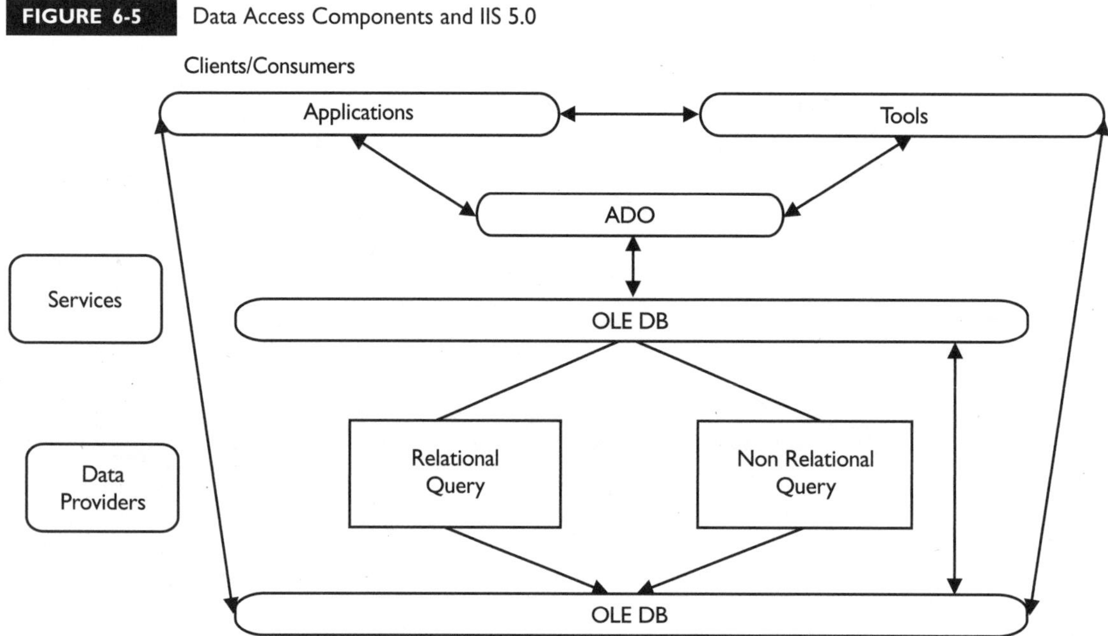

## Server/Server Communications

On a dynamic Web site, where content is continually being developed and updated, the process of replicating content from a staging server to a live site encounters numerous obstacles. Whether it is an issue of content accuracy or the time it takes for replication, your site is at risk. The Content Replication component of MCIS overcomes these obstacles by providing reliable and secure movement of large amounts of data across a network—even through a corporate firewall. Content Replication automatically replicates file-based content from one or more remote content servers to multiple destination content servers and can be used in a variety of applications, including production server staging, production server mirroring, and large and/or complex replication scenarios. Of course, not everything great about Web database access is free. Before you start combining databases and HTML, you should consider some important issues, discussed in this section.

### Dynamic Pages Versus Static Pages

How much of your site really needs data access? How often does your content change? Dynamic solutions, especially if they involve accessing a database, are slower than plain, static HTML pages. If you display data that does not change regularly, you can improve performance (for your server and your client) by converting dynamic pages to HTML.

### Server Load

Be sure you have sufficient server resources to handle the increased demands of database access. Consider memory, CPU speed, Internet connection speed, disk subsystems, and other critical hardware factors. If you are expecting heavy database traffic, you might need to separate your Web server and Database Management System (DBMS) onto two or more computers. In addition, use existing database and performance management tools to help you measure and balance your server load.

### Tool Support

The tools used to develop Web-based applications sometimes are not updated as fast as the technology changes. Research and choose your tools carefully before you implement a large-scale database project.

### Client Presentation

How will users access the data on your site? Will they be able to add to it or modify it? Will the users have their own copies of the data, or will they have access to the information only while online? Using Microsoft Data Access Components (MDAC), information can either be manipulated on the server as part of a server-side query or be bundled as a package and transmitted to the client. Choosing how the information will be presented to the user is perhaps the hardest decision you will have to make. Often, a hybrid approach is best.

### Database Scalability and Reliability

Determine how much the database is likely to grow. On average, how often will users access it? What kinds of tasks will they perform? What is your Web site's overall growth estimate—in terms of both content and readership?

### Data Warehousing and Online Analytical Processing

A *data warehouse* is often used as the basis for a decision-support system. It has even been called a *business intelligence system.* The design goal is to conquer the issues encountered when an organization attempts to perform an analysis using the same database that is used to perform Online Transaction Processing (OLTP).

Typically, OLTP systems are designed to manage transaction processing and minimize disk storage requirements by using a series of related and normalized tables. However, when users need to analyze their data, a number of problems often prohibit them from accessing the information:

- Application databases are often segmented across multiple servers, making it difficult for users to find the data in the first place.
- Users are unable to make ad hoc queries due to the complexities of the tables.
- Security restrictions could prevent users from accessing the detailed data they need.

Data warehousing offers a solution to these problems. Data warehousing is an approach to storing data in which assorted data sources from across the enterprise are all transferred to a common data store. Online analytical processing (OLAP) is the technology that enables client applications to process the data. Data warehouses (combined with OLAP) provide the following benefits:

- Differences among data structures across multiple databases can be resolved.

- Frequently queried data is amassed and the results are stored as "cubes," which are table-like in structure and enable quicker response time to ad hoc queries.

OLAP is a powerful tool for creating new views of data, based on a rich array of ad hoc functions.

### Component Object Model Extension

Component Object Model Extension (COM+) extends the functionality of applications running on Windows 2000 Server and IIS 5.0. Transactions are easily managed with COM+. Further benefits include:

- **Distributed application framework** Noninvasive; usually fewer than five lines of code are needed to make the object transaction aware.
- **Simplified programming** COM objects usually have the ability to participate in transactions without modification.
- **Components** Any language that supports the COM objects can have applications built to use the services.
- **Recovery and restart** COM+ applications are automatically restarted if they stop.
- **Scalability** Applications perform extremely well in high-usage environments.
- **Security** Automatically enforces user roles and Windows 2000 security.
- **Transactions** COM+ applications inherit the reliability of automatic distributed transactions.

**CERTIFICATION OBJECTIVE 6.02**

## Calculating Server Capacity

Inadequate server architecture can cause bottlenecks to plague the network. This section focuses on calculating memory, CPU, cost, and flexibility to avoid such bottlenecks. You need to understand how each component of the server affects the other. The section serves as a checklist of IIS Web server hardware tuning.

## Memory

Choosing a server with enough memory is imperative when you are running IIS 5.0. Make certain that you purchase the quickest ECC-supported memory for the chipset and bus of your motherboard. It is not a good idea to mix and match memory.

Remember the following when planning memory requirements for IIS 5.0:

- Inetinfo.exe takes 2.5MB of RAM just to start.
- Each client connection uses 10KB of RAM.
- Each log file takes 64KB.
- The IIS file and object cache can be 1MB to infinite in size.

exam Watch

***Because Exam 70-226 focuses on skills needed to set up and maintain highly available Web solutions using IIS 5.0 and Windows 2000, it is imperative that you be intimately familiar with the more advanced aspects of clustering, setting up fault tolerant hard drives, and monitoring and troubleshooting performance issues such as CPU and memory bottlenecks.***

Remember the following rules when planning for memory on the IIS 5.0 server:

1. You can never have enough RAM.
2. You should size your server for tomorrow, not today.
3. There are limits to the amount of RAM that the operating system can support. (And in this case, the versions of Windows support different amounts of RAM.)
4. If Intel makes server extensions, Rule 3 may be adjusted somewhat.
5. If your budget can afford it, refer back to Rule 1.

### Information on Monitoring Memory

This section is a brief review of the most important memory-monitoring techniques. Many performance-monitoring tools measure memory use systemwide and according to each process. These tools include Task Manager as well as System Monitor, which is usually referred to as *Perfmon* (Perfmon.msc, supplanting the older Perfmon.exe). These are Windows 2000 Server administrative tools built into Windows 2000 Server. The Windows 2000 Server Resource Kit includes tools such as Process

Monitor (Pmon.exe), Performance Data Log Service (PerfLog), Process Explode (Pview.exe), and Process Viewer (Pviewer.exe). PerfLog and PerfMon can measure memory use over a specific amount of time. PerfMon can read and log data from performance counters built into IIS 5.0 and the Windows 2000 operating system.

When IIS 5.0 receives a static file request, it sends the file handle to be cached in RAM. As more file requests are received, instead of going to the hard drive, IIS uses the files in cache to request the file again. As IIS 5.0 requests various files, older, cached files are purged to make room for the new files.

### Using System Monitor to View Memory Bottlenecks

Counters can be used to view bottlenecks in memory. Table 6-6 shows some available counters.

IIS 5.0 is well integrated with the Windows 2000 operating system. For this reason, IIS 5.0 services derive many benefits from the system architecture, including the Windows 2000 Server security model, RPC communication, messaging, the file systems, and other operating system services. Thus, monitoring memory for IIS 5.0 begins with monitoring overall server memory, particularly on a multipurpose server.

Monitoring the physical memory of a server running IIS 5.0 involves measuring the size of the areas in physical memory used by IIS 5.0 and assuring that enough space is available to contain the elements IIS 5.0 needs to store. The physical memory space should be sufficient for normal operation and for routine peaks in demand; however, your site might also encounter occasional spikes. If it does, you must decide how much degradation in performance (if any) you will allow at those times. Routine peaks on most sites reach about twice the average amount of utilization, whereas spikes can easily be a full order of magnitude beyond the average.

The Windows 2000 virtual memory system is designed to be self-tuning. The Virtual Memory Manager and Cache Manager within Windows 2000 adjust the size

**TABLE 6-6** Objects and Counters to View Memory Bottlenecks on a Server

| Object | Counter | Possible Bottleneck If Meets Criteria |
|---|---|---|
| Memory | Available bytes | Value near or under 4MB and pages/sec high |
| Memory | Pages second | High values not good if accompanied by low available bytes indicator |
| Paging file | % usage | If large, consider adding RAM to system; size of pagefile multiplied by % of pagefile in use |

of the file system cache, the working sets of processes, the paged and nonpaged memory pools, and the paging files on disk in order to produce the most efficient use of available physical memory. Similarly, the IIS 5.0 service regulates the size of the IIS object cache. Therefore, the primary purpose of monitoring memory in a Windows 2000-based server running IIS 5.0 is to make sure that the server has enough physical memory, not to adjust the size of each memory component, as might be the case with other operating systems.

***ASP files are cached in RAM and, unless limits are set on the number of cached files, they do not expire.***

Memory shortages frequently show up as or appear to be problems in other components. Therefore, when your server has a problem, it is a good idea to check memory before anything else.

**EXERCISE 6-2**

CertCam 6-2

## Installing MetaEdit Utility

In this exercise, you learn how to install the MetaEdit utility. Do the following:

1. Log in to the domain as Administrator.
2. Download the self-extracting file, MtaEdt2.1, that can be found at www.microsoft.com/technet/download/default.asp and then extract the files it contains.
3. Click Yes if you agree with the license request.
4. Accept the default setup installation for the file, or you may choose to change the directory. Click the large setup button to continue.
5. Select the program group to add the MetaEdit 2.1 icon or accept the default. Click OK. Click Continue when the installation has completed.
6. The installation is now complete and the utility is ready for use.

### Monitoring Available Memory

Compare the total physical memory that is available to Windows 2000 with the available memory remaining when you are running all server services. To gather more reliable results, log this value over time, making certain to include periods of peak activity. The system attempts to keep the amount of available bytes at 4MB or more, but it is sensible to keep at least 5 percent of memory (rather than a specific number of MB) available for peak use.

To track available memory, log the Computername\Memory\Available Bytes counter. Remember, Computername is not the one in Perfmon; it merely refers to the name of the computer you are running.

exam Watch

***Remember, if you are monitoring paging and you see a high rate of disk paging, this is indicative of a memory shortage.***

See the following bullets for information regarding memory shortage information when monitoring your IIS Web server.

- **Monitor paging** Continuous high rates of disk paging indicate a memory shortage.
- **Number of hard page faults** If a process requests a page in memory and the system cannot find it at the requested location, a page fault has occurred. The system also counts a page fault on a file access if the requested page is not found in the file system cache and must be retrieved from storage. The page fault counters do not distinguish between hard and soft faults, so you must combine counter information to deduce the number of hard faults.

on the Job

***If the page is elsewhere in memory, the fault is called a*** *soft page fault.* ***If the page must be retrieved from disk, the fault is called a*** *hard page fault.*

To track paging, log the following counters: Memory\Page Faults/sec, Memory\Cache Faults/sec, and Memory\Page Reads/sec. The first two of these track working sets and the file system cache. The Page Reads counter helps you track hard page faults: a high rate of page faults coupled with a high rate of page reads (these also show up in the Disk counters) indicates a high rate of hard faults.

### Monitoring the File System Cache

The working set of the file system is the *file system cache*, an area set aside in physical memory where the file system stores its frequently used and recently used data. The system reserves about 50 percent of physical memory for the file system cache. If the system detects that it is running out of memory, it trims the cache. IIS 5.0 functions like a dedicated file server, and a large and effective file system cache is essential to its overall performance.

### Monitoring the Paged and Nonpaged Memory Pool Sizes

The system's memory pools hold objects created and used by applications and the operating system. The contents of the memory pools are accessible only in privileged mode. On servers running IIS 5.0, threads that service connections are stored in the nonpaged pool, along with other objects used by the service, such as file handles. To monitor the pool space used directly by IIS 5.0, log the Computername\Process\Pool Paged Bytes: Inetinfo and Computername\Process\Pool Nonpaged Bytes: Inetinfo counters. To monitor the pool space for all processes on the server, log the Computername\Memory\Pool Paged Bytes and Computername\Memory\Pool Nonpaged Bytes counters.

### Tuning TCP Sockets

IIS 5.0 socket allocation is on a per-port basis, whereas in IIS 4.0, TCP sockets allocation is on a per-Web-site basis. Therefore, if you were an ISP using IIS 4.0 with thousands of sites on one server, the overall server would experience performance issues. With IIS 5.0, despite the number of Web sites you place on any particular port, they all share the sockets allocated to that port. Remember that if you place a large number of sites on one port, performance could still suffer. If you have a mission-critical site, you can avoid the risk of performance issues by disabling socket pooling for that particular site. Use the MetaEdit tool to change related Metabase entry MD_DISABLE_SOCKET_POOLING. As an alternative to the command line, you can change Metabase settings with Metabase Editor, which is distributed on the Resource Kit companion CD. The Metabase settings can be changed by the following switches at the command prompt: /LM/W3SVC/X (*X* relates to the number of the site). This causes the site to revert to IIS 4.0 behavior. If you choose to disable socket pooling, you should do so only at the site level, so that other less critical sites can continue to take advantage of this feature. Scripting may only be used to set this property. It is not available in the IIS snap-in. To disable global socket pooling, use the following command at the command prompt:

```
c:\inetpub\adminscripts\cscript adsutil.vbs set w3svc\disablesocketpooling true
```

The command prompt will reply:

```
disablesocketpooling : (BOOLEAN) True
```

***If pooling is enabled and you set bandwidth throttling for a site in the pool, the setting affects all the other sites as well. For this reason, it is a good idea to disable pooling for any throttled site(s).***

### Tuning Inetinfo.exe

Inetinfo.exe is a single process but is multithreaded. This means that the process is referred to as Inetinfo.exe. Inetinfo.exe provides a cache of objects associated with Web, SMTP, FTP services, and ASPs. To improve the performance of the Inetinfo process, you can tune the process to stay in RAM for faster access time. Depending on the RAM installed on your Windows 2000 server, there are two ways to configure this. Figure 6-6 shows you how to maximize data throughput for file sharing. Follow the same method and, depending on the amount of RAM in your system, you could choose Maximize Data Throughput for Network Applications under File and Printer Sharing for Network Properties.

Table 6-7 shows which option to use, based on RAM and file system cache settings.

Performance Monitor is used to view cache activity in IIS 5.0. Select the Performance object and choose the Internet Information Services Global tab. You can use the following counters to view cache activity in IIS 5.0:

- Cache File Handles
- Cache Flushes
- Cache Hits
- Cache Hits %
- Cache Misses
- Directory Listings
- Objects

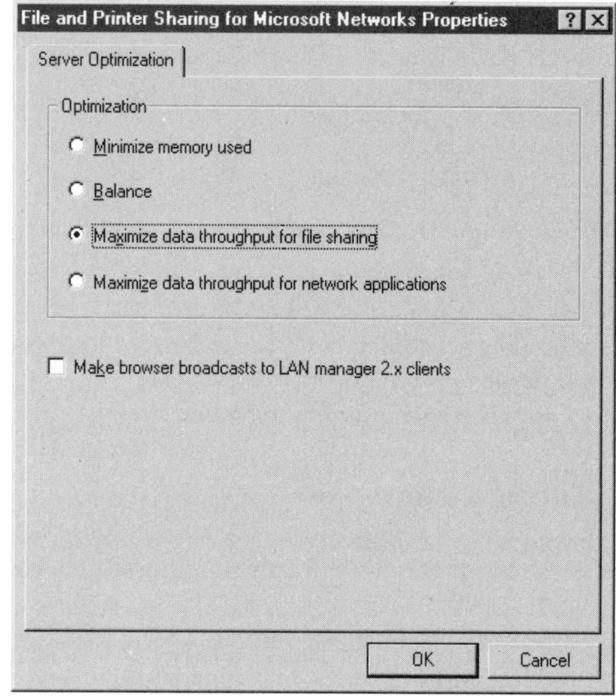


**FIGURE 6-6** Changing the Options for Server Performance

The Cache Hits % counter should be as high as possible. If you see a low value, it could mean that the server cannot retrieve enough files from cache. Either your cache is too small or many different files are being requested by clients.

## Increasing the Pagefile Size for Better Performance

Windows 2000 can dynamically increase the size of a pagefile up to the maximum setting on the Properties setting for the pagefile. Figure 6-7 shows the configuration

**TABLE 6-7** Maximizing Inetinfo.exe for Performance

| File System Cache Maximum | Server RAM | Server Optimization |
|---|---|---|
| 432MB | 1GB | Maximize data throughput for file sharing |
| 960MB | 2GB | Maximize data throughput for file sharing |
| Less than 432MB | Less than 1GB | Maximize data throughput for network applications |

**FIGURE 6-7**

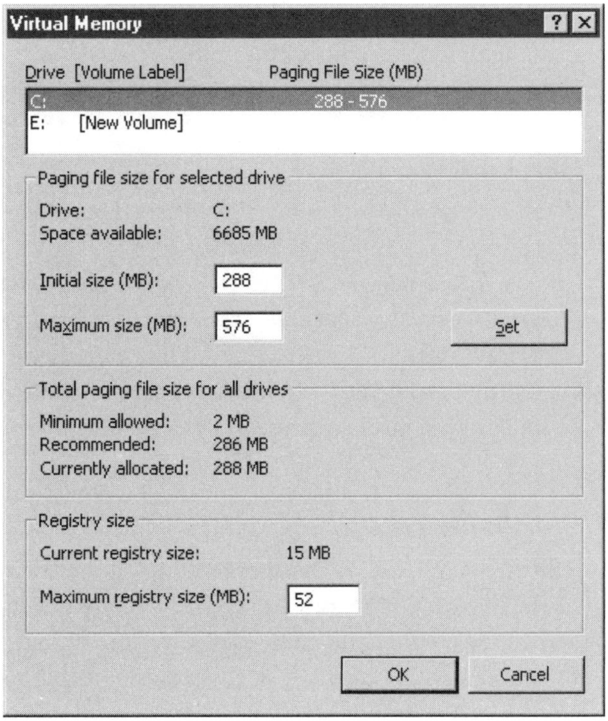

Changing a Server's Pagefile Settings

settings for pagefile. You can locate this setting by choosing Start | Settings | Control Panel | System | Advanced | Performance Options | Change. It is recommended that you set the pagefile's maximum size to twice that of the available RAM on the server, up to 4GB. For additional information regarding the pagefile size, please see the knowledge base article Q171793 on the Microsoft site at http://support.microsoft.com.

***Avoid placing the pagefile on RAID 5 or the second partition. Because RAID 5 is write intensive, it would cause the disk performance to be slower than usual. If you place the pagefile on the second partition and the hard disk drive is split in half, the disk heads must move across the hard drive to access the pagefile.***

## Removing Unnecessary Services

If you are running only IIS 5.0 on a server and nothing else, why would you need to have remote access services running in the background? Unless you are using these services for some type of remote administration, it is a good idea not to have them running. Use the Services icon in the Control Panel to disable a service. If you simply stop the service, the service will start again the next time you reboot.

### Screen Savers

Black-background screen savers are best when you are securing the system console. Some screen savers that are installed with Windows 2000 are memory intensive. You can use Task Manager to view the amount of RAM a screen saver uses by selecting a screen saver such as OpenGL and open Task Manager by pressing CTRL-ATL-DEL. View the Available Bytes counter for a few moments. Take note of the value, then change the screen saver to a blank background and view the counter again. Be aware of using screen savers that use 3D objects; they have a high CPU usage.

## Active Service Pages

ASPs are server-side Web pages residing on the Web server that are used to create interactive sites. ASPs can also create Web applications, dynamic server-side scripts, and COM components to be used with the combination of HTML pages. Because the script is Web based, the Web server does all the work.

### New in ASP

IIS 5.0 includes enhancements to make ASPs easier to use to write scripts or develop Web pages or applications:

- **ASP self-tuning** ASP can now detect when external resources block requests. If the CPU becomes overburdened, ASP cuts back the number of threads.
- **Error handling** You can trap errors using the Server.GetLastError method. The error is trapped in a new .ASP page.
- **Encoded scripts** ASP now supports script encoding that makes the code on the page appear in unreadable ASCII text. This prevents others from stealing the code from the Web page. For more information, visit Windows Script Technologies at http://msdn.microsoft.com/scripting/.

Microsoft IIS 5.0 has implemented many additional new features in IIS 5.0. The Microsoft site has further information: www.microsoft.com/windows2000/server/evaluation/features/web.asp.

### ASP Tuning

IIS 5.0 has made significant improvements over IIS 4.0 in terms of handling ASP queuing:

- The IIS template cache limit was set to unlimited in IIS 4.0; in IIS 5.0 it is set to 256 files. Although the limit can be adjusted, do not set this limit to 0.
- The script engine cache limit was set to 30 in IIS 4.0. In IIS 5.0, it is 120.
- The ProcessorThreadMax setting in IIS 4.0 was 10. In IIS 5.0, it is by default 25.

If the IIS template cache were set to –1, as it was in IIS 4.0, the cache would grow increasingly large. If a Web site had a great deal of ASP content, the IIS template cache had a tendency to fill the entire RAM in the server. Never set the limit on the IIS template cache to 0; doing so would cause no hits on the IIS script engine cache. The IIS script engine cache hits provide better performance than the IIS template cache. Unless you have only static pages, your performance would suffer. The same rules apply for the script engine cache limit and the ProcessorThreadMax settings as they did for the IIS template cache.

## CPU

The CPU processes instructions received by the computer. Clock speeds are usually viewed in MHz. The data bus can carry 16, 32, or 64 bits of data round trip. You can verify your processor bottleneck by a high CPU percentage utilization. If your usage is high, you can do one of the following:

- Upgrade the processor.
- Move applications that require high processor usage to another server.
- Replicate the site on another server.
- Add additional CPUs if possible.

Make certain that you have the proper CPUs sized for the version of Windows 2000 on which you will run IIS 5.0. (If you are running plain Win2K Server on a platform with eight CPUs, you lose out.) Adding CPUs to your server will not automatically double the capacity, but it will give you a sizable processing increase.

A note on the CPU utilization issue: Sometimes CPU utilization is very high due to a software error; sometimes this can be addressed by applying the latest drivers or updates and patches to the server. Table 6-8 shows the number of CPUs supported by OS edition.

When IIS 5.0 is installed, it runs Web applications at a medium application level. This allows the applications to run in an isolated process. In the event that a Web application crashes, it will not interfere with the entire IIS Web site. The application-tuning setting is found by right-clicking Web Site, then clicking Properties | Home Directory Tab | Application Protection. Table 6-9 shows the application protection level, performance level, and description of the settings.

The list below represents some tuning tips for your IIS 5.0 Web Server for enhanced performance.

- Throttling processes
- Controlling where Web server processes are executed
- Tuning the IIS queue size
- Optimizing ASPs for CPU
- A new feature in Windows 2000 is job objects, which have two main functions:
  - Account for CPU time usage
  - Throttle CPU usage

The accounting aspect of job objects allows you to account for CPU usage time. With throttling, you can limit the CPU time that any application is using to 10 percent.

**TABLE 6-8** Software Edition and CPU Support

| Software Edition | CPUs Supported |
|---|---|
| Windows 2000 Professional | 2 |
| Windows 2000 Server | 4 |
| Windows 2000 Advanced Server | 8 |
| Windows 2000 Datacenter Server | 32 (this is not sold stand-alone, it must be purchased bundled) |

**TABLE 6-9** Minimum RAM Requirements Based on a Pentium-Class CPU

| Number of CPUs | Minimum RAM |
| --- | --- |
| 1 | 256MB |
| 4 | 512MB |
| 6 | 1.5GB |
| 8 | 2.0GB |

**Accounting Scope** The following rule applies to the accounting scope: Only Object-Oriented Programming (OOP) applications are accounted, pooled OOP apps are not accounted. This is on a per Web site basis. Common Gateway Interface (CGI) applications are also accounted. This rule also applies to CPU throttling. To turn on extended logging use the MMC console. When using the MMC console log the Process Event, Total User Time and Total Kernel Time.

## Cost

*Transaction Cost Analysis (TCA)* attempts to diminish the vagueness of capacity planning by providing a structure for estimating each resource cost as a function of a usage profile, service mix, or hardware configuration. Hardware resources include CPU, RAM, system bus, cache, disk subsystem, and network. With the TCA approach, the potential for overestimating hardware is reduced because the entire workload range is measured. TCA also captures all overhead present during runtime, such as the operating system.

The requirements for performing TCA include:

- Usage profile
- Instrumentation
- Performance monitoring tool
- Load-generation tools that support all network protocols invoked by the services under analysis
- Load generation and usage profile scripts
- Configuration tool

## FROM THE CLASSROOM

### A Word About IIS 5.0 Tuning

Tuning IIS 5.0 for optimal performance is an ongoing process. In addition to tuning your Web site, you must have a good disaster recovery plan in place. To get the most performance out of your IIS 5.0 server, ask yourself the following questions:

- What is the use of this server?
- Does my hardware meet the requirements needed for good, solid performance?
- Is the server running other services such as e-mail? If, so is the hardware sized for additional resources that the service is using?

Items to do first to begin Tuning for Performance:

- Establish a baseline first during normal operations.
- Establish a baseline during heavy traffic times.
- Use the WCAT tool to stress-test the Web server.
- Use Performance Monitor to check performance during peak times.
- Create a daily or weekly to-do list (depending on traffic) to check performance.
- Keep all service packs and hot fixes up to date.
- Back up the Metabase before and after any changes.
- Back up the entire server daily (this is not really an option, it is a *must*).
- Create two emergency repair disks (ERDs) before and after any type of change and put the date on them.
- Have a good disaster recovery plan in place.
- Create an identical IIS 5.0 server in your lab and have a mock disaster occur. Time yourself as to how long it takes to recover your information. (Do not perform this step on your production IIS 5.0 server—it could have career-limiting effects!)

Finally, do not forget documentation. Document your IIS 5.0 server to aid other administrators in understanding the configuration so they may assist you in the future. Sometimes you will forget the configuration parameters yourself, so do keep notes.

*—Jada Brock-Soldavini, MCSE*

Microsoft has a great link for using TCA to get a cost ratio based on CPU usage. It is a complex topic that could consume a book or, at a minimum, a few chapters in itself. The document is based on high-usage sites that use Commerce Server. Visit www.microsoft.com/TechNet/comm/cataltca.asp.

### Usage Profile

When dealing with the usage profile, you need to assess the expected profile for each service, gathering user behavior and site profile information. To get started with this information, you can view the transaction logs of similar services. After you've gathered this information, you can use the information to establish a baseline.

### Site Profile

The effectiveness and flexibility of your capacity-planning model depends on a careful assessment of the expected usage profile for each service. This usage profile consists of both individual and aggregated user behavior and site profile information. Analysis of transaction logs of similar services provides a helpful starting point for defining this profile. Characteristics derived from this profile are used to establish baselines. A site profile can be defined by the following information:

- Services deployed
- Number of concurrent users for each service
- Expected deployment configuration

This deployment configuration should include the servers on which each software component will reside.

### Instrumentation

Although instrumentation to enable measurement of resource utilization is often already built into an operating system, the metrics to measure the performance of service transaction characteristics must also be defined and then built into the analytical tools. You can use counters with Performance Monitor to view analytical information. These counters include queue lengths, context switching, out-of-memory paging, network utilization, and latencies. In particular, when you use multiple-disk RAID arrays, the average disk queue length per array should not exceed the number of physical disks per array.

### Load-Generation Tool

Before load testing your Web server, restart it to get rid of caches and to restore the system to a steady state for data collection. Run each monitor long enough to generate an estimate of the load. In addition to collecting measurements of resource utilization and throughput, you should also monitor counters that help isolate points of contention in the system.

The concurrent connections should start small and increase incrementally up to a maximum of *N*. Then the transaction throughput begins to decline from its maximum at *T(max)*. The decline in throughput is due to factors such as high rates of context switching, queues, and out-of-memory paging.

**ISP Example** An ISP is interested in deploying a Web hosting platform that supports browsing of subscriber Web pages through the Internet. The platform will also provide subscribers with the use of FTP services to control file transfer of these Web pages from and to the host site. The services required to support this scenario consist of Web (HTTP), FTP, directory (for example, LDAP), and database (for example, SQL Server) services. The Web and FTP services are now configured on front-end servers; the directory and database services may each reside on separate back-end servers. All transactions by FTP will only "delete," "get," "open," and "put" to generate the most important load in amassed hits. Only these services should be monitored. The transactions for this analysis of HTTP will consist of "delete," "get," "open," and "put" for FTP and "get" for HTTP. The size and types of files transferred or deleted using FTP and the Web page size requested using HTTP are important transaction parameters.

**EXERCISE 6-3**

CertCam 6-3

## Customizing Error Messages to Point to a URL

In this exercise, you learn how to customize an error message by mapping to the URL www.testiis.com an error code bad request. Do the following:

1. Verify that you are logged in to the domain as administrator.
2. Create a file that contains the custom error message and place it in a directory.
3. In the IIS snap-in, select the Web site, virtual directory, directory, or file you would like to customize HTTP errors and then click Properties.

4. Select Custom Errors.
5. Select the HTTP error that you would like to change; use 400 Bad Request as the example.
6. Click Edit Properties.
7. Select URL from the drop-down list.
8. Type the URL www.testiis.com.
9. Click OK.

   Figure 6-8 shows the Error Mapping Properties sheet.

---

**CERTIFICATION OBJECTIVE 6.03**

# Calculating Cluster Size

Clustering allows software packages for multiple hard drives to connect together and appear as one. Software fault-tolerant disk sets may not be used for cluster storage. Dual, redundant RAID controllers should be used. Each cluster network must have one of four roles:

- Node-to-node communication (private networks)
- Client-to-cluster communication

**FIGURE 6-8**

Mapping an Error Code to a URL in IIS 5.0

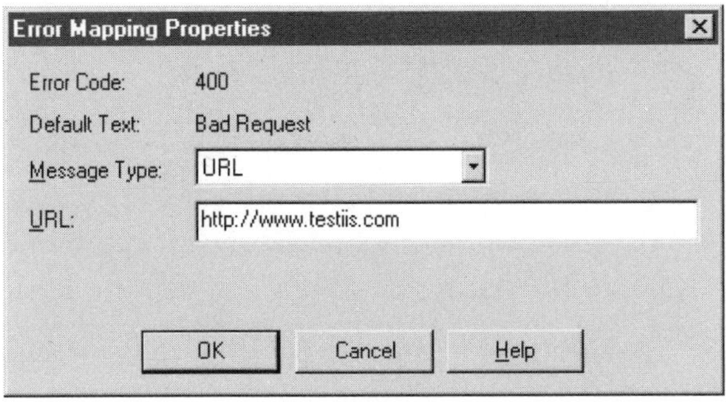

Error Mapping Properties

Error Code: 400

Default Text: Bad Request

Message Type: URL

URL: http://www.testiis.com

OK Cancel Help

- Both node-to-node communications and client-to-cluster communication
- No cluster-related communication

IIS 5.0 is designed to integrate with the Cluster Services feature of Windows 2000 Advanced Server and the Microsoft Content Replication System (CRS) feature of Microsoft Site Server.

Three types of clustering technology are used in Windows 2000:

- Network Load Balancing
- Component Load Balancing
- Cluster Services

exam Watch

***Note that only Windows 2000 Advanced Server and Windows 2000 Datacenter Server support back-end clusters.***

Cluster Services allow you to build back-end clusters with two nodes. If you are using Windows 2000 Datacenter, you can build up to four nodes. Node failure is detected through a heartbeat method. All nodes exchange heartbeats; if one node misses five heartbeats in a row, the other nodes believe it has failed. The nodes then regroup and recalculate membership in the cluster. If the node cannot be reached, it is kicked out of the cluster. Applications also use the heartbeat method.

## EXERCISE 6-4

### Installing Network Load Balancing

1. Log on to the domain controller with domain administrative privileges.
2. Click Start | Settings | Network and Dial-Up Connections | Local Area Connections.
3. Click Properties. Network Load Balancing should be visible but not checked.
4. If Network Load Balancing is not listed, you are not using Microsoft Windows 2000 Advanced Server or it was previously uninstalled and needs to be reinstalled.
5. Check the Network Load Balancing box and click Properties.

Windows 2000 Datacenter Server supports up to four nodes. It supports only Fibre Channel. Keep this in mind if you plan to deploy this type of clustering. Because disks can become a single point of failure with this configuration, you need to use a rights storage system. Since Windows 2000 does not support software rights, you must use a hardware resource called a *quorum resource* to guarantee that only one node owns a disk at any particular time.

**Server Clusters** Applications can run on a server cluster if they meet the following conditions:

- TCP/IP is the only protocol used.
- The application must be able to specify where its data is stored.
- Clients connecting on a server cluster must be permitted to reconnect in the event of a failure on the network.

### Fault Tolerance

If one node stops working, another server node should immediately pick up the load, and users should not notice any disruption. This process is called a *failover*. *Failback* means that the failed server node has been placed back online and has picked up the load.

***The IIS snap-in must be used to configure Web or FTP properties. You cannot stop and start the sites with the IIS snap-in, however. You must use the cluster administrator on a clustered server.***

### Clustering IIS 5.0

Use the Cluster Administrator tool and select the group into which you want to add the resource. A *group* in clustering technology is a unit of failover within the environment.

**EXERCISE 6-5**

### Using the Cluster Administrator Tool

1. Log on to the domain controller with domain administrative privileges.
2. Choose Start | Programs | Administrative Tools, and select Cluster Administration Tool.

3. Click the file, then click New, then click Resource.
4. Enter a name and description for the resource.
5. Select Resource Type IIS Server Instance from the drop-down box.
6. From the selection field, select the node in the cluster to which you want to make the resource available.
7. Click Next, then Add. Click Next, then select WWW.
8. Select a server from the drop-down list.
9. Select OK.

---

### Network Load Balancing Clusters

Network Load Balancing, or NLB, is an active-active and a shared-nothing solution. The term *active-active* means that no node sits idle; *shared-nothing* means that no servers completely share their disk subsystems. NLB is software-based and works by installing a virtual NIC adapter on each Web server. Only one IP address is advertised to the Internet, and when a response is received, depending on your configuration, a response is sent to the cluster. Refer to the following checklist before installing NLB on your server:

- IP addresses must be static. Dynamic Host Configuration Protocol (DHCP) cannot be used.
- Each host in a cluster must belong to the same subnet.
- TCP/IP is the only protocol that should be added to this adapter.
- If you are using multiple network adapter cards, make certain that NLB installs on one adapter only. This makes the adapter the cluster adapter.
- Port rules and cluster parameters must be set identically on all clustered hosts.

This section does not cover the specifics of setting up the NLB adapter. You must enter an IP address, all hosts must be on the same subnet, enter the Internet name, and a remote password. The Remote Control Box must be checked to enable remote control from other machines.

***If the cluster host is connected to a hub to receive requests, all traffic is automatically sent to all switch ports. This is referred to as flooding switch ports.***

## Manageability

The Cluster Administrator utility can be installed on computers running Windows NT Service Pack 3 or later and Windows 2000. The tool may be used to remotely manage a cluster. You can use the utility to monitor the status of the cluster on a routine basis. The Cluster Administrator also allows you to view the two resource groups: cluster group and disk group. The *cluster group* is essential for connectivity to a cluster. The *disk group* is created for each disk resource on the cluster. A concern when using clustering is keeping the data replicated. The command-line utility Iissync.exe can be used for managing data within a clustered environment.

## Application Scalability

The Cluster Application Wizard is used to configure applications to run on a cluster. Applications must be TCP/IP based and must be able to specify where the application data is stored. Any application that is run on a server must be able to store its data in a specific location. The client machine must be configured to retry to connect to the network in the event of a failover. Applications are put into two separate groups. Either applications support the cluster application programming interface (API) or they do not.

### Cluster-Aware Applications

Cluster-aware applications can register with the cluster service to receive status information. These applications support the cluster API. Supporting the cluster API means that the application calls the computer on which it is running to determine its name.

### Cluster-Unaware Applications

Cluster-unaware applications do not support the cluster API. They can still be used in a cluster and configured to failover.

## Cost

When you are planning, it is important to consider all the potential costs discussed in this section.

### Disk Planning

Each node must have enough available disk space to store permanent copies of all applications and other resources required to run all groups. While you're planning, calculate each node as though it were running all resources alone. Add allowances to the disk space so that if a failure occurs, any other node can efficiently run the application.

### CPU Requirements for Clustering

Plan for a failover when sizing your CPU. Make sure that each node in the cluster has enough capacity when a failure occurs. If you do not plan for adequate CPU speed and a failover occurs, the node that picks up the failure would be pushed to its limits.

### RAM Requirements for Clustering

When sizing your server for clustering, make certain that you have enough RAM installed on all nodes. The same rule that applies to the CPU requirements applies to the RAM requirements. Additionally, remember to set your paging files appropriately for each node in the cluster.

***A bug occurs when you try to uninstall Microsoft Cluster Services when running IIS 5.0. All IIS resources, including SMTP and NNTP, must be removed before you uninstall Microsoft Cluster Service. If you do not follow this procedure, you will not be able to stop or start the previously clustered IIS sites. The fix is to type the following at the command prompt:***

```
Inetpub\AdminScripts\adsutil.vbs set <service name>/<instance id>/ClusterEnabled 0
```

CERTIFICATION OBJECTIVE 6.04

# Calculating Storage Requirements

When you are planning to install IIS 5.0, calculating enough storage is a necessity. Not only must you plan for the Web and FTP services, applications, overhead, and Windows 2000 operating system—you must also plan for disk redundancy. Table 6-10 shows the basic disk capacity needed by application type.

## RAID Level

RAID is a solution for disk optimization. Windows 2000 continues to support the soft implementation of RAID—and now it no longer requires you to reboot the server. The newer disks support the mirror set, the stripe set, and so on, without requiring a reboot. Keep the following points in mind if you use RAID to improve disk performance:

- In a growing environment, hardware implementation of RAID is a more popular option.
- The more cache on your disk drives and disk controllers, the better your disk performance.

Realize that the IIS cache parameter also affects performance. In other words, if you have a server that is a dedicated to the Web, changing in the registry the amount

**TABLE 6-10** IIS 5.0 Server Disk Capacity Requirements by Application Type

| Application | Disk Storage Capacity Needed |
|---|---|
| Windows 2000 operation system requirement and IIS 5.0 | Over 500MB |
| Pagefile.sys file | 2GB |
| Web server application | 3GB |
| Server-based firewall | 30MB |
| Web content e-commerce and intranet | 10GB |

of variable RAM set aside for IIS cache pages can increase performance. Choosing which RAID level to use when planning your Web site is very important. You are not only dealing with fault-tolerance issues, but also various RAID levels can affect your Web server's performance. View the different RAID levels as described in the following discussion so that you get a better understanding of what they do in terms of fault tolerance and performance.

There are actually two different types of fault tolerance: RAID levels and mirrored volumes. RAID is good for redundancy, but in an environment in which information is frequently updated, mirrored volumes could be a better solution. This section discusses in detail RAID levels only. Table 6-11 provides a guide to using various RAID levels in specific situations.

exam Watch

***Know your RAID levels inside and out. Know which ones offer fault tolerance and which ones do not. Remember which ones have the best performance and which have the slowest or fastest read and write access.***

## RAID 0

RAID 0 is called *disk striping* because of its use of a *stripe set.* Data is divided into blocks, then spread into a fixed order among all disks in the array.

RAID 0 improves read/write performance by spreading operations across multiple disks so that operations can be performed independently and simultaneously. It has no fault tolerance.

## RAID 1

RAID 1 is known as *disk mirroring* because of its use of a *mirror set.* Disk mirroring provides a redundant, identical copy of a selected disk. All data written to the primary disk is written to the mirror disk.

**TABLE 6-11** Choosing the Right RAID Level

| Requirement | Choose This RAID Level |
|---|---|
| Need security | RAID 5 supports NTFS and FAT. |
| Need good read and write performance | Disk mirroring has good read and write performance. |
| Need to support large number of hard disks | RAID 5 supports up to 32 hard disks. |
| Need lower usage of system memory | Disk mirroring uses less memory than RAID. |

RAID 1 provides fault tolerance and generally improves read performance (but could degrade write performance).

### RAID 2

RAID 2 is not as efficient as other RAID levels, so it is not used very much. This level adds redundancy using an error correction method that spreads parity across all disks. It also employs a disk-striping strategy that breaks a file into bytes and spreads it across multiple disks. RAID 2 offers only a nominal improvement in disk utilization and read/write performance over mirroring (RAID 1).

### RAID 3

RAID 3 uses the same striping method as RAID 2, but the error correction method requires only one disk for parity data. Use of disk space varies with the number of data disks.

RAID 3 provides some read/write performance improvement.

### RAID 4

This level employs striped data in much larger blocks or segments than RAID 2 or RAID 3. RAID 4 holds user data separate from error-correction data. Its error-correction method requires only one disk for parity data.

RAID 4 is not as efficient as other RAID levels and is not generally used.

### RAID 5

RAID 5, also called *disk striping with parity,* has similarities to RAID 4 in that it stripes the data in large blocks across the disks in an array. The major difference is that it writes the parity across all the disks. Data redundancy is provided by the parity information. The data and parity information is then arranged on the disk array so that the two are always on different disks. Striping with parity offers better performance than disk mirroring (RAID 1).

RAID 5 is the most popular RAID method.

### Level 10 (1+0)

RAID 1+0 is also known as *mirroring with striping.* This level uses a striped array of disks that is then mirrored to another identical set of striped disks. The striped array of disks is then mirrored using another set of five striped disks. RAID 1+0 provides the performance benefits of disk striping with the disk redundancy of mirroring.

RAID 1+0 provides the highest read/write performance of any RAID level and uses twice as many disks.

## Redundancy

Most high-traffic sites cannot afford to be down for even a little while. Some financial institutions require a 99.9 percent or better uptime. Most places might not be that inflexible, but consider building a Web farm using NLB or the Cluster Services included with Windows 2000. A well-designed server farm can be scaled to accommodate increased site traffic and site performance in a cost-effective manner. A high-performance, highly scalable server farm requires fewer consolidated servers. The following are several techniques for achieving a highly scalable site.

### Architecture Enhancement

Building and deploying an application improves the efficiency of the server farm. The intention here is to identify operations with similar workload factors and then dedicate servers to each type of operation. This technique enables the servers to execute trivial processes with greater capacity, serving a higher number of concurrent users per server.

### Scaling Out

*Scaling horizontally* or *out* increases capacity by adding servers to the server farm. When you scale the server farm horizontally, you add the difficulty of distributing the load evenly across multiple severs. For this reason, this method must be dealt with using load-balancing techniques. Such techniques enable the load balancer to make a response to users' requests from any server available without losing the users' sessions.

### Scaling Up

*Scaling vertically* or *up* means increasing the capacity by upgrading hardware on the server. This could mean adding CPUs with more processing power, adding large amounts of RAM, or running the operating system on SMP servers to improve the

Input/Output (I/O) throughput of the IIS 5.0 server. This method simplifies management of a site, but the hardware cost is higher than with other methods.

## CERTIFICATION SUMMARY

Baselining your IIS 5.0 Web server for proper capacity planning is the first step in setting up and optimizing your Web server for peak performance. You must choose the proper Internet connection based on the file types requested by clients. Utilizing various monitors included with IIS 5.0 and Windows 2000 and mathematical algorithms, you can determine various capacities at which your network can function properly.

Before you begin base lining your server, you must have an idea of the volume of traffic the site will handle as well as the file sizes and types requested from clients. Make sure that you measure your current performance level for a long enough time to capture an accurate picture of activity taking place on the server. Examine all portions of the server and look for prospective bottlenecks. Correct each bottleneck issue one at a time, then re-examine the server to see if the changes have improved performance. It is not a good idea to correct multiple problems at once because it could cause an adverse effect on the server and would make it difficult to know specifically what has caused the problem. Monitoring performance on an IIS 5.0 server is an ongoing process because Web sites continually change based on Web content and traffic accessing the site.

Review the capacity-planning checklist:

- Type of site implemented
- Purpose of the site
- Complexity of the site (will you use SQL, ASP, CGI?)
- Current size and future anticipated customer expansion numbers
- Find the bottlenecks
- Determine the functions of each machine in the site: mail, SMTP, and WWW
- Make a network diagram of your site and identify the slow links
- Create a user profile for each page that answers the following questions: How long do users stay on the page? Does the page generate database activity? What objects are on the page?

- Define client-side and server-side objects
- Do a test, then another test, and then another—all in a lab environment; use WCAT and load stress objects until they begin to stress, then retune if possible
- Look for Dr. Watson errors, Inetinfo failures in the event logs, and STOP errors

Before you begin to audit your network, keep in mind not to cause your server more than necessary overhead. Running multiple copies of System Monitor, for example, can place a heavy load on the server. Be cautious when using the tools mentioned in this chapter. Exam 70-226 focuses on creating and maintaining highly available Web servers using IIS 5.0 and Windows 2000 Server.

# ✓ TWO-MINUTE DRILL

## Calculating Network Capacity

- When monitoring network Traffic Management use the Network Monitor program.
- When performing a base line on the network use the following tools: Performance Monitor, Network Monitor, and Task Manager.
- Monitor Bandwidth use as well as Network traffic frequently. Both of these will change based on number of users accessing the web site and the type of information that is posted on the web site.

## Calculating Server Capacity

- Memory resources and bottlenecks
- Memory management
- Memory tuning

## Calculating Cluster Size

- Cluster roles
- Network Load Balancing (NLB) with the cluster software
- Managing a cluster in IIS 5.0

## Calculating Storage Requirements

- Calculating storage requirements in IIS 5.0
- Making the storage scalable
- Choosing a RAID level

# SELF TEST

The following questions will help you measure your understanding of the material presented in this chapter. Read all the choices carefully because there might be more than one correct answer. Choose all correct answers for each question.

## Calculating Network Capacity

1. You currently have an ISDN line connecting your site to the Internet. A new SQL database has just been implemented to allow customers to query inventory available for sale. The pages are not graphics intensive and mostly contain text only. Customers are calling the help desk saying that they are not able to access the site. You monitor the traffic on the site and realize that for a one-week time period, you receive around 18 hits per second. What can you do to correct this problem?
   - A. Add more memory to the server.
   - B. Add another processor to the server.
   - C. Upgrade the line to a T1.
   - D. Upgrade the line to a T3.
2. What does WCAT stand for?
   - A. Microsoft Web Capacity Analysis Tool
   - B. Microsoft Web Connections Analysis Tool
   - C. Microsoft Web Capacity Active Server Pages Tool
   - D. Microsoft Web Connections Active Server Page Tool
3. Your company has a large intranet site that holds legal filings. The ASPs on the search page continue to lock up and give an error message. You need to get an estimate of the volume placed on the site. What tool and which two counters can you use to find the traffic volume?
   - A. Netmon; Total Connection Attempts, Current Connections counters
   - B. Netmon; ASP Request Wait Time; Bytes Total counters
   - C. Perfmon; Total Connection Attempts, Current Connections counters
   - D. Perfmon; Web Request Wait Time, Web Bytes Total counters.

## Calculating Server Capacity

**4.** What does the phrase *NIC adapter that supports promiscuous mode* mean?

A. The NIC adapter does not pass frames as they are received.

B. The NIC adapter passes frames sent on the network.

C. The NIC adapter holds frames, then passes them forward.

D. The NIC adapter sends the frames to a predetermined address.

**5.** You have a process that is taking up a large amount of CPU. You need the process to run, but it can take a lower priority. How can you assign this task a lower priority?

A. Press CTRL+ALT+DEL, then click on the Task Manager tab. Right-click the file under Image Name and then Set the priority to Average.

B. Press CTRL+ALT+DEL, then click on the Task Manager tab. Right-click the file under Image Name and set the priority to Below Normal.

C. Press CTRL+ALT+DEL, then click on the Task Manager tab. Right-click the file under Image Name and set the priority to High.

D. Press CTRL+ALT+DEL, then click on the Task Manager tab. Right-click the file under Image Name and set the priority to Low.

## Calculating Server Size

**6.** How much RAM does each client connection take on an IIS 5.0 Server?

A. 10MB RAM per connection

B. 100KB of RAM per connection

C. 10KB RAM per connection

D. 1KB RAM per connection

**7.** You have four CPUs in your IIS 5.0 server. What is the minimum amount of RAM you should have installed?

A. 256MB

B. 512MB

C. 1.5GB

D. 2.0GB

8. What are features of using COM+ in Windows 2000 Server and IIS 5.0? COM+ applications are automatically restarted if they stop. (Choose all that apply).
   A. Windows 2000 Security is automatically enforced.
   B. Fewer lines of code are required to make the object transaction aware.
   C. It is scalable.
   D. A, B, and C.
   E. A, B, C, and D.
9. What does OLTP mean?
   A. Online Transferable Processing
   B. Online Transactional Programs
   C. Online Transferable Programs
   D. Online Transaction Processing
10. If you need to read data log over a period of time, which tool can you use?
    A. Pview.exe
    B. PerfLog.exe
    C. Pviewer.exe
    D. Perfmon.exe
11. If you are monitoring the paging files and see that the % Usage counter is considerably large, what algorithm can you use to figure out how much RAM you need to add to the system?
    A. Size of RAM multiplied by % of pagefile in use
    B. Size of pagefile multiplied by % of pagefile in use
    C. Size of pagefile multiplied by hard drive space available
    D. Size of RAM multiplied by % of hard drive space available
12. Why would you need to disable TCP sockets for a site in IIS 5.0? (Choose all that apply.)
    A. To increase hard disk drive performance in IIS 5.0
    B. For better performance of the Web site
    C. So that the site does not share common ports with other Web sites on the server
    D. So that the site shares common ports with other Web sites on the server

**13.** If you are running less than 1GB of RAM on your server, what should your file system cache maximum be set to, and how can you optimize the server performance? (Choose all that apply.)

A. File system cache maximum is less than 432MB; server optimization maximizes data throughput for file sharing.

B. File system cache maximum is 960MB; server optimization maximizes data throughput for network applications.

C. File system cache maximum is 960MB; server optimization maximizes data throughput for file sharing.

D. File system cache maximum is less than 432MB; server optimization maximizes data throughput for network applications.

## Calculating Cluster Size

**14.** Choose the types of clustering technology used in Windows 2000 Server.

A. NIC Load Balancing, Component Load Balancing, and Cluster Services

B. Network Load Balancing, Component Load Balancing, and Cluster Services

C. Network Load Balancing, CPU Load Balancing, and Cluster Services

D. Network Load Balancing, Cluster Load Balancing, and Cluster Services

**15.** You have Microsoft Cluster Services installed. You notice that a node has missed five heartbeats. What is the first thing you should do next?

A. Reboot the server.

B. Take down the server to which the node belongs.

C. Install a new disk drive on the clustered node.

D. Do nothing.

**16.** You need to set up a server with the highest amount of fault tolerance and an average write performance on the disk drives. Which RAID option should you use?

A. RAID 0

B. RAID 1

C. RAID 5

D. RAID 1+0

17. What is the main function of job objects in Windows 2000 and IIS 5.0? (Choose all that apply.)

    A. Account for RAM usage

    B. Throttle RAM usage

    C. Account for CPU usage

    D. Throttle CPU usage

## Calculating Storage Requirements

18. You are planning to purchase a server that will have only Windows 2000 and IIS 5.0 running on it. How much disk space at a minimum should be available?

    A. 10GB

    B. 30GB

    C. 2GB

    D. More than 500MB

19. Which RAID option would you choose if you needed to support up to 32 hard disk drives with fault tolerance?

    A. RAID 0

    B. RAID 1

    C. RAID 5

    D. RAID 1+0

# LAB QUESTION

Two companies have merged. You have been hired as a consultant to merge their e-commerce SQL Server systems into one single system using a single database solution. The companies have created a hot-selling product that is in great demand and its sales are enormous.
Your objectives are as follows:

- Database availability must be 24 x 7.
- They expect 150,000 visits per day to the site.
- They expect 250 total transactions per second.
- They need a fast logging system for the SQL server.
- Customers are external and internal.
- Customers will be placing orders. Only two administrators will be completing scheduled maintenance on the server.
- Growth is expected because the company hopes to expand at a minimum of 17 percent each year.
- The ultimate goal is scalability.

You purchase a server from a well-known manufacturer with the proper warranty and service in case it is needed in the future. The server configuration is as follows:

- Windows 2000 Server
- SQL 2000 Server
- Four 750MHz CPUs; four more available on board
- A 2MB Level 2 cache
- 1.5GB of RAM ECC SDRAM, up to 8GB available on board
- I/O card configuration, one Fibre Channel adapter (slot 0) on board
- Two single-channel, full-duplex 3Com 100BaseTX Network adapter cards

The software configuration is as follows:

- Partition is on drive C: and includes:
  - Windows 2000 software

    - SQL 2000 software
    - System management software
    - Pagefile
- H: drive is configured for IIS 5.0
- I: drive is configured for Database 1 (RAID 5):
    - Fibre Channel attached RAID 1 of 2
- J: drive logs for Database 1:
    - Fibre Channel attached RAID 1 of 2
- K: drive is configured for Database 2 (RAID 5):
    - Fibre Channel attached RAID 2 of 2
- L: drive logs for Database 2:
    - Fibre Channel attached RAID 2 of 2
- P: drive is configured to hold the pagefile

# SELF TEST ANSWERS

## Calculating Network Capacity

1. ☑ C. If the traffic shows a hit rate of 18 pages per second, a T1 line will suffice for now. Since the pages accessed are mostly text files and not graphic files, the download speed will be faster. Remember that fewer graphics makes the page download more quickly.
☒ A is incorrect because adding more memory to the server will not help the hits-per-second time. **B** is incorrect because adding another processor to the server will only enhance server performance—it will not make the page download more quickly due to the ISDN line installed. **D** is incorrect because a T3 line is not what the site needs based on traffic monitoring.

2. ☑ A. WCAT is the Microsoft Web Capacity Analysis Tool used to stress-test an IIS Web server for capacity planning.
☒ B, Microsoft Web Connections Analysis Tool; **C**, Microsoft Web Capacity Active Server Pages Tool; and **D**, Microsoft Web Connections Active Server Page Tool are not valid tools in IIS 5.0.

3. ☑ C. The correct tool is Performance Monitor and the Total Connections and Current Connections counters. The Total Connections counter also includes connection requests that have failed. Run the log and get a baseline for the traffic over a period of time. At a minimum, run the log long enough to collect the data for the traffic. Do not run the counters continuously or you will experience an added load to your Web server.
☒ A and **B** are incorrect because Netmon is a tool used to analyze traffic on the network and view packets, frames, and the like. It does not use counters as Perfmon does. **D** is incorrect, even though the Perfmon tool is correct. However, the two counters—Web Request Wait Time and Web Bytes Total—are incorrect.

## Calculating Server Capacity

4. ☑ B. A *NIC adapter that supports promiscuous mode* means that the adapter passes frames that are sent over the network. Network Monitor needs this information to analyze the packets as they are sent over the network.
☒ A is incorrect because a NIC adapter that supports promiscuous mode does not keep the frames and does not pass them on to another address. **C** is incorrect because a NIC adapter that supports promiscuous mode does not hold the frames and then pass them on to another

address. **D** is incorrect because a NIC adapter that supports promiscuous mode does not send the frame to a predetermined address.

5. ☑ **D.** Using the Task Manager in Windows 2000, you can reassign the process to a lower priority. Some processes may be stopped using this method; however, other system processes cannot be stopped or reassigned.
☒ **A** is incorrect because, if you set the priority to average, it will still take up more processor usage than using the low setting. **B** is incorrect because, if you set the processor to Below Normal, it is not the lowest setting available to reassign the task. **C** is incorrect because, if you set the priority to High, it will take precedence over other processes. Remember also that if the system reboots, the settings will be lost.

## Calculating Server Size

6. ☑ **C.** A client connection takes up 10KB of RAM per connection. It is imperative that you have configured enough memory on your IIS 5.0 server.
☒ **A** is incorrect because 10MB would be an enormous amount of RAM to use for client connections. **B** and **D** are incorrect for RAM used in IIS 5.0.

7. ☑ **B.** With four CPUs installed on your IIS 5.0 server, you should have at a minimum 512MB of RAM installed for better performance. Take into account if you have other services such as NNTP, SMTP, or SQL running on the server.
☒ **A** is incorrect because 256MB is recommended for an IIS 5.0 server that has one CPU installed. **C** is incorrect because 1.5GB is recommended for an IIS 5.0 server that has six CPUs installed. **D** is incorrect because 2.0GB is recommended for an IIS 5.0 server that has eight CPUs installed.

8. ☑ **D.** COM+ offers many advantages when used with Windows 2000 and IIS 5.0. It is noninvasive, simplified programming; it works easily with applications; it is scalable, secure, and reliable.
☒ **A** and **B** are incorrect because they are not complete answers. **E** is incorrect because COM+ is also scalable.

9. ☑ **D.** OLTP stands for *Online Transaction Processing*. This means that these systems are designed to manage transaction processing and minimize disk storage requirements by using a series of related and normalized tables.
☒ **A**, **B**, and **C** are incorrect because these keywords do not exist in Windows 2000 or IIS 5.0.

**10.** ☑ **D.** Perfmon can read and log data from performance counters over a period of time. It uses the performance counters built into IIS 5.0 and the Windows 2000 operating system.
☒ **A** is incorrect because Pview.exe is used to list every process running on a machine. **B** is incorrect because PerfLog.exe captures data and writes it to a file. **C** is incorrect because Pviewer.exe is used to view running processes.

**11.** ☑ **B.** You can use the algorithm size of pagefiles multiplied by the % of the pagefile in use to figure if RAM needs to be added to a IIS 5.0 server.
☒ **A, C,** and **D** are incorrect because you would not use these algorithms to figure out whether or not you need to add additional RAM to an IIS 5.0 server. Memory problems in IIS 5.0 wreck havoc on performance. That is why Microsoft has built-in counters available to allow you to monitor your performance.

**12.** ☑ **B** and **C.** By disabling TCP sockets for a Web site using IIS 5.0, you are telling that site not to share socket allocation on a per-port basis. This allows the site to function like the IIS 4.0 Web sites in that all TCP sockets were assigned on a per-Web-site basis. By turning this feature off for a particular Web site in IIS 5.0, you are increasing the site's performance.
☒ **A** is incorrect because disabling the TCP sockets in IIS 5.0 will not improve the hard disk performance. **D** is incorrect because disabling the TCP sockets in IIS 5.0 will not allow them to share TCP ports on a per-port basis; it will allow them to share TCP Ports on a per-Web-site basis.

**13.** ☑ **D.** The file system cache maximum is less than 432MB; the server optimization maximizes data throughput for network application. This setting is under the File and Printer Sharing Network Properties; it improves the Inetinfo.exe process.
☒ **A** is incorrect because maximizing the server throughput for file sharing is not recommended to improve performance on a system that has less than 1GB of RAM. **B** is incorrect because the File system cache maximum is more than 432 MB. This setting will not help the Inetinfo performance based on the file system cache and RAM installed. **C** is incorrect because the maximum for the file system cache is too high; in addition, you would not maximize data throughput to file sharing based on the file system cache maximum and installed server RAM.

## Calculating Cluster Size

**14.** ☑ **B.** Network Load Balancing, Component Load Balancing and Cluster Service are the tree clustering technologies used in Windows 2000 server. They can only be used with Windows 2000 Advanced Server and Windows 2000 Datacenter Server.
☒ **A** is incorrect because there is no such thing as NIC load balancing as a clustering

technology for Windows 2000 Server. **C** is incorrect because there is no such thing as CPU load balancing as a clustering technology for Windows 2000 Server. **D** is incorrect because there is no such thing as cluster load balancing as a clustering technology for Windows 2000 Server.

**15.** ☑ **D.** Do nothing. The nodes in the cluster will automatically regroup and recalculate the membership in the cluster. If the node cannot be reached, it will be automatically kicked out of the cluster.
☒ **A** is not a valid option for Cluster Services. **B** is incorrect because it is not the first thing you should do when a failure has been detected in Microsoft Cluster Services. **C** is incorrect because it is not the first thing you should do when a failure has been detected in Microsoft Cluster Services. The node might have experienced a glitch rather than a complete hardware failure.

**16.** ☑ **D.** RAID 1+0 is the best to use for performance and redundancy. RAID 1+0 is known as *mirroring with striping*. This level of RAID uses a striped array of disks that are then mirrored to another identical set of striped disks.
☒ **A** is incorrect because RAID 0 is disk striping without fault tolerance. This level improves read/write performance but does not provide fault tolerance. **B,** RAID 1, is incorrect because it is also known as *disk mirroring* due to its use as a mirror set. Disk mirroring provides a redundant identical copy if a selected disk. This is slower for write performance. **C** is incorrect because RAID 5 this is the most popular method and it does provide fault tolerance, but it does not mirror the drives as RAID 1+0 does.

**17.** ☑ **C** and **D.** Job objects are new in Windows 2000. Their primary function is to allow you to account for and throttle CPU usage. You can throttle the CPU time any application is using, up to 10 percent.
☒ **A** and **B** are incorrect because these accounting features are available only to CPU usage and throttling, not RAM.

## Calculating Storage Requirements

**18.** ☑ **D.** At a minimum, more than 500MB is required to run just Windows 2000 and IIS 5.0 server. Of course, depending on what is installed on the server, more is better. Hard drive space capacity works hand in hand with RAM usage and performance.
☒ **A** is incorrect because 10GB is needed if you are running Windows 2000, IIS 5.0, Web content e-commerce, and intranet files. **B** is incorrect because 30GB is needed if you are running Windows 2000, IIS 5.0, and a server-based firewall. **C** is incorrect because 2GB is required if you are running Windows 2000, IIS 5.0, and a pagefile.sys file on the server.

**19.** ☑ C. RAID 5 supports up to 32 hard disk drives in a server.
☒ A is incorrect because RAID 0 does not provide fault tolerance. **B** is incorrect because RAID 1 mirrors disks but does not support up to 32 disk drives. **D** is incorrect because RAID 1+0 is the most fault tolerant; however, it does not support up to 32 disk drives. You must use twice as many drives for this RAID option.

# LAB ANSWER

Stress test after installation:

- Use the WCAT utility and stress-test the environment.
- Run the Perfmon tool to analyze performance on the server. Tune the IIS 5.0 server accordingly, following best practices described in this chapter. Use the tables provided to add counters when using Performance Monitor.

You have met all the requirements that needed to be met for this client. The server is expandable, the drives are redundant and, after the stress-testing on the server, it has been tuned. You will create best-practices guidelines for the two network administrators to follow so that they can continue to monitor and tune the server.

MCSE
MICROSOFT CERTIFIED SYSTEMS ENGINEER

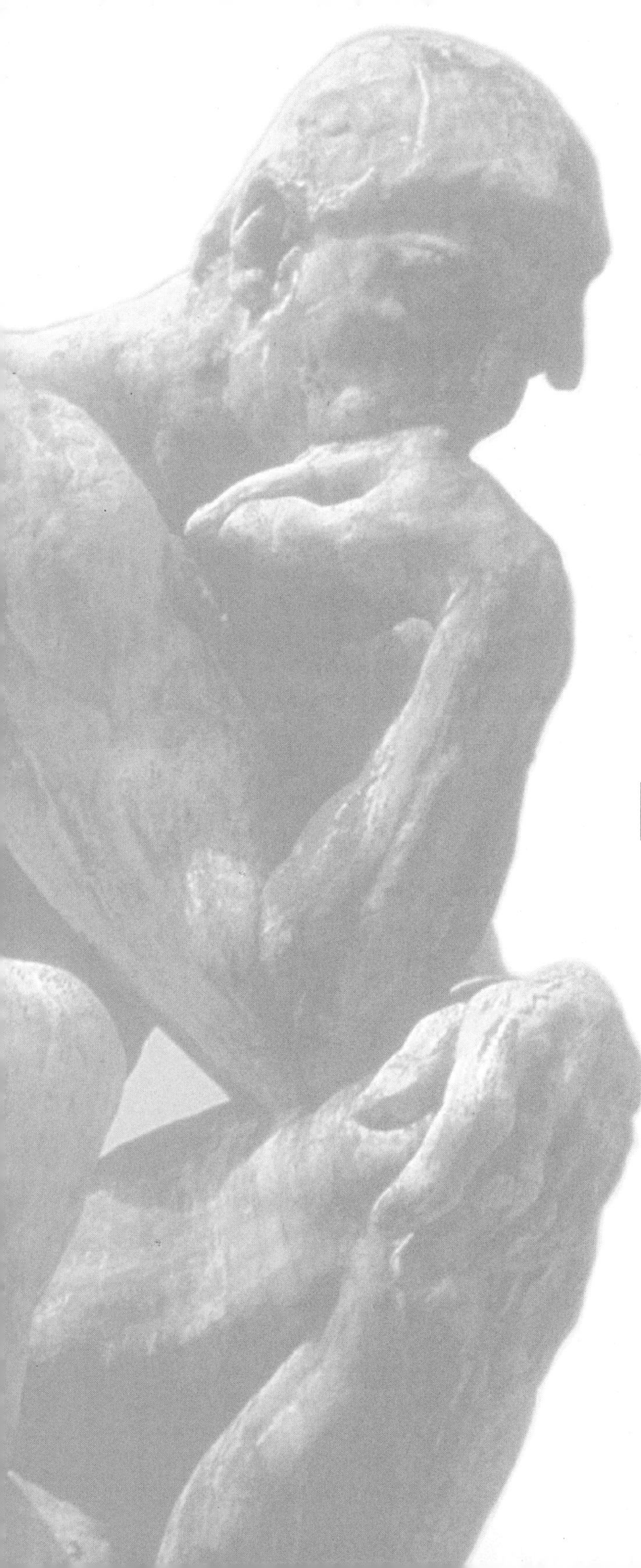

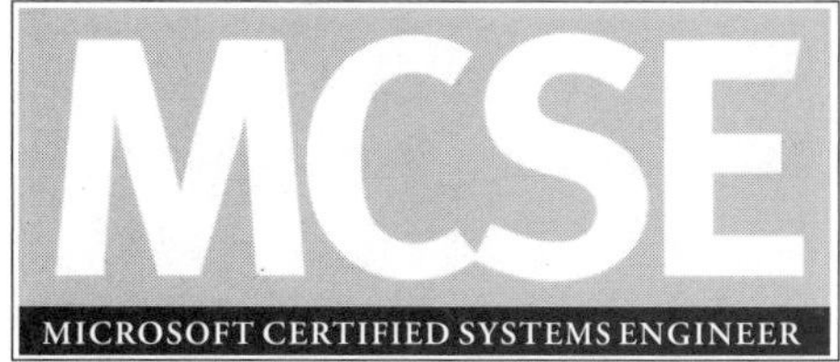

# 7

# Planning Directory Services

## CERTIFICATION OBJECTIVES

| | |
|---|---|
| 7.01 | Designing Upgrade Strategies for Networks, Servers, and Clusters |
| 7.02 | Designing Directory Services |
| ✓ | Two-Minute Drill |
| Q&A | Self Test |

Upgrading to Windows 2000 takes a little more effort than simply inserting an installation CD and clicking through the default options. Doing so could give you a functional network, but it wouldn't give you an effective one. To create a network that suits your organization's needs, you must design directory services and develop a strategy for upgrading the network, servers, and clusters.

A *directory service* is a component that stores information about objects and their attributes in a database. In Windows 2000, the directory service is called Active Directory (AD). It allows users to use a single logon to access resources on the network, and it allows administrators to work with objects that represent resources on the network. Because domains, user accounts, and other elements of the network are represented in AD, it is important that you design this structure properly.

When you decide to upgrade your network, it is important to look at the existing domain and determine the impact that Active Directory will have on it. Planning networks, servers, and clusters under Windows 2000 is different from planning for Windows NT. For example, as we'll see in this chapter, the network structure is designed differently in Windows 2000 networks than in networks running NT. In addition, special consideration—such as which server to upgrade first and the modes available to run Windows 2000—also have an impact on your network's design. By planning the upgrade in advance, you will be able to successfully create an efficient, effective network.

## CERTIFICATION OBJECTIVE 7.01

# Designing Upgrade Strategies for Networks, Servers, and Clusters

The process of designing upgrade strategies for networks, servers, and clusters will be affected by a variety of factors. Your strategy will depend on the operating systems currently being used, your network's current structure, and how you envision your future network. These factors will shape your strategy and determine the form of your overall network.

Windows 2000 allows you to upgrade from Windows NT 3.51 Server, Windows NT 4.0, and previous versions of Windows 2000. If you are upgrading from earlier versions of Windows NT, you need to upgrade to NT 4.0 before upgrading to Windows 2000. The alternative is to perform a clean install, but that will cause you to lose any account information stored on the server. The same is true if other operating systems are currently running on your server, because no other operating systems can be upgraded to Windows 2000 Server.

When you upgrade from Windows NT 3.51 or 4.0, you don't need to worry about which Service Pack is running on the server. The Windows 2000 installation supports all the Service Packs for these operating systems. Therefore, it isn't necessary to update your operating system to a particular Service Pack number before upgrading your server.

exam Watch

***To upgrade to Windows 2000, the server must be running Windows NT Server 3.51, Windows NT Server 4.0, or a previous version of Windows 2000. A trick to remembering what Windows 2000 Server supports for upgrades is remembering that Windows 2000 was originally designated as Windows NT 5.0. By remembering that Windows 2000 is built on NT technology, it makes sense that it can be upgraded only from previous versions of NT.***

When you are developing a strategy, it is also important to determine the current structure of your NT network and then decide whether changes will be made to it. In some cases, you need to upgrade the servers on your network only to Windows 2000; you don't have to worry about changing the domain structure. This is what's known as an *in-place upgrade*. In other cases, you should restructure the domain. The domains can be changed by combining some of them into a single domain; others might be split into separate domains. Additionally, you could use a combination of these methods for your upgrade strategy. As we'll see in the sections that follow, each of these methods has its own benefits and disadvantages.

## Scaling Up

*Scaling up* is a term that is used to describe the process of increasing the capabilities of a server by upgrading a server's operating system and hardware. When a server is scaled up, additional devices are added to it so that it can support an organization's increasing needs. This process may include adding such components as larger hard disks, more memory, additional CPUs or network adapters, and so forth. Such upgrades might be necessary for the server to be upgraded to Windows 2000 or to maintain or improve the network's performance.

When upgrading to Windows 2000, you might need to add new hardware to support the new operating system and any additional software you're installing. As you should know, all programs have minimal hardware requirements, including the amount of memory, free hard disk space, the CPU speed and type, and so forth. If such requirements aren't met, the operating system and any additional services and software might not function as expected.

The minimal hardware requirements for Windows 2000 Server are shown in Table 7-1. As additional software is added to the server, the amount of memory, hard disk space, and other requirements could increase to accommodate performance. As such, the hardware on your server should exceed these requirements so that it performs well as additional services, components, and other software are added.

When scaling up, it is common to perform an in-place upgrade. An in-place upgrade is the easiest upgrade solution because the domain structure remains

**TABLE 7-1** Windows 2000 Server Minimum Requirements

| Hardware | Minimum Requirements |
|---|---|
| CPU | 133MHz Pentium or higher. Windows 2000 Server supports a maximum of eight CPUs per computer. |
| Memory (RAM) | 128MB of RAM; 256MB is recommended. Windows 2000 Server supports up to a maximum of 8GB of RAM. |
| Hard disk | 1GB of free hard disk space. Additional hard disk space is needed as more components are installed or if installation is performed over the network. Network installations require an additional 100–200MB of free disk space. In addition, if FAT is the file system used, you'll need an additional 100–200MB of free disk space. The amount of free disk space required also increases if an upgrade instead of a clean install is performed. As AD is added to the server during the upgrade, user accounts could expand by as much as a factor of 10. Therefore, more disk space is required if a significant number of accounts are used. |
| Monitor | VGA or higher resolution. |
| Keyboard | Keyboard must be present to enter information. |
| Pointing device | Mouse or other pointing device is needed to select options. |
| Additional requirements for CD installations | CD-ROM or DVD drive. A 3.5-inch floppy disk drive is also required if your computer can't boot from the CD-ROM or DVD drive. |
| Additional requirements for network installation. | Network adapter card is required to connect to the network. The card must be compatible with Windows 2000, which can be determined by viewing the hardware compatibility list. An accessible server with the Setup files is also needed. |

unchanged. Any existing trust relationships and accounts are preserved when scaling up to Windows 2000 Server, so you don't need to recreate them as part of your upgrade strategy.

When performing this type of upgrade, you begin by selecting the domain you want to upgrade. As we'll see later in this chapter, different types of domain structures can exist on your Windows NT network. Some networks can consist of a single domain, in which all resources and user accounts are contained in one domain. In other cases, you might have one or more domains storing user accounts and others containing only resources. Depending on your company's needs, you might decide to incrementally upgrade your network. This is often the case when the business can't afford to upgrade all the servers at once or if NT Servers are required by certain applications used on your network. If you perform an incremental upgrade of the network, you will upgrade only certain domains and leave others as they are.

Once you've decided on the domains you'll upgrade, you should then perform a complete backup of your existing domain information. Backups are essential; they enable you to restore the data if problems occur during the upgrade. If the upgrade fails, data on the server could be lost. As a precaution, performing a full backup of all servers allows you to protect the information and restore it if necessary.

## FROM THE CLASSROOM

### What to Upgrade First

One of the biggest problems of any undertaking is deciding where to start. When it comes to determining which server to upgrade first, you're relieved of this decision because the Primary Domain Controller (PDC) is the first server that you have to upgrade to Windows 2000.

The PDC stores a master copy of the domain's user-account database. AD uses this database when it is installed to transfer information on user accounts and various other elements of your domain.

However, this might not be the only server that has a copy of this information. Backup Domain Controllers (BDCs) might exist on your network and have copies of the user-account database that are also used for authenticating users. It is wise that you synchronize the BDCs on your network prior to upgrading the PDC so that they have up-to-date information on user accounts.

*—Michael Cross, MCSE, MCP+I, MCPS, CNA*

As an additional line of defense against failed upgrades, you should take a BDC offline during the upgrade. This way, if the upgrade of your PDC fails, you can promote one of the BDCs to a PDC and be able to keep your network functioning. You would remove the upgraded PDC from the network, bring the BDC online again, and promote it to a PDC. In doing so, you are rolling back the upgrade so that your network is as it was before you began upgrading to Windows 2000.

Once the PDC is upgraded, you would then begin upgrading the BDCs in the domain. If several BDCs are being used, you don't need to upgrade them all at once. BDCs can be upgraded incrementally as needed and will continue to function while other servers are running Windows 2000 Server on the network. When the BDCs are upgraded, however, it is important that the PDC you upgraded is online. The upgraded PDC will be used as a template by the BDCs being upgraded and must be available on the network so that they can connect to the domain controller and obtain information.

### DNS Servers

DNS servers are used to resolve hostnames to IP addresses, and vice versa, so that Windows 2000 Servers and other hosts can be found on a network. DNS, short for the *Domain Name System*, is commonly associated with the Internet. However, whether your network or Web server is connected to the Internet or simply used for a local intranet, DNS is essential to Windows 2000.

DNS is highly integrated with Active Directory, and Windows 2000 networks require DNS to function. For a server to be upgraded to Windows 2000 Server, DNS must be present on the network. If a DNS server doesn't exist on the network, the DNS service will be installed on the first Windows 2000 Server on your network.

When using DNS, you need to plan ahead and determine how you will create the namespace for your domains. DNS is a distributed database, and the namespace serves as a naming scheme that provides a hierarchical structure to it. The database is indexed by name, which requires you to name each domain on your network. As a hierarchy, these domains can be either parent or child domains. For example, you could create a domain called syngress.com and then add domains below it called sales.syngress.com or finance.syngress.com. This scheme provides a structure to the domains making up the network while providing administrative barriers.

The domain name you use will depend on whether your server is an Internet Web server or if the network connected to the Internet. Domain names used for

Internet sites must be registered so that each name is unique. You can't simply make up a name, because your name could conflict with existing domain names for other sites. If your network isn't connected to the Internet, you may use registered domain names or use names that you create yourself. However, you still need to keep the names you use unique so that each domain in the namespace can be identified.

on the Job

***It is important that you give domains names that are meaningful so that users will be able to identify the purpose, location, or functionality of a particular domain. In addition, you should realize that domain names aren't case sensitive, so www.syngress.com and www.SYNGRESS.com are the same. The same applies to child domain names. You cannot name one child domain SALES.syngress.com and another sales.syngress.com.***

Another guideline to follow is to keep the number of child domains small so that the hierarchy remains manageable. As the number of domains in a hierarchy increases, it takes longer for DNS to resolve the names, and it becomes more complex for users to remember. For example, if a host is several levels down and has the name www.web.apps.dev.syngress.com, DNS has to work through each level in the domain name to resolve the host. This complexity also makes it more difficult for users to remember the name, possibly deterring them from visiting the site. Under no circumstances should you make the namespace more than three or four levels deep.

Domain names should be short and must use standard characters. Each domain can have up to 63 characters in its name; the total length of the fully qualified domain name (the combination of the host and domain name) cannot exceed 255 characters. However, you should remember that users will not want to type 255 characters into a Web browser to access a site, so your domain name should be significantly shorter than this length. The characters making up this name can contain letters (A–Z and a–z), numbers (0–9), and the hyphen (-). Unicode characters (required for languages such as Spanish, French, and German) are also supported.

## DHCP Servers

DHCP, the *Dynamic Host Configuration Protocol*, is used to assign IP addresses on a TCP/IP network. This saves administrators from having to physically visit each computer and statically assign an IP address to each host on the network. With DHCP, an IP address, a subnet mask, a default gateway, a DNS server address, and a WINS server address can automatically be added to a computer's configuration. The IP address assigned to a DHCP client is assigned from a pool of addresses for that network and is requested by the client when it connects to the DHCP server.

When upgrading to Windows 2000, you need to disable the DHCP service before you perform the upgrade. If it isn't disabled, the DHCP database won't be properly converted to Windows 2000. Once the upgrade has been performed, you then need to authorize the DHCP Server service in AD or the service won't start. Authorization isn't automatically granted simply because a server that previously served as a DHCP server has been upgraded. Later in this section, we discuss DHCP servers and their placement on the network.

## Scaling Out

In addition to scaling up, you can *scale out.* To illustrate the differences between the two scaling methods, think of a city. In a city, you can "scale up" by making higher and newer buildings without changing the actual size or shape of the city as a whole. If a city were to "scale out," new buildings would be built outward from the city center and the city's size and shape would expand. New areas would be developed, and old areas would be demolished and merged. This same dichotomy applies to networks, which can either be upgraded (as we saw in the last section) or completely restructured.

As we'll see in the next section, a Windows NT network can use one of several different domain structures. In many cases, you might find that multiple domains are required because of Windows NT capacity limits. Windows NT supported only up to 40,000 user accounts per domain. This limitation might have forced you to use multiple Windows NT domains so that the network could support a high number of users. Windows 2000 uses Active Directory, which theoretically supports up to 10 million objects. Therefore, you might need only a single domain in a Windows 2000 network, as opposed to the multiple domains required in a Windows NT network.

Another reason that Windows NT environments used multiple domains was due to the administrative barriers those domains provided. Windows 2000 supports multiple domains, but it is more likely that new sites will be created to break a network into well-connected subnets. Subnets are like mini-networks, where each subnet uses a different pool of IP addresses. This structure allows the smaller sites to work as individual units while still being part of the Windows 2000 network as a whole.

Sites can be used when a network spans large geographical areas or when more computers are used on the network than current IP addressing can support. Although each site on a network doesn't require domain controllers, you can add a DC to a site if performance is an issue. Users will be able to log on to DCs in other sites, but you might want to add a DC to a site if users are complaining that it takes significant time to be authenticated and access resources.

## Planning Strategies to Upgrade NT Domains to Windows 2000

To properly plan a strategy for upgrading NT domains to Windows 2000, you need to understand the different domain models used on NT networks. The domain models are used to determine how an NT domain is structured. These models affect how upgrading occurs and will change if you perform domain restructuring. There are four NT domain models:

- Single-domain model
- Single-master domain model
- Multiple-master domain model
- Complete trust model

In the sections that follow, we review each of these models and discuss issues that will impact your upgrade strategy.

### The Single-Domain Model

The *single-domain model* is the model on which all the other NT domain models are built. As shown in Figure 7-1, this model consists of only one domain, in which all the accounts and resources reside. Because all the users, groups, and computers are contained in one domain, there is no need for trust relationships with other domains. This is a major difference from the other models we discuss in this chapter.

The single-domain model is commonly used in NT environments. It is easy to implement and provides centralized management of user accounts and resources. All the servers are contained in one domain, making the domain easier to administer. Such servers in this domain structure include a PDC, an optional number of BDCs, and any number of member or standalone servers that serve resources (files, applications, and the like) to clients on the network.

**FIGURE 7-1**

The Single-Domain Model

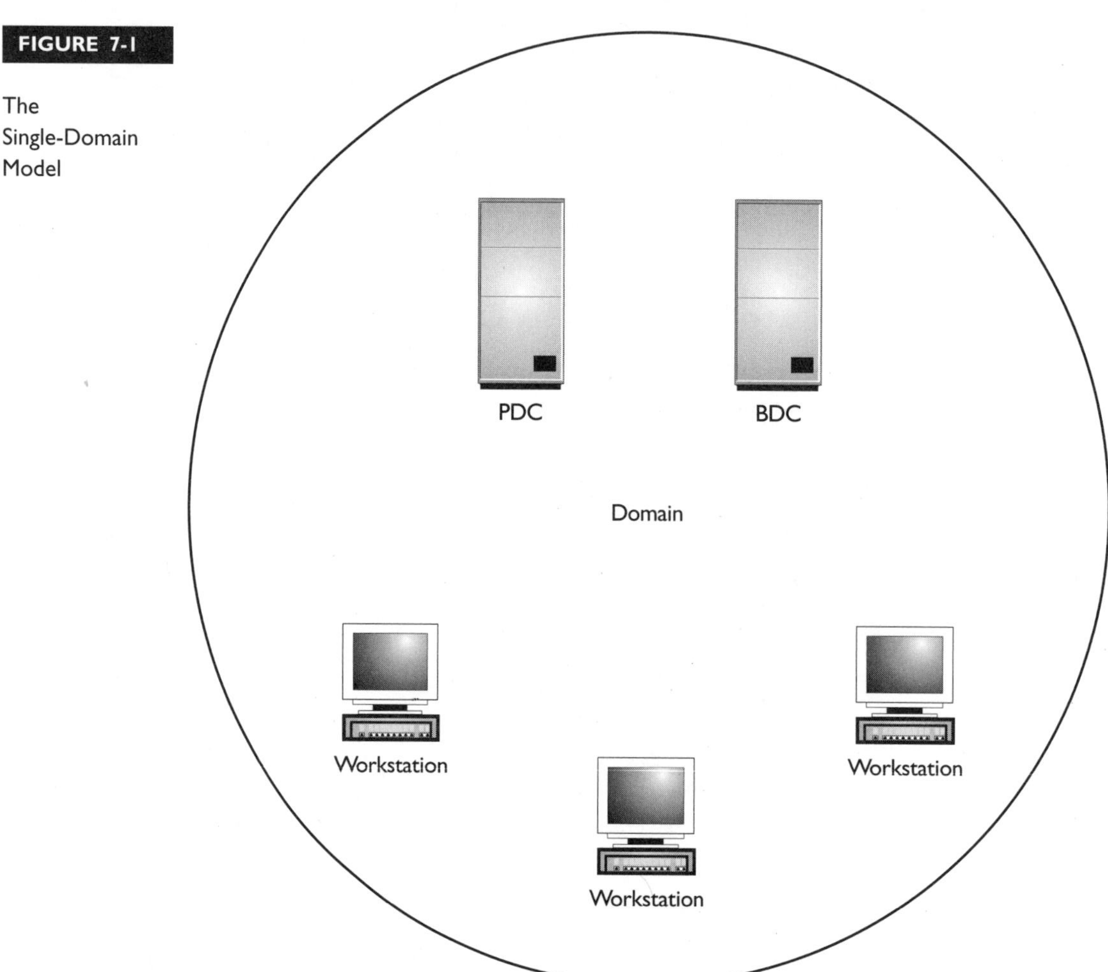


This model is the easiest to upgrade to Windows 2000, since everything is contained in a single domain structure. To upgrade this model, you would scale up the network by performing an in-place upgrade. Once the PDC and other servers are upgraded to Windows 2000 Server, the domain upgrade is complete.

## The Single-Master Domain

The *single-master domain model*, also called the *master domain model*, consists of one domain containing user accounts and one or more other domains containing resources, as shown in Figure 7-2. The single domain containing the user accounts is called a *master domain* or *account domain.* Other domains containing resources are referred to as *resource domains.*

In the figure, arrows show the direction of trust relationships between the domains. An NT trust relationship is made up of two parts: the trusted domain and the trusting domain. The trusted domain contains the user accounts that allow users to log on and then use the resources in this domain and other trusting domains. The trusting domain allows a trusted domain's users access to its resources. In the master domain model, the master domain is trusted, whereas the resource domains are

**FIGURE 7-2** The Single-Master Domain Model

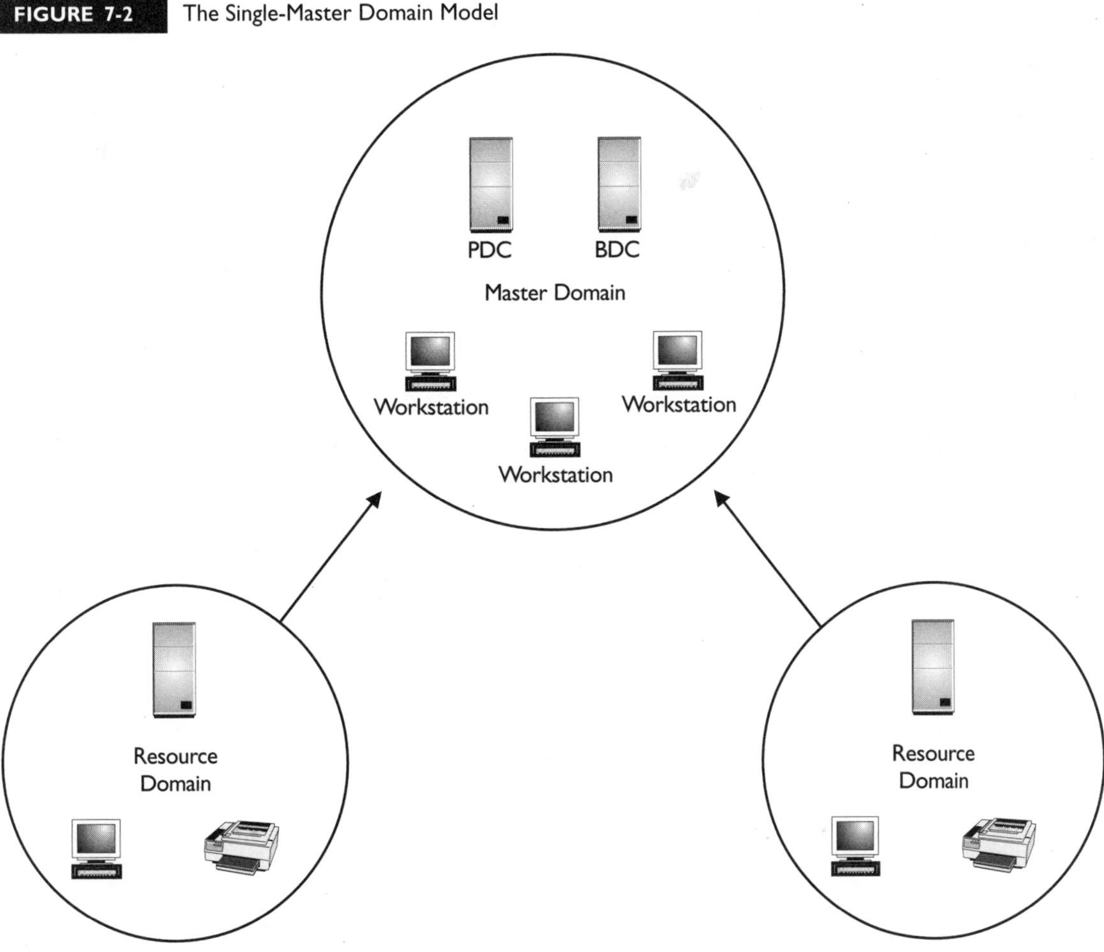

trusting. Because all domains trust the master domain, the resource domains recognize all the users and groups in this domain. This setup allows users to log on to the master domain and then access resources in the resource domains.

In Windows 2000, trust relationships are different from those in Windows NT. A Windows NT trust relationship is always one-way. The trusting domain allows access to the trusted domain, but the trusted domain won't allow access to the trusting domain. For both domains to trust one another, two one-way trusts need to be established. In Windows 2000, however, the trusts are two-way. If a trust relationship is established between two domains, both domains trust one another.

Another difference between trust relationships in NT and 2000 is the way trusts are handled between domains. In NT, the trust relationship only exists between two domains, and is non-transitive. Non-transitive means that the trust between the two domains doesn't extend to other domains. In other words, if Domain A trusts Domain B, and Domain B trusts Domain C, that doesn't mean that Domain C trusts Domain A as a result. The trust relationship exists only between two domains and doesn't extend to other domains. In Windows 2000, however, trust relationships are transitive and do extend to other domains. If we were to reconsider the previous example in Windows 2000, all the domains would trust one another.

The master domain model is similar to the single-domain model in that a single Security Accounts Manager (SAM) database is used. Although the master domain model uses multiple domains, the account domain stores all the user-account information. This master domain centralizes accounts, allowing the administrator to add, delete, and modify users and groups with ease. Each resource domain can be a department of a company or the geographical location of a branch office. You can use organizational units for this functionality in Windows 2000, allowing you to organize objects into different units in Windows 2000. The information in the SAM is transferred into Active Directory when the PDC in this domain is upgraded.

Another difference between the domain models before and after an upgrade is evident in the groups that are used. In Windows 2000, universal groups allow you to set access permissions for users, regardless of which domain they are a part of in the enterprise network. This means that when you add users to a universal group, it doesn't matter where in the network they are located. If you use native mode, which we'll discuss later, you can use a universal group anywhere in the same forest. However, universal groups are a new addition to Windows 2000; this type of group wasn't available in Windows NT.

In Windows NT, combinations of local and global groups were used with the master domain model. Local groups reside in the local accounts database of Windows NT or 2000 servers and workstations and allow you to control the access of members of these groups to that machine. The master domain model can contain either user accounts or global groups. *Global groups* are group accounts that are maintained by a PDC and contain members from that particular domain. The reason that global groups are so important to the master domain model is that they were the only group in Windows NT that could cross a trust relationship. As mentioned, in Windows 2000, universal groups can now be used because they have the ability to cross from one domain to another.

## The Multiple-Master Domain Model

The *multiple-master domain model* is also known as the *multimaster domain model.* Unlike the previously discussed models, the multimaster domain model has two or more account domains that contain user-account information. Because the two previous models used one account domain, they are limited by Windows NT's 40,000-user account limit. The multimaster domain model spreads these accounts across multiple account domains, meaning that with each account domain, the number of possible users can increase by 40,000. As mentioned earlier, this restriction no longer exists in Windows 2000; Active Directory can theoretically support more than 10 million objects.

As shown in Figure 7-3, the multimaster domain model is similar to the master domain model in that it is broken up into account and resource domains. The resource domains have a one-way trust with each of the master domains, allowing access to the various resources available in these domains. Where the multimaster domain model differs from the master domain model is that two or more account domains are used and connected to one another using two one-way trusts. In this way, the account domains trust one another, allowing them to access one another's accounts and resources.

The trust relationships between the domains provide the method in which users are able to log on to their accounts and then access resources. To calculate how many relationships are required in the NT environment, the following formula is used:

```
M * (M - 1) + (R * M)
```

In this formula, *M* is the number of master domains, and *R* is the number of resource domains. To illustrate, let's say that there were two master domains and

**FIGURE 7-3** The Multimaster Domain Model

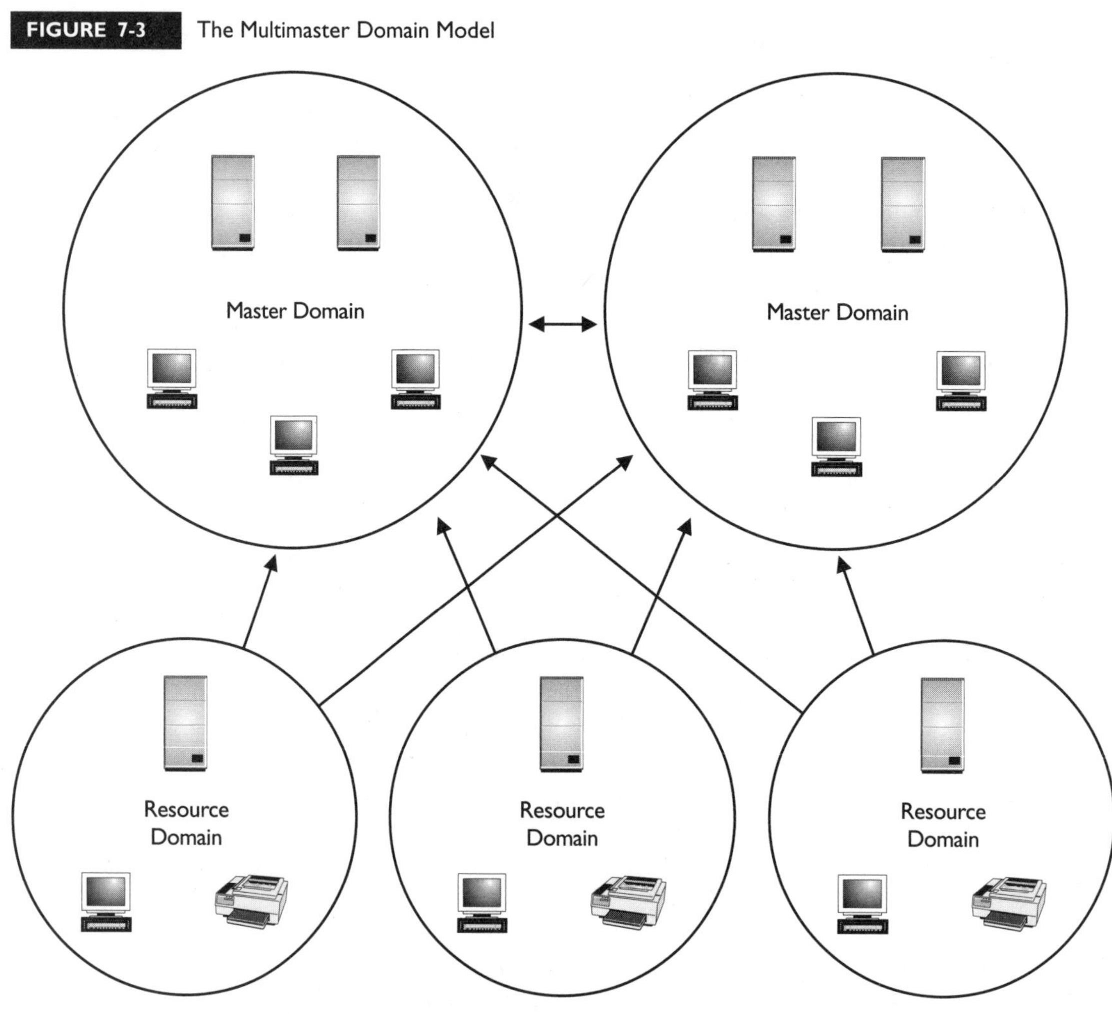


three resource domains. This would make the equation 2 * (2 - 1) + (3 * 2), which equals 8.

As mentioned in the previous section, Windows 2000 uses two transitive trusts, which means that this complex number of trust relationships is no longer required. If you wanted to retain the same number of domains after upgrading to Windows 2000, you'd require a minimal number of trusts. However, only one trust is needed between each domain. In addition, because trusts are automatic in Windows 2000, you wouldn't need to manually create them. In the case of the eight trust relationships required for the five domains in Figure 7-3, a minimum of four trusts would be required rather than the eight trusts required by the NT environment.

Generally, however, you wouldn't bother keeping so many domains on your Windows 2000 network. Since this type of domain model is used to accommodate more than 40,000 users on an NT environment, and Windows 2000 supports millions of objects, you could merge all or some of these domains into a single one.

exam Watch

***Remember to stress simplicity in designing domains for a network. There is no need to create new domains to support more than 40,000 users. If you create as few domains as possible, less administrative work is required.***

## The Complete Trust Model

The *complete trust model* is the final domain model used in NT environments. As shown in Figure 7-4, this model consists of multiple domains that have two one-way trust relationships with one another. The domains can access each other's resources because of this relationship structure.

Like the multimaster domain model, the complete trust model uses multiple SAM databases. This structure allows the model to exceed the 40,000-user limitation of a single NT domain, which no longer exists in Windows 2000. However, the similarities end there, because the complete trust model doesn't use resource domains. It resembles a series of single-domain models, with two one-way trusts connecting them.

The trust relationships in the complete trust model can become incredibly complex. This is shown by the following formula, which calculates the number of trusts required in such a domain structure:

```
n * (n - 1)
```

In this formula, *n* is the number of domains. For example, let's say that we had five domains that required complete trusts between them. With this formula, we would multiple 5 * (5 - 1), which equals 20. In other words, you need to create 20 one-way trusts to allow the domains to trust one another.

As with the multimaster model, fewer trust relationships are required after upgrading the network to Windows 2000. Trust relationships in Windows 2000 are two-way and transitive, so fewer relationships need to be created to connect the domains. In a network with five domains, you need to create a minimum of four trust relationships to connect the domains. With one trust relationship connecting

**FIGURE 7-4**

The Complete Trust Model

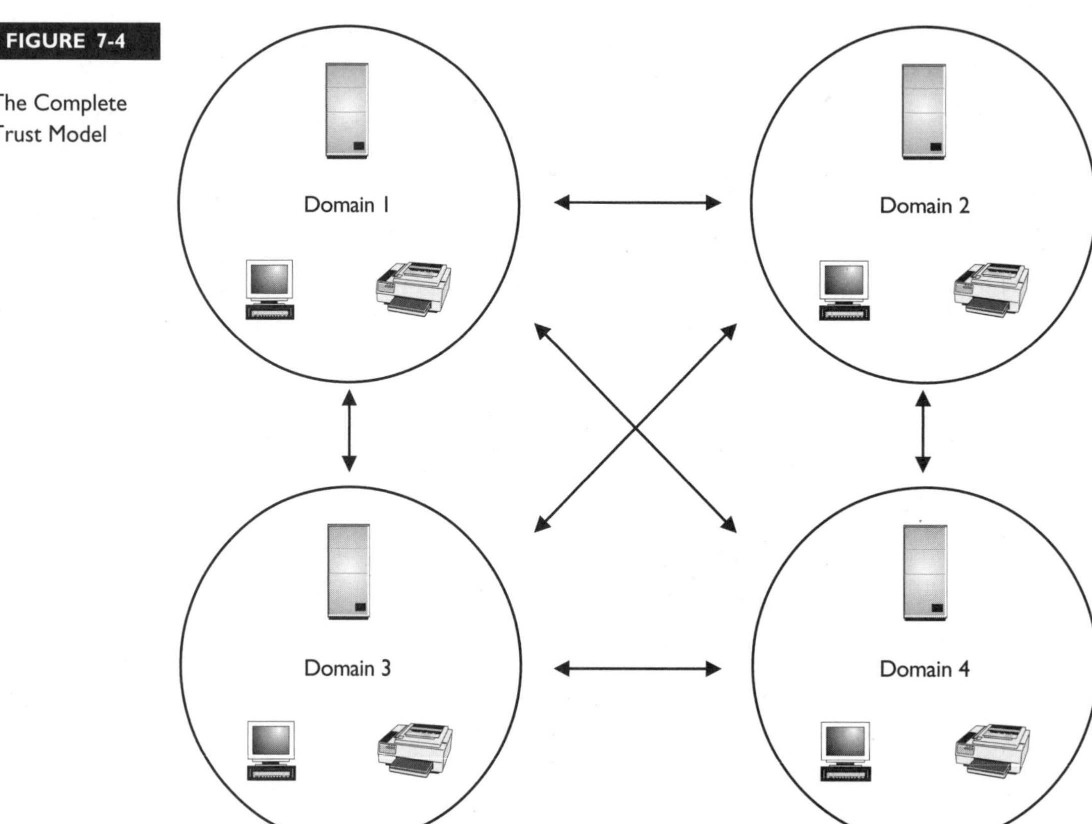


to the next, this network would provide the same result as a complete trust in Windows NT environments.

Complete trust relationships are often used when companies have multiple locations spread across a large geographic region. In such cases, you may consider creating a root domain, using child domains for various segments of the company. As shown in Figure 7-5, this would require you to create a tree based on geographic locations or departments. Each child domain would be able to maintain its own resources, but you would be able to centrally manage user accounts through Active Directory. We'll discuss this topic in more detail in the sections that follow, when we look at designing directory services.

**FIGURE 7-5**

Directory Tree Based on Geographic Locations

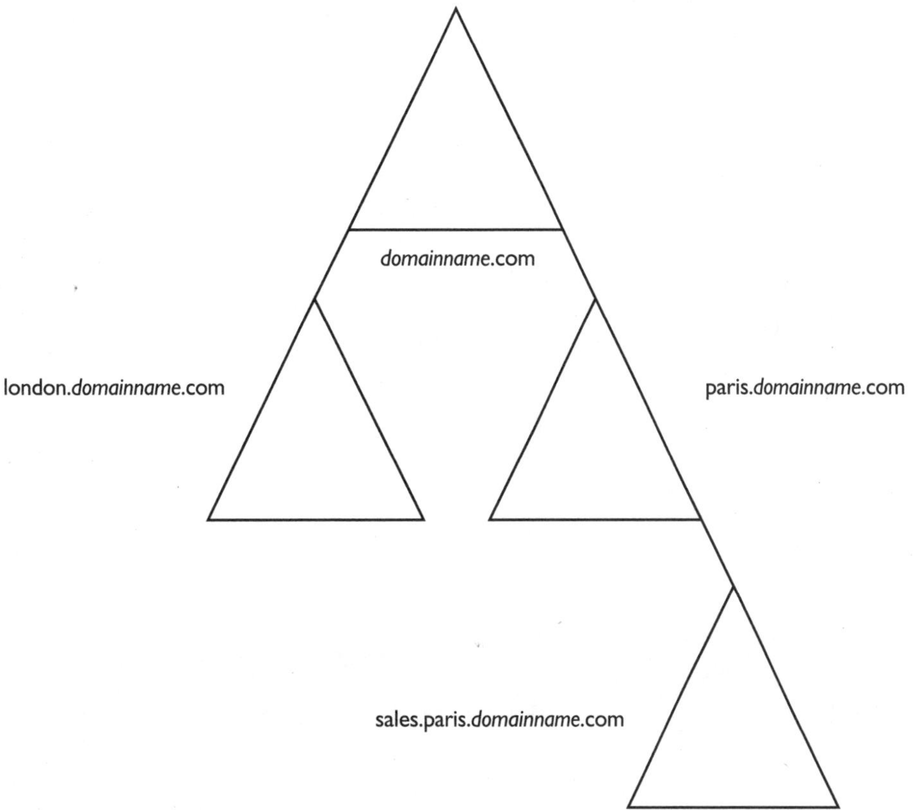


## Upgrading a PDC

When an NT domain is upgraded to Windows 2000, you need to upgrade the PDC first. There is only one PDC in each Windows NT domain. The PDC maintains the master copy of the domain's user-account database and is used to authenticate users. When you upgrade the PDC, AD will be installed on the machine, and information in the Windows NT account database and SAM will be transferred into AD.

Once the PDC is upgraded to a Windows 2000 domain controller, it will be fully backward compatible, which means that it can still function as a PDC. Windows 2000 will emulate a PDC for the other Windows NT 4.0 Servers and workstations that are running on the network. This allows your network to continue functioning as it was before, even though the PDC is the only server that has been upgraded at this time.

After upgrading the PDC, you can begin upgrading other servers on your network. Windows NT Servers may be designated for several roles, but the roles have changed somewhat in Windows 2000. Windows NT 4.0 has one PDC per domain, BDCs, member servers, and standalone servers. In Windows 2000, no domain controllers are designated as primary or backup servers; all domain controllers are considered equal. The roles in a Windows 2000 network are domain controllers, member servers, and standalone servers.

exam watch

***The first server that must be upgraded to Windows 2000 Server must be the PDC. You shouldn't attempt to upgrade any other server on the network before the PDC has been successfully upgraded.***

Now that you have a better idea of what should be included in your strategy to upgrade networks, servers, and clusters, here are some possible scenario questions and their solutions.

| SCENARIO & SOLUTION | |
|---|---|
| My network has two domains because there are 75,000 users. How many domains will I need if I upgrade to Windows 2000? | Windows 2000 isn't limited to 40,000 users per domain, as is the case with Windows NT 4.0. As such, if capacity is the only deciding factor, you could have all the users in one domain. |
| What roles can I designate to servers on a Windows 2000 network? | Servers can be designated as domain controllers, member servers, or standalone servers. |
| I have two domains with Windows NT 4.0 servers running in each. Which servers should I upgrade first in my domains? | Upgrade the PDC in each domain first. There will be one PDC in each domain on your network. The PDC should always be upgraded before any other servers on your network. |

## Switching to Native Mode

Windows 2000 domains can run in one of two modes: native mode and mixed mode. A major difference between these two modes is the type of domain controllers that can operate in the domain. *Mixed mode* allows Windows NT 3.51 or 4.0 BDCs to continue operating in the domain. In *native mode*, however, only Windows 2000 domain controllers can operate in the domain.

As we saw in the previous section, when a domain is upgraded to Windows 2000, the PDC is the first server that is upgraded. This leaves BDCs as the only remaining Windows NT domain controllers running on the network. To support the BDCs, the domain runs in mixed mode. The Windows 2000 domain controller will run as a PDC emulator and provide the same functionality as the Windows NT PDC. This allows the BDC to replicate to the Windows 2000 DC as it did to a Windows NT PDC.

When native mode is used, Windows NT BDCs cannot run in the domain, because Windows 2000 Server won't provide PDC emulation. Only Windows 2000 DCs can be used. When this mode is used, a number of features that aren't available in mixed mode will suddenly become available. For example, you will be able to nest groups and use Kerberos authentication. When you use native mode, AD will be used exclusively, and all DCs will have a master copy of AD, which can be updated by all DCs.

It is important to realize that switching from mixed mode to native mode is a one-way, one-time action. Once you've switched the domain from mixed mode to native mode, there is no way to undo the switch and revert to mixed mode. You need to ensure that at no time in the future will Windows NT BDCs be needed in the domain. Once the switch is performed, they can't be added to the domain, and existing ones will be unable to function as BDCs.

on the job

***Never switch to native mode unless you're sure that you won't be using any Windows NT BDCs on the network. Switching from mixed mode to native mode is a one-way switch and can't be undone. Once the domain is switched to native mode, you can't switch back to mixed mode.***

It is also important to realize that the various modes that can be used apply only to DCs. If native mode or mixed mode is used, it doesn't matter whether you have clients running Windows NT Workstation, Windows 9x, or Windows 2000. These clients can continue to run regardless of the mode used.

You can use native mode to make it easier to administer your Web infrastructure by enabling the use of universal groups. This type of group has the scope of the entire forest and allows you to add members from any domain. Once users are added, you can then assign access to resources in any domain so that users from one domain can access resources in another domain. This allows users of the domain used for your Web site to access data and other resources in other domains.

**EXERCISE 7-1**

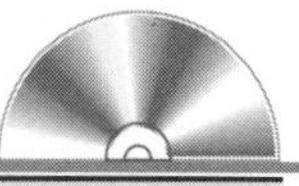


### Switching from Mixed Mode to Native Mode

1. From the Start menu, select Programs | Administrative Tools and then click Active Directory Domains and Trusts.
2. When Active Directory Domains and Trusts opens, right-click the domain and select Properties.
3. When the Properties dialog box appears, click the General tab.
4. Click the Change Mode button.
5. Once you've clicked the Change Mode button, a warning will appear, telling you that once the switch to native mode takes place, you will not be able to switch back. To switch to native mode, click the Yes button on the warning box. (If you wanted to stay in mixed mode, you would click No on the warning box.)
6. Click OK to close the Properties box. Your network will now run in native mode.

**CERTIFICATION OBJECTIVE 7.02**

## Designing Directory Services

Directory services are used to store information about objects and their attributes. To better understand the directory service in Windows 2000, let's look at another type of directory you're familiar with: a telephone book. A phone directory contains objects such as names of businesses and residents of a community. These objects have *attributes*, which are characteristics of the object, such as a name, phone number, and address. Similarly, in Windows 2000, the directory contains objects such as user accounts, servers, domains, and so forth. The directory service allows you to view and modify elements of your network so that the network is easier to manage and more effective to use.

## Active Directory

In Windows 2000, the directory service is called Active Directory. Through AD, you can organize, manage, and control access to any resources on your network. This includes user accounts, workstations, servers, Web access, shared files, printers, and any other elements making up your network. AD is the means through which you perform many of the administrative functions in a Windows 2000 environment, and in many ways it determines a user's abilities and experiences with the network.

Through AD, users are able to perform a single logon to access multiple servers and use the resources they are permitted to access. In Windows NT, a user would need to log on to each server on which he or she needed to access resources. This process could become frustrating or problematic if the user needed to access a significant number of servers. The exception to this rule is if a trust relationship exists or if a username and password are identical on user's local machine, allowing pass-through authentication. In Windows 2000, Active Directory enables users to log on once and only once to access everything you've given the user permissions to use.

AD also provides centralized administration, allowing network administrators to control the accounts and resources through any domain controller. Active Directory is integrated with Windows 2000 Server and distributed among the various DCs installed in your Windows 2000 environment. Unlike Windows NT, all the DCs in Windows 2000 act as peers, so administrators are able to modify AD through any DC. Changes to AD are then replicated to other DCs.

In Active Directory, you should organize objects effectively, because AD grows as your organization grows. Active Directory can consist of millions of objects, and although it is highly scalable, it can become a nightmare to manage if you haven't designed it properly. To put this idea into perspective, let's compare AD to a file structure. You might have thousands of files on your server, but imagine if they were all stored in just a few directories. They would become difficult to manage, just as AD would if it were poorly designed as a mishmash of millions of objects. As such, you should spend time planning your AD structure so that it can grow effectively as your company expands.

As we'll see in the sections that follow, AD has a number of units of organization that are used in designing directory services. These units make up AD's hierarchical structure and can be designed to reflect the organizational or geographical structure of your company.

## Forest Design

A *forest* is part of Active Directory's logical structure, which is used to mirror the logical structure of your company. This could reflect how your company is organized or geographically laid out. When users view Active Directory, they see the logical structure, allowing them to follow a structure that is familiar to them. This structure shields them from the network's physical structure, which is transparent to them.

As shown in Figure 7-6, Active Directory's logical structure is made up of forests, trees, domains, and organizational units. These elements are used to provide administrative boundaries and are integral parts of the overall design of a Windows 2000 network. When you upgrade or install a Windows 2000 network, it will consist of at least one forest, one tree, and one domain. A forest is the largest unit of organization in Active Directory and contains one or more trees. A *tree* is the next largest unit and contains one or more domains with contiguous namespaces. Finally, *organizational units* are containers in the domain that provide a method of organizing groups of users, groups, and resources. We discuss trees, domains, and organizational units in greater detail in the sections that follow.

A forest is automatically created when Active Directory is installed and you create the first domain on your Windows 2000 network. This first domain, known as the *forest root,* contains a schema container and configuration container that are used by all domains that are created in this forest. The *schema* is used to define the objects and attributes that are stored in Active Directory. The schema determines what objects can be used in AD and the characteristics that can be modified. The *configuration container,* on the other hand, is used to store information about the network's physical topology, the sites, the services, and other parameters used by Active Directory.

Because domains make up trees and trees make up the forest, the first tree is created when the first domain is created. Additional trees that use a different naming structure can also be added to the forest, which is useful when companies want to merge different networks so that these networks can communicate with one another. The various trees are part of the same forest, so they are able to communicate with one another through implicit two-way transitive trust relationships.

**FIGURE 7-6** Logical Structure of Active Directory

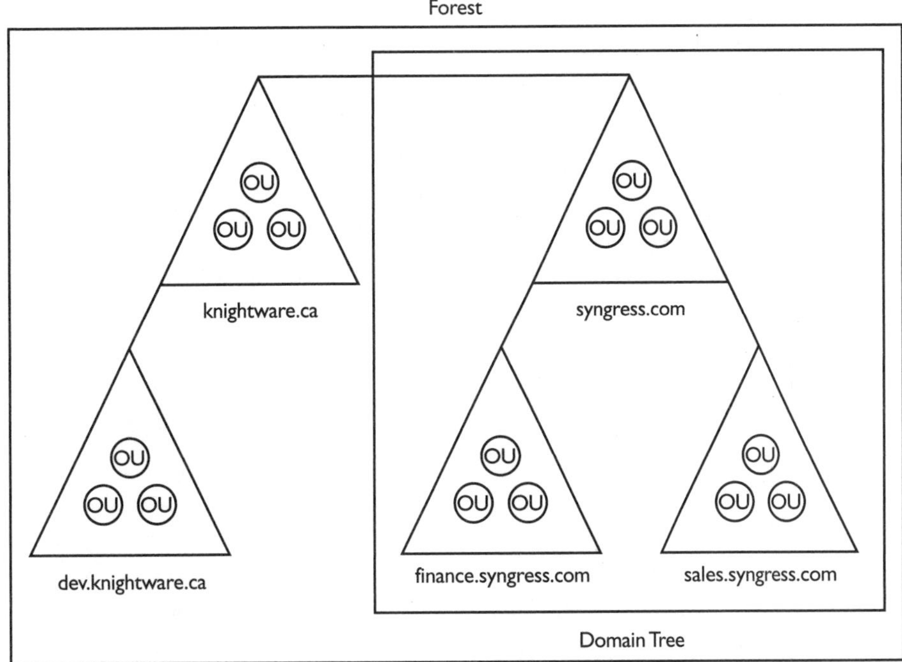


As with any of the elements making up AD's logical structure, one rule remains clear: The simpler the design, the better the design. You should try to keep the number of forests, domain trees, domains, and so forth to a minimum. As you make your design more complex, it will take more resources, planning, and effort to maintain it.

However, there are always exceptions to the rule, and having multiple forests could be useful in specific circumstances. One such instance is when two networks run separately from one another but need to exchange information. For example, two companies could join together for a particular project or merge into a partnership that requires them to run autonomously of one another for legal reasons. In such a case, two forests could be created with a trust relationship connecting them.

Another reason for creating multiple forests is when test labs are used in an organization. A test lab is a mockup of your production network that is used to test new operating systems or applications before they're put on the actual network. If problems occur with this test-lab software, it won't impact your production network. In addition, any changes that these programs make to the schema won't affect your production network, because each forest has its own schema, configuration container, and global catalog.

In a Web infrastructure, separate forests can be used for security purposes. If you create separate forests, you'll be able to have a public global catalog for Internet users and a private global catalog for local network users. Another reason for separate forests would be to have different schemas. When different schemas are used, different sets of information would be available to public and private users. This might be important if you need to implement a schema for Web applications and another for line-of-business applications.

## Domain Design and DNS Names

As mentioned, the first domain created in your AD environment is the forest root. It also designates the root domain name for your domain tree. A *domain tree* is the next largest organizational unit beneath a forest and contains one or more domains that share a contiguous namespace and hierarchical naming structure. For example, if your root domain is syngress.com, you could have child domains called finance.syngress.com and sales.syngress.com beneath it. Each of the child domains resides below the root domain in the hierarchy and has a name built on the root domain's name. Because of the importance of the first domain on your Windows 2000 network, you need to pay particular attention to domain design and DNS names, since they will affect any other domains created beneath them.

As you've seen by the examples in this section, Active Directory domain names use the Domain Naming Service (DNS) and use the same naming schemes that are seen on the Internet. In fact, if a company has an Internet presence, it generally uses the domain name of its Web site as the domain name for its Windows 2000 root domain. It is important that you choose the name for your root domain carefully, because it cannot be changed later without reinstalling AD.

The domain tree can consist of the root domain or the root domain and a series of child domains beneath it. Generally, it is best to limit the number of domain trees created in a forest, because administration requirements increase proportionately. If you use a single tree, you won't need to maintain trust relationships with other trees, fewer domain controllers will be required, and less planning will be involved.

Another problem with multiple trees is that domains can't be renamed or moved between trees and forests. Instead, you need to remove the domain. This requires downgrading DCs to member servers and then upgrading them to DCs in a new domain in a different tree. In this process, accounts are lost, so you need to recreate any users and groups in the domain. If the domain is a parent domain, you need to remove any child domains beforehand.

It is also easiest if you use a single domain for your network, but certain situations might require you to create additional domains. One reason to use multiple domains is that domains serve as administrative barriers in Windows 2000. Account policies are set at the domain level and can't be applied to other domains in a tree. For example, you might want to specify that passwords expire after a period of time. If a single domain is used, you couldn't have the passwords for one group expiring after 30 days and another group expiring after 90 days. To do so, you need to have multiple domains and implement separate policies for the users in each domain.

Another example of how domains can be used as an administrative barrier is demonstrated in the use of groups that are used for network administration. Administrative rights don't flow through the transitive trusts that are created between parent and child domains. As such, administrators in one domain won't have administrative rights to another domain. One group that is commonly used for administrative purposes is Domain Admins. Even if a member of this group doesn't have access to files or folders, he or she can take ownership and grant him- or herself permissions. This practice could cause problems in a single domain if access to certain information needed to be limited but you also needed users to be members of this group for other administrative duties. To deal with this situation, you could create a new domain with a minimal number of users as members of the Domain Admins group. If any users needed to provide an administrative role to other domains, you could use the Enterprise Administrators group, which has an administrative scope of the entire forest.

exam Watch

***Administrative rights don't flow through the transitive trusts that are created between parent and child domains. The exception to this rule is if the user is a member of the Enterprise Administrators group. The administrative scope of the Enterprise Administrators group is the entire forest, which allows members to serve in an administrative capacity anywhere in the forest.***

Another reason for multiple domains occurs when an organization needs to separate divisions of the company into various domains. This is common when a company has subsidiaries or divisions that have their own IT staff and require their own policies. For example, a large computer company could have one division that specializes in hardware and another that specializes in software. In this situation, the two divisions might need to exchange information, but they are largely autonomous of one another.

Another situation in which multiple domains could be required is when replication is an issue. Active Directory information is replicated to other DCs, allowing them to have identical copies of AD. If a link between two locations is slow or unreliable, the traffic generated by this replication could be an issue. By creating different domains, the entire AD database won't be replicated. Instead, changes to the schema, configuration container, and global catalog are replicated between domains. This results in less traffic being generated due to replication.

## Organizational Unit Design

The final element of Active Directory's logical structure that we'll discuss is the *Organizational Unit*, or *OU*. The OU is the smallest unit of organization in Active Directory and is used to create and maintain a logical structure that reflects your business's structure. OUs are containers that store and organize various objects in AD. To put them into perspective, you could compare them to folders that are used to organize a file system. Each folder can be nested within another folder, allowing you to create a structure that suits your needs. The major difference is that, instead of files, you're using OUs to group together users, groups, computers, and other organizational units.

OUs are limited to storing objects from the domain in which the OU resides. You can't place users, groups, computers, or OUs from other domains inside an OU. However, unlike domains, which can't be renamed or moved from one tree or forest to another, OUs are more flexible and allow movement and renaming.

OUs aid in structuring Active Directory to mirror the structure of your business. You can create OUs that represent a particular geographical location, department, or other component of your company. Users, groups, computers, and other OUs in this location or department can then be added to the OU. When designing the structure of OUs, you should try to keep the structure as flat as possible, for two reasons. First, managing OUs that are nested deeply in one another can become confusing. Second, it will take longer for users to authenticate when logging in. Since OUs can be nested and users might be part of different levels of OUs, Active Directory checks and applies group policies at each level.

Using OUs, you can delegate administration to users. This allows you to delegate administrative control of particular OUs to specific users and groups, thus limiting membership to commonly used groups such as Domain Admins. Earlier in this chapter, we mentioned how the Domain Admins group is commonly used for network administration and that this fact is a common reason for creating multiple domains. With OUs, you don't need to assign large numbers of users to predefined groups so that they can provide administration support to a particular area of your network.

Because OUs can be nested, you can delegate administration at any level of the domain structure. A person can be given the administrative scope that suits his or her needs. You can give the person authority over a domain, groups of OUs in a domain, or a single OU. This flexibility allows you to control administrative privileges at a granular level.

To delegate authority, the Delegation of Control Wizard is used. This wizard takes you step by step through the process of delegating administration over an OU by allowing you to select who is to delegate control. You then select which objects and OUs the users are to have authority over and their permissions to view and modify objects. Once completed, you will have delegated control over an OU to a particular user or group.

### Site Design

Unlike the other elements we've discussed so far, sites aren't part of the Active Directory namespace. Although forests, trees, and OUs are all part of Active Directory's *logical structure*, sites are part of its *physical structure*. As mentioned earlier in this chapter, a site is one or more IP subnets that are well connected and that represent a physical partitioning of Active Directory. In other words, they need fast and reliable links connecting them to other areas of the network, such as other sites.

WANs use sites to improve network performance by decreasing network traffic. Sites allow you to manage AD replication by enabling you to schedule when replication occurs and specify which protocol is to be used for replication. When Active Directory is replicated between sites, you can use either Remote Procedure Calls (RPCs) or the Simple Mail Transfer Protocol (SMTP). When AD is replicated within a domain, however, this choice isn't available; only RPCs are used. From this fact, you can see that sites provide greater flexibility for replicating AD.

on the Job

***Replication within a domain uses RPCs, whereas replication between domains uses the SMTP or RPCs. You have the choice of which protocol to use to replicate AD between domains, but you can only use RPCs for replication within a domain.***

Network traffic can also be lowered through the use of sites by allowing users to log on to DCs within a site. If a request is made of a service and a DC is available in the site, the request will be made to the local site rather than a remote DC. Through this ability, users are able to log on to a local DC instead of needing to log on to a DC in another location. This practice lowers network traffic because users don't have to be authenticated by communicating over a link between their locations and another that has its own DC.

Now that we've looked at the elements making up the physical and logical structure of Active Directory, here are some possible scenario questions and their solutions.

| SCENARIO & SOLUTION | |
|---|---|
| On which DC are modifications to Active Directory made? | All of them. AD is distributed among the various DCs installed in your Windows 2000 environment. Because all the DCs in Windows 2000 act as peers, administrators are able to modify AD through any DC. |
| What is the benefit of using the Enterprise Admins over the Domain Admins group? | The Domains Admins group has the scope of the domain, whereas the Enterprise Administrators group has the scope of the entire forest, which allows them to serve in an administrative capacity anywhere in the forest. |
| What objects can be placed inside an organizational unit? | Users, groups, computers, or other OUs can be stored inside an OU. |

## LDAP

LDAP is the Lightweight Directory Access Protocol. It is the primary access protocol for Active Directory, allowing clients to communicate with AD during logons or when searching for resources. For example, if you wanted to search for a particular user object in Active Directory, you could use LDAP to communicate with the server and query AD for this information. In using LDAP, the client is able to access directory data on a server, query and modify data in Active Directory, and share directory data.

LDAP is an open Internet standard, which is a major reason it is used by most directory services today. LDAP is also designed for use on networks running TCP/IP, which is the most commonly used protocol on networks. This makes LDAP highly interoperable with Active Directory and other directory services on the market.

## EXERCISE 7-2

CertCam 7-2

### Querying Active Directory Using LDAP

1. From the Windows Start menu, select Search, and then click For People.
2. When the Find People dialog box appears, select Active Directory from the "Look in" drop-down list.
3. In the Name field, type **Administrator**, and then click the Find Now button. LDAP will be used to query Active Directory for this user.
4. When the results of your search appear in a listing, select Administrator from the list, and then click the Properties button. LDAP will be used to return the information on this account.
5. A dialog box appears with the properties of the Administrator's user account. Review the results and then click OK to exit the Properties dialog box. Click Close to Exit the For People dialog box.

## Availability

If servers and resources are unavailable, a user's ability to do his or her work is adversely affected. This means a loss of time on projects as productivity drops to zero. It also means a loss of money because the company is still paying users for their time, even though they're unable to do their jobs. If an Internet server falls into the mix, the cost of downtime can reach the thousands or even millions of dollars because customers on the Internet are unable to purchase products online. The prospect of a nightmare scenario like this one makes availability a primary goal of your network's design.

In the sections that follow, we look at the purposes of various servers and how their placement on the network can improve availability. We also look at issues dealing with site replication, which ensures that all servers have the same Active Directory information. Site replication enables servers to authenticate users, give them the proper access, and provide the proper services and resources.

## Global Catalog Server Placement

As mentioned earlier, Active Directory is made up of objects and attributes representing elements of your network. Due to the fact that AD will grow as your organization grows, querying it can take considerable time . For this reason, the GC and Global Catalog Servers were incorporated into Windows 2000 networks.

The GC stores all the objects contained in Active Directory but stores only a subset of attributes. Because all the attributes for objects aren't stored in the GC, the GC is smaller than AD, allowing for quicker searches for objects and attributes. Furthermore, because the GC holds less information than AD, GC replication is faster and produces less traffic than a full AD replication.

Global Catalog Servers are DCs that have also been designated as GC servers and are an important part of an Active Directory environment. There is one GC server per domain. Because DCs store a copy of AD, the GC server has a complete replica of the domain in which it is located and a partial replica of other domains in the forest. Because it keeps a partial replica of other domains, users are able to query the GC about objects in these domains.

The GC is created on the first DC in the forest root, when Active Directory is installed. As additional sites and domains are created, additional GC servers are also created. However, these additional GC servers are based on the sites that are created. If two sites are created, each has a GC server. However, if two domains are created in the same site, only one GC server is needed. This GC server will have the attributes of objects in both domains, so multiple GCs aren't required.

**on the job**

***To add attributes to or remove default attributes from the GC, you need to be a member of the Schema Admins group. This group can use the Schema Manager to add and remove the attributes of object classes that are to be included in the GC. If you are not a member of this group, you can't add and remove these attributes from the GC.***

## Domain Controller Placement

DCs are Windows 2000 servers that have been designated in this role. Each DC stores a copy of AD and provides the ability to interface with it. Because all user accounts are stored in AD, each domain requires a DC so that users can be authenticated and access resources.

Although each domain requires a DC, it is common for two to be used to increase performance so that users will be able to log on to either domain. Having multiple DCs is also important for availability. If a DC in one site is down or a DC doesn't exist in that site, users will still be able to log on to a DC in another site. However, because the users will have to log on across the link between the sites, network traffic will increase and performance will degrade. Furthermore, if the link between these sites goes down as well, users will be unable to log on and will be cut off from the network.

Multiple DCs also provide an element of fault tolerance because DCs store all the information about that domain. If a single DC is used and the DC is lost, all information about that domain is also lost. This means that users will be unable to log on to the domain until the domain is completely rebuilt. If two DCs are used, the domain will continue to function if one of the DCs fails.

## DNS Server Placement

DNS, the Domain Name System, is used in Windows 2000 for name resolution. DNS servers are used to resolve the names of the DCs to IP addresses. This relieves the user from having to remember IP addresses, so that only computer and domain names are used. DNS servers are also vital to Windows 2000 networks because clients use DNS to locate DCs. Without DNS servers, users would be unable to locate a DC and log on to the network.

For Active Directory to be installed on the first Windows 2000 server in a forest, the DNS service must already be running on the network. Although any number of DNS servers can be used, the DNS server needs to support server resource records (SRV RRs). AD uses SRV RRs to locate DCs. If a DNS server that supports SRV RRs isn't found when AD is installed, the installation wizard gives you the option of installing the Windows 2000 Domain Name Service, which allows the server to operate as a DNS server on the network.

Windows 2000 DNS supports dynamic updates of the DNS database. DNS has traditionally used a static database, in which the administrator manually entered names and IP addresses. This isn't the case with dynamic updates, in which the client or a Dynamic Host Configuration Protocol (DHCP) server automatically updates the DNS server. If DHCP is used on your TCP/IP network, a DHCP server automatically assigns an IP address to a client and can update the DNS server. In other words, the DHCP server tells the DNS server that a particular computer is using a particular IP address.

It is recommended that you place a DNS server in each site on your Windows 2000 network. If the link for a site without a DNS server goes down, users in this site will be unable to find DCs and therefore will be unable to log on to the network. This also improves network performance because DNS queries can be made to the local DNS server rather than making the query across the link.

Installing DNS at each site can be done in one of two ways. First, you can install the DNS service or a DNS server program that supports SRV RRs on a server at each site. The other way is to integrate DNS with Active Directory. DNS uses a zone file that is stored on the DNS server's hard disk and contains information on that domain. When the Windows DNS server is integrated into AD, information from the DNS zone file is stored in AD. Because every DC stores a copy of AD, each DC can act as a DNS server.

## Managing Site Replication

*Replication* is the act of updating other servers with up-to-date information. For example, AD is regularly replicated across the network so that all DCs have identical copies. If replication did not occur, each server would have different information and would be unable to function properly after a period of time.

Because servers replicate by copying information over the network, it is important to realize that the act of replication has an impact on bandwidth. Copying this data causes network traffic and can have an impact on performance. This can be a problem, but you can deal with replication issues in a number of ways.

One method of lowering the impact of replication is to limit the number of DCs on your network. As the number of DCs on a network increases, the amount of replication traffic also increases. DCs replicate AD to other servers, so the more DCs, the more that are involved in the replication process. By limiting the number of DCs on your network, you'll have fewer DCs that need to transfer updates of the AD database.

This problem increases if there are slow links connecting sites. If a slow link connects two sites, it takes longer for the data to transfer from one site to another, eating up bandwidth. This situation can cause problems for users because it will take longer for servers to fulfill their requests. When slow links connect two sites, you should schedule replication to occur at times when few (if any) users are on the network.

These problems can also occur when GC servers replicate the GC. Although DCs replicate only within a domain, GC servers replicate between domains in a forest. This increases the scope over which replication takes place. If a considerable number of DCs act as GC servers, network traffic can increase significantly. GCs contain information from all domains in a forest, so all this data must be replicated to every domain in the forest.

You can also limit the traffic from replicating the GC by limiting the number of domains on your network. If a network consists of a single domain, every DC will already have a copy of AD. If you make each DC a GC server, traffic won't increase from replication, because each of them will receive updated information when AD is replicated.

As mentioned earlier, the DNS server can be integrated into AD so that it contains the zone file. When AD is replicated, the zone file is replicated with it, so each DC receives updates to DNS entries. This increases the size of AD when it is replicated. To deal with this problem, you can implement incremental zone transfers. When you perform an incremental zone transfer, the entire DNS database isn't replicated to other DNS servers. Instead, only changes to individual records are transferred.

## Authentication

Windows 2000 uses DCs for authentication. Users log on to a DC to acquire access to services and resources on the network. This makes DCs a vital component of your infrastructure, because users are unable to use the network without them.

It is recommended that you use multiple DCs for each site on your network. If you use two or more DCs, users will be able to log on to a local DC, even if one of them is down. At the very least, one DC should exist in each site of your network. If a slow link connects a site without a DC to another site, performance problems can occur. This is especially true during peak hours, when users must compete to connect to a remote DC to be authenticated.

If an unreliable link connects two or more sites, the need for a DC in each site is even more important. If users are unable to connect to the remote site, they can't be authenticated and will be unable to use the network. Therefore, a DC in each site will allow users to log on to the network, even if the link is down.

GC servers are another important authentication issue. Because the GC contains information from every domain in the network, it becomes a requirement when native mode is used. If you use native mode, you should designate multiple GCs so that users can log on to the network if one of them is down. When users log on to the network in native mode, the DC will query the GC server. This allows the GC to determine if users are members of universal groups. A *universal group* contains members from any domain in a forest, allowing users to perform actions with specified access in any domain. If a GC is unavailable, the DC will have no idea whether the user is a member of a universal group and if the user should be allowed or denied access to resources. Unless users are members of the Domain Admins group, they won't be able to log on to the domain.

## Sizing

Determining the number of DCs and GC servers required for a site can be difficult. To aid in this aspect of planning your network, the Active Directory Sizer Tool can be used. Using this tool, you can enter information about your network and view recommendations about the placement of DCs, GC servers, and bridgehead servers on your network. Once you've worked through the process, this tool will also provide an estimate of AD's size if these changes are made.

on the Job

***The Active Directory Sizer Tool is available on the Server Utilities CD in the Technet subscription, or you can download it for free from Microsoft's Web site. To acquire this tool from Microsoft's Web site, visit www.microsoft.com/windows2000/downloads/deployment/sizer/default.asp.***

Now that you have a better understanding of designing directory services, here are some possible scenario questions and their solutions.

| SCENARIO & SOLUTION | |
|---|---|
| What is LDAP? | LDAP is short for Lightweight Directory Access Protocol. It is the primary access protocol for Active Directory. |
| I have one DC in my domain, and it has completely failed. Although we used disk fault tolerance, each of the disks was damaged. What can I do to fix this problem? | Rebuild the domain. Since there is only one DC in this domain, all the information about this domain was lost when the server failed. Unfortunately, the domain needs to be rebuilt. |

# CERTIFICATION SUMMARY

In this chapter we discussed information dealing with upgrading a network to Windows 2000. In doing so, we learned about the various models you can encounter when upgrading. These models consist of the single-domain model, the single-master domain model, the multimaster domain model, and the complete trust model. We saw that during the upgrade it is vital that you upgrade the PDC first and that you switch from mixed mode to native mode after the upgrade is complete to activate certain Windows 2000 features.

We also discussed issues dealing with designing directory services. In Windows 2000, the directory service is called Active Directory. When designing AD, you need to consider the logical and physical structure of directory services. Logical structures include such elements as a forest, domain, and organizational units. The physical structure deals with elements such as sites. We also saw that a number of different server types might appear on your network, including domain controllers, global catalog servers, and DNS servers. Together, these form the shape that your AD will take and determine its availability on the network.

# TWO-MINUTE DRILL

## Designing Upgrade Strategies for Networks, Servers, and Clusters

- ❑ You can upgrade to Windows 2000 Server from Windows NT 3.51 Server, Windows NT 4.0 Server, and previous versions of Windows 2000 Server.
- ❑ The first Windows NT 4.0 Server that you must upgrade in a domain is the Primary Domain Controller (PDC).
- ❑ You should synchronize the Backup Domain Controllers (BDCs) on your network prior to upgrading the BDCs. The PDC stores a master copy of the domain's user-account database; BDCs store copies of this information. If you synchronize BDCs on your network prior to upgrading the PDC, the BDCs will have up-to-date information on user accounts.
- ❑ Windows 2000 doesn't have the capacity limits of Windows NT, so multiple domains might not be required. Windows NT only supported up to 40,000 user accounts per domain, but Active Directory theoretically supports up to 10 million objects. This means that the number of users won't dictate the number of domains on your network.
- ❑ You will encounter four different NT domain models when you upgrade or restructure domains. They are the single domain model, the single-master domain model, the multiple-master domain model, and the complete trust model.
- ❑ Trust relationships in Windows NT are one-way and nontransitive. In Windows 2000, they are two-way and transitive.
- ❑ In native mode, Windows NT BDCs cannot exist in the domain. Switching from mixed mode to native mode is a one-time, one-way action that cannot be undone.

## Designing Directory Services

- ❑ Active Directory is the directory service for Windows 2000. AD can be made up of millions of objects that represent elements of your network.

- ❑ You should design directory services with simplicity in mind. This means that you should limit your design to the minimum number of forests, trees, and domains that your organization requires.
- ❑ A forest is the largest unit of organization in Active Directory and contains one or more trees.
- ❑ A tree is made up of domains that use a contiguous namespace. Domains are used to organize AD objects and provide an administrative boundary for the network.
- ❑ Organizational Units (OUs) are the smallest units of organization in Active Directory and are used to create and maintain a logical structure that reflects your business's structure. OUs serve as containers to group users, groups, computers, and other OUs.
- ❑ A site is one or more IP subnets that are well connected and that represent a physical partitioning of Active Directory.
- ❑ The GC stores all the objects contained in AD but only stores a subset of attributes. Access to the GC is provided through DCs that have been designated as GC servers.
- ❑ Windows 2000 Servers can be designated as DCs. DCs store a copy of Active Directory and provide authentication and access to resources.
- ❑ DNS, the Domain Name System, is used in Windows 2000 for name resolution. DNS servers are used to resolve DCs' names to IP addresses.

# SELF TEST

The following questions will help you measure your understanding of the material presented in this chapter. Read all the choices carefully because there might be more than one correct answer. Choose all correct answers for each question.

## Designing Upgrade Strategies for Networks, Servers, and Clusters

1. You are planning to upgrade your network so that all servers are running Windows 2000 Server. Which of the following operating systems can you upgrade to Windows 2000 Server? (Choose all that apply.)

   A. Windows NT 3.51 Server

   B. Windows NT 4.0 Workstation

   C. Windows NT 4.0 Server, running Service Pack 4

   D. Linux

2. You are upgrading the servers in your Windows NT domain to Windows 2000. You have one PDC and one BDC. Prior to the upgrade, you synchronize the BDC with the PDC and then take the BDC offline. During the PDC upgrade, the upgrade fails and you are unable to restart the server. What will you do?

   A. Upgrade the BDC to a Windows 2000 domain controller.

   B. Bring the BDC online, and then promote it to a PDC.

   C. Demote the PDC to a BDC, and then promote the BDC to a PDC.

   D. Bring the PDC back online, and then restore the information to the PDC from the information that was synchronized with the BDC.

3. You have successfully upgraded the PDC on your Windows NT network and are now preparing to upgrade other Windows NT servers to Windows 2000. Which of the following must be done for this task to be successful?

   A. The PDC must be online for the BDCs to be upgraded properly.

   B. The BDCs must be designated as member or standalone servers because there is no BDC designation and there can only be one DC in a domain.

   C. All BDCs must be upgraded at the same time.

   D. You must determine whether you want the remaining servers to act as BDCs, member servers, or standalone servers.

**4.** You are upgrading a Windows NT environment that has 110,000 users. Capacity limitations are the only issue that's determining the number of domains being used. On this network, there are three PDCs, six BDCs, and three member servers. Based on this information, what is the minimum number of domains your network will require after upgrading to Windows 2000?

A. One

B. Two

C. Three

D. Six

**5.** You are preparing to upgrade your Windows NT network to Windows 2000. There is one PDC, one BDC, and a member server in a domain, with no trust relationships with other domains. The network is spread over several floors of a single building, and no users have been complaining about performance. There are 1500 users on your network; the users are split into three shifts over a five-day work week. The company itself is open seven days a week, and users are on the network at all times. Which of the following is the best method of upgrading this domain model to Windows 2000?

A. Perform an in-place upgrade.

B. Upgrade the PDC, the BDC, and the member server to Windows 2000, and then upgrade the trust relationships so that they are transitive.

C. Restructure the domain so that it is split into two separate domains.

D. Restructure the domain so that it is merged into a single-domain structure.

**6.** You are planning to upgrade a network to Windows 2000. Currently, the network runs Windows NT 4.0 Servers and uses a single Security Account Manager (SAM). The domain has a PDC and a BDC as well as two member servers in two other domains that serve applications and files to users. Which of the following domain models are being used?

A. Single-domain model

B. Single-master domain model

C. Multimaster domain model

D. Complete trust model

**7.** Your Windows NT domain consists of three domains. Domain A trusts Domain B, and Domain B trusts Domain C. Domain A is a trusted domain, and Domain B is the trusting domain in the first relationship. Domain B is the trusted domain, and Domain C is the trusting domain in the second relationship. After upgrading the entire network Windows 2000, which of the following is true?

A. Domain B will trust Domain A, and Domain C will trust Domain B, but Domain C won't trust Domain A.

B. Domain A will trust Domain B, and Domain B will trust Domain C, but Domain A won't trust Domain C.

C. All trust relationships will need to be recreated because Windows 2000 won't preserve the trusts between the domains.

D. All domains will trust one another.

8. Your NT environment consists of three domains in a complete trust relationship. You want to enable users to cross domains and access resources in each of the domains after upgrading these domains to Windows 2000. Which of the following will be true?

   A. Since the formula M * (M - 1) + (R * M) would be used to calculate the trusts, there would be 15 trust relationships.

   B. Since the formula n *(n - 1) would be used to calculate the trusts, there would be six trust relationships.

   C. Since trust relationships in Windows 2000 are one-way and nontransitive, only two trust relationships would need to exist to establish the minimal trusts.

   D. Since trust relationships in Windows 2000 are two-way and transitive, only two trust relationships would need to exist to establish the minimal trusts.

9. Which of the following servers in your Windows NT environment should you upgrade to Windows 2000 first?

   A. Primary Domain Controller

   B. Backup Domain Controller

   C. Member server

   D. Standalone server

10. Your network consists of two domains. The first domain runs a mixture of Windows 2000 DCs and Windows NT BDCs, whereas the second domain runs only Windows 2000 DCs. Each of the domains runs in the default mode it was in at the time it was upgraded to Windows 2000, and all clients in both domains run Windows NT Workstation. You want to implement group nesting and Kerberos authentication in the second domain. Which of the following will you do?

A. Switch the second domain from mixed mode to native mode.

B. Switch the second domain from native mode to mixed mode.

C. Nothing. Because one of the domains is still running Windows NT BDCs, you cannot switch modes.

D. Nothing. Because the clients in the second domain are still using Windows NT Workstations, you cannot switch modes.

## Designing Directory Services

11. An automotive company has just entered into a temporary partnership with an engine manufacturer. Over the next two years, the two companies will be attempting to develop a better engine design for a new car that's being developed. Both companies are running Windows 2000 Server in native mode. Each company has its own IT staff and runs autonomously of the other. During the partnership, however, certain members of each organization will need to access data stored in the other company. Which of the following will you do to help these companies meet their needs?

    A. Create a new tree for one company under the other company's forest. This will allow both companies to run autonomously while exchanging information.

    B. Create an organizational unit in the root domain of your company. This will allow both companies to run autonomously while exchanging information.

    C. Create a child domain under your root domain. This will allow both companies to run autonomously while exchanging information.

    D. Have the network running as multiple forests, with each company running under its own forest.

12. A year after designing directory services for your network, you decide that you don't like the placement of a domain. This domain has one child domain beneath it. Which of the following needs to be considered in your choice to move the domain?

    A. The domain must be moved to a different forest because it can't be renamed or moved between trees.

    B. The domain must be moved to a different tree because it can't be renamed or moved between forests.

    C. The child domain must be moved with the parent domain.

    D. The domain can't be renamed or moved between trees or forests.

13. Which group would you need to add users to if you wanted the member users to perform administrative duties anywhere in a forest?

A. Domain Admins

B. Enterprise Admins

C. Forest Admins

D. Domain Enterprise

14. Which of the following objects can be contained in an organizational unit? (Choose all that apply.)

A. Users

B. Organizational Units

C. Sites

D. Computers

15. You have two sites on your network. Which protocol can you use for replication between these sites?

A. Remote Procedure Calls

B. SMTP

C. SNMP

D. Remote Procedure Calls or SMTP

E. Remote Procedure Calls or SNMP.

16. Which of the following contains network objects and a subset of their attributes, which can be queried by clients?

A. Active Directory

B. Global Catalog

C. Domain Name Service

D. Domain Name Server

17. You have designated a domain controller as a Global Catalog server in each domain in your network. Which of the following is stored on the GC server? (Choose all that apply.)

A. A complete replica of the local domain

B. A partial replica of other domains in the forest

C. A complete replica of all domains in the forest

D. A partial replica of all domains in the forest

18. You have three sites called SiteA, SiteB, and SiteC. SiteA has a DC that allows local users to log on to the local domain. It is connected to SiteC using a slow connection. SiteB also has a DC, which is connected to SiteC using a T1 connection. Due to construction on the building, the T1 line has been broken, and SiteB has lost its link to SiteC. Users in SiteC are now complaining about performance. What can you do to improve performance and prevent performance from degrading in this way in the future?

A. Install a T1 connection between SiteA and SiteB.

B. Install a redundant dial-up connection between SiteB and SiteC.

C. Install a DC in SiteC.

D. Install another DC in SiteA.

19. Your network runs Windows 2000 servers and consists of two domains. Each domain currently has one DC. One of these DCs is designated as a GC server and runs in native mode. The other DC is designated as a DNS server and runs in mixed mode. During the middle of the workday, the GC server in the domain running in native mode fails. What impact will this situation have on the network?

A. Users will be unable to log on.

B. It will have no impact on the network. Users will log on to the other domain.

C. Users will use the DNS server to locate the other DC to log on.

D. The other DC will act as a GC server for both domains.

20. You are planning to add DCs and additional GC servers to your network but want to determine the impact this will have on the size of Active Directory. Which of the following tools would you use to determine the impact?

A. Active Directory Domains and Trusts

B. Active Directory Installation Wizard

C. Active Directory Sizer Tool

D. Active Directory Users and Computers

# LAB QUESTION

As shown in Figure 7-7, your network consists of four domains running Windows NT 4.0 Server. Each domain has a PDC and a BDC, and two have member servers. You are preparing to upgrade these servers to Windows 2000.

Once the domain upgrade is completed, you plan to have a Windows NT 4.0 BDC continuing to run Windows NT 4.0 Server with Internet Information Server 4.0. This will allow you to provide intranet HTML content to each domain as you become more familiar with the Internet Information

**FIGURE 7-7**

Lab Network

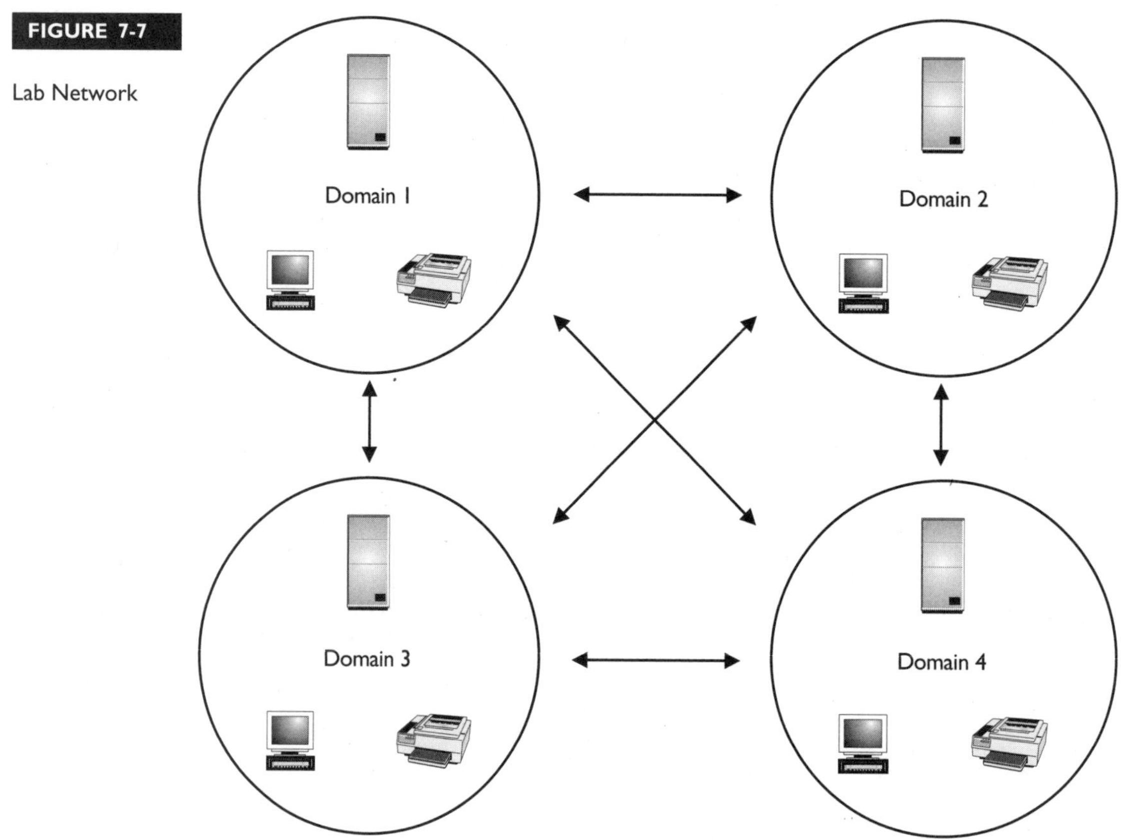

Services in Windows 2000 Server. Answer the following questions:

1. What type of Windows NT domain structure is used in this network?
2. After you perform an in-place upgrade of servers in each of the domains, what will happen to accounts and trust relationships between the domains?
3. How many PDCs will exist on the network after the upgrade is complete?
4. What mode will you use on Windows 2000 DCs in each of the domains?

# SELF TEST ANSWERS

## Designing Upgrade Strategies for Networks, Servers, and Clusters

1. ☑ A and C. Windows NT 3.51 Server and Windows NT 4.0 Server can each be upgraded to Windows 2000. All the service packs for these operating systems are supported, so it doesn't matter which service packs have been applied to the server's operating system.
   ☒ B is incorrect because Windows 2000 supports only upgrades from Windows NT 3.51 Server, Windows NT 4.0 Server, and previous versions of Windows 2000. **D** is incorrect because only Windows NT 3.51 Server, Windows NT 4.0 Server, and previous versions of Windows 2000 can be upgraded. No other operating systems can be upgraded to Windows 2000. If you are running another operating system, such as Linux, you need to do a clean install of Windows 2000.

2. ☑ **B.** Bring the BDC online, and then promote it to a PDC. By taking the BDC offline during the upgrade, you can promote it to a PDC if PDC upgrade fails. In this situation, the upgraded PDC won't restart, so it is removed from the network. As such, you only need to bring the BDC online again and promote it to a PDC. In doing so, you are rolling back the upgrade so that your network is as it was before you began upgrading to Windows 2000.
   ☒ A is incorrect because if you upgrade the BDC to Windows 2000 and this upgrade fails as well, both servers will be ruined. If that happens, all information contained on these servers will be lost. **C** is incorrect because the PDC is already offline. All that is required is that you promote the BDC to a PDC. **D** is incorrect because the question states that the server can't be restarted and because the PDC cannot be restored through the BDC.

3. ☑ **A.** The PDC must be online for the BDC to be upgraded properly. The BDCs being upgraded will use the upgraded PDC as a template. Therefore, the upgraded PDC must be available on the network so the BDCs can connect to the DC and obtain information.
   ☒ B is incorrect because—although the "primary" and "backup" designations don't exist in Windows 2000—there can be more than one DC in a Windows 2000 domain. **C** is incorrect because you don't need to upgrade all BDCs at once. They can be upgraded incrementally over time. **D** is incorrect because there is no backup domain controller designation in Windows 2000.

4. ☑ **A.** One. Multiple domains were required due to Windows NT's capacity limits. Windows NT only supported up to 40,000 user accounts per domain. This limitation would have caused three domains to be used, as indicated by the fact the Windows NT network used three PDCs. Because Active Directory theoretically supports up to 10 million objects and has been tested to

support 1 million objects, only a single domain would be needed after upgrading to Windows 2000.

☒ B, C, and D are all incorrect because only a single domain is needed.

**5.** ☑ **A.** Upgrade the domain model by performing an in-place upgrade. The domain model described in this question is a single-domain model. Everything is contained within a single domain structure, so once the PDC and other servers are upgraded to Windows 2000 Server, the domain upgrade is complete.

☒ **B** is incorrect because this domain model doesn't use trust relationships. A single-domain model consists of only one domain, in which all the accounts and resources reside. Because all the users, groups, and computers are contained in one domain, there is no need for trust relationships with other domains. **C** is incorrect because there is no reason to split the domain into two or more domains. The domain isn't spread over a wide geographical area, and performance isn't an issue. Even on a Windows NT network, there aren't enough users to justify splitting the network into different domains. **D** is incorrect because the domain is already a single-domain structure.

**6.** ☑ **B.** Single-master domain model. This model consists of one domain containing user accounts and one or more other domains containing resources. The single domain containing the user accounts is called a *master domain* or *account domain.* Other domains containing resources are referred to as *resource domains.*

☒ **A** is incorrect because the single-domain model consists of only a single domain. **C** is incorrect because the multimaster domain consists of two or more account domains. It has two or more SAM databases. There is one SAM for each account domain used in the multimaster domain model. **D** is incorrect because the complete trust model consists of multiple domains that trust one another. Because the domain described in the question has one SAM database and each domain in a complete trust has its own SAM database, the domain in this question can't be a complete trust.

**7.** ☑ **D.** All domains will trust one another. In Windows 2000, trust relationships are two-way and transitive. The term *two-way* means that if a trust relationship is established between two domains, both domains trust one another. *Transitive* means that trust relationships extend to other domains. As such, since Domain A and Domain B have a trust relationship, and Domain B has a trust relationship with Domain C, it follows that Domain A will trust Domain C (and vice versa) after the network is upgraded.

☒ **A** and **B** are incorrect because trust relationships are two-way and transitive in Windows 2000. Therefore, all the domains will trust one another. **C** is incorrect because trust relationships between domains are preserved after upgrading to Windows 2000.

**8.** ☑ **D.** Since trust relationships in Windows 2000 are two-way and transitive, only two trust relationships would need to exist to establish the minimal trusts. One trust would be established between the first and second domain and between the second and third domains. This would allow users to cross the domains and access resources in each of them.
☒ **A** is incorrect because this formula is used to calculate the number of trust relationships used in a multimaster domain model. In the formula M * (M - 1) + (R * M), *M* is the number of master domains, while *R* is the number of resource domains. Since there are no resource domains in a complete trust relationship, this formula couldn't be used even when the environment was running on Windows NT. **B** is incorrect because trust relationships in Windows 2000 are two-way and transitive. For that reason, the formula n * (n - 1) wouldn't apply. In this formula, *n* is the number of domains. You would need to use this formula to calculate one-way, nontransitive trusts, which aren't used in Windows 2000 networks. **C** is incorrect because in Windows 2000, trusts are not one-way and nontransitive.

**9.** ☑ **A.** Primary Domain Controller. When an NT domain is upgraded to Windows 2000, the PDC must be upgraded first. The PDC maintains the master copy of the domain's user-account database and is used to authenticate users. When you upgrade the PDC, AD is installed on the machine, and information in the Windows NT account database and SAM is transferred into AD.
☒ **B, C,** and **D** are incorrect because the PDC is the first server that must be upgraded to Windows 2000.

**10.** ☑ **A.** Switch the second domain from mixed mode to native mode. In doing so, you will be able to use a number of features that aren't available in mixed mode, such as group nesting and Kerberos authentication.
☒ **B** is incorrect because the domain will already be running in mixed mode due to the fact that the modes haven't been switched since the domain was upgraded. **C** is incorrect because the second domain is running Windows 2000 DCs exclusively. No NT BDCs exist in the second domain. **D** is incorrect because it doesn't matter if users are running NT clients. Native mode and mixed mode apply only to DCs.

## Designing Directory Services

**11.** ☑ **D.** Have the network running as multiple forests, with each company running under its own forest. With each company running under a different forest with a trust relationship connecting them, each company will be able to maintain its own network yet will be able to exchange information.
☒ **A, B,** and **C** are incorrect because in each choice the domain, OU, or tree will be under

your forest or the other company's forest. In each case, your network will continue to be removed from the other company's network.

**12.** ☑ **D.** The domain can't be renamed or moved between trees or forests. The only way to change the domain in this way is to remove and recreate it. Before you can do so, the child domain must be removed.
☒ **A** is incorrect because a domain can't be renamed or moved between forests. **B** is incorrect because a domain can't be renamed or moved between trees. **C** is incorrect because a domain can't be renamed or moved between trees or forests. Therefore, the child domain can't be moved with or without the parent domain.

**13.** ☑ **B.** Enterprise Admins. The Enterprise Administrators group has an administrative scope of the entire forest.
☒ **A** is incorrect because the Domain Admins group is limited to the domain in which the group is located. Administrative rights don't flow through the transitive trusts that are created between parent and child domains and can't be used in different domains in a forest. So, administrators in one domain won't have administrative rights to another domain. **C** and **D** are incorrect because these groups don't exist in Windows 2000.

**14.** ☑ **A, B,** and **D.** Users, Organizational Units, and computers. Of the various objects existing in Active Directory, only users, groups, computers, and other OUs can be added to an Organizational Unit.
☒ **C** is incorrect because sites can't be added to an Organizational Unit.

**15.** ☑ **D.** Remote procedure calls or SMTP. When replication occurs between sites, you can use either RPCs or the Simple Mail Transfer Protocol.
☒ **A** and **D** are incorrect because either RPCs or SMTP can be used. **B** is incorrect because SNMP is the Simple Network Management Protocol and isn't used for replication. **C** and **E** are incorrect because RPCs are used when AD is replicated within a domain.

**16.** ☑ **B.** Global Catalog. The GC contains all the objects contained in Active Directory but stores only a subset of attributes. Because all the attributes for objects aren't stored in the GC, this makes the GC smaller than Active Directory and thereby quicker to query.
☒ **A** is incorrect because AD contains network objects and all their attributes. **C** and **D** are incorrect because DNS is used for resolution of domain names to IP addresses and vice versa.

**17.** ☑ **A** and **B.** The GC contains a complete replica of the local domain and a partial replica of other domains in the forest. The GC server has a complete replica of the domain in which it is located and a partial replica of other domains in the forest. Because the GC keeps a partial replica of other domains, users are able to query the GC about objects in other domains.

☒ C is incorrect because only a partial replica of other domains is stored in the GC. **D** is incorrect because a complete replica of the local domain is stored in the GC.

**18.** ☑ **C.** Install a DC in SiteC. This step will allow users to log on to the local DC rather than over the network. This will improve availability and performance. If a DC in SiteC is down, users will still be able to log on to a DC in another site. If the link between these sites goes down, users will be able to log on locally.
☒ **A** is incorrect because if the link between SiteB and SiteC is down, users will still have to connect to SiteA over a slow connection. Improving the connection between SiteA and SiteB will do nothing for SiteC. **B** is incorrect because this step will do nothing to improve performance. SiteC will still have to connect over a slow link. **D** is incorrect because SiteC will still need to connect to SiteA over a slow connection, which is the reason for the bottleneck.

**19.** ☑ **A.** Users will be unable to log on. A GC is required for users to log on to a domain running in native mode. When users log on to the network in native mode, the DC will query the GC server. This allows the GC to determine whether or not users are members of universal groups. A universal group contains members from any domain in a forest, allowing users to perform actions with specified access in any domain. If a GC is unavailable, the DC will have no idea whether the user is a member of a universal group and if they should be allowed or denied access to resources. For this reason, users won't be able to log on to the domain.
☒ **B** and **C** are incorrect because users will be unable to log on if the GC server in that domain is unavailable. **D** is incorrect because the DC won't act as a GC server for both domains.

**20.** ☑ **C.** Active Directory Sizer Tool. This tool provides an estimate as to the size of the Active Directory if changes are made to the network. Such changes would include the addition of DCs and GC servers.
☒ **A** is incorrect because Active Directory Domains and Trusts is used to manage trust relationships between domains, change the mode from mixed to native, and various other tasks. It isn't used to determine the size of AD after changes are made. **B** is incorrect because the Active Directory Installation Wizard is used to install AD. **D** is incorrect because Active Directory Users and Computers is used to add, delete, and modify user and computer accounts; manage DCs and OUs, and various other tasks. It isn't used to determine the size of AD after changes are made.

# LAB ANSWER

1. Complete trust. The network shows a complete trust relationship between the domains making up this network.
2. Any existing trust relationships and accounts are preserved when scaling up to Windows 2000 Server, so you don't need to re-create them as part of your upgrade strategy.
3. None. In Windows 2000, only DCs are used. There are no DCs with the designation of "primary" or "backup."
4. Mixed mode, which allows you to run Windows NT BDCs on the network with Windows 2000 DCs.

MCSE
MICROSOFT CERTIFIED SYSTEMS ENGINEER

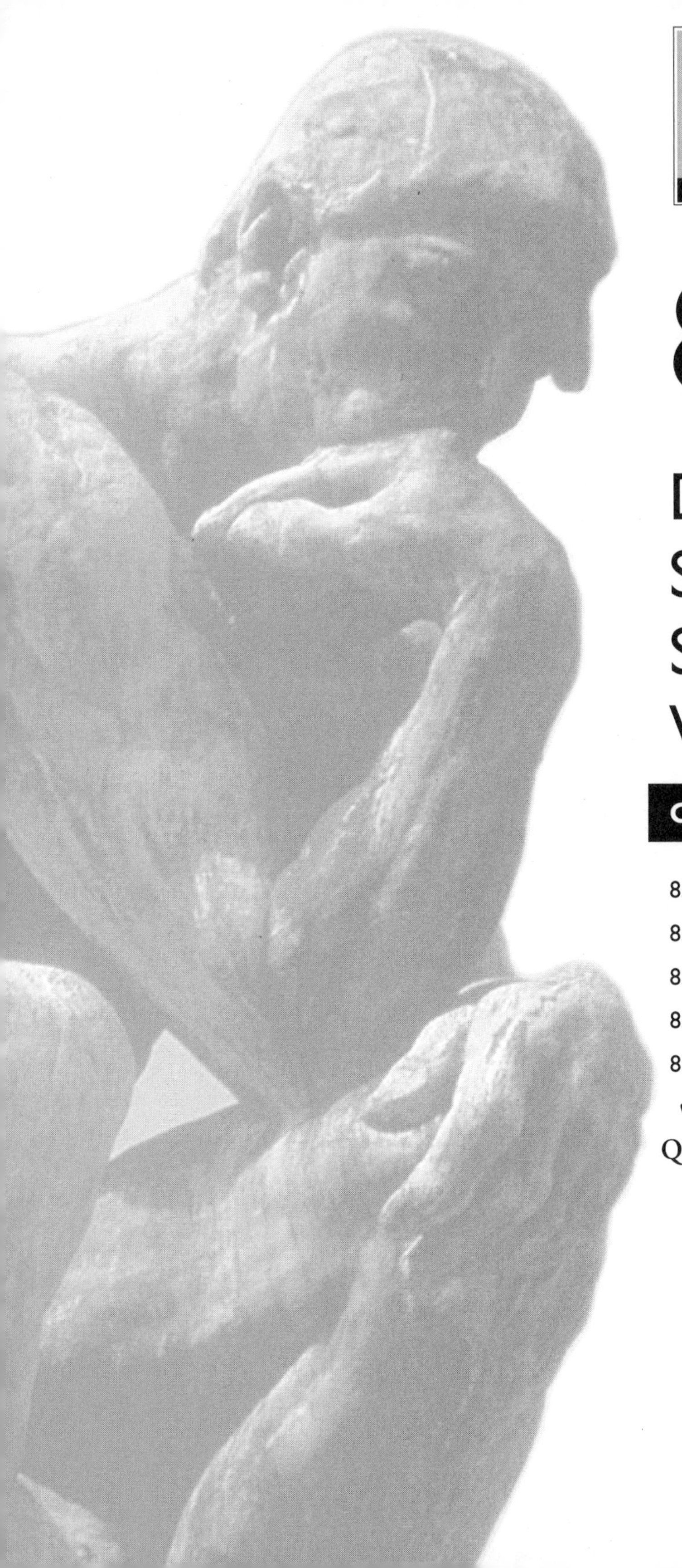

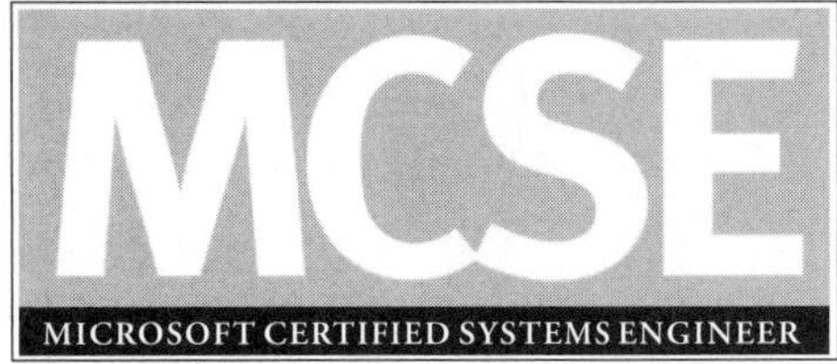

# 8

# Designing Security Strategies for Web Solutions

## CERTIFICATION OBJECTIVES

| | |
|---|---|
| 8.01 | Designing an Authentication Strategy |
| 8.02 | Designing an Authorization Strategy |
| 8.03 | Designing an Encryption Strategy |
| 8.04 | Designing a Firewall Strategy |
| 8.05 | Designing a Security Auditing Strategy |
| ✓ | Two-Minute Drill |
| Q&A | Self Test |

Almost all companies have Web sites or even Internet connections that allow their employees to access the Internet from company intranets. With a connection from a private company network to a public network, security is always an issue. Good security measures can be very important in keeping a company safe from external attacks by hackers who attempt to access confidential internal data.

Such attacks can be stopped by the use of a firewall as well as secure authentication procedures that require users on the public network, the Internet, to prove their identities to the private network, or intranet.

To prevent hackers from monitoring and deciphering data being passed over the Internet from one office to another, the data can be encrypted to allow only the sender and receiver to determine the true contents. A company can employ various methods and combinations of methods to provide the best security measures to protect its private network. This chapter examines these methods, the first of which is authentication.

**CERTIFICATION OBJECTIVE 8.01**

# Designing an Authentication Strategy

In a corporate Web site, some pages might contain confidential information that requires only specific users be able to access the data; other pages will contain general information that any user can access without verification of identity. There are many ways to provide authentication of users' identities to verify that these users do indeed have security rights to access a Web page or even a whole Web site. These authentication methods are as follows:

- Certificates
- Anonymous access
- Directory Services authentication
- Digest authentication
- Windows Integrated Authentication

- Kerberos
- Authenticode

Let's look at these methods in more detail.

## Certificates

A *certificate* is a kind of "driver's license" for the Internet. A certificate verifies the user's or company's identity to other users and/or companies that are not actual members of the domain by having an Active Directory user account. Certificates for the Internet are assigned by a *Certificate Authority (CA)*, which verifies the certificate owner's identity to others on the Internet.

Sometimes corporate Internet users must be verified for access to critical and confidential information, especially if a user is accessing the information remotely and using either a direct-dial connection to the Internet or an Internet Service Provider (ISP). Certificates can also be used to encrypt transferred data between two hosts on the Internet or an intranet. The certificate is used as an encryption key; on the receiving end of the transmission, the certificate is used as a decryption key.

The Windows 2000 Server family can provide certificates to authorize intranet access to a user, whether the user is accessing the network locally or remotely. The Certificate Service, an add-on service, is not enabled by default but can be easily added for use by the domain. The service is the Microsoft Certificate Service (MCS). Exercise 8-1 shows how to install the service.

Note that it's easy to remove the Certificate Service, but doing so will not allow for the certificates to be properly verified. Certificate Services should be removed only when certificates are no longer needed.

**EXERCISE 8-1**

CertCam 8-1

### Installing Microsoft Certificate Services

1. Go to Start | Settings and then select Control Panel.
2. In the Control Panel Window, open Add/Remove Programs.
3. In Add/Remove Programs, select the Add/Remove Windows Components on the left side of the screen.

4. Once the Windows Component Wizard has determined which components are currently installed, the wizard will display a list of components that can be added or removed. (Note that the services already installed have a check mark next to the service name or group.)
5. The second option on the list is Certificate Services. Select Certificate Services and then click the Details button.
6. Once the details of the Certificate Services group have been displayed, you have the option of choosing Certificate Services CA and/or Certificate Services Web Enrollment Support. (Note that the Certificate Services CA is the Certificate Authority Services, and the Web Enrollment Support option allows the Certificate server to take requests for a certificate, which can then be forwarded to a Certificate Server.)
7. Select the options you need and then press OK. (Make sure that the Certificate Services CA option is selected for this exercise. If the Certificate Services CA option is selected, the Web Enrollment option is also selected.)
8. You are then prompted with a message that the server cannot be renamed or removed from the domain. Select Yes to continue, and then click OK.
9. Select Next to continue the Add/Remove Components Wizard. At this screen, you are prompted to select the type of CA this server will be, as explained in the following list and Figure 8-1:
   - **Enterprise root CA** This certificate server will be the main certificate server in a domain environment, requiring access to Active Directory as well as the currently logged-on user having Domain Administrator rights. The enterprise root CA approves or denies the request for a certificate immediately based on rules set by the administrator. This server publishes the authorized certificates in Active Directory as well as those certificates that have been revoked in the Certification Revocation List (CRL).
   - **Enterprise subordinate CA** This certificate server is a client to the enterprise root CA. The subordinate CA submits requests for certificates to the enterprise root CA and awaits response regarding whether to approve or deny the request. Initially, the request can be put in a pending state until approval or denial. The parent CA can be another subordinate CA, an enterprise root CA, or even a third-party company, such as VeriSign.

- **Standalone root CA** This is the same as the enterprise root CA but without the requirement for Active Directory. A standalone root CA allows you to install a certificate server within a workgroup. This requires the user who is installing the service to have Administrative rights on the local PC.
- **Standalone subordinate CA** This is the same as the enterprise subordinate CA, except for the need for an enterprise root CA. This option does require a standalone root CA.

**FIGURE 8-1** Various Certificate Server Hierarchies

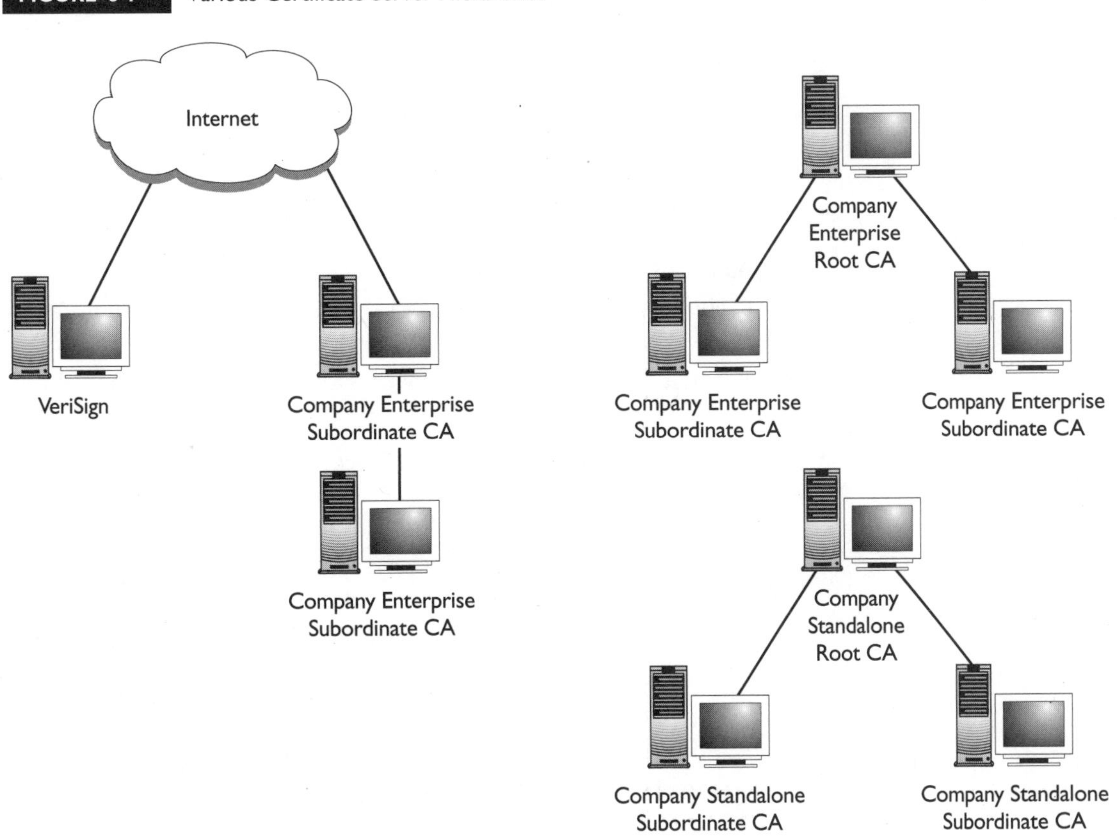

10. Once you have selected a certificate server type, the next screen allows you to specify the private and public key pair. You are allowed to choose the cryptographic service provider (CSP) that is the manufacturer of the algorithm type used to encrypt data. You can also choose the hash algorithm that is used to do the actual encryption. You can even specify a key length. The longer the key, the more secure the encryption, but more resources are used to encrypt and decrypt the information. You are also given the option to import existing keys to let the older key algorithms coexist with the new algorithms until the older certificates expire.
11. The next screen prompts you to enter the information pertaining to the certificate service. This screen not only allows you to enter the company information; you can also specify a default expiration on all certificates issued. The default is initially set to two years. Once all data is entered, press Next.
12. In the next window, you specify the location of the certificate database and the logs, as well as the shared folder in which to store the configuration data for subordinate CAs to download information. Click Next to proceed.
13. If the Internet Information Services (IIS) are running, a message appears to prompt you to allow the IIS to be stopped temporarily while the certificate services are configured and started. Select OK. (Note that at this point, if any of the Windows 2000 Service Packs are installed, the service pack source files will be asked to get the updated certificate services files as well as the Microsoft Server CD.)
14. Once all files are copied, the final screen of the Windows Components Wizard will be displayed. Press Finish.
15. Select Close on the Add/Remove Programs window and close the Control Panel.

The Certificate Service should now be installed and running, as should the IIS, which was shut down in Step 13. Once Certificate Service is installed, Administrative Tools should have an option called Certificate Authority for managing certificates. To actually create and revoke certificates, you should add the Certificates snap-in to the Microsoft Management Console (MMC). The snap-in is not added to any preconfigured MMC under Administrative Tools.

### Designing a Hierarchical Certificate Server System

The hierarchical design of certificate servers is quite a simplistic one. It must have one root CA, whether an enterprise root CA or a standalone root CA, if your company wants to issue its own certificates. Under the root CA, you can have multiple subordinate CAs that will be enterprise CAs if the root is also an enterprise CA; you can have standalone subordinate CAs if the root is a standalone root CA. The subordinate CAs submit the requests for a certificate to the root CA and wait for the response of the root CA to signify if the certificate is approved or denied.

The root CA, whether enterprise or standalone, is the most trusted CA in the hierarchy. All subordinates are trusted if their certificates were issued by the root CA. Since the whole hierarchy is dependent on the root CA, it is very important to keep the root CA functioning. Once a root CA is created, the subordinates will be directed to the root CA or another subordinate, which will point to the root CA for authentication of the CA's validity.

It is imperative that the root CA be accessible at all times to sustain the certificate security structure. The root CA should be implemented as a cluster or with some type of hardware failover to prevent failure of the root CA.

If the job of maintaining a certificate server is too great a task, use a third party's services and direct your subordinate CA to the third-party server. This strategy allows the subordinate to act as a "middle man" while the third party manages the certificates.

In a multiple-location intranet, a subordinate could be placed at each "branch" or remote site that is pointing to the enterprise certificate server at headquarters, or even a third-party certificate server.

### Using Certificates for Web Site Access

If you selected the Web Enrollment Support option when installing the Certificate Services, the certificate server will be accessible remotely via Web browsers, connecting the certificate server to remotely request certificates. The default Web page to connect to is http://*servername*/certserv, where *servername* is the name of the certificate server. Once connected, you will open a Web page as shown in Figure 8-2.

As you can see from the figure, you have three choices:

- Retrieve the CA certificate or revocation list.
- Request a certificate.
- Check on a pending certificate.

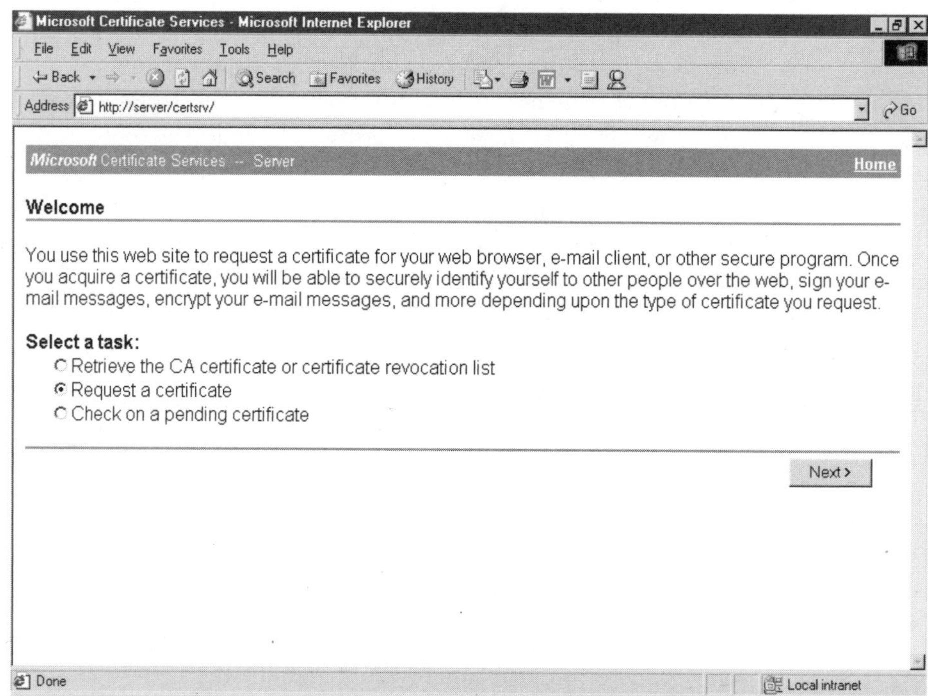


**FIGURE 8-2** Certificate Request from the Web Site Main Page

If you want to request a certificate, select Request a Certificate and then select Next. On the next screen, you can choose either an e-mail protection certificate with which to validate e-mail messages or a Web browser certificate to use to verify identity to a Web site, as shown in Figure 8-3.

The Advanced Request options enable us to request a certificate using a form, make a renewal request, or request a smart-card certificate, as shown in Figure 8-4.

After specifying the certificate type, the next screen allows you to enter your information that will be bound to the certificate, as shown in Figure 8-5. The More Options button allows you to specify the type of algorithm you are requesting for your certificate. The default algorithm is Microsoft Base Cryptographic Provider v1.0.

After this screen, if the root CA were set to authorize certain certificates automatically, this request would be authorized and immediately available for installation, as shown in Figure 8-6. If the request was not authorized immediately and set for pending, you would be presented with the screen shown in Figure 8-7.

If the certificate were authorized immediately and the option shown was as in Figure 8-6, and you were selecting the option to install the certificate immediately, you would be given a screen stating that the certificate was installed successfully.

**FIGURE 8-3**

Certificate Type Request from the Web Site

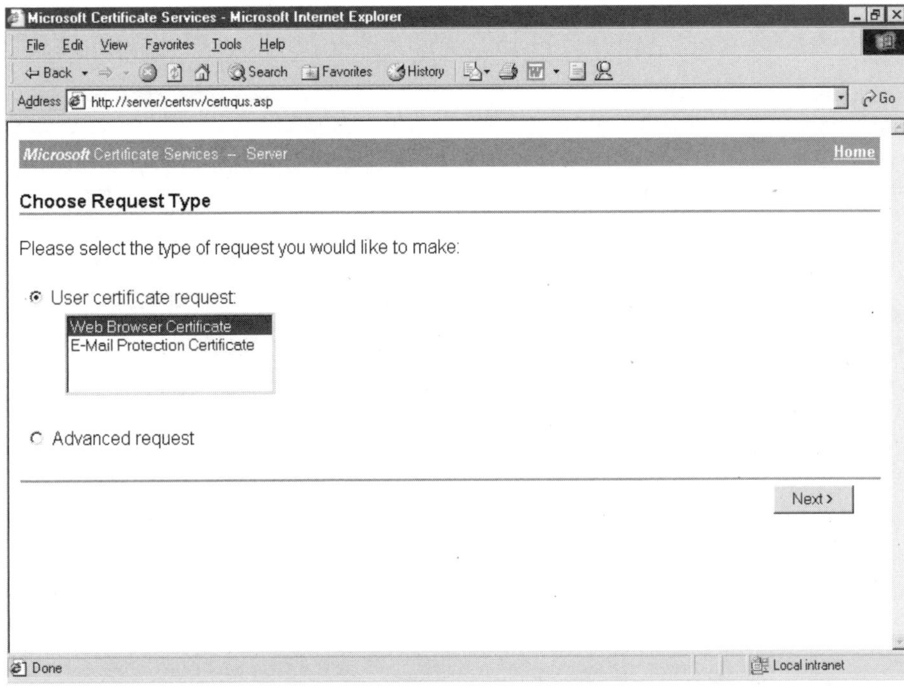


**FIGURE 8-4**

Advanced Certificate Request from the Web Site

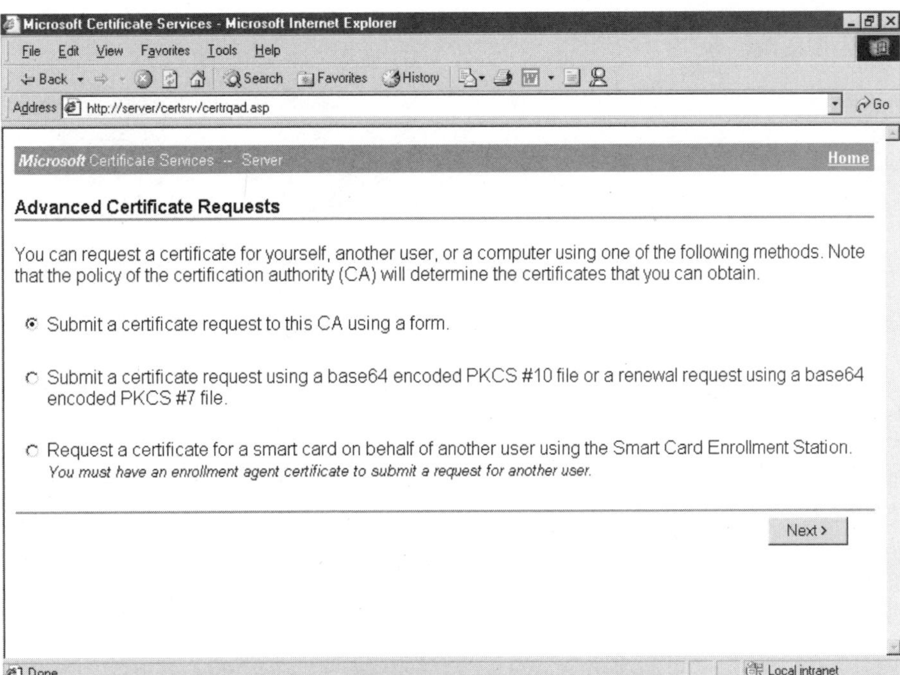

**FIGURE 8-5**

Certificate Request for Identity from the Web Site

Microsoft Certificate Services - Microsoft Internet Explorer
File Edit View Favorites Tools Help
Back Search Favorites History
Address http://server/certsrv/certrqbi.asp?type=0
Go
Microsoft Certificate Services -- Server
Home
Web Browser Certificate - Identifying Information
Please fill in the following identifying information that will go on your certificate:
Name:
E-Mail:
Company:
Department:
City:
State:
Country/Region:
More Options >>
Submit >
Done
Local intranet

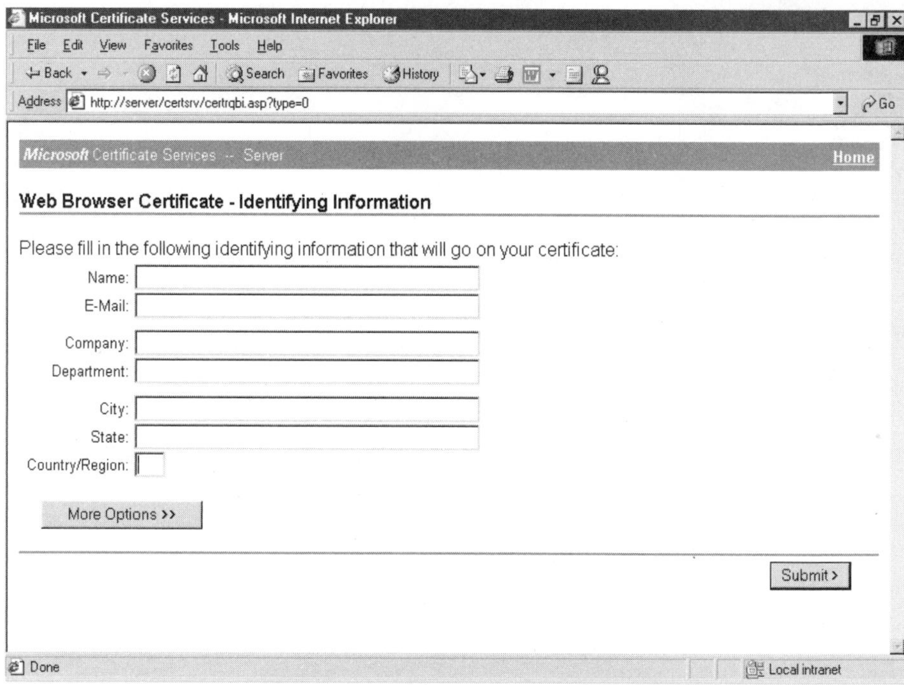

**FIGURE 8-6**

Authorized Certificate Request

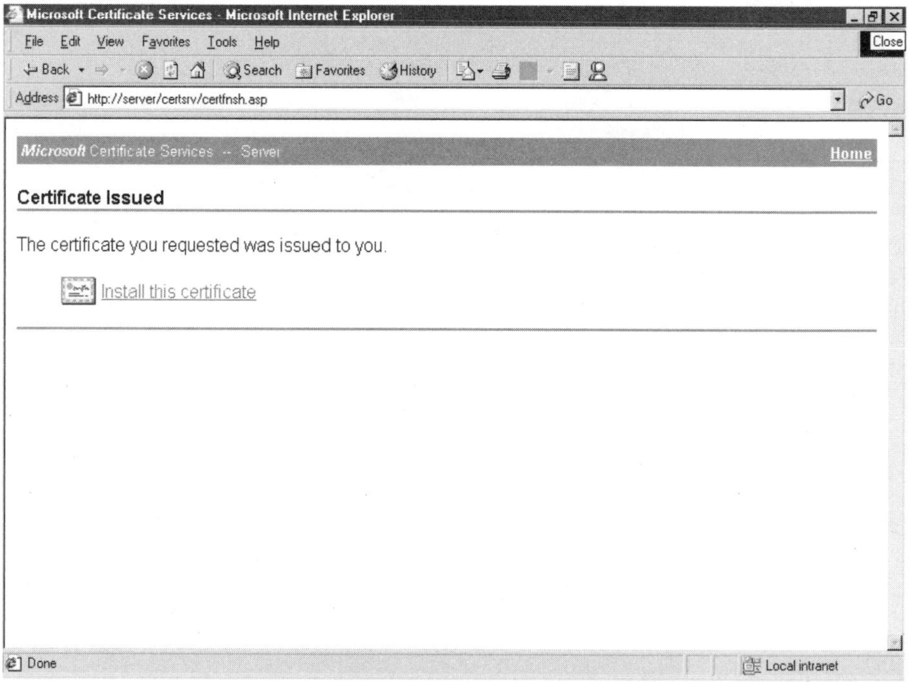

Microsoft Certificate Services - Microsoft Internet Explorer
File Edit View Favorites Tools Help
Close
Back Search Favorites History
Address http://server/certsrv/certfnsh.asp
Go
Microsoft Certificate Services -- Server
Home
Certificate Issued
The certificate you requested was issued to you.
Install this certificate
Done
Local intranet

**FIGURE 8-7**

Pending Certificate Request

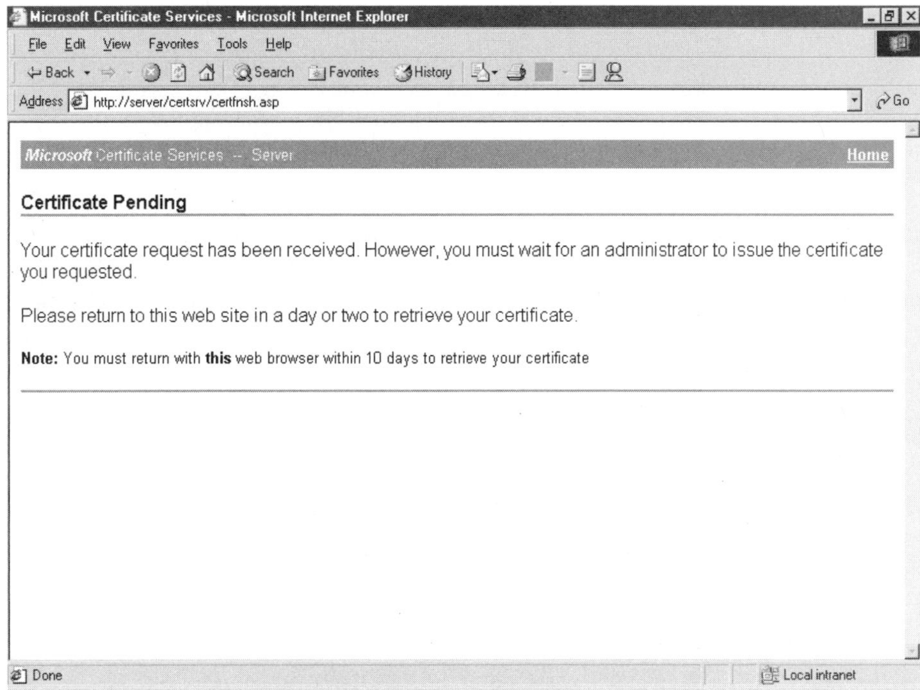
Microsoft Certificate Services - Microsoft Internet Explorer
File Edit View Favorites Tools Help
Back Search Favorites History
Address http://server/certsrv/certfnsh.asp
Go
Microsoft Certificate Services -- Server
Home
Certificate Pending
Your certificate request has been received. However, you must wait for an administrator to issue the certificate you requested.
Please return to this web site in a day or two to retrieve your certificate.
Note: You must return with this web browser within 10 days to retrieve your certificate
Done
Local intranet

## Anonymous Access

When Windows 2000 is installed, the IIS is installed by default. These services allow for the use of World Wide Web (WWW), File Transfer Protocol (FTP), Network News Transfer Protocol (NNTP), and Simple Mail Transfer Protocol (SMTP) services on the server. These services allow *anonymous access*, which is access by any user without the user having to supply credentials for authentication.

Anonymous access is granted by mapping users to the anonymous user account that is created when IIS is installed. The account is named IUSR_*servername* by default and should not be deleted or renamed. The account should not be changed in any way, except for security permissions for access to files or Web pages. Changing file security permissions for the IUSR_*servername* account in effect changes the permissions for the anonymous user and prevents the user from accessing specific files or even Web pages; in the reverse, it could allow the user to access files and Web sites that the user has no right to access.

For anonymous access to work correctly, the IUSR_*servername* account needs to have Log on Locally privileges, which are granted by default. Without this permission, anonymous users could not access the IIS.

Anonymous access should be used only in nonsecure environments for areas that require no type of accounting for the users accessing the IIS server. If, for example, the Web site has a page that anyone is allowed to view, such as a home page for a bank, it can be set for anonymous access. Anonymous access is fine for an intranet Web site that is not accessible from the Internet, as long as the Web content is not secure for a company's employees to view. If some of the content is secure for only specific individuals, you need to use Directory Services authentication.

## Directory Services

*Directory Services authentication* allows Web site visitors to be authenticated to the user list in Active Directory. This check can be performed in three ways:

- Basic authentication
- Digest authentication
- Windows Integrated Authentication

If anonymous access is disabled, any Directory Services authentication types are used. If the NT File System (NTFS) permissions are set on the actual Hypertext Markup Language (HTML) files, anonymous access cannot be used.

### Basic Authentication

*Basic authentication* prompts the user who is accessing the Web site for a username and password, as shown in Figure 8-8.

The user enters the username and password once and selects the OK button. The username and password are sent to the specified domain controller for validation against the Active Directory user account.

The main issue with basic authentication is that the username and password are sent across the network to the validation server as clear text. Anyone using some type of packet analyzer can read the username and password. For this reason, basic authentication should not be used over the Internet, but it's useful on the local intranet to keep security risks at a minimum.

**FIGURE 8-8**

Basic Authentication Validation Login Screen

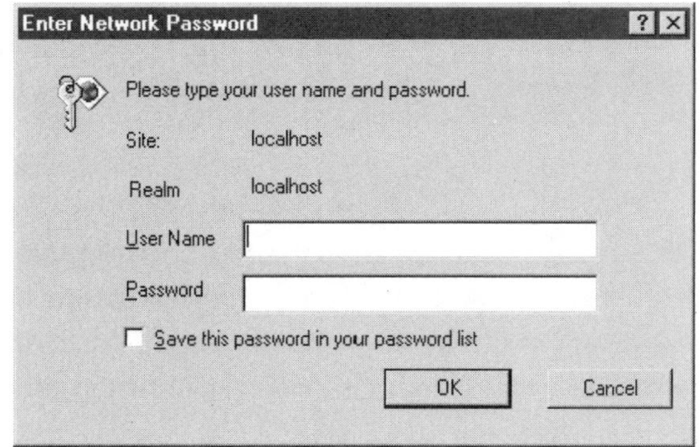


### Digest Authentication

*Digest authentication* requires that the Web server be a domain controller, because the username and password must be checked locally to confirm a match of those credentials sent from the user.

When a user contacts a Web site that has digest authentication enabled, the Web server sends a string of information. This string of information is used with the username and password that the user enters in the dialog box, as shown in Figure 8-8, and is encrypted or hashed. Once encrypted, the resulting information is sent to the Web server, which performs the same information on the server side using the string that was sent with the username and password that are in Active Directory. If the resulting hash is identical to the hash sent by the user, the logon is validated.

This authentication method is more secure and best used over the Internet or nonsecure networks. The hash values can be sent through proxy servers and firewalls.

### Windows Integrated Authentication

Windows Integrated Authentication is based on the single logon method used with all Windows networks. Once a user has logged in and been validated by the domain controller, the user receives a *token,* which is a list of all security groups in which the user is a member.

When accessing a Web site, the token can be verified to allow access to a Web page or a whole Web site. Since the token has already been issued, the username and password do not need to be sent over the network; only the token needs to be verified. For Internet Explorer Web browser users, this type of authentication requires at least IE version 2.0 to support the Windows authentication.

## FROM THE CLASSROOM

### Digest Authentication Hashing

A *hashing algorithm* is a formula that is used to take the username, password, and string that were sent to the user's PC to come up with another value or set of values. The server can then perform the same algorithm and determine that the username and password are identical.

For example, let's assume that the server sent a string to the user who was attempting to access a Web site that has digest authentication enabled. The string sent was *jKhdkHj*. Now assume that the username entered was *JBuse*, but we will convert this to all lowercase. The password entered was *Eilly*, and passwords are case sensitive. If we convert the letters of these three strings to their ASCII values and add them all up, we get 1718. If the algorithm then divides that number by 127, we get 13.527559055118110236220472440945. The server side produces the same number if the username and password are the same in Active Directory.

Now, let's assume that the username and password are correct in Active Directory, but the user enters the password as *eilly* instead of *Eilly*. We would get a value of 1750 on the client side and 1780 on the server side. After dividing by 127, the values would still be different, and the user would not be authenticated.

Needless to say that the algorithm used in this example is extremely basic; the algorithm Windows uses is much more complex. Furthermore, note that the initial string sent to the user is different every time and is randomly generated. This prevents someone from capturing the hashed data and being able to use it to force entry into the system later.

*—Jarret W. Buse, MCT, MCSE+I, CCNA, A+, Network+*

A drawback of this authentication method is that the user must have a user account for the domain in which the Web server exists. If this Web site is connected to the Internet, it will be extremely secure by using standard Windows logon security. If the number of users is few, user accounts could be created, but if a lot of users need authenticated access to a Web site, Windows Integrated Authentication would be out of the question. This is because a user account would have to be created for each. A single generic account could be used, but this would reduce the Web site's security by having multiple people log on as a single user and not allowing for proper auditing of the users' activities.

Now that you understand the various Windows authentication types, let's look at some scenarios and solutions so we know when to use each one.

| SCENARIO & SOLUTION | |
|---|---|
| What if my Web site users will access from my local intranet domain as well as through VPNs with no security requirements? | Basic authentication should be used. |
| What if my Web site users will be from my local intranet domain as well as from remote domains, with no proxy servers? | Windows Integrated Authentication requires that users have a domain account. This authentication method does not work with proxy servers. |
| What if my Web site users will be from my local intranet domain as well as from remote domains connecting over the Internet through proxy servers? | Digest authentication should be used for encryption purposes as well as for the ability to be used with proxy servers. |

**exam watch** ***Make sure that you know when to employ each type of authentication strategy.***

## Kerberos

The name *Kerberos* is taken from Greek mythology; Cerberos is the three-headed dog that guards the gates of Hades. Kerberos is the encryption scheme used to protect data and prevent it from being decrypted and read, especially the username and password that are being authenticated on nonlocal trusted domains.

Kerberos is also the Windows standard to authenticate systems and users on a domain. The Kerberos standard is an open standard that anyone is allowed to use. It has been implemented in a number of other systems.

Kerberos uses mutual authentication—that is, it identifies the user and the network services to which users are making requests for resources. For example, when a user logs on to the network, the username and password are verified and the user is issued a *Ticket-Granting Ticket (TGT)*, which is an encrypted set of information containing the user's encrypted password. The TGT is issued by the Key Distribution Center (KDC), which has access to all user accounts and their passwords. When a user wants to access a resource on a domain controller, the user's PC sends a copy of the TGT to the Ticket-Granting Service (TGS). If the TGT is accepted, the TGS grants the user a service ticket that shows that the bearer has been granted rights to the resource. Later, when the user wants to access the same resource, the service ticket is sent instead; this ticket grants access and does not require the whole Kerberos authentication method to occur again.

Any client machines need to be placed on a network for access if a domain controller, especially one that hosts a Web site, should support Kerberos version 5. By allowing the client to support Kerberos, the authentication is encrypted (a process that is discussed later in this chapter) to help enhance security.

## Authenticode

*Authenticode* is used to digitally "sign" a software package that is needed for viewing a Web site. For example, if you need a special viewer or ActiveX control to be able to view certain graphics or sounds on a Web site, you are prompted with a window to specify whether the program code should be downloaded and installed. You also have the choice of signifying whether the software manufacturer should always be trusted. If the manufacturer should be trusted, a check box can be checked to allow for no further prompts when a software program that is signed by the same company is to be downloaded. This control, if downloaded, is installed only on the local computer, and the trust setting is also set for only the local computer. A good example of the Authenticode method is the Macromedia Shockwave software that enables users to view moving graphics with sounds on the Internet.

Authenticode is a digital signature that can show whether the software package was altered or corrupted from its original state. This information is helpful to determine whether or not the software package has a virus or has been altered and could cause problems when installed. The software package, even if signed, could still be harmful to a system due to software bugs or incompatibilities with the user's system. New Authenticode version 2.0 also uses timestamps to allow for software programs to expire after a certain amount of time, requiring a new digital signature.

CERTIFICATION OBJECTIVE 8.02

# Designing an Authorization Strategy

Once a user has been authenticated, the user must be *authorized* to view a Web page or Web site. If the user does not have the authority or security clearance to see confidential data, the data should not be sent to the user's Web browser.

Many types of authorization can be used to enable permissions to view Web pages. These authorization types can be implemented in tandem to provide more security for confidential information.

## Group Membership

As with all resource access in Windows, you can provide access to resources by granting group membership to many users and granting user access to Web pages based on the user's group. This method allows all members of a group to have the same permissions assigned to them. If a user is a member of multiple groups, all rights from all the user's groups will be combined to provide higher access. Permissions can be placed on the individual HTML files and on the directory in which the Web site files exist by using NTFS permissions. These permissions can be set not only for the Web site but also for the FTP site.

These permissions are best used to create a finer degree of permission for users within your domain. This finer granularity is extremely useful in an intranet, especially when a database front end can be accessed and manipulated through the Web server. We discuss actual file security settings in more detail in the following section.

## Access Control Lists

An *Access Control List (ACL)* is a listing or setting of security options on an individual file or directory. As shown in Figure 8-9, you can see the default securities set on the WWWROOT directory, where all Web pages and sites that are hosted on a server are stored.

Here, permissions can be granted or denied. If you set a permission to be denied, any group in which the user belongs that has the permission granted will be overridden.

**FIGURE 8-9**

Default Permissions on the WWWROOT Directory

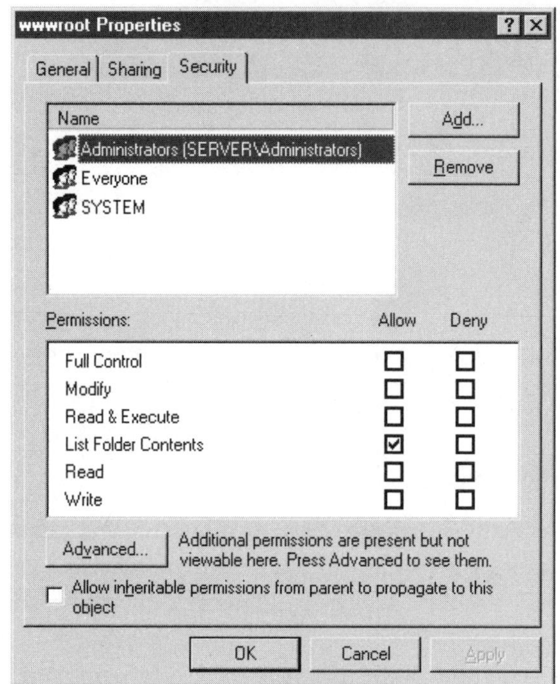


These permissions can be set on all files individually as well as whole directories. When permissions are set on a directory, by default the permissions are inherited by all files and folders within the directory. These permissions can also be overridden by clearing the "Allow inheritable permissions from parent to propagate to this object" option, allowing the permissions from a directory not to be inherited by the subfolders and files within the directory on which the permissions are set. If a user should complain that he or she does not have access to a particular file, you can access the file's Properties and select the Security tab. The user will be listed, and if selected, the user's effective permissions will be shown for that specific file.

This ability allows for granular security settings, especially on an intranet, since the user and group accounts from the domain directory or a Security Accounts Management (SAM) database on a standalone server are used.

exam Watch

***Be sure that you understand NTFS permissions and the inheritance feature.***

## IP Blocking

*Internet Protocol (IP) blocking* can be enabled to block or grant access based on a single IP address, whole subnets, and even by domain name. This function can be useful to grant access to all users except specific computers, subnets, or domains. The option also works the other way so that all users except the listed computers, subnets, or whole domains can be denied access.

These options can be useful on an intranet to provide security and authorization only for those computers within the domain or subnet. If only certain users, such as administrators, should be able to access a particular page, the access for the single page could be limited to the IP addresses of the administrator PCs or even servers. If certain pages are limited to servers and the company servers are located in a locked room, the Web pages will be very secure.

An ISP could have a Web site on the Internet accessible only to its customers. The Web site could be limited to the subnet the ISP is able to use. This setup would mean that only the ISP's customers could access the page.

## Web Content Zones

The *Web content zone* type of authorization is enabled on a Web server for a specific Web site but is more useful on the client side than it is on the server side. This setting allows you to specify the contents of your Web site to allow for clients to determine whether the site can be trusted or completely barred from being viewed.

To enable ratings for Web content, look at Exercise 8-2.

**EXERCISE 8-2**

### Editing Content Rating

1. Open the Internet Information Services from the Administrative Tools.
2. Expand the contents below your IIS server name.
3. Right-click the Web site to set ratings and select Properties.
4. Select the HTTP Headers tab.
5. Under the Edit Ratings section, select the Edit Ratings button.
6. To view the descriptions of the settings, select the More Info button.

(Note: These steps take you to the Recreational Software Advisory Council (RSAC) Web site to give you more information. The actual Web site is www.rsac.org/ratingsv01.html).

7. Once you have viewed the information, you can go back to the IIS properties screen and select the Ratings Questionnaire button.

   (Note: This step takes you to the RSAC Web site to fill out a questionnaire for the Web content of your site. The actual Web site is www.rsac.org/ratingsv01.html).

8. Once at the RSCA Web site, you can choose to read more information or fill out the questionnaire. Once the questionnaire is filled out, you will be assigned a label to include on you home page as a metatag. This tag will be read by the Web site visitors' browsers and will determine if the page is allowable. The tag will not be visible to the browsers' users.

The questionnaire covers such areas of Web content as nudity, sexual materials, violence, and language. Each of these areas is broken down to determine if there is any specific content to warrant placing a specific rating on the site. For example, the violence section of the questionnaire asks if there is fighting and then goes into a greater degree of what is actually shown. Content can then be explained to some extent, such as is the fighting related to a sport such as football. This method helps prevent a Web site on sports activities from being blocked by adults on their Web browsers and allows violent content not related to sports to be blocked to prevent children from seeing it.

The metatag label can be obtained for a whole site, a branch of the site, or an individual page. This can allow specific areas to be viewed while blocking some parts of the Web site from Web browsers with content ratings enabled.

Content zones are more of an authorization for specific age groups of maturity. Note that not all parents or adults will enable content ratings on their Web browsers. If the contents ratings are not enabled on a Web browser, the content labels will do nothing to prevent viewing Web site. Furthermore, if your site has no label, a Web browser filters out your site and does not allow viewing. Adding a label to your Web site allows it to be viewed by all visitors as long as the label does not specify that the site contains questionable material for young viewers.

***Note that you should use a label on your site. If you don't, your site will not be accessible by Web browsers that have content ratings enabled. It might also be a good idea to enable content ratings on Web browsers with your company to prevent employees from accessing Web sites that should not be visited on company time.***

## CERTIFICATION OBJECTIVE 8.03

# Designing an Encryption Strategy

You can *encrypt* data being transmitted between two devices on a network, whether the network is an intranet or the Internet. *Encryption* is the means by which data is transformed to a nonreadable format for the data's protection. With encryption, anyone who intercepts the data with ill intent cannot easily read it.

Encryption is managed by using an algorithm to transform the data into meaningless information but still allow the data to be recovered by processing the information through an algorithm to *decrypt* the data to its original readable form. No matter which method of encryption is used, this security technique is meant to enhance all other security measures that can keep a Web site as well its content secure while being transferred over the network.

Encryption can be managed and used in several ways for encryption of more than just Web content. Let's look at a few of those methods.

## IPSec

*IPSec,* or *IP Security,* is an encryption method that still uses standard IP packets to transmit the encrypted data. This method allows the transmission media and all devices in between to need to be able to manage only Transmission Control Protocol/Internet Protocol (TCP/IP) packets. This means that the devices between the sending and receiving hosts, which include routers, switches, and hubs, need no modifications to be able to receive and transmit data packets.

IPSec is enabled on Windows 2000 machines from the MMC. After opening an MMC console, go to Add/Remove Snap-in to add the IP Security Policy Management snap-in. A window then appears, prompting you to select the computer that the snap-in will manage. You can choose local computer, local domain, remote domain, or another computer. Once a choice is selected, you can open the IPSec Policy Manager to manage the IP Security features you will employ for the computer or domain you selected.

Once the console is open, you can click "IP Security Policies on *computer/domain.*" *computer/domain* is the choice you selected previously. In the right pane, you have three choices: Client, Secure Server, or Server:

- **Client (Respond Only)** This option allows a client computer to respond to a server only if IPSec is enabled on the server. If IPSec is not enabled, normal, nonencrypted transmissions will occur.
- **Secure Server (Requires Security)** This option is used on a server when the server requires secure transmissions only. If the client computer does not have IPSec enabled, transmissions will be refused.
- **Server (Request Security)** This option allows a server to request IPSec be used, but if the client does not have IPSec enabled, the server allows normal, nonencrypted transmissions.

exam Watch

***Know when each of the policy templates should be used and what the outcome will be for IPSec use.***

To enable one of the policies, right-click the policy and select Assign. This action enables the default policy, which includes all ports and all IP traffic. The policy can be edited by right-clicking the policy and selecting Properties.

The Policy Properties window appears. On the General tab, you will see a list of current rules. You can select a rule and then select the Edit button to change the default or existing rules. The rules can be set to require or request IPSec for the rule as well as permit without requiring or requesting IPSec. The packets can be filtered to allow only certain ports as well as access from and to specific IP addresses or subnets. The connection type can be set to the local LAN, any network, or remote access. The rule can also be applied to a VPN or standard connection.

The final setting can determine how the encryption will occur, such as Kerberos version 5.0, a certificate, or a pre-shared key.

When a Web site has very confidential data that requires very secure transmissions for the data being sent between the client and the server, IPSec policies should be used, since they can enforce the use of IPSec to verify that both ends of the transmission are secure.

## Secure Sockets Layer

*Secure Sockets Layer (SSL)* is used as an encryption scheme between a Web server and a Web browser client to encrypt data transmissions between the two. SSL is a security protocol for TCP/IP that uses port 443 and Hypertext Transfer Protocol Secure (HTTPS) instead of HTTP on port 80.

On a Web site that uses SSL, the Web address start with https:// instead of http://. When the address starts with https://, you know that the data being transferred between the client and Web server is encrypted and secure. In addition, a lock icon appears as closed on the browser status bar. You can see an example of SSL when you place an online order on a Web site, such as syngress.com, and you enter your personal information on the checkout page, which should be secure so that no one can intercept the information and use your credit card numbers or other personal information.

SSL causes a lag in the Web page rendering and data transmission due to time required to encrypt and decrypt the data. SSL should be used only on pages where confidential data is being transferred to or from the client or server. If a whole Web site were to be based on SSL encryption, major overhead would be placed on the Central Processing Unit (CPU). As a result, the Web site would appear to be slow, causing users to avoid visiting the site.

SSL is usually needed only over the Internet. If a company has internal issues of security, however, SSL could be used in an intranet.

on the job

***Be prepared to use SSL or some other means when deploying an e-commerce Web site. You should also secure the database that contains all the customer data for preventing unauthorized access of customer information.***

## Certificates

As discussed previously, a certificate authenticates that its bearer is who he or she claims to be and should be used to allow the user access and to grant specific security permissions.

A certificate also supplies encryption via a private key within it. The private key is used to encrypt your data that is to be sent to another computer. During the handshaking process, two PCs exchange a public key, which does no one any good without the accompanying private keys. Once data that is encrypted with private keys is exchanged, the public keys can decrypt the data.

Certificates are good for user verification, but with certificates come an extra overhead of maintenance. Each certificate eventually expires and must be reissued. In addition, an administrator must keep track of the certificates and be ready to revoke a certificate when the bearer should no longer need to use the certificate for access to a Web site. This can cause a security issue if someone is fired and the administrator is not immediately notified so that the certificate can be revoked. Certificates do require a bit of time and effort to maintain and keep secure and up to date.

## Encrypting File System

*Encrypting File System (EFS)* is a new feature of Windows 2000 that allows for the encryption of files on a server. The partition must, of course, be NTFS to support the new feature.

EFS works by using certificates to authenticate users and allow them the option of enabling the EFS attribute on a file or folder. If a folder is encrypted, all files within the folder are, by default, encrypted also. EFS cannot work on a disk with disk compression enabled.

For EFS to work, the user who wants to encrypt a file must have a valid certificate, and for added safety, a user or group should be set as a *recovery agent*—a user or group that has the rights to use a second certificate to decrypt the encrypted files and restore the data to a readable format. This is needed in situations in which a user might encrypt a file and then lose his job, but the person taking his place needs the data file to resume his job responsibilities.

To use EFS, the partition must be NTFS (the Windows 2000 NTFS, or NTFS 5), and the system requires that the user encrypting the file has Write Attributes, Create Files/Write Data, and List Folder/Read Data permissions.

To encrypt a file, perform the steps shown in Exercise 8-3.

**EXERCISE 8-3**

### Encrypting a File

1. Select the file or folder and right-click, selecting Properties from the drop-down list.

2. On the General tab, select the Advanced button. This button brings up the Advanced Properties window, as shown in Figure 8-10.
3. In the Advanced Properties window, select the box next to the "Encrypt contents to secure data" check box to enable EFS.
4. Select the OK button and then select OK or Apply on the file/folder Properties window.
5. If you have chosen to encrypt a file, a window will appear to ask if you want to encrypt the file or the whole folder in which the file resides. Select either option and choose OK.

At this point, the person who encrypted the file is the only person who can read the file. A recovery agent, which you should create initially, could decrypt the file, but that takes a little work. The person who encrypted the file is able to open the file as normal, and all decryption is transparent to the person who encrypted the file. Even if the file is opened and temporary files are created, the temporary files are also encrypted.

To decrypt the file completely, the user can simply perform the same steps they took to encrypt the file, but clear the check box next to "Encrypt contents to secure data."

Using EFS allows for file contents to be readable only by the user who encrypts the file. This security measure is beneficial for access to remote files that are

**FIGURE 8-10**

File Properties Advanced Attributes

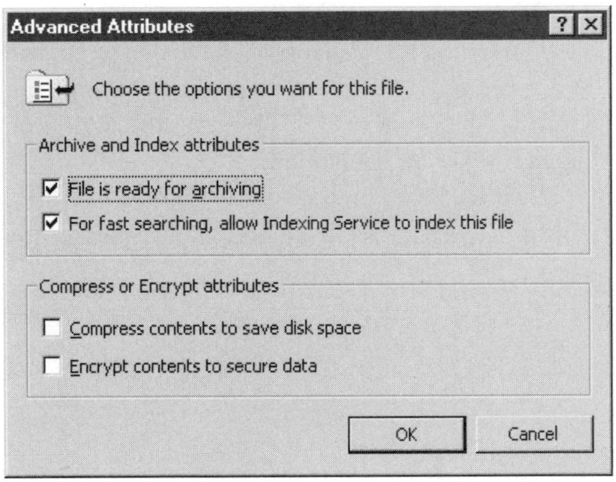

intended for use by only one person. A user can encrypt shared files on a Web server; the user is then able to remotely access the files through the Web server and be the only user able to open the files.

Note that EFS only encrypts the data on the server hard disk and not over the network media. The server decrypts the file before sending it to the user.

---

## Layer 2 Tunneling Protocol

*Layer 2 Tunneling Protocol (L2TP)* is actually a combination of PPTP and Layer-2 Forwarding (L2F), allowing for data encryption over a point-to-point tunnel. L2TP works only with TCP/IP, but is intended to work with Internetworking Packet Exchange/Sequenced Packet Exchange (IPX/SPX), Frame Relay, X.25, and Asynchronous Transfer Mode (ATM) networks. L2TP packets are transmitted as User Datagram Protocol (UDP) packets.

L2TP and IPSec together make a VPN, providing the highest level of security with a secure and encrypted connection over a public network. When remote users will be connecting to a Web site for confidential data exchange, the connection is best established as VPN for the highest level of security.

## Point-to-Point Tunneling Protocol

*Point-to-Point Tunneling Protocol (PPTP)* is used to encapsulate IP, IPX, or NetBEUI packets as TCP/IP packets and send them over a TCP/IP network, such as the Internet. PPTP allows a connection to be made from one point to another and, when used with IPSec, creates a VPN similar to L2TP but uses TCP packets instead of UDP packets. PPTP makes the secure connection between two PCs but requires IPSec for encryption.

L2TP is a better protocol for a VPN, but PPTP can be used just the same. The only difference is that PPTP does not use header compression, whereas L2TP does.

CERTIFICATION OBJECTIVE 8.04

# Designing a Firewall Strategy

When users on your intranet connect directly to the Internet, there is a problem of external, unauthorized users gaining access to the internal network and being able to access internal data. The Internet is merely an extension of the intranet; without proper procedures and equipment, unwanted users will be able to access your internal network. Firewall methods are employed to keep unauthorized Internet users from gaining access to an intranet. Let's look at some firewall strategies.

## Packet Filters

*Packet filters* are used to stop specific packets from entering or exiting the intranet to or from the Internet. Packets can be filtered based on port, protocol, destination, or source address. For example, a filter could be enabled such that only packets sent on port 80 could pass the filtering device. This filter would limit all requests except HTTP requests.

Packets can also be filtered based on inbound or outbound destinations. For instance, a PING could be allowed for outbound but not inbound access. This filter would allow internal users to PING hosts on the intranet, but no one on the Internet could PING a host on the intranet.

Another packet filter option that can be used for inbound and outbound access is to allow DHCP to be passed outbound. This option allows DHCP clients that are external to the intranet to be given IP addresses when a request is received.

This is very useful in keeping the network secure from specific points of interest. If the external users need access to a Web server only for HTTP requests and not for HTTPS or even FTP, only port 80 will not be filtered out and denied. This can keep the intranet secure as long as other means are used in conjunction with IP filters to make sure only authorized persons are accessing the Web site.

exam Watch

***You might want to know some of the well-known port designations.***

## Proxy Servers

Proxy Server is now known as *Internet Security and Acceleration Server (ISA)*. This product not only provides a firewall solution by allowing the use of packet filtering, but it can also be used to prevent specific internal users from accessing the Internet.

Proxy servers allow caching of previously visited Web sites. When another user requests a page previously visited by another user on the intranet, the page can be retrieved from the cache instead of reconnecting to the Web site and retrieving the page again. This feature can also be used for FTP sites as well.

Proxy servers help increase speed but also enhance security for an intranet connection to the Internet. For more information on Proxy Server or, specifically, the ISA server, see any documentation on Microsoft Exam 70-227.

on the Job

***Make sure that the proxy server has quite a bit of disk space to provide for better caching. The more Web pages that are cached, the better the response time for users accessing the Internet.***

## Protocol Settings

Using private addresses on an intranet makes it impossible to access the intranet from the Internet. Every IP class has a "reserved" range of addresses that are not usable on the Internet. If these addresses are used on an intranet, anyone can emulate an intranet address from the Internet since the address is not valid on the Internet.

The addresses that are used as private addresses are listed in Figure 8-11. These addresses can be used on an intranet only and cannot be used to pass the gateway device to the Internet if the private intranet is connected to the Internet.

If the intranet is connected to the Internet and the intranet IP addresses are from the private IP address ranges, a proxy server or Network Address Translation (NAT) must be used for Web pages to be requested from the Internet.

## Network Address Translation

*Network Address Translation (NAT)* is a method to protect the internal network from external attacks. NAT keeps the intranet addresses from being seen on the Internet. If a person wants to gain access to an intranet, he or she can watch for the IP addresses being used on the intranet by capturing data packets exiting the

**FIGURE 8-11** Private Addresses for Private Intranets

| | Private IP Address | | |
|---|---|---|---|
| Class A | 10.0.0.0 | to | 10.255.255.255 |
| Class B | 172.16.0.0 | to | 172.31.255.255 |
| Class C | 192.168.0. | to | 192.168.255.255 |

intranet. Once those IP addresses are determined, the person would be able to emulate a valid address. The firewall implementations might allow the hacker's data packets to pass through from the Internet to the intranet and allow access.

Whenever a request is sent to the Internet, the requesting user's IP address is part of the packet and allows the response to be sent back to the user. NAT allows the gateway to translate the intranet addresses to an Internet address. This method is the same as Proxy Server, which changes the requester's IP address to the address of the proxy server. NAT allows the translation of many addresses to a single address or even a few addresses. The NAT server translates the requests to the NAT external IP address with a specific port address such that the NAT address can translate the response packet back to the internal address.

As shown in Figure 8-12, if an intranet uses the private Class C address of 192.168.0.0 and has a single Internet address of 193.128.3.4, the internal users send a request to the Internet and the IP address is changed to 193.128.3.4 and port XX.

**FIGURE 8-12** NAT Example

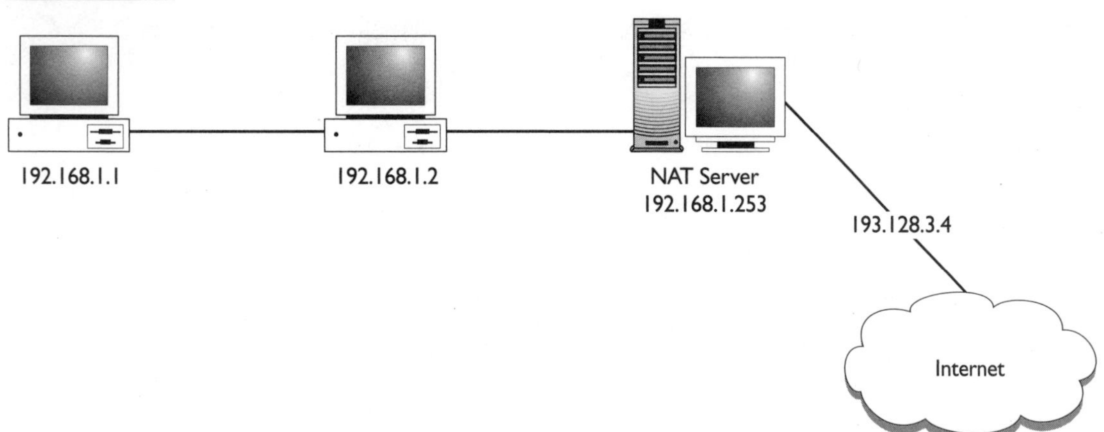

For example, let's say that we are using a workstation with an intranet address of 192.168.1.1. If we submit a request to the Internet for www.syngress.com, the packet is sent to the gateway or NAT server. The packet is examined to see that the source IP address is 192.168.1.1 and will be assigned an external address and port, which will be 193.128.3.4, and we assume the port address will be 2500. The source address will be changed to the translated address and sent on the Internet. The Web site, www.syngress.com, receives the request and submits the response to the destination address of 193.128.3.4, port address 2500, which is sent back to the NAT server. The NAT server checks its address table and determines that the address 193.128.3.4 and port 2500 were mapped to the internal workstation with an address of 192.168.1.1. The packet is changed to change the IP address back to the workstation address and is sent on the intranet to the workstation that sent the request. This process occurs for all translated packets sent to our workstation address, and we will eventually receive the all of the packets sent from the Syngress Web server to generate the Web page we requested.

on the Job

***NAT can be used to help keep Internet costs down. A company has to lease only a single IP address for multiple users to gain access to the Internet instead of providing a leased address for each user.***

Now let's look at some scenarios and solutions related to designing a firewall strategy. Then Exercise 8-4 walks us through the NAT installation process.

| SCENARIO & SOLUTION | |
|---|---|
| What if my company has one Internet address and 100 users with no need for performance? | Use NAT. It does not cache information. |
| What if my company has one Internet address and 100 users and needs performance? | Use a proxy server for caching ability to enhance performance. |
| What if my company has 10 Internet addresses and 100 users and has no need for increased performance? | Use a NAT server and let it map the 100 users to 10 Internet addresses. |
| What if my company has 10 Internet addresses and 100 users and needs performance? | Use multiple proxy servers. Performance is increased by caching ability. |

**EXERCISE 8-4**

### Installing NAT

1. Open the Routing and Remote Access tool under Administrative Tools.
2. In the left pane, right-click the server that will be the NAT server.
3. On the drop-down menu, select Configure and Enable Routing and Remote Access.
4. When the wizard starts, click Next.
5. On the next window, select Internet Connection Server, and then select Next.
6. The next window allows you to set up a router with the NAT Routing Protocol. Select Next.
7. The last window asks for the Internet connection type on which the NAT will occur. Designate the connection type.

## Perimeter Networks

A *demilitarized zone*, or *DMZ*, is a perimeter network that is used to separate an intranet from the Internet. This type of setup allows for double firewalls by putting the servers that will be accessed by Internet users and possibly intranet users on a separate network. This strategy allows for the possibility of using separate protocols. The DMZ can even use a protocol like IPX/SPX and allow for protocol translation at either the firewall or gateway.

As shown in Figure 8-13, there are two firewalls: the server with the address of 192.168.1.253 on the intranet the server with the address 193.128.3.4 on the Internet side. The DMZ consists of a Web server and data server that could be an SQL server used to supply information for Active Server Pages. The DMZ could consist of a third TCP/IP subnet or even IPX/SPX. This structure would help prevent the address spoofing of a hacker trying to use an intranet address to gain access by making the servers believe that the hacker is internal and not external to the network. This method is useful for companies that want to keep their intranets

**FIGURE 8-13** DMZ Example

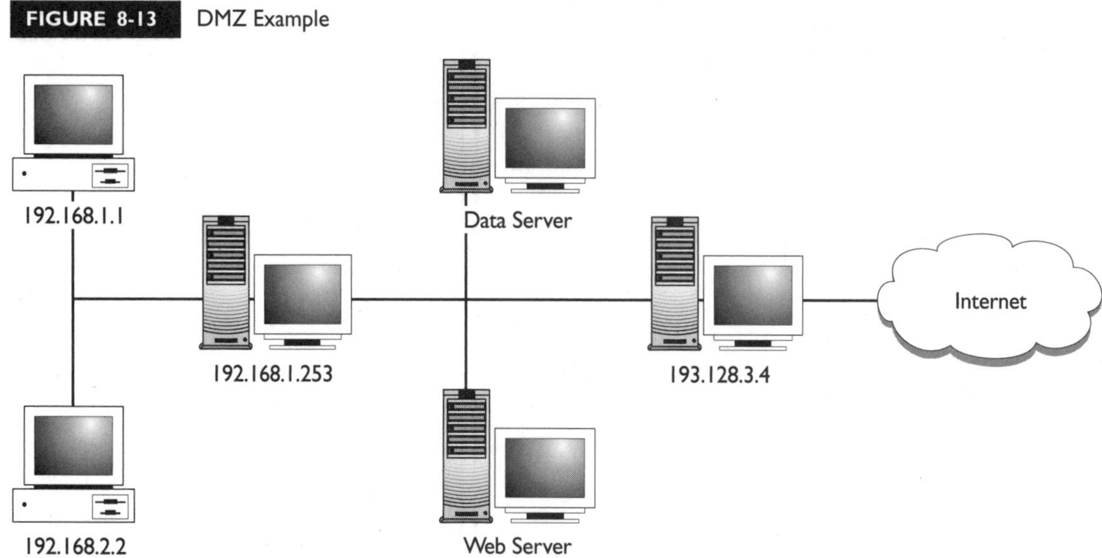


separate from the Internet as well as separating the network with the servers being accessed by the Internet.

## CERTIFICATION OBJECTIVE 8.05

# Designing a Security Auditing Strategy

Having a security strategy in place is not enough to detect nonauthorized users trying to gain access to your intranet. If a nonauthorized person keeps attempting to gain access but the administrator is unaware of the attempts and never does anything to take precautions, the hacker could eventually find a security hole in the setup to eventually gain access to the intranet. It is very important to have auditing enabled to track and monitor intranet entry attempts and even determine if a security hole has been found so that you can "fix" the hole and prevent further intrusion.

on the job

***When using auditing of any sort, always remember to monitor the logs daily to make sure that some event is not occurring or recurring over a period of days, when it could have been stopped. Security is extremely important to most Web sites and should not be taken lightly.***

## Intrusion Detection

When any security, authorization, or authentication method is used, it usually carries a method of logging events or notifying an administrator when an event occurs that is defined as not allowed, such as a user trying to log in and failing to enter the correct password.

When an event occurs such as an incorrect password entered, notification needs to be sent to someone in a position to respond to this alert of a possible security breach. If a person should learn of a valid username for an intranet user, that person can attempt to guess the password or use programs that use a *dictionary attack*, which is a program that draws on a database of words to guess a password. If the program strikes on the correct password, the unauthorized user could gain access to the intranet as often as he or she wants. Most networks allow a user to attempt a login a specified number of times with an invalid password before the user account is locked out and cannot log in, even with a valid password.

Once an intrusion has been detected, proper means should be taken to verify that the unauthorized access should stop. If an authorized user leaves on vacation, for example, some high-security networks actually disable the user account until the user returns, to prevent someone else from attempting to use the account or guess a password. Some networks also require passwords to be changed every three months to prevent unauthorized users from guessing a password. Even if a password should be correctly guessed, the unauthorized use of the account will no longer be possible after the password is changed.

Exercise 8-5 shows you how to enable logon auditing.

**EXERCISE 8-5**

### Enabling Logon Auditing

1. Open the Domain Controller Security Policy window.
2. Expand Local Policies, and select Audit Policy.

3. In the right pane, double-click Audit Account Logon Events.
4. In the window that opens, select whether to audit successes or failures of logon attempts, and select OK.
5. When you're done, close the Domain Controller Security Policy window.

---

## Security

Audit logs and any auditing information should be kept secure. If unauthorized people should access or see the items being audited, they could be able to determine a different way to access the network so that they are not audited. They could even determine which areas are more critical for monitoring.

If events are stored in the Event Log, only administrators and server operators can view the logs. These people are the users who already have access to the servers and user accounts.

## Performance

Some security audits consume server resources, such as disk storage, memory, and CPU. Some special hardware devices can be implemented instead of using built-in Windows auditing.

If a Windows system performs its own auditing, use a separate disk and controller to keep the logs and event audits so as to not interfere with operating system disk resources. If a special hardware device should be used, the device's performance will be better than that of a Windows server. For instance, a Cisco router could be used to integrate NAT into an intranet and operate at a faster speed, delivering better translation performance than a Windows server that is managing the translations by software.

## Denial of Service

*Denial of Service* occurs when a system is overloaded with requests; in attempting to handle these requests, the system cannot respond to any new requests. If your Web server should become overloaded with requests from the Internet, no one will be able to access your Web site. Your Web server will most likely crash due to being overburdened.

A good example of a denial-of-service situation is the *PING of Death.* When a PING command is sent, it requires that the receiving host submit the packet back to the requester. If the PING packet that is sent is incomplete, the host waits for the rest of the packet, causing the host to leave a connection open to the requester. If the requester should send a flood of PING requests, the Web server will eventually run out of connections and fail. If a flood of large PING packets is sent, the Web server could be overrun with large amounts of data it is trying to receive and retransmit at the same time.

You can install patches to cause a Web server not to accept these packets and even refuse PING requests completely. This security measure can also be managed with IP filtering.

exam Watch

***You need to know how a denial of service is caused and how to prevent it.***

## Logging

By *logging,* we can track unauthorized events such as requests from a domain name that is set to be filtered or even specific IP addresses. When these events occur, the administrator will should recognize that someone is trying to access the Web site or intranet from a forbidden location. Logging can help the administrator determine where attacks are coming from and choose a course of action. Logs should record the source IP address of the person that is attempting unauthorized access and can track and find the person and possibly be able to press charges or alert them to quit.

Logging can determine not only unauthorized attempts but also authorized access that is being blocked due to improper settings of security policies. Logs can help track down problems so that you can troubleshoot these issues.

You can also use logging to determine access trends, to find times when authorized access might be at a high usage point to determine that a Web server is overutilized and requires more resources such as memory or processors.

## Data Risk Assessments

Every network administrator should assess his or her network and determine if there are any holes in the implemented security plan. They should watch manufacturer Web sites to determine updates for fixing security holes.

In addition, some security sites issue information to warn of potential access to intranets through specific hardware and software vendor equipment. For example, the Web site astalavista.box.sk is a security site that can be used to search for security holes for specific equipment such as routers and switches. If your company employs a router for its gateway, you can search this Web site for known ways to bypass the router or switch. You will also be able to determine a fix or at least be able to consult the router or switch manufacturer for a fix.

You can also consult security companies to check your Web site for holes and try to access your network or Web server without having proper access rights or authority.

## CERTIFICATION SUMMARY

With security being so important to network administrators and Web site hosts, it is crucial that administrators be familiar with the many ways to implement security features, such as those we have seen in this chapter.

Authentication is used to verify users' identities. Authorization checks authorize users' access permissions. If you used no authentication and authorization for specific users, anyone could access your Web site (unless anonymous access is granted).

Once users are approved to use and access Web sites and Web pages, you face the problem of securing the data you are trying to protect while it is in transit over the network media. Such security requires data encryption—formatting the data in such a way to prevent the data from being readily viewed.

Firewalls are necessary to prevent specific traffic from entering or leaving your intranet. They help prevent unwanted activity from occurring on your network. Firewalls can help minimize unwanted network traffic, such as FTP requests to a Web site that does not host an FTP site.

Auditing is a necessity in most cases to track events occurring on a Web site that should not be occurring and allow for monitoring successful or attempted security breaches.

All these security methods, used in a combination to suit your company Web site, will help protect your data and your local intranet.

# TWO-MINUTE DRILL

## Designing an Authentication Strategy

- ❑ A certificate does not require a user account but can be mapped to a user account.
- ❑ Anonymous access should be used only when it is acceptable for anyone to access your Web site.
- ❑ Directory Services can be used to validate usernames and passwords to the database of domain user accounts.

## Designing an Authorization Strategy

- ❑ Group membership can be used to grant access to multiple users at once.
- ❑ Be careful using IP blocking so that you do not block IP addresses that might be needed.
- ❑ Do not grant more permissions than are necessary for someone to access your Web site. Extraneous permissions can allow users to modify or delete things they should not be allowed to alter. Only grant users the bare requirements to accomplish the task they need to accomplish.

## Designing an Encryption Strategy

- ❑ Create VPNs between remote offices to keep access secure between sites. You can also allow individuals accessing your network to use VPNs to access your Web site.
- ❑ Remember that not all users want to connect through the Internet. PPTP can be used for direct connections.
- ❑ Use SSL when creating an e-commerce site.

## Designing a Firewall Strategy

- ❑ Do not filter out all packets unless you must. Allow only the protocols that are needed to pass through.
- ❑ Use proxy servers to enhance Internet access response time.

- ❑ Use NAT when Internet response time is not an issue.

## Designing a Security Auditing Strategy

- ❑ Be aware when intruders attempt to breach your security and fix any holes that might exist when they are found, not after intruders find and exploit them.
- ❑ Always log events such as improper password logon attempts.
- ❑ Implement a fix for Denial of Service.

# SELF TEST

The following questions will help you measure your understanding of the material presented in this chapter. Read all the choices carefully because there might be more than one correct answer. Choose all correct answers for each question.

## Designing an Authentication Strategy

1. Your company wants to allow access to your Web site for employees only. Your supervisors want to allow access to specific individuals who are part of the company but will be consulting on the Web site design and layout. The consultants need no more access to the network than just the Web site. Which authentication method should you employ for these users?

   A. Allow anonymous access.

   B. Create user accounts for the consultants to log in to the Web site.

   C. Assign the consultants a certificate.

   D. Make sure the consultants use Kerberos.

2. Your company wants to allow access to your Web site by anyone. Which authentication method should you employ for these users?

   A. Allow anonymous access.

   B. Create a user account for everyone to log in to the Web site.

   C. Assign certificates.

   D. Make sure EFS is used on the Web server.

3. Your supervisors want to create a Web site for employees only to allow the exchange of ideas by posting comments to the Web page. Verification needs to occur to make sure that only employees can access the Web page. This specific Web page will be implemented on the Web server that is accessed by Internet users but located on the intranet. Which authentication method should be employed for employees to be verified?

   A. Anonymous access

   B. Basic authentication

   C. Digest authentication

   D. Windows Integrated Authentication

4. Which of the following use Active Directory for authentication? (Choose all that apply.)

   A. Anonymous access

B. Basic authentication

C. Digest authentication

D. Windows Integrated Authentication

## Designing an Authorization Strategy

5. Your company wants to give employees in three departments within your domain access to a specific Web page on the company intranet site. How would you accomplish this task?

   A. Create three distribution groups, assigning proper permissions to the three groups.

   B. Create one distribution group, and assign proper permissions to the group.

   C. Create three security groups, assigning proper permissions to the three groups.

   D. Create one security group, and assign proper permissions to the group.

6. You have had some complaints from some employees who cannot view your corporate Web site with their default browsers. After you install another browser, the Web site is easily accessed. What could have caused this problem?

   A. Group membership authorization

   B. IP blocking

   C. ACLs

   D. Web content zones

7. Your company has two physical subnets. One is Ethernet and the other is Token Ring. The users on the Ethernet network have full access to the intranet Web site, whereas the Token Ring network users do not. The Token Ring network users can access all servers except the Web server. What could be causing the problem?

   A. Group membership authorization

   B. IP blocking

   C. ACLs

   D. Web content zones

8. When using IP blocking, which of the following values would be valid? (Choose all that apply.)

   A. 10.1.1.1

   B. 10.0.0.0, 255.0.0.0

   C. www.mynet.net

   D. Server1

## Designing an Encryption Strategy

9. In allowing remote users to access a Web server, what kind of security can you use to verify that only a single user can access a data file and if someone else gains access, that person cannot view the contents?

    A. IPSec

    B. SSL

    C. Certificates

    D. EFS

10. Which security protocol should be used to verify that a customer placing an order on an e-commerce site will not have her credit card number stolen by anyone monitoring the data traffic?

    A. IPSec

    B. SSL

    C. Certificates

    D. EFS

11. Which of the following Web sites are encrypted? (Choose all that apply.)

    A. http://www.amazon.com

    B. https://www.syngress.com

    C. http://www.mcsin.net

    D. https://www.jwb.net

12. When setting up an IPSec policy, you want your Web server to require all clients to use IPSec or else the connection will be refused. What method will you use?

    A. Client

    B. Secure client

    C. Server

    D. Secure server

## Designing a Firewall Strategy

13. A remote user has been trying to download a file from your Web server, where the file is stored. You have granted the user access to the file and made sure the file exists and is the correct file

for the user. The user calls to say that he gets a "Connection refused" message every time the connection starts. You are able to download the file from the intranet through the Web server with no problem. What could be causing the problem? (Choose all that apply.)

A. Packet filters

B. Proxy servers

C. NAT server

D. DMZ

14. A user calls to complain that his IP address does not work on the Internet at home the way it does at work. He tried to use the same Internet address at home in the evening since he was not using it at work, so why did this happen? (Choose all that apply.)

A. The problem is caused by the public address.

B. The problem is caused by the private address.

C. The DMZ at work enables the address to work.

D. The user does not have a proxy server at home.

15. A company has 500 users who access the Internet. The company wants to enhance the performance of Web requests for its employees. The company leases two Internet addresses for connecting to the Internet. How should the company implement a firewall?

A. Have one ISA server and one NAT server.

B. Have two ISA servers.

C. Have two NAT servers.

D. Have one proxy server with two IP addresses.

16. The supervisor of your company wants to completely separate the Web server from the rest of the network to be certain that intruders who target the Web server can never reach the rest of the main data servers. What would you deploy to comply with your supervisor's wishes?

A. Packet filters

B. Proxy servers

C. NAT server

D. DMZ

### Designing a Security Auditing Strategy

**17.** Which of the following is caused by PINGs?

A. Address spoofing

B. Denial of service

C. Dictionary attack

D. Guessed password

**18.** How often should security audit logs be checked?

A. Every day

B. Once a week

C. Once a month

D. Once a year

**19.** How often should an administrator determine security risks for a network or Web server?

A. Always

B. Sometimes

C. Seldom

D. Never, until it is required

## LAB QUESTION

Your company has a Web server that is used for an online catalog and to place orders. The clients have complained about the speed of the Web server and that it takes a long time to load the online catalog. Speed has not been a major issue in terms of placing orders, however. Some employees need access to the Web server for changing catalog content and checking the status of orders, but for the most part, most employees do not need access to the Web server. It has been suggested that, for the sake of security and performance, the Web server be placed on a different subnet. The company has two leased IP addresses but is not concerned about performance for the regular employees, only security. How could this network be configured?

# SELF TEST ANSWERS

## Designing an Authentication Strategy

1. ☑ C. For access to the Web site without also gaining access to the network, certificates, not user accounts, should be used.
   ☒ A, B, and D are incorrect because the certificate allows Web site access without allowing access to the whole intranet. Anonymous access allows anyone to access the Web site. If the consultants have user accounts, they could log on to and access the intranet. Kerberos is the authentication method used by certificates.

2. ☑ A. For anyone to have standard access to the Web site, use anonymous access.
   ☒ B, C, and D are incorrect because if everyone had a user account, the overhead for the administrator would be tremendous. Certificates would also be a tremendous task if thousands of people accessed the Web site. EFS is needed only for protecting specific files, not allowing full access.

3. ☑ D. For best results, use Windows Integrated Authentication so users do not have to log on to the Web server, since they are most likely already logged on to the domain.
   ☒ A, B, and C are incorrect because anonymous access would not verify the employees' identities. Basic authentication would work but would require another logon. Digest authentication is used when the media is not secure.

4. ☑ B, C, and D. All usernames and passwords entered in the logon windows will be validated against Active Directory.
   ☒ A is incorrect because anonymous access allows access to anyone, even users not in Active Directory. There is no verification except for the presence and rights for anonymous access.

## Designing an Authorization Strategy

5. ☑ D. You should create only one security group to assign permissions to the group.
   ☒ A, B, and C are incorrect because distribution groups are not used to assign permissions, and using three separate groups would create a little more overhead for the administrator.

6. ☑ D. If the Web site had no label and the content settings were enabled in the default browser, the Web site could not be viewed.
   ☒ A, B, and C are incorrect because if the problem were group membership, IP blocking, and ACLs, the other browser would have the same problem.

7. ☑ **B.** The most likely reason is that the whole subnet is being blocked by IP blocking.
☒ **A, C,** and **D** are incorrect because group membership and ACL settings would require previous planning and settings to disable the Token Ring users from accessing the Web server. Web content zones could be the problem, but again, that's highly unlikely. If the company employed standards for browser setup, all users would have the problem.

8. ☑ **A, B,** and **C.** IP blocking can use an IP address, a subnet, or a domain name.
☒ **D** is incorrect because Server1 is a NetBIOS name, not a DNS name.

## Designing an Encryption Strategy

9. ☑ **D.** EFS allows for only the person who encrypted a file to access it and readily be able to view it.
☒ **A, B,** and **C** are incorrect because IPSec, SSL, and certificates are used to encrypt data over the network media. EFS only encrypts data on a hard disk.

10. ☑ **B.** SSL is used to encrypt data transfer between the Web site and the Web user for specific pages—usually only the pages that require personal information.
☒ **A, C,** and **D** are incorrect because IPSec can be used, but usually in setting up a VPN that would require some configuration on the user's side. Certificates could be used, but they require major overhead to create and distribute to all users who will access the Web site. EFS is used for encrypting files on the Web server hard disks.

11. ☑ **B** and **D.** When a Web page uses the SSL encryption method, the protocol used is HTTPS.
☒ **A** and **C** are incorrect because they use the standard HTTP, which is not SSL enabled.

12. ☑ **D.** Secure server requires that all transmissions use IPSec or be refused.
☒ **A, B,** and **C** are incorrect because these do not require but only request that IPSec be used. Secure client is not a valid option since it does not exist.

## Designing a Firewall Strategy

13. ☑ **A** and **B.** Packet filters are stopping FTP from entering the intranet. This could be enabled on the proxy server or some other firewall product.
☒ **C** and **D** are incorrect because the NAT server and DMZ do not filter out protocols. If the problem were with the DMZ, the problem should exist on the intranet as well.

14. ☑ **B** and **D.** The user has a private address that is being translated to a public address for use on the Internet. This could be because the user does not have NAT or a proxy server to translate the address.

☒ A and C are incorrect because if the user were using a public address, it would work when connecting to the Internet. The DMZ has nothing to do with addresses working or not working.

**15.** ☑ **B.** For performance enhancements, a proxy server of some sort should be used to gain caching ability. Windows 2000 has an add-on product called ISA that is the Windows 2000 version of Proxy Server and should be employed with two servers working together. If one should fail, the other would still be operational.
☒ A, C, and D are incorrect because NAT servers do not provide for request enhancements.

**16.** ☑ **D.** The DMZ is a separate network from the rest of the intranet. The DMZ is a network between the Internet and the intranet.
☒ A, B, and C are incorrect because these do separate the network into different areas of accessibility.

## Designing a Security Auditing Strategy

**17.** ☑ **B.** A denial of service is caused by a server being flooded with PING requests, causing the server to be unable to respond to regular requests.
☒ A, C, and D are incorrect. Address spoofing occurs when a person attempts to make it appear as though he or she is using an IP address that is valid to a network. A dictionary attack is done via a list of passwords through which a software program sorts to guess a password for a specific user. A guessed password simply gives someone access to a network; it does not cause a denial of service.

**18.** ☑ **A.** Any audit log should be checked daily for the proactive maintenance of the network, whether it is security or otherwise.
☒ B, C, and D are incorrect because they are too intermittent to be able to catch a problem before it becomes too severe to contain. If someone is breaking into your network server, at some point the hacker will steal data, causing damage or creating his or her own username for complete and full access at all times.

**19.** ☑ **A.** Security issues should always be at the top of an administrator's agenda. The administrator should take a proactive role in securing the Web site and network instead of waiting for a security breach to occur.
☒ B, C, and D are incorrect because the security of the network and Web site is too important to wait for something to happen or to not to make security a priority.

# LAB ANSWER

First, a DMZ that has the Web server should be created. A proxy server should also be in the DMZ. The proxy server will help enhance a little speed for Internet users. (Proxy servers can cache files both ways.) The database server should be placed on the regular network to keep it more secure. The DMZ should be set as a gateway for users who require access to the Web server, and a NAT server should be used for all other users as their gateway to the Internet. This setup requires an IP address for the NAT server and one for the proxy server. See Figure 8-14 for a diagram of the network.

**FIGURE 8-14** Lab Network Diagram

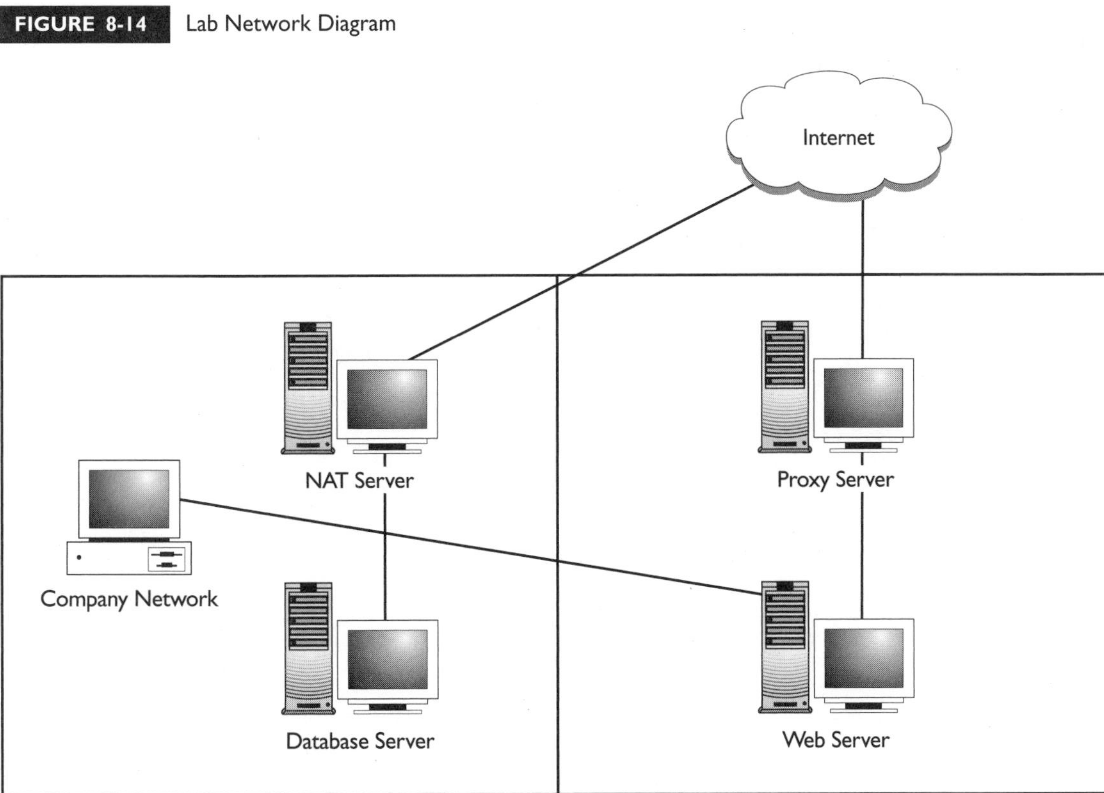

MCSE

MICROSOFT CERTIFIED SYSTEMS ENGINEER

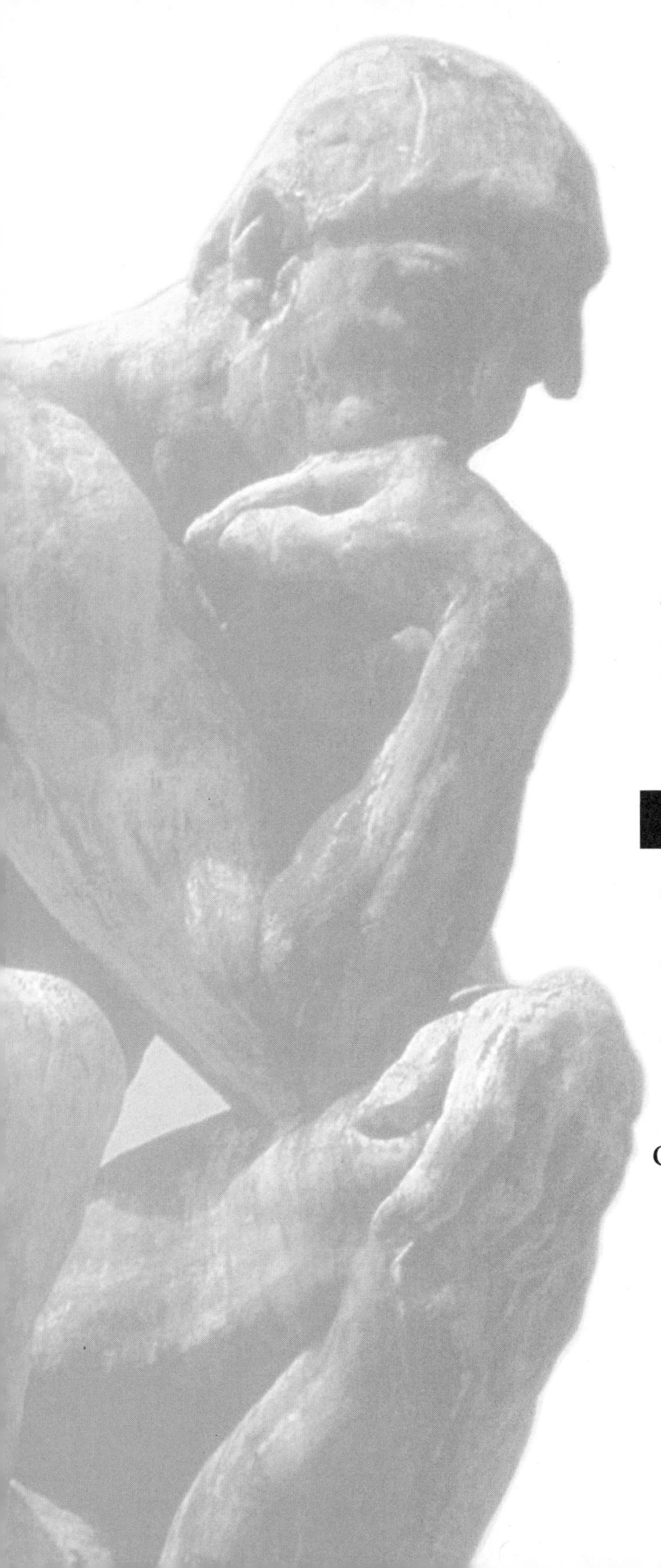

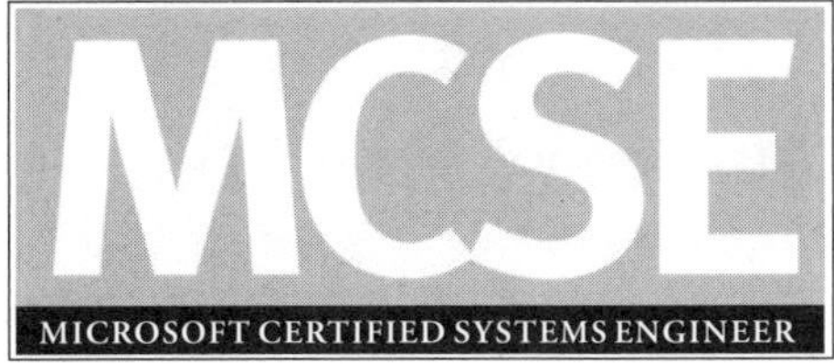

# 9

# Designing Application and Service Infrastructures

## CERTIFICATION OBJECTIVES

| | |
|---|---|
| 9.01 | Designing a Microsoft Exchange Messaging Web Integration Strategy |
| 9.02 | Designing a Database Web Integration Strategy |
| 9.03 | Designing Content and Application Topology |
| ✓ | Two-Minute Drill |
| Q&A | Self Test |

Most Internet Web sites do not stand alone. That is, they do not function without communicating with other applications. Applications, including electronic messaging, can enhance a Web site's capabilities. They can also be the main reason for the Web site's creation. This chapter discusses the principles of design surrounding the integration of Microsoft Exchange Server, as well as applications, with a Web site.

CERTIFICATION OBJECTIVE 9.01

## Designing a Microsoft Exchange Messaging Web Integration Strategy

Microsoft Exchange 2000 Server provides users with the ability to view and send messages through a mail client or browser, keep a personal calendar, and chat and send instant messages to other users, while at the same time providing a variety of other features. Microsoft Exchange 2000 Server is integrated with Microsoft Internet Information Services (IIS), and works with common Internet mail protocols, including Simple Mail Transfer Protocol (SMTP) and Post Office Protocol (POP). With Microsoft Exchange 2000 Server, network users are able to share information with one another, or, if connected to the Internet, with Internet users.

In smaller organizations, Exchange Server 2000 is capable of running on a single Windows 2000 Server. In organizations that use multiple servers, however, Microsoft recommends configuring Exchange to use a Front-End/Back-End topology. The topology shown in Figure 9-1 is set up so that Exchange Server 2000 runs on multiple servers on the network. The Front-End server that runs Exchange Server 2000 is configured to work as a proxy and receives requests from clients. When the Front-End server receives a request, it uses LDAP (Lightweight Directory Access Protocol) to query Active Directory (AD). Through this query, the Front-End server determines which Back-End server (which is an Exchange Server that is configured normally) has a requested resource.

When both Front-End and Back-End servers are used, the Front-End server can be placed either on or behind the server that acts as a firewall. The firewall can then be configured so that only the Front-End server accepts traffic from the Internet.

**FIGURE 9-1**

Front-End/ Back-End Topology

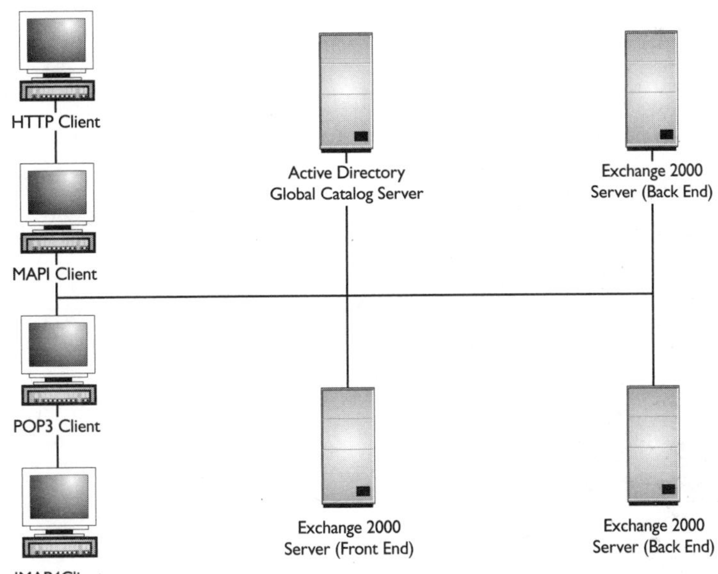


Neither the Back-End server, nor the AD server that contains user information, accept such traffic. This particular topology provides security, as hackers are unable to access user information from the Exchange Server.

Another benefit of this topology is that it can be configured to use a single namespace. For example, if Outlook Web Access (OWA), which is discussed in the next section, is utilized, users are able connect to their mailboxes via a Universal Resource Locator (URL) such as http://mail. This does not require users to know which server stores their mailbox. Without such a configuration, users would need to know the name of the server and would need to enter specific URLs such as http://*servername*/exchange to access their mailboxes. With OWA, users simply connect to the Front-End server, which then passes along their requests using AD. This process is transparent to users.

Two methods may be used to determine how many Front- and Back-End servers are required to configure such a topology. First, there is a general rule of employing one Front-End server for every Back-End server. However, this is not accurate enough because it does not take into consideration the number of users for each Back-End server, which protocols are being used, or how the servers will be used. To determine the accurate number of Front-End and Back-End servers needed for your network, use the Exchange Server 2000 Capacity and Topology Calculator.

The Exchange Server 2000 Capacity and Topology Calculator determines the number of users that can be supported by a single Exchange Server. It also determines the number of servers required by your network. This tool is available, free of charge, from Microsoft's Web site at http://www.microsoft.com/Exchange/techinfo/planning/2000/ExchangeCalculator.asp. Information on how to use the Exchange Server 2000 Capacity and Topology Calculator is shown in Exercise 9-1.

exam Watch

***Don't expect to see questions that deal directly with the Exchange Server 2000 Capacity and Topology Calculator. You may, however, be asked to calculate the capacity and topology for a Front-End/Back-End topology, and it is important that you understand the proper method of calculation.***

**EXERCISE 9-1**

## Using Exchange Server 2000 Capacity and Topology Calculator

1. Log on to the Internet, and using your Web browser, go to http://www.microsoft.com/Exchange/techinfo/planning/2000/ExchangeCalculator.asp
2. Click on the link to download the Calculator.
3. When the calculator has loaded, it appears in a separate Web browser, as shown in Figure 9-2. Answer each question by entering information into the boxes. This input will provide the information used to calculate predicted resource utilization, transaction rates for Post Office Protocol 3 (POP3), Internet Message Access Protocol 4 (IMAP4), Messaging Application Programming Interface (MAPI), dependent clients such as Outlook, and Outlook Web Access clients.
4. Review the calculations and close the browser window when finished.

**FIGURE 9-2** Exchange Server 2000 Capacity and Topology Calculator

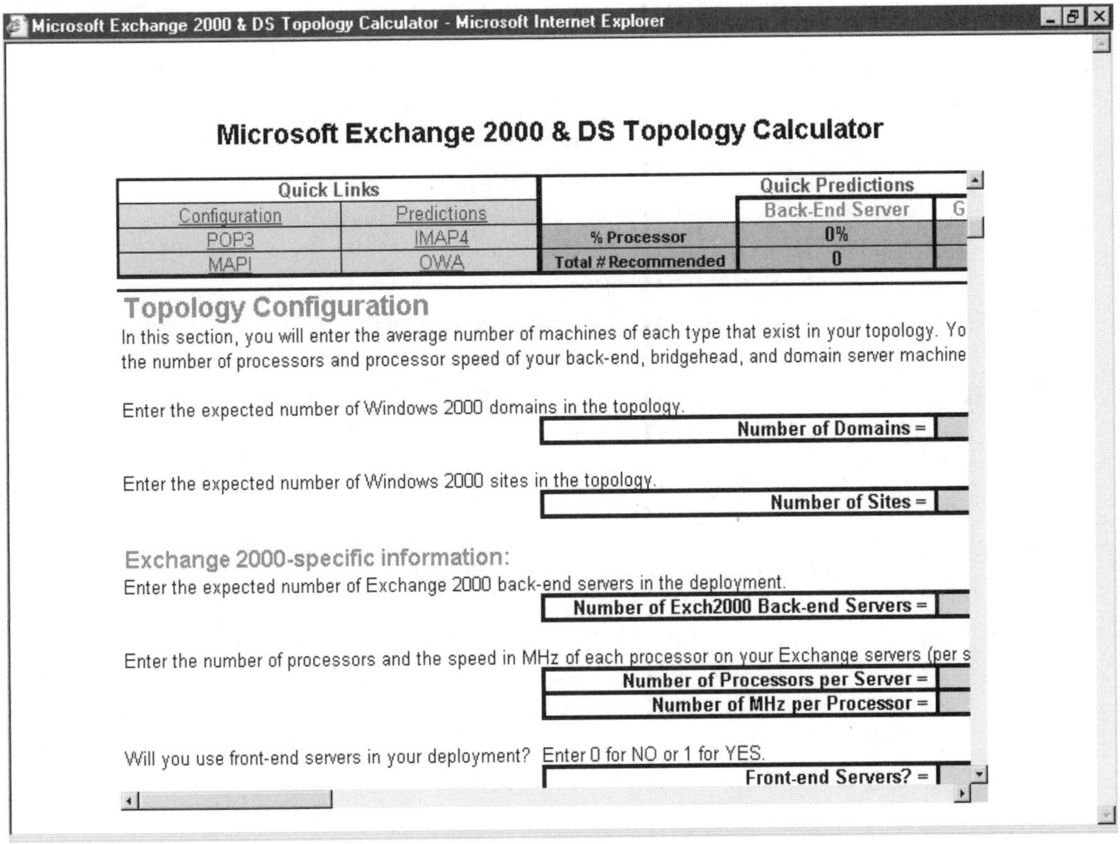

Microsoft Exchange 2000 & DS Topology Calculator - Microsoft Internet Explorer

**Microsoft Exchange 2000 & DS Topology Calculator**

| Quick Links | | | Quick Predictions | |
|---|---|---|---|---|
| | | | Back-End Server | G |
| Configuration | Predictions | | | |
| POP3 | IMAP4 | % Processor | 0% | |
| MAPI | OWA | Total # Recommended | 0 | |

Topology Configuration

In this section, you will enter the average number of machines of each type that exist in your topology. Yo
the number of processors and processor speed of your back-end, bridgehead, and domain server machine

Enter the expected number of Windows 2000 domains in the topology.
Number of Domains =

Enter the expected number of Windows 2000 sites in the topology.
Number of Sites =

Exchange 2000-specific information:
Enter the expected number of Exchange 2000 back-end servers in the deployment.
Number of Exch2000 Back-end Servers =

Enter the number of processors and the speed in MHz of each processor on your Exchange servers (per s
Number of Processors per Server =
Number of MHz per Processor =

Will you use front-end servers in your deployment? Enter 0 for NO or 1 for YES.
Front-end Servers? =

## Browser Access

With Exchange set up on the network, users will need a way to access messages on the Exchange server(s). Although a number of different clients can be used for this purpose, the client must support the following:

- SMTP
- POP3
- IMAP4 (Internet Message Access Protocol version 4)

If the client supports these protocols, it can access messages in Exchange 2000's message store. Although this allows for the use of a wide variety of clients, Microsoft does have recommendations for which clients to use under certain circumstances.

Two of the major clients Microsoft recommends for use with Exchange are Outlook 2000 and Outlook Express. Each is primarily an e-mail program, but there are some major differences between the two. Outlook 2000 is recommended for use with Exchange 2000 and provides HyperText Markup Language (HTML) e-mail, iCalendar, and various other features. Outlook 2000 runs in two modes: Corporate/Workgroup mode and Internet mode. In Internet mode, Outlook 2000 only provides e-mail functionality and limited group scheduling. In Corporate/Workgroup mode, which is also called MAPI mode, Outlook 2000 allows you to use all of the scheduling and collaboration features present in Exchange. Outlook Express is considered a somewhat watered-down version of Outlook. It doesn't provide all of the collaborative and scheduling features that Outlook provides, but it does provide e-mail, news, and some other features. It is available for free with Internet Explorer 4.0 and later. Because Outlook 2000 and Outlook Express need to be installed and configured, you are prevented from accessing Exchange from computers that don't use Outlook or Outlook Express.

exam Watch

***Outlook 2000 and Outlook Express are not the same program. Outlook Express is designed for Internet messaging, and (unlike Outlook 2000) doesn't support MAPI. Outlook Express does, however, support POP3, IMAP4, and HTTP. Older versions support POP3 and IMAP4. As an Internet client, you will need to run one of these Internet messaging protocols on the server, or Outlook Express will be unable to be used with Exchange.***

Outlook Web Access (OWA) differs from Outlook 2000 and Outlook Express in that it allows users to access their e-mail, personal calendar, group scheduling, contacts, and collaboration applications through a Web browser, regardless of the computer being used, or the platform on which the browser is running. This may be particularly important to an organization with users who need to access their mail and other items in Exchange from remote locations or from computers that don't support programs such as Outlook or Outlook Express.

As shown in Figure 9-3, OWA is designed to have an appearance that's similar to Outlook 2000. Through an HTML interface, users are able to access their inbox, calendar, contacts, and options through icon shortcuts on the left of the screen. Messages, the personal calendar, and information related to the shortcut you've chosen to follow appear in the main window. This allows users who are familiar with Outlook to use OWA with little to no training. In terms of your organization, this decreases time and costs associated with training and waiting for users to get used to the new program.

exam Watch

***Outlook Web Access allows users to view their e-mail, personal calendar, and interact with other Exchange 2000 features through a browser. The user logs on to OWA through a Web page and interacts with Exchange 2000 through other Web pages that mimic the look and functionality of Outlook 2000.***

**FIGURE 9-3** Outlook Web Access Calendar

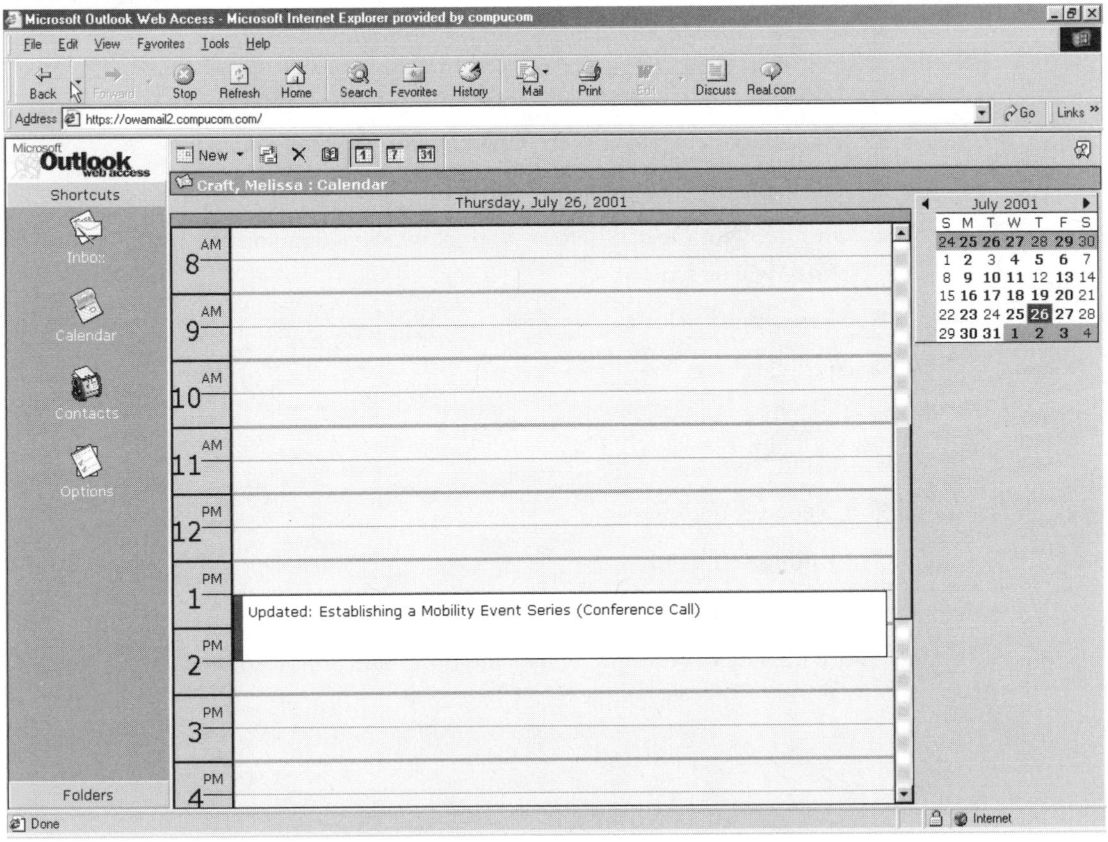

The deciding factor in whether or not a legitimate user is able to connect to Exchange 2000 is the browser he or she is using. OWA supports browsers that are compliant with HTML 3.2 and European Computer Manufacturers Association (ECMA) script standards. This includes, but isn't limited to, Microsoft Internet Explorer 4.0 and later, as well as Netscape Navigator 4.0 and later. Because earlier versions and browsers aren't fully compliant and may not be able to function, it is recommended that any browsers that will access your OWA site support HTML 3.2 and ECMA script standards.

Although Outlook Web Access provides the ability to connect to Exchange 2000, and performs many of the functions associated with Microsoft Outlook, there are limitations to OWA. Certain features in Outlook cannot be performed in OWA. These include:

- Tasks
- Journal
- Rules
- The ability to view e-mail and use other features offline
- The ability to copy between public folders and mailbox folders
- The ability to enter and edit text directly in Calendar view
- The "Do Not Deliver Before" option, which allows you to control when e-mail will be sent
- User-defined fields in Contacts
- Spell-checking
- Expiration options
- Reminders
- Telephony options
- Printing templates

Remember that OWA isn't a replacement for the Outlook client, but is an alternative method of accessing e-mail and other functions associated with Outlook.

on the job

***Outlook Web Access should be considered as an alternative to other methods of accessing Exchange 2000 Server, but shouldn't be the only method available. Outlook 2000 offers significantly more features than OWA. With this in mind, clients such as Outlook 2000 and Outlook Express should be installed on all machines used on a regular basis by certain users.***

## Wireless Access Protocol (WAP) Gateways

WAP is the wireless application protocol that allows wireless devices to access the Internet. Such devices include cell phones, palmtops, radio transceivers, and other wireless devices that can be used for acquiring e-mail, viewing newsgroups, browsing the Web, and chatting through Internet Relay Chat (IRC). Through WAP, Web applications are able to access network resources without being physically connected to a network.

The WAP protocol is not part of the Transmission Control Protocol/Internet Protocol (TCP/IP) protocol suite, which is the standard protocol for communicating over the Internet. Because it is different from TCP/IP, devices that use WAP are unable to communicate directly with Web servers. For a WAP device to successfully access resources such as e-mail, newsgroups, or other features offered by Exchange, the protocol must be translated from the WAP format into a format used by the Web server, network server, or other network-capable devices. To do this, a WAP gateway must be implemented as part of the topology.

Generally, the content server to which devices will connect is a Web server that uses HyperText Transfer Protocol (HTTP) to communicate with clients. The WAP gateway translates the binary language used by the Wireless Application Protocol into HTTP. This allows the remote wireless devices to connect to the internal local area network (LAN) or to public resources available on the content server.

**CERTIFICATION OBJECTIVE 9.02**

# Designing a Database Web Integration Strategy

Data is the most vital resource available in any network environment. The inability to access a company's data causes downtime, results in a loss of productivity, and costs a business valuable money in one way or another. For instance, with employees unable to work, the business continues to pay them despite little or no productivity. In terms of an e-commerce site, customers may be unable to utilize the information they need, and more importantly, they may not be able to access data that allows them to purchase items. For these reasons, the availability of data is vital to any organization's network.

When integrating data with a Web application, there are two basic reasons why the application is unable to access data. First, some piece of hardware or software has malfunctioned or failed, which prevents the data from being accessed. This may be the Web application itself, or a service or component that provides access to the data source. The second reason is that a server's load has become so great that it is unable to respond to client requests. In this situation, downtime is avoidable by implementing redundancy, so that the data is available to the application.

When designing your database Web integration strategy, there are a number of ways to ensure that your data is available. One of the most common methods is to create a Web server farm. A Web server farm consists of multiple Windows 2000 Servers running Internet Information Services (IIS), which together provide an organization's presence on the Web or intranet. The Internet or intranet site is distributed to all of the servers, including the Web applications that you wish to be made available to users. Each of these servers is combined into a single virtual server so that the client views these servers as a single site.

In addition to making the site highly available, you can carry this over to the data that is integrated with your site's Web applications. For example, SQL Server databases can be placed on multiple servers, which are also viewed as single servers by the user and other computers. This is done through clustering. Like Web server farms, clustering groups of servers together allows data to be distributed among multiple machines, which means that Web applications can still access data if one server fails, or experiences high workloads or other problems.

Distributed File System (DFS) is an additional method of distributing data among multiple machines. With this method, files are distributed among multiple servers, but accessed only through a single share. These files can be replicated, so servers in different locations have a local copy of data. DFS is automatically installed with Windows 2000 Server.

## Database Access and Authentication

The ability to access data is impacted by the authentication methods configured in a Web application. If a user does not have permission to use a database or application, he or she will be unable to view and/or modify that data. This access is dependent on different levels of security and authentication in the server, application, or database.

Most database software enables a developer to implement some form of security, whether it be a password protecting a database, or requiring the database administrator to specify which users and groups can perform certain database functions. For example, in a SQL server database, you may set up certain accounts or groups to be allowed to use a particular database. If the user or group isn't given access through SQL Server, and/or is unable to give the proper password, access is denied. Such access, however, is dependent on the capabilities of the database software, and must be determined by reading its documentation.

Internet Information Services employs a number of authentication methods that can be used to control user access. These methods are integrated with Windows 2000 Server and Active Directory. With these methods, you can control who is allowed to access certain areas of your site, such as those areas offering Web applications. This includes both Internet and intranet users. The authentication methods and information related to each of them are shown in Table 9-1.

**TABLE 9-1** Internet Information Server 5.0 Authentication Methods

| Authentication Method | Description | Type of Browser Required | Additional Information |
|---|---|---|---|
| Anonymous | This is the authentication used for guest users, such as those who require general access to a site. This authentication uses the user account IUSR_computername. | All browsers are supported with this method. | General users of your site use this authentication. For this reason, the IIS_computername account should not be given high levels of access. |
| Basic | With this method, the user must enter a username and password that matches a valid Windows 2000 user account. The username and password is sent unencrypted as clear text to the server | Most browsers on the market support basic authentication. | This is a common method used to access low-level site areas. It is often used on membership areas of a site. |

**TABLE 9-1** Internet Information Server 5.0 Authentication Methods *(continued)*

| Authentication Method | Description | Type of Browser Required | Additional Information |
|---|---|---|---|
| Basic/SSL | With this method, the user must enter a username and password that matches a valid Windows 2000 user account. The username and password is sent using SSL encryption | Browsers must be SSL 2.0 and 3.0 compliant. | This method is commonly used for secure and semi-secure site areas. It is often used on membership areas of a site |
| Integrated Windows Authentication | Like Basic and Basic/SSL, this method also requires a valid Windows 2000 password. However, this method doesn't display a dialog box for users to enter the information. Instead, the information is transmitted through Internet Explorer. | Requires Microsoft Internet Explorer 2.0 or later. | Secure Web sites use this method, which was called "Windows Challenge/Response" in Windows NT. |
| Client Certificates | Client certificates and a private key are used to authenticate users. | Browsers must be certificate compatible. Those that are must have a copy of the client certificate and the public key. | Used by secure Web sites. |
| Digest | Hashing technologies are used to transmit information about the user. | Only available to users running Microsoft Internet Explorer 5 or later, who are accessing a Windows 2000 domain. | Extremely secure Web sites use this method. However, the site must be running Windows 2000 Server. |
| Fortezza | Client certificates and a private key are used to authenticate users. This is stored in a smart card on the user's machine. | Browser must be Fortezza compliant and have a smart card reader. The user must have a smart card containing the necessary information to log on to the site. | Extremely secure sites. |

## XML

XML is an acronym for the eXtensible Markup Language. It allows you to access structured data and display it on a Web page. XML is a subset of the Standard Generalized Markup Language (SGML), and is used to generate text files used by other applications (such as browsers accessing Web pages) to view, modify, and/or use data. The XML text file is processed by other programs, which control how the data is used.

In a number of ways, XML is similar to Hypertext Markup Language (HTML), which is the language used to create Web pages. Each of these languages uses markup symbols, or tags, to indicate the contents of the page being displayed. The difference between the two is that HTML uses tags to indicate the contents of a Web page (i.e. text and graphics formatting), while XML allows you to delimit data appearing in the file. For example, in an XML file, you might use a markup tag called "cost" to indicate that data on prices would follow this tag.

## ODBC

ODBC is an acronym for Open Database Connectivity. It is an Application Program Interface (API) that allows you to access various types of data, including relational and nonrelational databases, text, and other types of data sources. Using this open standard, developers are able to create applications that access data sources, without having the proprietary information about the database being accessed.

With ODBC, a driver or module is needed to access a particular database. This driver or database can be obtained from the manufacturer of the data source, or may be available through the ODBC drivers that were installed with the operating system. Because ODBC is commonly used and promoted by Microsoft, a number of common drivers are installed with Windows 9x, 2000, ME, and NT. Updated drivers can be acquired from Microsoft's Web site, or from the database manufacturer.

## ADO

ADO is short for ActiveX Data Objects. This is another Application Program Interface (API), which exposes a set of functions to access data sources. ADO allows you to develop client-side and server-side applications to access data from both relational and nonrelational databases.

ADO is a language-neutral object model, which serves as an object-based interface to OLE DB (which we'll discuss next). Because it is an interface, it is considered a "data consumer." Rather than accessing the data directly, it indirectly accesses the data through OLE DB.

## OLE DB

OLE DB is an open specification that allows you to access data. It is a low-level API that allows you to access relational and nonrelational databases, text, hierarchical data sources, and other types of data sources. It does this by exposing methods for reading and writing data, which can then be used to view and modify the data.

With OLE DB, there are consumers and providers. The data provider is a component or data source that serves data to the consumer. The data consumer is a component or interface that connects with the provider to acquire the data. Between the two, a Web application can connect to a data source, issue a command, process the results, and return these results to the user.

on the job

***Originally, OLE was an acronym for "Object Linking and Embedding," while DB was an acronym for "database." Despite the origins of the name, OLE DB no longer stands for anything, as Microsoft no longer attributes any meaning to the letters making up OLE DB.***

Now that you have a better idea of issues related to designing database Web strategies, here are some possible scenario questions and their answers.

| SCENARIO & SOLUTION | |
|---|---|
| How do I use ADO in a Web application? | ADO is an object-orientated method of accessing data. Using various objects, you can access data sources. |
| Fortezza uses smart cards. What are these cards and how can I use them for authentication? | Smart cards are small cards that contain data, and are read through a smart card reader. This reader is a device that can be attached to a computer. It reads the information on the card, which can contain the username, password, access levels, and other information about the user. |

CERTIFICATION OBJECTIVE 9.03

# Designing Content and Application Topology

In Chapter 3 we discussed a number of topologies that focus mainly on securing your Internet Information Server. In this section, we discuss content and application topology issues that improve the availability and performance of sites using Web applications on intranets and the Internet. This information should not be considered an alternative to what was discussed in Chapter 3, but something that can be added to previously discussed topologies.

Web server farms are an important part of creating an effective content and application topology. Creating a Web server farm implements clustering, so that a group of Web servers appears as a single Web site to clients. This spreads requests across multiple servers and improves the reliability and performance of the site.

There are two different types of Web server clusters to implement. The first is Active/Active, in which multiple servers are both independent and redundant. The second is Active/Passive, in which multiple servers provide the same service, but only one of these provides that service at any given time. When a problem occurs, the other servers act as spares to the server or service that fails. In the paragraphs and sections that follow, we discuss each of these types of server clusters in greater detail.

## Scaling Out

Scaling out is the process of adding additional servers to a site. Rather than every request going to a single server, a client's request may go to one of several different servers. This improves the availability of content and applications on the site, because if a single IIS or data server fails, clients can still use other servers with identical content.

Scaling out improves a site's ability to handle its workload. It allows the requests sent to a server to be referred to other servers. In doing so, the load placed on an individual server is decreased. This is something we'll see in the section that follows, as the techniques used in scaling out are related to load balancing.

***Scaling out is the opposite of scaling up, which involves upgrading not only a server's operating system and software, but also its hardware. When scaling up, the CPU, memory, and other hardware is upgraded to meet the needs of network demands.***

## Load Balancing

Load balancing distributes client requests for Web applications and services across multiple machines, so that one server doesn't have to carry the workload by itself. There are several methods of load balancing Web applications and servers so that one server doesn't have to process and respond to every request. By splitting this work across several servers, the performance of a Web application can improve dramatically, as more server resources are available with each server added.

As we've seen with other topologies used in this chapter, Active/Active server clusters allow you to combine multiple servers so that they appear as a single site to a client. Rather than going to multiple servers, the user connects to a single server, and client requests are then passed on to other servers. The server that initially responds to the client's request is the Front-End server, while the content and application servers that these requests are passed on to are the Back-End servers. When dealing with Web servers, this is called a server cluster, server farm, or Web farm.

In an Active/Active server cluster, load balancing can also be performed through round-robin Domain Name System (DNS). With this method, DNS servers split requests between multiple servers by using multiple DNS resource records (RR). For each domain name the client tries to access, there are multiple 'A' records that are revolved in DNS. Each RR lists a domain name and an IP address for different Web servers in the cluster. Clients requesting a particular resource are given different IP addresses. Rather than one server responding to all of the requests, each request is sent to a different server in the cluster.

It is debatable as to whether round-robin DNS is actually a form of load balancing, because it doesn't take into consideration the load placed on each individual server in the cluster. Load balancing is meant to send requests to servers with the least amount of work, or experiencing the least amount of network traffic. This isn't the case with round-robin DNS, as it will pass along requests on a rotating basis, without taking those factors into consideration. Despite this, it is an effective method of splitting requests among multiple servers.

As we saw in Chapter 3, Windows 2000 Advanced Server includes a Network Load Balancing service that works with server clusters. This isn't limited to Web servers, but can also be used with other servers running on a Windows 2000 network. This means you can use Network Load Balancing for database servers, such as SQL Server or others, providing the resources you want to make available through IIS. When a request is sent to a cluster, it is distributed to different servers making up the cluster.

## Fault Tolerance

Clustering provides fault tolerance because there is more than one server present with the resources that users need to access. In an Active/Active server cluster, multiple servers will provide the same content and applications. If one of these servers goes down, requests can still be passed along to other servers in the cluster.

In discussing the load-balancing methods in the previous section, it is important to realize that round-robin DNS provides no fault tolerance. It is configured to use a set of IP addresses for servers. If one of the servers fails, DNS will continue to use its IP address in the rotation. In other words, even though the server is no longer available, round-robin DNS will continue to use that IP address so that requests for resources may be passed to it.

## Staging Content

A common misconception in Web development is the belief that once you've created your content, you merely need to deploy it by posting it on your intranet or the World Wide Web. However, an important step is missing between these two events—staging content. When content is staged, it is tested and refined.

Testing is a procedure of ensuring that your Web pages appear as expected, and that Web applications run properly. A basic element of testing is making sure the Web page appears as expected when viewed through different browsers on different machines. Some components may not run on certain browsers, and certain code won't be recognized because it is designed for a particular browser. Because of this, you need to inspect each Web page to see whether or not it appears as planned. You should also test performance to see if the Web page or application runs sluggishly. It may do so due to increased traffic at certain times of the day, or because so much content appears on a page that it loads slowly at lower bandwidths. Finally, you should test each application and element of a page to see that it responds properly. Be sure to test all hyperlinks and make sure that applications return the expected output.

If your content passes testing, it can then be placed on the site. Otherwise, it must be refined. This may require you to remove graphics to improve speed, break content into multiple pages, or reprogram applications so that they run properly.

on the Job

***Managing content is an ongoing job of creation, staging, and deployment. Once you've created your content, it must be tested and refined, and only then should it be made available to users of the intranet or Internet. Once this has been completed, you begin creating new content and start the process all over again!***

## State Management

State management is the process of managing connections to different servers so that each client request is connected to other client requests. This can be difficult when Web server clusters are involved, due to the nature of the protocols used to access Web pages. HTTP, the Hypertext Transfer Protocol, transfers Web pages from the server to the client, and passes certain requests from the client to the server. Unfortunately, HTTP is a stateless protocol, which means that it is unable to maintain a connection to a server. This prevents the Web page from distinguishing one user's request from another. It also prevents the Web server from recognizing what pages have already been sent to a user.

One method of state management is the use of cookies, which are blocks of information a Web server stores on a client computer. The information in the cookie may contain a user's preferences, logon information, or other data that a Web application may need at a later time. Each cookie is limited to 4,096 bytes, so if a significant amount of information is required by your application, multiple cookies or other methods altogether may be needed.

State management may also be obtained through software and hardware. State management through software may include storing information about a session in a database that may reside on the Front-End server or another server on the network. The Back-End server can access this information as needed. Hardware state management may be used if hardware load balancing is used by a cluster. Algorithms are used to map servers in a Web farm and to keep track of client IP addresses, ports, and other information that is acquired by reading information in packets transmitted between the client and server.

## Service Placement

Every Web server provides services that are accessed by the public. Aside from certain exceptions (such as the World Wide Web Publishing Service that serves Web pages), many of the services available through a Web server are optional, and may be installed as your needs dictate. These services include, but aren't restricted to, File Transfer Protocol (FTP), e-mail, and news services.

Where these services are placed affects the loads placed on servers and therefore, the performance of your site. If your site is particularly active and certain services are commonly used, it is wise to split them among different servers. For example, one server could provide the Web page content of your site, another could be an FTP server, another could be a news server, and yet another could be your site's mail server. Rather than every user accessing a single server, each would instead use a different one. This would split your site's load across multiple servers, even when clustering isn't used.

## Log Shipping

Log shipping is a method of keeping data between servers consistent so that the same data is accessible in the event that the main server becomes unavailable. Some server applications require separate add-on components for this functionality, however, others – such as SQL Server 2000 – have built-in log shipping. This allows Web applications to continue accessing data from other servers when problems arise.

When log shipping is used with SQL Server, transaction logs are applied on a scheduled basis from one server to another SQL Server. If the main SQL Server fails, the Web application can use the other SQL Server. Information on the secondary server would be slightly out of date, depending on how long it had been since the last scheduled log shipping (which is when the transaction logs would be applied to this server).

Now that you have a better idea of designing content and applications, here are some possible scenario questions and their answers:

| SCENARIO & SOLUTION | |
|---|---|
| What is the difference between scaling out and scaling up? | Scaling out is a process of adding additional servers to a network. This is different from scaling up, which involves upgrading servers. |
| Why is state management an issue for Web servers? | HTTP is a stateless or connectionless protocol, and is thereby unable to maintain information dealing with the user's session. State management allows a server to revisit information about the user, such as user preferences or pages the user has already visited. |

## CERTIFICATION SUMMARY

More and more, Web sites rely on communicating with other applications. This not only applies to services and other software running on servers, but also to Web applications that are custom created for your site. When designing your site, messaging will allow your Web applications (and users of your site) to have a more fulfilling experience.

In this chapter, we discussed Web integration strategies and topologies for Exchange, databases, and content. We saw the importance of keeping the site, as well as your applications, highly available. To achieve this goal, you can utilize clustering, use topologies that improve performance and availability, and use various tools and applications that work with these designs and strategies. Doing so will allow you to create Internet and intranet sites that can withstand a variety of problems, while providing users with the functionality they need.

## Designing a Microsoft Exchange Messaging Web Integration Strategy

- ❑ Microsoft Exchange 2000 Server provides users with the ability to view and send messages through a mail client or browser. It also provides other features such as a personal calendar, chat features, and instant messaging.
- ❑ In a Front-End/Back-End topology, the Front-End server running Exchange Server 2000 is configured to work as a proxy, and receives requests from clients. It then queries Active Directory to determine which Back-End server has a requested resource. The Back-End server is an Exchange Server that is configured normally.
- ❑ The Exchange Server 2000 Capacity and Topology Calculator allows you to determine how many users can be supported by a single Exchange Server, and how many servers are required by your network.
- ❑ Clients using Outlook Web Access must support SMTP (Simple Mail Transfer Protocol), POP3 (Post Office Protocol version 3), and IMAP4 (Internet Message Access Protocol version 4).
- ❑ WAP is the Wireless Application Protocol, which allows wireless devices to access the Internet.

## Designing a Database Web Integration Strategy

- ❑ A Web server farm consists of multiple Windows 2000 Servers running Internet Information Services, which together provide an organization's presence on the Web or intranet.
- ❑ Internet Information Services offers a variety of authentication methods, including Anonymous, Basic, Basic/SSL, Integrated Windows Authentication, Client Certificates, Digest Authentication, and Fortezza.
- ❑ XML is an acronym for the eXtensible Markup Language. It allows you to access structured data and display it on a Web page.
- ❑ ODBC is an acronym for Open Database Connectivity. It is an Application Program Interface (API) that allows you to access various types of data,

including relational and nonrelational databases, text, and other types of data sources.

- ADO is short for ActiveX Data Objects, and is an Application Program Interface (API), which exposes a set of functions to access data sources.
- OLE DB is a low-level API that allows you to access relational and nonrelational databases, text, hierarchical data sources, and other types of data sources.

## Designing Content and Application Topology

- Web farms are groups of Web servers that the client views as being a single Web server. The fact that requests are passed on to other servers in the cluster is transparent to the user.
- Scaling out is a process of adding additional servers to a site.
- Load balancing distributes client requests for Web applications and services across multiple machines, so that one server doesn't have to carry the workload by itself.
- Round-robin DNS is a process of using DNS servers to split requests between multiple servers by using multiple DNS resource records (RR).
- Staging content involves testing and refining the content that will be deployed to your site.

## SELF TEST

The following questions will help you measure your understanding of the material presented in this chapter. Read all the choices carefully because there might be more than one correct answer. Choose all correct answers for each question.

### Designing a Microsoft Exchange Messaging Web Integration Strategy

1. An Exchange 2000 Front-End server receives a request from a client. Which of the following protocols will this server use to query Active Directory and to determine which Back-End server has a requested resource?

   A. LDAP

   B. WAP

   C. SMTP

   D. IPX

2. You are implementing Exchange 2000 Servers on your network, using a Front-End/Back-End topology. Your supervisor asks you how many Front-End and Back-End servers will be required for this configuration. He wants an estimate, and doesn't want you to give firm numbers based on the number of users and other factors. Which of the following will you tell him?

   A. One Back-End server for every Front-End server

   B. One Front-End server for every two Back-End servers

   C. One Front-End server for every four Back-End servers

   D. One Back-End server for every four Front-End servers

3. Which of the following protocols must be supported for a client to access messages from Microsoft Exchange 2000? (Choose all that apply.)

   A. LDAP

   B. SMTP

   C. NNTP

   D. POP3

4. A user calls you and complains that her e-mail client doesn't allow her to use all of the collaboration and scheduling features offered through the Exchange 2000 Servers used on the

network. In evaluating what she can use, you find that she can only access e-mail and limited group scheduling. The client she is using is Outlook 2000. What is most likely the reason for this problem?

A. Internet mode is being used.

B. Corporate/Workgroup mode is being used.

C. Outlook 2000 isn't able to access such features because those features aren't available through the Exchange 2000 Server.

D. Outlook 2000 doesn't have these modes, and has less functionality than Outlook Express.

**5.** A user complains that he is unable to access e-mail through Outlook Web Access (OWA). You find he is using Netscape Navigator as an Internet browser. Which of the following is the probable reason that he is unable to use OWA?

A. The version of Netscape Navigator being used is older than version 4.0.

B. The version of Netscape Navigator being used is later than version 4.0, which doesn't support HTML 3.2 or ECMA script standards.

C. OWA only works with Microsoft Internet Explorer 4.0 or later. The user must use IE to access OWA.

D. OWA isn't accessed with a browser.

**6.** Which of the following protocols must use a gateway when wireless devices use Web applications to access e-mail and resources without physically being connected to the network?

A. WAP

B. IPX

C. HTML

D. ZAP

## Designing a Database Web Integration Strategy

**7.** Your Web site resides on a single Web server running IIS 5.0. A Web application accesses data from a SQL Server database, and displays it to users. The SQL Server runs on another Windows 2000 Server. There is concern that users will be unable to access the data if one of these servers fails. Which of the following will ensure that this data is available? (Choose all that apply.)

A. Create a Web server farm, so that the Web server resides on several servers.

B. Create a cluster of servers, so that the SQL Server runs on several servers.

C. Implement DFS so that the SQL Server database resides on several servers.

D. Implement Fortezza.

**8.** You have added a Web application for sales people to access data through your Web site. You want to implement an encrypted method of authentication that doesn't require users to enter a username and password into a dialog box when accessing the application, which resides in a secure area of your Web site. Which of the following authentication methods will you use?

A. Windows Challenge/Response

B. Anonymous

C. Integrated Windows Authentication

D. Basic/SSL

**9.** Using the authentication method from the previous question, some users begin to complain that they can't access the Web application located in a secure area of your site. Which of the following is a possible reason for this? (Choose all that apply.)

A. Browsers previous to Microsoft Internet Explorer 2.0 are unable to work with this authentication method.

B. Netscape Navigator users require a special plug-in to use this authentication method.

C. Browsers other than Netscape Navigator and Microsoft Internet Explorer are unable to use this method of authentication.

D. Browsers other than Microsoft Internet Explorer are unable to use this method of authentication.

**10.** You have decided to access data through a Web application using a markup language. This will be incorporated into the Web page to display data from a separate data source. Which of the following will you use to create this Web application?

A. ADO

B. OLE DB

C. ODBC

D. XML

**11.** Which of the following is a low-level Application Program Interface that allows you to access relational and nonrelational databases, text, hierarchical data sources, and other types of data sources. (This may be used with other methods of accessing data.)

A. ADO

B. OLE DB

C. ODBC

D. XML

12. Methods listed as choices in the previous question use data providers and data consumers. Which of the following defines the difference between the two? (Choose all that apply.)

A. Data consumers are components or data sources that access data directly.

B. Data providers are components or data sources that access data directly and serve it to data providers.

C. Data providers are components or data sources that access data directly and serve it to data consumers.

D. Data consumers are components or interfaces that connect to a data source indirectly to access data.

## Designing Content and Application Topology

13. Which of the following cluster topologies uses multiple servers with identical services, but only one of these servers is available at a given time?

A. Active

B. Passive

C. Active/Passive

D. Active/Active

14. At present, your site uses a single server to provide Web content and access to Web applications. You have decided to scale out your site. Which of the following will you do?

A. Add additional servers to your site to improve performance and reliability.

B. Add additional memory to the existing Web server.

C. Upgrade all of the hardware on the existing Web server.

D. Upgrade all of the software on the existing Web server.

15. Which of the following uses DNS servers to distribute the load of client requests between multiple servers?

A. DHCP

B. DNS

C. Round-robin DNS

D. Exchange 2000

**16.** Which of the following load balancing methods provides no fault tolerance?

A. Clustering

B. Windows Network Load Balancing

C. Round-robin DNS

D. Fortezza

**17.** Which of the following is involved when staging content? (Choose all that apply.)

A. Creating content

B. Testing content

C. Refining content

D. Deploying content

**18.** You have decided to use cookies for state management for your Web application. The amount of information the application needs retained is 8000 bytes in size. You decide to use cookies so that this information can be reviewed by the application when needed. How many cookies will you need to create so that the application can use all of this information?

A. 1

B. 2

C. 3

D. None. Cookies aren't used for state management.

**19.** Your Web site is located on a single server. You want to improve performance and reliability, but don't want to implement clustering. Which of the following will you do?

A. Create a Web farm.

B. Separate the services so they are on different servers.

C. Create a Web server cluster.

D. Nothing. To improve availability and performance, clustering has to be used.

**20.** You have implemented log shipping on a SQL Server that is used with a Web application. The last time transaction logs were applied was five minutes ago. What will happen if the SQL Server used by your application fails?

A. The application will be unable to access the data.

B. The Web application will use the up-to-date data on the second SQL Server.

C. The Web application will fail, and a second Web application using the other SQL Server will be started.

D. The Web application will be redirected to use the second SQL Server, but data on that server will be slightly out-of-date.

# LAB QUESTION

Your network has ten servers running Windows 2000 Server. Of these servers, one of them works as an Exchange 2000 Front-End Server, while another four work as Exchange 2000 Back-End Servers. There is a Web server that provides content to Internet users, and allows certain users to access resources on the local network. On this Web server, there is a Web application that requires users with smart cards to authenticate themselves.

There are a large number of users who need to access the network over the Internet, and view the internal e-mail that's sent to them by other users of the intranet. Unfortunately, they don't have access to their own computers, and thereby can't configure their own e-mail information into an e-mail client program.

1. What can these remote users use to access their e-mail over the Internet?
2. When users access their e-mail using Outlook 2000, which is installed on their workstations, which of the Exchange 2000 Servers will the client connect with?
3. What authentication method is being used to access the Web application?

# SELF TEST ANSWERS

## Designing a Microsoft Exchange Messaging Web Integration Strategy

1. ☑ **A.** LDAP is the Lightweight Directory Access Protocol. When the Front-End server receives a request, it uses LDAP to query Active Directory. Through this query, the Front-End server determines which Back-End server (which is an Exchange Server that is configured normally) has a requested resource.
   ☒ **B**, **C**, and **D** are incorrect because WAP, SMTP, and IPX aren't protocols that are used by Exchange 2000 Front-End Servers to query Active Directory.

2. ☑ **C.** One Front-End server for every four Back-End servers. To determine an accurate number of Front-End and Back-End servers for your network, it is ideal to use the Exchange Server 2000 Capacity and Topology Calculator. However, estimations may be achieved by using the general rule of using one Front-End server for every four Back-End servers used.
   ☒ **A**, **B**, and **D** are incorrect because the estimated number of Front-End and Back-End servers can be acquired using the general rule of "one Front-End server for every four Back-End servers used."

3. ☑ **B** and **D.** For clients to access messages on an Exchange 2000 Server, the following protocols must be supported by the client: SMTP (Simple Mail Transfer Protocol), POP3 (Post Office Protocol version 3), and IMAP4 (Internet Message Access Protocol version 4). If the client supports these protocols, it can access messages in Exchange 2000's message store.
   ☒ **A** is incorrect because LDAP is the Lightweight Directory Access Protocol, which isn't required to access messages on the Exchange 2000 Server. **C** is incorrect, because NNTP is the Network News Transfer Protocol, and also isn't required to access messages on Exchange 2000 Server. NNTP is used to view newsgroups. Although these protocols aren't required, clients that can be utilized to access messages may support them. For example, Outlook 2000 and Outlook Express both support LDAP and NNTP.

4. ☑ **A.** Internet mode is being used. In Internet mode, Outlook 2000 will only provide e-mail functionality and limited group scheduling. To access the features this user wants, Outlook 2000 needs to be in Corporate/Workgroup mode (which is also called MAPI mode). This will allow the user to access all of the scheduling and collaboration features in Exchange.
   ☒ **B** is incorrect because Corporate/Workgroup mode allows the user to access all of the scheduling and collaboration features in Exchange. This isn't the case when Internet mode is used, as Outlook 2000 will only be able to provide e-mail functionality and limited group scheduling. **C** is incorrect because these features are available through Exchange 2000 Server

when being accessed by an Outlook 2000 client running in Corporate/Workgroup mode. **D** is incorrect because Outlook Express has less features than Outlook 2000 and doesn't have Internet and Corporate/Workgroup modes.

5. ☑ **A.** The version of Netscape Navigator being used is older than version 4.0. OWA supports browsers that are compliant with HTML 3.2 and ECMA (European Computer Manufacturers Association) script standards. This includes, but isn't limited to, Microsoft Internet Explorer 4.0 and later and Netscape Navigator 4.0 and later.
   ☒ **B** is incorrect because Netscape Navigator version 4.0 or later supports HTML 3.2 or ECMA script standards, which are necessary to use OWA. **C** is incorrect because OWA works with browsers that are compliant with HTML 3.2 and ECMA (European Computer Manufacturers Association) script standards. This includes both Microsoft Internet Explorer 4.0 and later and Netscape Navigator 4.0 and later. **D** is incorrect because OWA is accessed through a browser.

6. ☑ **A.** WAP. WAP is the Wireless Application Protocol. It is used by wireless devices, such cell phones, palmtops, radio transceivers, and other wireless devices used for acquiring e-mail, viewing newsgroups, browsing the Web, and chatting through IRC (Internet Relay Chat). Through this protocol, Web applications can access network resources without being physically connected to a network.
   ☒ **B** is incorrect because IPX isn't necessary for wireless devices to access e-mail on a local network. **C** is incorrect because HTML isn't a protocol. It is a markup language used to create Web pages. **D** is incorrect because there is no protocol used by wireless devices called ZAP.

## Designing a Database Web Integration Strategy

7. ☑ **A** and **B.** Create a Web server farm, so that the Web server resides on several servers, and create a cluster of servers, so that the SQL Server runs on several servers. Web server farms make sites more available by having a single site located on several IIS servers. Like Web server farms, clustering groups of servers together allows data to be distributed among multiple machines. This means that Web applications can still access data if one server fails, experiences high workloads, or encounters some other problem.
   ☒ **C** is incorrect because implementing DFS allows you to distribute data over several servers, but won't ensure that users are able to access data on the SQL Server or that the Web server software will be available. **D** is incorrect because Fortezza isn't used to make data more available, but is instead used for authentication. Fortezza uses client certificates, and a private key is used to authenticate users.

**8.** ☑ C. Integrated Windows Authentication. Integrated Windows Authentication allows users to access secure areas of a site by sending encrypted information about the user. In doing so, the user isn't required to enter a username and password into a dialog box.
☒ A is incorrect because Windows Challenge/Response authentication was the term used for Integrated Windows Authentication in Windows NT. It isn't called that in Windows 2000. **B** is incorrect because anonymous authentication allows general users into areas of your site. It isn't used for secure areas of a site. **D** is incorrect because Basic/SSL requires the user to enter a username and password into a dialog box.

**9.** ☑ A and **D**. The previous question used Integrated Windows Authentication. Browsers previous to Microsoft Internet Explorer 2.0 are unable to work with this authentication method. This means that only Microsoft Internet Explorer browsers (versions 2.0 and later) are able to access the secure area of the site.
☒ B is incorrect because Microsoft Internet Explorer 2.0 or later is required. Other browsers cannot use Integrated Windows Authentication. **C** is incorrect because browsers other than Microsoft Internet Explorer 2.0 or later are unable to use this method of authentication. As such, Netscape Navigator cannot be used.

**10.** ☑ D. XML. XML is the eXtensible Markup Language. It allows you to access structured data, and display it on a Web page. It is used to generate text files that are used by other applications (such as browsers accessing Web pages) to view, modify, and/or use data. The XML text file is processed by other programs, which control how the data is used.
☒ A, **B**, and **C** are incorrect because ADO, OLE DB, and ODBC aren't markup languages.

**11.** ☑ B. OLE DB is a low-level API that allows you to access relational and nonrelational databases, text, hierarchical data sources, and other types of data sources. It does this by exposing methods for reading and writing data, which can then be used to view and modify the data.
☒ A, **B**, and **C** are incorrect because none of these are low-level APIs that can be used with other methods to access data.

**12.** ☑ C and **D**. Data providers are components or data sources that access data directly and serve it to data consumers. Data consumers are components or interfaces that connect to a data source indirectly to access data. Between the two, a Web application can connect to a data source, issue a command, process the results, and return these results to the user.
☒ A is incorrect because data consumers aren't data sources, and don't access data directly. **B** is incorrect because data providers don't provide data to other data providers.

## Designing Content and Application Topology

**13.** ☑ C. Active/Passive. In an Active/Passive topology, multiple servers provide one service, but only one of these provides that service at any given time. When a problem occurs, the other servers act as spares to the server or service that failed.
☒ **A** and **B** are incorrect because there is an Active/Passive and an Active/Active topology, but there isn't an Active topology or a Passive topology. **D** is incorrect because an Active/Active topology has multiple servers that are independent and redundant. With this topology, all of the servers are active.

**14.** ☑ **A.** Add additional servers to your site to improve performance and reliability. Scaling out is a process of adding servers to the site, so that services, content, and data can be split among servers.
☒ **B, C,** and **D** are incorrect because each of these is an element involved in scaling up a Web site.

**15.** ☑ C. Round-robin DNS. With this method, DNS servers split requests between multiple servers by using multiple DNS resource records (RR). For each domain name the client tries to access, there are multiple 'A' records that are revolved in DNS. Each RR lists a domain name and IP address for different Web servers in the cluster. Clients requesting a particular resource are given different IP addresses. Rather than one server responding to all of the requests, each request is sent to a different server in the cluster.
☒ **A** is incorrect because DHCP is the Dynamic Host Configuration Protocol. It is used to dynamically assign IP addresses to hosts on a TCP/IP network. **B** is incorrect because DNS is the Domain Name System, which is used to resolve IP addresses and host names. While DNS is used in round-robin DNS, it isn't the only element involved. **C** is incorrect because Exchange 2000 isn't used in round-robin DNS.

**16.** ☑ C. Round-robin DNS. Round-robin DNS provides no fault tolerance. It is configured to use a set of IP addresses for servers. If one of the servers fails, DNS will continue to use its IP address in the rotation. In other words, even though the server is no longer available, round-robin DNS will continue to use that IP address, so that requests for resources may be passed to it.
☒ **A** and **B** are incorrect because clustering and Windows Network Load Balancing both provide fault tolerance. If one server fails, another server can still respond to client requests. **D** is incorrect because Fortezza is an authentication method and isn't used in load balancing.

**17.** ☑ **B and C.** Testing and refining content. Staging content involves testing and refining the content that is created before it is deployed to the Web.
☒ **A** is incorrect because creating content occurs before staging content. **D** is incorrect because deployment occurs after content is staged.

**18.** ☑ **B.** 2. Each cookie is limited to 4,096 bytes, so the information contained in this file is limited. As such, if a significant amount of information is required by your application, multiple cookies or other methods may be needed. In the case of this application, two would be needed.

☒ **A, C,** and **D** are incorrect because the minimum number of cookies required would be two.

**19.** ☑ **B.** Separate the services so they are on different servers. By separating the services, one server would provide the Web page content of your site, another would be an FTP server, another would be a news server, and yet another would be your site's mail server. Rather than each user accessing a single server, users would instead be using different servers.

☒ **A** is incorrect because a Web farm is another term for a cluster of Internet Information Servers. **C** is incorrect because clusters aren't to be used. **D** is wrong because there are other methods to improve availability and performance other than clustering.

**20.** ☑ **D.** The Web application will be redirected to use the second SQL Server, but data on that server will be slightly out-of-date. When log shipping is used with SQL Server, transaction logs are applied from one server to another SQL Server on a scheduled basis. If the main SQL Server fails, the Web application can use the other SQL Server. Information on the secondary server would be slightly out-of-date, depending on how long it has been since the last scheduled log shipping (which is when the transaction logs would be applied to this server).

☒ **A** is incorrect because if the main server fails, the Web application can be redirected to use the other SQL Server. **B** is incorrect because the second SQL Server will have data that is slightly out-of-date. **C** is incorrect because the original Web application will be redirected to use the second SQL Server.

# LAB ANSWER

1. Outlook Web Access. This allows users to access their e-mail using a browser.
2. The Front-End server. Requests will be passed from this server to Back-End servers, which hold the user's mailbox and other information they may wish to access with the client.
3. Fortezza. This method uses client certificates, and a private key is used to authenticate users. This is stored in a smart card on the user's machine.

# 10

# Designing Component Data Objects for Web Solutions

## CERTIFICATION OBJECTIVES

10.01 Designing an *n*-Tier, Component-Based Topology

10.02 Designing an Application Management and Monitoring Strategy

✓ Two-Minute Drill

Q&A Self Test

This chapter explores how to use Internet Information Services 5.0 (IIS 5.0) to create *n*-tier component-based topology. It also includes details as to how to design an application management and monitoring strategy in the Windows 2000 environment. The IIS 5.0 Web server software program is an excellent program to use to reach potential clients and consumers who use the Internet for purchases or information. Applications for transactions as well as database access via the Web can be created in a rapid and scalable environment.

Detailed in this chapter are the following concepts: Component Object Model (COM), Distributed Component Object Model (DCOM), Component Object Model + (COM+), Component Load Balancing (CLB), COM component location, Web caches, Active Server Pages (ASP) versus Internet Server Application Program Interface (ISAPI), and Web stress and analysis in the IIS 5.0 environment.

**CERTIFICATION OBJECTIVE 10.01**

## Designing an *n*-Tier, Component-Based Topology

This chapter deals with *n*-tier application design, but before we jump into a discussion of *n*-tier topologies, let's take a quick look at two-tier (client/server) applications.

The client/server application is a simple design that enables clients to input information using the following scenario: Information is input using a client interface, the information is processed, and then the status is reported back to the client. The client machine processes the information, and the server transmits the data to the client machine. Although this seems a fairly straightforward and simple method of processing application requests, it has a downside, which is that unless specific rules are put into place regarding the type of processing the application employs, the server must trust the client machine in order to open the connection so the request can be processed. This can be a somewhat difficult task to manage on a large-scale basis.

## *n*-Tier Application Design

*n*-Tier application processing is also referred to as *multitiered application design*. The major difference between the two-tier and the *n*-tier design types is that in the latter, the tasks are grouped into various stages instead of between just the client and the server machines. This type of architecture gives developers and programmers the option to divide various computing tasks across the application. Typically, an application can be broken into three basic tiers for improved functionality. These tiers are listed in Table 10-1.

Dividing the application into layers isolates each area of functionality. This is because applications will not always reside in the same location within the network. The ASP and SQL Server Database could reside on one server running IIS 5.0, or they could be on separate servers in the network. In addition, the Microsoft Component Object (COM) could reside on a server and make task requests to more numerous servers. Figure 10-1 shows the basic flow of *n*-tier applications.

### Windows DNA

The architecture that Microsoft uses to build *n*-tier solutions is referred to as simply a *Web solution platform*. It was previously referred to as the Windows Distributed interNet Applications Architecture, or Windows DNA. The Web solutions platform provides a standard by which developers and programmers create and build solutions for e-commerce applications and corporations. The architecture uses

**TABLE 10-1** Various Levels of n-Tier Applications

| Tier Level | Function to the Application | Uses |
|---|---|---|
| Client tier | Topmost level of *n*-tier application. Client's Web browser is used to interact with the Web or data server over the Internet. | Data retrieval by client machine, data entry, request queries from data on the server. |
| Middle tier | This is the business logic tier. It is used to perform specific tasks and can be a simple design or a more complex design. | Active Server Pages (ASP), Microsoft Component Object Model (COM). |
| Third tier | This is the tier level from which the application requests specific tasks. | Exchange Mail Server, SQL database, or any transactional type of data. |

**FIGURE 10-1** The Basic Flow of n-Tier Applications

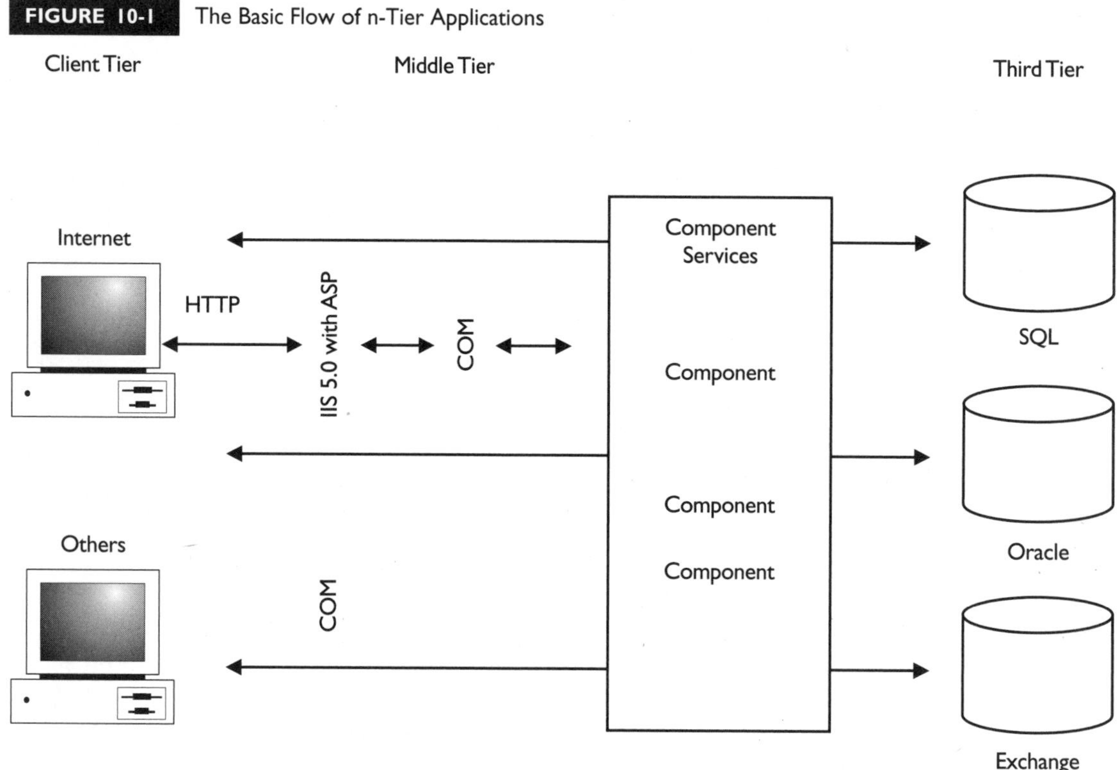


services such as ActiveX controls, Dynamic Hypertext Markup Language (DHTML), COM components, scripting on the client and server side, database access, and data access. COM components allow different applications to share and use these components easily. Microsoft has also crafted a new technology that is called .Net.

## .NET

In order to implement the Web solution platform, Microsoft has developed a new business strategy called .Net. .Net is a combination of desktop computing and the Internet. Its overall function is to provide clients (both individuals and businesses) with application and computing devices that work seamlessly with a Web browser. .Net is so new to the market that Microsoft has not completed some of its details, but the .Net platform will include servers, services, such as Web-based data storage, and device software.

The .Net platform should provide some of the following services:

- An online subscription service
- Data storage that is centralized
- E-mail, fax, and telephone integration
- A greater use of Extensible Markup Language (XML) in Web sites
- User information that automatically updates with other computing devices

Developers should find the .Net suite an easy way to build reusable code to increase productivity and reduce the number of programming errors.

## Client Tier

The client-side tier consists of many types of applications, such as the following:

- Client browser
- Client-side scripting
- ActiveX controls
- HTML
- Cascading style sheets

When developing full-scale applications to use the Internet, you would not want to use strictly client-side technologies, because not all browsers support some of these technologies. In addition, if you have the client machine doing most of the work, you are not taking part in the full functionality of enterprise applications.

## Middle Tier

Middle-tier technologies discussed in this section include the following:

- Common Gateway Interface (CGI) applications
- ISAPI extensions and filters
- ASP
- Process isolation

**CGI Applications** CGI applications are most widely used on UNIX systems to create executable programs that run on the Web server. Arguments following the question mark in the URL are passed to the CGI application as environment strings. These applications do not work as well in the Windows environment because each time CGI is run, a separate process is opened. Each of these processes requires its own memory space and system resources. For this reason, ISAPI was written specifically for IIS 5.0 as an alternative to CGI.

**ISAPI Extensions** An ISAPI extension is a runtime Dynamic Link Library (DLL) and is usually loaded in the same memory address space occupied by IIS 5.0. ISAPI extensions are more complex than CGI applications but they use an easy Application Programming Interface (API). However, they do have a drawback: They are harder to maintain than CGI. If any changes are made to the HTML page returned by an ISAPI extension, the page must be recompiled and linked. ISAPI extensions in a separate process can be stopped and restarted without affecting the server process.

**ISAPI Filters** ISAPI filters can also be created using ISAPI. These filters can grab specific server events before the server itself handles them. ISAPI filters can also cut down server performance if they are poorly written. In IIS 5.0, ISAPI filters can be loaded for the Web server as a whole or for specific sites, but they cannot be run out of process.

**Third Tier** The Internet is changing our expectations about the availability of information. As online commerce and electronic publishing become increasingly common, sites that provide a high level of interactivity will replace those that are static. Interactivity and complexity call for information to be stored in a way that makes it easy to manipulate and modify. This is the central role of the database in today's Web applications.

**Data Publishing Considerations** Make certain you have sufficient server resources to handle the increased demands of database access. The following are some good practices to remember when publishing data to the Web:

- Stress test your server and create a baseline that will allow for estimating the RAM usage, CPU speed, Internet connection speed, disk subsystems, and other hardware issues.
- Determine how much the database is likely to grow.
- Estimate how much will it be accessed by clients.
- Determine the tasks the client will perform on the site.

**ODBC and OLE DB** Open Database Connectivity (ODBC) is a way to retrieve information in different databases. The great thing about ODBC is that if developers are using it with their applications, they do not have to change the applications as long as an ODBC driver is in place. As long as an ODBC driver is in place for a particular back end, the ODBC-enabled front end can access the database.

ODBC developers either write applications that are on a server, also known as *Back-End,* or ODBC enabled *Front-End* or *client* desktop programs. The main differences between the two are listed here:

- *Back-End* refers to the database management system (DBMS) application that resides on a server used by numerous clients to store data that is accessed. The advantages to this type of ODBC use is that the application usually runs faster, has better security, and is typically backed up more frequently than an application that resides on the client desktop.
- *Front-End* refers to the client desktop application. This is the program that the client sees on his or her computer desktop machine.

Object Link Embedding and Database (OLE DB) was designed to provide another standard for accessing data. OLE DB is a set of routines or methods used to read and write data. An application using OLE DB would use this request sequence:

1. Initialize OLE.
2. Connect to a data source.
3. Issue a command.
4. Process the results.
5. Release the data source object and uninitialize OLE.

*Note:* At this time, Microsoft no longer ascribes these meanings to the letters OLE and DB.

Table 10-2 illustrates the differences between ODBC and OLE DB.

**ADO and RDS** Advanced Data Objects (ADO) and Remote Data Service (RDS) use OLE DB providers to communicate with local and remote data sources, respectively. Any application that uses ADO objects gets its data indirectly from OLE DB. If there is an OLE DB provider for it, the data is accessible through ADO. RDS is a feature of ADO that facilitates client-side programming by optimizing the transfer of data between the client and the ADO components in the middle tier of a Web application. RDS uses ADO as a programming interface between the code and the data exposed by the underlying OLE DB provider.

**ADC** The Advanced Data Connector (ADC) is considered the "father" of RDS. The RDS technology used to access remote data is inherited from ADC. Because ADC was formerly less flexible, it was blended in with ADO to provide a standard for accessing remote data. ADC is now obsolete because RDC has replaced ADC programming. Instead of ADC, use RDS when you need to provide a common programming model for accessing either local or remote data. RDS objects are installed with Microsoft Internet Explorer 4.0 and later versions on the client machine. They are also shipped with Microsoft Data Access Components (MDAC).

**RDO** Remote Data Objects (RDO) was designed to access remote ODBC relational data sources and to add a thin object layer to the ODBC application programming interface (API). RDO performance is, in most cases, close to that of the ODBC API.

Now that you have a better understanding of ADO and RDO, here are some real-world scenarios and solutions.

**TABLE 10-2**

ODBC versus OLE DB

| | |
|---|---|
| ODBC | Used to access relational databases; can be either front-end or back-end driven. |
| OLE DB | Used to communicate with any data source, including relational and nonrelational data. |

| SCENARIO & SOLUTION | |
|---|---|
| I need an easy object model. Should I use ADO or RDO? | Use ADO. |
| I need access to a large variety of data stores. Should I use ADO or RDO? | Use RDO. |

## COM

COM components are simply blocks of reusable code that can be used to perform a task or series of tasks. This type of component enables Web programmers and developers to encapsulate business logic into reusable code. Components are contained in either Dynamic Link Library (.DLL) files or executable (.EXE) files. COM components can be created with any COM-compliant programming language such as ASP, C++, Java, and Visual Basic. Remember, the threading model of a component can affect IIS 5.0 performance.

on the Job

***If you are using Microsoft Application Center 2000, it does not automatically deploy and synch COM+ applications. You can use the Deployment Wizard to deploy the application, or you must stop and restart the Web Services.***

## DCOM

Distributed COM, also known as DCOM, is a protocol that allows software components to communicate over a network. DCOM has a few strengths that make it stand out from the crowd. DCOM is based on the most widely used component technology today. It is an open technology that runs on multiple platforms. DCOM is the best networking technology to extend component applications across the Internet.

DCOM is simply a low-level extension of the Component Object Model, the core object technology within Microsoft ActiveX. You can find the ActiveX Web site at www.microsoft.com/activex/default.htm. Major development tools vendors such as Borland, IBM, Oracle, Microsoft, Sybase, and Symantec all sell development tools for software that produce ActiveX components. All these tools and the applications employ DCOM, making it a widely supported component that is flexible and multiplatform enabled. DCOM works as an adhesive for applications that run across the Web with technologies such as TCP/IP, Java, and HTTP. Microsoft is openly licensing DCOM technology to other software companies to run on all the major operating systems. This includes UNIX-based servers and systems. All these factors will give businesses and developers the ability to support cross-platform applications.

### DCOM and the Internet

Microsoft added DCOM to the ActiveX Server technology back in 1996. It allows developers to create applications in a more cost-effective and speedy environment. Table 10-3 presents some examples of the ActiveX Server services.

The simplicity of DCOM working with the Internet makes it an ideal technology for linking components for applications that span platforms.

## COM+

COM+ was created to improve some limitations of COM. Many of COM+'s improved functions make COM applications and components easier to build and services easier for programmers to create.

***If you are using Microsoft Application Center 2000, it does not automatically deploy and synch COM+ applications. You can use the Deployment Wizard to deploy the application, or you must stop and restart the Web Services.***

### COM+ Server-Side Installations

If databases, IIS configuration, or data files require installation from a COM+ application, they must be installed outside the Component Services Administration utility.

**TABLE 10-3** ActiveX Server Services Support

| Service | Purpose |
|---|---|
| Transactions | Rollback and recovery for component-based applications if a system fails. |
| Server Scripting | Component applications can be integrated with Web-based applications. |
| Queuing | Reliable store-and-forward queues. |

### COM+ Client-Side Installations

If a COM+ application for the server has been installed and the need arises to access it remotely, you can use either DCOM or message queuing. The Component Services Administration tool can also be used to export the COM+ application .MSI file. The .MSI file contains the registration information that enables you to remotely connect to the classes in a COM+ application through DCOM.

### COM+ and Active Server Pages in IIS 5.0

If you had IIS 4.0 and upgraded your Windows NT Server with IIS 4.0, the Microsoft Transaction Services in IIS 4.0 are automatically upgraded to COM+. Applications in IIS 5.0 can be defined as a group of files or directories in a virtual server or directory. When applications run in IIS 5.0, they can be grouped together in various ways, as shown in Table 10-4.

exam watch

***Since COM+ manages the application, the application can be stopped and started without interfering with other applications. When you set up a virtual directory in IIS 5.0, it is set up by default as an application that runs outside on the IIS process.***

**Configuring an Application in IIS 5.0** The following exercise will show you how to configure component services in Windows 2000.

**TABLE 10-4** Processes in Which Applications May Run in IIS 5.0

| Process | Definition |
|---|---|
| In-process | Applications will run in the same address space as the INETINFO.EXE. This method is used by default in IIS 5.0. |
| Out-of-process | Applications will run as an isolated process in their own address space. The COM+ component manages this type of application. |
| Out-of-process and pooled | Applications will run as isolated processes in their own address space and can be pooled with other applications. |

## EXERCISE 10-1

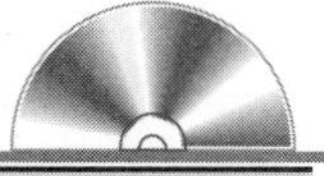


### Configuring Component Services in Windows 2000

1. To configure the Component Services in Windows 2000, click Start | Programs | Administrative Tools | Component Services. See Figure 10-2 for the Component Services page.
2. To add a new application, expand the Component Services folder by clicking the plus sign (+). Figure 10-3 shows this expanded folder.
3. To add an application, right-click the COM+ Applications folder.
4. Select New, then Application. This should open the COM Application Wizard installation screen. Figure 10-4 shows this screen. Click Next as shown in Figure 10-5. Click Create an Empty Application. Figure 10-6 shows this screen.

**FIGURE 10-2**

The Component Services Page

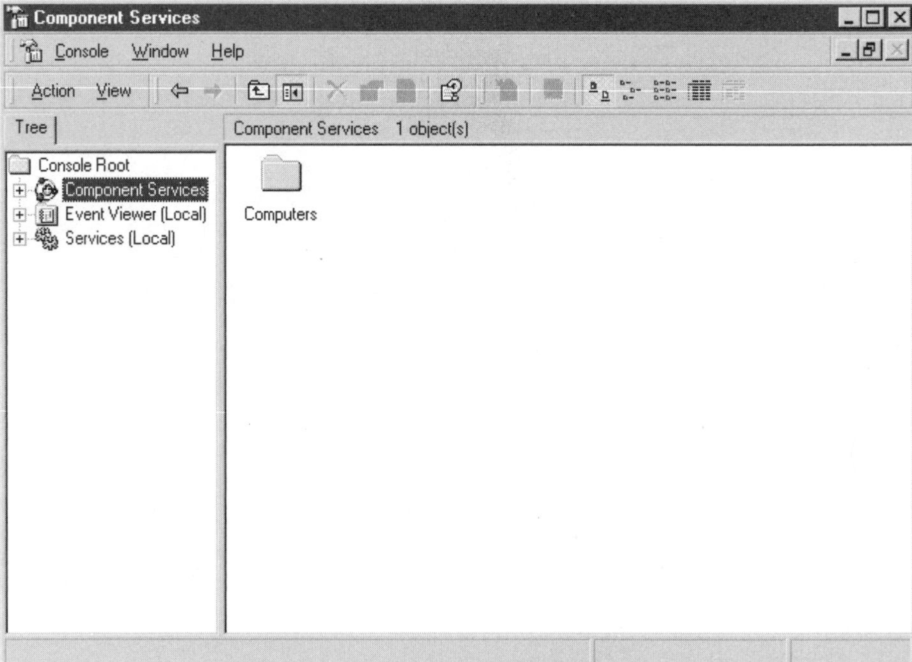

**FIGURE 10-3**

The Expanded Component Services Folder

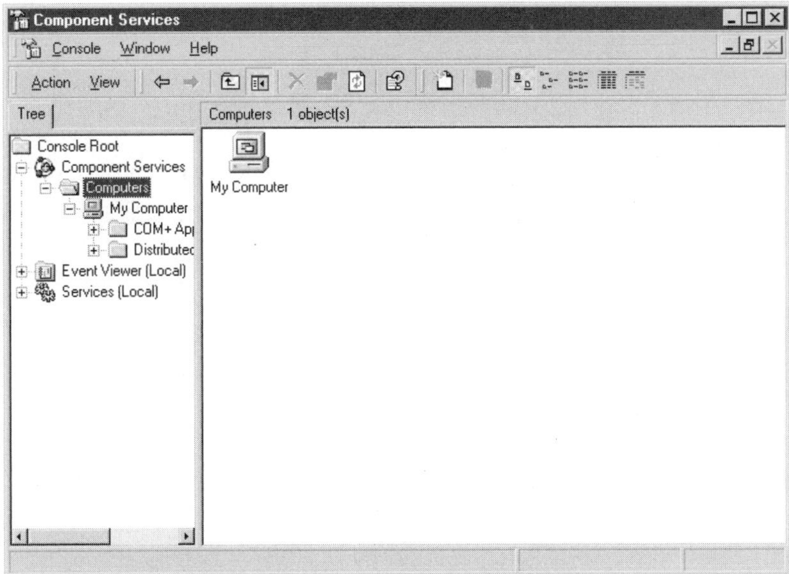


5. Enter the Application Name. Choose either Library or Server. (This choice controls whether the application runs in the calling process library or the

**FIGURE 10-4**

The COM Application Wizard Screen

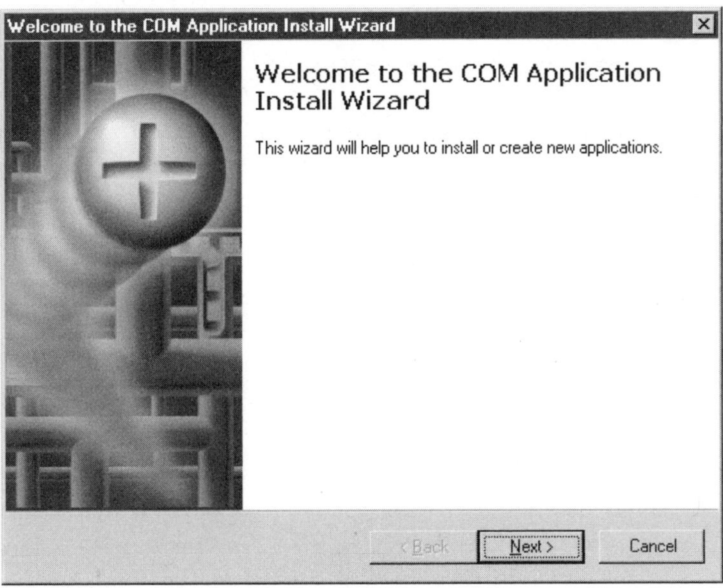

**FIGURE 10-5**

The Application Installation Screen Wizard

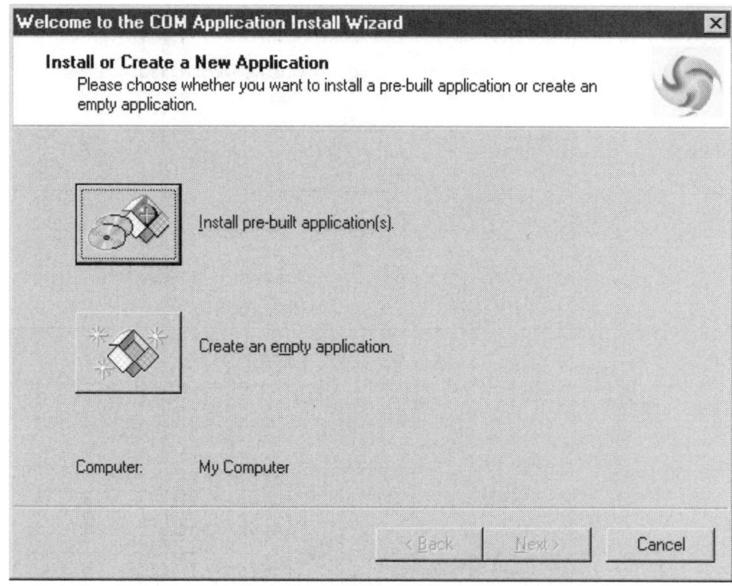


server process space.) Figure 10-6 shows where to enter the name for the new application.

**FIGURE 10-6**

Creating an Empty Application

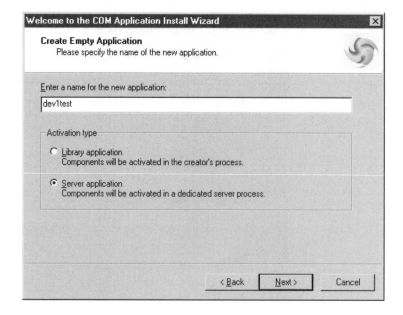

6. Choose Next. Choose This User and then select the valid user account for the application. Enter the password for the user, and click Next. Figure 10-7 shows where the account information is input for the chosen user.
7. Click Finish on the wizard's last screen to complete the application creation process. The Component Services manager updates its display to include your new applications folder, as shown in Figure 10-8.
8. To change the properties of the newly created application, right-click the application and choose Properties, then select the Advanced tab as shown in Figure 10-9.
9. This tab allows the developer to control various settings. The Leave Running When Idle option lets the application run even if other applications are executing nothing in any of its components. The Minutes Until Idle tab tells the application to shut down after so many minutes of being idle. The Disable Deletion tab can be used to prevent the application from being deleted. If you do not want anyone to change the application, you can select the Prevent Anyone from Changing the Application tab.
10. The Launch in Debugger option allows COM+ to load in a debugger. After you select the option, enter the correct debugger configuration in the Debugger path box.

**FIGURE 10-7**

Entering the Account Information for the Application

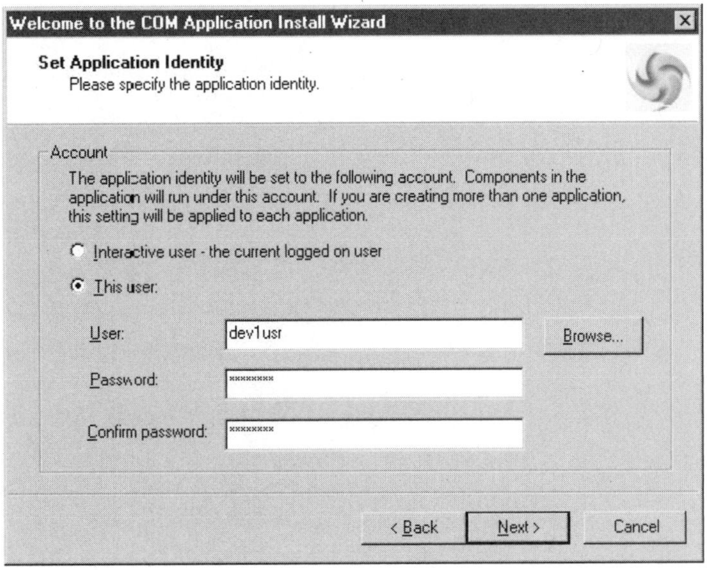

**FIGURE 10-8**

The Newly Created Application in Component Services

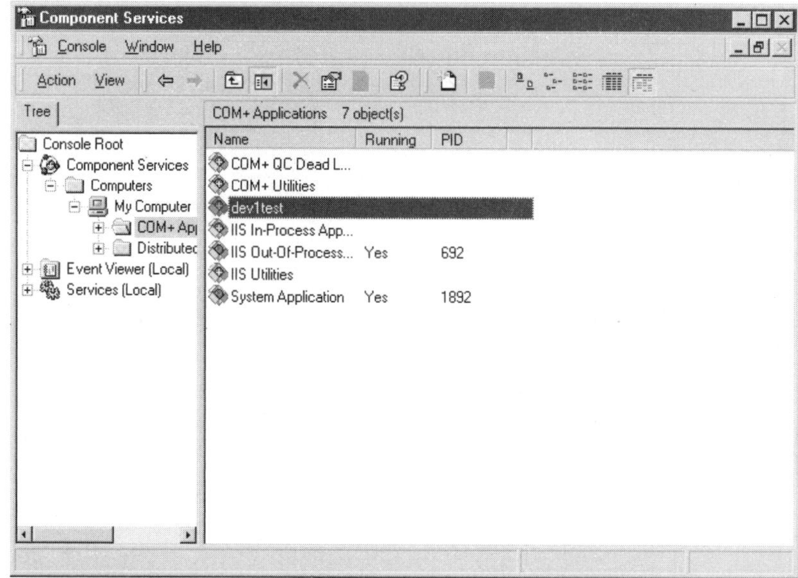


**FIGURE 10-9**

Advanced Properties Tab

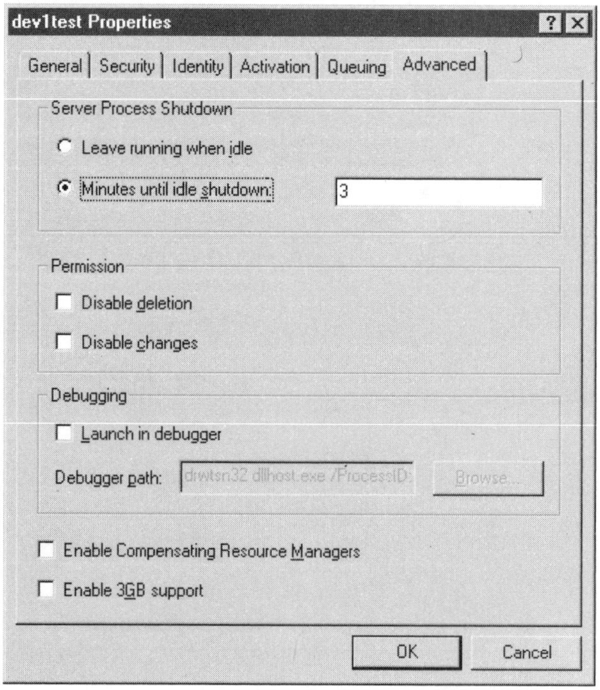

dev1test Properties

General | Security | Identity | Activation | Queuing | Advanced

Server Process Shutdown

Leave running when idle

Minutes until idle shutdown: 3

Permission

Disable deletion

Disable changes

Debugging

Launch in debugger

Debugger path: drwtsn32 dllhost.exe /ProcessID: Browse...

Enable Compensating Resource Managers

Enable 3GB support

OK Cancel

11. The final two options are used to control Advance features. The Enable Compensating Resource Managers option allows use of custom resource managers.

---

on the job

***Compensating Resource Manager (CRM) is a custom resource manager that provides functionality for a transactional resource, such as a file's participation in transactions. If a component deletes a file and the transaction terminates, COM+ won't roll back the deletion, because the file deletion isn't part of a transactional operation. The CRM will instead handle the rollback by restoring the file. The final option enables support for up to 3GB of memory on Windows 2000 Advanced Server.***

**Installing Components** When you must add components that contain event classes to Components Services, use the Add Component Wizard, as shown in Figure 10-10. Open the Components folder, and right-click it. Choose New Component, and click Next. Choose the type of component you want to install.

**FIGURE 10-10**

The COM Component Installation Wizard

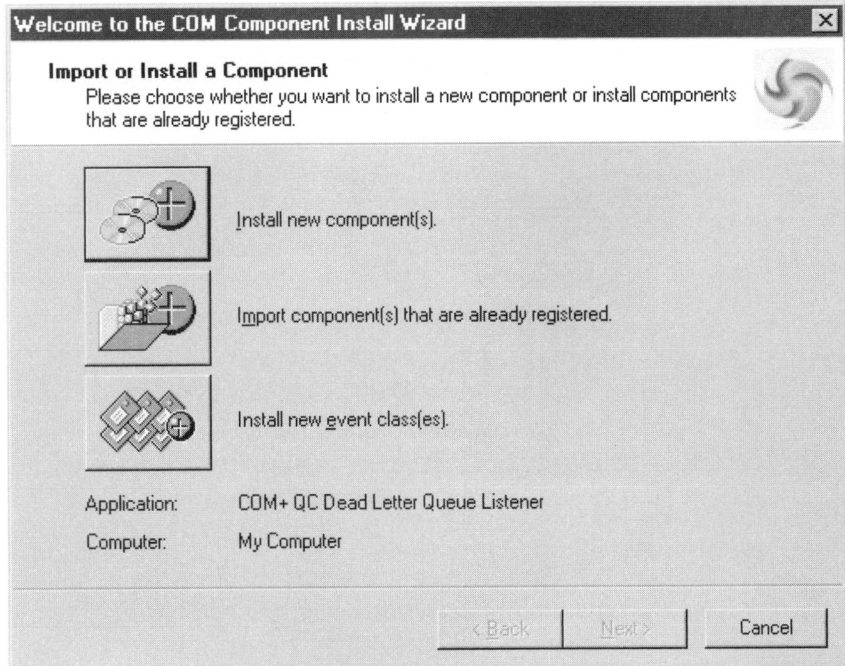

You can install a component that is not registered on your system, choose from all components registered on the system, or install a component that contains one or more event classes. For the sake of time, we will choose a component that already exists. Figure 10-11 shows the list of COM components that already exist and may be imported.

For this example, let's choose the AccessControlEntry from the list to import. After selecting the component, choose Next, then choose Finish. The component will show up in the right display panel. Figure 10-12 shows the newly imported component in the display panel.

Now you can set properties for each component by right-clicking the component and choosing Properties. The General tab allows you to enter a description for the class and displays the class identifier (CLSID) for the class with the full path to the executable file.

on the Job

***Since the description defaults to the class's program ID, it is not recommended that you alter this information.***

Figure 10-13 shows the General settings for the advanced properties of an imported component.

**FIGURE 10-11**

Importing an Already Existing Component

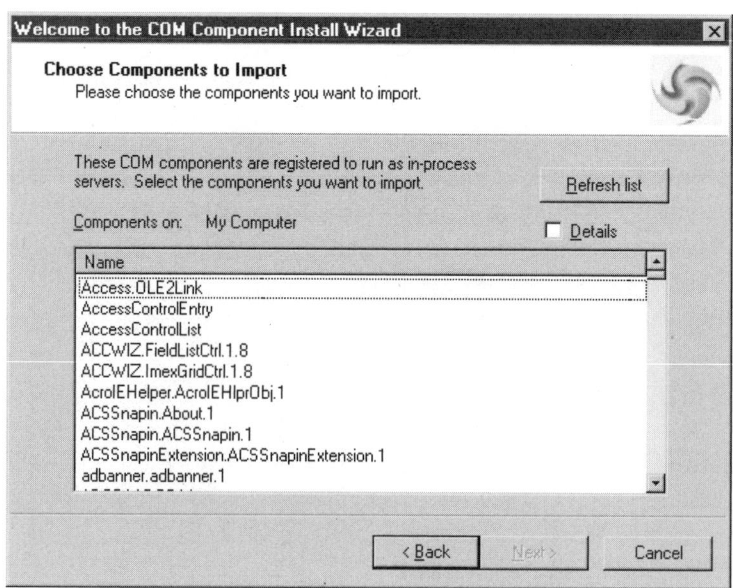

**FIGURE 10-12**

The Newly Added Component in the Display Panel in Component Services

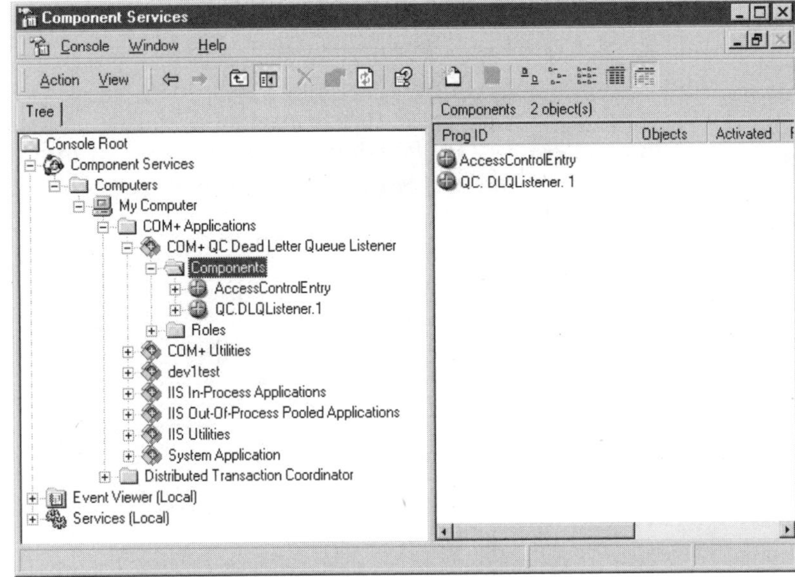


**FIGURE 10-13**

The General Settings Tab on the Advanced Settings of an Imported Component

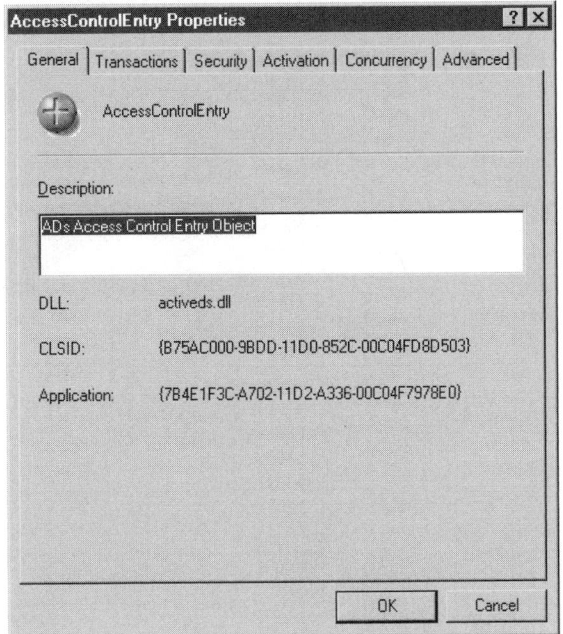

The Transactions tab controls class transactional settings. When this option is disabled, COM+ will not run the class in a transaction. This option removes almost the entire overhead of running a component in COM+.

on the Job

***This setting is very useful when you're using a class that doesn't need transactional support, but you want to manage it using COM+.***

The other transaction options are Not Supported, meaning that the class does not support transactions; Supported, meaning that the class supports but doesn't require a transaction; Required, which means that the class requires a transaction; and Requires New, meaning that the class requires a new transaction. Figure 10-14 shows the Transactions tab.

The Security tab includes the option to enforce component level access checks and the roles that are explicitly set for the selected items. Figure 10-15 shows this screen.

**FIGURE 10-14**

The Transactions Tab in Advanced Properties of Imported Components

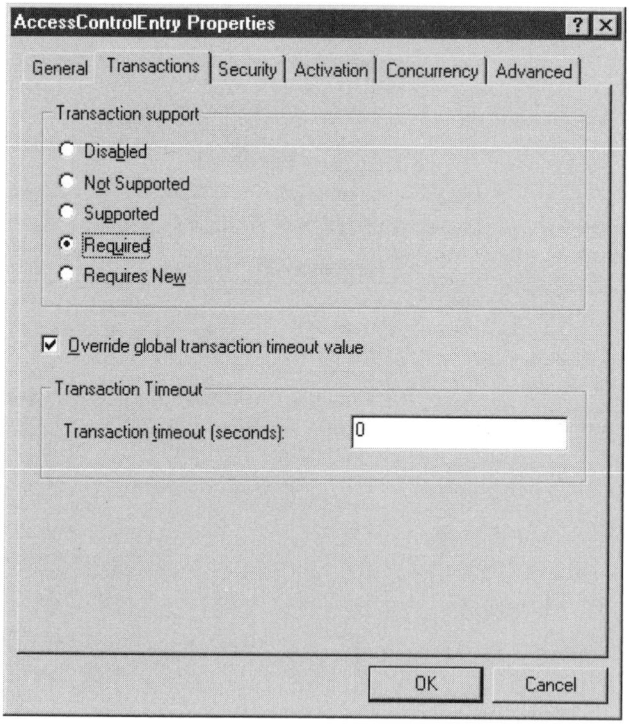

**FIGURE 10-15**

The Security Tab in Advanced Properties of Imported Components

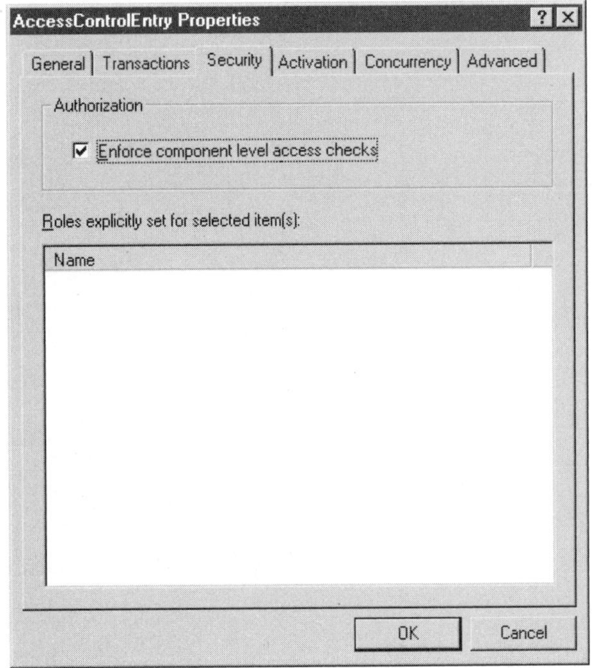


The Activation tab holds the Enable Object Pooling and the Enable Object Construction options. Enable Object Pooling allows for entering a minimum pool size, a maximum pool size, and a creation timeout in milliseconds. Figure 10-16 shows the Activation tab settings.

Object pooling is used to determine how COM+ handles the pool of pipeline objects. These properties include:

- **Minimum pool size** Minimum number of objects that are in the pool and minimum number of objects created when the application starts.
- **Maximum pool size** When the pool reaches this size, no other inactive or active objects can be created.
- **Creation request timeout** This option specifies how long a client can wait for an object from the pool before the request times out. The client would receive an E_TIMEOUT error message.

**FIGURE 10-16**

The Activation Tab in Advanced Properties of Imported Components

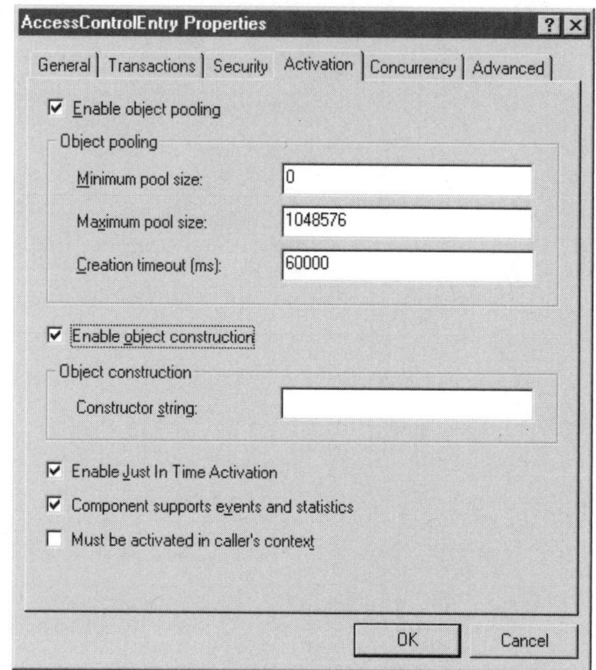


The Concurrency tab, shown in Figure 10-17, enables you to use synchronization on the component. Use this option if the settings for the COM application are to be synchronized.

Figure 10-18 shows the Advanced tab that allows for entries into the queuing exception class.

## Component Load Balancing

*Component Load Balancing*, or *CLB,* is used to enable the load balancing of COM+ components. CLB uses a routing list and a server response table to pass the COM+ application request through a COM+ cluster. After the COM+ member has created the component, no further involvement from the component is needed.

### Routing List

The *routing list* exists on every member of the Web tier cluster. If a location has no Web tier function, the routing list is located on a COM+ routing cluster.

**FIGURE 10-17**

The Concurrency Tab in Advanced Properties of Imported Components

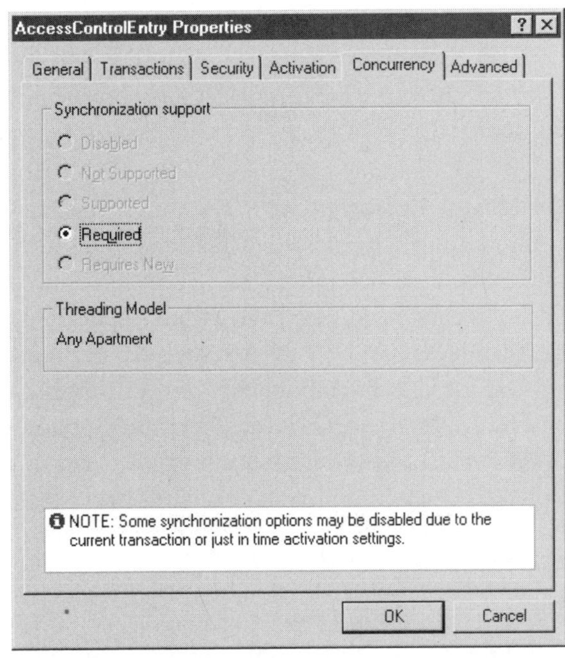


**FIGURE 10-18**

The Advanced Tab in Advanced Properties of Imported Components

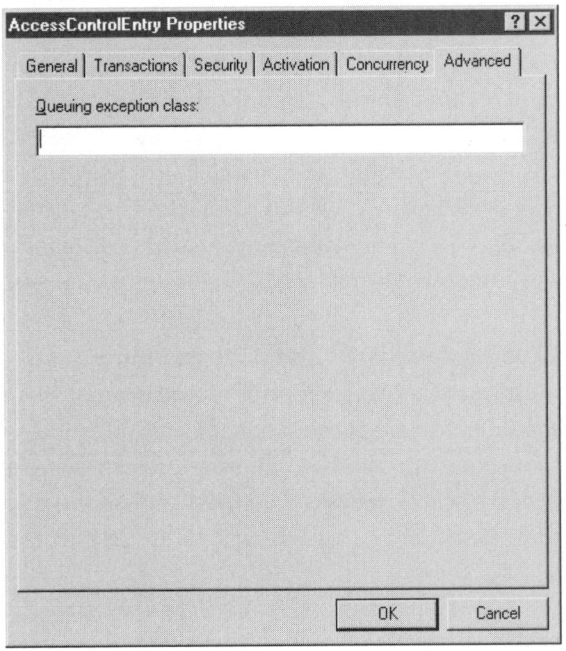

On the Web tier cluster controller, the routing list is created and synchronized with the other cluster members. An advantage of putting the routing list on each Web tier cluster member is that it would prevent a failure if a cluster member encountered a problem.

**Building a Routing List** The routing list is created on the Web tier cluster controller and automatically synchronized throughout the Web tier cluster. The list of COM+ cluster members can be added via the component Services tab on the Web tier cluster property page within Application Center software. Once installation has been completed, the Web tier software running on behalf of clients will use the COM+ components COM+ cluster.

The COM+ cluster is created with the Application Center Cluster Creation Wizard. Each cluster member must have the same copy of the COM+ component installed. Once created, the component needs to be aware of its existence within a CLB cluster.

### Response Time table

A heartbeat is taken each 200 milliseconds with the CLB software that is running on each Web tier cluster member. Then an in-memory table is built that lists the COM+ cluster members in order of response time. The slower the member's response, the lower the position it has in the table. The Web tier member uses the response timetable in a round-robin manner and passes incoming activation requests to the COM+ cluster members. When a request is received, the fastest COM+ cluster is used before any others, followed by the next fastest member, and so on. The table becomes full and the next request is routed via the first table entry. This process continues until the next scheduled response time update occurs, and activation then is reset to the beginning of the freshly load-balanced table.

**Cluster-Aware COM+ Components** To use CLB, COM+ components must be written to acknowledge the situation they are in. COM+ components should not retain per-component state information because it will affect the way transactions are handled. Transaction management is made more complex because per-component states cannot cross transaction boundaries. Component states need to be stored either in a DBMS or with the client, possibly in the form of a cookie.

**Setting Up the Clusters** Two clusters are required for CLB. One cluster holds the routing lists. Typically, as described previously, this cluster is on the Web tier cluster. The second cluster is the COM+ cluster.

**Deploying the COM+ Components to the COM+ Cluster** Using the Deployment Wizard enables administrators to install Application Center applications to other clusters. This wizard can be used to strategically manage the staging of clusters that are used to deploy updated content to production clusters.

exam watch

***COM+ components are not deployed, so try to avoid bringing the entire cluster down during component deployment. This task requires a phased deployment in which cluster members are taken offline, updated, and then brought back online.***

**Deploy the COM+ Components to the Web Tier Cluster** CLB requires that the COM+ component be installed on each Web tier cluster member. Use the Deployment Wizard to accomplish this task in the application. The COM+ component can be wrapped up in the Application Center application being deployed to the Web site.

**Mark the Web Tier COM+ Components as Supporting CLB** The COM+ components on the Web tier cluster need to be marked as supporting CLB. This is done through the Component Services Explorer, readily available through the Application Center snap-in. Mark the component by drilling to it through its COM+ containing application, selecting the Activation tab on the property page, and then selecting the "Component supports dynamic load balancing" check box.

CLB is a helpful technology for building distributed solutions. If performance is not an issue, it would be advisable to test and baseline CLB before going live.

**Performance** The following are two major items of importance when you are choosing whether or not to use CLB:

- **Throughput** The work that is done by the Web site.
- **Response time** How long it took to give the information back to the client.

Any call over the network will have a higher overhead and slower throughput than calls to software installed on the same computer. If throughput were at the top of your critical list, CLB would not be an advisable solution. It would be more advisable to install the COM+ components locally on the Web tier cluster members that would avoid all cross-network calls. CLB support is lost, but load balancing is still available through Network Load Balancing (NLB).

**Response Time** A slow Web site could make or break a company doing business on the Internet. If the COM+ architecture is used on the Web tier cluster, it could cause server performance to spiral downward. There are two possible solutions to remedy this situation:

- Move a COM+ component to a COM+ cluster tier. This action will lighten the workload for the Web tier cluster, and clients that are not using the COM+ technology would have improved performance.
- Move the routing lists to a separate COM+ routing cluster. This step would cause a much lighter workload because no CLB work would be taking place on the server. Note that this action would cause added network traffic, however.

Developers and Web architects should be aware of the limitations regarding use of CLB.

CERTIFICATION OBJECTIVE 10.02

## Designing an Application Management and Monitoring Strategy

The next section deals with managing applications and monitoring the IIS 5.0 server. It covers ISAPI versus ASP usage and stress testing your IIS 5.0 Web server with a handy tool from Microsoft.

on the Job

***As a best practices reminder before trying any of the following suggestions, make sure that you have a current emergency rescue disk and a current backup of your server.***

## Application Performance Optimization

When you use IIS 5.0 with applications, it is very important to test for performance levels before the server goes live. This is especially true if the HTML pages are custom written and not off-the-shelf software. When using ISAPI applications, the developer has a lower overhead because ISAPI runs faster than ASP. In retrospect, both ISAPI and ASP files run faster than CGI applications.

Now that you have an understanding of the various types of applications, let's look at some scenarios and solutions.

| SCENARIO & SOLUTION | |
|---|---|
| What do I use if I run applications on UNIX servers only? | Use CGI. |
| How can I lower the cost of expensive developer overhead? | Use ISAPI. |

To maximize performance for Web applications, an important task is to stress-test the applications before they go live on the site. When you're using more than one CPU on a production server, it is also important to stress-test on a test server with more than one CPU. This practice should allow developers to identify multiprocessor-balancing issues.

Microsoft has a helpful utility, called the Web Application Stress (WAS) tool, you can use to test. You can download this utility from the Microsoft Web Application Stress Tool site at the following URL: http://webtool.rte.microsoft.com/ or find it on the Windows 2000 Resource Kit companion CD. The CD also contains a tutorial and a knowledge base dedicated to the WAS utility.

The following are some best practices that you should consider when working with applications on an IIS 5.0 Server:

- Static files should be used when possible because known overhead is associated with them.
- If you must use applications, design them to push as much of the processing load as possible onto the client in order to avoid network slowdowns. Designing applications in this manner will also allow changes to appear to the client almost instantly.
- Turn debugging off on all production servers. If it is enabled, you must change the metabase property AppAllowDebugging to False.
- For all images, remember to set Expires headers to allow the images to be stored on the client side.
- Do not store apartment-threaded components in ASP Application and Session states. This includes all Microsoft Visual Basic components but not Java or most C++ objects.
- Use Secure Sockets Layer (SSL) only when necessary. Using the HTTPS protocol is much more expensive than standard HTTP. Be sure that the information being sent, such as credit card numbers or medical information, is sensitive enough to warrant the added expense.
- Process isolation will affect Web application performance as well.
- IIS 5.0 Web applications run in the out-of-process pool (medium protection) by default. It is safer to take the performance impact of process isolation than to risk server downtime and data loss that can be caused by a low-isolation application crashing the Inetinfo process.
- For enhancement, use Microsoft SQL Server 2000.
- Try to separate the database on a server from the Web service.
- Because performance degradation occurs when both SQL Server and IIS are on the same server, separate them on different machines.
- To minimize I/O on your database queries, create and maintain good indexes.
- Use stored procedures because they take less time to run and are easier to write than an ASP script designed to do the same task.
- In general, if an ASP script is more than 100 lines long, create a COM+ component to provide the same function. If the COM+ component is

written efficiently and debugged properly, it can offer 20 to 30 times the processing speed of a script for the same dynamic page.

### Testing the Web Application

Applications developed for the Internet need to be tested thoroughly. A developer would not want to put a shopping page with a cart out on the site without testing it for accuracy. The following section covers some methods of testing that can be performed on the Internet site application.

**Content Testing** Make certain that the site looks good and that the client or customer will find it easy to maneuver. Information on the site should be checked for proper spelling and grammar, and the content should be consistent and kept current.

**Browser Testing** Since not all browsers are compatible with all Web applications, it is a good idea to test the browser for compatibility. Table 10-5 shows common browsers and versions with the functions they support in Web pages.

**Visual Elements** This is very important. Try not to use outlandish fonts and styles on the site. Use standard size fonts when creating pages and applications for

**TABLE 10-5** Browser Types and Supported Functions

| Internet Browser | ActiveX | VBScript | JavaScript | Java Applets | Dynamic DHTML | Frames |
|---|---|---|---|---|---|---|
| Internet Explorer 4.0 and later | Enabled | Enabled | Enabled | Enabled | Enabled | Enabled |
| Netscape Navigator 4.0 and later | Disabled | Disabled | Enabled | Enabled | Enabled | Enabled |
| Netscape Navigator 3.0 | Disabled | Disabled | Enabled | Enabled | Disabled | Enabled |
| Microsoft Web TV | Disabled | Disabled | Disabled | Disabled | Disabled | Disabled |

Web use. Some font types do not display in all browsers. The fonts should be tested for compatibility issues before the application is launched.

on the Job

***Remember that the fewer the graphics, the faster the page will download on the client side. If you are selling items on your Internet site, remember this rule, because you would not want to lose potential sales because of a slow site.***

**Hyperlinks** Make certain that all hyperlinks work as they should. Broken links are frustrating to a client or consumer who is trying to reach an object or application that is not available. It is a good idea to have a procedure put into place for developers to test if they make changes to a source folder. In addition, check for links that were inadvertently left out when the application was posted to the Web site. You can use Microsoft Site Server 3.0 to check for broken links and to perform a series of other tasks on your Web site. You can find more information regarding this product at www.microsoft.com/catalog/display.asp?site=635&subid=22&pg=1.

**Graphical User Interface Testing** Here are some common ways that you can test your application with a GUI:

- Check to make sure that all shortcut keys are defined and work correctly.
- Check for the tab order. It should be from top left to bottom right.
- Check to make sure that the cursor is positioned on the first input field when the window is opened.
- Make sure that if any default button is specified, it works properly.
- Check the control buttons (push, radio, and list boxes) to make sure that they work.
- Test to make sure that multiple windows can be opened at the same time.
- Include a Help Menu for users.
- Test to make sure that the colors, fonts, and font widths are standard for the field prompts and displayed text.
- Test that the color of the field prompts and field background is standard in read-only mode.
- Test to make sure that vertical scrollbars or horizontal scrollbars do not appear unless required.

- Test to make sure that the various controls on the window are aligned correctly.
- Check the spelling of all the text displayed in the window, such as the window caption, status bar options, field prompts, pop-up text, and error messages.
- Test to make sure that all character or alphanumeric fields are left-justified and that the numeric fields are right-justified.
- Check for the display of defaults, if there are any.
- If using multiple windows, remain consistent with the design.

## Software Performance Testing

Software performance testing is an attempt to ensure that the software performs in accordance with specifications for response time, processing costs, storage use, and printed output.

The data on software performance is gathered during:

- Current and expected normal transactions
- Current and expected peak transactions
- Minimal transaction volumes

All interfaces are fully tested. This includes verifying the facilities and equipment and checking to make sure that the communication lines are performing to required standards. Table 10-6 shows what to test, the environment to be tested, and the tools to use for testing.

The number of simultaneous users that the server can successfully handle measures its capacity. An excessive load on the Web server causes performance to

**TABLE 10-6** The "What, Where, and How" of Testing

| What to Test | Environment | Tools or Techniques |
| --- | --- | --- |
| Data capture | Development environment | Test ASP and CGI scripts. |
| Transactions | User/system test environment | Simulate customer information. |
| Mathematical calculations | User environment | Use random data. |

nosedive. The main objective of stress testing is to determine the maximum number of clients that a server can handle.

### Load Testing Software

The testing technique used by most software is to simulate multiple logons. After a series of these multiple logons, the software calculates the optimum load factor for the Web server. The Web server software is then configured using this test data. As a result, if the traffic increases beyond the Web server's load capacity, the server stops entertaining further requests from online users. Visit the following URL for more information on Web performance testing: www.Webperfcenter.com.

As mentioned earlier, Microsoft has a Web Application Stress (WAS) utility that is designed to simulate multiple browsers requesting pages from a Web site. If enough client machines are used, this utility simulates many requests from clients to test the Web server for stress.

### Stress Testing

Running a Web server in a high-stress environment creates demands on system resources and causes stress to the server. When you're stress testing the IIS 5.0 server, you must write the tests to ensure that the system can process expected load. Stress tests are used to gradually increase the load on the server beyond the maximum design load until the system fails. This type of testing does two things. First, it tests the way a system behaves if it fails. Second, it determines if overloading the system will result in data or service loss to the client. It is particularly important that e-commerce sites stress-test their systems before they go live, because these types of systems generally exhibit performance degradation during peak times.

### Database Testing

The main purpose of testing a database is to create a baseline. No database stays consistent because it is not static, so the process is ongoing. If you create a database, you should also create a mirror and store it separately. Put the mirrored database through the testing, and leave the original alone. Continue until all tests are successful; then you can make changes on the original database.

The main reasons databases are tested are as follows:

- Search results accuracy
- Query response time

- Data integrity
- Data validity
- Recovery

## Recovery Testing

Another test that is performed on database software is the recovery test. This test involves forcing the system to fail in a variety of ways to ensure the following:

- The system recovers from faults and resumes processing within a predefined period of time.
- The system is fault-tolerant, meaning that processing issues do not stop the overall function of the system.
- Data recovery and restart are correct in case of autorecovery. Do not depend on human intervention in the case of autorecovery; doing so could waste valuable time.

## Acceptance Testing

Acceptance testing could demonstrate that the system does not exhibit the anticipated performance and functionality. This type of testing can be used to confirm that the system is ready for the live environment. It could be a good idea to conduct a survey of end users as to how well the site looks, functions, and performs.

## Regression Testing

Regression testing refers to retesting previously tested system components or functionality to ensure that they function properly, even after a change has been made to parts of the system. The various types of regression testing are as follows

- Client acceptance testing
- Content testing
- Database testing
- Security testing
- Server load
- Software testing

## FROM THE CLASSROOM

### Modifying the SSL Session Cache

When you access the Web server, an S channel holds the Secure Sockets Layer (SSL) session IDs and other SSL session information. The length of time that the SSL session information is cached must be known so that that the appropriate length can be set when developing load-balancing applications that identify separate users based on their SSL session numbers. Exercise 10-2 walks you through the process of modifying the SSL session information in the registry.

*—Jada Brock-Soldavini, MCSE*

Have the developer correct errors and then retest the system after the regression testing has been completed.

## Web Caches

IIS now has its own dedicated file cache. In previous versions, IIS shared its cache with the file system's cache. Since IIS 5.0 has its own file cache, it can ensure that it always has fast access to the most commonly requested pages.

**EXERCISE 10-2**

CertCam 10-2

### Modifying the SSL Session Information in the Registry

Warning: Use the registry editor at your own risk. Modifying registry entries could make the server unusable. Before you make changes to the registry, always create a current emergency repair disk and make certain that the registry is backed up and that the backup is available to restore if needed.

Let's modify the length of time that the SSL session information is cached by using the registry editor and changing the following keys:

1. Open the registry editor by clicking Start | Run and typing **Regedt32.exe**.

2. Drill down to the following key in the registry:

   [HKEY_LOCAL_MACHINE][System][CurrentControlSet][Control][SecurityProviders] [SCHANNEL]

3. On the Edit menu, select Add Value, type **ClientCacheTime**, and select the Data Type of REG_DWORD. Click OK. In the data field, type a decimal value in milliseconds. Click OK. Repeat Steps 2 and 3 to add the ServerCacheTime value. Exit the registry editor.

4. The following are the key locations and values:

   [HKEY_LOCAL_MACHINE] [System][CurrentControlSet] [Control]

   [SecurityProviders] [SCHANNEL] ClientCacheTime:REG_DWORD

5. Values are entered in milliseconds. The default is 2 minutes, which is 120000, and keys do not show up in the registry unless they are changed from their default. A value of 0 disables the secure connection caching. The key locations and values apply to all versions of the S channel. The shorter the interval, the better the overall management of the S channel cache.

---

## ASP Versus ISAPI

An ISAPI extension is a C++ or Visual Basic .DLL file that implements a specific API. This specific API allows the DLL to be plugged into a Web server, where it can process requests and produce HTML output that is returned to the client. The difference between ISAPI and ASP is that ASP is essentially interpreted and dynamically compiled by the server for every request to the page. With ISAPI, the code is precompiled and requires no translation overhead. By translating ASP code into equivalent ISAPI code, you can produce dramatic performance differences. Commonly, ISAPI code is 2 to 10 times greater than ASP in terms of page throughput. Conversations about ISAPI usually include the words *extension* or *filter*. Extensions and filters differ from each other. Extensions have become virtually obsolete, thanks to advances in ASP technology, but you can't replace ISAPI filters.

ISAPI filters literally filter each HTTP request to IIS. However, ISAPI filters have their drawbacks. A filter is invoked for every HTTP request, so you must be careful that you design the filter properly. Making sure that you allocate and deallocate memory correctly is crucial. If you've failed to deallocate even one byte, each HTTP request will cause IIS to consume an additional byte of memory. Furthermore, if the ISAPI filter is flawed, it can prevent IIS from servicing all HTTP requests.

There are three areas of information which are labeled as follows:

- Status
- Filter name
- Priority

The status will be green if IIS was able to load the ISAPI filter. *Priority* refers to the order in which ISAPI filters execute, which is especially important for ISAPI filters that process the same events. Filters that are listed with the same priority process sequentially in the order in which they appear. If you want an ISAPI filter to process across all Web site instances, add a filter to the master properties of the WWW Service. To add a filter to the master properties, right-click the machine name within the MMC, choose Properties, select WWW Service, and click Edit.

on the job

***At the time of this writing, Microsoft has a nifty Web page setup that developers and administrators can use that will help them sort out various .DLL conflicts. The URL for this site is http://support.microsoft.com/servicedesks/fileversion/dllinfo.asp?fr=0&sd=msdn. Use this site to sort by product only, file only, or product and file, as well as by various languages and .DLL filenames.***

## Process Isolation

With IIS 5.0, performance of out-of-process applications has improved over the previous version, especially for ASP. Applications that run in the Web services process (INETINFO.EXE) result in higher performance, but there is also a greater chance that the application could render the Web server unusable. It is recommended that the INETINFO.EXE run in its own process. That way mission-critical applications can be run with high protection and all other applications can run in medium protection. A best practice is to run ASP applications in medium protection and then configure any COM+ components as library applications instead of server applications.

If you decide to run your application as a separate process or with other applications in a single pooled process, you need to select High Isolated or Medium Pooled from the Application Protection drop-down list on the Home Directory or

Virtual Directory Properties sheet. Create an application directory first and designate it as either a Home Directory or a Virtual Directory. All new applications are run in medium protection by default. A large number of applications can be run at medium isolation, but only a few dozen applications can be run at high isolation because the processes take up system resources.

### Using Process Accounting

To turn on process accounting, click Start | Programs, then the Internet Services Manager. Select the Web site on which you want to set up process accounting. Open the site's property sheet, and click the Home Directory tab. Figure 10-19 shows this screen.

Next, click the Application Protection drop-down menu and choose the High (Isolated) settings. Figure 10-20 shows this menu.

On the site's Properties sheet, click the Web Site tab, and make sure Enable Logging is selected. Figure 10-21 shows this screen.

**FIGURE 10-19**

The Home Directory Tab in Internet Service Manager

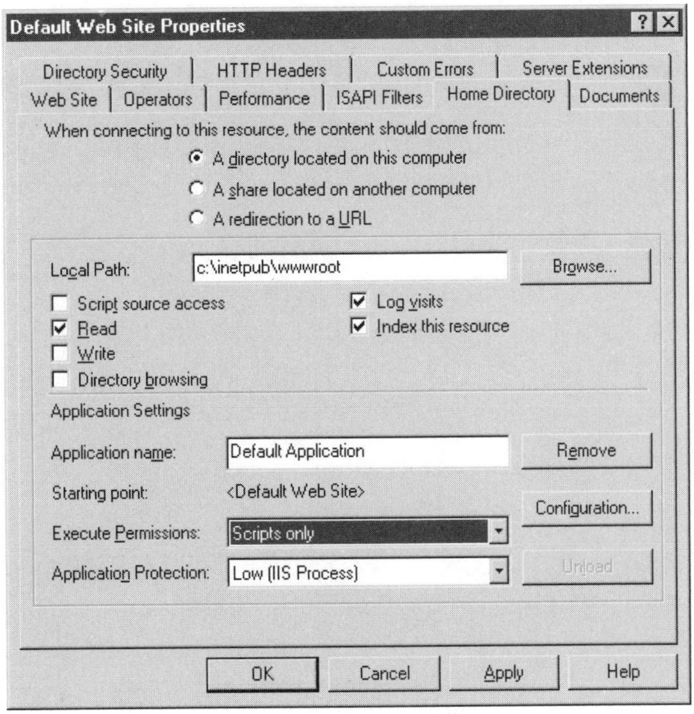

**FIGURE 10-20**

The Application Settings Box in Internet Services Manager

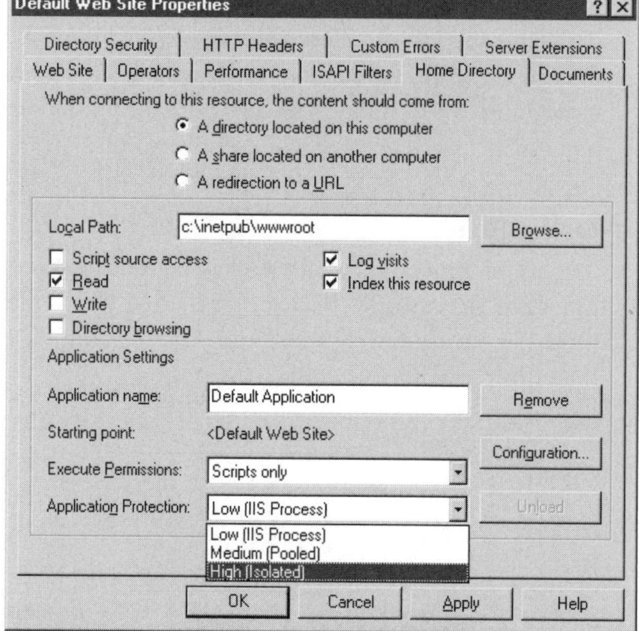


**FIGURE 10-21**

The Website Tab

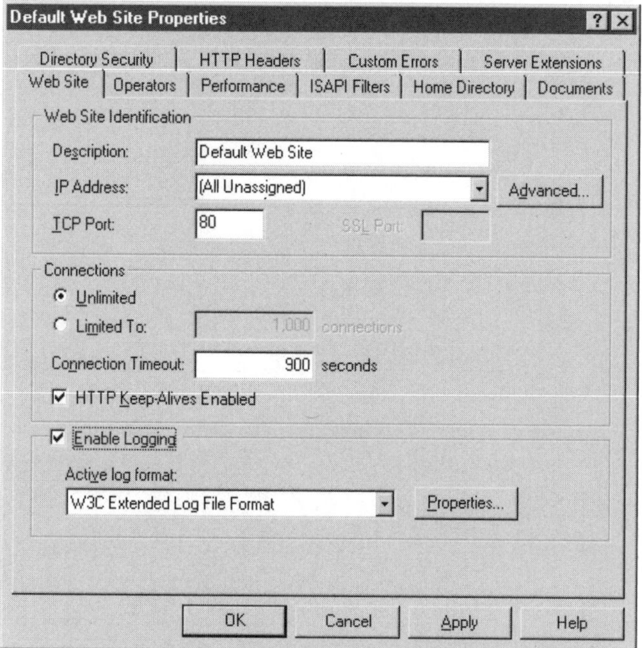

On the Web Site Properties sheet, click the Logging Properties button, and select Process Accounting. Figure 10-22 shows this screen.

The first two steps of this procedure set the Web site to run out-of-process. The last two steps turn on process accounting for the site.

## Limiting a Site's Resources

If a site is using more resources than it should, you can limit the site's resource consumption by running the site's applications out-of-process, then turning on process throttling. In ISM, choose the Site's Properties sheet, click Performance. Select Enable Process Throttling. In the Maximum CPU use box, enter the percentage of CPU resources dedicated to the site. Figure 10-23 shows this setting.

Choose the Enforce Limits button shown in Figure 10-24.

Once the site hits the limit, an action that has been previously defined will take place.

exam Watch

***In-process and pooled-process applications are not affected by processor throttling and are not included in process accounting statistics.***

**FIGURE 10-22**

Process Accounting for a Web Site in Internet Services Manager

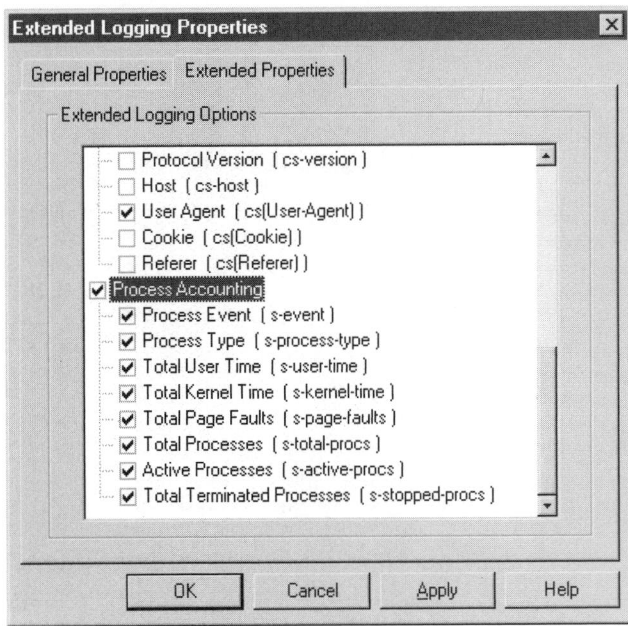

**FIGURE 10-23**

Enable Process Throttling for a Web Site in Internet Services Manager

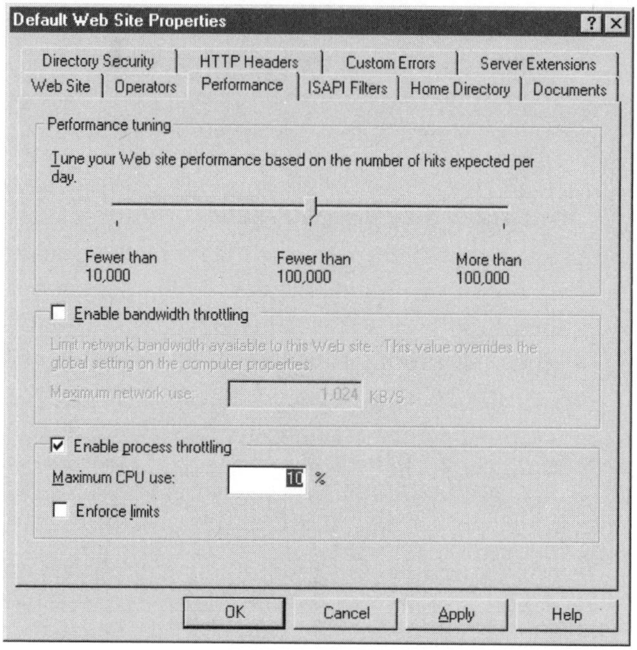

Default Web Site Properties

Directory Security | HTTP Headers | Custom Errors | Server Extensions

Web Site | Operators | Performance | ISAPI Filters | Home Directory | Documents

Performance tuning

Tune your Web site performance based on the number of hits expected per day.

Fewer than 10,000 | Fewer than 100,000 | More than 100,000

Enable bandwidth throttling

Limit network bandwidth available to this Web site. This value overrides the global setting on the computer properties.

Maximum network use: 1,024 KB/S

Enable process throttling

Maximum CPU use: 10 %

Enforce limits

OK | Cancel | Apply | Help

**FIGURE 10-24**

The Enforce Limits Setting

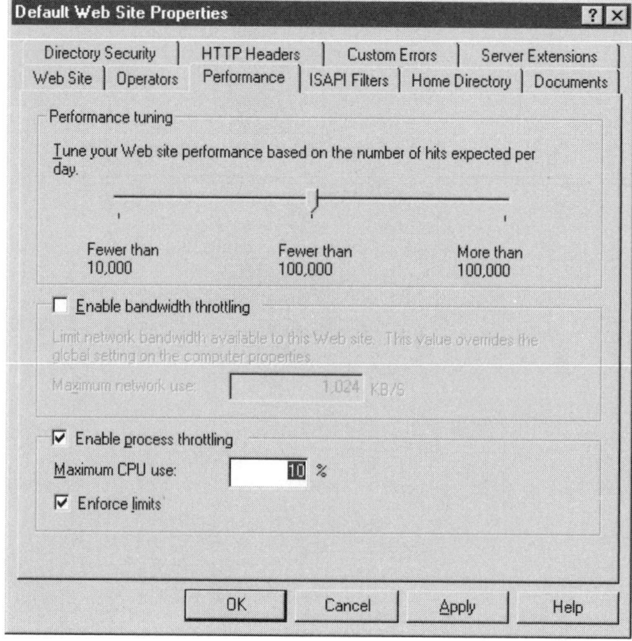

Use the following counters in Performance Monitor to determine if you need to use process throttling:

- Processor: % Processor Time.
- Web Service: Maximum CGI Requests.
- Web Service: Total CGI Requests.
- Enable process accounting so that Job Object counters are included in IIS logs.
- Examine the dllhost object counters to determine the number of out-of-process WAM and ISAPI requests.

Before you use PERFMON.EXE to monitor these processes, keep in mind that the throttled dllhost process is running at a lower priority, meaning that it will not respond quickly to requests from INETINFO.EXE. This could cause your server to become bogged down. Monitor the Web server before and after making any changes so that you can note its responsiveness.

## Web Stress and Analysis

Microsoft has a tool called Web Capacity Analysis Tool (WCAT) that is available online at www.microsoft.com/workshop/server/toolbox/wcat.asp. WCAT simulates various workloads on the IIS server. The ASP files on the Web server can be tested for response time and tuned accordingly. The IIS Resource Kit provides invaluable information on the performance tuning and design of your Web sites.. Here are some best practices for tuning:

- What is the cost of ASP dependencies outside of your Web server?
- Does any component slow performance?
- Determine the number of production servers that will be needed. Add more servers if necessary.
- Use application state for caching output in the ASPIIS Resource Kit. This section briefly covers how to stress your Web site.
- Create and modify the ProcessorThreadMax registry value.
- Use system DSNs only.
- Turn on buffering for all applications.

- Disable session state, if not used.
- Use OptionExplicit with VBScript.
- Make ADO free-threaded if you use SQL Server.
- Modify the metabase AspScriptEngineCacheMax value.

## CERTIFICATION SUMMARY

This chapter explored how to use Internet Information Services 5.0 (IIS 5.0) to create *n*-tier component-based topology as well as how to design an application management and monitoring strategy in the Windows 2000 environment. The IIS 5.0 Web server software program is an excellent one to use to reach potential clients and consumers who use the Internet for purchases or information. Applications for transactions as well as database access via the Web can be created in a rapid and scalable environment. Using the *n*-tier design structure, developers can create more dynamic Web resources.

Detailed in this chapter are the following concepts: COM, DCOM, COM+, Component Load Balancing, COM component location, Web caches, ASP versus ISAPI, and Web stress and analysis in the IIS 5.0 environment. Before implementing any of these on a live Web server, you should be cautious and plan, test, and view the results carefully. Hastily made decisions regarding any of these components on a live Web server could cause harm to overall server performance and end in customer dissatisfaction. Due to the growth in the number of users who have access to the Internet, businesses should be highly motivated to adopt the *n*-tier strategy and design structure. Application management design is a crucial portion of the success of the Web site and its performance structure. Poorly written applications that are not tuned and monitored for performance could cause clients to go to other competitive Web sites for their services.

# TWO-MINUTE DRILL

## Designing an *n*-Tier, Component-Based Topology

- COM applications and components are easier to build and to use to create services.
- COM components are simply defined as blocks of reusable code that can perform a task or series of tasks.
- DCOM is the best networking technology to extend component applications across the Internet.
- Software companies runing on all the major operating systems, including UNIX-based servers, use DCOM technology.
- Improved functions of COM+ are to make COM applications and components easier for developers to build.
- Component Load Balancing enables the load balancing of COM+ components.
- Before implementing CLB, remember that throughput and response time can be affected, leading to performance issues on the Web site.

## Designing an Application Management and Monitoring Strategy

- ISAPI runs faster than Active Server Pages.
- Both ISAPI and ASP files run faster than CGI applications.
- If using more than one CPU on a production server, stress test on a test server with more than one CPU for accurate results.
- Use the WAS tool to perform Web application stress testing on your server before going live.
- Process isolation affects Web application performance.
- Try to separate the database on a server from the Web service.
- Use stored procedures because they take less time to run and are easier to write than an ASP script designed to do the same task.

# SELF TEST

The following questions will help you measure your understanding of the material presented in this chapter. Read all the choices carefully because there might be more than one correct answer. Choose all correct answers for each question.

## Designing an *n*-Tier, Component-Based Topology

1. You work as a developer for a large corporation. You need to implement an *n*-tier design throughout the corporation. Which of the following are considered middle-tier technologies?

   A. CGI applications

   B. SQL Server

   C. Exchange Server mail

   D. Client Web browser retrieval from Web site

2. What are some issues that could arise if an ISAPI filter is not written well for use on a Web server?

   A. It could cause the server to reboot.

   B. It could slow response time on the Web server.

   C. It could cause the Web site to have performance degradation issues.

   D. A and C.

   E. B and C.

3. What is OLE DB used for in IIS 5.0? (Choose all that apply.)

   A. Accessing nonrelational data on the Web server

   B. Accessing relational data on the Web server

   C. Accessing remote data objects (RDO) on the Web server

   D. Accessing TCP/IP information on the Web server

4. What file types make up COM components? (Choose all that apply.)

   A. .ASP

   B. .EXE

   C. .DLL

   D. .CGI

**5.** When an application is run in the same address space as the INETINFO.EXE process, what is this called?

A. In-process

B. In-process pooled

C. Out-of-process

D. Out-of-process pooled

**6.** What tool is used to configure Component Sevices in Windows 2000?

A. Application Center

B. Application Services

C. Component Center

D. Component Services

**7.** You are setting up a COM component and need to remove some of the overhead associated with this component. What tab would you use after setup on the component, and what changes need to be made? (Choose all that apply.)

A. Advanced tab

B. Transactions tab

C. Click the Disabled box in the Advanced tab Properties

D. Click the Disabled box in the Transactions tab Properties

**8.** When using Component Load Balancing software, what is the default time in milliseconds between heartbeats?

A. 2

B. 5

C. 200

D. 500

**9.** How many clusters are required, at a minimum, for use with CLB?

A. Two

B. Three

C. Four

D. Any number may be used

10. You want to implement Web tier clustering. What tool is used to add members to the clustering tier?

   A. Internet Services Manager | Web Site | Properties

   B. Network Properties Page | Component Services tab on the Web Tier Cluster Property page

   C. Component Services Software | Component Services tab on the Web Tier Cluster Property page

   D. Application Center Software | Component Services tab on the Web Tier Cluster Property page

## Designing an Application Management and Monitoring Strategy

11. What happens to ISAPI filters that are listed with the same priority?

   A. They are processed at the same time.

   B. They are processed in the order in which they appear.

   C. They must have different levels of priority.

   D. The oldest one processes first.

12. What utility can be used to load-test your software before going to a live environment?

   A. Web Application Stress Test (WAST)

   B. Internet Application Stress Test (IAST)

   C. Web Stress Test (WST)

   D. Performance Monitor (PERFMON.EXE)

13. What is a benefit of using ISAPI over ASP?

   A. Ease of use for the developer

   B. Easy to manage

   C. Low overhead

   D. More reliable

14. What is the purpose of acceptance testing your IIS 5.0 Server?

   A. To check for database errors

   B. To check for system recovery in the event of a failure

   C. To check that the system is ready to go live

   D. To check for appearance issues and browser compatibility

**15.** You want to turn on isolated process accounting. Via what tool is this task completed?

A. Application Center

B. Internet Services Manager

C. Task Manager

D. Network Properties

**16.** Which of the following runs the slowest?

A. ASP

B. ISAPI

C. CGI

D. HTML

**17.** What would happen on your Web server if you placed your dllhost file at a low priority?

A. Nothing would happen.

B. The Web server would speed up.

C. The Web server would slow down.

D. This file cannot be placed at a priority level.

**18.** You work for an ISP. You are noticing that a particular site has an application that is using more processing power than it should be. What can you do to limit the site's processing power?

A. Stop and restart the site.

B. Install another CPU on the server.

C. Run the application in-process and turn on process throttling.

D. Run the application out-of-process and turn on process throttling.

**19.** Why should you use stored procedures instead of ASP scripting in IIS 5.0? (Choose all that apply.)

A. They take less time to run.

B. They are easier to write than a script designed to do the same task.

C. ASP is not as accepted as stored procedures.

D. Stored procedures have more functionality than ASP scripting.

**20.** Why is it important not to run a lot of high-process applications in IIS 5.0?

A. Security

B. Client memory

C. System resources

D. Fault tolerance

## LAB QUESTION

You are a developer for a large ISP that handles the hosting of many Web sites with IIS 5.0. Slow server response time is not an option for a few of your clients because they sell goods on the Internet and must remain up to speed. Most of your clients are smaller companies that simply do business on the Internet; they don't conduct e-commerce. You need to get a baseline for performance on the IIS 5.0 Server and target your applications that run the most. What can you do to meet these requirements for your client sites? Some sites are using more processing power than they should, and the more important sites are not getting their fair share of power. What can be done to improve overall performance on the IIS 5.0 Server for the Web sites?

# SELF TEST ANSWERS

## Designing an *n*-Tier, Component-Based Topology

1. ☑ **A.** A CGI application is considered a middle-tier technology. Also included as middle-tier technologies are ASP and ISAPI filters and extensions.
☒ **B** is incorrect because the SQL Server is considered a third-tier function. **C** is incorrect because the Exchange Server mail is considered a third-tier function. **D** is incorrect because clients' retrieval of information through their Web browsers occurs at the client-tier level.

2. ☑ **E.** If ISAPI filters are poorly written, they can cause performance degradation issues on the Web server and slow response time. All filters should be written and tested in a lab environment before they are used on a live Web server.
☒ **A** is incorrect because poorly written ISAPI filters would not typically cause the server to reboot. They could cause the need for the server to be rebooted. **D** is incorrect because badly written ISAPI filters would not cause the server to reboot, but they could cause performance issues.

3. ☑ **A** and **B.** OLE DB is used to communicate with any data source, including relational and nonrelational data.
☒ **C** is incorrect because RDO is used to access remote ODBC relational data sources and to add a thin object layer to the ODBC application programming interface. **D** is incorrect because OLE DB is not used to access TCP/IP information from the Web server.

4. ☑ **B** and **C.** COM components consist of either the Dynamic Link Library (.DLL) file type or an executable (.EXE) file type.
☒ **A** is incorrect because .ASP makes up the Active Server Pages file type. **D** is incorrect because the .CGI file is not a COM component file.

5. ☑ **A.** By default, applications are set to run in the same address space as the INETINFO.EXE process. This is called *in-process.* It is a good idea to change applications to other address spaces so that this process is not hindered in any way.
☒ **B** is incorrect because there is no such process as in-process pooled. **C** is incorrect because an out-of-process application is one that will be run as an isolated process in its own address space. The COM+ component manages this type of application. **D** is incorrect because an out-of-process pooled component is one that will be run as an isolated process in its own address space and can also be pooled with other applications.

6. ☑ **D.** The Component Services tool in Windows 2000 is used to configure COM services. You can access it by clicking Start | Programs | Administrative Tools and then Component Services.
   ☒ **A** is incorrect because the Application Center is used to administer Web tier information on the server. **B** is incorrect because no such tools exist in Windows 2000. **C** is incorrect because no such tool exists in Windows 2000.

7. ☑ **B** and **D.** The Transactions tab controls class transactional settings. When this option is disabled, COM+ will not run the class in a transaction. This option removes almost the entire overhead of running a component in COM+.
   ☒ **A** and **C** are incorrect because the Advanced tab is used to allows entries into the queuing exception class; it does not have a Disabled tab. It would not be suitable for taking the overhead off a COM component.

8. ☑ **C.** By default, it takes 200 milliseconds between each heartbeat with the CLB software. This number can be changed to a different level if needed.
   ☒ **A**, **B**, and **D** are all incorrect because they are not the default settings for heartbeat readings in CLB.

9. ☑ **A.** Two clusters are required for CLB. One cluster holds the routing lists, and the second cluster is the COM+ cluster.
   ☒ **B**, **C**, and **D** are incorrect because they are not the minimum number of clusters that can be used with CLB.

10. ☑ **D.** Using the Application Center Software | Component Services tab on the Web Tier Cluster Property page allows you to add members to the clustering tier.
    ☒ **A**, **B**, and **C** are all incorrect because they would not allow you to add members to the clustering tier.

## Designing an Application Management and Monitoring Strategy

11. ☑ **B.** The ISAPI filters will process in the order in which they appear in the list.
    ☒ **A**, **C**, and **D** are all incorrect because they do not apply to the ISAPI filter priority list.

12. ☑ **A.** The Web Application Stress Test (WAST) utility is designed to simulate multiple browsers that are requesting pages from a Web site. If enough client machines are used, this utility simulates many requests from clients to test the Web server for stress.
    ☒ **B** and **C** are incorrect because these do not exist. **D** is incorrect because Perfmon is used to monitor performance using specific counters.

**13.** ☑ C. Because ISAPI precompiles the code, it has no translation overhead as ASP does.
☒ A, B, and D are incorrect in relation to ISAPI versus ASP. ISAPI, if not written properly, can cause issues such as all HTTP requests not to be serviced.

**14.** ☑ C. Acceptance testing might demonstrate that the system does not exhibit the anticipated performance and functionality. It can be used to confirm that the system is ready for the live environment.
☒ A, B, and D are all incorrect because they are not part of the acceptance-testing process.

**15.** ☑ B. Click Start | Programs, then the Internet Services Manager. Select the Web site on which you want to set up process accounting. Open the site's Properties sheet, and click the Home Directory tab. Click the Application Protection drop-down menu and choose High (Isolated).
☒ A is incorrect because it is not used to turn on process accounting. C is incorrect because the Task Manager is used to view running processes. D is incorrect because process accounting cannot be turned on using the Network Properties function.

**16.** ☑ C. CGI runs the slowest because it opens a process for each request. Both ISAPI and ASP files run faster than CGI applications, with ISAPI the fastest.
☒ A is incorrect because ASP runs faster than CGI but slower and with more processing tasks than ISAPI. B is incorrect because ISAPI is the fastest of these options. D is incorrect because HTML is not really a process; it is used to access Web pages as a markup language.

**17.** ☑ C. If the dllhost file is placed at a low level, it will not answer HTTP requests in a fast manner.
☒ A is incorrect because it would cause requests not to be processed as quickly. B is incorrect because the server would not speed up if the dllhost file were placed at a lower priority. D is incorrect because the priority level can be changed on this file.

**18.** ☑ D. If a site is using more resources than it should, you can limit the site's resources by running the site's applications out-of-process, then turning on process throttling. In ISM, choose the site's Properties sheet, click Performance, and select Enable Process Throttling. In the Maximum CPU Use box, enter the percentage of CPU resources you want to dedicate to the site.
☒ A is incorrect because it would simply stop the site for a moment and not take care of the issue at hand. B is incorrect because it would not stop the application from running on more than its share of processing power. C is incorrect because the process should be run out-of-process.

**19.** ☑ **A** and **B**. Use stored procedures because they take less time to run and are easier to write than an ASP script designed to do the same task.
☒ **C** is incorrect because ASP scripting is accepted as readily as stored procedures. **D** is incorrect because ASP can perform the same functions as stored procedures.

**20.** ☑ **C**. All new applications are run in medium protection by default. A large number of applications can be run at medium isolation, but only a few dozen applications can be run at high isolation because the processes take up system resources.
☒ **A**, **B**, and **D** are all incorrect because they do not apply to running an application with the high process enabled in IIS 5.0

# LAB ANSWER

Since you need to establish a baseline for the sites, use Performance Monitor and track the results for a short period of time. (Doing so does affect overhead, so do not leave Performance Monitor on for long periods of time.) After the baseline has been completed but before any changes are made, make certain that you have a current ERD and a good backup for safety. Use the following counters in PERFMON.EXE to check for which site can be throttled:

- Processor: % Processor Time.
- Web Service: Maximum CGI Requests.
- Web Service: Total CGI Requests counters.
- Enable process accounting so that job object counters are included in IIS logs.
- Examine the dllhost object counters to determine the number of out-of-process WAM and ISAPI requests.

Once these tasks have been done, you can throttle each site using Internet Services Manager and choose the site's Properties sheet. Click Performance, and select Enable Process Throttling. In the Maximum CPU Use box, enter the percentage of CPU resources you want to dedicate to the site.

Next, you can isolate the most important applications to run with higher performance than the others. Remember not to isolate more than 10 to 12 at a higher process because it can cause performance degradation. In addition, remember not to make too many changes at one time; if you do have an issue arise, it could be difficult to figure out which change is causing the problem.

# A

# About the CD

This CD-ROM contains the CertTrainer software. CertTrainer comes complete with ExamSim, Skill Assessment tests, CertCam movie clips, the e-book (electronic version of the book), and Drive Time. CertTrainer is easy to install on any Windows 98/NT/2000 computer and must be installed to access these features. You may, however, browse the e-book directly from the CD without installation.

# Installing CertTrainer

If your computer CD-ROM drive is configured to autorun, the CD-ROM will automatically start up upon inserting the disk. From the opening screen you may either browse the e-book or install CertTrainer by pressing the *Install Now* button. This will begin the installation process and create a program group named "CertTrainer." To run CertTrainer use START | PROGRAMS | CERTTRAINER.

## System Requirements

CertTrainer requires Windows 98 or higher and Internet Explorer 4.0 or above and 600 MB of hard disk space for full installation.

# CertTrainer

CertTrainer provides a complete review of each exam objective, organized by chapter. You should read each objective summary and make certain that you understand it before proceeding to the SkillAssessor. If you still need more practice on the concepts of any objective, use the "In Depth" button to link to the corresponding section from the Study Guide or use the CertCam button to view a short .AVI clip illustrating various exercises from within the chapter.

Once you have completed the review(s) and feel comfortable with the material, launch the SkillAssessor quiz to test your grasp of each objective. Once you complete the quiz, you will be presented with your score for that chapter.

# ExamSim

As its name implies, ExamSim provides you with a simulation of the actual exam. The number of questions, the type of questions, and the time allowed are intended to be an accurate representation of the exam environment. You will see the screen shown in Figure A-1 when you are ready to begin ExamSim:

When you launch ExamSim, a digital clock display will appear in the upper left-hand corner of your screen. The clock will continue to count down to zero unless you choose to end the exam before the time expires.

There are three types of questions on the exam:

- **Multiple Choice** These questions have a single correct answer that you indicate by selecting the appropriate check box.
- **Multiple-Multiple Choice** These questions require more than one correct answer. Indicate each correct answer by selecting the appropriate check boxes.
- **Simulations** These questions simulate actual Windows 2000 menus and dialog boxes. After reading the question, you are required to select the appropriate settings to most accurately meet the objectives for that question.

**FIGURE A-1**

The ExamSim opening page

## Saving Scores as Cookies

Your ExamSim score is stored as a browser cookie. If you've configured your browser to accept cookies, your score will be stored in a file named *History*. If your browser is not configured to accept cookies, you cannot permanently save your scores. If you delete this History cookie, the scores will be deleted permanently.

# E-Book

The entire contents of the Study Guide are provided in HTML form, as shown in Figure A-2. Although the files are optimized for Internet Explorer, they can also be viewed with other browsers including Netscape.

# CertCam

CertCam .AVI clips provide detailed examples of key certification objectives. These clips walk you step-by-step through various system configurations and are narrated

**FIGURE A-2**

Study Guide contents in HTML format

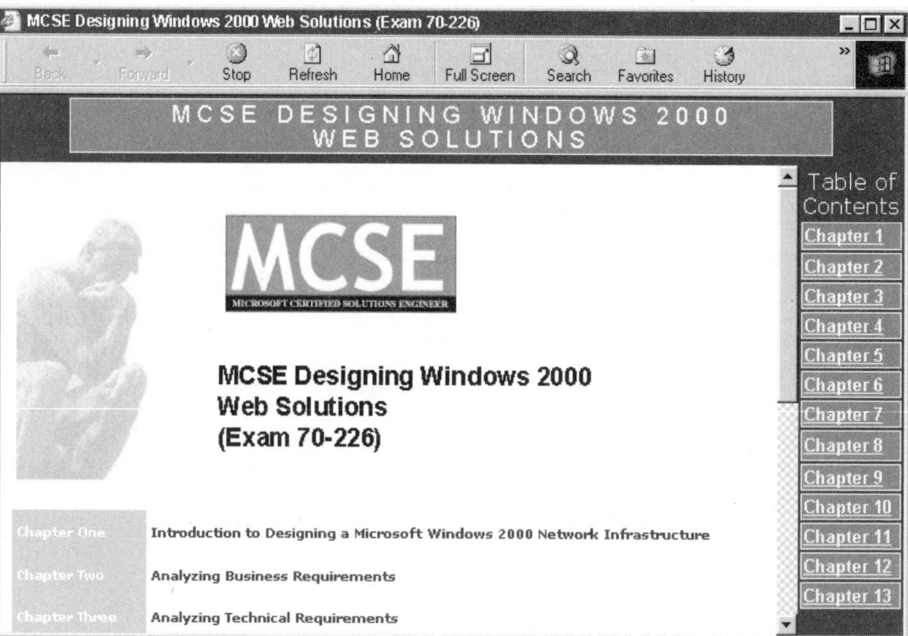

by George D. Hoffman, MCSE, MCT. You can access the clips directly from the CertCam table of contents (shown in Figure A-3) or through the CertTrainer objectives.

The CertCam .AVI clips are recorded and produced using TechSmith's Camtasia Producer. Since .AVI clips can be very large, ExamSim uses TechSmith's special AVI Codec to compress the clips. The file named tsccvid.dll is copied to your Windows\System folder when you install CertTrainer. If the .AVI clip runs with audio but no video, you may need to re-install the file from the CD-ROM. Browse to the "bin" folder and run TSCC.EXE.

# DriveTime

DriveTime audio tracks will automatically play when you insert the CD-ROM into a standard CD-ROM player, such as the one in your car or stereo. There is one

**FIGURE A-3**

The CertCam Table of Contents

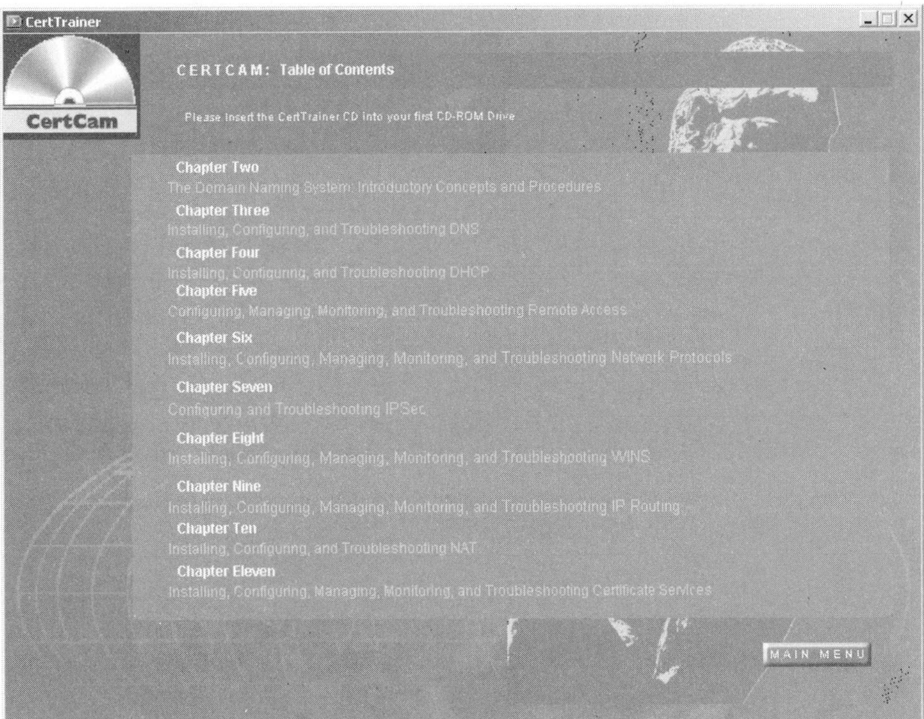

track for each chapter. These tracks provide you with certification summaries for each chapter and are the perfect way to study while commuting.

# Help

A help file is provided through a help button on the main CertTrainer screen in the lower right hand corner.

# Upgrading

A button is provided on the main ExamSim screen for upgrades. This button will take you to www.syngress.com where you can download any available upgrades.

MCSE

MICROSOFT CERTIFIED SYSTEMS ENGINEER

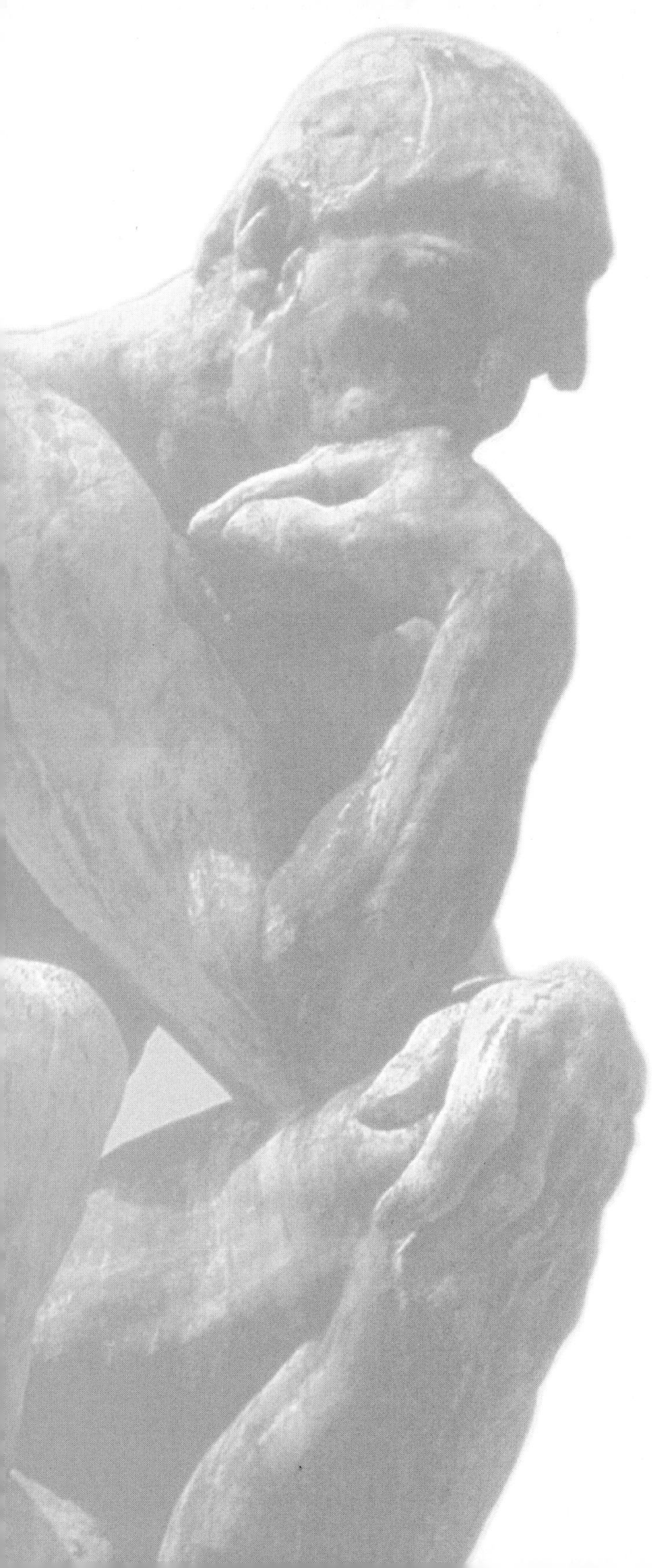

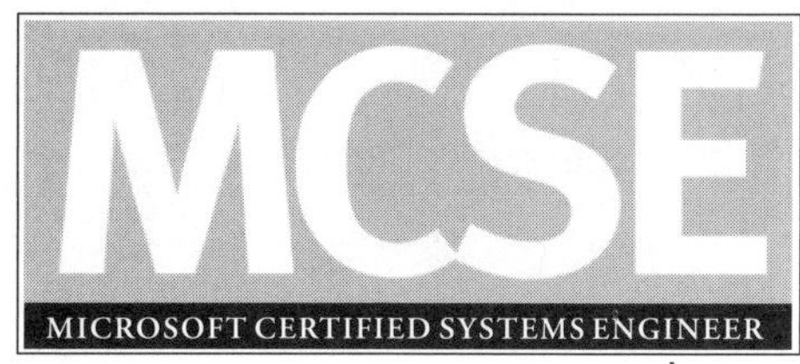

# B

# About the Web Site

At Access.Globalknowledge, the premier online information source for IT professionals (http://access.globalknowledge.com), you'll enter a Global Knowledge information portal designed to inform, educate, and update visitors on issues regarding IT and IT education.

## Get *What* You Want *When* You Want It

At the Access.Globalknowledge site, you can:

- Choose personalized technology articles related to your interests. Access a news article, a review, or a tutorial, customized to what you want to see, regularly throughout the week.
- Continue your education, in between Global courses, by taking advantage of chat sessions with other users or instructors. Get the tips, tricks, and advice that you need today!
- Make your point in the Access.Globalknowledge community by participating in threaded discussion groups related to technologies and certification.
- Get instant course information at your fingertips. Customized course calendars show you the courses you want, and when and where you want them.
- Obtain the resources you need with online tools, trivia, skills assessment, and more!

All this and more is available now on the Web at

http://access.globalknowledge.com.

Visit today!

# Glossary

**Access Control List (ACL)** The part of a security descriptor that allows or disallows access to the object based on permissions the owner of the object has set.

**Access token (or security token)** An object that uniquely identifies the user who has logged on to the network.

**Account lockout** A security feature that locks a user account if the number of failed logon attempts exceeds those specified in the account lockout policy. Locked accounts cannot log on to the network.

**Account policy** The account policy controls the way passwords work on all user accounts in a domain or on an individual computer. The policy defines minimum length of password, frequency of password change, and reuse of old passwords.

**ACL** *See* Access Control List.

**Active-active** In NLB, active-active is a state in which no node sits idle.

**Active Directory** Active Directory is the directory service available with Windows 2000 Server.

**Address Resolution Protocol (ARP)** An IP that maps Internet addresses dynamically to the actual addresses on a LAN.

**Administrator privilege** One of three privilege levels you can assign to a Windows NT user account. Guest and User are the other two privilege levels available.

**Alerts** Alerts are notifications that inform you when a particular performance threshold has been exceeded.

**Alert View** Alert View is used to monitor counters based on a threshold value rather than showing a continuous display of the value of the counter.

**Application log** The Application log provides information on events that are logged by various programs running on the system. These include both programs that are started by Windows 2000 Server when it boots up and applications that are started manually.

**Archive bit** An archive bit is an attribute of a file and is used to indicate whether or not files need to be backed up.

**ARP** *See* Address Resolution Protocol.

**Array** *See* Redundant Array of Inexpensive Disks.

**Array controller** An array controller is an interface card that connects to both hard disks using a SCSI cable and has the configuration information on the logical disk that is created.

**Auditing** Auditing tracks the activities of users by recording selected events in the security log.

**Audit policy** The audit policy defines the types of security events that will be logged for servers of a domain, or for an individual computer.

**Authentication** The process of validating the identity of a user for the purpose of accessing network resources.

**Automatic client configuration** Automatic client configuration (also known as *automatic IP addressing*) is an addressing technique used only by Windows 2000 Professional and Windows 98 clients when they are unable to contact a DHCP server. The clients automatically assign themselves an IP address in the range 169.254.0.0 with a subnet mask of 255.255.0.0.

**Automatic IP addressing** *See* Automatic client configuration.

**Automatic Private IP Addressing (APIPA)** A self-allocation process wherein a Windows 2000 client, which has been configured to obtain an IP address automatically and does not get a response from a DHCP server, allocates itself an address.

**Bandwidth** Bandwidth is the speed or data capacity of a network connection.

**Basic Input/Output System (BIOS)** The BIOS is a small chip inside the computer responsible for informing the processor(s) which devices are present in the system and how to communicate with those devices.

**BIOS** *See* Basic Input/Output System *and* NetBEUI.

**Boot partition** The volume that contains the Windows NT operating system and supporting files. The boot partition can be the same as the system partition (but does not *have* to be the same).

**Bottleneck** A condition that limits one part of the system from performing optimally.

**Broadcast packets** Broadcast packets can be employed to see if a computer on the local subnet is using a particular NetBIOS name. A computer sends out a name query broadcast packet containing the NetBIOS name for which it wants an IP address. If a computer using the queried name receives the packet, it replies with a name query response.

**Built-in groups** Default groups provided with Windows NT Server that have been granted a set of commonly used rights and capabilities for a particular group of users.

**Bus mastering** Bus mastering is a method of quickly moving large amounts of data to and from system memory. This method is a form of direct memory access, or DMA, which relies on special hardware to move data directly to and from system RAM without processor intervention. Bus mastering is the highest-performance DMA type.

**Cache memory** Memory that stores frequently accessed random access memory (RAM) locations and the addresses of where this data is stored.

**Capacity** Capacity refers to the number of users or transactions that can be supported.

**Central Processing Unit (CPU)** A CPU is a chip with a number of transistors and is used to move and calculate data within the personal computer (PC).

**Certificates** Certificates verify the user or company's identity to other users and/or companies that are not actual members of the same domain by having an Active Directory user account. Certificates are assigned by a Certificate Authority (CA), which will verify the certificate owner's identity to others on the Internet.

**Checkpoint Manager** The Checkpoint Manager is responsible for checking registry keys on a node whenever a resource is brought online and for writing data to the quorum resource when the resource goes offline. This ensures that the Cluster Services can recover from a resource failure.

**CLB** *See* Component Load Balancing.

**Client affinity** Feature that creates a direct one-to-one mapping between a particular client and server so that traffic from this client always goes to that particular server.

**Clusters** Clusters are groups of servers configured to work together as a single server or entity.

**COM Components** Blocks of reusable code that can be used to perform a task or series of tasks.

**Communications Manager** The Communications Manager uses remote procedure calls (RPCs) to maintain communication between nodes within a cluster. The Communications Manager provides guaranteed, one-time message delivery between nodes in their correct order and guarantees that any messages sent by offline nodes will be ignored.

**Component Load Balancing** Component Load Balancing (CLB) uses a routing list and a server response table to pass the COM+ application request through a COM+ cluster, enabling the load balancing of COM+ components.

**Component Object Model (COM)** Microsoft's component architecture software, it creates a structure to aid in constructing routines to be retrieved and executed.

**Configuration Database Manager** The Configuration Database Manager carries out the functions needed to maintain the cluster configuration database. All the information about the physical and logical objects in the cluster is contained in the configuration database. Any changes made to the configuration of the cluster—whether addition or subtraction of a node, relocation of a resource, or change in an IP address—are all written to the configuration database.

**Convergence** Convergence is a process used to stabilize a cluster if one server becomes unavailable or a new server is added to the cluster. The server with the highest priority is then designated the default host and handles client requests.

**Copy backup** Copies all selected files, but does not mark files as having been backed up.

**Cost** *See* Hop count.

**Counter logs** Counter logs obtain and store data collected by specified counters.

**Counters** Counters are items associated with resources and services on the system that are used to control the system elements that System Monitor is to watch.

**CPU** *See* Central Processing Unit.

**Daily backup** Copies all selected files that have been modified the day of the backup.

**Data backup** Data backups are copies of data written to a tape or other storage device. Using a backup program, files are archived to a medium that can be stored in another location.

**DC** *See* Domain controller.

**DDNS** See Dynamic Domain Name System.

**Demilitarized Zone** *Demilitarized zone* or *DMZ* refers to a place on a network where hosts are both visible to the Internet and separate from the rest of the network. Commonly, DMZs are used for securing Web, Internet mail, and FTP servers while giving them accessibility from the Internet. A DMZ is usually a separate network "grown" from a firewall or router interface that is not routed to or through an enterprise's private network.

**Default gateway** The intermediate device on the network that has knowledge of other networks. Packets destined for remote networks are passed through the default gateway.

**Default groups** Groups provided with Windows NT Server that have been granted a set of commonly used rights and capabilities for a particular group of users.

**Denial of Service attack** Type of attack where a system is overloaded with requests, is attempting to handle these requests, and cannot handle any new requests.

**Device driver** A program designed to enable a specific hardware device to communicate with the operating system.

**Dfs** *See* Distributed File System.

**DHCP** *See* Dynamic Host Configuration Protocol.

**DHCP IP address acquisition process** Four-phase process responsible for DHCP dynamic address allocation. The four phases are actually four "conversations" that take place between the client and the DHCP server. They are: Discover (DHCPDISCOVER), Offer (DHCPOFFER), Request (DHCPREQUEST), and Acknowledgment (DHCPACK). If the address assignment process is not successful, the fourth phase is a negative acknowledgment (DHCPNACK).

**Diagnostic tools** Diagnostic tools are used to troubleshoot your computer and detect possible problems. Such tools may be included with the computer itself, available through the operating system installed on it, or added separately as utilities and software packages.

**Dictionary attack** A dictionary attack is a program that will use a database of words to uncover a password. If the password is found, then the user can gain access to the Intranet as often he wishes.

**Differential backup** Copies those files created or changed since the last normal or incremental backup.

**Digital Audio Tape (DAT)** The DAT drive was created by Sony and Philips for recording music in a digital format, but was found to be useful for recording data in backups. With this method, data is stored on 4 mm tapes. DAT is not as fast as DLT, and doesn't provide as large a storage capacity. However, it is less expensive than DLT, which makes DAT a popular method of tape backup.

**Digital Data Storage (DDS)** The DDS format uses a process similar to that used in VCRs to store data on the DAT tape. It uses a helical scan, in which read/write heads spin diagonally across a DAT tape. Two read heads and two write heads are used. When data is written, the read heads verify that data has been written correctly to the tape. If it detects any errors, the data is rewritten.

**Directory database** The database of security information containing user account names, passwords, and security settings. Also called the Security Accounts Manager (SAM).

**Disabled** Filtering mode available in Network Load Balancing that serves to block all network traffic for an associated port rule from being handled by any cluster host.

**Disk quotas** Disk quotas are a feature of the Windows 2000 operating system whereby an administrator can limit the amount of storage space to a specified amount per user. This allocation of space can be performed only on volumes formatted with the NTFS file system.

**Disk striping with parity** Disk striping (with parity), also known as RAID5, provides the performance of RAID0, but with fault tolerance. Disk striping consists of data being written in stripes across a volume that has been created from areas of free space. These areas are all the same size and spread over an array of 3 to 32 disks. The primary benefit of striping is that disk I/O is split between disks, improving performance, although improvements do not exceed the I/O capabilities of the disk controllers. Fault tolerance functionality is added to disk striping with the addition of parity information in one of the stripes. The parity stripe is the exclusive OR (XOR) of all the data values for the data stripes in the stripe. If no disks in the stripe set with parity have failed, the new parity for a write can be calculated without having to read the corresponding stripes from the other data disks.

**Dispatcher** A dispatcher is typically software with multiple components that are meant to coordinate, monitor, and distribute TCP traffic to hosts on a network.

**Distributed File System (Dfs)** A network server component that allows files to span multiple file servers in order to better manage enterprise data and storage resources.

**DMZ** *See* Demilitarized zone.

**DNS** *See* Domain Name System.

**DNS name servers** The servers containing information about a portion of the DNS database, providing name resolution across the Internet.

**Domain** A collection of computers that share a common directory database. (2) A domain is also a partition of Active Directory that contains users, computers, servers, groups, and other resource objects.

**Domain controller** Domain controllers (DCs) are used to authenticate users. The first server designated as a DC on a new network creates the domain.

**Domain master browser** The domain master browser receives lists from every master browser in a network that consists of several subnets. The lists are used to produce a single list of all resources on the network. This single list is then copied back to the master browsers. There is only one domain master browser on a network.

**Domain Namespace** Naming scheme consisting of a hierarchical and logical tree structure on which DNS is based. This structure, stored as a database, is called the domain namespace.

**Domain Name System (DNS)** The service that provides domain name resolution for TCP/IP hosts.

**Dual-homed servers** Servers that can be equipped with two NICs to be used on the same network, advertising the same services.

**Duplexing** Of all the types of RAID, RAID1 (or mirroring) and RAID5 are the most often implemented. When configuring RAID1, two disks are installed, along with one or two controllers. When two controllers are used, it is called *duplexing*. Duplexing ensures fault tolerance not just with data, but also with the disk controller. With traditional mirroring, there is one disk controller. If the controller fails, the server is down until that component is replaced. Duplexing allows the use of a second controller.

**Dynamic Host Configuration Protocol (DHCP)** A protocol used to automatically assign IP addresses to computers on a network.

**Dynamic Domain Name System (DDNS)** Dynamic Domain Name System (DDNS) allows computers to register their own names and IP addresses mapping in a DNS server. This reduces administrative overhead.

**Dynamic Volumes** Dynamic volumes are a new type of disk partition supported by Windows 2000. Dynamic volumes are more flexible than traditional partitioning and support software-level RAID.

**EFS** *See* Encrypting File System.

**Encrypting File System (EFS)** A new feature of Windows 2000 that allows for the encryption of files on a server.

**Encryption** The process of making data indecipherable to protect it from unauthorized access and viewing.

**Ethernet** A networking protocol linking up to 1,024 nodes in a bus topology. Has been used by DEC and 3Com. *See also* Fast Ethernet.

**Event log** Most event logs are simply files of text written to the hard disk. Almost always, an event log is saved in the partition that is most easily available if the network operating system didn't boot. This is usually the system partition for the server. In the case of NetWare, you can find log information stored on the DOS partition.

**Event Log Manager** The Event Log Manager is responsible for replicating event log entries from one node to all other nodes in a cluster.

**Event Processor** The Event Processor's task is to facilitate communication between applications and Cluster Services components running on each node of a cluster. This is the mechanism that Cluster Services use to pass information about important events to all other components of a cluster.

**Event Viewer** Tool provided in Windows NT that can be used to monitor, troubleshoot, and optimize the system. Essentially contains three logs available for viewing: system, security, and application. Event Viewer can also be used to view logs on other computers.

**Extended Industry Standard Architecture** The Extended Industry Standard Architecture (EISA) bus is an updated version of the ISA bus, originally designed for use with the 80386, 80486, and Pentium processors. EISA buses, like PCI buses, are 32-bits wide and support multiprocessing.

**Extensible Markup Language (XML)** Programming language that allows Web developers to create customized tags allowing content to be organized and delivered more efficiently. Basically a simplified version of SGML, some believe it may one day replace HTML.

**Failover** Failover is the ability of the inactive unit of redundant components to take over the functions of the primary unit in the event of failure of the primary unit.

**Failover clustering** Arrangement in which client connections are only provided by a primary server in the cluster. If the primary server fails, the secondary server detects the failure and takes over the primary server's tasks.

**Failover Manager** The Failover Manager is responsible for starting and stopping resources, managing resource dependencies, and initiating failover of resource groups. The Failover Manager makes decisions on which resources to start, stop, or move based on the resource and system information it receives from the Node Manager and from Resource Monitors. The Failover Manager is also responsible for deciding resource group ownership.

**Fast Ethernet** A LAN access method that runs at 100 Mbps. Ethernet runs at 10 Mbps, and Gigabit Ethernet runs at 1000 Mbps.

**Fault tolerance** Fault tolerance is the ability of a component, or an entire system, to continue normal operations even in the event of a hardware or software failure. Usually, fault tolerance is implemented through redundant components. Thus, the disaster is prevented even though a failure has taken place. In Windows

NT, fault tolerance is provided by the Ftdisk.sys driver and is implemented via mirror and stripe sets.

**Fiber channel arbitrary loop (FC-AL) SANs** The most common fiber-channel-based SANs.

**File allocation table (FAT)** A list maintained by some operating systems to track segments of the disk. Both FAT and NTFS are supported in Windows NT.

**File level permissions** These can be assigned on an NTFS partition by anyone with Owner or Administrator access. By default, each file and folder has the group Everyone assigned the full control permission. When assigning file permissions, there are five levels to choose from: No access, Read, Change, Full Control, and Special Access.

**File system cache** The working set of the file system is the *file system cache*, an area set aside in physical memory where the file system stores its frequently used and recently used data.

**File Transfer Protocol (FTP)** Supports the transferring of files between local and remote computers. FTP is implemented as part of the Internet Information Service (IIS) in Windows NT.

**Firewall** A system that protects the boundary between two or more networks, and keeps intruders out of private networks.

**Flooding switch ports** When the cluster host is connected to a hub to receive requests, and all traffic is automatically sent to all switch ports.

**Forest** An Active Directory forest is the largest unit of Active Directory. It contains member domains, a common global catalog, plus a common schema and configuration.

**Full backup** Full backups are used to back up all directories and files on a volume, or all the volumes on a server. Depending on the amount of data being saved to a server, a full backup should be performed on a weekly or monthly basis. If tapes are filling quickly and important data is changing rapidly, then a full backup should be performed at least once a week. When a full backup is performed, the file is changed to indicate it has been backed up.

**Gateway** Translates different protocols for heterogeneous networks. Translates transport protocols or data formats.

**Gateway Services for NetWare (GSNW)** A service in Windows NT that allows Windows-based clients to access resources on a Netware server through the gateway.

**Global Catalog** The global catalog is the index of partial information about users, groups, and other resource objects that exists in every domain in a single forest.

**Global Update Manager** The Global Update Manager is used by the Configuration Database Manager to replicate cluster changes to the cluster configuration database across all nodes. Any node that does not commit the replicated information from the Global Update Manager to its configuration is forced out of the cluster and put offline.

**Graphical User Interface (GUI)** An interface on a computer screen that uses both words and pictures.

**Group** A *group* in clustering technology is a unit of failover within the environment.

**GUI** *See* Graphical User Interface.

**Hard page fault** A fault that occurs when a program needs data that is neither in its working set in the main memory nor anywhere else in physical memory, and yet data must be retrieved from the disk.

**Hashing Algorithm** The Hashing Algorithm is a formula used to take the username, password, and string sent to the user's PC and come up with another value or set of values that the Server can perform using the same algorithm, and determining that the username and password are identical.

**High-availability networks** High-availability networks are networks that serve customers with 99.999 percent reliability.

**Hop count** Distance measured between two points on the Internet by the number of routers you must traverse to arrive at the desired destination. This distance is also known as the *cost*.

**Host ID** The host ID identifies the specific host on the network.

**Host name** A host name is used to identify a computer to TCP/IP applications. It can be up to 255 characters long and can contain alphanumeric characters and hyphens. It can also be either a single word (or alias) or use the Domain Naming System; for example, www (an alias) or www.syngress.com (using DNS).

**Hyperlink** Hyperlinks are links in Web pages that take you to another HTML document or Web site, or to another spot in the same document. Though hyperlinks can sometimes appear as pictures, they are typically embedded in a document as text that has been underlined and colored (often in blue).

**Hypertext Markup Language (HTML)** A markup language using ASCII text files with embedded codes denoting formatting and hypertext links.

**Hypertext Transport Protocol (HTTP)** The protocol by which clients and servers communicate on the World Wide Web (WWW). It is an application level protocol.

**Incremental backup** Copies only those files created or changed since the last normal or incremental backup.

**Industry Standard Architecture** The Industry Standard Architecture, or ISA, bus is found in virtually all computers. Based on older IBM XT computer architecture, today it is being replaced by the PCI bus. Many computer systems, however, still use the ISA bus for slower peripherals that do not require the fast throughput the PCI bus provides.

**Input/Output (I/O) address** One type of computer resource is the I/O address. When the computer is started, the BIOS loads into RAM device-specific information about the existing devices, including their drivers and other rules of communication. Whenever the processor needs to communicate with a device in the computer, it first checks RAM for the entries pertaining to that device. Without an I/O address, components would appear nonexistent to the processor.

**Internet Authentication Service (IAS)** The Internet Authentication Service (IAS) is an authentication and registration service integrated with Windows NT security when installed. IAS works by checking the user's identity (when they log in to the system) against a user account database.

**Internet Protocol (IP)** The protocol used to execute the network layer of communications (layer three). This protocol accepts packets from layer 4 (transport layer) and sends them to layer 2 (data link layer). *See also* Transmission Control Protocol/Internet Protocol.

**Internet Information Server (IIS)** A file and application server that supports multiple Internet-related protocols including HTML and HTTP.

**Internet Protocol (IP)** The messenger protocol that is part of the TCP/IP suite of protocols, responsible for addressing and sending TCP packets over the network.

**Internet Protocol Security (IPSec)** Internet Protocol Security (IPSec), which is used in VPNs, is a method of securing data at the packet level. This means that data is secure as it is being transmitted across an internetwork.

**Internet service provider (ISP)** A company or institution that provides Internet access to remote users via dial-up or leased lines.

**Intersite replication** Type of replication that occurs between DCs in different sites. You should be aware of a number of other differences between the two. With intersite replication, data is always compressed, so the amount of data transferred is reduced 88 to 90 percent.

**Intranet** A TCP/IP network using Internet technology that is typically internal to a company and not connected directly to the Internet.

**Intrasite replication** Type of replication that occurs between DCs within a site. With intrasite replication, data that is replicated isn't compressed and, by default, replication occurs every five minutes.

**I/O address** *See* Input/Output address.

**IP** *See* Internet Protocol.

**IP address** An address used to identify each device on a network and to specify routing information. Each IP address on a network must be unique.

**IP blocking** IP blocking blocks or grants access based on a single IP address, whole subnets, or even domain names.

**IP router** A component connected to two or more physical TCP/IP networks that can deliver IP packets between networks.

**IPSec** *See* Internet Protocol Security.

**IPX/SPX** A set of transport protocols used by Novell NetWare networks. Windows NT implements this protocol using NWLink.

**Kerberos** Kerberos is a secure authentication method developed at the Massachusetts Institute of Technology (MIT). In the Kerberos method, a user is granted a ticket, which enables that user to access network resources and services.

**L2TP** See Layer 2 Tunneling Protocol.

**LAN** *See* Local area network.

**Layer 2 Tunneling Protocol (L2TP)** Layer 2 Tunneling Protocol (L2TP) is used for VPNs. It creates a tunnel through the Internet through which secure data can pass.

**LDAP** *See* Lightweight Directory Access Protocol.

**Lightweight Directory Access Protocol (LDAP)** Lightweight Directory Access Protocol (LDAP) is the primary access protocol for Active Directory.

**Linux** An Open Source implementation of Unix, which can run on many different hardware platforms. *See* Unix.

**Load weighting** Load weighting is the parameter that determines how much traffic a single cluster host is configured to filter or process for a particular port rule when a cluster is employing multiple host filtering mode.

**Local area network (LAN)** A system using high-speed connections over high-performance cables to communicate among computers within a few miles of each other.

**LogicalDisk** LogicalDisk exposes counters associated with local drives and storage volumes.

**Log Manager** The Log Manager works with the Checkpoint Manager to ensure that the recovery log on the quorum resource contains the most up-to-date configuration data and change checkpoints.

**Master boot record (MBR)** The MBR is an area on the hard disk that contains the partition table for the disk and a small amount of executable code to begin the boot process.

**Membership Manager** The Membership Manager helps maintain cluster membership as well as monitoring the health of member nodes in the cluster.

**Memory** Considered the primary storage area on a computer. *See also* Cache memory.

**Micro Channel Architecture** Micro Channel Architecture (MCA) was designed by IBM to replace the older AT bus. It competed with the EISA bus, but was a proprietary architecture. For a variety of reasons, it never became popular in the industry and is now seen only in older machines.

**Microsoft Management Console (MMC)** Windows 2000 provides the Performance Console as a method of monitoring performance on local and remote computers. This console is actually the Microsoft Management Console (MMC) with two snap-ins installed: System Monitor and Performance Logs and Alerts.

**Mirror set** For the selected disk, an identical copy of the data is written to a second disk called a shadow disk, providing fault tolerance.

**Mirroring** One of the more common ways to back up your data is to create a mirrored copy of the data on another disk. The mirroring system utilizes a code that duplicates everything written on one hard disk to another hard disk, making them identical. The best way to incorporate disk mirroring is at the hardware level with what is known as an array controller.

**MMC** *See* Microsoft Management Console.

**Modem** *See* Modulator/demodulator.

**Modulator/demodulator (modem)** Modems are responsible for transmitting data to and from the computer.

**Motherboard** The main component in computers, holding the processor as well as a host of other chips. These boards have many functions built into them, including parallel and serial ports, USB ports, memory, cache, power management, and BIOS (Basic Input/Output System).

**Multicast mode** Mode employed by NLB for handling network traffic. Multicast mode alleviates the need for a second NIC by assigning a Layer 2 multicast address to the cluster based on the primary IP address of the cluster. As a result, each cluster member retains its original address. Both the unicast and multicast MAC addresses are derived from the primary IP address of the cluster.

**Multimaster Replication** Replication, or synchronization, of the objects within the domain partitions and the global catalog is considered "multimaster." Each DC is considered a master, or authoritative, for the information in its partition. When the DCs replicate, the objects are updated between the DCs. If two DCs have conflicting updates for the same object, multimaster replication uses an algorithm to determine which update is the latest.

**Multiple host** Filtering mode available in Network Load Balancing that specifies multiple cluster hosts will handle the traffic for the particular port rule.

**(N-1)-way failover** In NLB (network load balancing), in a cluster with a number of hosts equaling *N*, all but one host must fail for load balancing to fail.

**Name resolution** Before the client computer can begin communicating with the destination computer, a name must be converted to an IP address. This process is called name resolution.

**NAT** See Network Address Translation.

**NetBEUI** A network protocol used in small networks. NetBEUI cannot be routed. *See* NetBIOS Extended User Interface.

**NetBIOS** NetBIOS (*Network Basic Input/Output System)* is used to provide file and printer sharing between computers. It is an application protocol rather than a network protocol and therefore relies on the presence of network protocols such as TCP/IP or NWLink to function. Within Windows NT 4.0, NetBIOS is an essential component because many network services use it. However, in a network that consists entirely of Windows 2000 computers, NetBIOS is not required.

**NetBIOS Extended User Interface (NetBEUI)** The transport layer for NetBIOS.

**Network adapter** *See* Network Interface Card.

**Network Address Translation (NAT)** Network Address Translation (NAT) enables a private network to use one set of IP addresses and translate them to a public IP address. This enables the network to have more hosts than the public IP address(es) set might support.

**Network administrator** Person responsible for establishing and maintaining a network. Tasks include: software installation, assigning passwords, making backups, system security, and restores when the system goes down.

**Network Fault Tolerance (NFT)** NFT occurs when you install two NICs; one is the active NIC, while the other only becomes active upon failure of the first NIC.

**Network Interface Card (NIC)** A network adapter is also referred to as a Network Interface Card (NIC). You can configure multiple NICs in a single server to access the same local area network if the hardware and the network operating system support it.

**Network Load Balancing (NLB)** NLB occurs when you install two or more NICs, all of which are active on the same LAN, simultaneously sharing the network traffic load.

**Network Monitor** A tool, available with Windows NT Server and Windows 2000 Server, that analyzes network traffic and can determine why certain computers are unable to communicate. The versions that come with these operating systems are limited to only analyzing activity on the local network segment.

**Network number** The network number identifies the network that any particular host is a part of.

**NFT** *See* Network Fault Tolerance.

**NIC** *See* Network Interface Card.

**NLB** *See* Network Load Balancing.

**Node** A member of a cluster.

**NT File System (NTFS)** A file system supported only in Windows NT that allows for greater management and control of file resources. All files are treated as objects with user-defined and system-defined attributes.

**Node Manager** The Node Manager runs on each node of the cluster and maintains a local list of the cluster member nodes. The Node Manager is also responsible for sending periodic heartbeat messages to the other members of the cluster to detect node failures. If a node detects a failure on another node, it broadcasts the failure to the other nodes in the cluster, and they perform what is known as a *regroup event* to verify their views of the cluster membership. The Node Manager orchestrates the moving of the resources hosted on that node to another active node or the redistribution of the resources among the surviving members of the cluster.

**Normal backup** Copies all selected files and marks each as having been backed up.

**NTFS** *See* NT File System.

**Object Manager** The Object Manager supports management of all cluster objects by allowing for search, creation, numbering, and reference counting on cluster objects.

**OEM** *See* Original Equipment Manufacturer.

**Open Systems Interconnection model (OSI)** Each layer of the TCP/IP model corresponds to one or more layers in the International Standards

Organization (ISO) seven-layer OSI model. TCP/IP layers are Application, Transport, Internet, and Network Interface. The OSI layers are Application, Presentation, Session, Transport, Network, Data Link, and Physical.

**Organizational Unit (OU)** An organizational unit (OU) is a container that can be nested into a tree within a domain. An OU can contain user, group, computer, and other objects as well as other OUs.

**Original Equipment Manufacturer (OEM)** A company that makes a product and then sells it to an authorized reseller, who either adds features to the product before reselling, renames it, or associates it with other products in their line.

**OU** *See* Organizational Unit.

**Packet filtering** Packet filtering is a function provided by routers that allows you to control what is permitted in and out of a network. You can specify which packets are routed from the internal network and which are allowed to pass on to the internal network from the Internet.

**Packet Internet Groper (PING)** *See* PING.

**Performance Monitor (PERFMON)** PERFMON is a tool used for monitoring performance issues on a Windows NT Server. It provides four methods of monitoring various components of NT: Report View, Chart View, Alert View, and Log View.

**Peripheral Component Interconnect** The Peripheral Component Interconnect, or PCI, is a bus type found in most computers today. Though the PCI bus is a 64-bit bus, it is often implemented as a 32-bit bus, and runs at a clock speed of 33MHz or 66MHz. Being a fairly fast bus type, many peripheral controllers utilize the PCI bus for faster throughput. As a result, PCI has become increasingly popular, making it the *de facto* standard today.

**PhysicalDisk** PhysicalDisk exposes counters for monitoring the physical hard disk.

**PING (Packet Internet Groper)** A command used to verify connections to one or more remote hosts (computers).

**Point-to-Point Tunneling Protocol (PPTP)** A secure networking technology that supports multiprotocol virtual private networks (VPNs).

**Point-to-Point Protocol (PPP)** A standard for dial-up telephone connections of computers to the Internet.

**POP3** *See* Post Office Protocol 3.

**Pop-up message** Pop-up messages are messages that will pop-up on a user's screen. Such messages may appear on every workstation, or be directed to a specific user. If you can designate where the pop-up message will appear, you may have the ability to direct the message to a specific IP address or user account.

**Post Office Protocol 3 (POP3)** Specific rules through which mail can be received from a mail server by a client machine.

**Primary domain controller (PDC)** In a Windows NT Server domain, a server that authenticates domain logons and maintains the directory database for a domain. This database is replicated to BDCs.

**Primary zone** A primary zone contains the records managed by the DNS server that is authoritative for those records.

**Protocol isolation topology** Protocol isolation topology separates the Internet from the internal network using separate protocols.

**Proxy server** Provides access to files from other servers by pulling them from either its local cache or from the remote server.

**Quorum resource** The quorum resource is a physical disk resource on the common storage resource for the cluster, which stores the list of services in the resource group, their configuration, and the members of the cluster that contribute to the resources group, as well as the configuration of the entire cluster.

**RAID** *See* Redundant Array of Inexpensive Disks.

**RAID0** Disk striping without parity. Data is spread across all disks in an array. No redundant information is stored on other disks, so no fault tolerance is provided.

**RAID1** Disk mirroring. Everything is duplicated on another hard disk. Windows 2000 Server supports disk mirroring.

**RAID2** Disk striping across multiple disks. Error-correction codes are maintained across all disks. RAID2 isn't as efficient as other levels of RAID that provide fault tolerance, and for that reason it isn't commonly used.

**RAID3** Disk striping across multiple disks. Error-correction codes are stored on one disk. Because all parity information is written to a single disk, it creates a write bottleneck, and all parity information will be lost if the disk containing that information fails.

**RAID4** Disk striping across multiple disks. This is similar to RAID3 but writes the information in larger blocks. Like RAID3, this level creates a write bottleneck, and all parity information will be lost if the disk containing that information fails.

**RAID5** Disk striping with parity. Data is written across all disks in the array, and parity information is also written across all disks in the array. Windows 2000 supports this level of RAID.

**RAID controller** A RAID controller handles the creation and regeneration of redundant information for the array.

**Random access memory (RAM)** The memory of a computer that is used while running applications or working on system files. Random access means various files and memory portions can be accessed instantly and directly, instead of having to search for the data's location, as is the case with other media such as magnetic tapes, for example, which have to be wound to the spot where the data resides. If not saved to the disk before computer shutdown, all information in RAM will be lost.

**Redundant Array of Inexpensive Disks (RAID)** A method of using disk drives in an array to provide fault tolerance and performance improvements. Windows NT supports three levels of RAID: 0, 1, and 5.

**Redundant components** Built-in components that eliminate the time spent repairing systems or replacing broken-down components

**Remote Access Service (RAS)** A service that provides remote network access to file and print services, e-mail, scheduling, and other network-based tasks.

**Remote troubleshooting** Remote troubleshooting refers to the ability to troubleshoot and resolve computer problems without having to sit at that computer. In many cases, one server on a network can be used to troubleshoot another server on the network. There are a number of services available for remote troubleshooting, such as Windows Remote Access Service (RAS) or third-party applications. These types of services provide the interface and tools for managing, configuring, and troubleshooting remote computers.

**Report View** Used to display the current value of counter data as text in a report format.

**Resource Monitors** Resource Monitors create the interface between the Cluster Services and resource dynamic link libraries (DLLs). When data is needed from a resource, Cluster Services make the request to the particular Resource Monitor for that resource, and the Monitor passes it on to the resource DLL. The reverse happens whenever a resource DLL needs to report an event to the Cluster Services. Many cluster-aware applications, such as Microsoft's DHCP Server, provide their own resource DLLs.

**Resources** The applications, disks, and other devices that participate in a cluster

**Rolling upgrade** A rolling upgrade is a process of upgrading cluster nodes, one node at a time, in such a way that services and resources offered by the cluster are always available, even though nodes being upgraded are not.

**Routing and Remote Access Service (RRAS)** The Routing and Remote Access Service enables routing over IP and IPX networks by connecting local area or wide area networks. It connects LANs or WANs without the use of other hardware.

**SACK** See Selective acknowledgments.

**SAN** See Storage Area Network.

**SCSI** *See* Small Computer System Interface.

**SDRAM** *See* Synchronous Dynamic RAM.

**Secondary zone** Secondary zones are copies of the primary DNS zone that balance out the DNS name queries for the hosts in the domain.

**Secure Sockets Layer (SSL)** A protocol used to provide secure data communications through data encryption and decryption. It utilizes public key cryptography and bulk data encryption.

**Security Accounts Manager (SAM)** A directory database that stores user account names, passwords, and security settings.

**Security identifier (SID)** A unique name used to identify a logged-on user.

**Security log** The Security log provides information on audited events. The events that are recorded in this log are determined by the audit policy that is created on your system.

**Security policy** In Windows NT Server, security policies consist of Account, User Rights, Audit, and Trust Relationship policies. They are managed via User Manager For Domains.

**Selective acknowledgments (SACK)** The ability to correctly identify and acknowledge packets that belong to a specific data transmission. SACK identifies that packets have been dropped or are out of sequence and facilitates their retransmission or re-sequencing and defragmentation.

**Server Message Block (SMB)** A file-sharing protocol that allows access to files on remote computer systems.

**Server topology** Server topology refers to the layout of servers on a Windows 2000 network.

**Shadow disk** The second disk in a mirror set that contains an exact copy of data on the primary disk, providing fault tolerance.

**Shared-nothing cluster architecture model** Model in which all devices common to the cluster are actually owned by one of the individual servers in the cluster.

**Simple Mail Transfer Protocol (SMTP)** Part of the TCP/IP suite of protocols that controls the exchange of e-mail.

**Simple Network Management Protocol (SNMP)** A protocol used to get and set status information about computers (hosts) on a TCP/IP network.

**Single host** Filtering mode available in Network Load Balancing that specifies that a single cluster host will handle network traffic for an associated port rule.

**Site** A site is a collection of well-connected IP subnets. Sites are defined by an administrator and can be configured to optimize traffic across heavily utilized, costly, low-bandwidth and wide area network (WAN) links.

**Sizing** Determining the number of Domain Controllers and Global Catalog servers required for a site.

**Small Computer System Interface (SCSI)** SCSI is the most prevalent (and preferred) interface in servers. SCSI is superior to other interfaces because it manages its own power, freeing the CPU from that type of overhead. SCSI also has its own basic input/output system (BIOS).

**Smart cards** Yet another method of providing some security to your network, smart cards are small plastic cards that have a microchip and/or a memory module embedded in them, which can store a significant amount of information. The cards are generally inserted into a special reader that reads information on the card, although some readers can scan the cards from a distance. They come in both disposable and reprogrammable formats.

**SMP** *See* Symmetric Multi-Processing.

**Snap-in** A snap-in is a module added to the MMC, allowing you to perform various functions through a central console program.

**Software RAID** Software RAIDs are implemented in the OS and take a larger toll on OS performance. They usually do not allow for Hot Swap functionality, so, if a drive fails, the server must be taken offline to replace it.

**Split-brain DNS** Split-brain DNS, or split DNS, refers to utilizing separate internal and external DNS views of a domain's network using internal and external DNS servers.

**Split DNS** *See* Split-brain DNS.

**SQL** *Structured Query Language (pronounced "S-Q-L" or "Sequel").* A language used to query, sustain, and produce relational databases.

**SQL Server** *Structured Query Language (SQL) Server.* A client/server relational database management system. SQL Server is often used with Unix, Vax, NetWare, and Windows NT and OS/2 servers.

**Storage Area Network (SAN)** Storage Area Network (SAN) is a dedicated high-speed network that consists of multiple storage devices interconnected with each other and with servers that access the data stored in the devices.

**Stripe set** A method of writing data across several physical disk drives to improve access times.

**Stripe set with parity** A method of writing data across several physical disk drives using parity. Parity is an algorithm used to regenerate data if any of the other data is lost.

**Striping** The striping of data is a way to spread the data across the disks. This can improve performance. To do striping properly, a minimum of three hard disks is needed. Three or more different hard disks all acting to get a piece of the data will make the input/output (I/O) faster. Striping also gives you the option of adding parity to the drive set. *See also* Disk striping with parity.

**Subnet** A portion of a network that shares a network address with other parts of the network, but has a distinct subnet number.

**Subnet mask** Component of a TCP/IP address, which, when used with the address, enables a user to determine whether a host belongs to a local or a remote network. The subnet mask consists of two parts: the network portion and the host portion. In the subnet mask, the network portion is the part that consists of all 1s, and the host portion is the part that contains all the 0s.

**Subsystem** Subsystems hold multiple disks, which can be configured as separate disk drives, or as a single RAID array, or some combination of these. *See also* Redundant Array of Inexpensive Disks.

**Symmetric Multi-Processing (SMP) units** Many server platforms support more than one processor. Symmetric indicates that these servers distribute a symmetrical load across the processors in the machine. Each vendor's SMP server platforms have different percentages of actual contributed processing power as more CPUs are added.

**Synchronous Dynamic RAM (SDRAM)** Synchronous DRAM is a generic name for various kinds of dynamic random access memory. SDRAM is synchronized with the CPU speed and thus provides better performance. SDRAM is rated in MHz rather than nanoseconds to more easily compare the CPU speed to the RAM speed. Mounted in 64-bit wide 168 pin DIMMs. SDRAM has an access time of eight nanoseconds to 12 nanoseconds.

**Syskey utility** This security tool utilizes a system key to highly encrypt the information contained in the Security Accounts Manager (SAM) database.

**System Area Network** A System Area Network is the network that a SAN runs over. It allows any server or cluster attached to it to access any of the components of the SAN.

**System default profile** The user profile that is loaded when Windows NT is running but no user is logged on.

**System Log** The System log provides information that is logged by Windows 2000 itself. This information is generated by components that run on the server and reports errors on various drivers and system software that failed to load on startup or experienced problems when running.

**System Monitor** System Monitor allows you to monitor resource utilization and network throughput. It provides a visual representation of the counters being watched, and allows viewing of real-time and previously logged data about areas of its system and network.

**System partition** The location of the hardware-specific files needed to load Windows NT.

**System policy** A policy created using the System Policy Editor to control the user work environment.

**Task Manager** A tool provided in Windows NT to help monitor and optimize performance. It can be used to view applications, processes, and performance.

**Tape backup** Tape backups are the most common method of backing up data. With this method, magnetic tapes are used to store data sequentially. These tapes are similar to those used in micro-cassette recorders, which require you to fast-forward and reverse the tape to find what you want. This sequential access to archived data makes it slow to restore data, as the device must cue up the tape to where the data are located. However, the cost to purchase such tapes is minimal, with each tape costing a few dollars. This makes tapes a popular method of data recovery.

**TCA** *See* Transaction cost analysis.

**TCP fast retransmit** A timer setting in TCP that waits for acknowledgments of packets passed down to IP. If an acknowledgment is not received in time, the packet is resent.

**TCP/IP** *See* Transmission Control Protocol/Internet Protocol.

**Trace logs** Trace logs are different from counter logs in that they don't obtain data at regular update intervals. Instead, they log data when certain events occur. For example, a trace log might gather data when a page fault occurs. It monitors the activities you specify, and when a page fault happens, it stores the information in a log file.

**Transaction cost analysis (TCA)** Process that attempts to diminish the vagueness of capacity planning by providing a structure for estimating each resource cost as a function of a usage profile, service mix, or hardware configuration.

**Transitive Trusts** Trusts between Active Directory domains are transitive so that if Domain A trusts Domain B, and Domain B trusts Domain C, then Domain A also trusts Domain C.

**Transmission Control Protocol/Internet Protocol (TCP/IP)** A suite of networking protocols that allows communication across interconnected networks.

**Unicast Mode** Mode employed by NLB for handling network traffic. In unicast mode, NLB changes the Media Access Control (MAC) address of its cluster adapter and uses the same changed address as the MAC address for all the network adapters for all the hosts in the cluster. This makes the entire cluster look like one host to the network and allows all the members of the cluster to receive all incoming packets at the network adapter level and pass them to NLB for filtering.

**Uninterruptible Power Supply (UPS)** A UPS is a large battery. In the event of a power failure, the UPS kicks in and supplies power to the server.

**Universal Serial Bus (USB)** USB technology allows the user to add multiple external peripherals (e.g., printers, hard disks, modems, scanners, and so on) to a single port, without the conflicts associated with serial and parallel connections of the past.

**Unix** Originally designed for minicomputers, then revised for use on mainframes and personal computers, Unix is a multiuser, multitask operating system compatible with several computer platforms.

**User default profile** The user profile that is loaded by a server when a user's specific profile cannot be loaded.

**VBScript** Scripting language based on the Visual Basic (VB) programming language, but is much simpler and is similar to JavaScript. Using VBScript, you can add scrollbars, buttons, and other interactive features to Web pages.

**Virtual private network (VPN)** A virtual network created using the Point-to-Point Tunneling Protocol (PPTP) that provides for secure network connectivity from a remote location.

**Virtual servers** Virtual servers are representations of each application or service that the servers in a cluster advertise to clients.

**VPN** See Virtual private network.

**WAN** *See* Wide Area Network.

**WCAT** *See* Web Capacity Analysis Tool.

**Web Capacity Analysis Tool (WCAT)** Tool provided by Microsoft that runs simulated workloads on client/server configurations. With WCAT, you can test how your IIS and network configuration respond to a variety of client requests for information. You can use results of these load tests to determine the server and network configuration for your Web server. WCAT is designed to evaluate how Internet servers respond to various client workload simulations.

**Wide Area Network (WAN)** A network using high-speed long-distance common-carrier circuits or satellites to cover a large geographic area.

**Windows Load Balancing Service** In Microsoft's Windows Load Balancing Service (WLBS), two or more servers work together to service the network traffic from the Internet.

**WLBS** *See* Windows Load Balancing Service.

**Zone** A group of domains managed from a single DNS is called a zone. A zone is a portion of the DNS database that is responsible for domains contained within it. Zones are classified as either primary or secondary.

# INDEX

## A



## B

## D

## N



## O



## P

## T

## W

## INTERNATIONAL CONTACT INFORMATION


**AUSTRALIA**
McGraw-Hill Book Company Australia Pty. Ltd.
TEL +61-2-9417-9899
FAX +61-2-9417-5687
http://www.mcgraw-hill.com.au
books-it_sydney@mcgraw-hill.com

**CANADA**
McGraw-Hill Ryerson Ltd.
TEL +905-430-5000
FAX +905-430-5020
http://www.mcgrawhill.ca

**GREECE, MIDDLE EAST, NORTHERN AFRICA**
McGraw-Hill Hellas
TEL +30-1-656-0990-3-4
FAX +30-1-654-5525

**MEXICO (Also serving Latin America)**
McGraw-Hill Interamericana Editores S.A. de C.V.
TEL +525-117-1583
FAX +525-117-1589
http://www.mcgraw-hill.com.mx
fernando_castellanos@mcgraw-hill.com

**SINGAPORE (Serving Asia)**
McGraw-Hill Book Company
TEL +65-863-1580
FAX +65-862-3354
http://www.mcgraw-hill.com.sg
mghasia@mcgraw-hill.com

**SOUTH AFRICA**
McGraw-Hill South Africa
TEL +27-11-622-7512
FAX +27-11-622-9045
robyn_swanepoel@mcgraw-hill.com

**UNITED KINGDOM & EUROPE (Excluding Southern Europe)**
McGraw-Hill Education Europe
TEL +44-1-628-502500
FAX +44-1-628-770224
http://www.mcgraw-hill.co.uk
computing_neurope@mcgraw-hill.com

**ALL OTHER INQUIRIES Contact:**
Osborne/McGraw-Hill
TEL +1-510-549-6600
FAX +1-510-883-7600
http://www.osborne.com
omg_international@mcgraw-hill.com

## Custom Corporate Network Training

**Train on Cutting Edge Technology** We can bring the best in skill-based training to your facility to create a real-world hands-on training experience. Global Knowledge has invested millions of dollars in network hardware and software to train our students on the same equipment they will work with on the job. Our relationships with vendors allow us to incorporate the latest equipment and platforms into your on-site labs.

**Maximize Your Training Budget** Global Knowledge provides experienced instructors, comprehensive course materials, and all the networking equipment needed to deliver high quality training. You provide the students; we provide the knowledge.

**Avoid Travel Expenses** On-site courses allow you to schedule technical training at your convenience, saving time, expense, and the opportunity cost of travel away from the workplace.

**Discuss Confidential Topics** Private on-site training permits the open discussion of sensitive issues such as security, access, and network design. We can work with your existing network's proprietary files while demonstrating the latest technologies.

**Customize Course Content** Global Knowledge can tailor your courses to include the technologies and the topics which have the greatest impact on your business. We can complement your internal training efforts or provide a total solution to your training needs.

**Corporate Pass** The Corporate Pass Discount Program rewards our best network training customers with preferred pricing on public courses, discounts on multimedia training packages, and an array of career planning services.

**Global Knowledge Training Lifecycle** Supporting the Dynamic and Specialized Training Requirements of Information Technology Professionals

- Define Profile
- Assess Skills
- Design Training
- Deliver Training
- Test Knowledge
- Update Profile
- Use New Skills

**College Credit Recommendation Program** The American Council on Education's CREDIT program recommends 53 Global Knowledge courses for college credit. Now our network training can help you earn your college degree while you learn the technical skills needed for your job. When you attend an ACE-certified Global Knowledge course and pass the associated exam, you earn college credit recommendations for that course. Global Knowledge can establish a transcript record for you with ACE, which you can use to gain credit at a college or as a written record of your professional training that you can attach to your resume.

# Registration Information

*In the US:*

CALL: 1 (888) 762-4442

FAX: 1 (919) 469-7070

VISIT OUR WEBSITE:

www.globalknowledge.com

MAIL CHECK AND THIS FORM TO:

Global Knowledge
Suite 200
114 Edinburgh South
P.O. Box 1187
Cary, NC 27512

*In Canada:*

CALL: 1 (800) 465-2226

FAX: 1 (613) 567-3899

VISIT OUR WEBSITE:

www.globalknowledge.com.ca

MAIL CHECK AND THIS FORM TO:

Global Knowledge
Suite 1601
393 University Ave.
Toronto, ON M5G 1E6

COURSE FEE: The fee covers course tuition, refreshments, and all course materials. Any parking expenses that may be incurred are not included. Payment or government training form must be received six business days prior to the course date. We will also accept Visa/MasterCard and American Express. For non-U.S. credit card users, charges will be in U.S. funds and will be converted by your credit card company. Checks drawn on Canadian banks in Canadian funds are acceptable.

COURSE SCHEDULE: Registration is at 8:00 a.m. on the first day. The program begins at 8:30 a.m. and concludes at 4:30 p.m. each day.

CANCELLATION POLICY: Cancellation and full refund will be allowed if written cancellation is received in our office at least six business days prior to the course start date. Registrants who do not attend the course or do not cancel more than six business days in advance are responsible for the full registration fee; you may transfer to a later date provided the course fee has been paid in full. Substitutions may be made at any time. If Global Knowledge must cancel a course for any reason, liability is limited to the registration fee only.

GLOBAL KNOWLEDGE: Global Knowledge programs are developed and presented by industry professionals with "real-world" experience. Designed to help professionals meet today's interconnectivity and interoperability challenges, most of our programs feature hands-on labs that incorporate state-of-the-art communication components and equipment.

ON-SITE TEAM TRAINING: Bring Global Knowledge's powerful training programs to your company. At Global Knowledge, we will custom design courses to meet your specific network requirements. Call 1 (919) 461-8686 for more information.

YOUR GUARANTEE: Global Knowledge believes its courses offer the best possible training in this field. If during the first day you are not satisfied and wish to withdraw from the course, simply notify the instructor, return all course materials, and receive a 100% refund.

REGISTRATION INFORMATION:

Course title ______________________________

Course location ____________________ Course date __________

Name/title ____________________ Company __________

Name/title ____________________ Company __________

Name/title ____________________ Company __________

Address __________ Telephone __________ Fax __________

City __________ State/Province __________ Zip/Postal Code __________

Credit card __________ Card # __________ Expiration date __________

Signature ______________________________

## LICENSE AGREEMENT

THIS PRODUCT (THE "PRODUCT") CONTAINS PROPRIETARY SOFTWARE, DATA AND INFORMATION (INCLUDING DOCUMENTATION) OWNED BY THE McGRAW-HILL COMPANIES, INC. ("McGRAW-HILL") AND ITS LICENSORS. YOUR RIGHT TO USE THE PRODUCT IS GOVERNED BY THE TERMS AND CONDITIONS OF THIS AGREEMENT.

**LICENSE:** Throughout this License Agreement, "you" shall mean either the individual or the entity whose agent opens this package. You are granted a non-exclusive and non-transferable license to use the Product subject to the following terms:
(i) If you have licensed a single user version of the Product, the Product may only be used on a single computer (i.e., a single CPU). If you licensed and paid the fee applicable to a local area network or wide area network version of the Product, you are subject to the terms of the following subparagraph (ii).
(ii) If you have licensed a local area network version, you may use the Product on unlimited workstations located in one single building selected by you that is served by such local area network. If you have licensed a wide area network version, you may use the Product on unlimited workstations located in multiple buildings on the same site selected by you that is served by such wide area network; provided, however, that any building will not be considered located in the same site if it is more than five (5) miles away from any building included in such site. In addition, you may only use a local area or wide area network version of the Product on one single server. If you wish to use the Product on more than one server, you must obtain written authorization from McGraw-Hill and pay additional fees.
(iii) You may make one copy of the Product for back-up purposes only and you must maintain an accurate record as to the location of the back-up at all times.

**COPYRIGHT; RESTRICTIONS ON USE AND TRANSFER:** All rights (including copyright) in and to the Product are owned by McGraw-Hill and its licensors. You are the owner of the enclosed disc on which the Product is recorded. You may not use, copy, decompile, disassemble, reverse engineer, modify, reproduce, create derivative works, transmit, distribute, sublicense, store in a database or retrieval system of any kind, rent or transfer the Product, or any portion thereof, in any form or by any means (including electronically or otherwise) except as expressly provided for in this License Agreement. You must reproduce the copyright notices, trademark notices, legends and logos of McGraw-Hill and its licensors that appear on the Product on the back-up copy of the Product which you are permitted to make hereunder. All rights in the Product not expressly granted herein are reserved by McGraw-Hill and its licensors.

**TERM:** This License Agreement is effective until terminated. It will terminate if you fail to comply with any term or condition of this License Agreement. Upon termination, you are obligated to return to McGraw-Hill the Product together with all copies thereof and to purge all copies of the Product included in any and all servers and computer facilities.

**DISCLAIMER OF WARRANTY:** THE PRODUCT AND THE BACK-UP COPY ARE LICENSED "AS IS." McGRAW-HILL, ITS LICENSORS AND THE AUTHORS MAKE NO WARRANTIES, EXPRESS OR IMPLIED, AS TO THE RESULTS TO BE OBTAINED BY ANY PERSON OR ENTITY FROM USE OF THE PRODUCT, ANY INFORMATION OR DATA INCLUDED THEREIN AND/OR ANY TECHNICAL SUPPORT SERVICES PROVIDED HEREUNDER, IF ANY ("TECHNICAL SUPPORT SERVICES"). McGRAW-HILL, ITS LICENSORS AND THE AUTHORS MAKE NO EXPRESS OR IMPLIED WARRANTIES OF MERCHANTABILITY OR FITNESS FOR A PARTICULAR PURPOSE OR USE WITH RESPECT TO THE PRODUCT. McGRAW-HILL, ITS LICENSORS, AND THE AUTHORS MAKE NO GUARANTEE THAT YOU WILL PASS ANY CERTIFICATION EXAM WHATSOEVER BY USING THIS PRODUCT. NEITHER McGRAW-HILL, ANY OF ITS LICENSORS NOR THE AUTHORS WARRANT THAT THE FUNCTIONS CONTAINED IN THE PRODUCT WILL MEET YOUR REQUIREMENTS OR THAT THE OPERATION OF THE PRODUCT WILL BE UNINTERRUPTED OR ERROR FREE. YOU ASSUME THE ENTIRE RISK WITH RESPECT TO THE QUALITY AND PERFORMANCE OF THE PRODUCT.

**LIMITED WARRANTY FOR DISC:** To the original licensee only, McGraw-Hill warrants that the enclosed disc on which the Product is recorded is free from defects in materials and workmanship under normal use and service for a period of ninety (90) days from the date of purchase. In the event of a defect in the disc covered by the foregoing warranty, McGraw-Hill will replace the disc.

**LIMITATION OF LIABILITY:** NEITHER McGRAW-HILL, ITS LICENSORS NOR THE AUTHORS SHALL BE LIABLE FOR ANY INDIRECT, SPECIAL OR CONSEQUENTIAL DAMAGES, SUCH AS BUT NOT LIMITED TO, LOSS OF ANTICIPATED PROFITS OR BENEFITS, RESULTING FROM THE USE OR INABILITY TO USE THE PRODUCT EVEN IF ANY OF THEM HAS BEEN ADVISED OF THE POSSIBILITY OF SUCH DAMAGES. THIS LIMITATION OF LIABILITY SHALL APPLY TO ANY CLAIM OR CAUSE WHATSOEVER WHETHER SUCH CLAIM OR CAUSE ARISES IN CONTRACT, TORT, OR OTHERWISE. Some states do not allow the exclusion or limitation of indirect, special or consequential damages, so the above limitation may not apply to you.

**U.S. GOVERNMENT RESTRICTED RIGHTS:** Any software included in the Product is provided with restricted rights subject to subparagraphs (c), (1) and (2) of the Commercial Computer Software-Restricted Rights clause at 48 C.F.R. 52.227-19. The terms of this Agreement applicable to the use of the data in the Product are those under which the data are generally made available to the general public by McGraw-Hill. Except as provided herein, no reproduction, use, or disclosure rights are granted with respect to the data included in the Product and no right to modify or create derivative works from any such data is hereby granted.

**GENERAL:** This License Agreement constitutes the entire agreement between the parties relating to the Product. The terms of any Purchase Order shall have no effect on the terms of this License Agreement. Failure of McGraw-Hill to insist at any time on strict compliance with this License Agreement shall not constitute a waiver of any rights under this License Agreement. This License Agreement shall be construed and governed in accordance with the laws of the State of New York. If any provision of this License Agreement is held to be contrary to law, that provision will be enforced to the maximum extent permissible and the remaining provisions will remain in full force and effect.

# GET CERTIFIED WITH HELP FROM THE EXPERTS

## MCSE Designing Windows® 2000 Web Solutions Study Guide

### A COMPLETE STUDY PROGRAM BUILT UPON PROVEN INSTRUCTIONAL METHODS

**Self-study features include:**

**Expert advice** on how to take and pass the test:

*"This test takes on a different format compared with the traditional MCSE exams. This exam's questions are based on case studies in order to test your performance capabilities."*

**Step-by-step Certification Exercises** focus on the specific skills most likely to be on the exam. The **CertCam** icon guides you to the video clip that demonstrates and explains this skill set on CD-ROM.

**Special warnings** that prepare you for tricky exam topics:

*"Take care to understand the differences between host priority and handling priority, and filtering modes and client affinity. The terms are very similar and should not be confused. The exam will probably include questions involving the differences between these terms."*

MCSE **On The Job Notes** present important lessons that help you work more efficiently:

*"Users see a cluster using NLB as though it were a single server. They only need to know a single IP address and/or hostname in order to access the resources provided by the cluster."*

**Two-Minute Drills** at the end of every chapter quickly reinforce your knowledge and ensure better retention of key concepts:

*"Cluster Service is available in two levels: two-node clusters in Windows 2000 Advanced Server and four-node clusters in Windows 2000 Datacenter Server."*

**Scenario & Solution** sections lay out problems and solutions in a quick-read format. For example:

I was considering using Recovery Console to repair my system, but the file system on the Windows 2000 Server uses FAT32. Will Recovery Console support FAT32?

*Yes. Recovery Console allows you to access the hard disk regardless of whether FAT16, FAT32, or NTFS is used as the file system.*

**Hundreds of realistic practice questions with answers** help prepare you for the real test.

**How much RAM does each client connection take on an IIS 5.0 Server?**

**A.** 10MB RAM per connection

**B.** 100KB of RAM per connection

**C.** 10KB RAM per connection

**D.** 1KB RAM per connection

☑ **C.** A client connection takes up 10KB of RAM per connection. It is imperative that you have configured enough memory on your IIS 5.0 server.

☒ **A** *is incorrect because 10MB would be an enormous amount of RAM to use for client connections.* **B** *and* **D** *are incorrect for RAM used in IIS 5.0.*